Frank Robbins'

JOHNNY HAZARD

VOLUME SEVEN: The Newspaper Dailies 1954-1956

Introduction by Daniel Herman

Hermes Press

Cover image: Paradise and Johnny Hazard with Gadzooks on his shoulder, based on an by image by Frank Robbins
Cover and book design by Daniel Herman and Sabrina Herman
First printing, 2019

Published by Hermes Press an imprint of Herman and Geer Communications, Inc.
2100 Wilmington Road
Daniel Herman, Publisher
Troy Musguire, Production Manager
Sabrina Herman, Managing Editor/Vice President
Alissa Fisher, Senior Graphic Designer
Kandice Hartner, Senior Editor
Brian Peck, Special Projects Editor
Benjamin Beers, Archivist
Neshannock, Pennsylvania 16105
(724) 652-0511
www.HermesPress.com; info@hermespress.com

LCCN Applied for 10 9 8 7 6 5 4 3 2 1 0
ISBN 978-1-61345-153-3
Image scanning by Kandice Hartner and Benjamin Beers; digital corrections by H + G Media and Alissa Fisher

Acknowledgements: This book would not be possible without the help, cooperation, patience, and kindness of many people. First and foremost in making this endeavor possible are all the folks at King Features: Ita Golzman and Frank Caruso. Additionally, and most importantly, the help and assistance of Randy Scott of Michigan State University's Special Collections was of paramount importance in making our continuing series of *Johnny Hazard* reprints possible. Randy and all the wonderful people at MSU gave us access to their collection of *Johnny Hazard* press proofs which were used as the source for this entire book. Also, special thanks to Art Lortie for supplying strips MSU didn't have and we couldn't find anywhere else!

Printed in China

contents

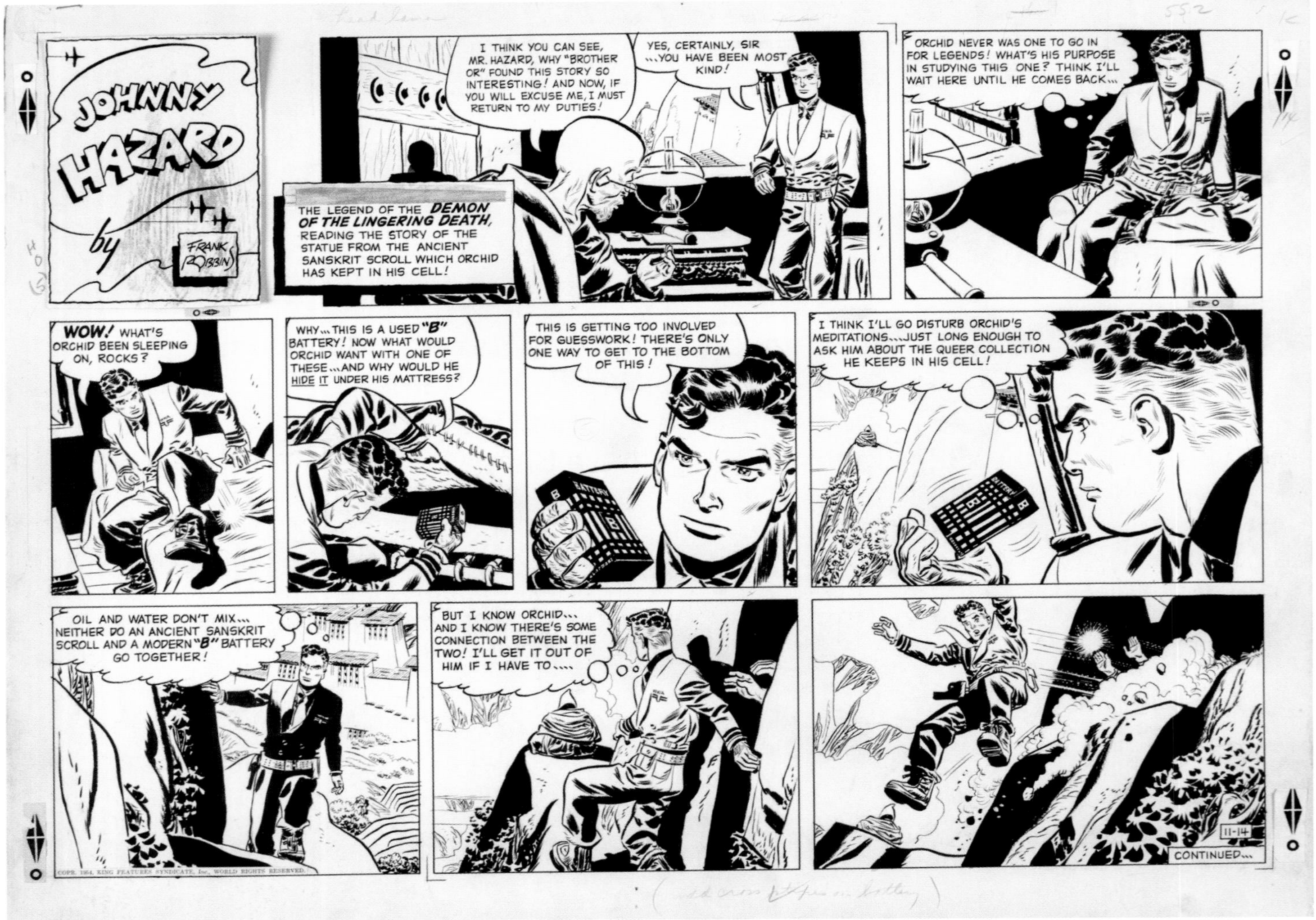
JOHNNY HAZARD
by FRANK ROBBINS
I THINK YOU CAN SEE, MR. HAZARD, WHY "BROTHER OR" FOUND THIS STORY SO INTERESTING! AND NOW, IF YOU WILL EXCUSE ME, I MUST RETURN TO MY DUTIES!
YES, CERTAINLY, SIR ...YOU HAVE BEEN MOST KIND!
THE LEGEND OF THE DEMON OF THE LINGERING DEATH, READING THE STORY OF THE STATUE FROM THE ANCIENT SANSKRIT SCROLL WHICH ORCHID HAS KEPT IN HIS CELL!
ORCHID NEVER WAS ONE TO GO IN FOR LEGENDS! WHAT'S HIS PURPOSE IN STUDYING THIS ONE? THINK I'LL WAIT HERE UNTIL HE COMES BACK...
WOW! WHAT'S ORCHID BEEN SLEEPING ON, ROCKS?
WHY... THIS IS A USED "B" BATTERY! NOW WHAT WOULD ORCHID WANT WITH ONE OF THESE... AND WHY WOULD HE HIDE IT UNDER HIS MATTRESS?
THIS IS GETTING TOO INVOLVED FOR GUESSWORK! THERE'S ONLY ONE WAY TO GET TO THE BOTTOM OF THIS!
BATTERY
I THINK I'LL GO DISTURB ORCHID'S MEDITATIONS... JUST LONG ENOUGH TO ASK HIM ABOUT THE QUEER COLLECTION HE KEEPS IN HIS CELL!
OIL AND WATER DON'T MIX... NEITHER DO AN ANCIENT SANSKRIT SCROLL AND A MODERN "B" BATTERY GO TOGETHER!
BUT I KNOW ORCHID... AND I KNOW THERE'S SOME CONNECTION BETWEEN THE TWO! I'LL GET IT OUT OF HIM IF I HAVE TO....
11-14
CONTINUED...
COPR. 1954, KING FEATURES SYNDICATE, Inc., WORLD RIGHTS RESERVED.

introduction

Johnny Hazard Continues...

Nineteen Fifty-four witnessed Alfred Hitchcock's *Rear Window* hold first place in the U.S. box office; Dwight D. Eisenhower was President; Marilyn Monroe married Joe Dimaggio; Senator "Tailgunner Joe" McCarthy continued to fuel the "Red Scare"; Elvis Presley released his first single, and the *Johnny Hazard* newspaper strip continued on, celebrating its first decade in print.

Indeed, the strip was on a roll with continuous action and adventure, more beautiful woman to confound and confront Johnny and even a parakeet as a main plot point of one of the continuities in this volume. *Johnny Hazard*

Frank Robbins' original artwork for the *Johnny Hazard* Sunday strip from November 11, 1954. This strip was created during the same period that the strips featured in this volume saw print.

boasted not only sense of humor, but impeccable pacing coupled with artist Frank Robbins' flawless composition and inking. Although Robbins has frequently been pigeonholed as a Caniff-inspired disciple, his art had always been individually distinctive. After ten years of strips the art had a personality, rhythm, and use of positive and negative space which is quickly discernible as being uniquely that of Frank Robbins.

The stories presented in this volume are classic B-movie action/adventure yarns which include all the elements found in the now classic films of the period. This book presents seven continuities: "What's My Name?" (June 21 - September 18, 1954; "A Little Birdie Told

A SHOW OF SPEED MAY BE NECESSARY, BUT...THIS IS INVITING DISASTER!

Me" (September 20 - December 25, 1954); "It's a Snap" (December 27, 1954 - May 21, 1955); "Death at the Opera" (May 23 - August 6, 1955); "There's No Hiding Place" (August 8 - October 22, 1955); "The Car Thief" (October 24, 1955 - January 21, 1956); and "Project Heat Barrier" (January 23 - April 21, 1956).

The stories in the volume take Johnny to the continent; Robbins' artwork captures the ambience of the locations and the period. These tales are populated by classic 1950s characters, vehicles, clothing, bad guys and, of course femme fatales.

The seven continuities presented here were created with a light touch that successfully mixes humor, slam bang fights and shoot outs, not to mention military hardware, planes, and fighter jets, and let's not forget Gadzooks (the parakeet), featured on the cover, who stars in the second storyline.

The stories presented in this volume are clearly rooted in the era when they were created, but, hold up very nicely sixty years hence their creation. While they represent the dramatic sensibilities of the period, these stories do not stray into political relevance or cross over into the toxic

Left: Original Frank Robbins artwork from a panel from the September 5, 1955 *Johnny Hazard* Sunday. Opposite page: Frank Robbins' original artwork for the *Johnny Hazard* daily strip from February 8, 1954. These strips were created during the same period that the strips featured in this volume saw print.

HYA, LI'L JAWN... WHERE YA BEEN ALL DAY? AH'M OVER AT TRECHAT'S PLACE... CAN YUH JOIN ME HERE PRONTO?
SORRY, LOW-NOON, CAN'T MAKE IT! MATTER OF FACT, I DON'T THINK I CAN SEE YOU ANY MORE!
2-8
I'VE GOT TO CHECK OUT OF PARIS... IMPORTANT BUSINESS! BUT LISTEN... ON A HUNCH I INVESTIGATED TRECHAT FOR YOU ...FOUND OUT HE'S OKAY!
FRANK ROBBINS
Copr. 1954, King Features Syndicate, Inc., World rights reserved.
SO LET HIM RUSTLE UP SOME PAINTINGS... BECAUSE I FOUND OUT HE'S ONE OF THE BIGGEST RUSTLERS IN ALL OF FRANCE! SO LONG, LOW-NOON!

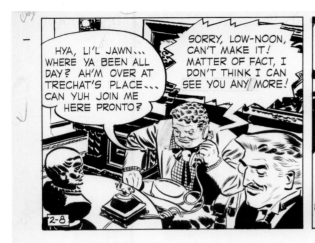

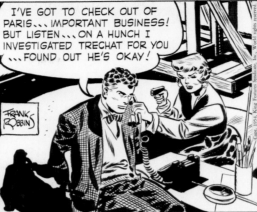

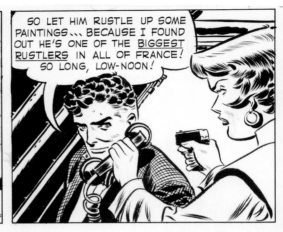

national climate of the 1950s, which was rarely reflected in mainstream entertainment. The exception, of course, was Walt Kelly's *Pogo* strip. That being said, good solid melodrama serves the distinctly important function of being diverting, which *Johnny Hazard* most certainly was.

The storytelling, camera angles, framing, and plot development is effortless and moves each story along without the reader considering the artwork involved in creating these strips, which is as it should be. The plots effortlessly flow drawing the audience along for the ride. However, if the reader stops and looks at each strip as a piece of art, Robbins' skill in creating the look of the world of Johnny Hazard is obvious. Indeed, these stories can be viewed on several levels which is why they continue to fascinate and attract an audience.

Robbins was a master of the medium and this reprint is demonstrative of his skill in creating a film in newspaper print.

—*Daniel Herman*

JOHNNY HAZARD

Chapter One: What's My Name?

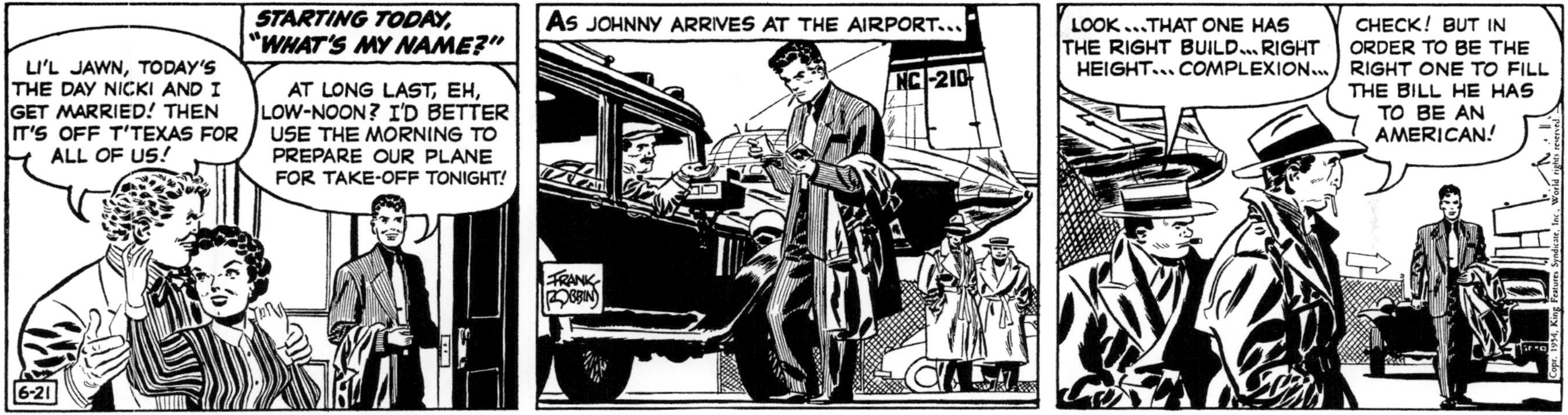
6-21
LI'L JAWN, TODAY'S THE DAY NICKI AND I GET MARRIED! THEN IT'S OFF T'TEXAS FOR ALL OF US!
STARTING TODAY, "WHAT'S MY NAME?"
AT LONG LAST, EH, LOW-NOON? I'D BETTER USE THE MORNING TO PREPARE OUR PLANE FOR TAKE-OFF TONIGHT!
AS JOHNNY ARRIVES AT THE AIRPORT...
NC-210
FRANK ROBBINS
LOOK...THAT ONE HAS THE RIGHT BUILD...RIGHT HEIGHT...COMPLEXION...
CHECK! BUT IN ORDER TO BE THE RIGHT ONE TO FILL THE BILL HE HAS TO BE AN AMERICAN!
Copr. 1954, King Features Syndicate, Inc., World rights reserved.

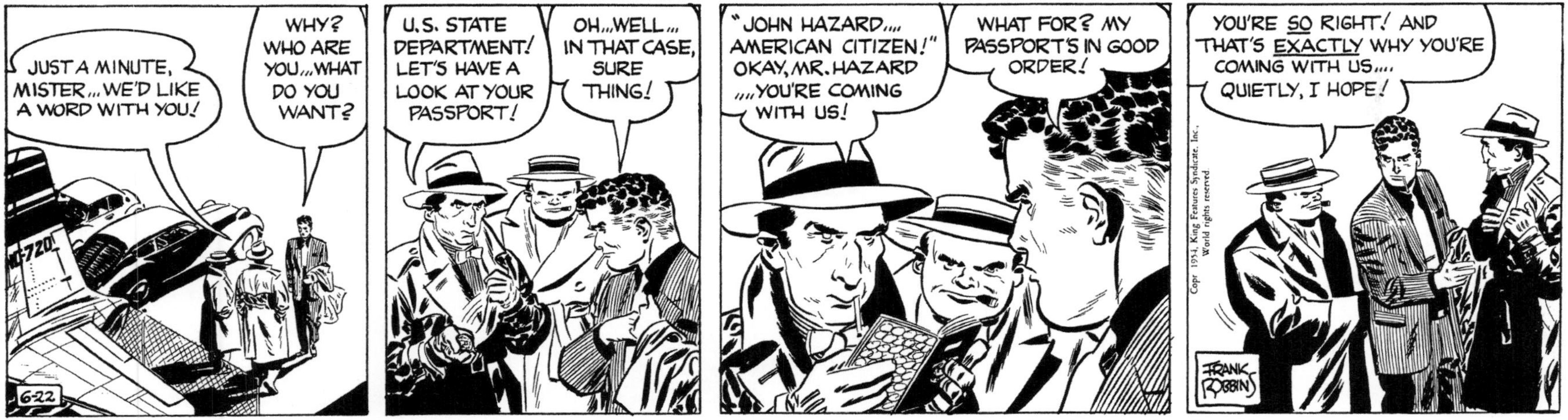
6-22
JUST A MINUTE, MISTER...WE'D LIKE A WORD WITH YOU!
WHY? WHO ARE YOU...WHAT DO YOU WANT?
NC-720
U.S. STATE DEPARTMENT! LET'S HAVE A LOOK AT YOUR PASSPORT!
OH...WELL... IN THAT CASE, SURE THING!
"JOHN HAZARD.... AMERICAN CITIZEN!" OKAY, MR. HAZARD ....YOU'RE COMING WITH US!
WHAT FOR? MY PASSPORT'S IN GOOD ORDER!
Copr 1954, King Features Syndicate, Inc. World rights reserved.
YOU'RE SO RIGHT! AND THAT'S EXACTLY WHY YOU'RE COMING WITH US.... QUIETLY, I HOPE!
FRANK ROBBINS

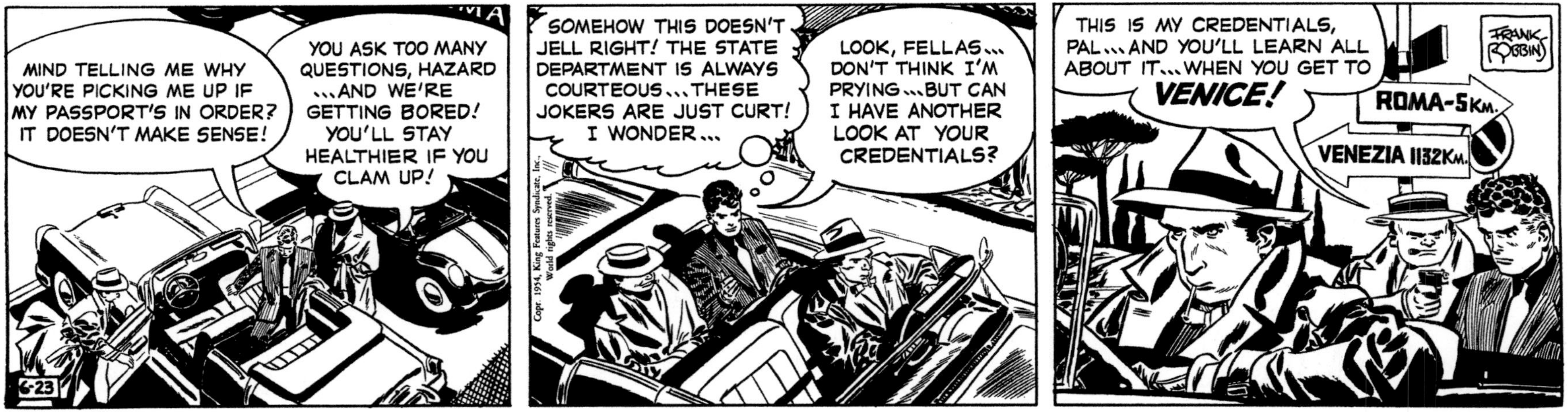
MA
6-23
MIND TELLING ME WHY YOU'RE PICKING ME UP IF MY PASSPORT'S IN ORDER? IT DOESN'T MAKE SENSE!
YOU ASK TOO MANY QUESTIONS, HAZARD ...AND WE'RE GETTING BORED! YOU'LL STAY HEALTHIER IF YOU CLAM UP!
SOMEHOW THIS DOESN'T JELL RIGHT! THE STATE DEPARTMENT IS ALWAYS COURTEOUS...THESE JOKERS ARE JUST CURT! I WONDER...
LOOK, FELLAS... DON'T THINK I'M PRYING...BUT CAN I HAVE ANOTHER LOOK AT YOUR CREDENTIALS?
Copr. 1954, King Features Syndicate, Inc., World rights reserved.
FRANK ROBBINS
THIS IS MY CREDENTIALS, PAL...AND YOU'LL LEARN ALL ABOUT IT...WHEN YOU GET TO VENICE!
ROMA-5KM.
VENEZIA 1132KM.

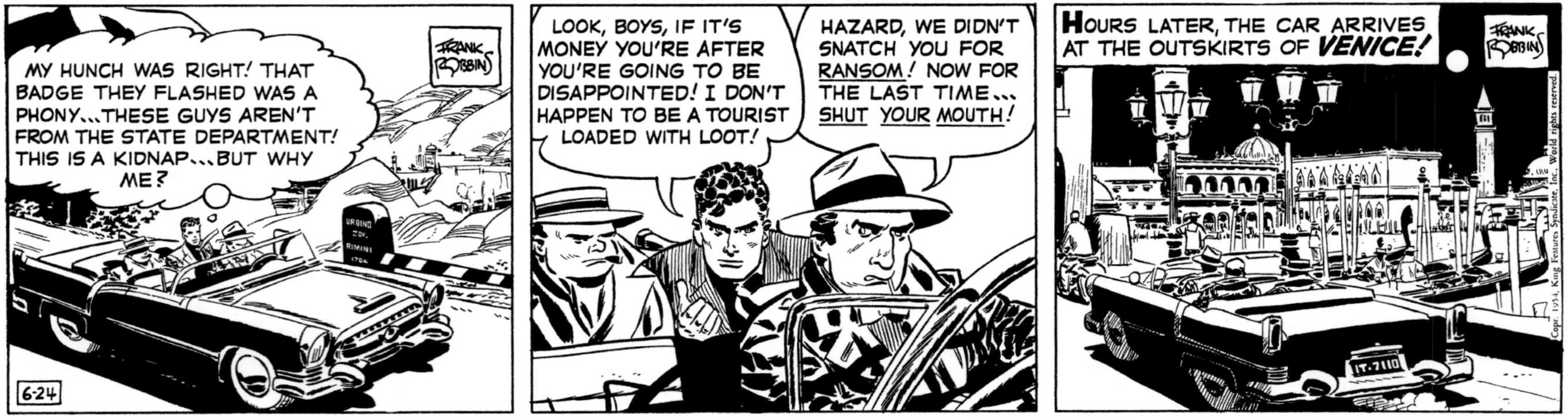
FRANK ROBBINS
MY HUNCH WAS RIGHT! THAT BADGE THEY FLASHED WAS A PHONY...THESE GUYS AREN'T FROM THE STATE DEPARTMENT! THIS IS A KIDNAP...BUT WHY ME?
URBINO ZOV. RIMINI
6-24
LOOK, BOYS, IF IT'S MONEY YOU'RE AFTER YOU'RE GOING TO BE DISAPPOINTED! I DON'T HAPPEN TO BE A TOURIST LOADED WITH LOOT!
HAZARD, WE DIDN'T SNATCH YOU FOR RANSOM! NOW FOR THE LAST TIME... SHUT YOUR MOUTH!
HOURS LATER, THE CAR ARRIVES AT THE OUTSKIRTS OF VENICE!
FRANK ROBBINS
Copr. 1954, King Features Syndicate, Inc., World rights reserved.
IT-7110

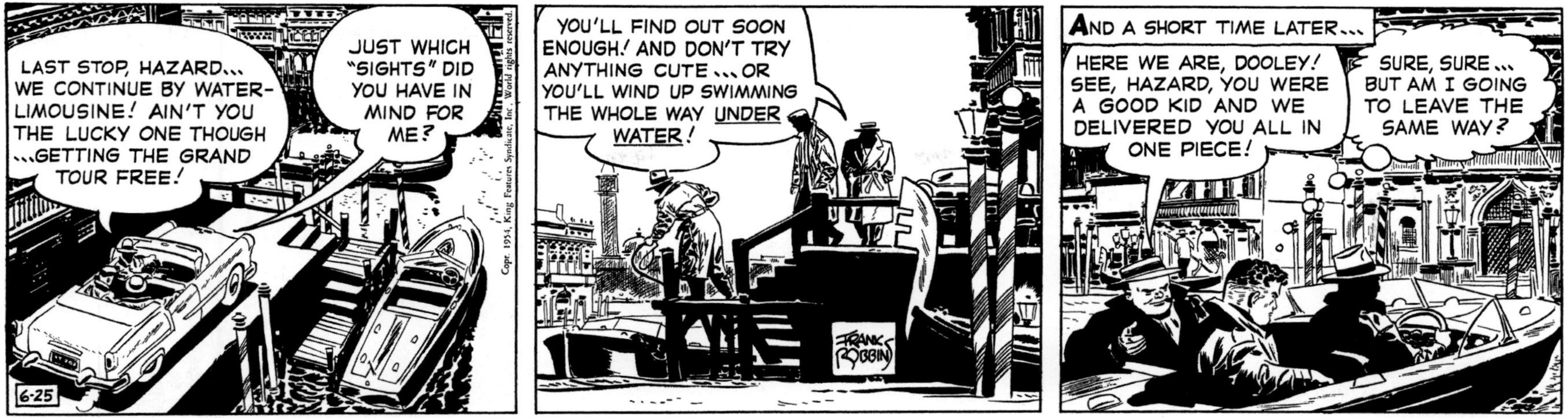
LAST STOP, HAZARD... WE CONTINUE BY WATER-LIMOUSINE! AIN'T YOU THE LUCKY ONE THOUGH ...GETTING THE GRAND TOUR FREE!
JUST WHICH "SIGHTS" DID YOU HAVE IN MIND FOR ME?
Copr. 1954, King Features Syndicate, Inc. World rights reserved.
6-25
YOU'LL FIND OUT SOON ENOUGH! AND DON'T TRY ANYTHING CUTE ... OR YOU'LL WIND UP SWIMMING THE WHOLE WAY UNDER WATER!
FRANK ROBBINS
AND A SHORT TIME LATER...
HERE WE ARE, DOOLEY! SEE, HAZARD, YOU WERE A GOOD KID AND WE DELIVERED YOU ALL IN ONE PIECE!
SURE, SURE... BUT AM I GOING TO LEAVE THE SAME WAY?

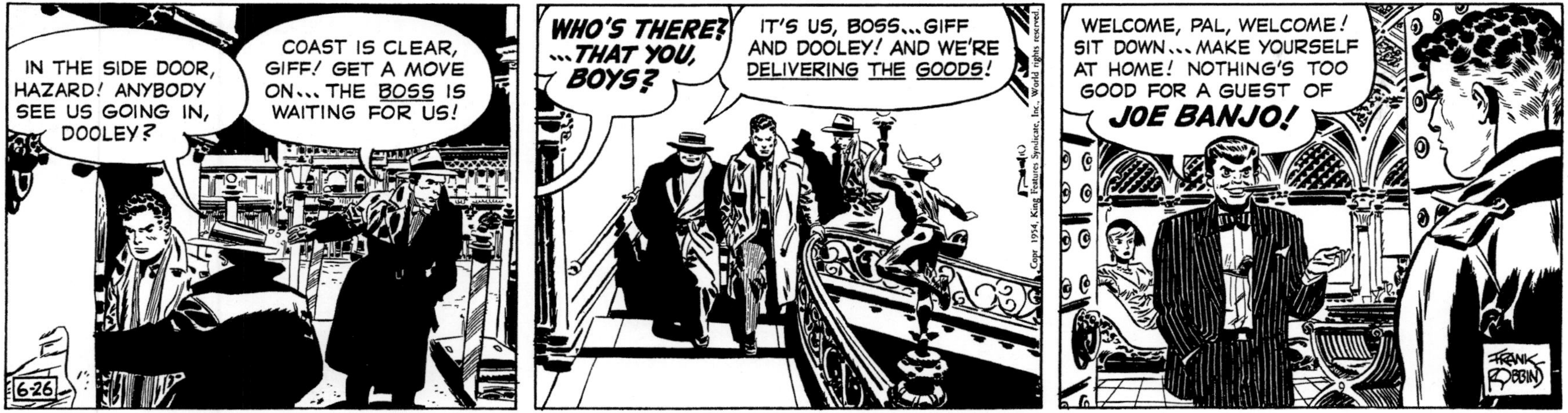
IN THE SIDE DOOR, HAZARD! ANYBODY SEE US GOING IN, DOOLEY?
COAST IS CLEAR, GIFF! GET A MOVE ON... THE BOSS IS WAITING FOR US!
6-26
WHO'S THERE? ...THAT YOU, BOYS?
IT'S US, BOSS...GIFF AND DOOLEY! AND WE'RE DELIVERING THE GOODS!
Copr. 1954, King Features Syndicate, Inc. World rights reserved.
WELCOME, PAL, WELCOME! SIT DOWN... MAKE YOURSELF AT HOME! NOTHING'S TOO GOOD FOR A GUEST OF JOE BANJO!
FRANK ROBBINS

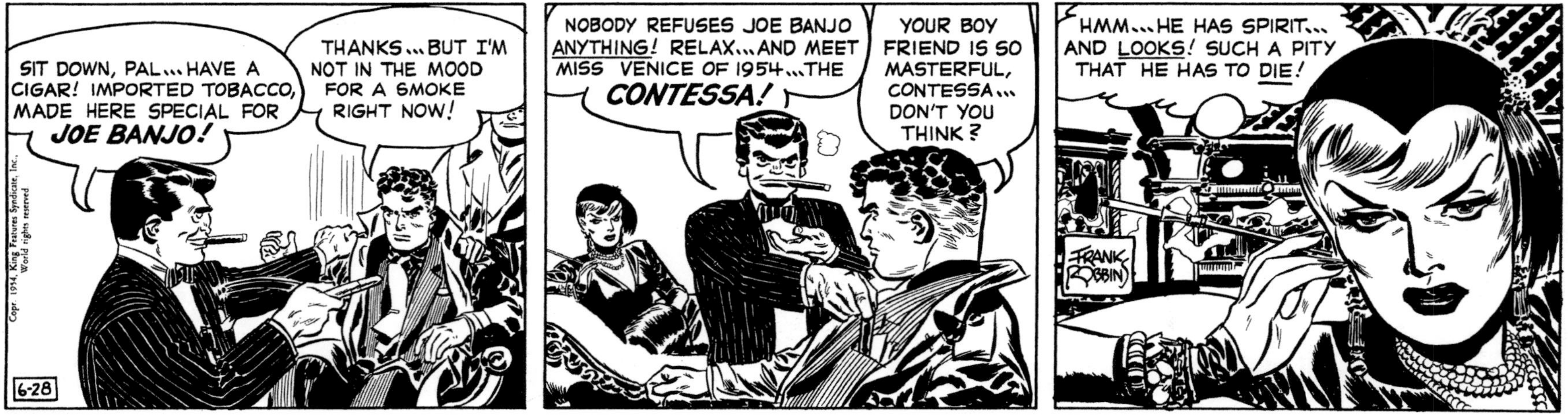
6-28
Copr. 1954, King Features Syndicate, Inc., World rights reserved
SIT DOWN, PAL... HAVE A CIGAR! IMPORTED TOBACCO, MADE HERE SPECIAL FOR JOE BANJO!
THANKS... BUT I'M NOT IN THE MOOD FOR A SMOKE RIGHT NOW!
NOBODY REFUSES JOE BANJO ANYTHING! RELAX... AND MEET MISS VENICE OF 1954... THE CONTESSA!
YOUR BOY FRIEND IS SO MASTERFUL, CONTESSA... DON'T YOU THINK?
HMM... HE HAS SPIRIT... AND LOOKS! SUCH A PITY THAT HE HAS TO DIE!
FRANK ROBBINS

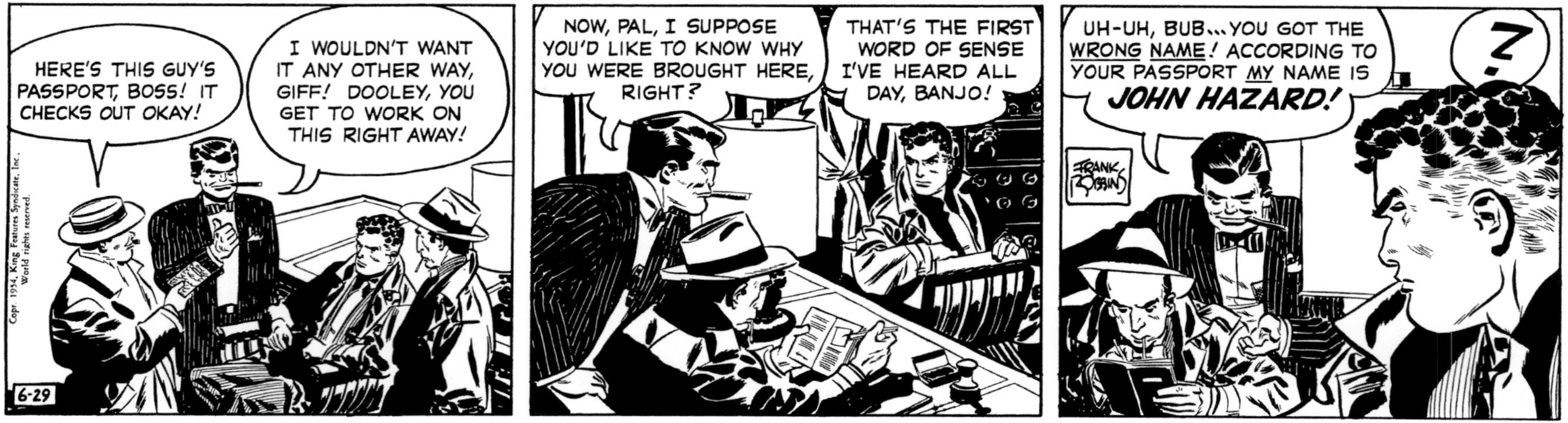
6-29
Copr. 1954, King Features Syndicate, Inc., World rights reserved.
HERE'S THIS GUY'S PASSPORT, BOSS! IT CHECKS OUT OKAY!
I WOULDN'T WANT IT ANY OTHER WAY, GIFF! DOOLEY, YOU GET TO WORK ON THIS RIGHT AWAY!
NOW, PAL, I SUPPOSE YOU'D LIKE TO KNOW WHY YOU WERE BROUGHT HERE, RIGHT?
THAT'S THE FIRST WORD OF SENSE I'VE HEARD ALL DAY, BANJO!
UH-UH, BUB... YOU GOT THE WRONG NAME! ACCORDING TO YOUR PASSPORT MY NAME IS JOHN HAZARD!
?
FRANK ROBBINS

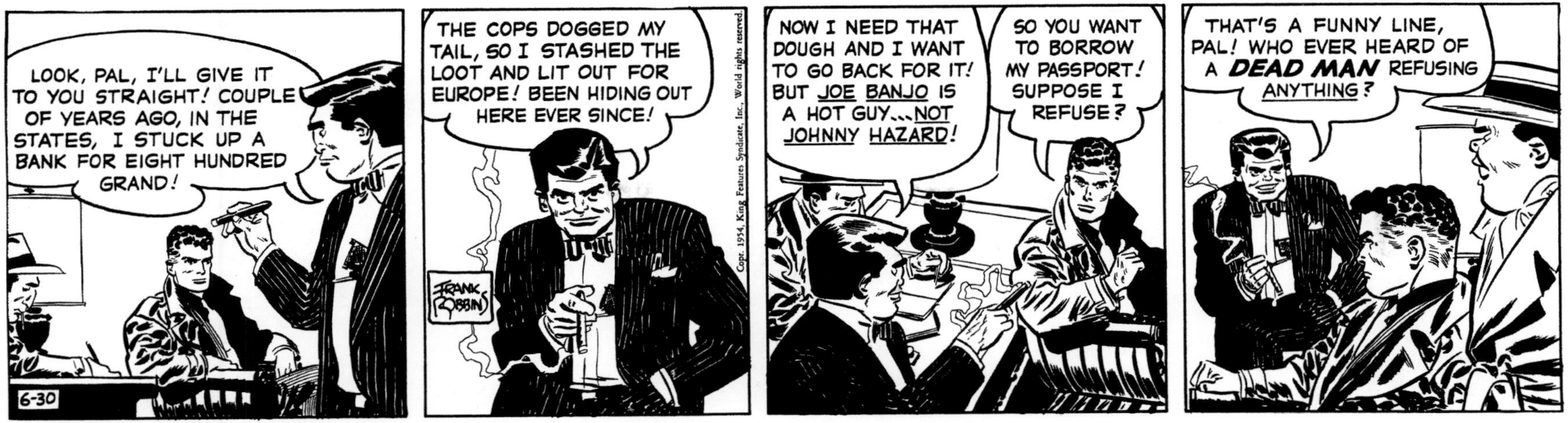
6-30
LOOK, PAL, I'LL GIVE IT TO YOU STRAIGHT! COUPLE OF YEARS AGO, IN THE STATES, I STUCK UP A BANK FOR EIGHT HUNDRED GRAND!
THE COPS DOGGED MY TAIL, SO I STASHED THE LOOT AND LIT OUT FOR EUROPE! BEEN HIDING OUT HERE EVER SINCE!
FRANK ROBBINS
Copr. 1954, King Features Syndicate, Inc., World rights reserved.
NOW I NEED THAT DOUGH AND I WANT TO GO BACK FOR IT! BUT JOE BANJO IS A HOT GUY... NOT JOHNNY HAZARD!
SO YOU WANT TO BORROW MY PASSPORT! SUPPOSE I REFUSE?
THAT'S A FUNNY LINE, PAL! WHO EVER HEARD OF A DEAD MAN REFUSING ANYTHING?

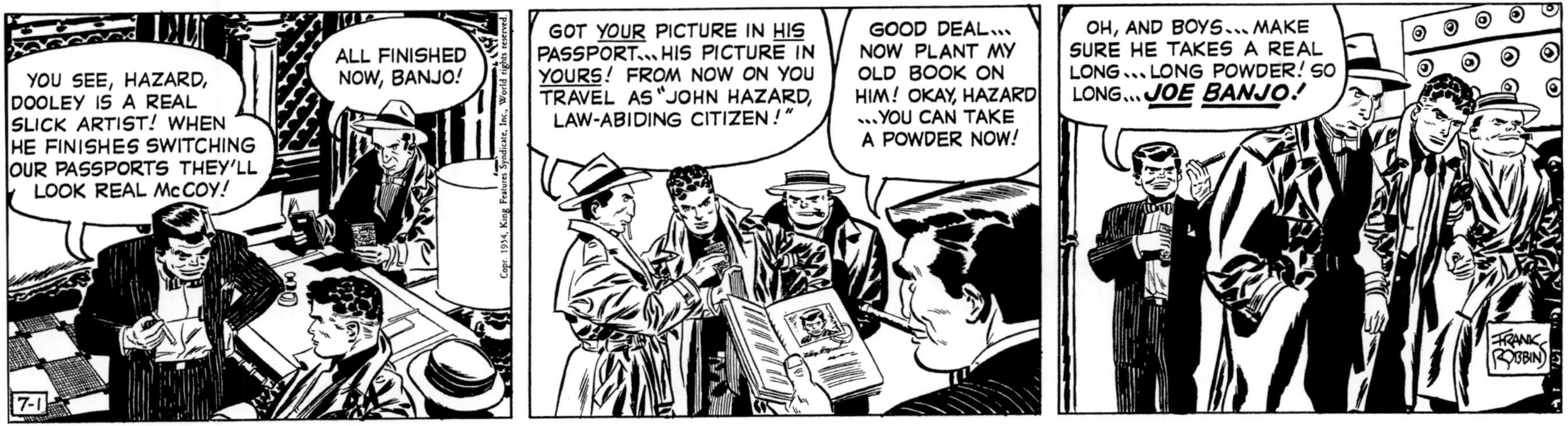
7-1
YOU SEE, HAZARD, DOOLEY IS A REAL SLICK ARTIST! WHEN HE FINISHES SWITCHING OUR PASSPORTS THEY'LL LOOK REAL McCOY!
ALL FINISHED NOW, BANJO!
Copr. 1954, King Features Syndicate, Inc., World rights reserved.
GOT YOUR PICTURE IN HIS PASSPORT... HIS PICTURE IN YOURS! FROM NOW ON YOU TRAVEL AS "JOHN HAZARD, LAW-ABIDING CITIZEN!"
GOOD DEAL... NOW PLANT MY OLD BOOK ON HIM! OKAY, HAZARD ...YOU CAN TAKE A POWDER NOW!
OH, AND BOYS... MAKE SURE HE TAKES A REAL LONG... LONG POWDER! SO LONG... JOE BANJO!
FRANK ROBBINS

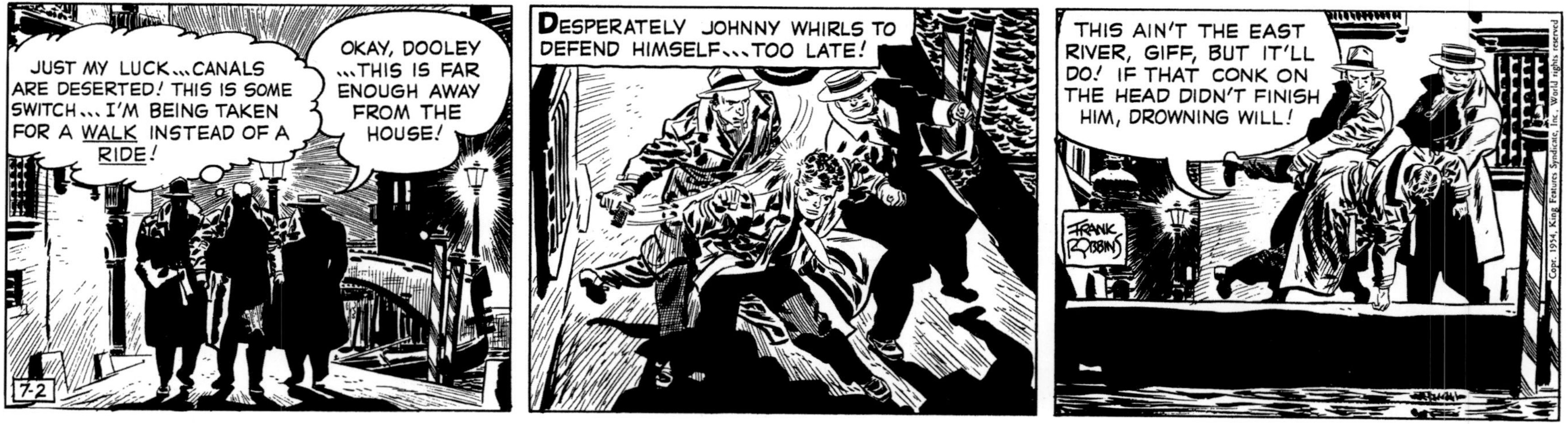
JUST MY LUCK ... CANALS ARE DESERTED! THIS IS SOME SWITCH ... I'M BEING TAKEN FOR A WALK INSTEAD OF A RIDE!
OKAY, DOOLEY ... THIS IS FAR ENOUGH AWAY FROM THE HOUSE!
7-2
DESPERATELY JOHNNY WHIRLS TO DEFEND HIMSELF ... TOO LATE!
THIS AIN'T THE EAST RIVER, GIFF, BUT IT'LL DO! IF THAT CONK ON THE HEAD DIDN'T FINISH HIM, DROWNING WILL!
FRANK ROBBINS
Copr. 1954, King Features Syndicate, Inc., World rights reserved

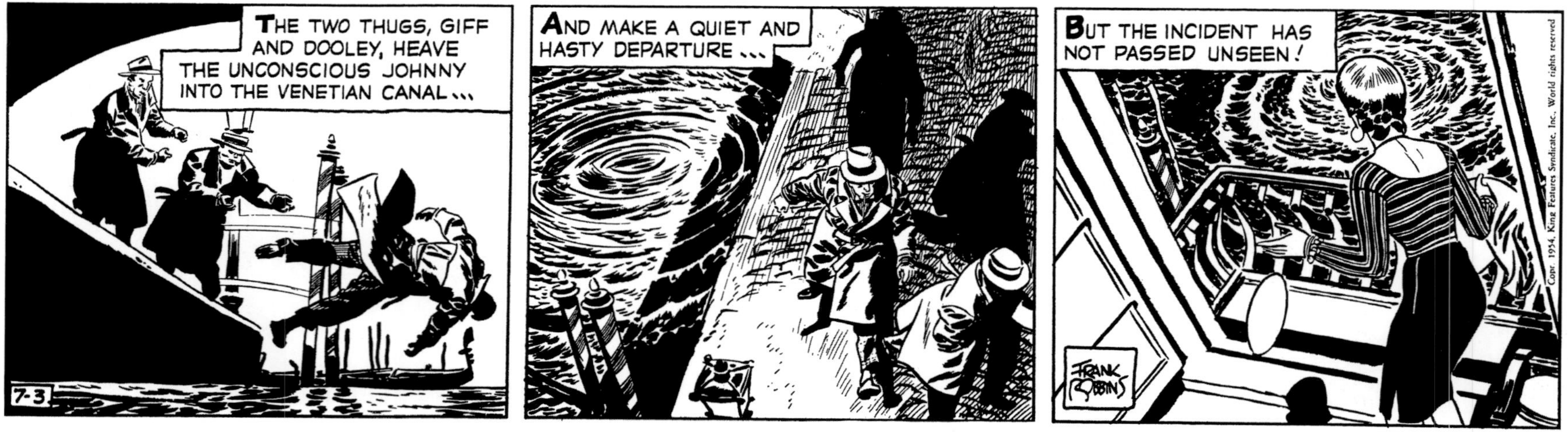
THE TWO THUGS, GIFF AND DOOLEY, HEAVE THE UNCONSCIOUS JOHNNY INTO THE VENETIAN CANAL ...
7-3
AND MAKE A QUIET AND HASTY DEPARTURE ...
BUT THE INCIDENT HAS NOT PASSED UNSEEN!
FRANK ROBBINS
Copr. 1954, King Features Syndicate, Inc., World rights reserved

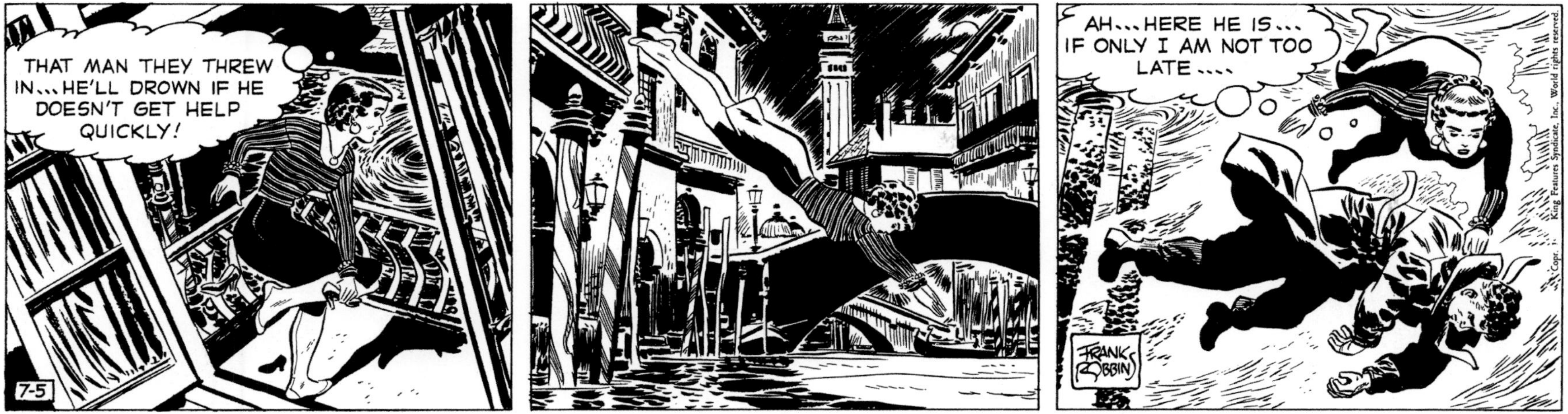
THAT MAN THEY THREW IN... HE'LL DROWN IF HE DOESN'T GET HELP QUICKLY!
7-5
AH... HERE HE IS... IF ONLY I AM NOT TOO LATE....
FRANK ROBBINS
Copr. 1954, King Features Syndicate, Inc., World rights reserved.

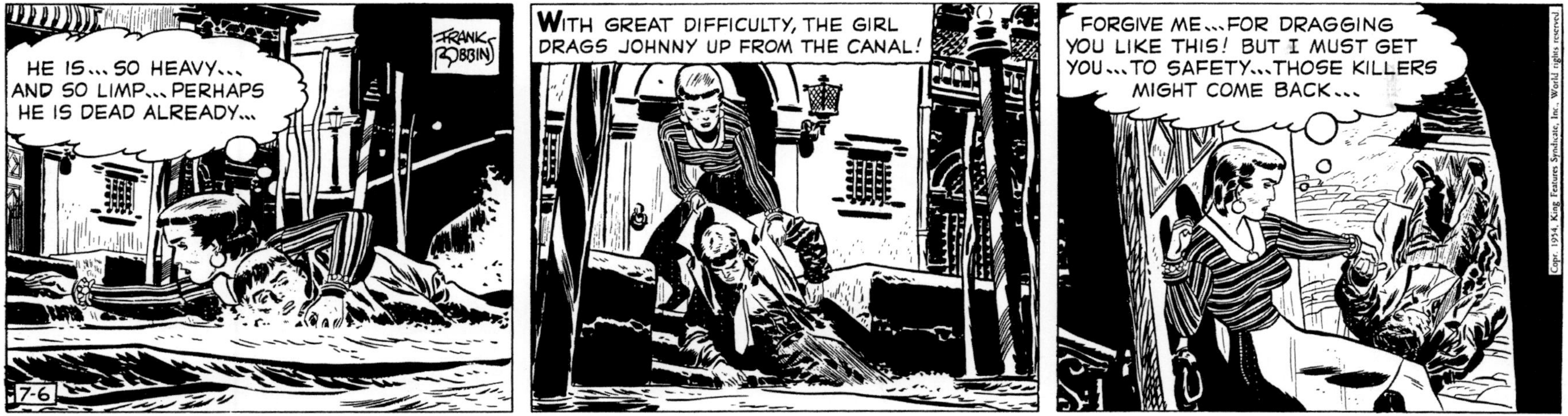
HE IS... SO HEAVY... AND SO LIMP... PERHAPS HE IS DEAD ALREADY...
FRANK ROBBINS
7-6
WITH GREAT DIFFICULTY, THE GIRL DRAGS JOHNNY UP FROM THE CANAL!
FORGIVE ME... FOR DRAGGING YOU LIKE THIS! BUT I MUST GET YOU... TO SAFETY... THOSE KILLERS MIGHT COME BACK...
Copr. 1954, King Features Syndicate, Inc., World rights reserved

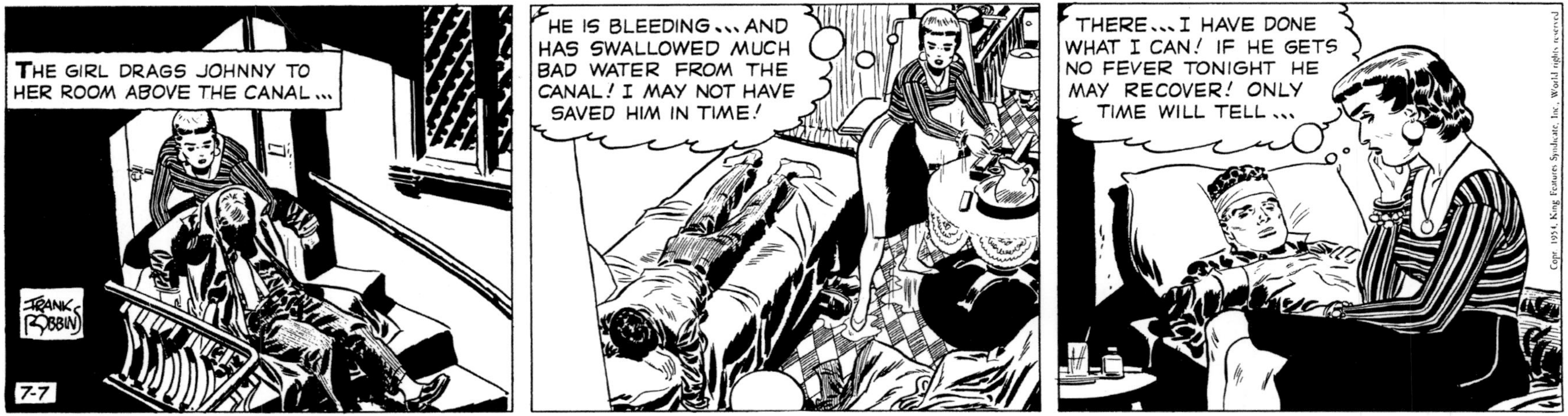
THE GIRL DRAGS JOHNNY TO HER ROOM ABOVE THE CANAL...
FRANK ROBBINS
7-7
HE IS BLEEDING... AND HAS SWALLOWED MUCH BAD WATER FROM THE CANAL! I MAY NOT HAVE SAVED HIM IN TIME!
THERE... I HAVE DONE WHAT I CAN! IF HE GETS NO FEVER TONIGHT HE MAY RECOVER! ONLY TIME WILL TELL...
Copr. 1954, King Features Syndicate, Inc., World rights reserved

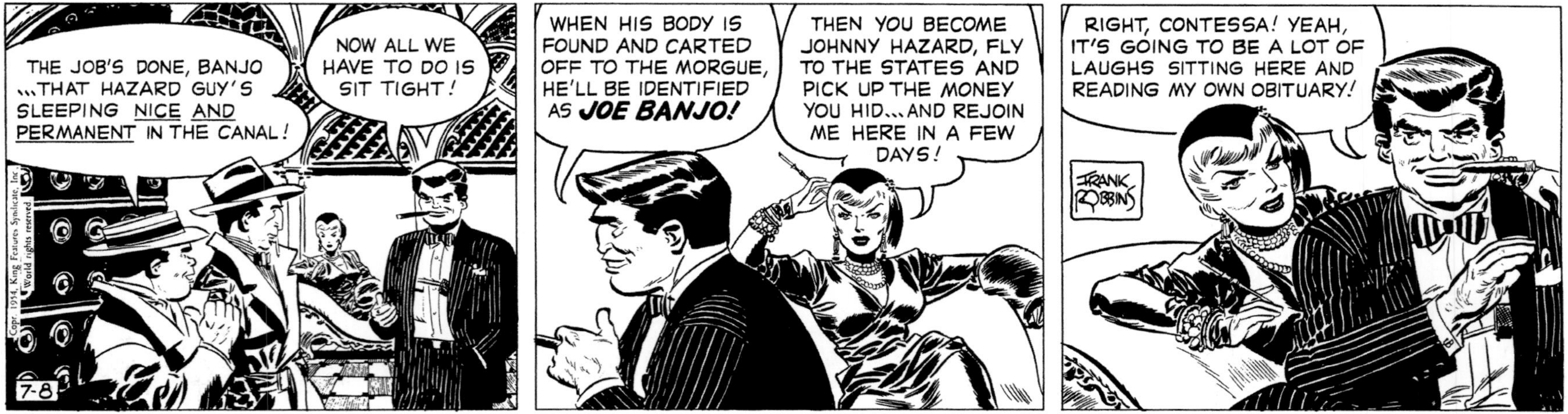
THE JOB'S DONE, BANJO ...THAT HAZARD GUY'S SLEEPING NICE AND PERMANENT IN THE CANAL!
NOW ALL WE HAVE TO DO IS SIT TIGHT!
Copr. 1954, King Features Syndicate, Inc., World rights reserved
7-8
WHEN HIS BODY IS FOUND AND CARTED OFF TO THE MORGUE, HE'LL BE IDENTIFIED AS JOE BANJO!
THEN YOU BECOME JOHNNY HAZARD, FLY TO THE STATES AND PICK UP THE MONEY YOU HID... AND REJOIN ME HERE IN A FEW DAYS!
RIGHT, CONTESSA! YEAH, IT'S GOING TO BE A LOT OF LAUGHS SITTING HERE AND READING MY OWN OBITUARY!
FRANK ROBBINS

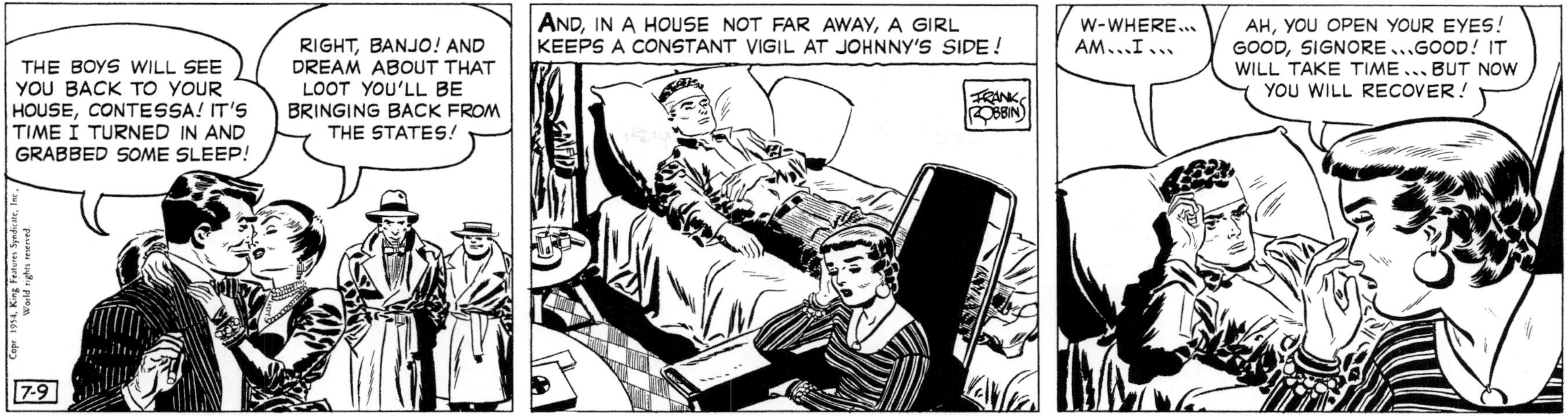
THE BOYS WILL SEE YOU BACK TO YOUR HOUSE, CONTESSA! IT'S TIME I TURNED IN AND GRABBED SOME SLEEP!
RIGHT, BANJO! AND DREAM ABOUT THAT LOOT YOU'LL BE BRINGING BACK FROM THE STATES!
Copr 1954, King Features Syndicate, Inc., World rights reserved.
7-9
AND, IN A HOUSE NOT FAR AWAY, A GIRL KEEPS A CONSTANT VIGIL AT JOHNNY'S SIDE!
FRANK ROBBINS
W-WHERE... AM...I...
AH, YOU OPEN YOUR EYES! GOOD, SIGNORE...GOOD! IT WILL TAKE TIME... BUT NOW YOU WILL RECOVER!

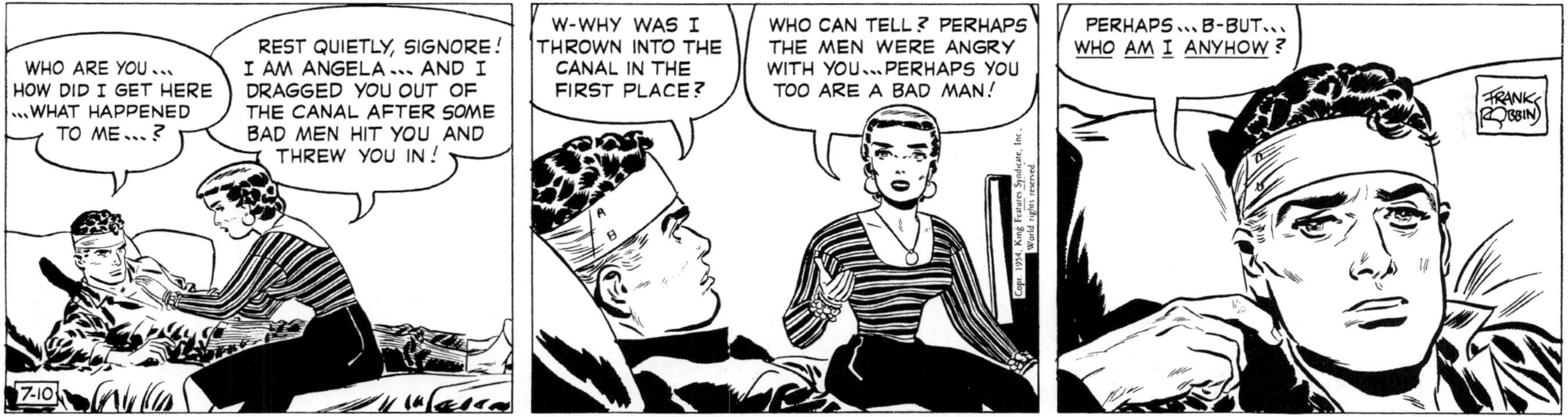
WHO ARE YOU... HOW DID I GET HERE ...WHAT HAPPENED TO ME...?
REST QUIETLY, SIGNORE! I AM ANGELA... AND I DRAGGED YOU OUT OF THE CANAL AFTER SOME BAD MEN HIT YOU AND THREW YOU IN!
7-10
W-WHY WAS I THROWN INTO THE CANAL IN THE FIRST PLACE?
WHO CAN TELL? PERHAPS THE MEN WERE ANGRY WITH YOU...PERHAPS YOU TOO ARE A BAD MAN!
Copr. 1954, King Features Syndicate, Inc., World rights reserved.
PERHAPS... B-BUT... WHO AM I ANYHOW?
FRANK ROBBINS

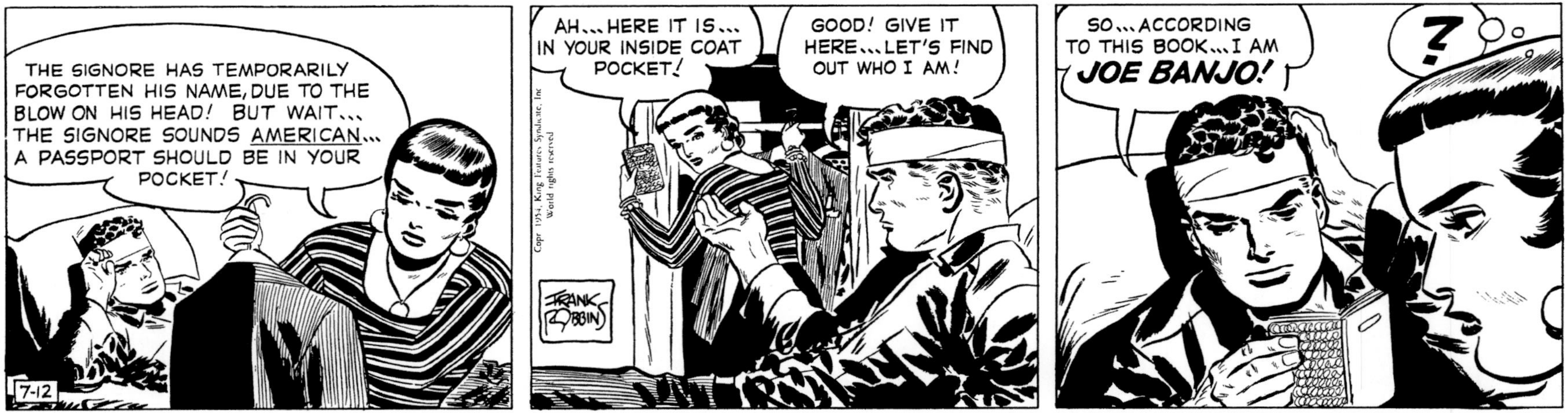
THE SIGNORE HAS TEMPORARILY FORGOTTEN HIS NAME, DUE TO THE BLOW ON HIS HEAD! BUT WAIT... THE SIGNORE SOUNDS AMERICAN... A PASSPORT SHOULD BE IN YOUR POCKET!
7-12
AH... HERE IT IS... IN YOUR INSIDE COAT POCKET!
GOOD! GIVE IT HERE... LET'S FIND OUT WHO I AM!
Copr 1954, King Features Syndicate, Inc World rights reserved
FRANK ROBBINS
SO... ACCORDING TO THIS BOOK... I AM JOE BANJO!
?

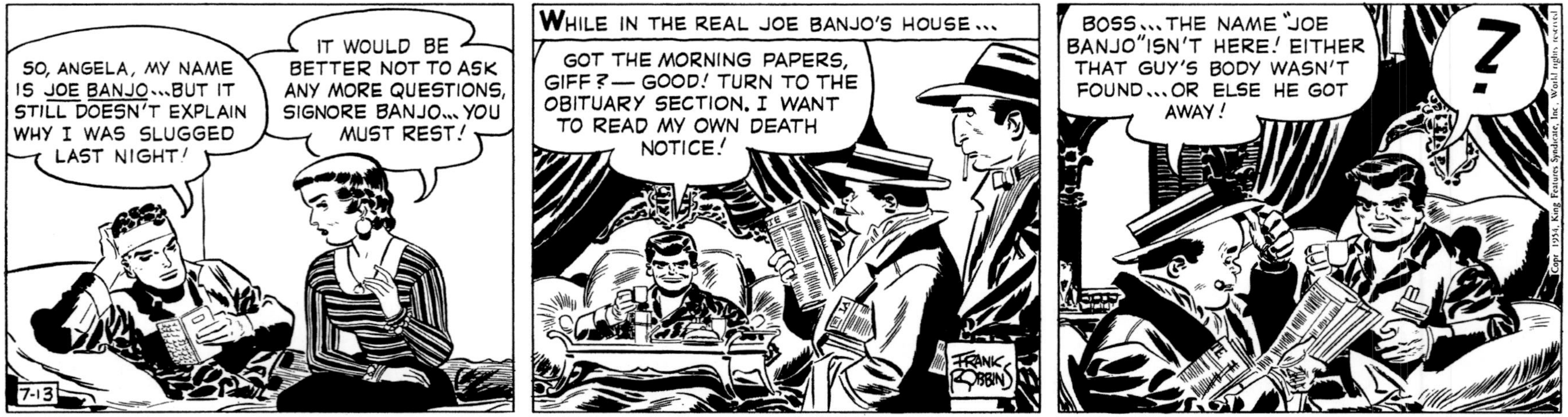
SO, ANGELA, MY NAME IS JOE BANJO... BUT IT STILL DOESN'T EXPLAIN WHY I WAS SLUGGED LAST NIGHT!
IT WOULD BE BETTER NOT TO ASK ANY MORE QUESTIONS, SIGNORE BANJO... YOU MUST REST!
7-13
WHILE IN THE REAL JOE BANJO'S HOUSE...
GOT THE MORNING PAPERS, GIFF? — GOOD! TURN TO THE OBITUARY SECTION. I WANT TO READ MY OWN DEATH NOTICE!
FRANK ROBBINS
BOSS... THE NAME "JOE BANJO" ISN'T HERE! EITHER THAT GUY'S BODY WASN'T FOUND... OR ELSE HE GOT AWAY!
?
Copr 1954, King Features Syndicate, Inc, World rights reserved

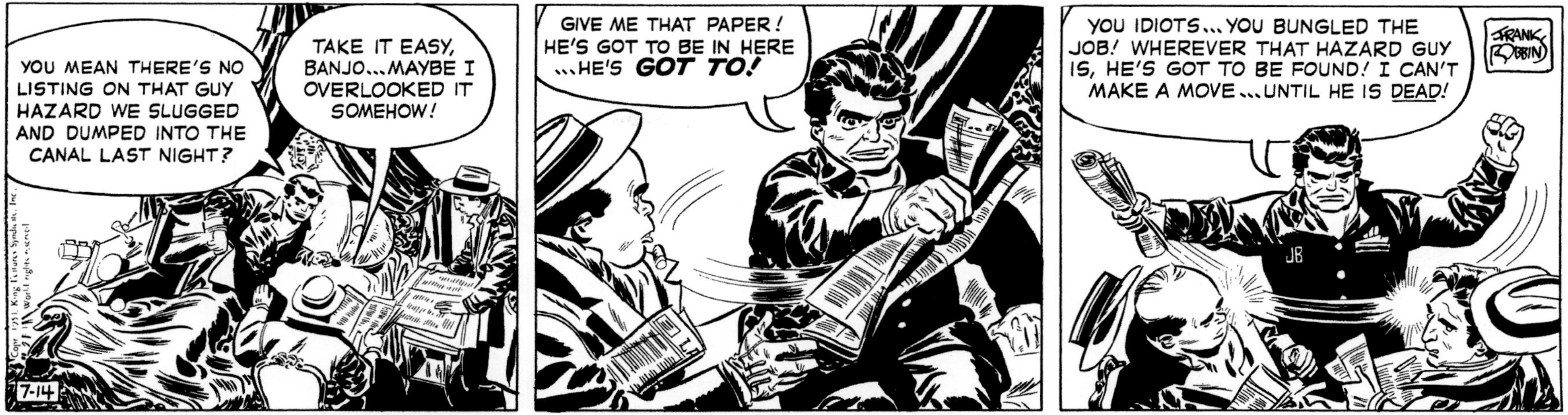
YOU MEAN THERE'S NO LISTING ON THAT GUY HAZARD WE SLUGGED AND DUMPED INTO THE CANAL LAST NIGHT?
TAKE IT EASY, BANJO... MAYBE I OVERLOOKED IT SOMEHOW!
7-14
GIVE ME THAT PAPER! HE'S GOT TO BE IN HERE ...HE'S **GOT TO!**
YOU IDIOTS... YOU BUNGLED THE JOB! WHEREVER THAT HAZARD GUY IS, HE'S GOT TO BE FOUND! I CAN'T MAKE A MOVE... UNTIL HE IS DEAD!
FRANK ROBBINS
JB

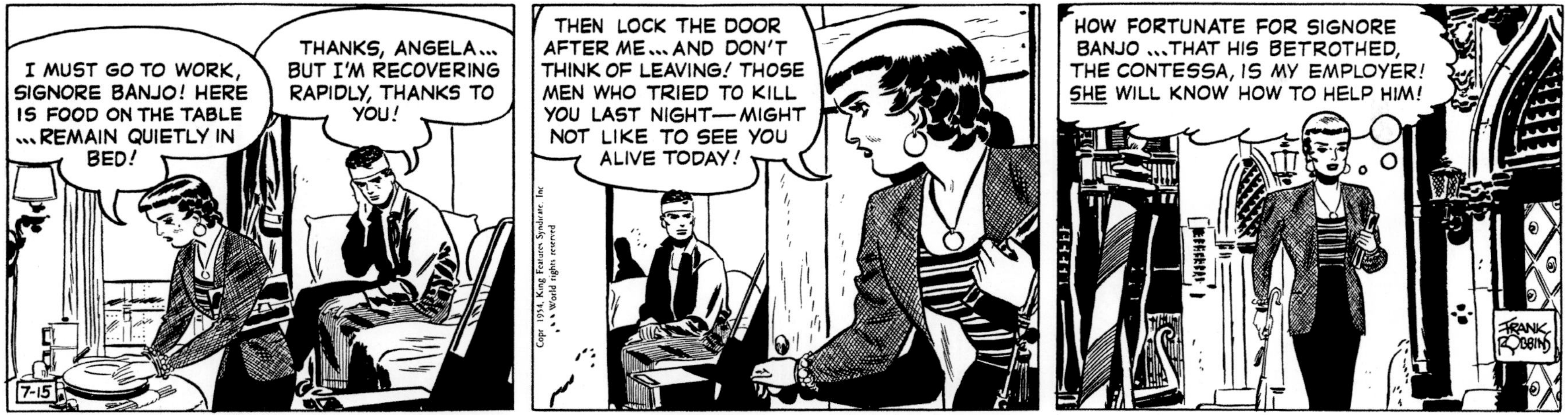
I MUST GO TO WORK, SIGNORE BANJO! HERE IS FOOD ON THE TABLE ...REMAIN QUIETLY IN BED!
THANKS, ANGELA... BUT I'M RECOVERING RAPIDLY, THANKS TO YOU!
7-15
THEN LOCK THE DOOR AFTER ME... AND DON'T THINK OF LEAVING! THOSE MEN WHO TRIED TO KILL YOU LAST NIGHT—MIGHT NOT LIKE TO SEE YOU ALIVE TODAY!
Copr 1954, King Features Syndicate, Inc World rights reserved
HOW FORTUNATE FOR SIGNORE BANJO ...THAT HIS BETROTHED, THE CONTESSA, IS MY EMPLOYER! SHE WILL KNOW HOW TO HELP HIM!
FRANK ROBBINS

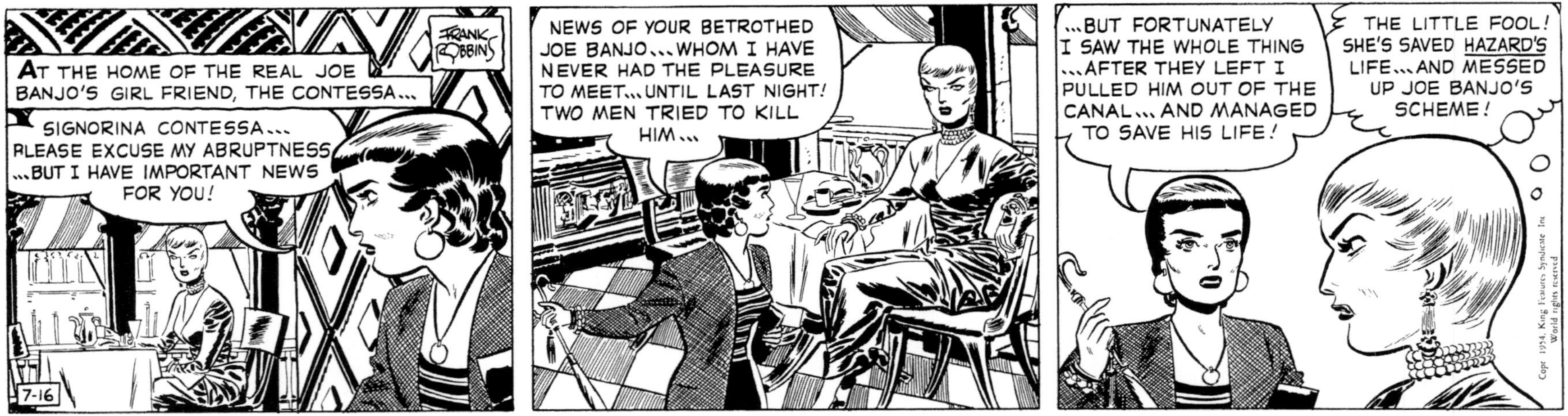
FRANK ROBBINS
AT THE HOME OF THE REAL JOE BANJO'S GIRL FRIEND, THE CONTESSA...
SIGNORINA CONTESSA... PLEASE EXCUSE MY ABRUPTNESS ...BUT I HAVE IMPORTANT NEWS FOR YOU!
7-16
NEWS OF YOUR BETROTHED JOE BANJO... WHOM I HAVE NEVER HAD THE PLEASURE TO MEET... UNTIL LAST NIGHT! TWO MEN TRIED TO KILL HIM...
...BUT FORTUNATELY I SAW THE WHOLE THING ...AFTER THEY LEFT I PULLED HIM OUT OF THE CANAL... AND MANAGED TO SAVE HIS LIFE!
THE LITTLE FOOL! SHE'S SAVED HAZARD'S LIFE...AND MESSED UP JOE BANJO'S SCHEME!
Copr 1954, King Features Syndicate, Inc World rights reserved

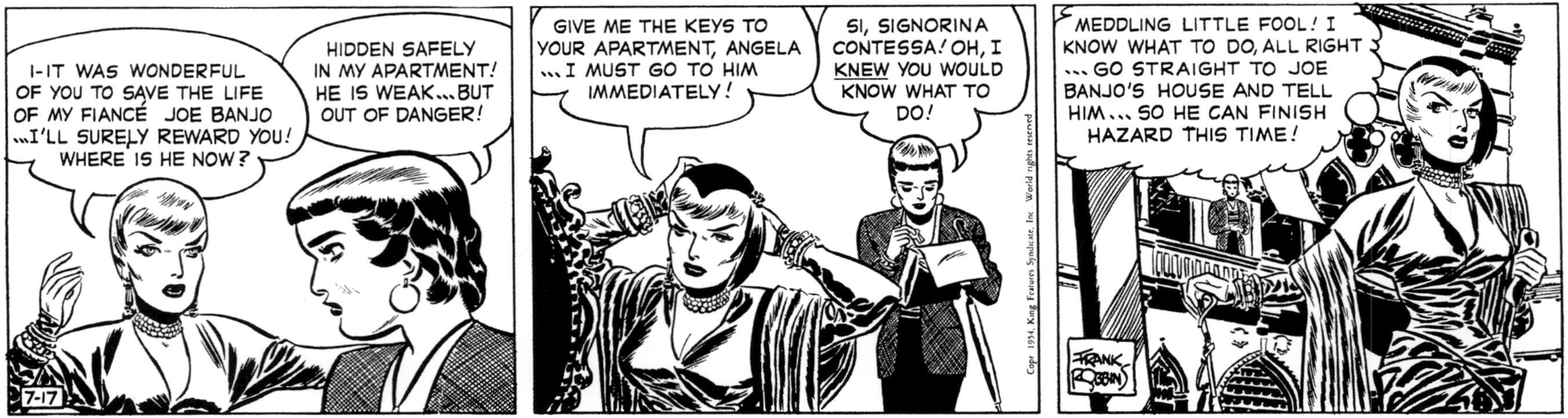
I-IT WAS WONDERFUL OF YOU TO SAVE THE LIFE OF MY FIANCÉ JOE BANJO ...I'LL SURELY REWARD YOU! WHERE IS HE NOW?
HIDDEN SAFELY IN MY APARTMENT! HE IS WEAK...BUT OUT OF DANGER!
7-17
GIVE ME THE KEYS TO YOUR APARTMENT, ANGELA ...I MUST GO TO HIM IMMEDIATELY!
SI, SIGNORINA CONTESSA! OH, I KNEW YOU WOULD KNOW WHAT TO DO!
Copr 1954, King Features Syndicate, Inc World rights reserved
MEDDLING LITTLE FOOL! I KNOW WHAT TO DO, ALL RIGHT ...GO STRAIGHT TO JOE BANJO'S HOUSE AND TELL HIM... SO HE CAN FINISH HAZARD THIS TIME!
FRANK ROBBINS

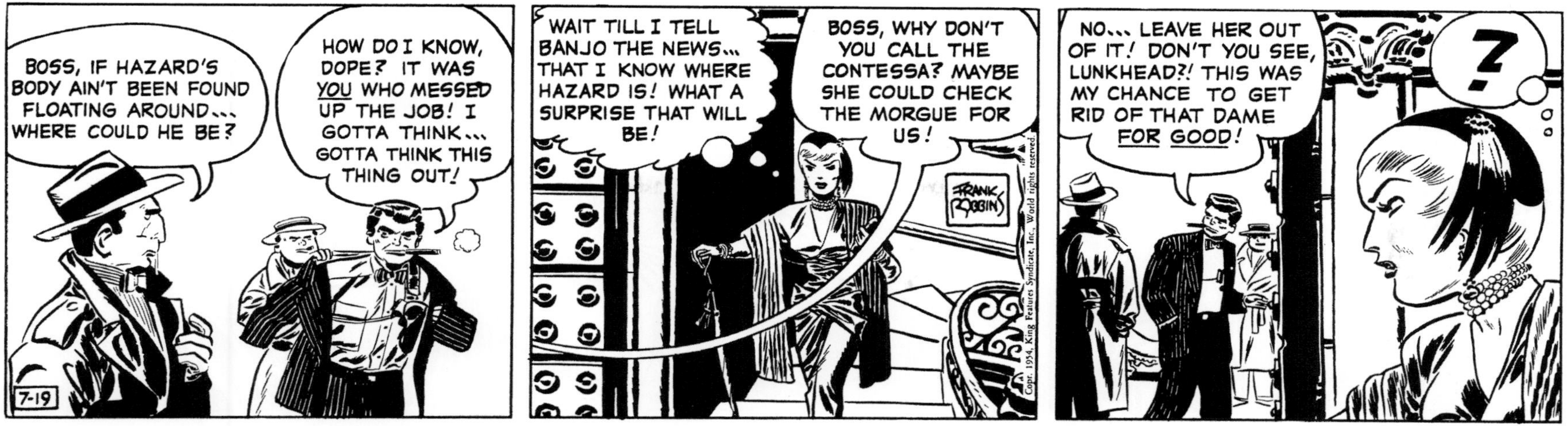
BOSS, IF HAZARD'S BODY AIN'T BEEN FOUND FLOATING AROUND... WHERE COULD HE BE?
HOW DO I KNOW, DOPE? IT WAS YOU WHO MESSED UP THE JOB! I GOTTA THINK... GOTTA THINK THIS THING OUT!
7-19
WAIT TILL I TELL BANJO THE NEWS... THAT I KNOW WHERE HAZARD IS! WHAT A SURPRISE THAT WILL BE!
BOSS, WHY DON'T YOU CALL THE CONTESSA? MAYBE SHE COULD CHECK THE MORGUE FOR US!
FRANK ROBBINS
Copr. 1954, King Features Syndicate, Inc., World rights reserved.
NO... LEAVE HER OUT OF IT! DON'T YOU SEE, LUNKHEAD?! THIS WAS MY CHANCE TO GET RID OF THAT DAME FOR GOOD!
?

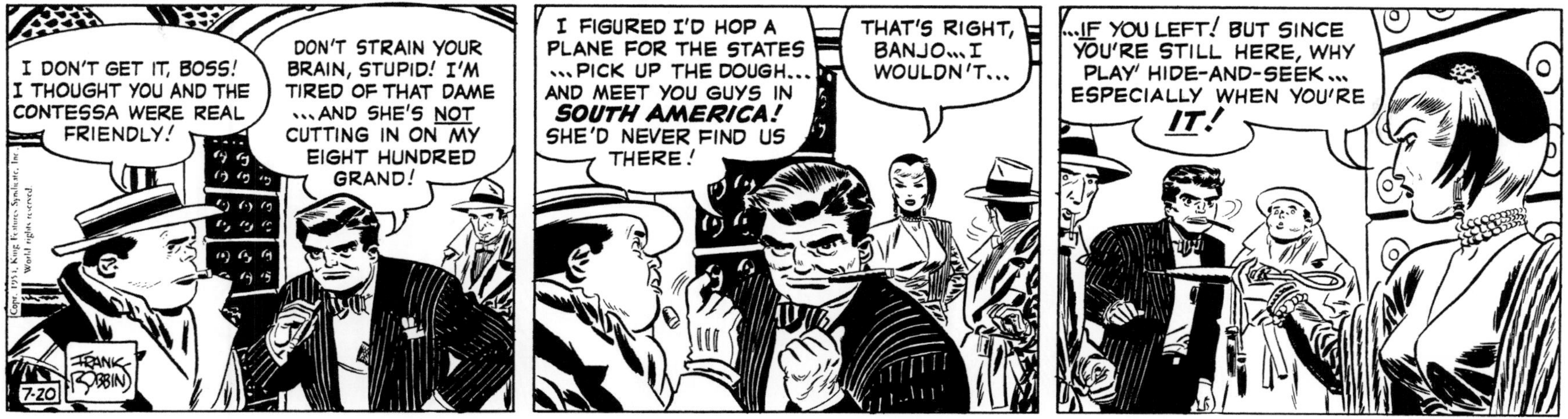
I DON'T GET IT, BOSS! I THOUGHT YOU AND THE CONTESSA WERE REAL FRIENDLY!
DON'T STRAIN YOUR BRAIN, STUPID! I'M TIRED OF THAT DAME ...AND SHE'S NOT CUTTING IN ON MY EIGHT HUNDRED GRAND!
Copr. 1954, King Features Syndicate, Inc. World rights reserved.
FRANK ROBBINS
7-20
I FIGURED I'D HOP A PLANE FOR THE STATES ...PICK UP THE DOUGH... AND MEET YOU GUYS IN SOUTH AMERICA! SHE'D NEVER FIND US THERE!
THAT'S RIGHT, BANJO... I WOULDN'T...
...IF YOU LEFT! BUT SINCE YOU'RE STILL HERE, WHY PLAY HIDE-AND-SEEK... ESPECIALLY WHEN YOU'RE IT!

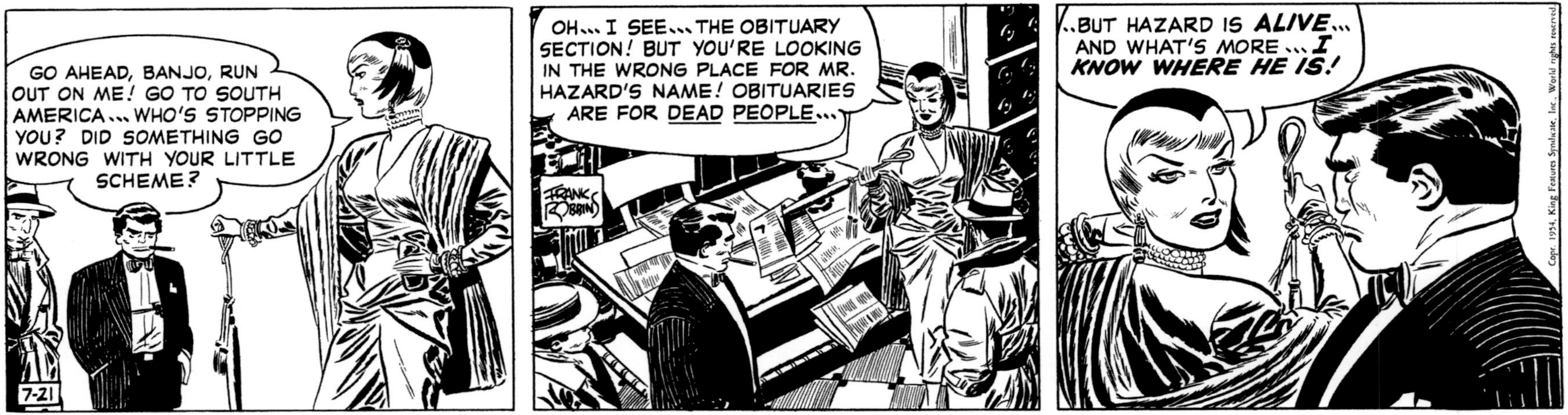
GO AHEAD, BANJO, RUN OUT ON ME! GO TO SOUTH AMERICA ... WHO'S STOPPING YOU? DID SOMETHING GO WRONG WITH YOUR LITTLE SCHEME?
7-21
OH... I SEE... THE OBITUARY SECTION! BUT YOU'RE LOOKING IN THE WRONG PLACE FOR MR. HAZARD'S NAME! OBITUARIES ARE FOR DEAD PEOPLE...
FRANK ROBBINS
..BUT HAZARD IS ALIVE... AND WHAT'S MORE ... I KNOW WHERE HE IS!
Copr. 1954, King Features Syndicate, Inc., World rights reserved

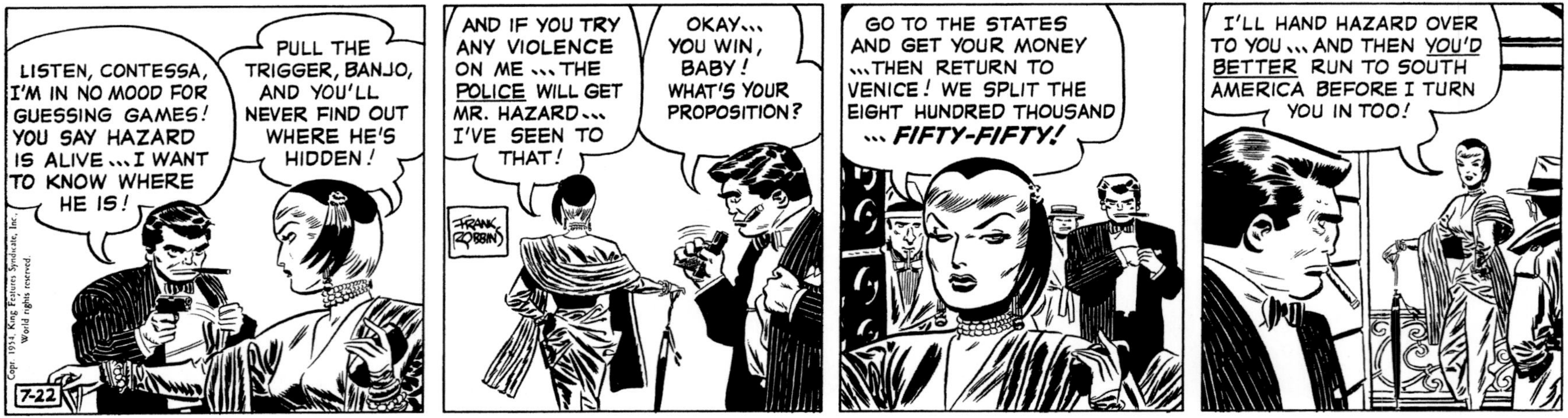
LISTEN, CONTESSA, I'M IN NO MOOD FOR GUESSING GAMES! YOU SAY HAZARD IS ALIVE ... I WANT TO KNOW WHERE HE IS!
PULL THE TRIGGER, BANJO, AND YOU'LL NEVER FIND OUT WHERE HE'S HIDDEN!
Copr. 1954, King Features Syndicate, Inc. World rights reserved.
7-22
AND IF YOU TRY ANY VIOLENCE ON ME ... THE POLICE WILL GET MR. HAZARD... I'VE SEEN TO THAT!
OKAY... YOU WIN, BABY! WHAT'S YOUR PROPOSITION?
FRANK ROBBINS
GO TO THE STATES AND GET YOUR MONEY ...THEN RETURN TO VENICE! WE SPLIT THE EIGHT HUNDRED THOUSAND ... FIFTY-FIFTY!
I'LL HAND HAZARD OVER TO YOU ... AND THEN YOU'D BETTER RUN TO SOUTH AMERICA BEFORE I TURN YOU IN TOO!

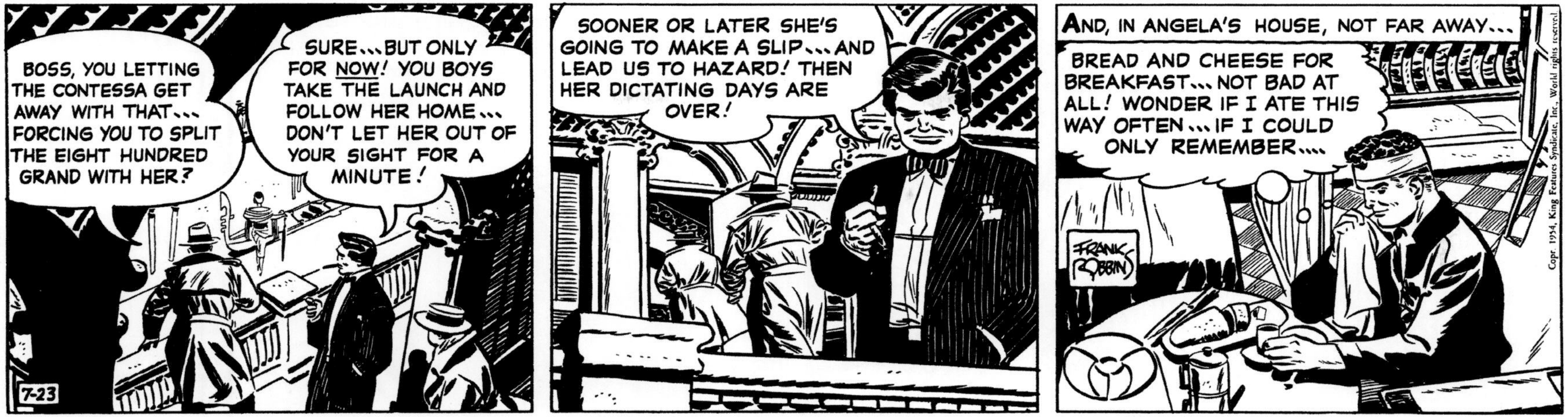
BOSS, YOU LETTING THE CONTESSA GET AWAY WITH THAT... FORCING YOU TO SPLIT THE EIGHT HUNDRED GRAND WITH HER?
SURE...BUT ONLY FOR NOW! YOU BOYS TAKE THE LAUNCH AND FOLLOW HER HOME... DON'T LET HER OUT OF YOUR SIGHT FOR A MINUTE!
7-23
SOONER OR LATER SHE'S GOING TO MAKE A SLIP... AND LEAD US TO HAZARD! THEN HER DICTATING DAYS ARE OVER!
AND, IN ANGELA'S HOUSE, NOT FAR AWAY...
BREAD AND CHEESE FOR BREAKFAST... NOT BAD AT ALL! WONDER IF I ATE THIS WAY OFTEN... IF I COULD ONLY REMEMBER....
FRANK ROBBIN
Copr. 1954, King Features Syndicate, Inc., World rights reserved.

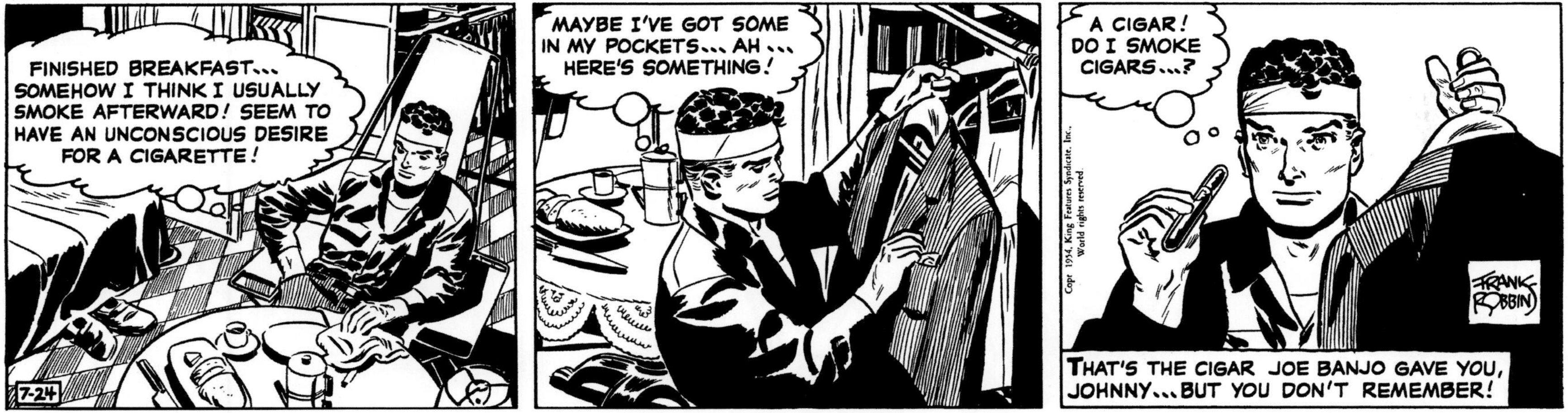
FINISHED BREAKFAST... SOMEHOW I THINK I USUALLY SMOKE AFTERWARD! SEEM TO HAVE AN UNCONSCIOUS DESIRE FOR A CIGARETTE!
7-24
MAYBE I'VE GOT SOME IN MY POCKETS... AH ... HERE'S SOMETHING!
Copr 1954, King Features Syndicate, Inc., World rights reserved.
A CIGAR! DO I SMOKE CIGARS...?
FRANK ROBBIN
THAT'S THE CIGAR JOE BANJO GAVE YOU, JOHNNY...BUT YOU DON'T REMEMBER!

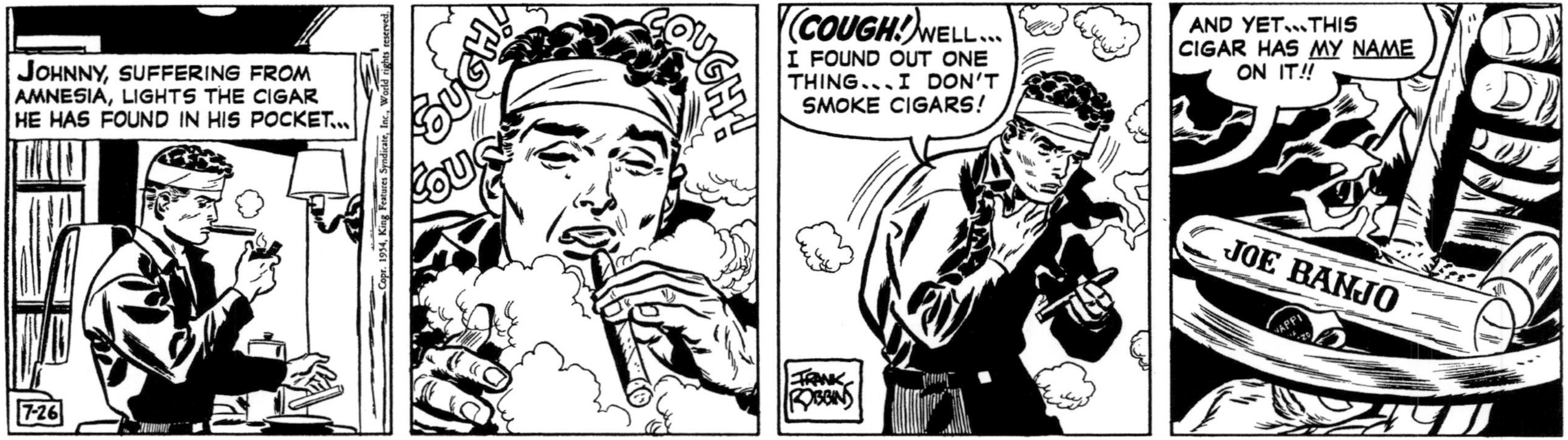
JOHNNY, SUFFERING FROM AMNESIA, LIGHTS THE CIGAR HE HAS FOUND IN HIS POCKET...
Copr. 1954, King Features Syndicate, Inc., World rights reserved.
7-26
COUGH! COUGH! COUGH!
(COUGH!) WELL... I FOUND OUT ONE THING... I DON'T SMOKE CIGARS!
FRANK ROBBINS
AND YET...THIS CIGAR HAS MY NAME ON IT!!
JOE BANJO

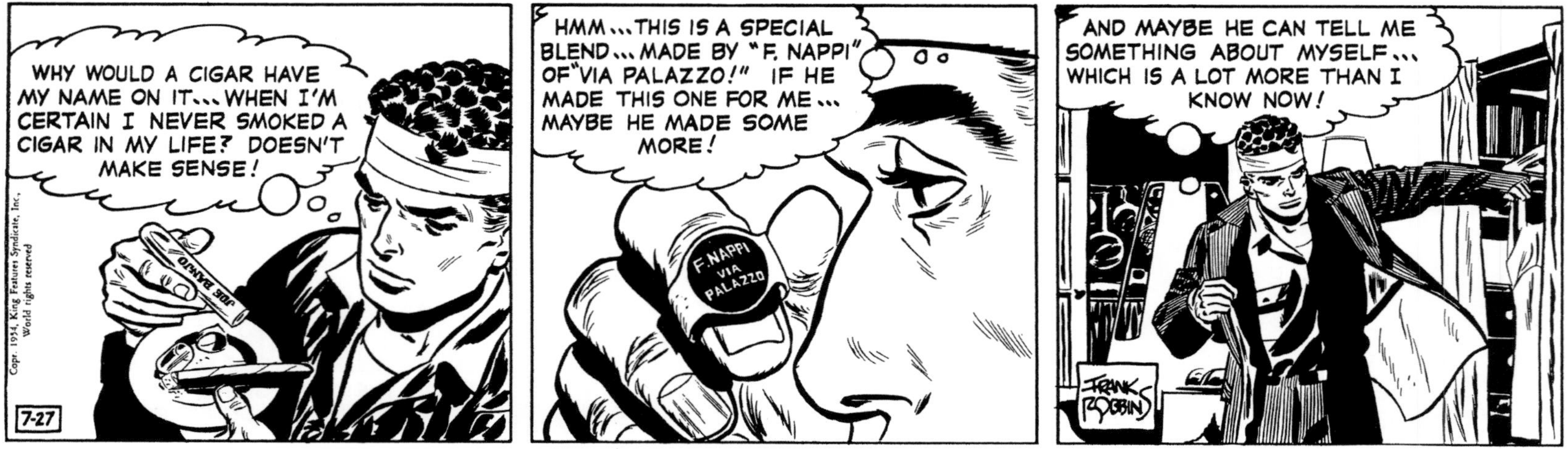
WHY WOULD A CIGAR HAVE MY NAME ON IT...WHEN I'M CERTAIN I NEVER SMOKED A CIGAR IN MY LIFE? DOESN'T MAKE SENSE!
JOE BANJO
Copr. 1954, King Features Syndicate, Inc., World rights reserved
7-27
HMM...THIS IS A SPECIAL BLEND...MADE BY "F. NAPPI" OF "VIA PALAZZO!" IF HE MADE THIS ONE FOR ME... MAYBE HE MADE SOME MORE!
F. NAPPI VIA PALAZZO
AND MAYBE HE CAN TELL ME SOMETHING ABOUT MYSELF... WHICH IS A LOT MORE THAN I KNOW NOW!
FRANK ROBBINS

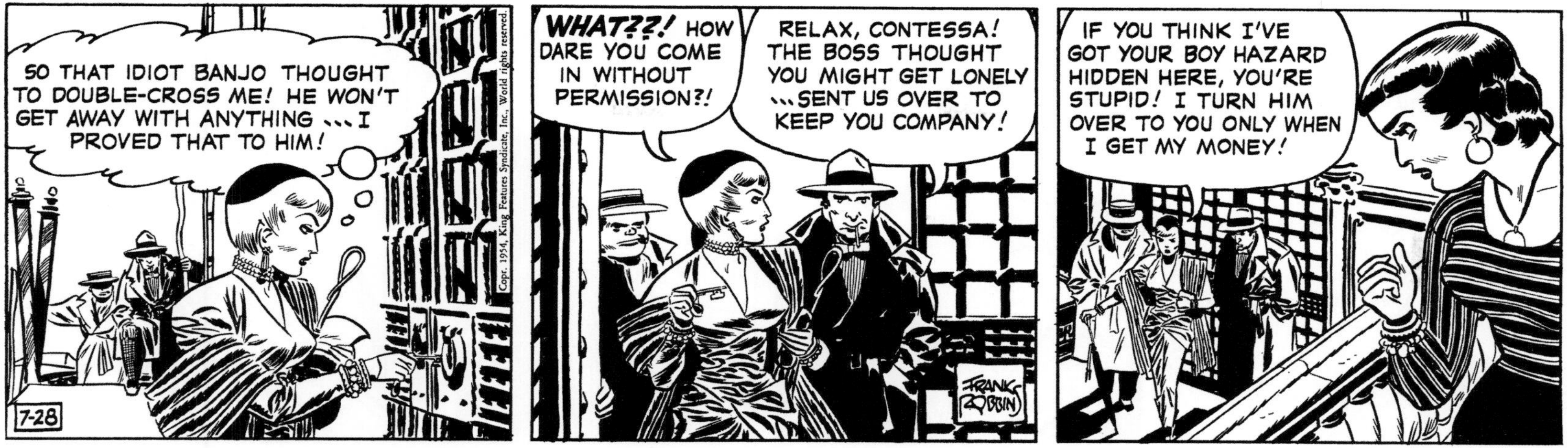
SO THAT IDIOT BANJO THOUGHT TO DOUBLE-CROSS ME! HE WON'T GET AWAY WITH ANYTHING ... I PROVED THAT TO HIM!
7-28
Copr. 1954, King Features Syndicate, Inc., World rights reserved.
WHAT??! HOW DARE YOU COME IN WITHOUT PERMISSION?!
RELAX, CONTESSA! THE BOSS THOUGHT YOU MIGHT GET LONELY ... SENT US OVER TO KEEP YOU COMPANY!
FRANK ROBBINS
IF YOU THINK I'VE GOT YOUR BOY HAZARD HIDDEN HERE, YOU'RE STUPID! I TURN HIM OVER TO YOU ONLY WHEN I GET MY MONEY!

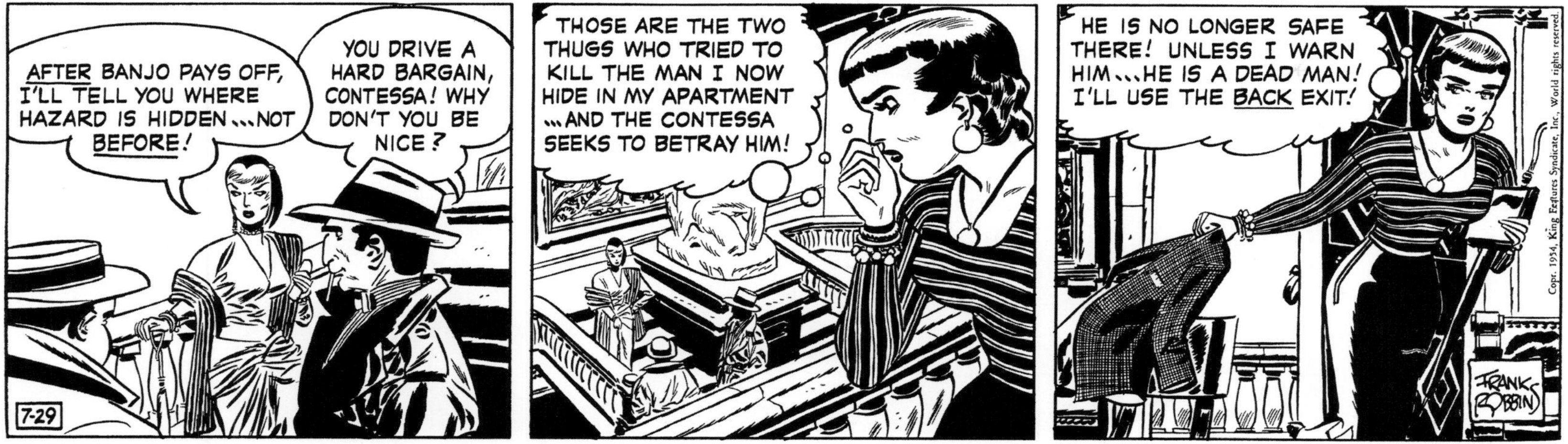
AFTER BANJO PAYS OFF, I'LL TELL YOU WHERE HAZARD IS HIDDEN ... NOT BEFORE!
YOU DRIVE A HARD BARGAIN, CONTESSA! WHY DON'T YOU BE NICE?
7-29
THOSE ARE THE TWO THUGS WHO TRIED TO KILL THE MAN I NOW HIDE IN MY APARTMENT ... AND THE CONTESSA SEEKS TO BETRAY HIM!
HE IS NO LONGER SAFE THERE! UNLESS I WARN HIM ... HE IS A DEAD MAN! I'LL USE THE BACK EXIT!
Copr. 1954, King Features Syndicate, Inc., World rights reserved.
FRANK ROBBINS

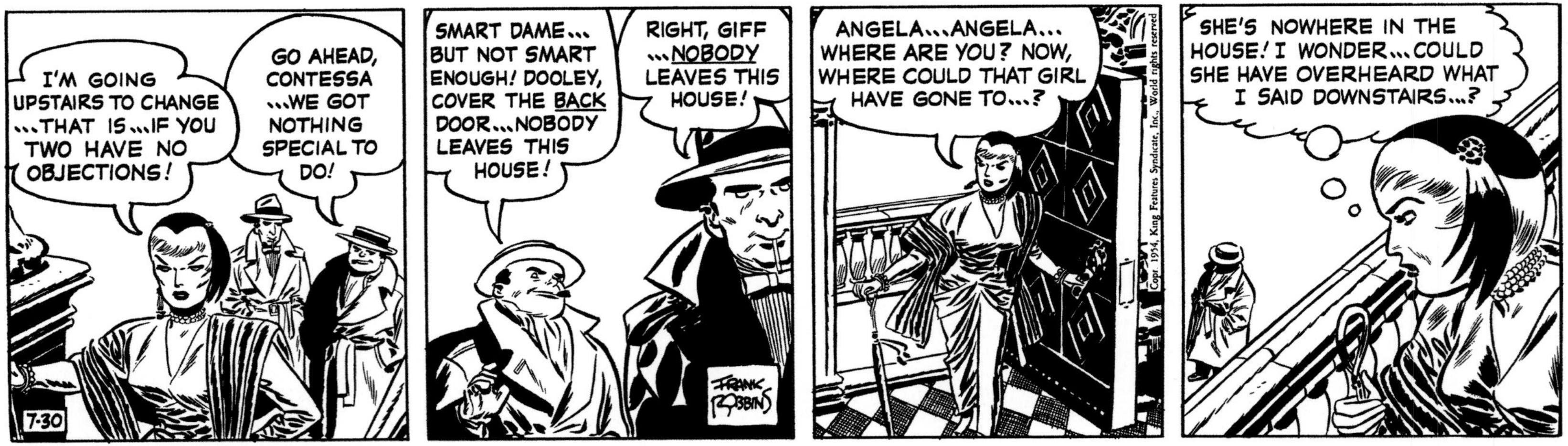
7·30
I'M GOING UPSTAIRS TO CHANGE ...THAT IS...IF YOU TWO HAVE NO OBJECTIONS!
GO AHEAD, CONTESSA ...WE GOT NOTHING SPECIAL TO DO!
SMART DAME... BUT NOT SMART ENOUGH! DOOLEY, COVER THE BACK DOOR...NOBODY LEAVES THIS HOUSE!
RIGHT, GIFF ...NOBODY LEAVES THIS HOUSE!
FRANK ROBBINS
ANGELA...ANGELA... WHERE ARE YOU? NOW, WHERE COULD THAT GIRL HAVE GONE TO...?
Copr. 1954, King Features Syndicate, Inc., World rights reserved
SHE'S NOWHERE IN THE HOUSE! I WONDER...COULD SHE HAVE OVERHEARD WHAT I SAID DOWNSTAIRS...?

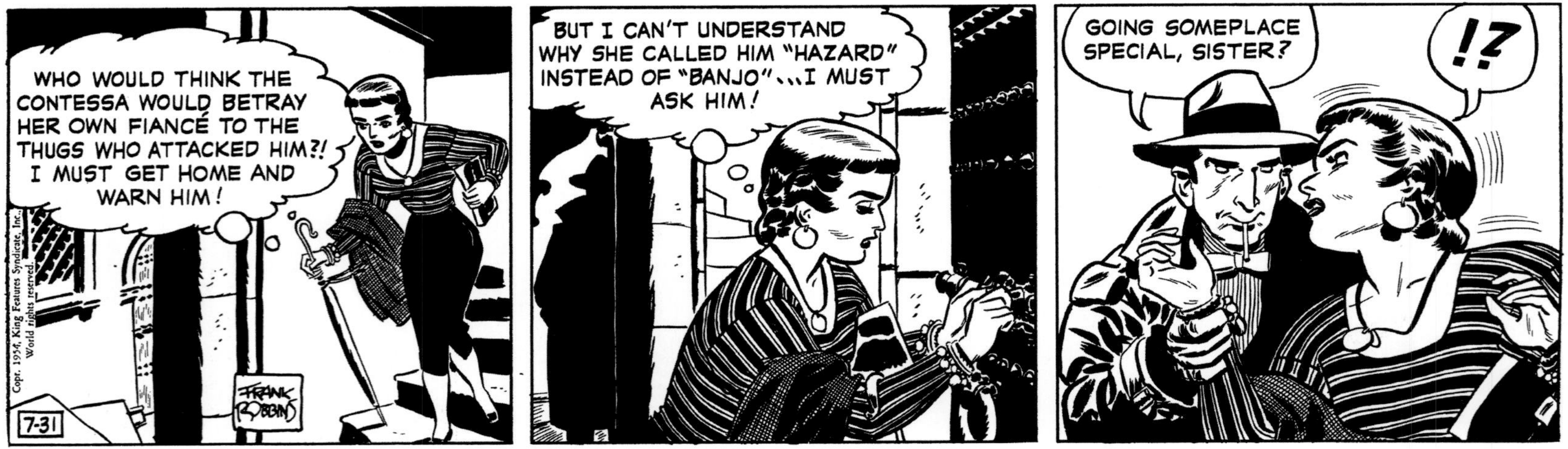
WHO WOULD THINK THE CONTESSA WOULD BETRAY HER OWN FIANCÉ TO THE THUGS WHO ATTACKED HIM?! I MUST GET HOME AND WARN HIM!
Copr. 1954, King Features Syndicate, Inc., World rights reserved.
FRANK ROBBINS
7·31
BUT I CAN'T UNDERSTAND WHY SHE CALLED HIM "HAZARD" INSTEAD OF "BANJO"...I MUST ASK HIM!
GOING SOMEPLACE SPECIAL, SISTER?
!?

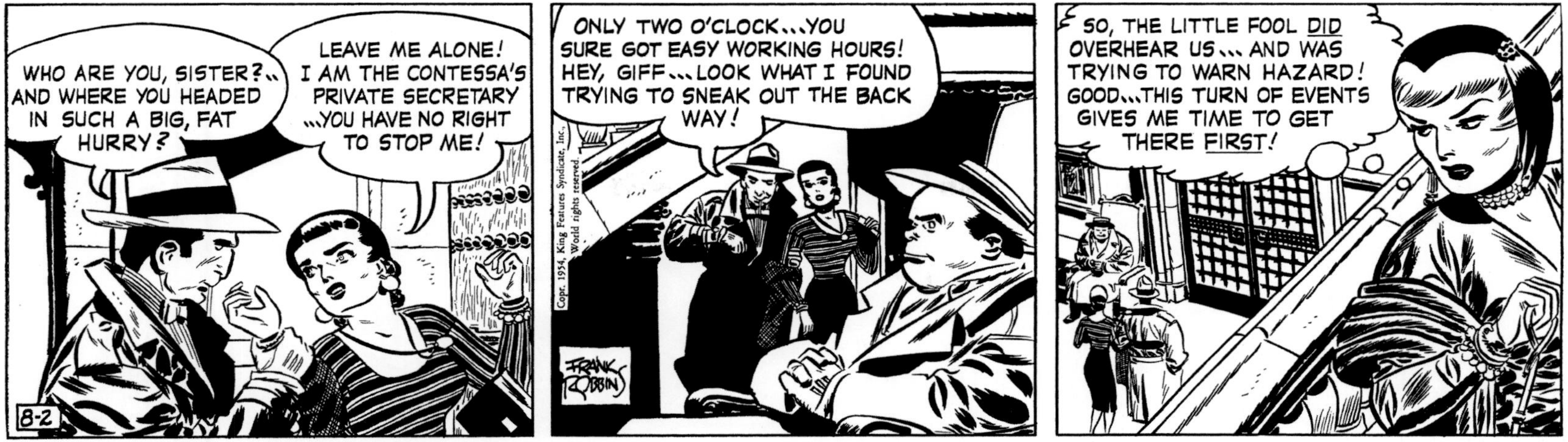
WHO ARE YOU, SISTER?.. AND WHERE YOU HEADED IN SUCH A BIG, FAT HURRY?
LEAVE ME ALONE! I AM THE CONTESSA'S PRIVATE SECRETARY ...YOU HAVE NO RIGHT TO STOP ME!
8-2
ONLY TWO O'CLOCK...YOU SURE GOT EASY WORKING HOURS! HEY, GIFF...LOOK WHAT I FOUND TRYING TO SNEAK OUT THE BACK WAY!
Copr. 1954, King Features Syndicate, Inc., World rights reserved.
FRANK ROBBINS
SO, THE LITTLE FOOL DID OVERHEAR US... AND WAS TRYING TO WARN HAZARD! GOOD...THIS TURN OF EVENTS GIVES ME TIME TO GET THERE FIRST!

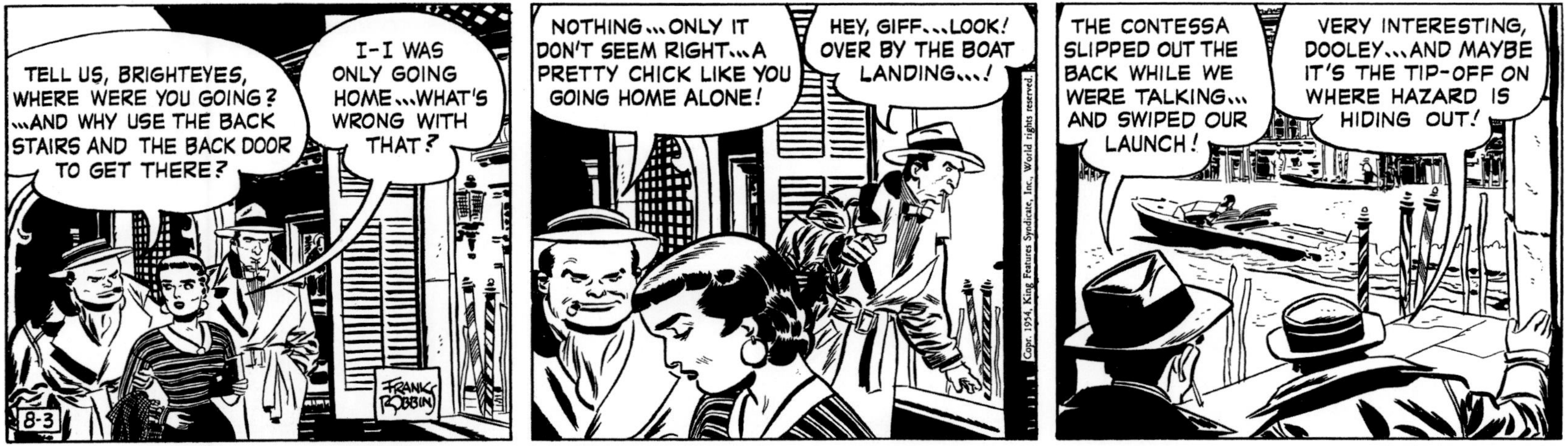
TELL US, BRIGHTEYES, WHERE WERE YOU GOING? ...AND WHY USE THE BACK STAIRS AND THE BACK DOOR TO GET THERE?
I-I WAS ONLY GOING HOME...WHAT'S WRONG WITH THAT?
8-3
FRANK ROBBINS
NOTHING...ONLY IT DON'T SEEM RIGHT...A PRETTY CHICK LIKE YOU GOING HOME ALONE!
HEY, GIFF...LOOK! OVER BY THE BOAT LANDING...!
Copr. 1954, King Features Syndicate, Inc., World rights reserved.
THE CONTESSA SLIPPED OUT THE BACK WHILE WE WERE TALKING... AND SWIPED OUR LAUNCH!
VERY INTERESTING, DOOLEY...AND MAYBE IT'S THE TIP-OFF ON WHERE HAZARD IS HIDING OUT!

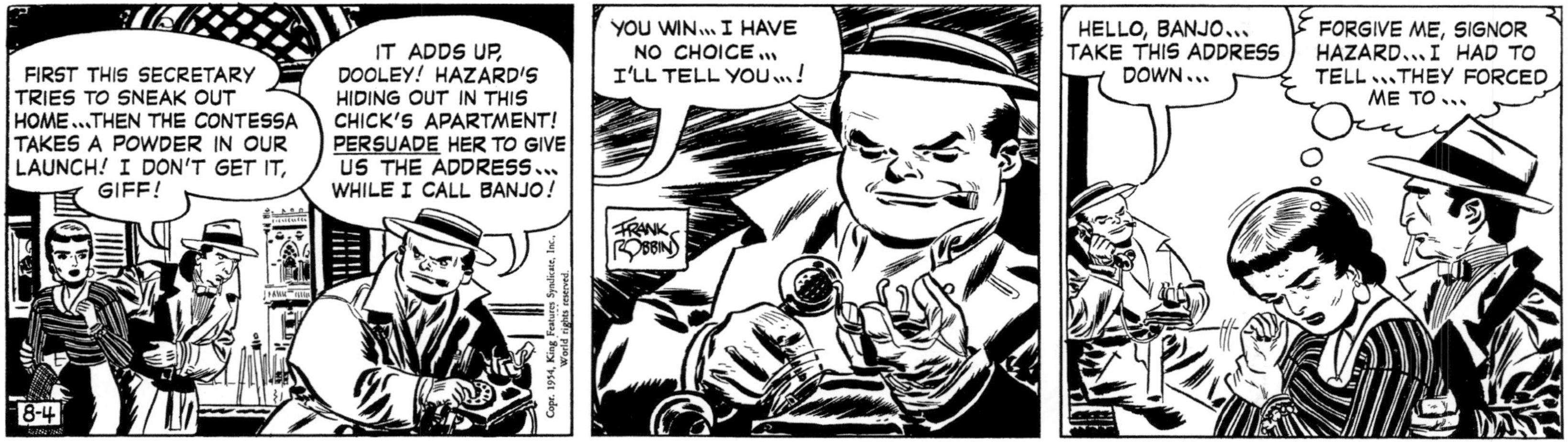

FIRST THIS SECRETARY TRIES TO SNEAK OUT HOME...THEN THE CONTESSA TAKES A POWDER IN OUR LAUNCH! I DON'T GET IT, GIFF!
IT ADDS UP, DOOLEY! HAZARD'S HIDING OUT IN THIS CHICK'S APARTMENT! PERSUADE HER TO GIVE US THE ADDRESS... WHILE I CALL BANJO!
8-4
Copr. 1954, King Features Syndicate, Inc., World rights reserved.
YOU WIN... I HAVE NO CHOICE... I'LL TELL YOU...!
FRANK ROBBINS
HELLO, BANJO... TAKE THIS ADDRESS DOWN...
FORGIVE ME, SIGNOR HAZARD... I HAD TO TELL...THEY FORCED ME TO...

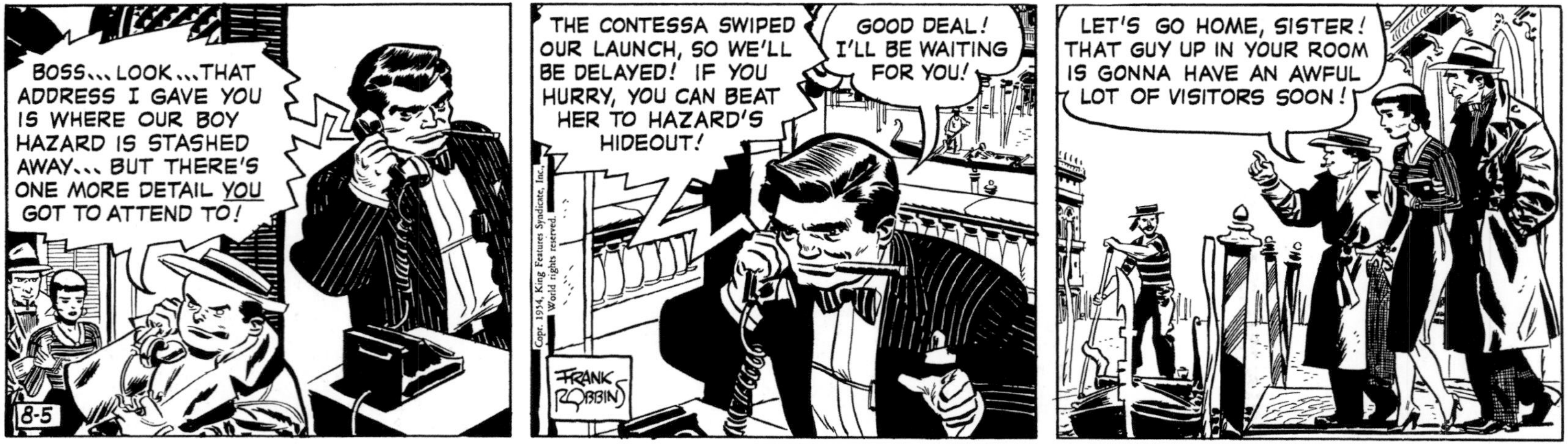

BOSS... LOOK...THAT ADDRESS I GAVE YOU IS WHERE OUR BOY HAZARD IS STASHED AWAY... BUT THERE'S ONE MORE DETAIL YOU GOT TO ATTEND TO!
8-5
THE CONTESSA SWIPED OUR LAUNCH, SO WE'LL BE DELAYED! IF YOU HURRY, YOU CAN BEAT HER TO HAZARD'S HIDEOUT!
GOOD DEAL! I'LL BE WAITING FOR YOU!
Copr. 1954, King Features Syndicate, Inc., World rights reserved.
FRANK ROBBINS
LET'S GO HOME, SISTER! THAT GUY UP IN YOUR ROOM IS GONNA HAVE AN AWFUL LOT OF VISITORS SOON!

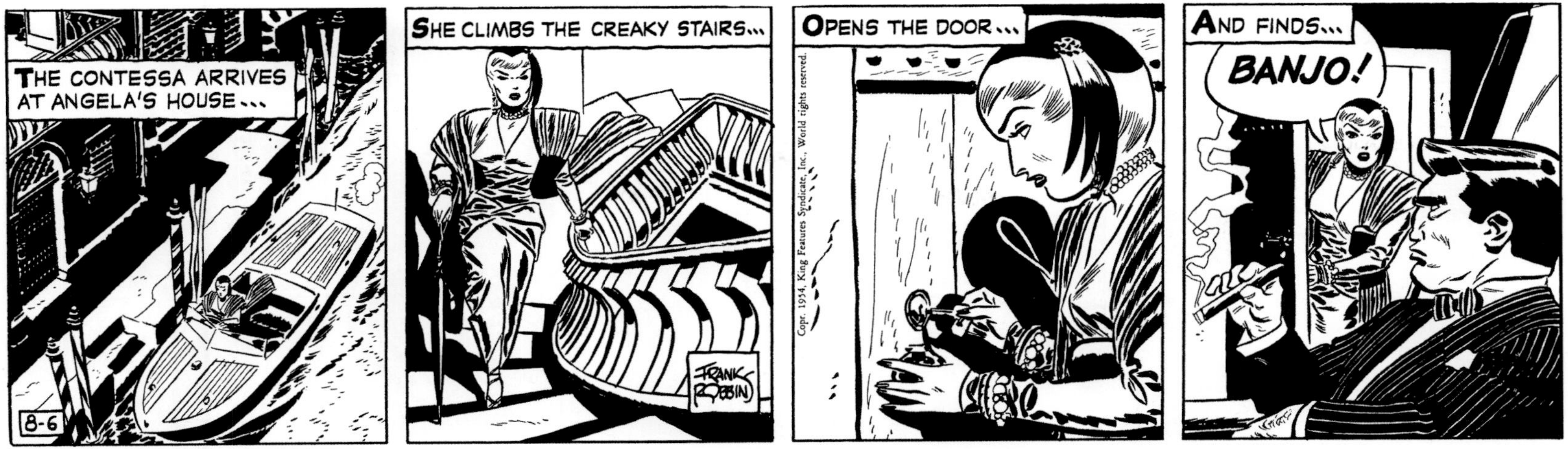
THE CONTESSA ARRIVES AT ANGELA'S HOUSE...
8-6
SHE CLIMBS THE CREAKY STAIRS...
FRANK ROBBINS
OPENS THE DOOR...
Copr. 1954, King Features Syndicate, Inc., World rights reserved.
AND FINDS...
BANJO!

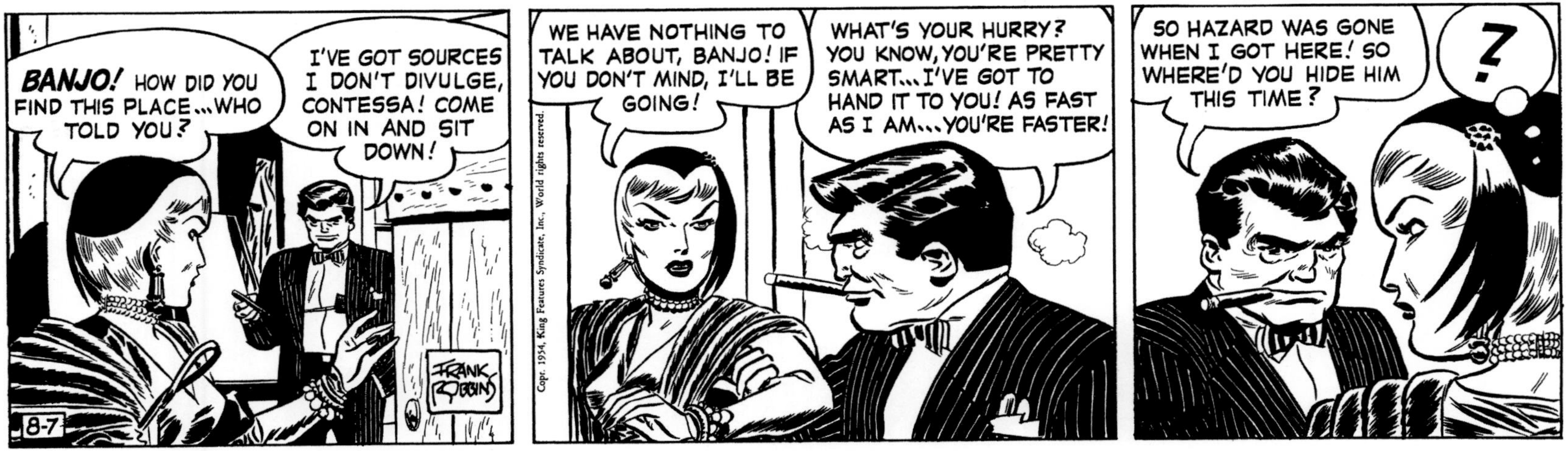
BANJO! HOW DID YOU FIND THIS PLACE...WHO TOLD YOU?
I'VE GOT SOURCES I DON'T DIVULGE, CONTESSA! COME ON IN AND SIT DOWN!
FRANK ROBBINS
8-7
Copr. 1954, King Features Syndicate, Inc., World rights reserved.
WE HAVE NOTHING TO TALK ABOUT, BANJO! IF YOU DON'T MIND, I'LL BE GOING!
WHAT'S YOUR HURRY? YOU KNOW, YOU'RE PRETTY SMART...I'VE GOT TO HAND IT TO YOU! AS FAST AS I AM...YOU'RE FASTER!
SO HAZARD WAS GONE WHEN I GOT HERE! SO WHERE'D YOU HIDE HIM THIS TIME?
?

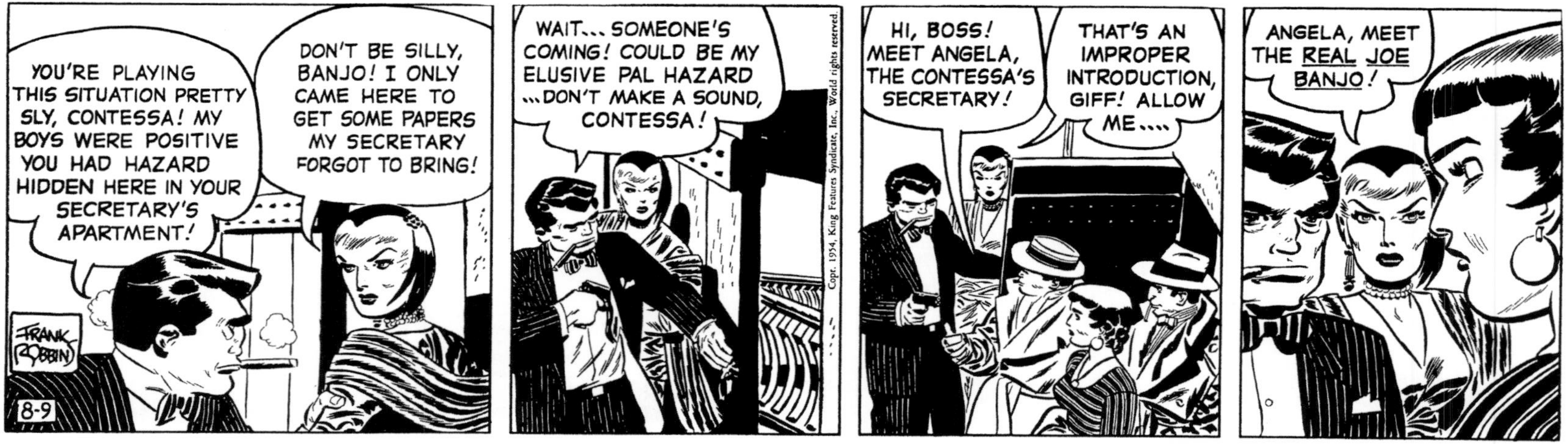
YOU'RE PLAYING THIS SITUATION PRETTY SLY, CONTESSA! MY BOYS WERE POSITIVE YOU HAD HAZARD HIDDEN HERE IN YOUR SECRETARY'S APARTMENT!
DON'T BE SILLY, BANJO! I ONLY CAME HERE TO GET SOME PAPERS MY SECRETARY FORGOT TO BRING!
FRANK ROBBINS
8-9
WAIT... SOMEONE'S COMING! COULD BE MY ELUSIVE PAL HAZARD ...DON'T MAKE A SOUND, CONTESSA!
Copr. 1954, King Features Syndicate, Inc., World rights reserved.
HI, BOSS! MEET ANGELA, THE CONTESSA'S SECRETARY!
THAT'S AN IMPROPER INTRODUCTION, GIFF! ALLOW ME....
ANGELA, MEET THE REAL JOE BANJO!

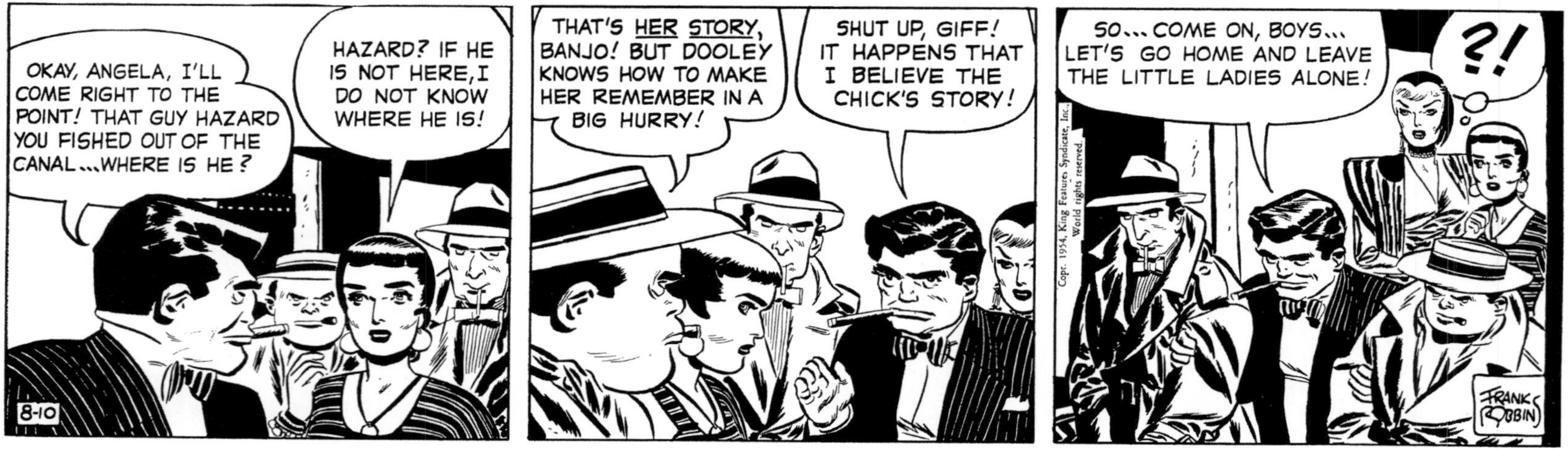
OKAY, ANGELA, I'LL COME RIGHT TO THE POINT! THAT GUY HAZARD YOU FISHED OUT OF THE CANAL...WHERE IS HE?
HAZARD? IF HE IS NOT HERE, I DO NOT KNOW WHERE HE IS!
8-10
THAT'S HER STORY, BANJO! BUT DOOLEY KNOWS HOW TO MAKE HER REMEMBER IN A BIG HURRY!
SHUT UP, GIFF! IT HAPPENS THAT I BELIEVE THE CHICK'S STORY!
Copr. 1954, King Features Syndicate, Inc., World rights reserved.
SO... COME ON, BOYS... LET'S GO HOME AND LEAVE THE LITTLE LADIES ALONE!
?!
FRANK ROBBINS

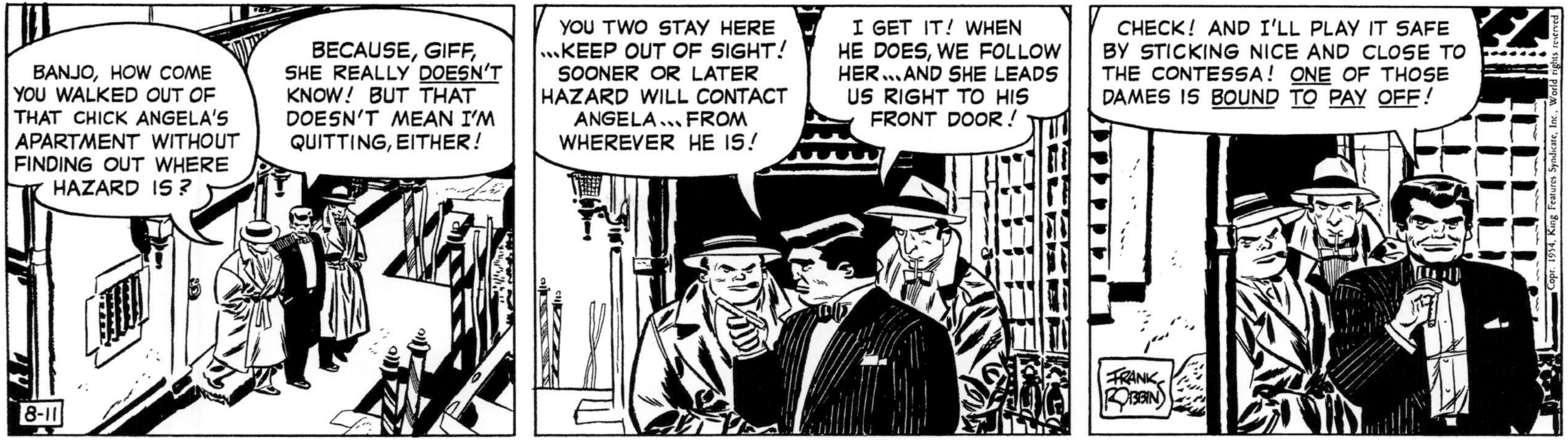
8-11
BANJO, HOW COME YOU WALKED OUT OF THAT CHICK ANGELA'S APARTMENT WITHOUT FINDING OUT WHERE HAZARD IS?
BECAUSE, GIFF, SHE REALLY DOESN'T KNOW! BUT THAT DOESN'T MEAN I'M QUITTING, EITHER!
YOU TWO STAY HERE ...KEEP OUT OF SIGHT! SOONER OR LATER HAZARD WILL CONTACT ANGELA... FROM WHEREVER HE IS!
I GET IT! WHEN HE DOES, WE FOLLOW HER...AND SHE LEADS US RIGHT TO HIS FRONT DOOR!
CHECK! AND I'LL PLAY IT SAFE BY STICKING NICE AND CLOSE TO THE CONTESSA! ONE OF THOSE DAMES IS BOUND TO PAY OFF!
FRANK ROBBINS
Copr. 1954, King Features Syndicate, Inc., World rights reserved.

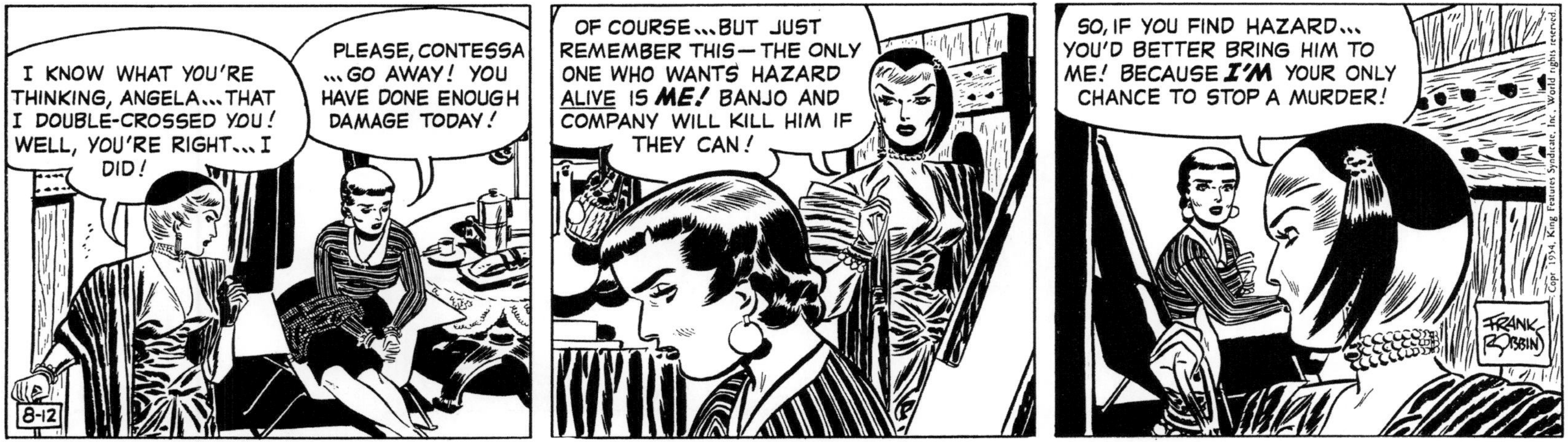
8-12
I KNOW WHAT YOU'RE THINKING, ANGELA... THAT I DOUBLE-CROSSED YOU! WELL, YOU'RE RIGHT... I DID!
PLEASE, CONTESSA ...GO AWAY! YOU HAVE DONE ENOUGH DAMAGE TODAY!
OF COURSE... BUT JUST REMEMBER THIS—THE ONLY ONE WHO WANTS HAZARD ALIVE IS ME! BANJO AND COMPANY WILL KILL HIM IF THEY CAN!
SO, IF YOU FIND HAZARD... YOU'D BETTER BRING HIM TO ME! BECAUSE I'M YOUR ONLY CHANCE TO STOP A MURDER!
FRANK ROBBINS
Copr. 1954, King Features Syndicate, Inc., World rights reserved.

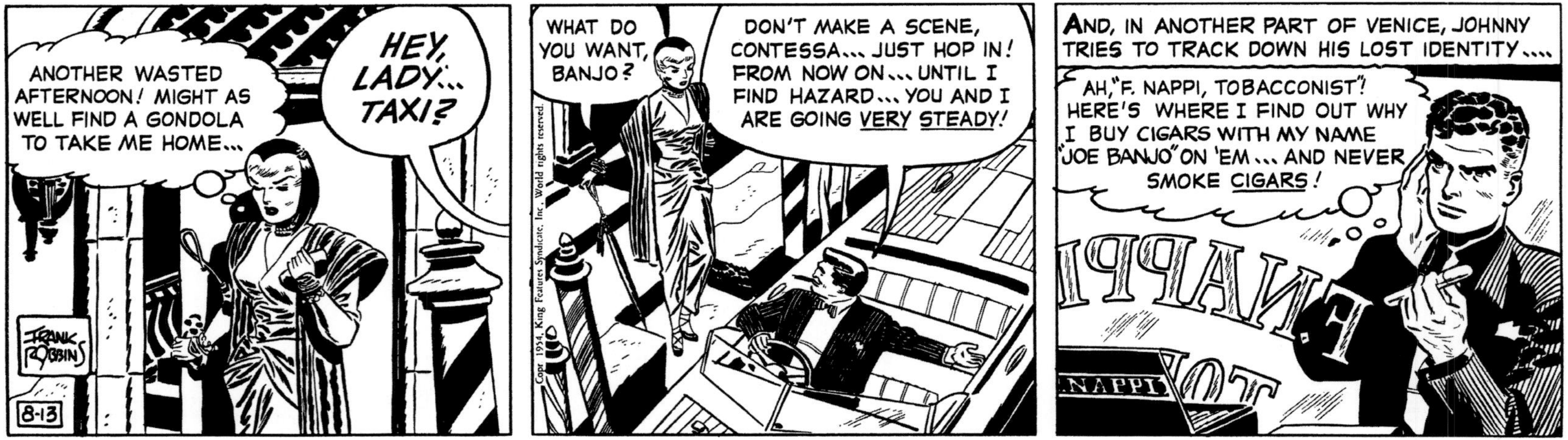
ANOTHER WASTED AFTERNOON! MIGHT AS WELL FIND A GONDOLA TO TAKE ME HOME...
HEY, LADY... TAXI?
FRANK ROBBINS
8-13
WHAT DO YOU WANT, BANJO?
DON'T MAKE A SCENE, CONTESSA... JUST HOP IN! FROM NOW ON... UNTIL I FIND HAZARD... YOU AND I ARE GOING VERY STEADY!
Copr. 1954, King Features Syndicate, Inc., World rights reserved.
AND, IN ANOTHER PART OF VENICE, JOHNNY TRIES TO TRACK DOWN HIS LOST IDENTITY....
AH, "F. NAPPI, TOBACCONIST"! HERE'S WHERE I FIND OUT WHY I BUY CIGARS WITH MY NAME "JOE BANJO" ON 'EM... AND NEVER SMOKE CIGARS!
F. NAPPI

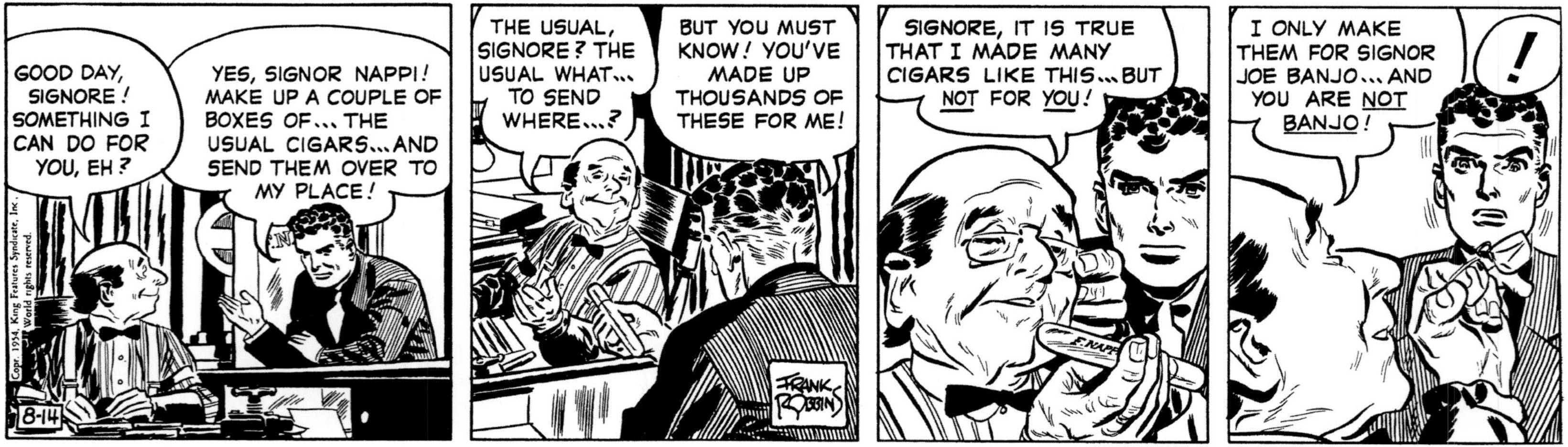
GOOD DAY, SIGNORE! SOMETHING I CAN DO FOR YOU, EH?
YES, SIGNOR NAPPI! MAKE UP A COUPLE OF BOXES OF... THE USUAL CIGARS...AND SEND THEM OVER TO MY PLACE!
Copr. 1954, King Features Syndicate, Inc., World rights reserved.
8-14
THE USUAL, SIGNORE? THE USUAL WHAT... TO SEND WHERE...?
BUT YOU MUST KNOW! YOU'VE MADE UP THOUSANDS OF THESE FOR ME!
FRANK ROBBINS
SIGNORE, IT IS TRUE THAT I MADE MANY CIGARS LIKE THIS...BUT NOT FOR YOU!
I ONLY MAKE THEM FOR SIGNOR JOE BANJO... AND YOU ARE NOT BANJO!
!

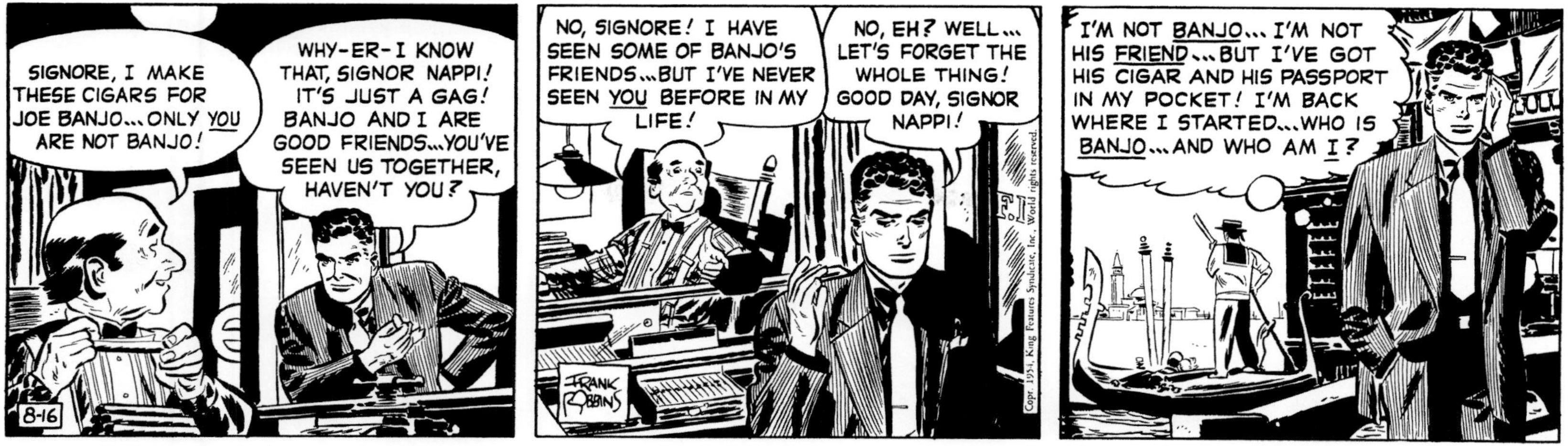
8-16
SIGNORE, I MAKE THESE CIGARS FOR JOE BANJO...ONLY YOU ARE NOT BANJO!
WHY-ER-I KNOW THAT, SIGNOR NAPPI! IT'S JUST A GAG! BANJO AND I ARE GOOD FRIENDS...YOU'VE SEEN US TOGETHER, HAVEN'T YOU?
NO, SIGNORE! I HAVE SEEN SOME OF BANJO'S FRIENDS...BUT I'VE NEVER SEEN YOU BEFORE IN MY LIFE!
NO, EH? WELL... LET'S FORGET THE WHOLE THING! GOOD DAY, SIGNOR NAPPI!
FRANK ROBBINS
Copr. 1954, King Features Syndicate, Inc. World rights reserved.
I'M NOT BANJO... I'M NOT HIS FRIEND...BUT I'VE GOT HIS CIGAR AND HIS PASSPORT IN MY POCKET! I'M BACK WHERE I STARTED...WHO IS BANJO...AND WHO AM I?

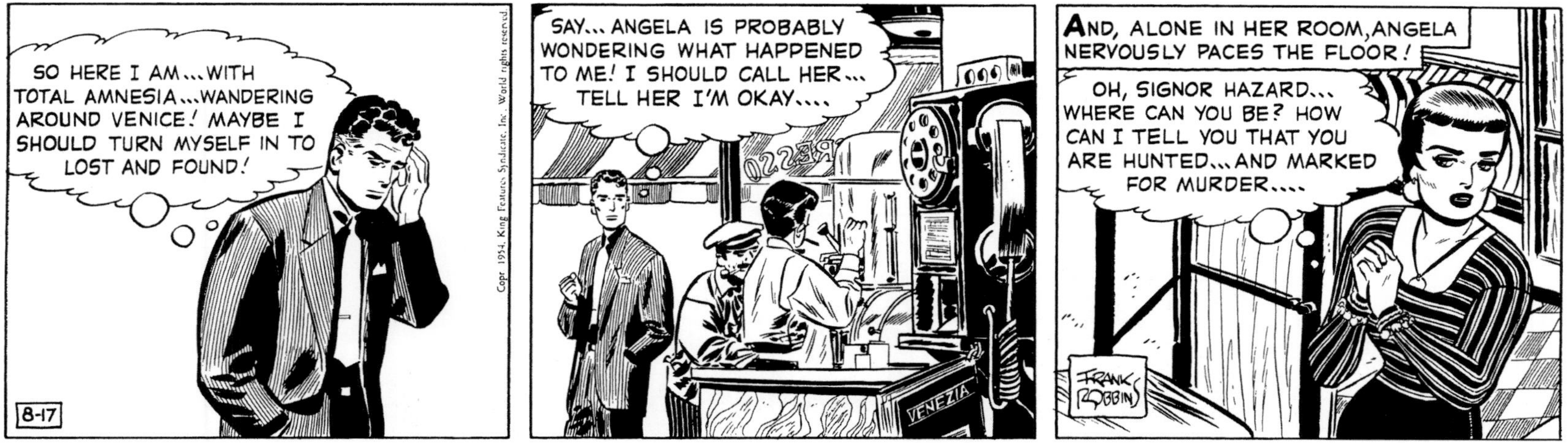
8-17
SO HERE I AM...WITH TOTAL AMNESIA...WANDERING AROUND VENICE! MAYBE I SHOULD TURN MYSELF IN TO LOST AND FOUND!
Copr. 1954, King Features Syndicate, Inc. World rights reserved.
SAY... ANGELA IS PROBABLY WONDERING WHAT HAPPENED TO ME! I SHOULD CALL HER... TELL HER I'M OKAY....
VENEZIA
AND, ALONE IN HER ROOM, ANGELA NERVOUSLY PACES THE FLOOR!
OH, SIGNOR HAZARD... WHERE CAN YOU BE? HOW CAN I TELL YOU THAT YOU ARE HUNTED...AND MARKED FOR MURDER....
FRANK ROBBINS

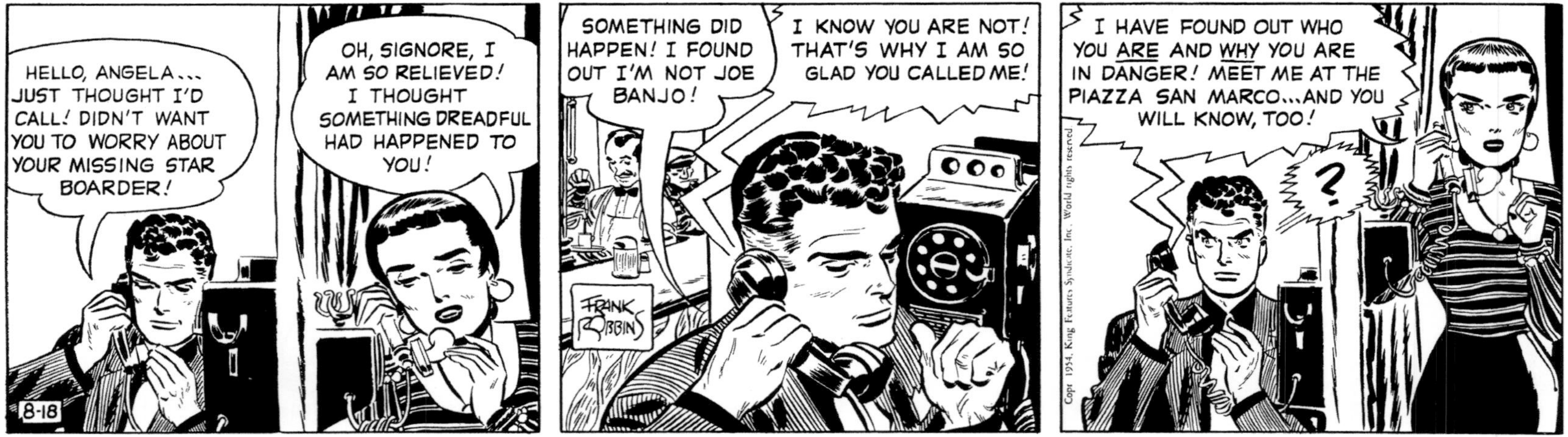
HELLO, ANGELA... JUST THOUGHT I'D CALL! DIDN'T WANT YOU TO WORRY ABOUT YOUR MISSING STAR BOARDER!
8-18
OH, SIGNORE, I AM SO RELIEVED! I THOUGHT SOMETHING DREADFUL HAD HAPPENED TO YOU!
SOMETHING DID HAPPEN! I FOUND OUT I'M NOT JOE BANJO!
I KNOW YOU ARE NOT! THAT'S WHY I AM SO GLAD YOU CALLED ME!
FRANK ROBBINS
I HAVE FOUND OUT WHO YOU ARE AND WHY YOU ARE IN DANGER! MEET ME AT THE PIAZZA SAN MARCO...AND YOU WILL KNOW, TOO!
?
Copr 1954, King Features Syndicate, Inc., World rights reserved

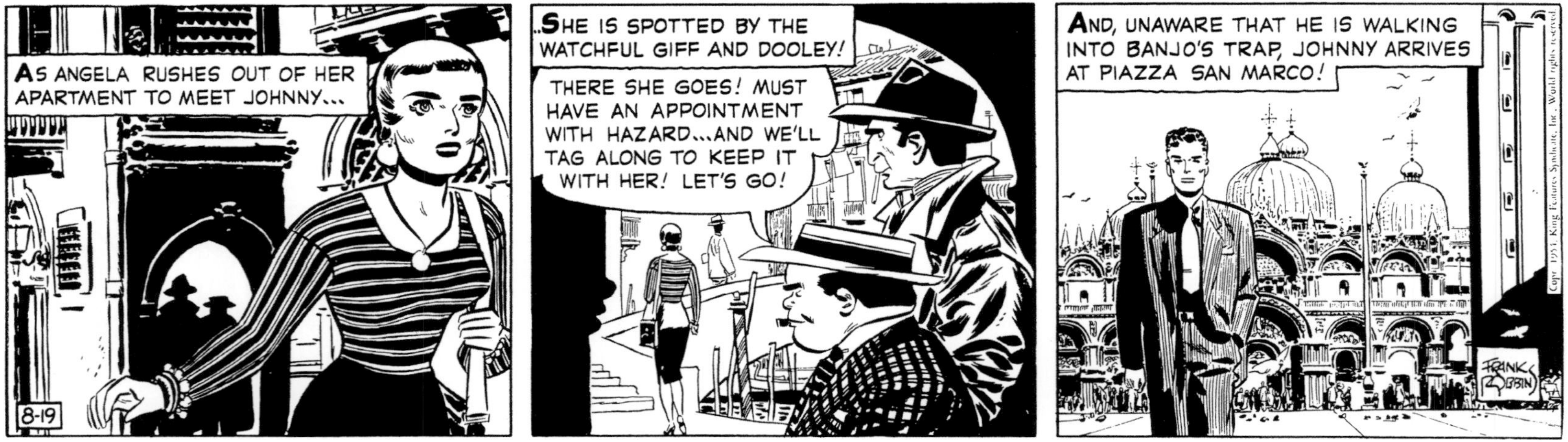
AS ANGELA RUSHES OUT OF HER APARTMENT TO MEET JOHNNY...
8-19
..SHE IS SPOTTED BY THE WATCHFUL GIFF AND DOOLEY!
THERE SHE GOES! MUST HAVE AN APPOINTMENT WITH HAZARD...AND WE'LL TAG ALONG TO KEEP IT WITH HER! LET'S GO!
AND, UNAWARE THAT HE IS WALKING INTO BANJO'S TRAP, JOHNNY ARRIVES AT PIAZZA SAN MARCO!
FRANK ROBBINS
Copr 1954, King Features Syndicate, Inc., World rights reserved

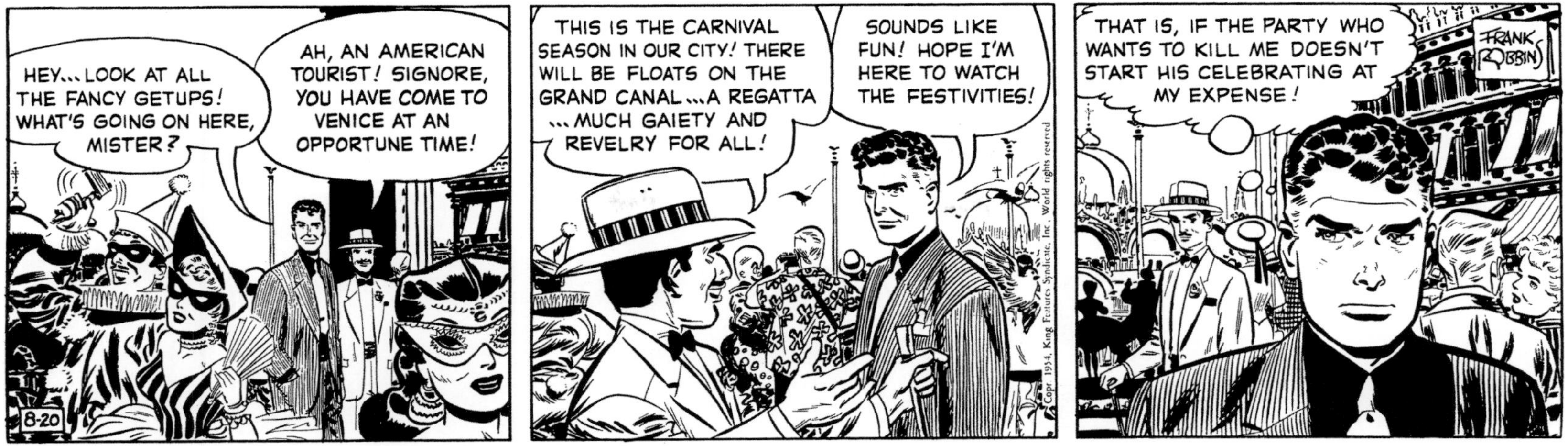

HEY... LOOK AT ALL THE FANCY GETUPS! WHAT'S GOING ON HERE, MISTER?
AH, AN AMERICAN TOURIST! SIGNORE, YOU HAVE COME TO VENICE AT AN OPPORTUNE TIME!
8-20
THIS IS THE CARNIVAL SEASON IN OUR CITY! THERE WILL BE FLOATS ON THE GRAND CANAL ... A REGATTA ... MUCH GAIETY AND REVELRY FOR ALL!
SOUNDS LIKE FUN! HOPE I'M HERE TO WATCH THE FESTIVITIES!
Copr. 1954, King Features Syndicate, Inc. World rights reserved
THAT IS, IF THE PARTY WHO WANTS TO KILL ME DOESN'T START HIS CELEBRATING AT MY EXPENSE!
FRANK ROBBINS

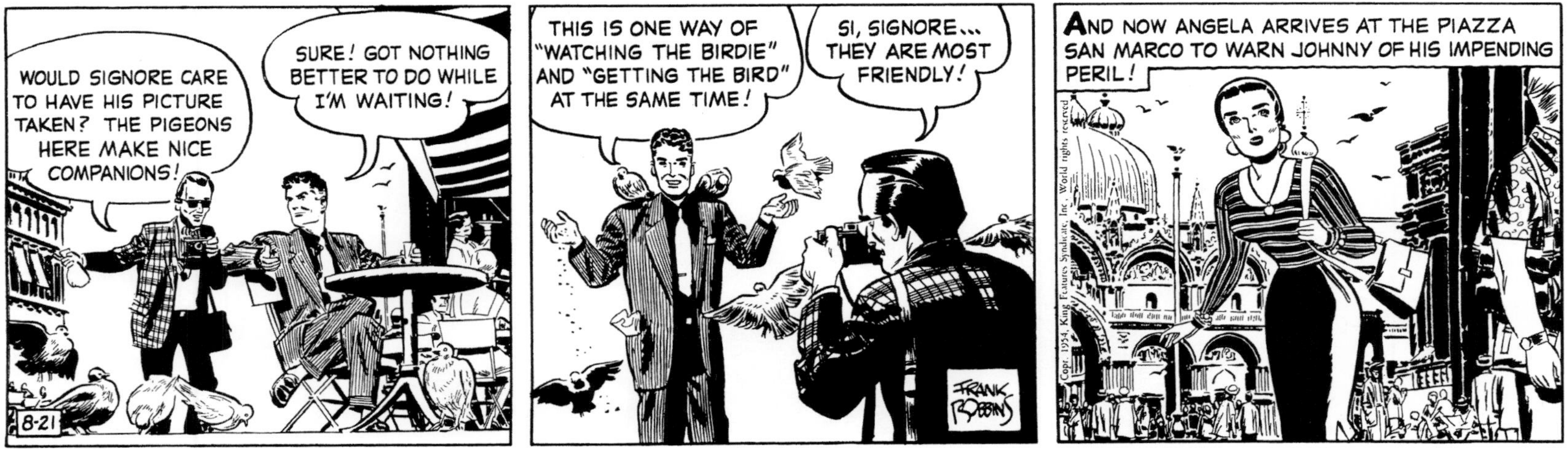

WOULD SIGNORE CARE TO HAVE HIS PICTURE TAKEN? THE PIGEONS HERE MAKE NICE COMPANIONS!
SURE! GOT NOTHING BETTER TO DO WHILE I'M WAITING!
8-21
THIS IS ONE WAY OF "WATCHING THE BIRDIE" AND "GETTING THE BIRD" AT THE SAME TIME!
SI, SIGNORE... THEY ARE MOST FRIENDLY!
FRANK ROBBINS
AND NOW ANGELA ARRIVES AT THE PIAZZA SAN MARCO TO WARN JOHNNY OF HIS IMPENDING PERIL!
Copr. 1954, King Features Syndicate, Inc. World rights reserved

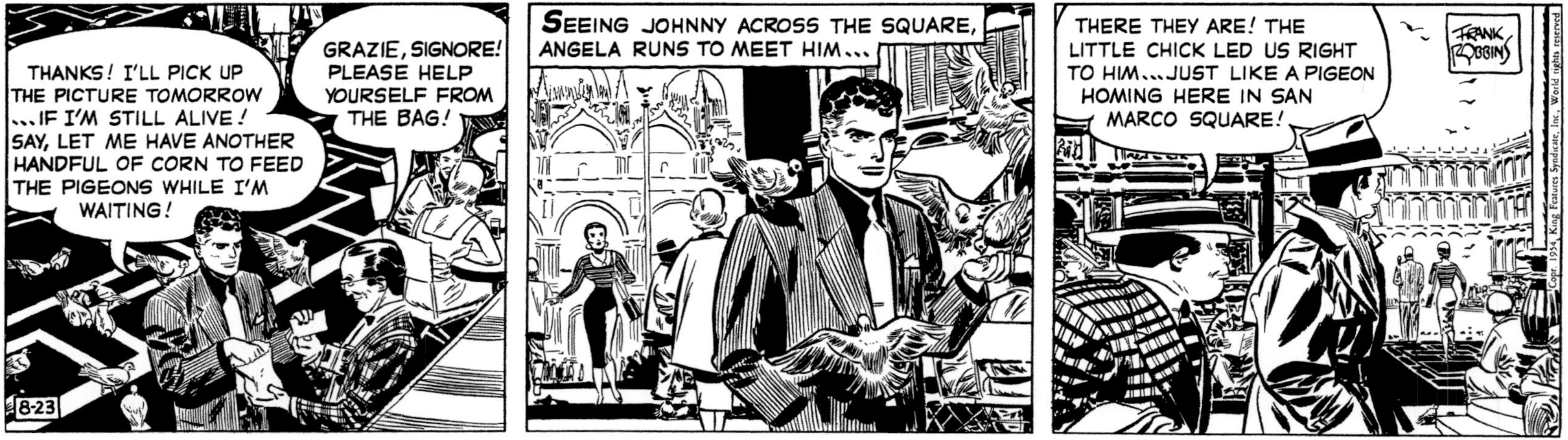
8-23
THANKS! I'LL PICK UP THE PICTURE TOMORROW ...IF I'M STILL ALIVE! SAY, LET ME HAVE ANOTHER HANDFUL OF CORN TO FEED THE PIGEONS WHILE I'M WAITING!
GRAZIE, SIGNORE! PLEASE HELP YOURSELF FROM THE BAG!
SEEING JOHNNY ACROSS THE SQUARE, ANGELA RUNS TO MEET HIM...
THERE THEY ARE! THE LITTLE CHICK LED US RIGHT TO HIM...JUST LIKE A PIGEON HOMING HERE IN SAN MARCO SQUARE!
FRANK ROBBINS
Copr. 1954, King Features Syndicate, Inc., World rights reserved

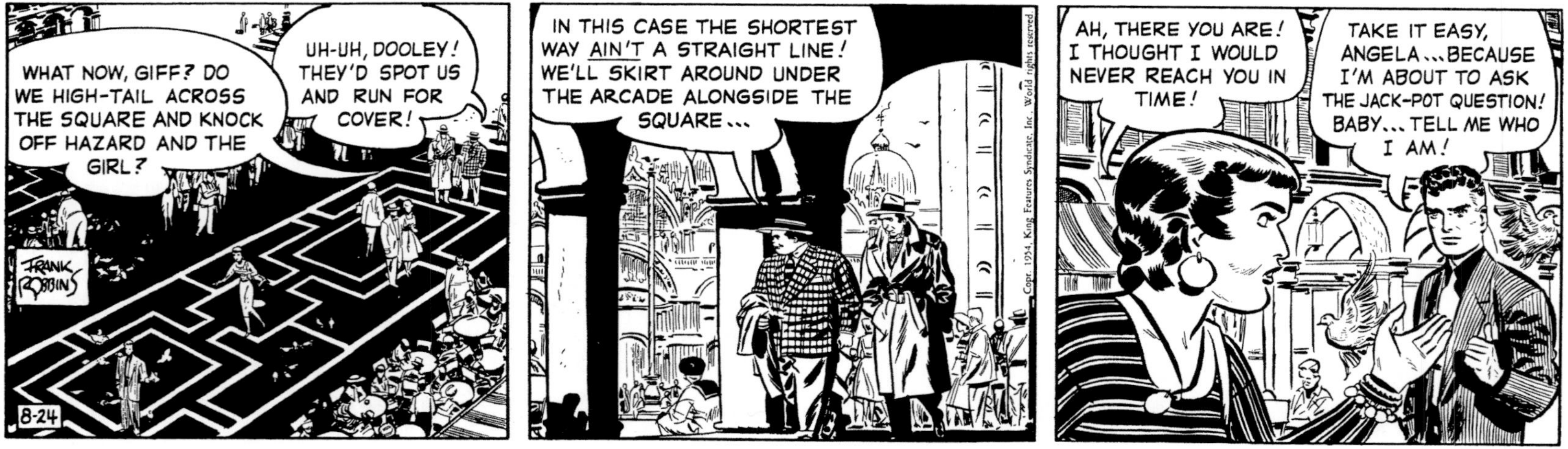
8-24
WHAT NOW, GIFF? DO WE HIGH-TAIL ACROSS THE SQUARE AND KNOCK OFF HAZARD AND THE GIRL?
UH-UH, DOOLEY! THEY'D SPOT US AND RUN FOR COVER!
FRANK ROBBINS
IN THIS CASE THE SHORTEST WAY AIN'T A STRAIGHT LINE! WE'LL SKIRT AROUND UNDER THE ARCADE ALONGSIDE THE SQUARE...
Copr. 1954, King Features Syndicate, Inc., World rights reserved
AH, THERE YOU ARE! I THOUGHT I WOULD NEVER REACH YOU IN TIME!
TAKE IT EASY, ANGELA...BECAUSE I'M ABOUT TO ASK THE JACK-POT QUESTION! BABY...TELL ME WHO I AM!

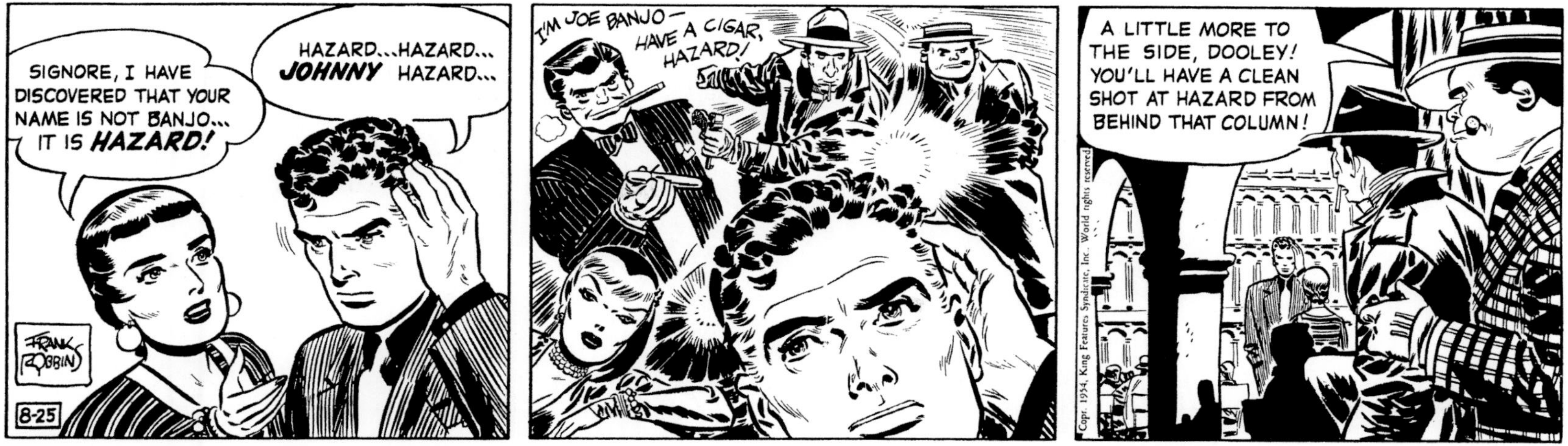
SIGNORE, I HAVE DISCOVERED THAT YOUR NAME IS NOT BANJO... IT IS HAZARD!
HAZARD...HAZARD... JOHNNY HAZARD...
FRANK ROBBINS
8-25
I'M JOE BANJO— HAVE A CIGAR, HAZARD!
A LITTLE MORE TO THE SIDE, DOOLEY! YOU'LL HAVE A CLEAN SHOT AT HAZARD FROM BEHIND THAT COLUMN!
Copr. 1954, King Features Syndicate, Inc. World rights reserved.

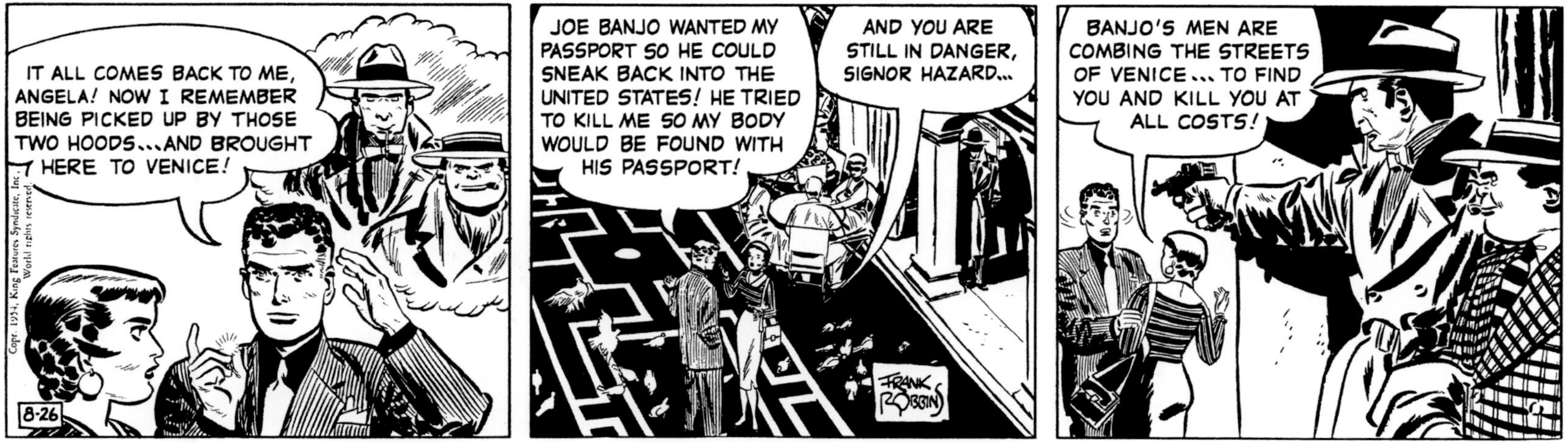
IT ALL COMES BACK TO ME, ANGELA! NOW I REMEMBER BEING PICKED UP BY THOSE TWO HOODS...AND BROUGHT HERE TO VENICE!
Copr. 1954, King Features Syndicate, Inc. World rights reserved.
8-26
JOE BANJO WANTED MY PASSPORT SO HE COULD SNEAK BACK INTO THE UNITED STATES! HE TRIED TO KILL ME SO MY BODY WOULD BE FOUND WITH HIS PASSPORT!
AND YOU ARE STILL IN DANGER, SIGNOR HAZARD...
FRANK ROBBINS
BANJO'S MEN ARE COMBING THE STREETS OF VENICE... TO FIND YOU AND KILL YOU AT ALL COSTS!

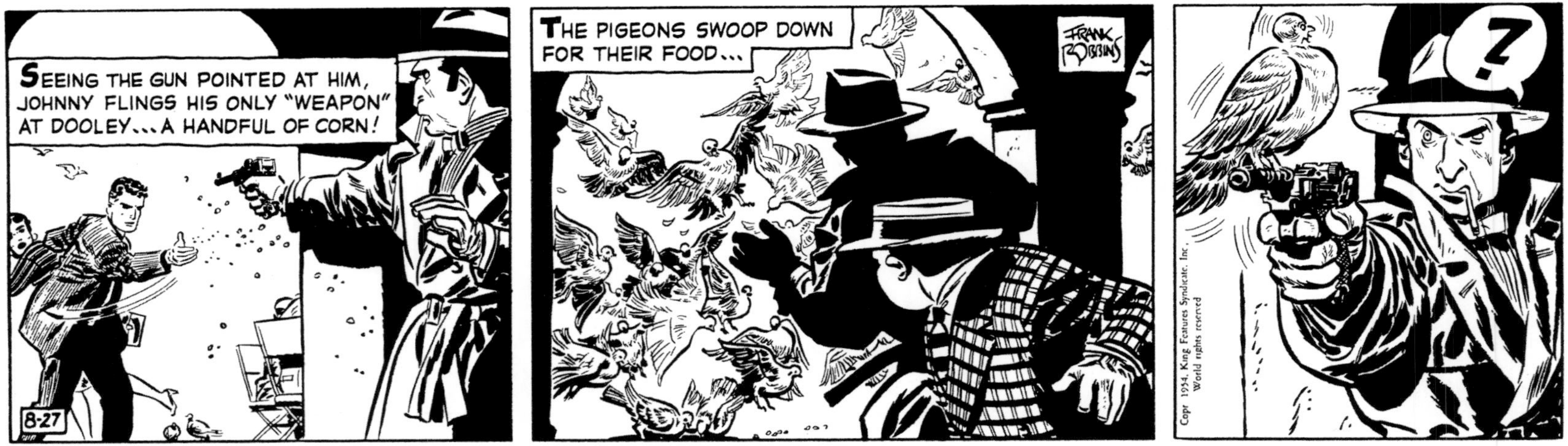
SEEING THE GUN POINTED AT HIM, JOHNNY FLINGS HIS ONLY "WEAPON" AT DOOLEY... A HANDFUL OF CORN!
8-27
THE PIGEONS SWOOP DOWN FOR THEIR FOOD...
FRANK ROBBINS
Copr 1954, King Features Syndicate, Inc. World rights reserved
?

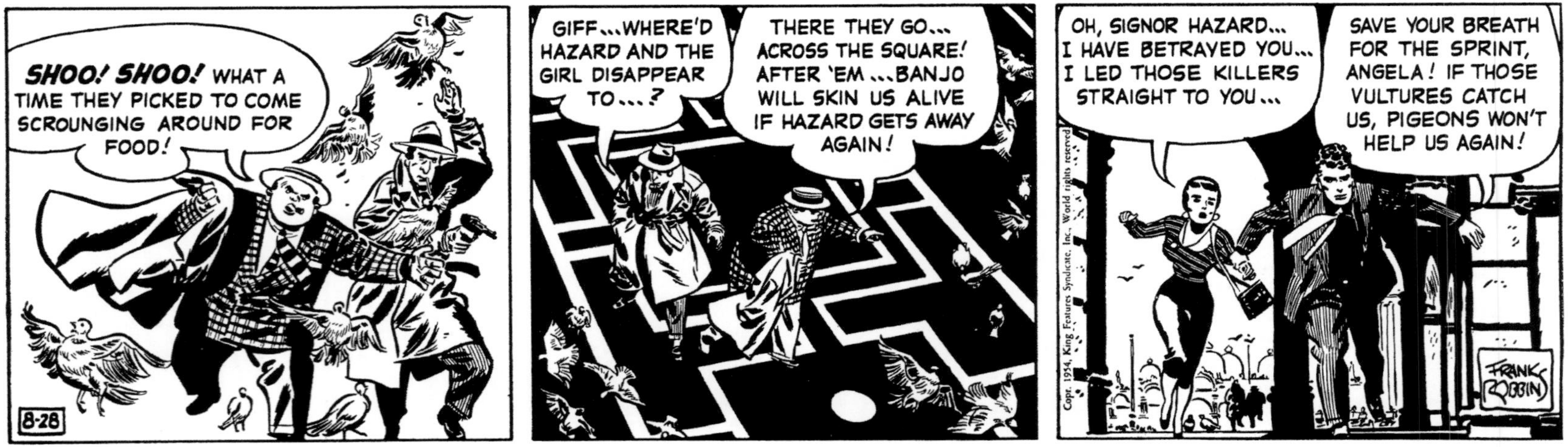
SHOO! SHOO! WHAT A TIME THEY PICKED TO COME SCROUNGING AROUND FOR FOOD!
8-28
GIFF...WHERE'D HAZARD AND THE GIRL DISAPPEAR TO...?
THERE THEY GO... ACROSS THE SQUARE! AFTER 'EM ...BANJO WILL SKIN US ALIVE IF HAZARD GETS AWAY AGAIN!
Copr. 1954, King Features Syndicate, Inc., World rights reserved
OH, SIGNOR HAZARD... I HAVE BETRAYED YOU... I LED THOSE KILLERS STRAIGHT TO YOU...
SAVE YOUR BREATH FOR THE SPRINT, ANGELA! IF THOSE VULTURES CATCH US, PIGEONS WON'T HELP US AGAIN!
FRANK ROBBINS

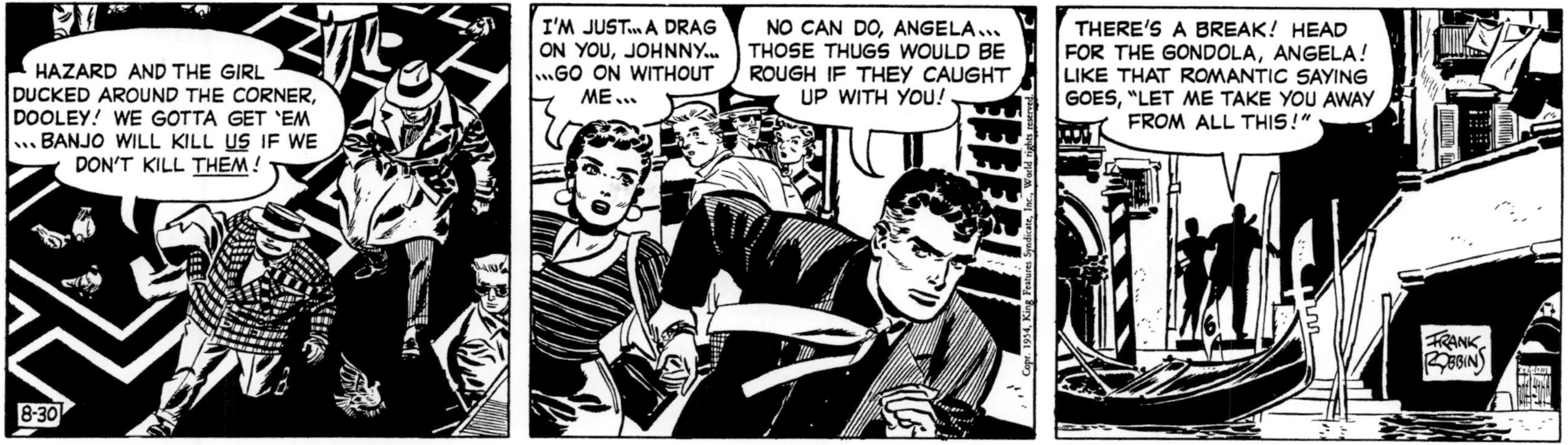
HAZARD AND THE GIRL DUCKED AROUND THE CORNER, DOOLEY! WE GOTTA GET 'EM ... BANJO WILL KILL US IF WE DON'T KILL THEM!
8-30
I'M JUST... A DRAG ON YOU, JOHNNY... ...GO ON WITHOUT ME...
NO CAN DO, ANGELA... THOSE THUGS WOULD BE ROUGH IF THEY CAUGHT UP WITH YOU!
Copr. 1954, King Features Syndicate, Inc., World rights reserved.
THERE'S A BREAK! HEAD FOR THE GONDOLA, ANGELA! LIKE THAT ROMANTIC SAYING GOES, "LET ME TAKE YOU AWAY FROM ALL THIS!"
6
FRANK ROBBINS

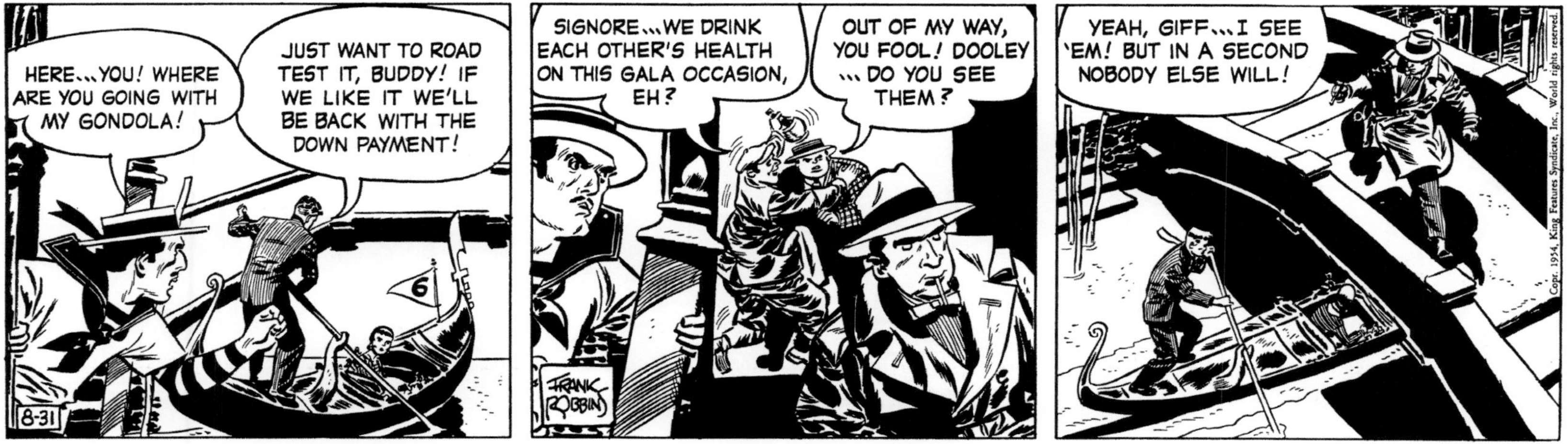
HERE... YOU! WHERE ARE YOU GOING WITH MY GONDOLA!
JUST WANT TO ROAD TEST IT, BUDDY! IF WE LIKE IT WE'LL BE BACK WITH THE DOWN PAYMENT!
6
8-31
SIGNORE... WE DRINK EACH OTHER'S HEALTH ON THIS GALA OCCASION, EH?
OUT OF MY WAY, YOU FOOL! DOOLEY ... DO YOU SEE THEM?
FRANK ROBBINS
YEAH, GIFF... I SEE 'EM! BUT IN A SECOND NOBODY ELSE WILL!
Copr. 1954, King Features Syndicate, Inc., World rights reserved.

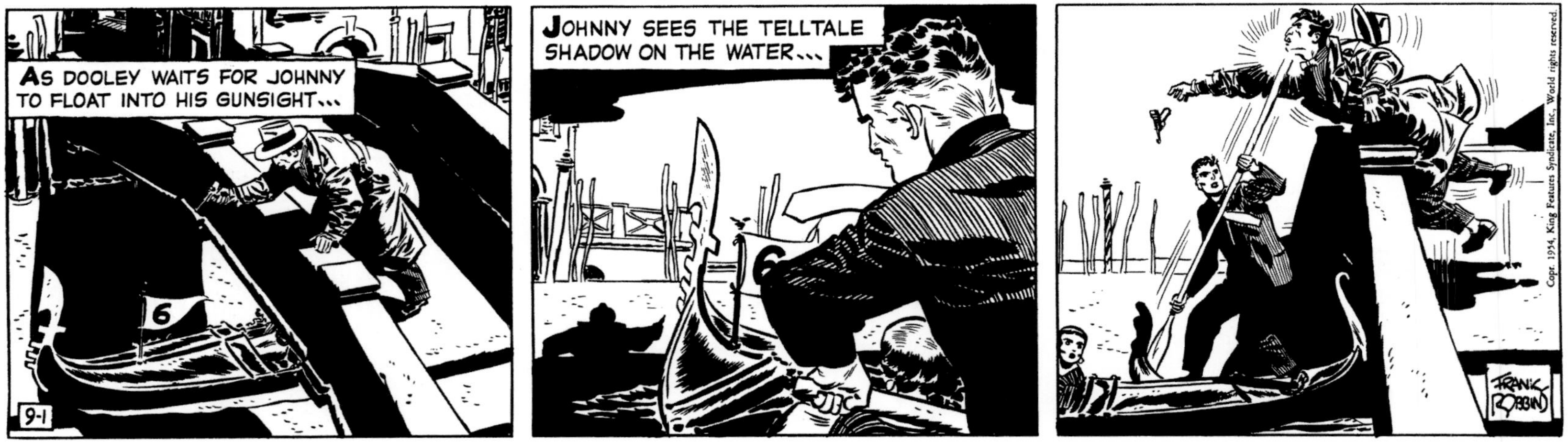
AS DOOLEY WAITS FOR JOHNNY TO FLOAT INTO HIS GUNSIGHT...
9-1
JOHNNY SEES THE TELLTALE SHADOW ON THE WATER...
Copr. 1954, King Features Syndicate, Inc., World rights reserved.
FRANK ROBBINS

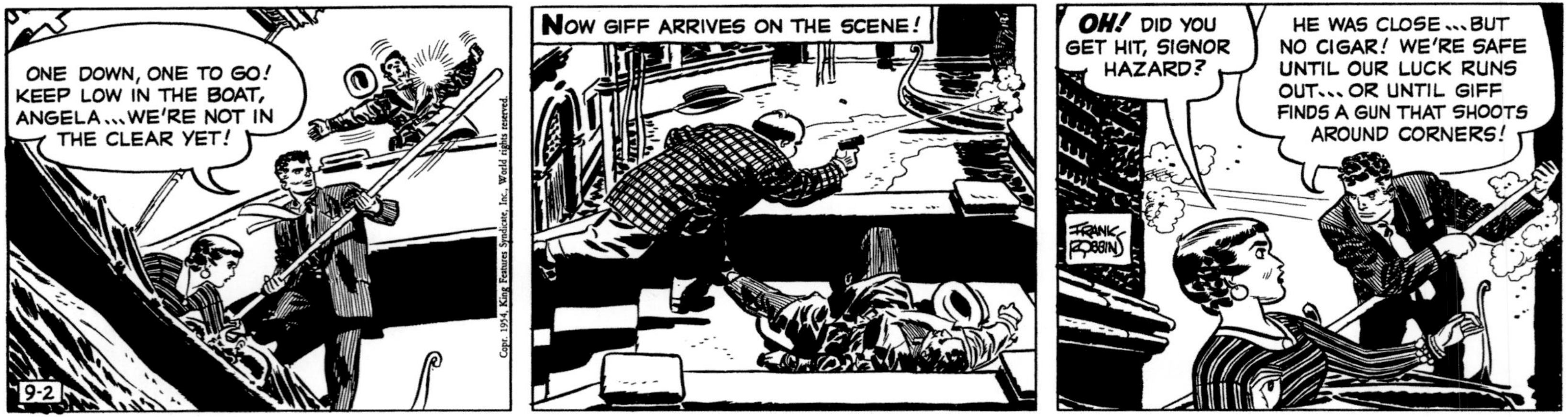
ONE DOWN, ONE TO GO! KEEP LOW IN THE BOAT, ANGELA...WE'RE NOT IN THE CLEAR YET!
9-2
Copr. 1954, King Features Syndicate, Inc., World rights reserved.
NOW GIFF ARRIVES ON THE SCENE!
OH! DID YOU GET HIT, SIGNOR HAZARD?
HE WAS CLOSE...BUT NO CIGAR! WE'RE SAFE UNTIL OUR LUCK RUNS OUT...OR UNTIL GIFF FINDS A GUN THAT SHOOTS AROUND CORNERS!
FRANK ROBBINS

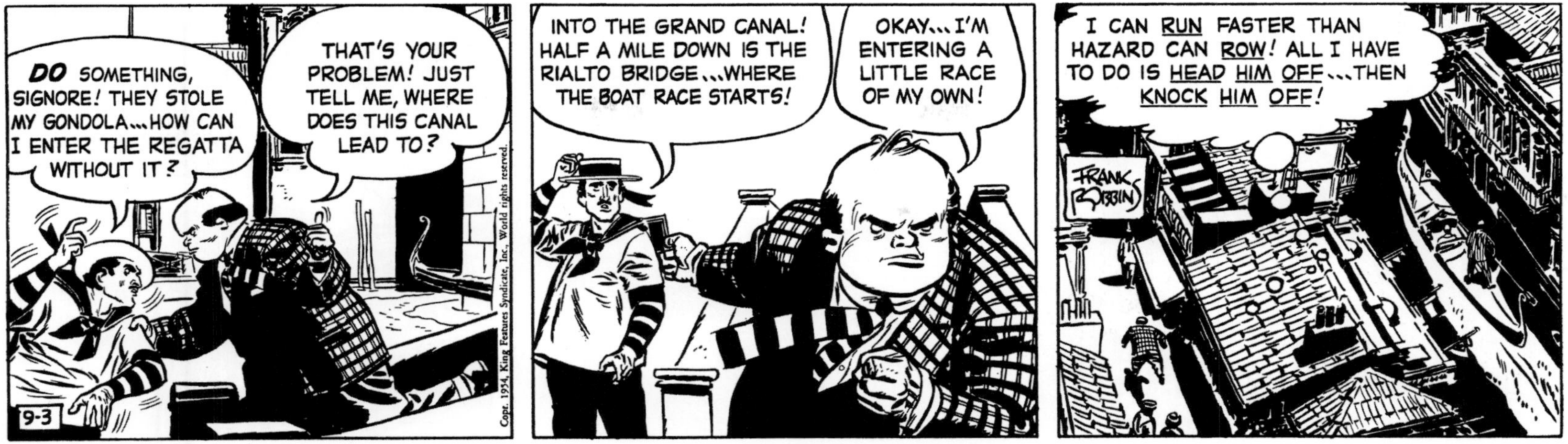

DO SOMETHING, SIGNORE! THEY STOLE MY GONDOLA...HOW CAN I ENTER THE REGATTA WITHOUT IT?
THAT'S YOUR PROBLEM! JUST TELL ME, WHERE DOES THIS CANAL LEAD TO?
9-3
Copr. 1954, King Features Syndicate, Inc., World rights reserved.
INTO THE GRAND CANAL! HALF A MILE DOWN IS THE RIALTO BRIDGE...WHERE THE BOAT RACE STARTS!
OKAY...I'M ENTERING A LITTLE RACE OF MY OWN!
I CAN RUN FASTER THAN HAZARD CAN ROW! ALL I HAVE TO DO IS HEAD HIM OFF...THEN KNOCK HIM OFF!
FRANK ROBBINS

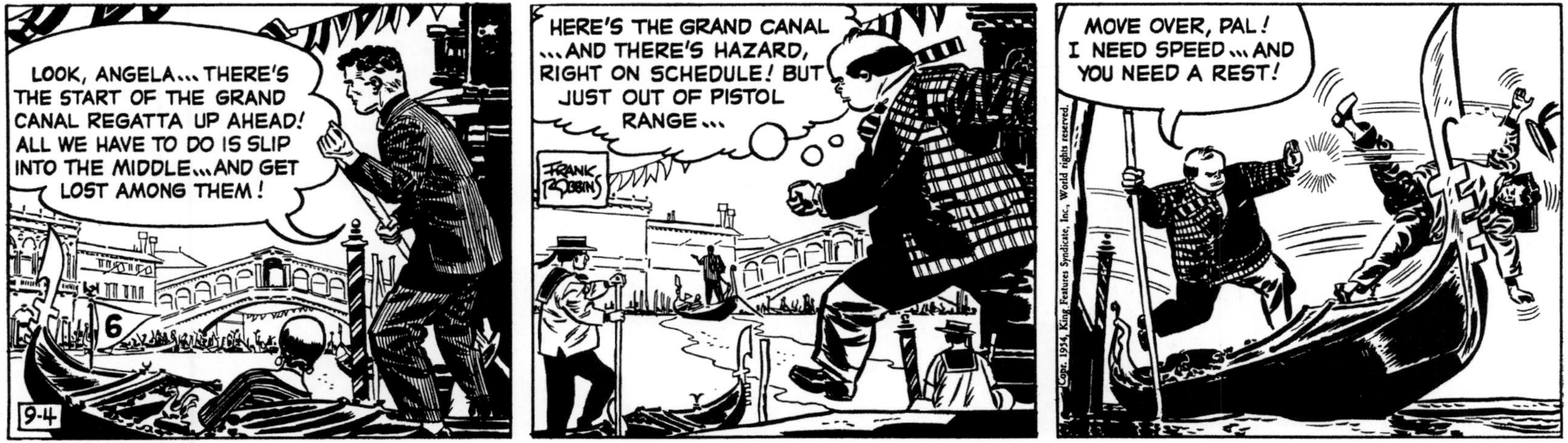

LOOK, ANGELA...THERE'S THE START OF THE GRAND CANAL REGATTA UP AHEAD! ALL WE HAVE TO DO IS SLIP INTO THE MIDDLE...AND GET LOST AMONG THEM!
6
9-4
HERE'S THE GRAND CANAL ...AND THERE'S HAZARD, RIGHT ON SCHEDULE! BUT JUST OUT OF PISTOL RANGE...
FRANK ROBBINS
MOVE OVER, PAL! I NEED SPEED...AND YOU NEED A REST!
Copr. 1954, King Features Syndicate, Inc., World rights reserved.

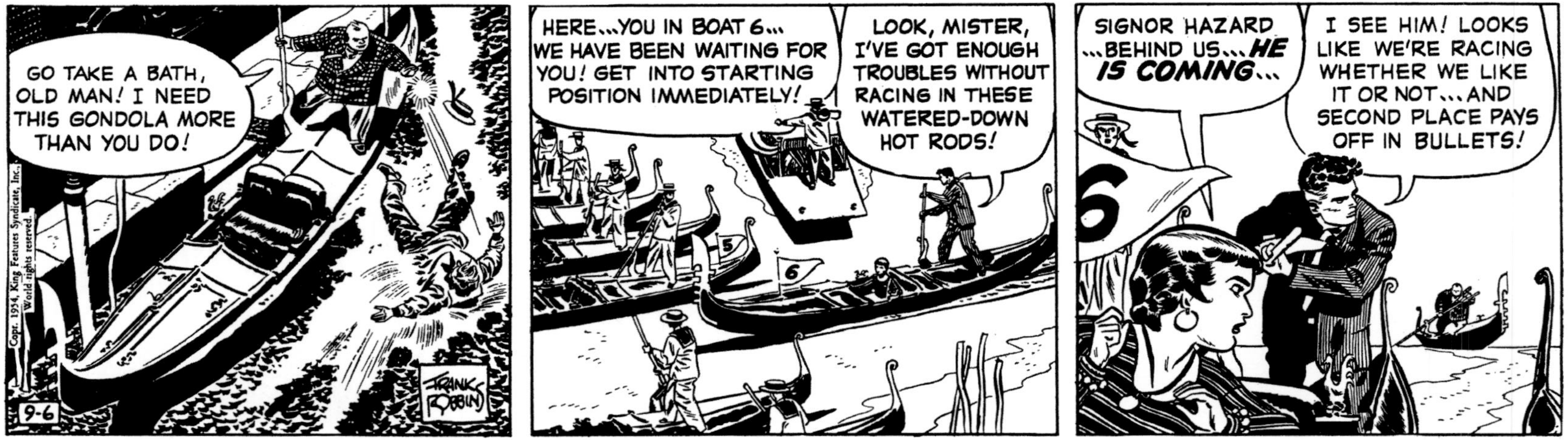
GO TAKE A BATH, OLD MAN! I NEED THIS GONDOLA MORE THAN YOU DO!
Copr. 1954, King Features Syndicate, Inc., World rights reserved.
9-6
FRANK ROBBINS
HERE...YOU IN BOAT 6... WE HAVE BEEN WAITING FOR YOU! GET INTO STARTING POSITION IMMEDIATELY!
LOOK, MISTER, I'VE GOT ENOUGH TROUBLES WITHOUT RACING IN THESE WATERED-DOWN HOT RODS!
5
6
SIGNOR HAZARD ...BEHIND US... **HE IS COMING**...
I SEE HIM! LOOKS LIKE WE'RE RACING WHETHER WE LIKE IT OR NOT...AND SECOND PLACE PAYS OFF IN BULLETS!

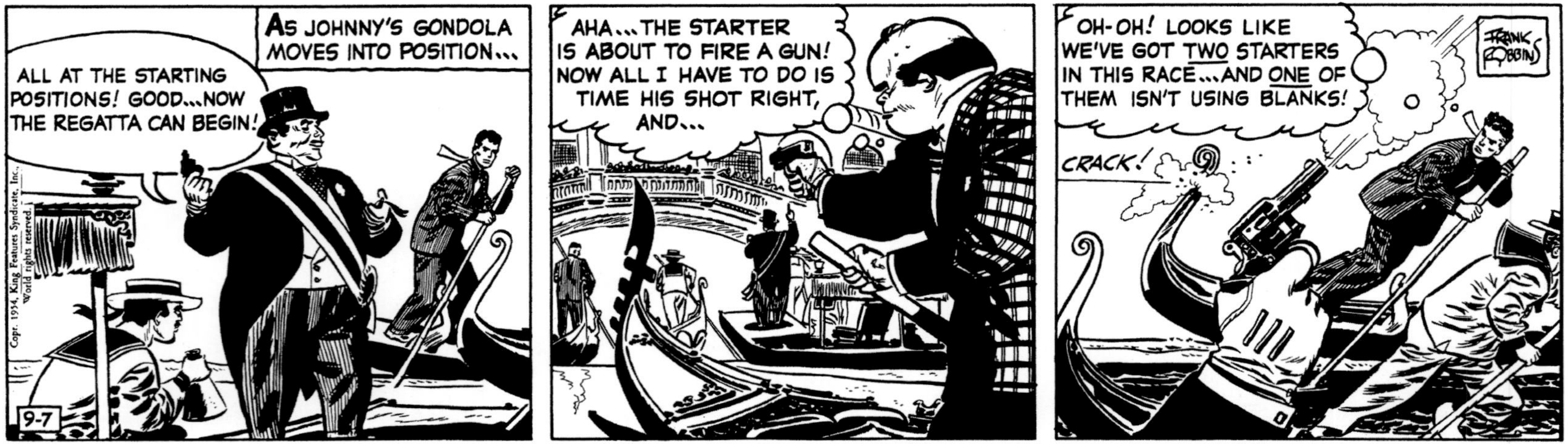
AS JOHNNY'S GONDOLA MOVES INTO POSITION...
ALL AT THE STARTING POSITIONS! GOOD...NOW THE REGATTA CAN BEGIN!
Copr. 1954, King Features Syndicate, Inc., World rights reserved.
9-7
AHA...THE STARTER IS ABOUT TO FIRE A GUN! NOW ALL I HAVE TO DO IS TIME HIS SHOT RIGHT, AND...
OH-OH! LOOKS LIKE WE'VE GOT TWO STARTERS IN THIS RACE...AND ONE OF THEM ISN'T USING BLANKS!
FRANK ROBBINS
CRACK!

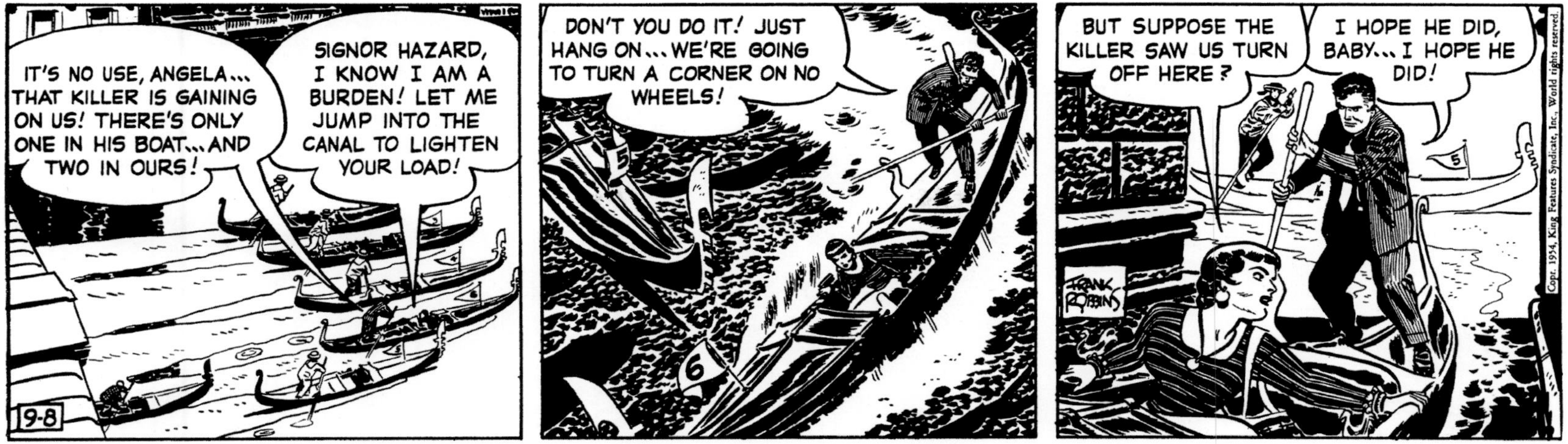
IT'S NO USE, ANGELA... THAT KILLER IS GAINING ON US! THERE'S ONLY ONE IN HIS BOAT... AND TWO IN OURS!
SIGNOR HAZARD, I KNOW I AM A BURDEN! LET ME JUMP INTO THE CANAL TO LIGHTEN YOUR LOAD!
9-8
DON'T YOU DO IT! JUST HANG ON... WE'RE GOING TO TURN A CORNER ON NO WHEELS!
6
BUT SUPPOSE THE KILLER SAW US TURN OFF HERE?
I HOPE HE DID, BABY... I HOPE HE DID!
5
FRANK ROBBINS
Copr. 1954, King Features Syndicate, Inc., World rights reserved.

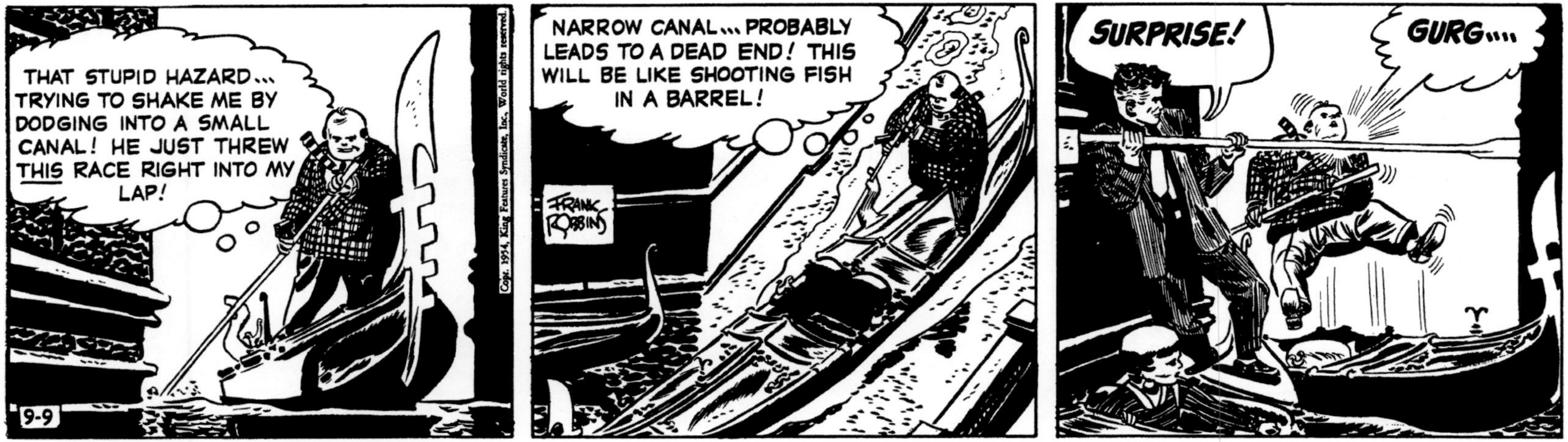
THAT STUPID HAZARD... TRYING TO SHAKE ME BY DODGING INTO A SMALL CANAL! HE JUST THREW THIS RACE RIGHT INTO MY LAP!
9-9
Copr. 1954, King Features Syndicate, Inc., World rights reserved.
NARROW CANAL... PROBABLY LEADS TO A DEAD END! THIS WILL BE LIKE SHOOTING FISH IN A BARREL!
FRANK ROBBINS
SURPRISE!
GURG....

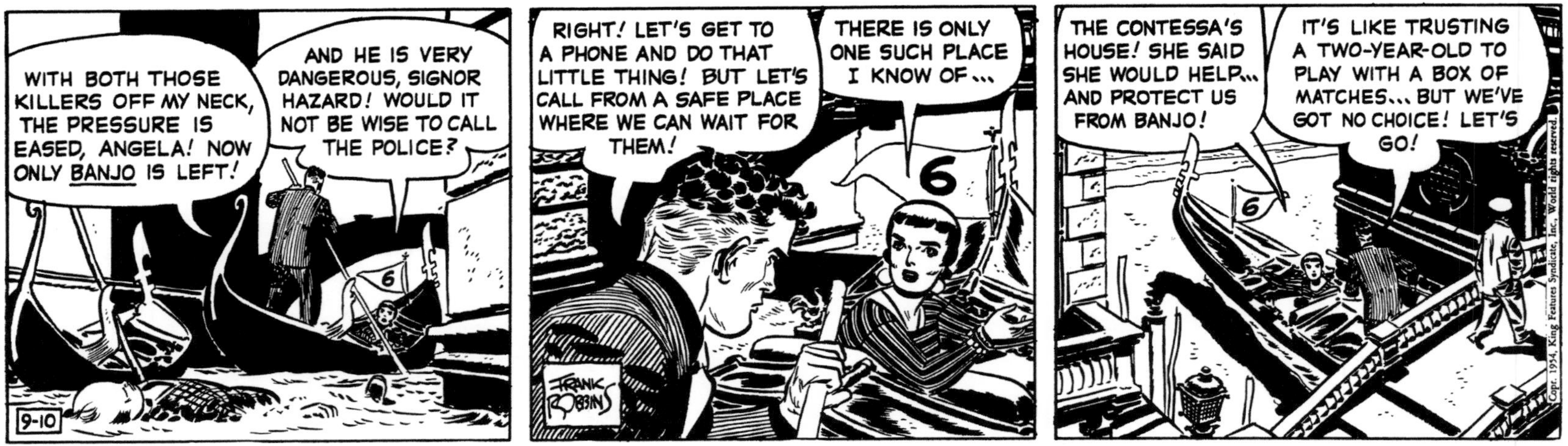
9-10
WITH BOTH THOSE KILLERS OFF MY NECK, THE PRESSURE IS EASED, ANGELA! NOW ONLY BANJO IS LEFT!
AND HE IS VERY DANGEROUS, SIGNOR HAZARD! WOULD IT NOT BE WISE TO CALL THE POLICE?
RIGHT! LET'S GET TO A PHONE AND DO THAT LITTLE THING! BUT LET'S CALL FROM A SAFE PLACE WHERE WE CAN WAIT FOR THEM!
THERE IS ONLY ONE SUCH PLACE I KNOW OF...
FRANK ROBBINS
THE CONTESSA'S HOUSE! SHE SAID SHE WOULD HELP... AND PROTECT US FROM BANJO!
IT'S LIKE TRUSTING A TWO-YEAR-OLD TO PLAY WITH A BOX OF MATCHES... BUT WE'VE GOT NO CHOICE! LET'S GO!
Copr. 1954, King Features Syndicate, Inc., World rights reserved.

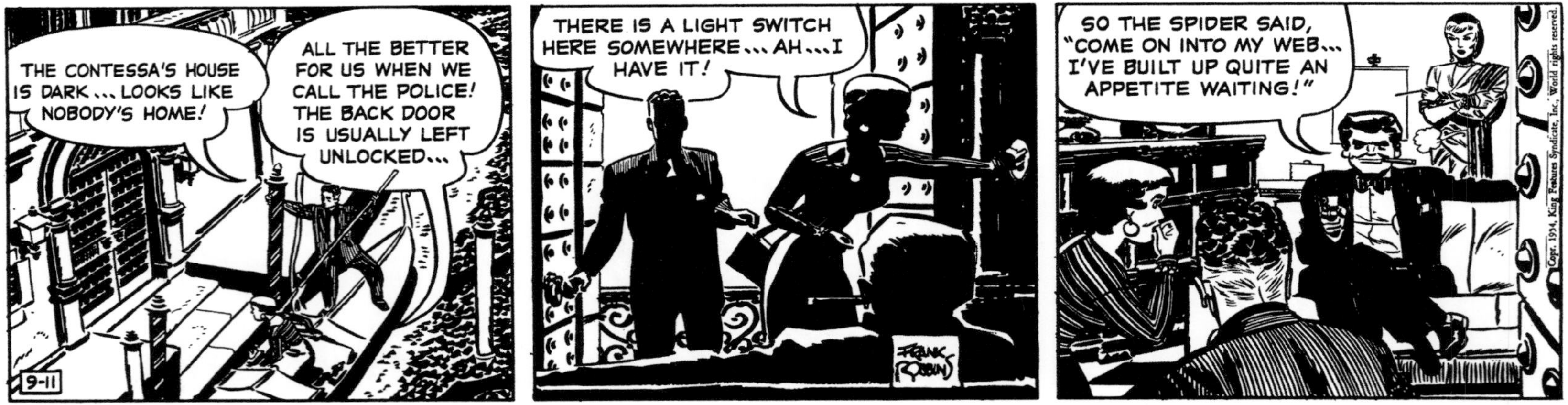
9-11
THE CONTESSA'S HOUSE IS DARK... LOOKS LIKE NOBODY'S HOME!
ALL THE BETTER FOR US WHEN WE CALL THE POLICE! THE BACK DOOR IS USUALLY LEFT UNLOCKED...
THERE IS A LIGHT SWITCH HERE SOMEWHERE... AH... I HAVE IT!
FRANK ROBBINS
SO THE SPIDER SAID, "COME ON INTO MY WEB... I'VE BUILT UP QUITE AN APPETITE WAITING!"
Copr. 1954, King Features Syndicate, Inc., World rights reserved.

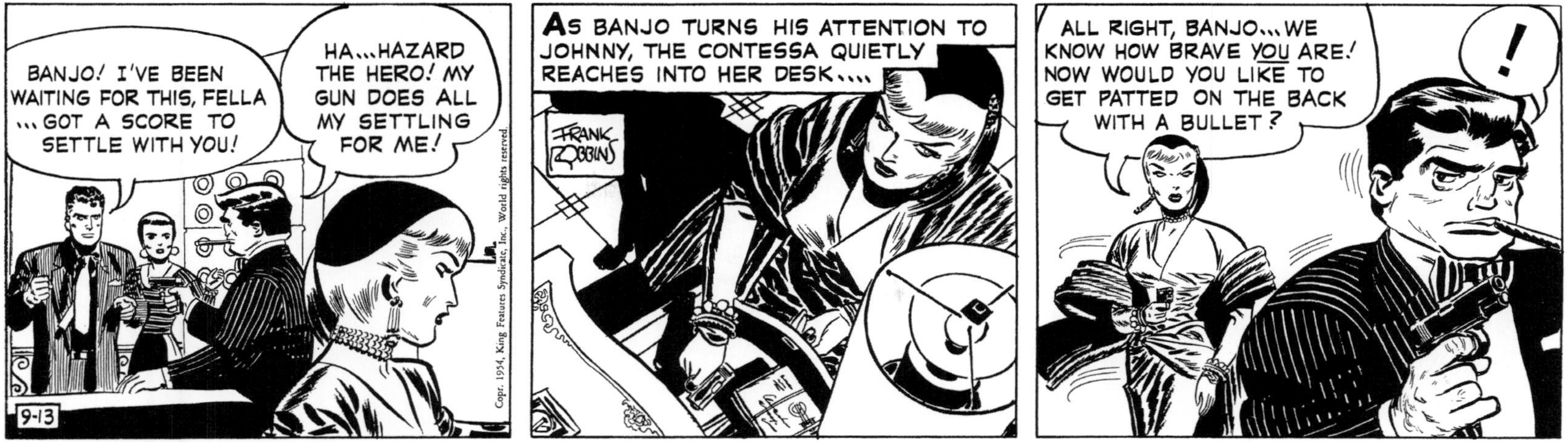

9-13
BANJO! I'VE BEEN WAITING FOR THIS, FELLA ... GOT A SCORE TO SETTLE WITH YOU!
HA...HAZARD THE HERO! MY GUN DOES ALL MY SETTLING FOR ME!
Copr. 1954, King Features Syndicate, Inc., World rights reserved.
AS BANJO TURNS HIS ATTENTION TO JOHNNY, THE CONTESSA QUIETLY REACHES INTO HER DESK....
FRANK ROBBINS
ALL RIGHT, BANJO... WE KNOW HOW BRAVE YOU ARE! NOW WOULD YOU LIKE TO GET PATTED ON THE BACK WITH A BULLET?
!

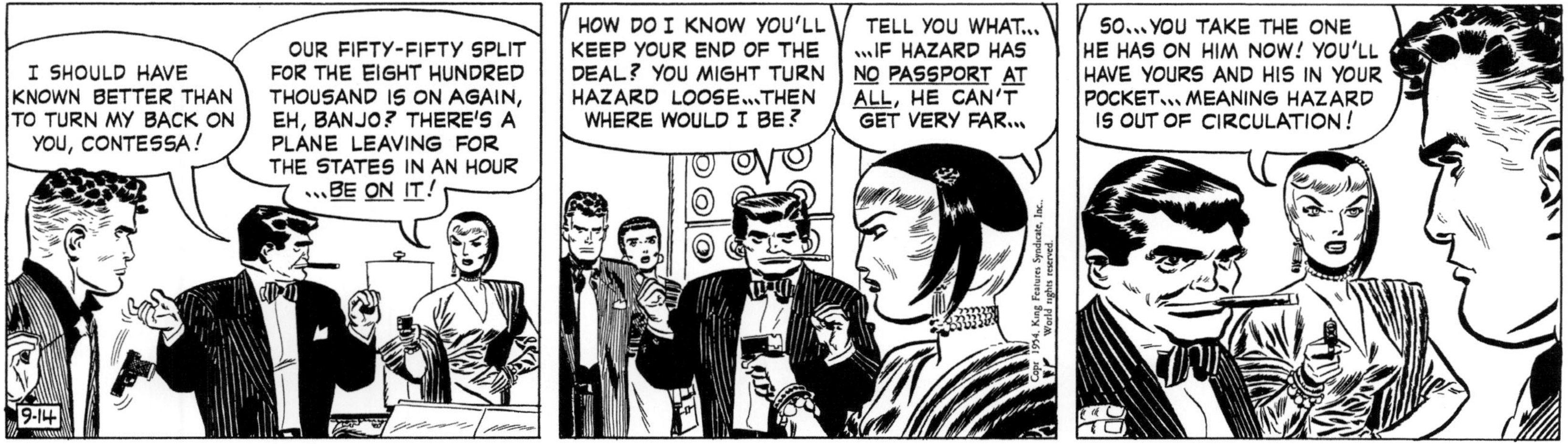

9-14
I SHOULD HAVE KNOWN BETTER THAN TO TURN MY BACK ON YOU, CONTESSA!
OUR FIFTY-FIFTY SPLIT FOR THE EIGHT HUNDRED THOUSAND IS ON AGAIN, EH, BANJO? THERE'S A PLANE LEAVING FOR THE STATES IN AN HOUR ...BE ON IT!
HOW DO I KNOW YOU'LL KEEP YOUR END OF THE DEAL? YOU MIGHT TURN HAZARD LOOSE...THEN WHERE WOULD I BE?
TELL YOU WHAT... ...IF HAZARD HAS NO PASSPORT AT ALL, HE CAN'T GET VERY FAR...
Copr. 1954, King Features Syndicate, Inc., World rights reserved.
SO...YOU TAKE THE ONE HE HAS ON HIM NOW! YOU'LL HAVE YOURS AND HIS IN YOUR POCKET... MEANING HAZARD IS OUT OF CIRCULATION!

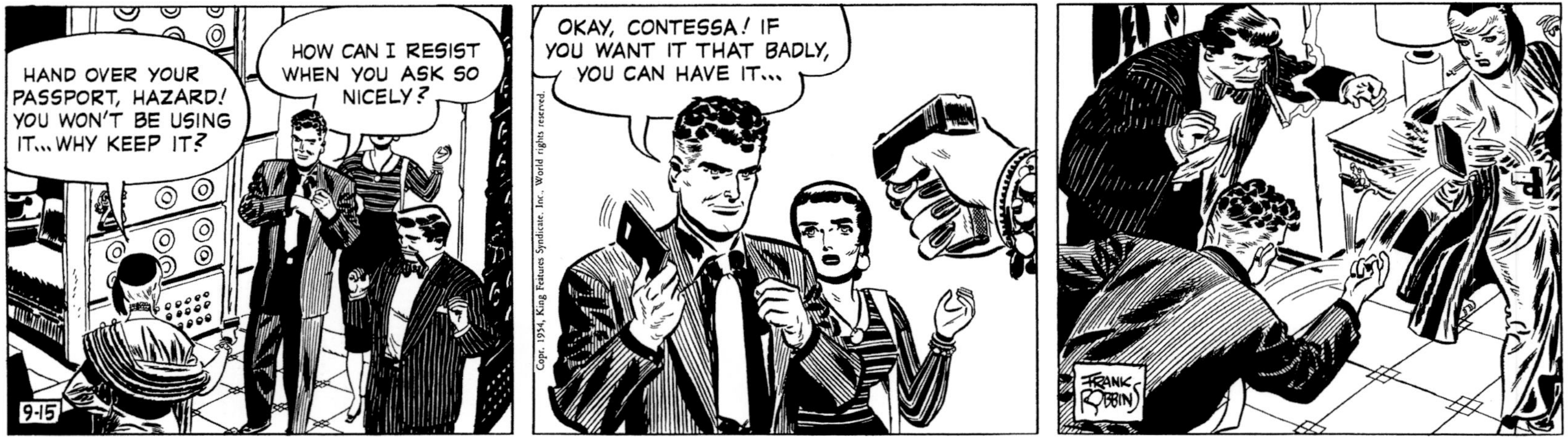
9-15
HAND OVER YOUR PASSPORT, HAZARD! YOU WON'T BE USING IT... WHY KEEP IT?
HOW CAN I RESIST WHEN YOU ASK SO NICELY?
Copr. 1954, King Features Syndicate, Inc. World rights reserved.
OKAY, CONTESSA! IF YOU WANT IT THAT BADLY, YOU CAN HAVE IT...
FRANK ROBBINS

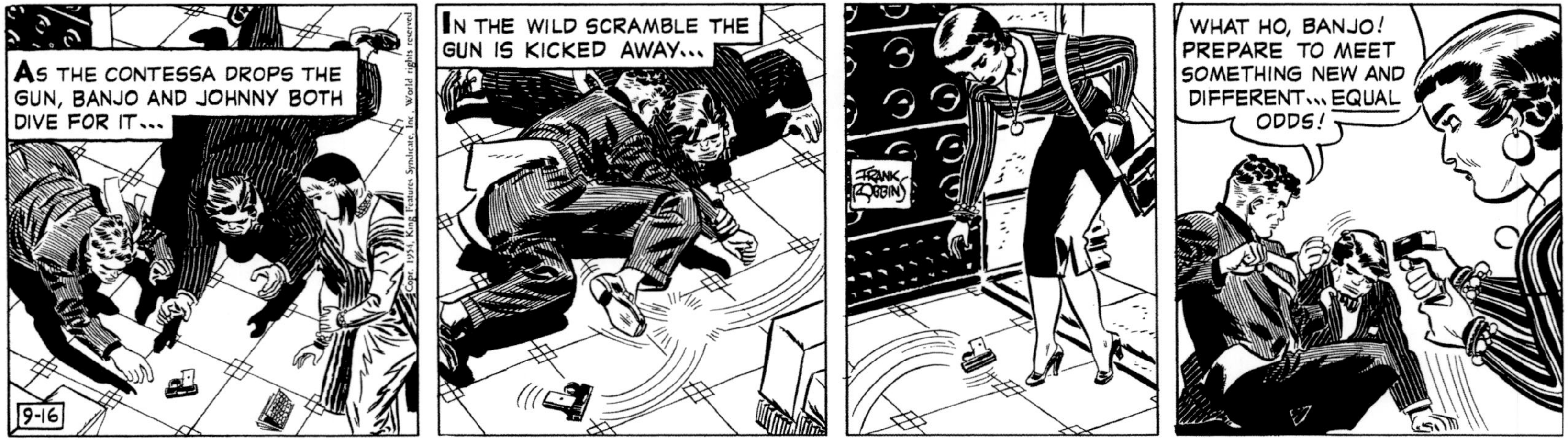
9-16
AS THE CONTESSA DROPS THE GUN, BANJO AND JOHNNY BOTH DIVE FOR IT...
Copr. 1954, King Features Syndicate, Inc. World rights reserved.
IN THE WILD SCRAMBLE THE GUN IS KICKED AWAY...
FRANK ROBBINS
WHAT HO, BANJO! PREPARE TO MEET SOMETHING NEW AND DIFFERENT... EQUAL ODDS!

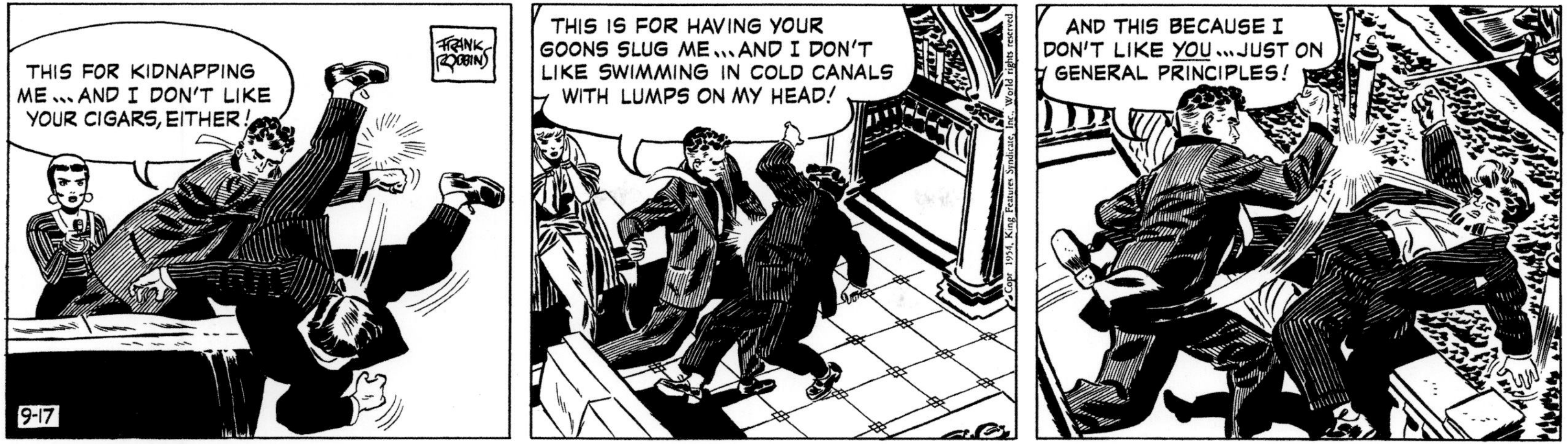
FRANK ROBBINS
THIS FOR KIDNAPPING ME ... AND I DON'T LIKE YOUR CIGARS, EITHER!
9-17
THIS IS FOR HAVING YOUR GOONS SLUG ME ... AND I DON'T LIKE SWIMMING IN COLD CANALS WITH LUMPS ON MY HEAD!
Copr 1954, King Features Syndicate, Inc., World rights reserved
AND THIS BECAUSE I DON'T LIKE YOU ... JUST ON GENERAL PRINCIPLES!

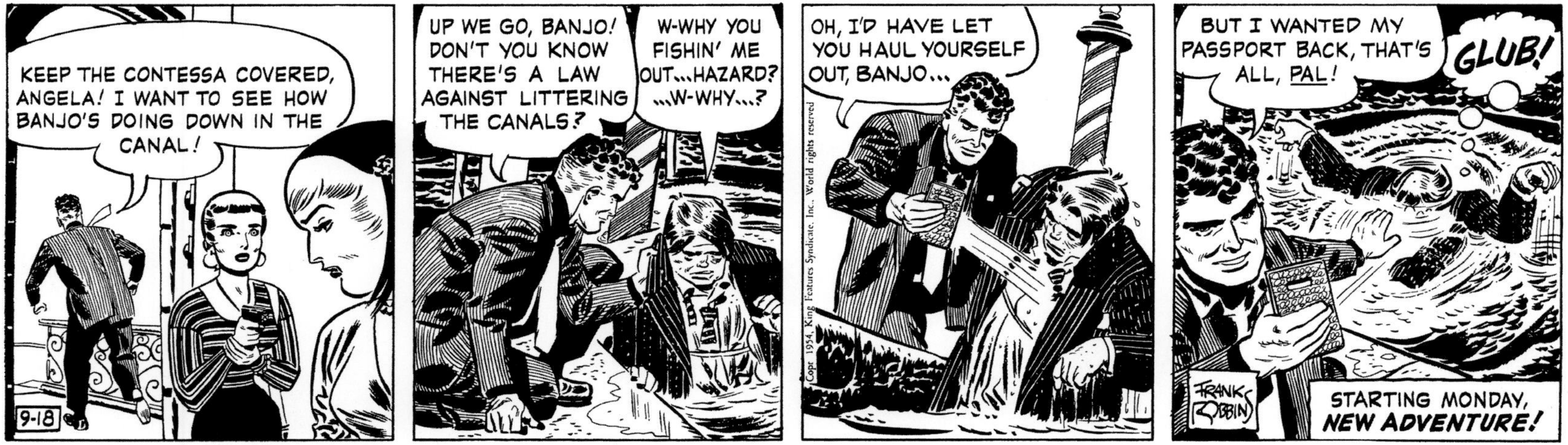
KEEP THE CONTESSA COVERED, ANGELA! I WANT TO SEE HOW BANJO'S DOING DOWN IN THE CANAL!
9-18
UP WE GO, BANJO! DON'T YOU KNOW THERE'S A LAW AGAINST LITTERING THE CANALS?
W-WHY YOU FISHIN' ME OUT...HAZARD? ...W-WHY...?
OH, I'D HAVE LET YOU HAUL YOURSELF OUT, BANJO...
Copr 1954, King Features Syndicate, Inc., World rights reserved
BUT I WANTED MY PASSPORT BACK, THAT'S ALL, PAL!
GLUB!
FRANK ROBBINS
STARTING MONDAY, NEW ADVENTURE!

JOHNNY HAZARD

Chapter Two: A Little Birdie Told Me

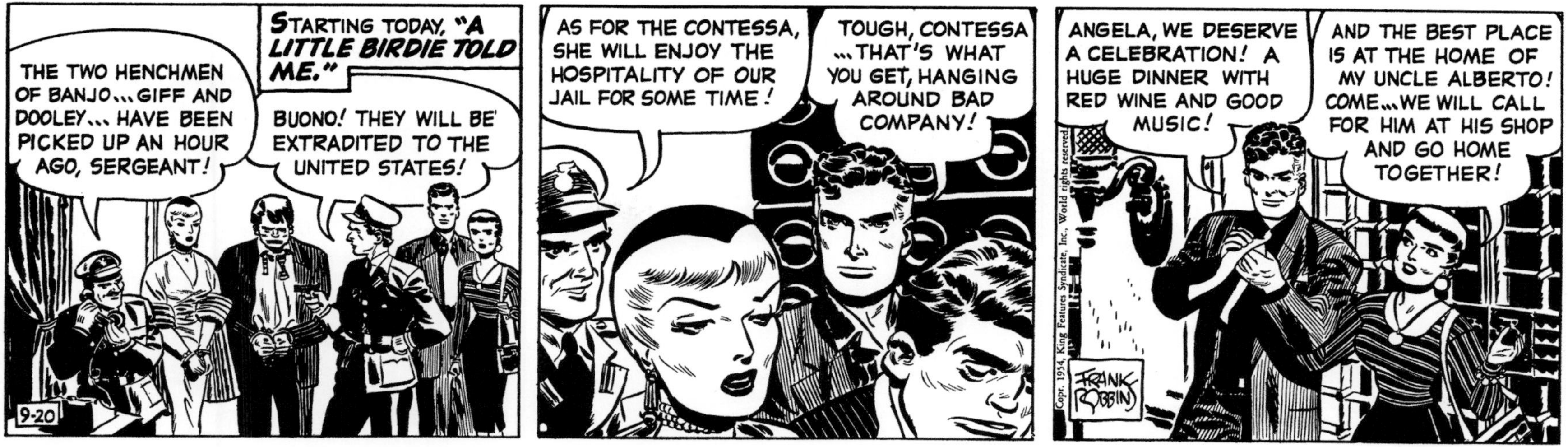
STARTING TODAY, "A LITTLE BIRDIE TOLD ME."
THE TWO HENCHMEN OF BANJO...GIFF AND DOOLEY... HAVE BEEN PICKED UP AN HOUR AGO, SERGEANT!
BUONO! THEY WILL BE' EXTRADITED TO THE UNITED STATES!
9-20
AS FOR THE CONTESSA, SHE WILL ENJOY THE HOSPITALITY OF OUR JAIL FOR SOME TIME!
TOUGH, CONTESSA ...THAT'S WHAT YOU GET, HANGING AROUND BAD COMPANY!
ANGELA, WE DESERVE A CELEBRATION! A HUGE DINNER WITH RED WINE AND GOOD MUSIC!
AND THE BEST PLACE IS AT THE HOME OF MY UNCLE ALBERTO! COME...WE WILL CALL FOR HIM AT HIS SHOP AND GO HOME TOGETHER!
Copr. 1954, King Features Syndicate, Inc., World rights reserved
FRANK ROBBINS

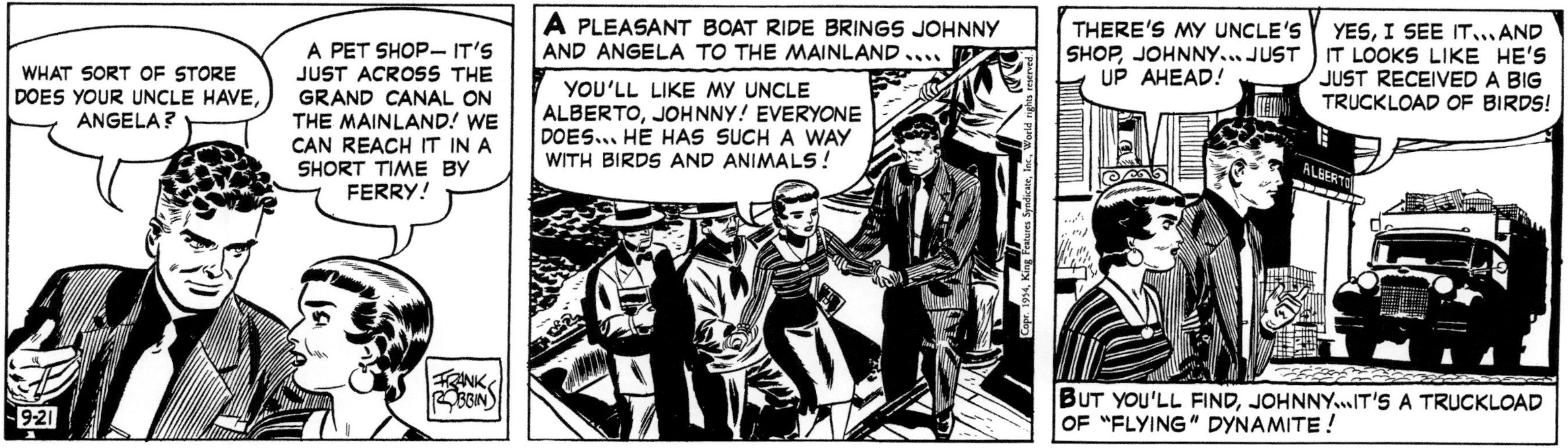
WHAT SORT OF STORE DOES YOUR UNCLE HAVE, ANGELA?
A PET SHOP— IT'S JUST ACROSS THE GRAND CANAL ON THE MAINLAND! WE CAN REACH IT IN A SHORT TIME BY FERRY!
9-21
FRANK ROBBINS
A PLEASANT BOAT RIDE BRINGS JOHNNY AND ANGELA TO THE MAINLAND....
YOU'LL LIKE MY UNCLE ALBERTO, JOHNNY! EVERYONE DOES... HE HAS SUCH A WAY WITH BIRDS AND ANIMALS!
Copr. 1954, King Features Syndicate, Inc., World rights reserved.
THERE'S MY UNCLE'S SHOP, JOHNNY... JUST UP AHEAD!
YES, I SEE IT...AND IT LOOKS LIKE HE'S JUST RECEIVED A BIG TRUCKLOAD OF BIRDS!
ALBERTO
BUT YOU'LL FIND, JOHNNY...IT'S A TRUCKLOAD OF "FLYING" DYNAMITE!

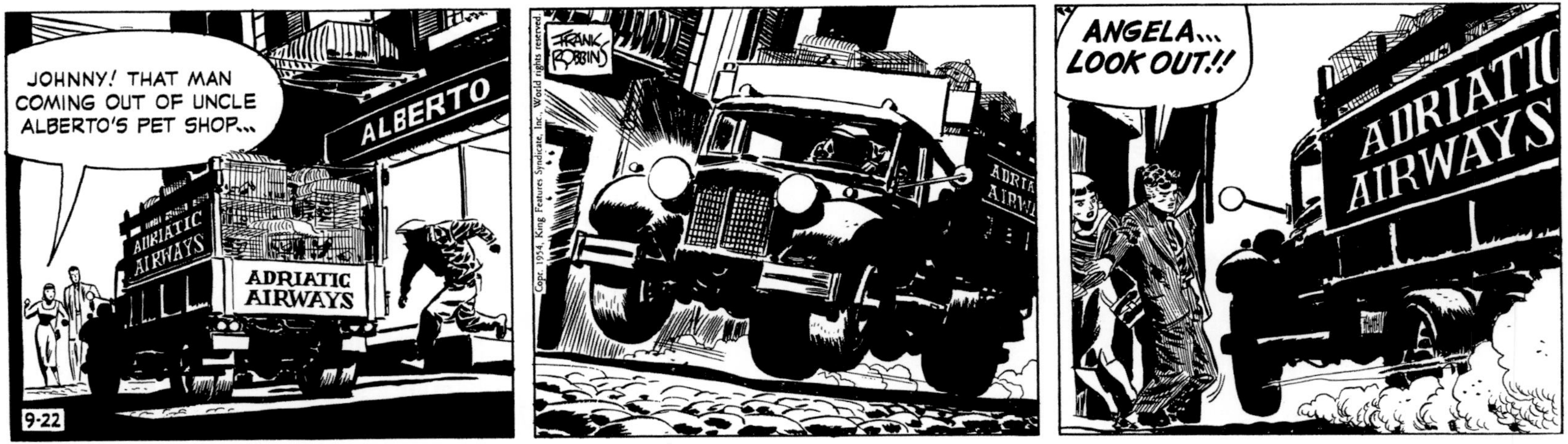
9-22
JOHNNY! THAT MAN COMING OUT OF UNCLE ALBERTO'S PET SHOP...
ALBERTO
ADRIATIC AIRWAYS
ADRIATIC AIRWAYS
FRANK ROBBINS
Copr. 1954, King Features Syndicate, Inc., World rights reserved.
ANGELA... LOOK OUT!!
ADRIATIC AIRWAYS

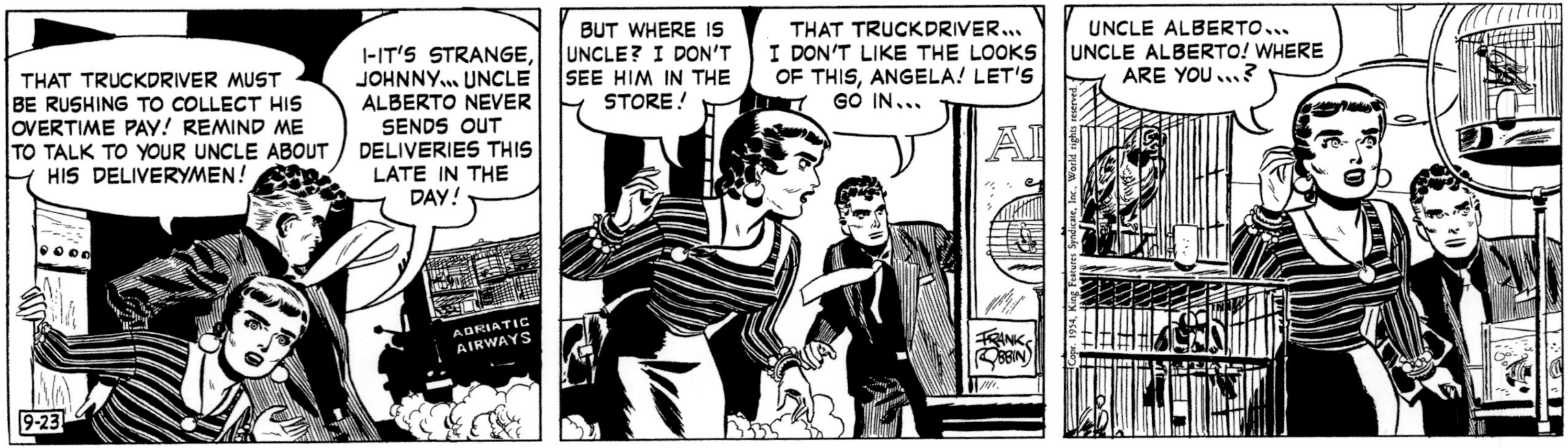
9-23
THAT TRUCKDRIVER MUST BE RUSHING TO COLLECT HIS OVERTIME PAY! REMIND ME TO TALK TO YOUR UNCLE ABOUT HIS DELIVERYMEN!
I-IT'S STRANGE, JOHNNY... UNCLE ALBERTO NEVER SENDS OUT DELIVERIES THIS LATE IN THE DAY!
ADRIATIC AIRWAYS
BUT WHERE IS UNCLE? I DON'T SEE HIM IN THE STORE!
THAT TRUCKDRIVER... I DON'T LIKE THE LOOKS OF THIS, ANGELA! LET'S GO IN...
FRANK ROBBINS
UNCLE ALBERTO... UNCLE ALBERTO! WHERE ARE YOU...?
Copr. 1954, King Features Syndicate, Inc., World rights reserved.

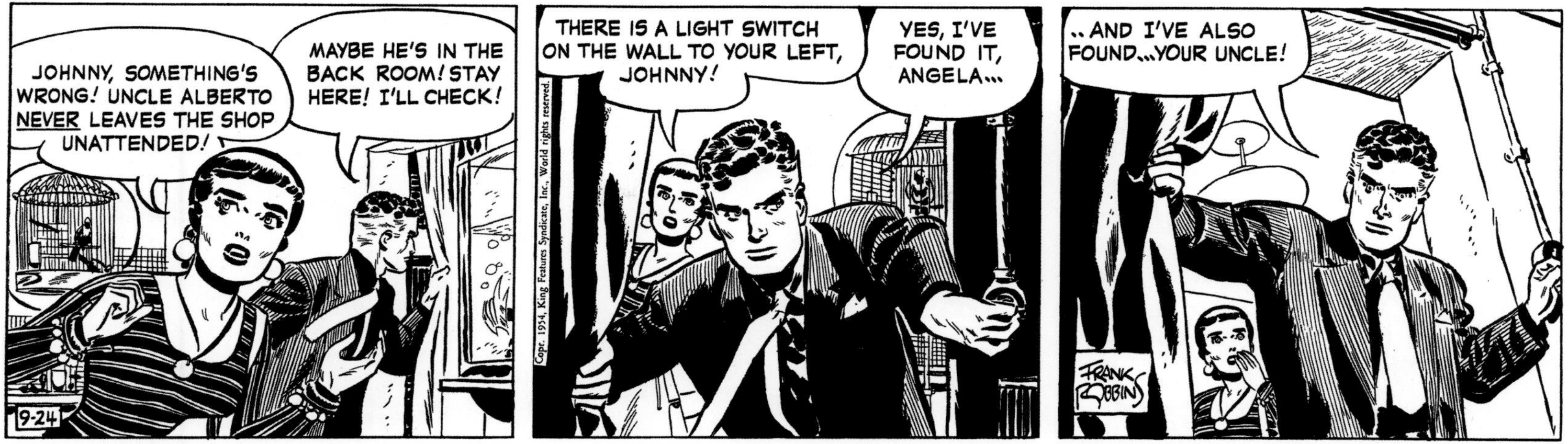
JOHNNY, SOMETHING'S WRONG! UNCLE ALBERTO NEVER LEAVES THE SHOP UNATTENDED!
MAYBE HE'S IN THE BACK ROOM! STAY HERE! I'LL CHECK!
THERE IS A LIGHT SWITCH ON THE WALL TO YOUR LEFT, JOHNNY!
YES, I'VE FOUND IT, ANGELA...
..AND I'VE ALSO FOUND...YOUR UNCLE!
9-24
Copr. 1954, King Features Syndicate, Inc., World rights reserved.
FRANK ROBBINS

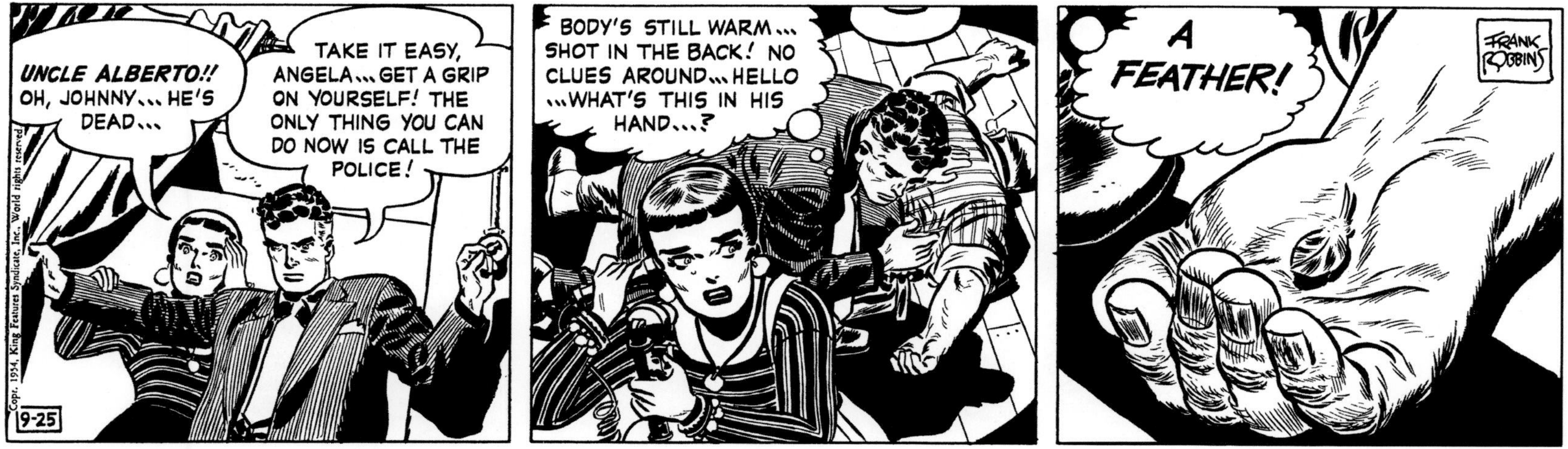
UNCLE ALBERTO!! OH, JOHNNY... HE'S DEAD...
TAKE IT EASY, ANGELA...GET A GRIP ON YOURSELF! THE ONLY THING YOU CAN DO NOW IS CALL THE POLICE!
BODY'S STILL WARM... SHOT IN THE BACK! NO CLUES AROUND... HELLO ...WHAT'S THIS IN HIS HAND...?
A FEATHER!
9-25
Copr. 1954, King Features Syndicate, Inc., World rights reserved
FRANK ROBBINS

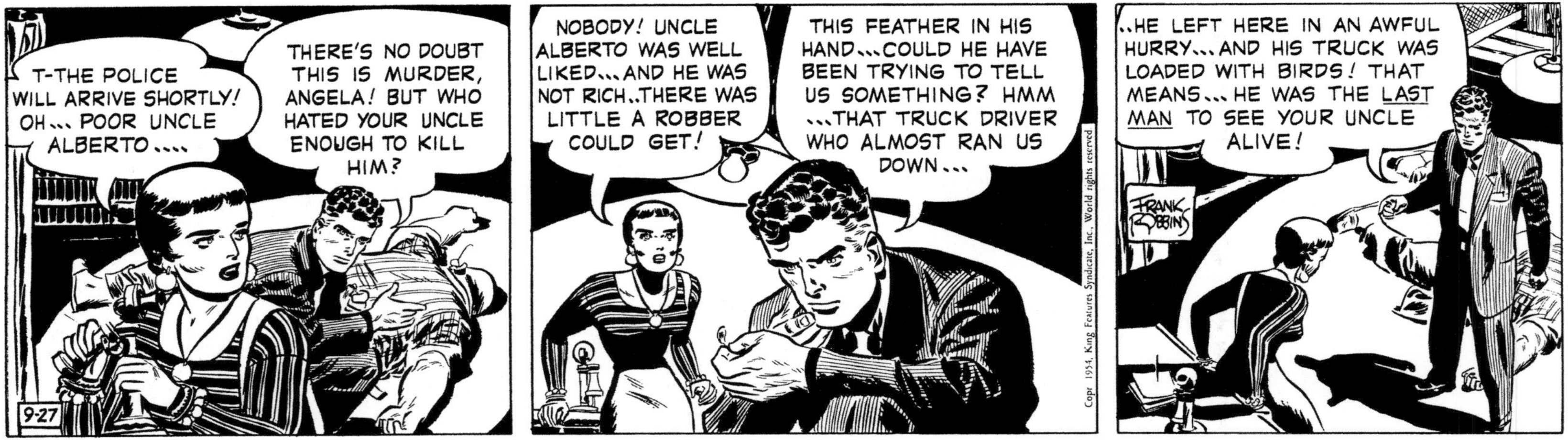
T-THE POLICE WILL ARRIVE SHORTLY! OH... POOR UNCLE ALBERTO....
THERE'S NO DOUBT THIS IS MURDER, ANGELA! BUT WHO HATED YOUR UNCLE ENOUGH TO KILL HIM?
9-27
NOBODY! UNCLE ALBERTO WAS WELL LIKED...AND HE WAS NOT RICH..THERE WAS LITTLE A ROBBER COULD GET!
THIS FEATHER IN HIS HAND...COULD HE HAVE BEEN TRYING TO TELL US SOMETHING? HMM ...THAT TRUCK DRIVER WHO ALMOST RAN US DOWN...
Copr 1954, King Features Syndicate, Inc, World rights reserved
..HE LEFT HERE IN AN AWFUL HURRY...AND HIS TRUCK WAS LOADED WITH BIRDS! THAT MEANS...HE WAS THE LAST MAN TO SEE YOUR UNCLE ALIVE!
FRANK ROBBINS

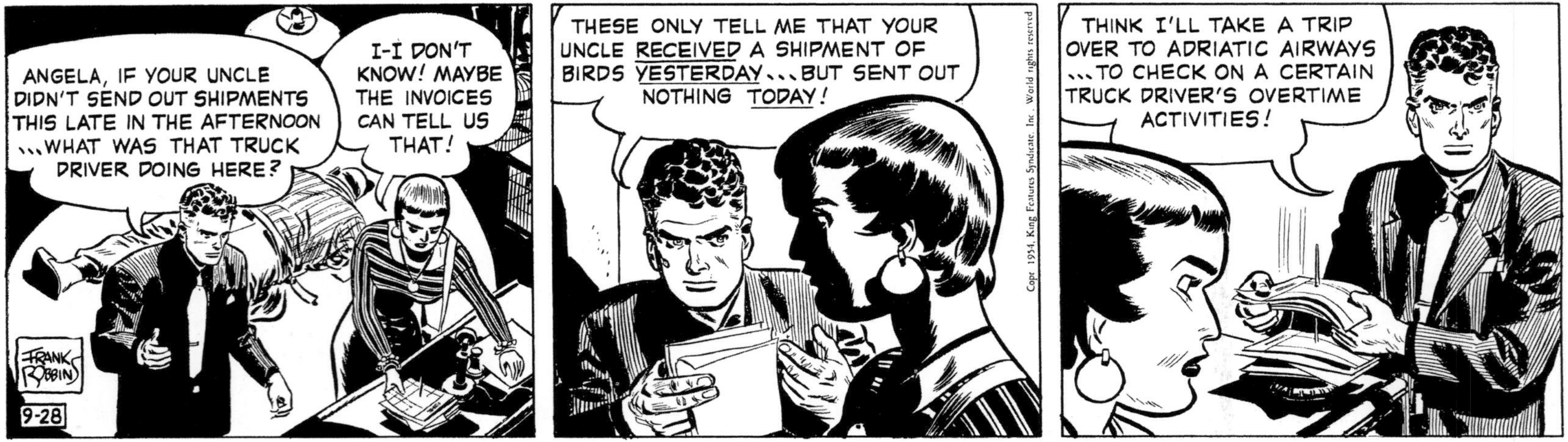
ANGELA, IF YOUR UNCLE DIDN'T SEND OUT SHIPMENTS THIS LATE IN THE AFTERNOON ...WHAT WAS THAT TRUCK DRIVER DOING HERE?
I-I DON'T KNOW! MAYBE THE INVOICES CAN TELL US THAT!
FRANK ROBBINS
9-28
THESE ONLY TELL ME THAT YOUR UNCLE RECEIVED A SHIPMENT OF BIRDS YESTERDAY...BUT SENT OUT NOTHING TODAY!
Copr 1954, King Features Syndicate, Inc. World rights reserved
THINK I'LL TAKE A TRIP OVER TO ADRIATIC AIRWAYS ...TO CHECK ON A CERTAIN TRUCK DRIVER'S OVERTIME ACTIVITIES!

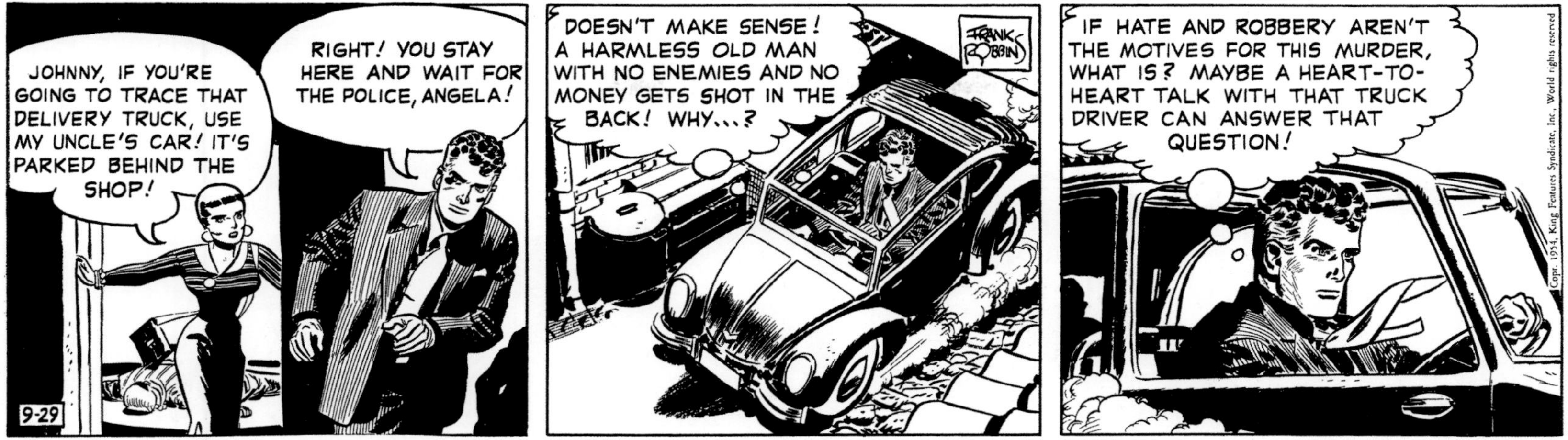
9-29
JOHNNY, IF YOU'RE GOING TO TRACE THAT DELIVERY TRUCK, USE MY UNCLE'S CAR! IT'S PARKED BEHIND THE SHOP!
RIGHT! YOU STAY HERE AND WAIT FOR THE POLICE, ANGELA!
FRANK ROBBINS
DOESN'T MAKE SENSE! A HARMLESS OLD MAN WITH NO ENEMIES AND NO MONEY GETS SHOT IN THE BACK! WHY...?
IF HATE AND ROBBERY AREN'T THE MOTIVES FOR THIS MURDER, WHAT IS? MAYBE A HEART-TO-HEART TALK WITH THAT TRUCK DRIVER CAN ANSWER THAT QUESTION!
Copr. 1954, King Features Syndicate, Inc., World rights reserved

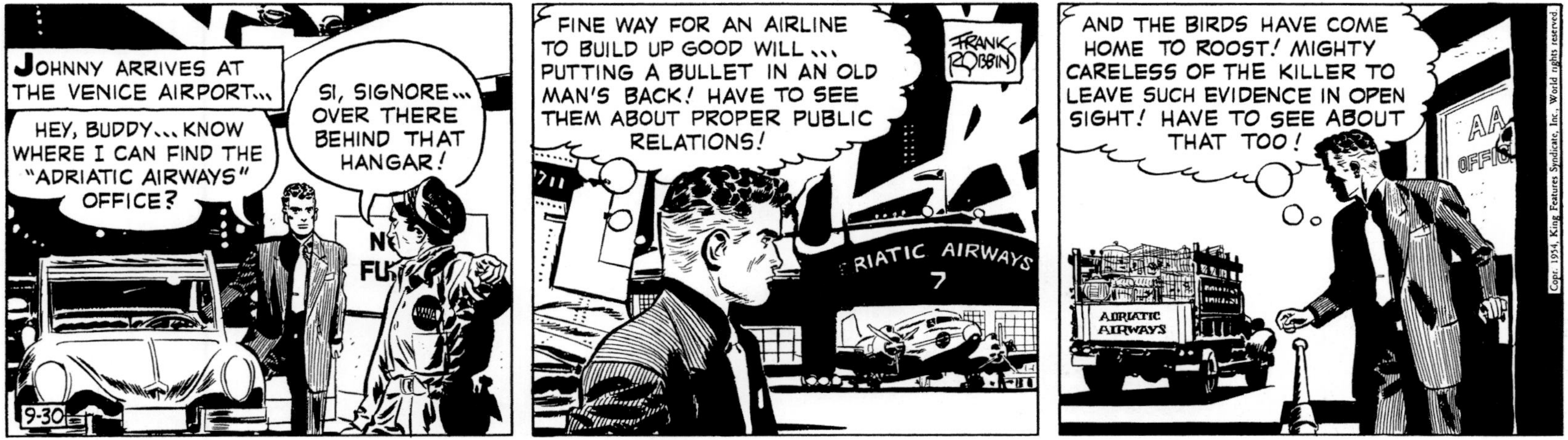
9-30
JOHNNY ARRIVES AT THE VENICE AIRPORT...
HEY, BUDDY... KNOW WHERE I CAN FIND THE "ADRIATIC AIRWAYS" OFFICE?
SI, SIGNORE... OVER THERE BEHIND THAT HANGAR!
FRANK ROBBINS
FINE WAY FOR AN AIRLINE TO BUILD UP GOOD WILL... PUTTING A BULLET IN AN OLD MAN'S BACK! HAVE TO SEE THEM ABOUT PROPER PUBLIC RELATIONS!
RIATIC AIRWAYS
7
AND THE BIRDS HAVE COME HOME TO ROOST! MIGHTY CARELESS OF THE KILLER TO LEAVE SUCH EVIDENCE IN OPEN SIGHT! HAVE TO SEE ABOUT THAT TOO!
ADRIATIC AIRWAYS
Copr. 1954, King Features Syndicate, Inc., World rights reserved

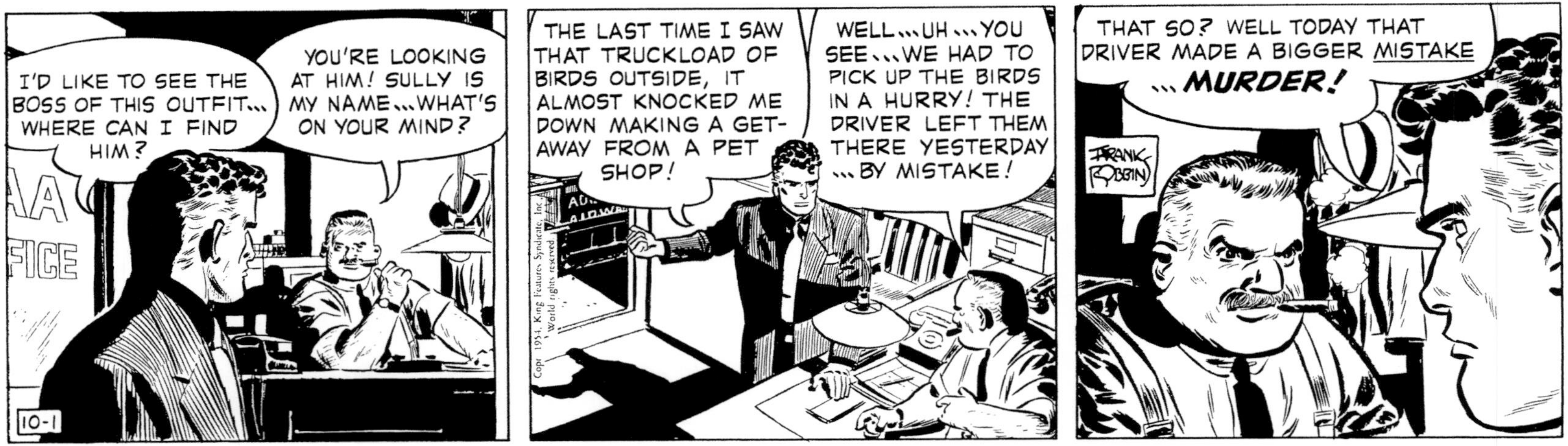
I'D LIKE TO SEE THE BOSS OF THIS OUTFIT... WHERE CAN I FIND HIM?
YOU'RE LOOKING AT HIM! SULLY IS MY NAME... WHAT'S ON YOUR MIND?
10-1
THE LAST TIME I SAW THAT TRUCKLOAD OF BIRDS OUTSIDE, IT ALMOST KNOCKED ME DOWN MAKING A GET-AWAY FROM A PET SHOP!
WELL... UH... YOU SEE... WE HAD TO PICK UP THE BIRDS IN A HURRY! THE DRIVER LEFT THEM THERE YESTERDAY ... BY MISTAKE!
Copr. 1954, King Features Syndicate, Inc., World rights reserved
THAT SO? WELL TODAY THAT DRIVER MADE A BIGGER MISTAKE ... MURDER!
FRANK ROBBIN

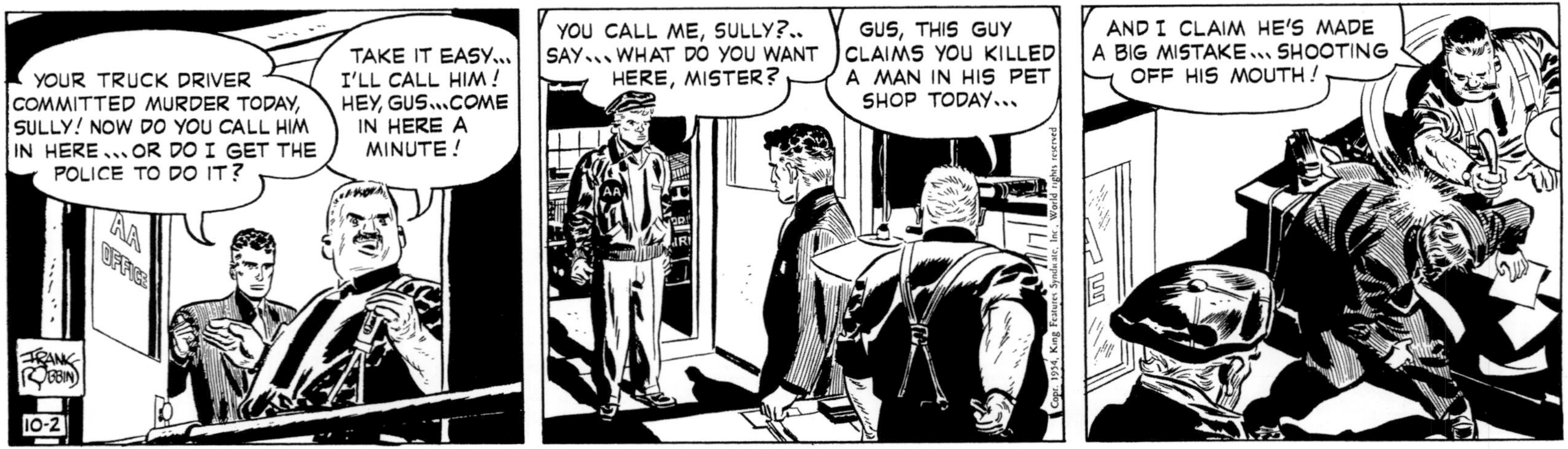
YOUR TRUCK DRIVER COMMITTED MURDER TODAY, SULLY! NOW DO YOU CALL HIM IN HERE... OR DO I GET THE POLICE TO DO IT?
TAKE IT EASY... I'LL CALL HIM! HEY, GUS... COME IN HERE A MINUTE!
AA OFFICE
FRANK ROBBIN
10-2
YOU CALL ME, SULLY?.. SAY... WHAT DO YOU WANT HERE, MISTER?
GUS, THIS GUY CLAIMS YOU KILLED A MAN IN HIS PET SHOP TODAY...
Copr. 1954, King Features Syndicate, Inc., World rights reserved
AND I CLAIM HE'S MADE A BIG MISTAKE... SHOOTING OFF HIS MOUTH!

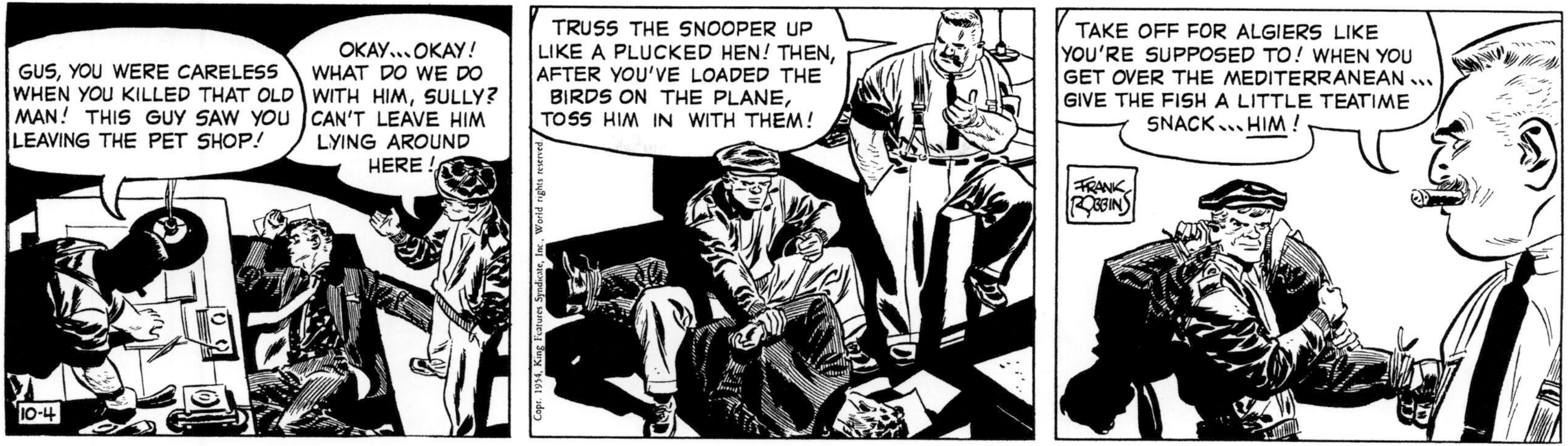
GUS, YOU WERE CARELESS WHEN YOU KILLED THAT OLD MAN! THIS GUY SAW YOU LEAVING THE PET SHOP!
OKAY...OKAY! WHAT DO WE DO WITH HIM, SULLY? CAN'T LEAVE HIM LYING AROUND HERE!
10-4
TRUSS THE SNOOPER UP LIKE A PLUCKED HEN! THEN, AFTER YOU'VE LOADED THE BIRDS ON THE PLANE, TOSS HIM IN WITH THEM!
Copr. 1954, King Features Syndicate, Inc., World rights reserved
TAKE OFF FOR ALGIERS LIKE YOU'RE SUPPOSED TO! WHEN YOU GET OVER THE MEDITERRANEAN... GIVE THE FISH A LITTLE TEATIME SNACK...HIM!
FRANK ROBBINS

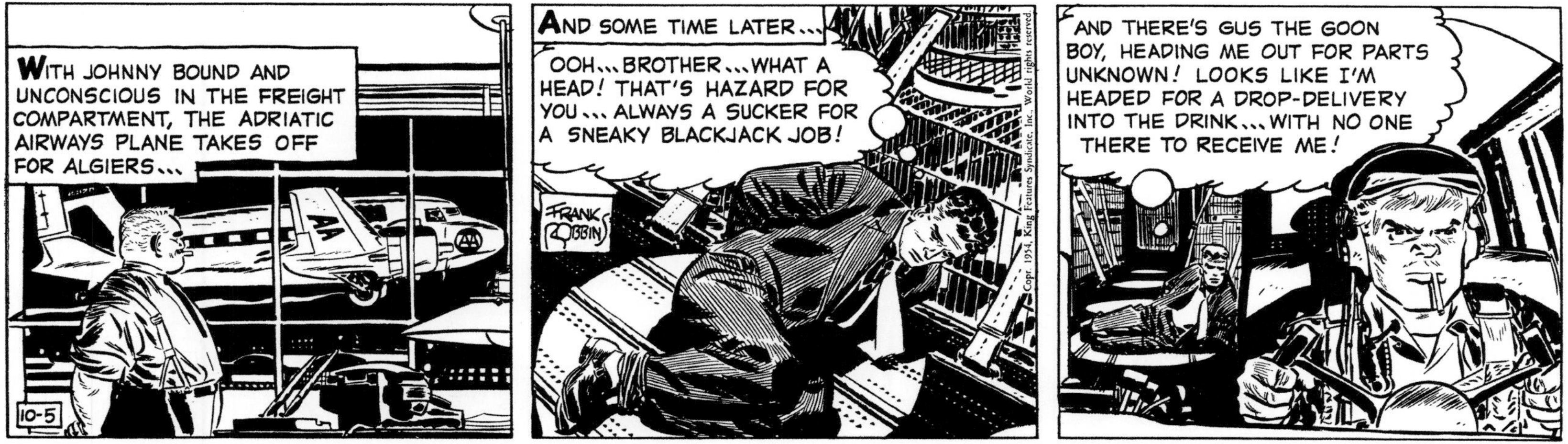
WITH JOHNNY BOUND AND UNCONSCIOUS IN THE FREIGHT COMPARTMENT, THE ADRIATIC AIRWAYS PLANE TAKES OFF FOR ALGIERS...
AA
10-5
AND SOME TIME LATER...
OOH...BROTHER...WHAT A HEAD! THAT'S HAZARD FOR YOU... ALWAYS A SUCKER FOR A SNEAKY BLACKJACK JOB!
FRANK ROBBINS
Copr. 1954, King Features Syndicate, Inc., World rights reserved
AND THERE'S GUS THE GOON BOY, HEADING ME OUT FOR PARTS UNKNOWN! LOOKS LIKE I'M HEADED FOR A DROP-DELIVERY INTO THE DRINK...WITH NO ONE THERE TO RECEIVE ME!

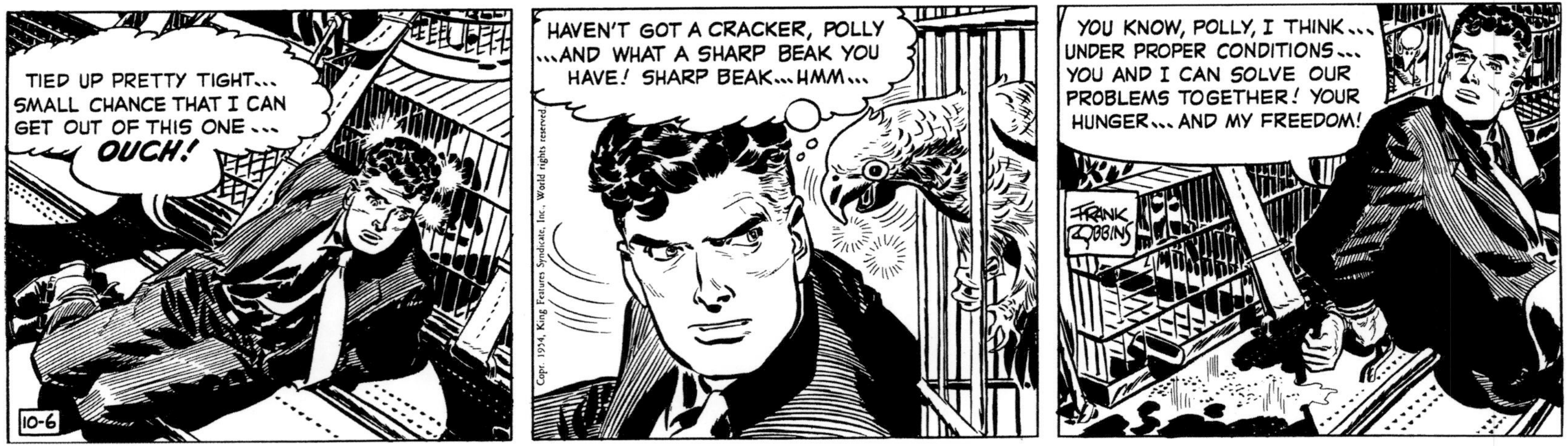
TIED UP PRETTY TIGHT... SMALL CHANCE THAT I CAN GET OUT OF THIS ONE ... OUCH!
10-6
HAVEN'T GOT A CRACKER, POLLY ...AND WHAT A SHARP BEAK YOU HAVE! SHARP BEAK... HMM...
Copr. 1954, King Features Syndicate, Inc., World rights reserved.
YOU KNOW, POLLY, I THINK... UNDER PROPER CONDITIONS... YOU AND I CAN SOLVE OUR PROBLEMS TOGETHER! YOUR HUNGER... AND MY FREEDOM!
FRANK ROBBINS

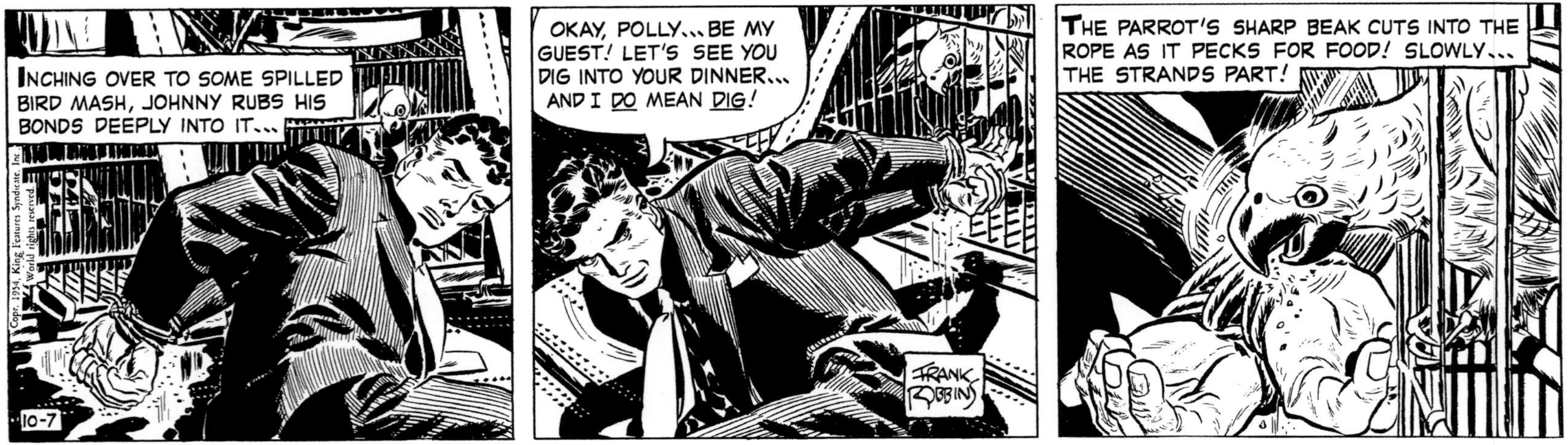
INCHING OVER TO SOME SPILLED BIRD MASH, JOHNNY RUBS HIS BONDS DEEPLY INTO IT...
Copr. 1954, King Features Syndicate, Inc., World rights reserved.
10-7
OKAY, POLLY... BE MY GUEST! LET'S SEE YOU DIG INTO YOUR DINNER... AND I DO MEAN DIG!
FRANK ROBBINS
THE PARROT'S SHARP BEAK CUTS INTO THE ROPE AS IT PECKS FOR FOOD! SLOWLY... THE STRANDS PART!

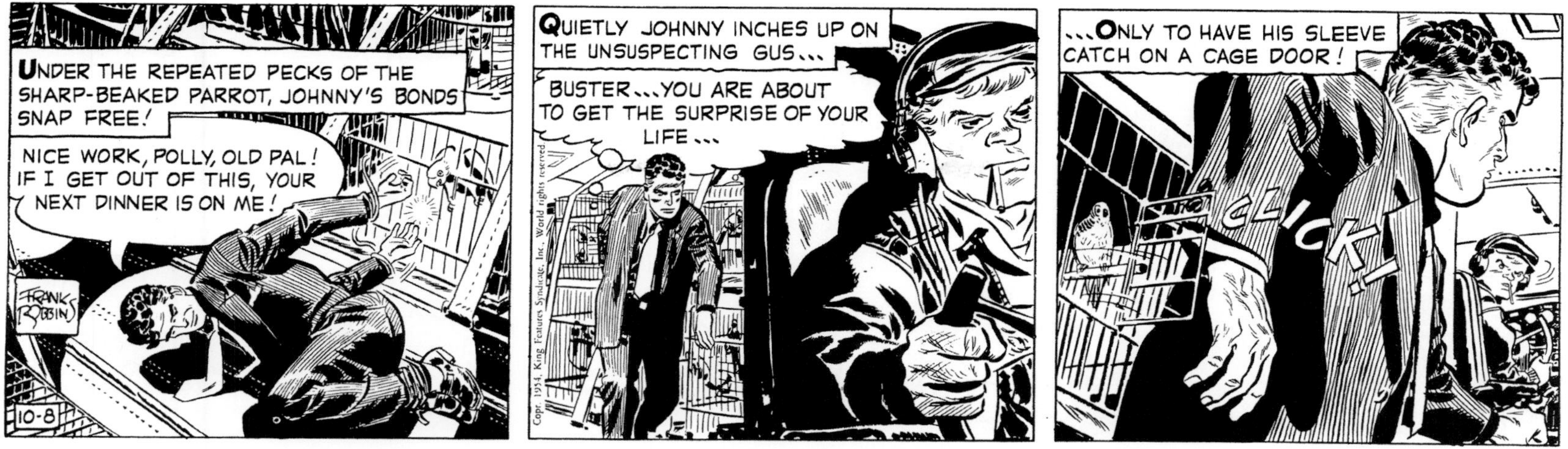
UNDER THE REPEATED PECKS OF THE SHARP-BEAKED PARROT, JOHNNY'S BONDS SNAP FREE!
NICE WORK, POLLY, OLD PAL! IF I GET OUT OF THIS, YOUR NEXT DINNER IS ON ME!
FRANK ROBBINS
10-8
QUIETLY JOHNNY INCHES UP ON THE UNSUSPECTING GUS...
BUSTER...YOU ARE ABOUT TO GET THE SURPRISE OF YOUR LIFE...
Copr. 1954, King Features Syndicate, Inc., World rights reserved
...ONLY TO HAVE HIS SLEEVE CATCH ON A CAGE DOOR!
CLICK!

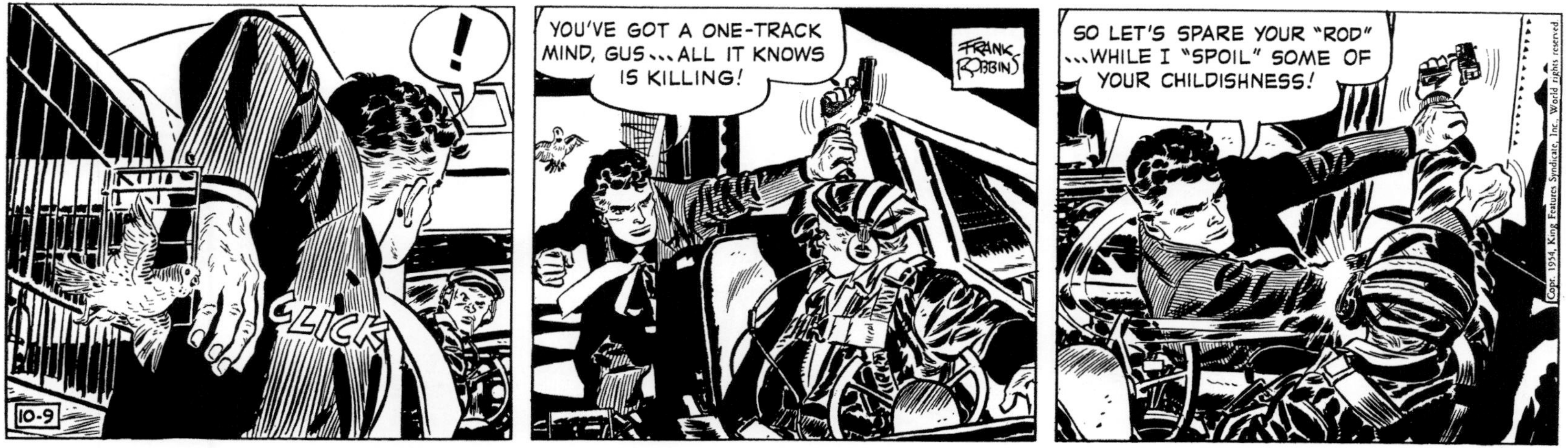
!
CLICK
10-9
YOU'VE GOT A ONE-TRACK MIND, GUS...ALL IT KNOWS IS KILLING!
FRANK ROBBINS
SO LET'S SPARE YOUR "ROD" ...WHILE I "SPOIL" SOME OF YOUR CHILDISHNESS!
Copr. 1954, King Features Syndicate, Inc., World rights reserved

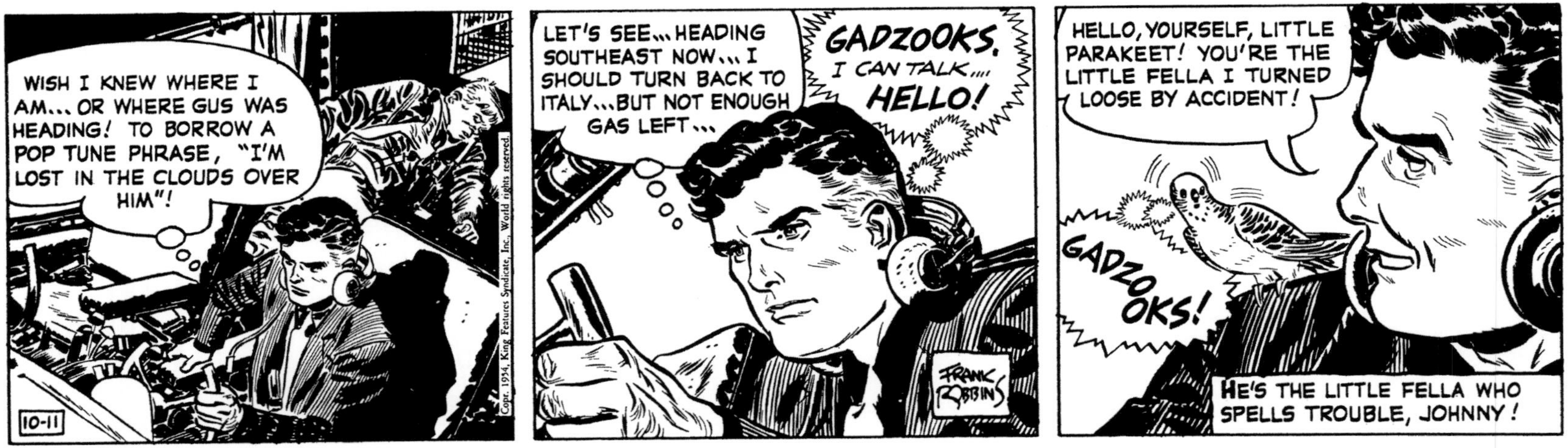
WISH I KNEW WHERE I AM... OR WHERE GUS WAS HEADING! TO BORROW A POP TUNE PHRASE, "I'M LOST IN THE CLOUDS OVER HIM"!
10-11
Copr. 1954, King Features Syndicate, Inc., World rights reserved.
LET'S SEE... HEADING SOUTHEAST NOW... I SHOULD TURN BACK TO ITALY... BUT NOT ENOUGH GAS LEFT...
GADZOOKS. I CAN TALK.... HELLO!
FRANK ROBBINS
HELLO, YOURSELF, LITTLE PARAKEET! YOU'RE THE LITTLE FELLA I TURNED LOOSE BY ACCIDENT!
GADZOOKS!
HE'S THE LITTLE FELLA WHO SPELLS TROUBLE, JOHNNY!

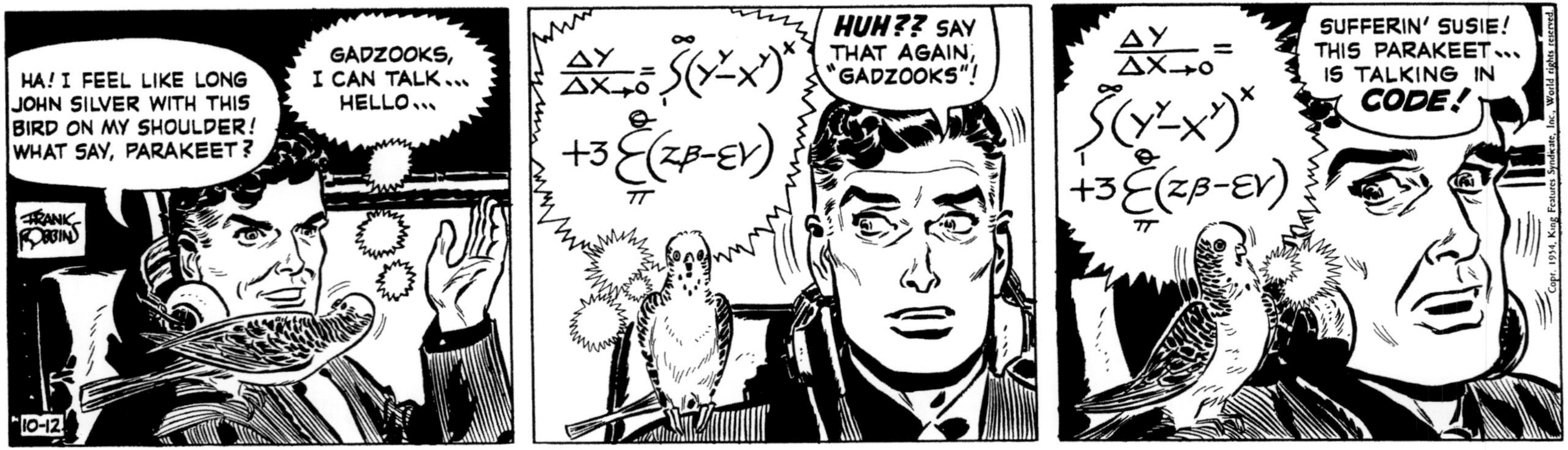
HA! I FEEL LIKE LONG JOHN SILVER WITH THIS BIRD ON MY SHOULDER! WHAT SAY, PARAKEET?
GADZOOKS, I CAN TALK... HELLO...
FRANK ROBBINS
10-12
$\frac{\Delta Y}{\Delta X_{\to 0}} = \int_1^\infty (Y^Y - X^Y)^X$
$+3 \sum_\pi^\theta (Z\beta - \varepsilon V)$
HUH?? SAY THAT AGAIN, "GADZOOKS"!
$\frac{\Delta Y}{\Delta X_{\to 0}} =$
$\int_1^\infty (Y^Y - X^Y)^X$
$+3 \sum_\pi^\theta (Z\beta - \varepsilon V)$
SUFFERIN' SUSIE! THIS PARAKEET... IS TALKING IN CODE!
Copr. 1954, King Features Syndicate, Inc., World rights reserved.

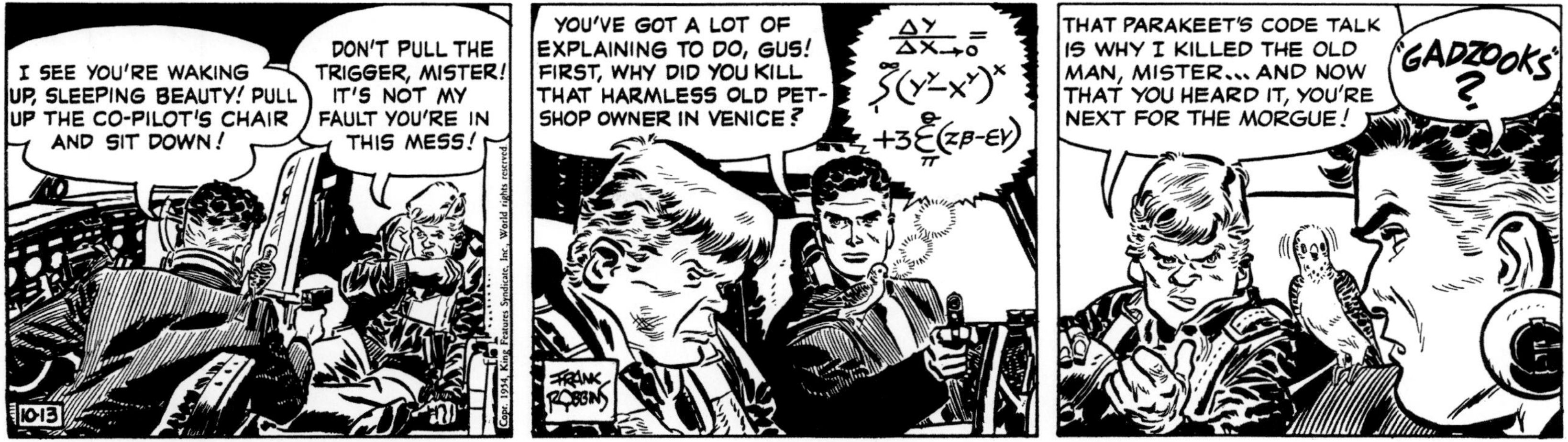
I SEE YOU'RE WAKING UP, SLEEPING BEAUTY! PULL UP THE CO-PILOT'S CHAIR AND SIT DOWN!
DON'T PULL THE TRIGGER, MISTER! IT'S NOT MY FAULT YOU'RE IN THIS MESS!
10-13
Copr. 1954, King Features Syndicate, Inc., World rights reserved
YOU'VE GOT A LOT OF EXPLAINING TO DO, GUS! FIRST, WHY DID YOU KILL THAT HARMLESS OLD PET-SHOP OWNER IN VENICE?
$\frac{\Delta Y}{\Delta X \to 0} = \sum (Y^Y - X^Y)^X + 3 \sum (Z\beta - \varepsilon Y)$
FRANK ROBBINS
THAT PARAKEET'S CODE TALK IS WHY I KILLED THE OLD MAN, MISTER... AND NOW THAT YOU HEARD IT, YOU'RE NEXT FOR THE MORGUE!
"GADZOOKS"?

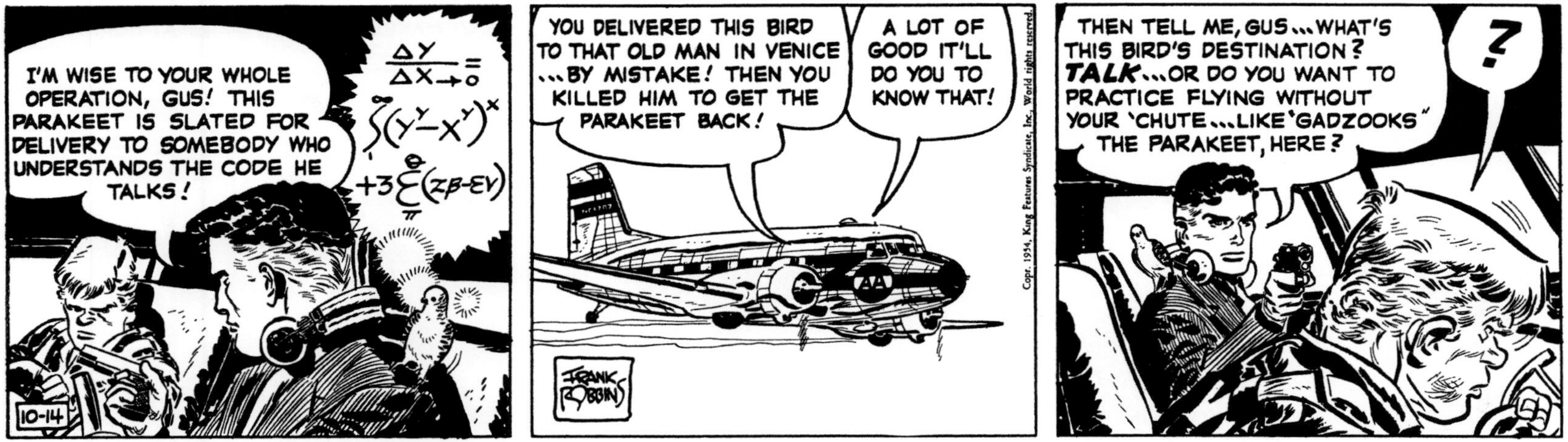
I'M WISE TO YOUR WHOLE OPERATION, GUS! THIS PARAKEET IS SLATED FOR DELIVERY TO SOMEBODY WHO UNDERSTANDS THE CODE HE TALKS!
$\frac{\Delta Y}{\Delta X \to 0} = \sum (Y^Y - X^Y)^X + 3 \sum (Z\beta - \varepsilon Y)$
10-14
YOU DELIVERED THIS BIRD TO THAT OLD MAN IN VENICE ...BY MISTAKE! THEN YOU KILLED HIM TO GET THE PARAKEET BACK!
A LOT OF GOOD IT'LL DO YOU TO KNOW THAT!
Copr. 1954, King Features Syndicate, Inc., World rights reserved.
FRANK ROBBINS
THEN TELL ME, GUS... WHAT'S THIS BIRD'S DESTINATION? TALK...OR DO YOU WANT TO PRACTICE FLYING WITHOUT YOUR 'CHUTE...LIKE "GADZOOKS" THE PARAKEET, HERE?
?

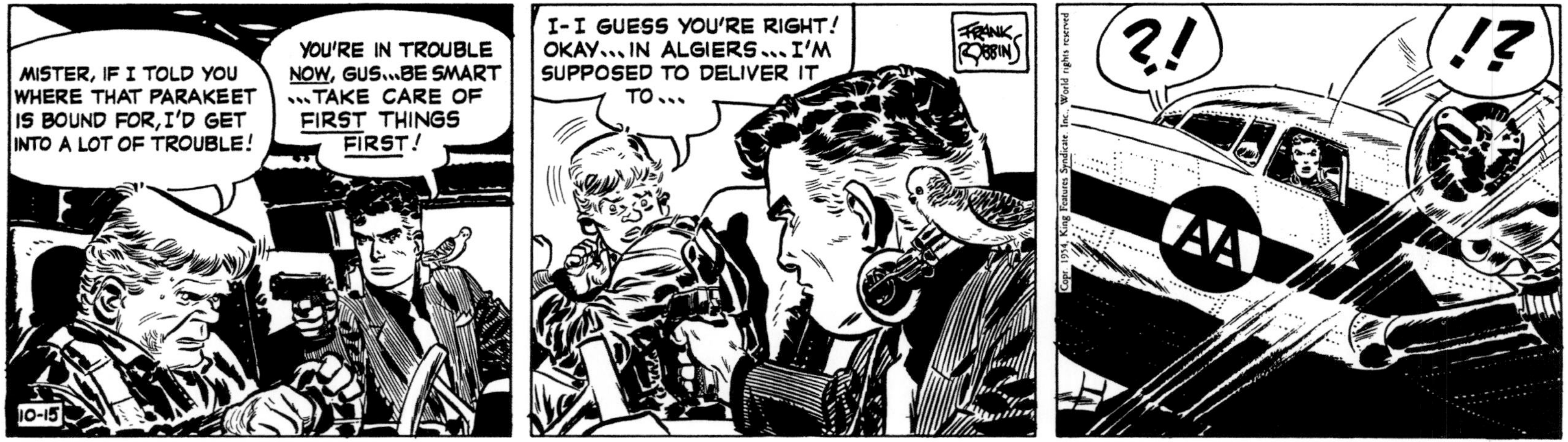
10-15
MISTER, IF I TOLD YOU WHERE THAT PARAKEET IS BOUND FOR, I'D GET INTO A LOT OF TROUBLE!
YOU'RE IN TROUBLE NOW, GUS...BE SMART ...TAKE CARE OF FIRST THINGS FIRST!
I-I GUESS YOU'RE RIGHT! OKAY... IN ALGIERS... I'M SUPPOSED TO DELIVER IT TO...
FRANK ROBBINS
?!
!?
AA
Copr. 1954, King Features Syndicate, Inc., World rights reserved

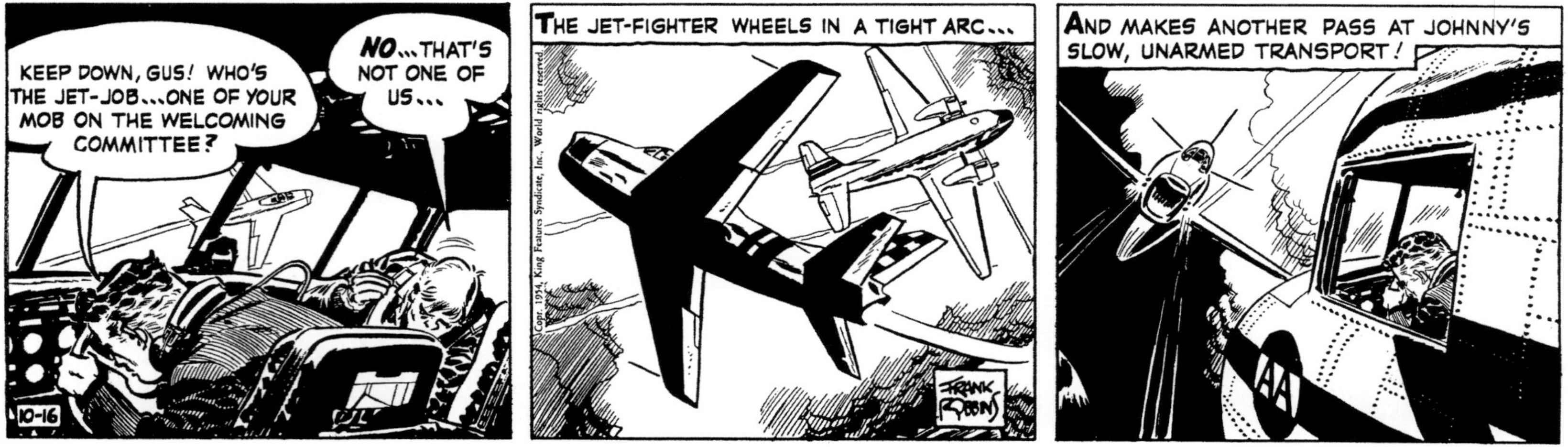
KEEP DOWN, GUS! WHO'S THE JET-JOB...ONE OF YOUR MOB ON THE WELCOMING COMMITTEE?
NO...THAT'S NOT ONE OF US...
10-16
THE JET-FIGHTER WHEELS IN A TIGHT ARC...
Copr. 1954, King Features Syndicate, Inc., World rights reserved.
FRANK ROBBINS
AND MAKES ANOTHER PASS AT JOHNNY'S SLOW, UNARMED TRANSPORT!
AA

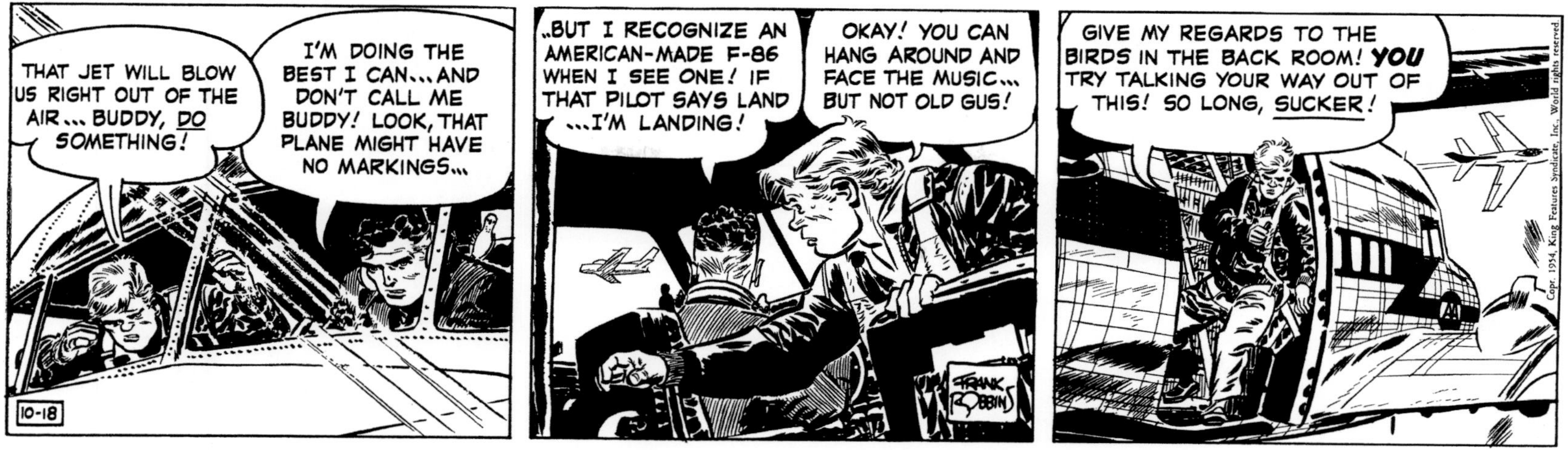
THAT JET WILL BLOW US RIGHT OUT OF THE AIR... BUDDY, DO SOMETHING!
I'M DOING THE BEST I CAN... AND DON'T CALL ME BUDDY! LOOK, THAT PLANE MIGHT HAVE NO MARKINGS...
10-18
..BUT I RECOGNIZE AN AMERICAN-MADE F-86 WHEN I SEE ONE! IF THAT PILOT SAYS LAND ...I'M LANDING!
OKAY! YOU CAN HANG AROUND AND FACE THE MUSIC... BUT NOT OLD GUS!
FRANK ROBBINS
GIVE MY REGARDS TO THE BIRDS IN THE BACK ROOM! YOU TRY TALKING YOUR WAY OUT OF THIS! SO LONG, SUCKER!
Copr. 1954, King Features Syndicate, Inc., World rights reserved.

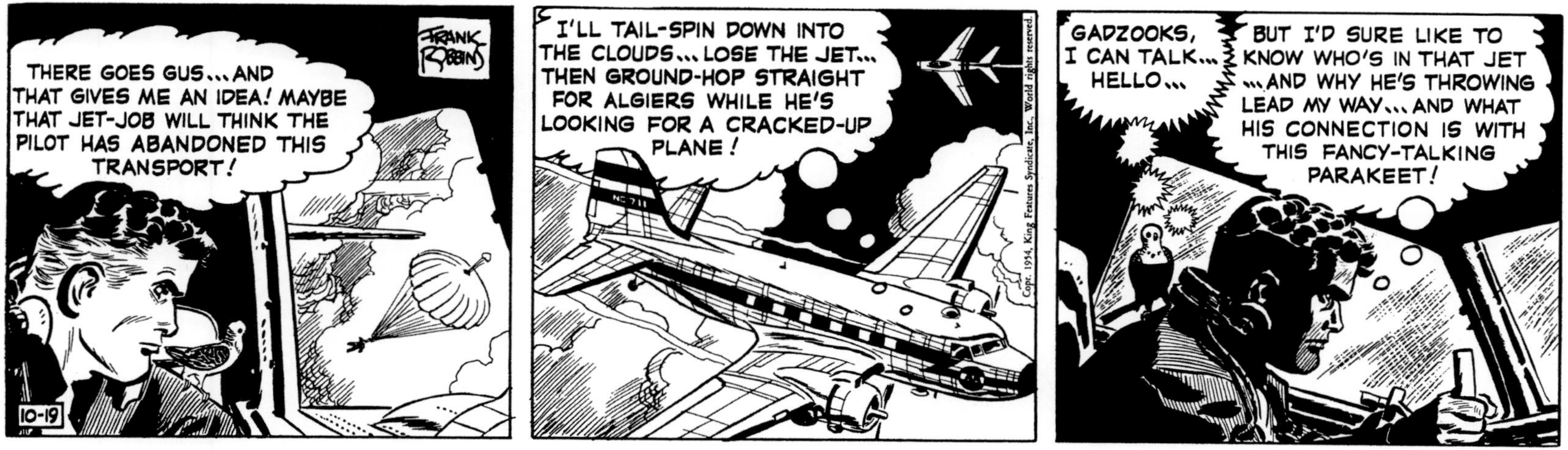
FRANK ROBBINS
THERE GOES GUS... AND THAT GIVES ME AN IDEA! MAYBE THAT JET-JOB WILL THINK THE PILOT HAS ABANDONED THIS TRANSPORT!
10-19
I'LL TAIL-SPIN DOWN INTO THE CLOUDS... LOSE THE JET... THEN GROUND-HOP STRAIGHT FOR ALGIERS WHILE HE'S LOOKING FOR A CRACKED-UP PLANE!
Copr. 1954, King Features Syndicate, Inc., World rights reserved.
GADZOOKS, I CAN TALK... HELLO...
BUT I'D SURE LIKE TO KNOW WHO'S IN THAT JET ...AND WHY HE'S THROWING LEAD MY WAY... AND WHAT HIS CONNECTION IS WITH THIS FANCY-TALKING PARAKEET!

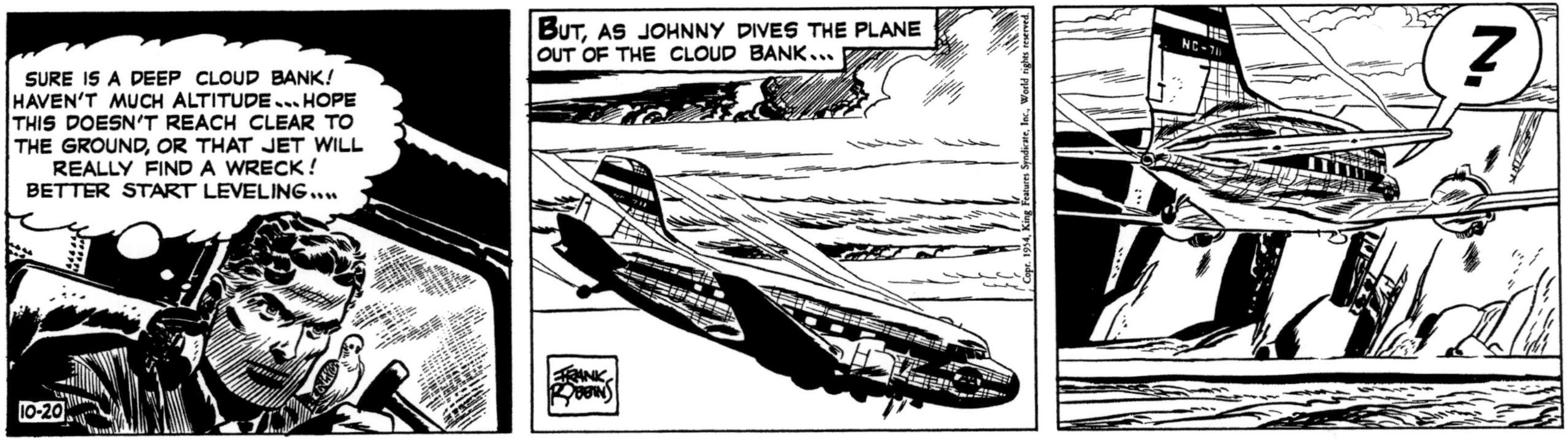
10-20
SURE IS A DEEP CLOUD BANK! HAVEN'T MUCH ALTITUDE... HOPE THIS DOESN'T REACH CLEAR TO THE GROUND, OR THAT JET WILL REALLY FIND A WRECK! BETTER START LEVELING....
BUT, AS JOHNNY DIVES THE PLANE OUT OF THE CLOUD BANK...
FRANK ROBBINS
Copr. 1954, King Features Syndicate, Inc., World rights reserved.
NC-711
?

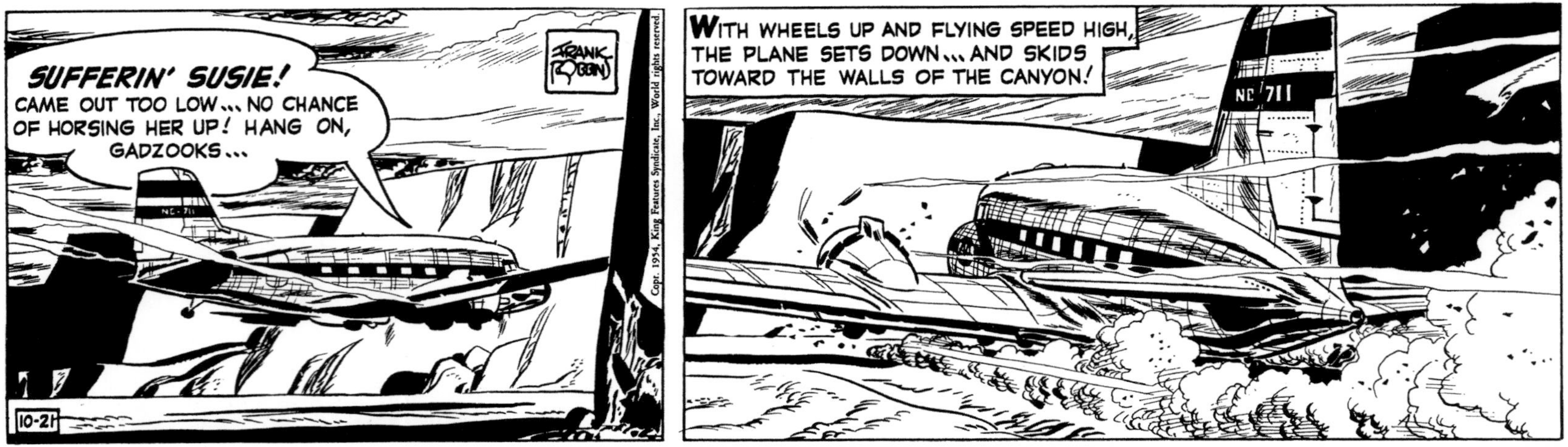
SUFFERIN' SUSIE!
CAME OUT TOO LOW... NO CHANCE OF HORSING HER UP! HANG ON, GADZOOKS...
FRANK ROBBINS
Copr. 1954, King Features Syndicate, Inc., World rights reserved.
NC-711
10-21
WITH WHEELS UP AND FLYING SPEED HIGH, THE PLANE SETS DOWN... AND SKIDS TOWARD THE WALLS OF THE CANYON!
NC 711

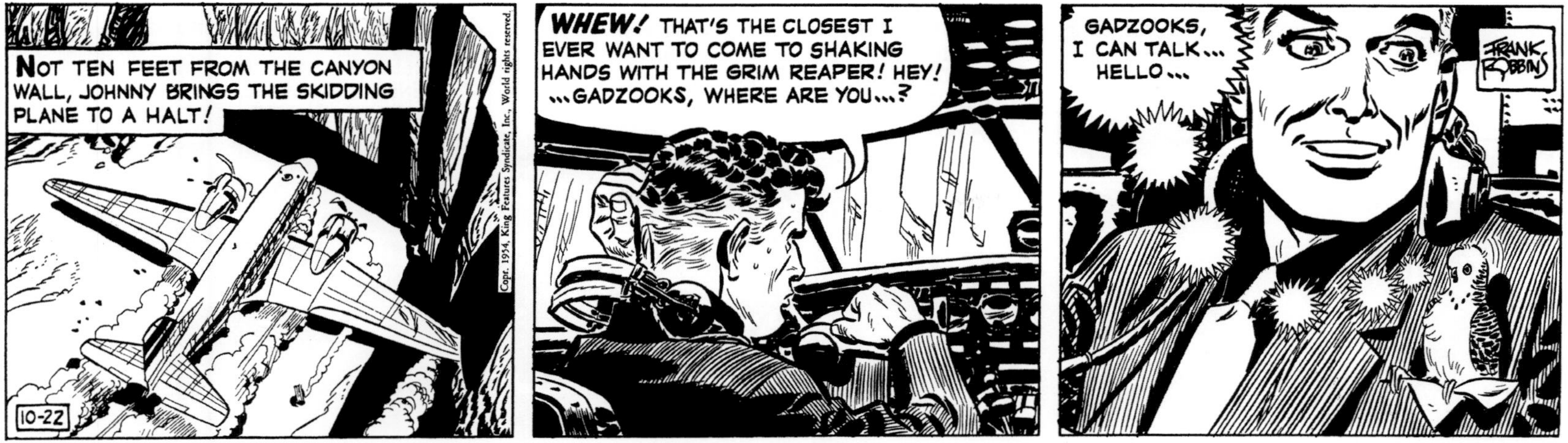
NOT TEN FEET FROM THE CANYON WALL, JOHNNY BRINGS THE SKIDDING PLANE TO A HALT!
10-22
Copr. 1954, King Features Syndicate, Inc., World rights reserved.
WHEW! THAT'S THE CLOSEST I EVER WANT TO COME TO SHAKING HANDS WITH THE GRIM REAPER! HEY! ...GADZOOKS, WHERE ARE YOU...?
GADZOOKS, I CAN TALK... HELLO...
FRANK ROBBINS

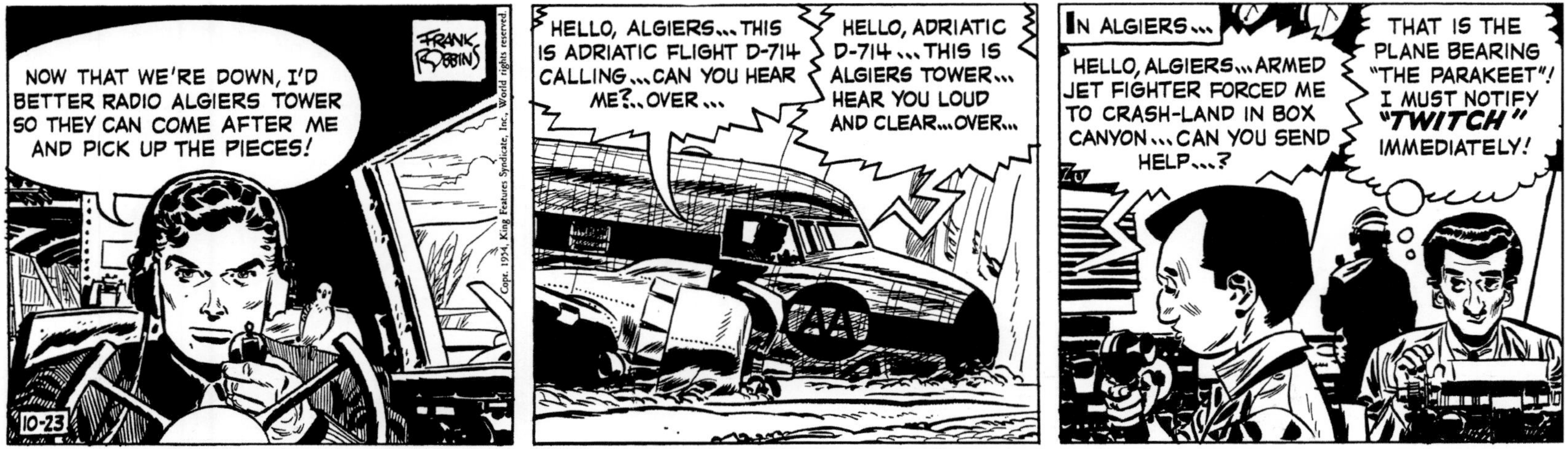
FRANK ROBBINS
NOW THAT WE'RE DOWN, I'D BETTER RADIO ALGIERS TOWER SO THEY CAN COME AFTER ME AND PICK UP THE PIECES!
10-23
Copr. 1954, King Features Syndicate, Inc., World rights reserved.
HELLO, ALGIERS... THIS IS ADRIATIC FLIGHT D-714 CALLING... CAN YOU HEAR ME?.. OVER...
HELLO, ADRIATIC D-714 ... THIS IS ALGIERS TOWER... HEAR YOU LOUD AND CLEAR... OVER...
IN ALGIERS...
HELLO, ALGIERS... ARMED JET FIGHTER FORCED ME TO CRASH-LAND IN BOX CANYON... CAN YOU SEND HELP...?
THAT IS THE PLANE BEARING "THE PARAKEET"! I MUST NOTIFY "TWITCH" IMMEDIATELY!

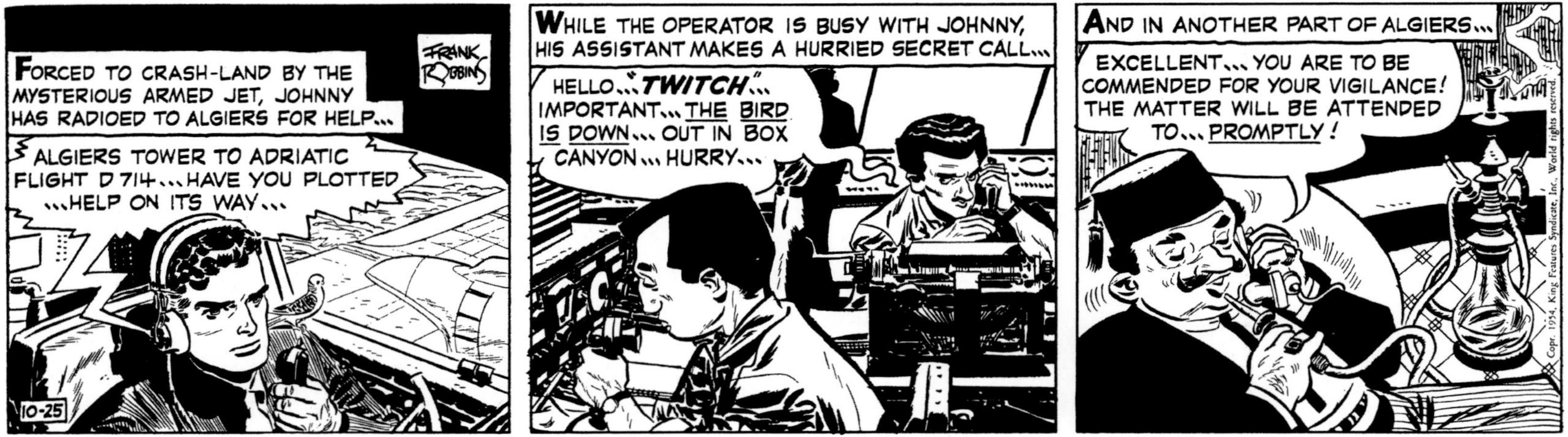
FRANK ROBBINS
FORCED TO CRASH-LAND BY THE MYSTERIOUS ARMED JET, JOHNNY HAS RADIOED TO ALGIERS FOR HELP...
ALGIERS TOWER TO ADRIATIC FLIGHT D 714... HAVE YOU PLOTTED ...HELP ON ITS WAY...
10-25
WHILE THE OPERATOR IS BUSY WITH JOHNNY, HIS ASSISTANT MAKES A HURRIED SECRET CALL...
HELLO..."TWITCH"... IMPORTANT... THE BIRD IS DOWN... OUT IN BOX CANYON... HURRY...
AND IN ANOTHER PART OF ALGIERS...
EXCELLENT... YOU ARE TO BE COMMENDED FOR YOUR VIGILANCE! THE MATTER WILL BE ATTENDED TO... PROMPTLY!
Copr. 1954, King Features Syndicate, Inc., World rights reserved.

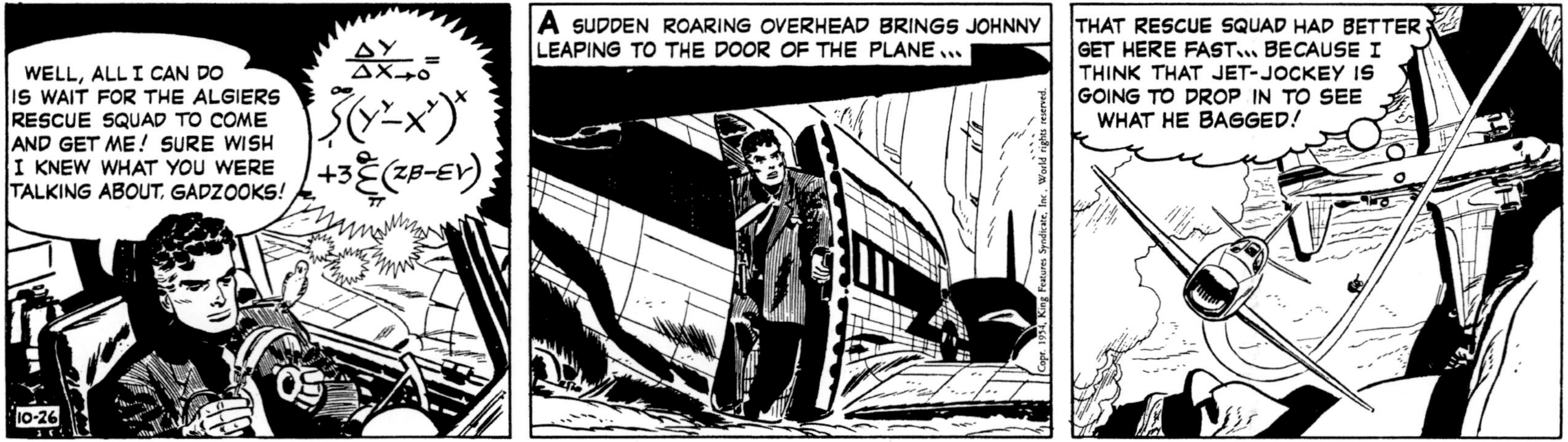
WELL, ALL I CAN DO IS WAIT FOR THE ALGIERS RESCUE SQUAD TO COME AND GET ME! SURE WISH I KNEW WHAT YOU WERE TALKING ABOUT, GADZOOKS!
10-26
A SUDDEN ROARING OVERHEAD BRINGS JOHNNY LEAPING TO THE DOOR OF THE PLANE...
Copr. 1954, King Features Syndicate, Inc., World rights reserved.
THAT RESCUE SQUAD HAD BETTER GET HERE FAST... BECAUSE I THINK THAT JET-JOCKEY IS GOING TO DROP IN TO SEE WHAT HE BAGGED!

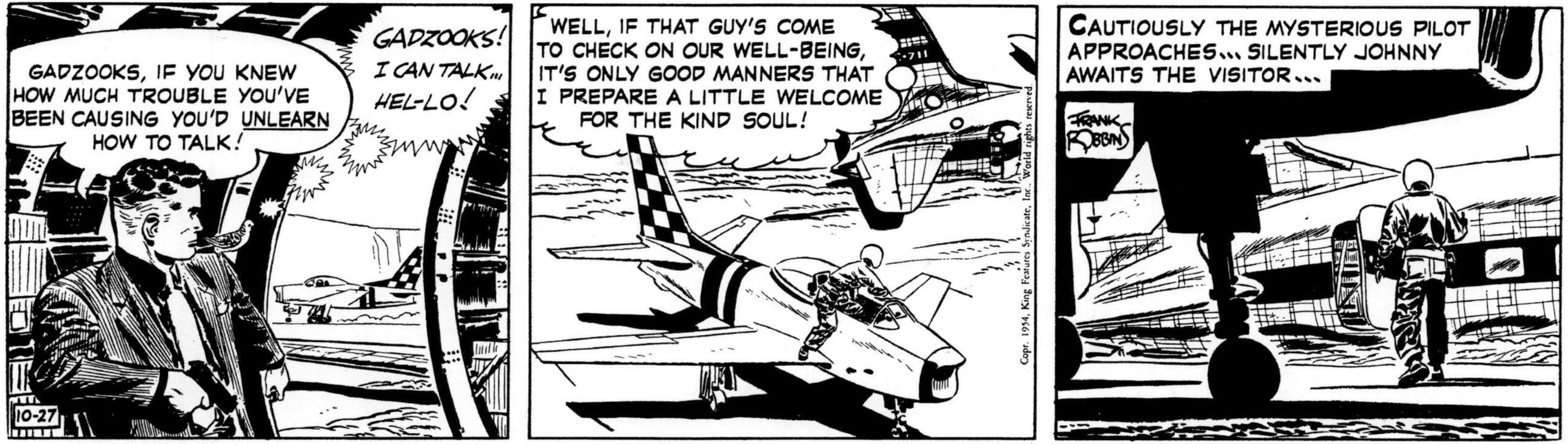
10-27
GADZOOKS, IF YOU KNEW HOW MUCH TROUBLE YOU'VE BEEN CAUSING YOU'D UNLEARN HOW TO TALK!
GADZOOKS! I CAN TALK... HEL-LO!
WELL, IF THAT GUY'S COME TO CHECK ON OUR WELL-BEING, IT'S ONLY GOOD MANNERS THAT I PREPARE A LITTLE WELCOME FOR THE KIND SOUL!
Copr. 1954, King Features Syndicate, Inc., World rights reserved.
CAUTIOUSLY THE MYSTERIOUS PILOT APPROACHES... SILENTLY JOHNNY AWAITS THE VISITOR...
FRANK ROBBINS

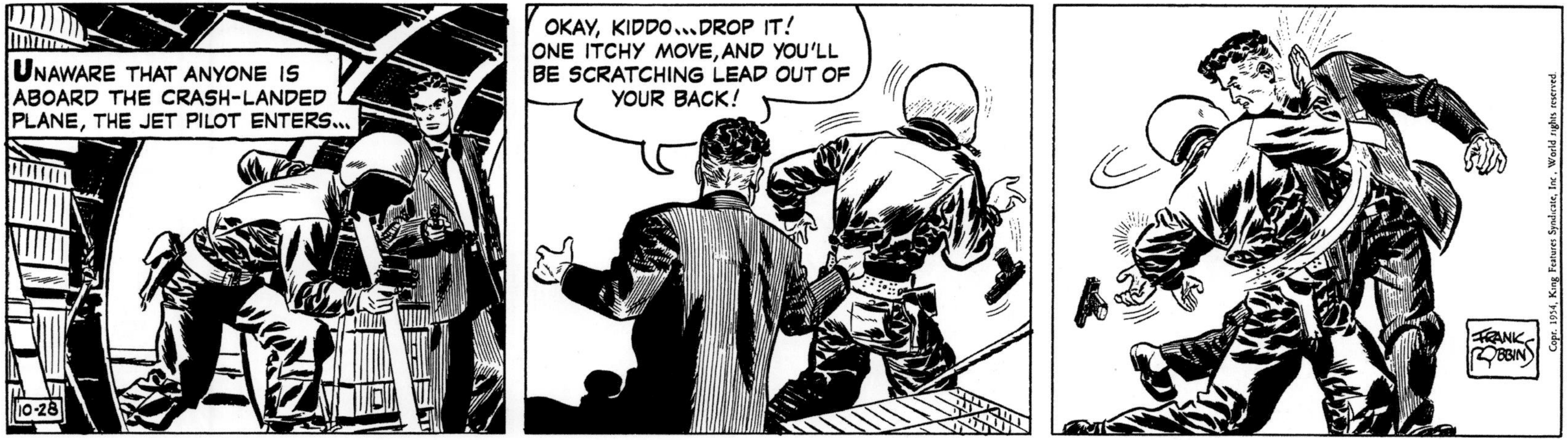
10-28
UNAWARE THAT ANYONE IS ABOARD THE CRASH-LANDED PLANE, THE JET PILOT ENTERS...
OKAY, KIDDO...DROP IT! ONE ITCHY MOVE, AND YOU'LL BE SCRATCHING LEAD OUT OF YOUR BACK!
FRANK ROBBINS
Copr. 1954, King Features Syndicate, Inc., World rights reserved.

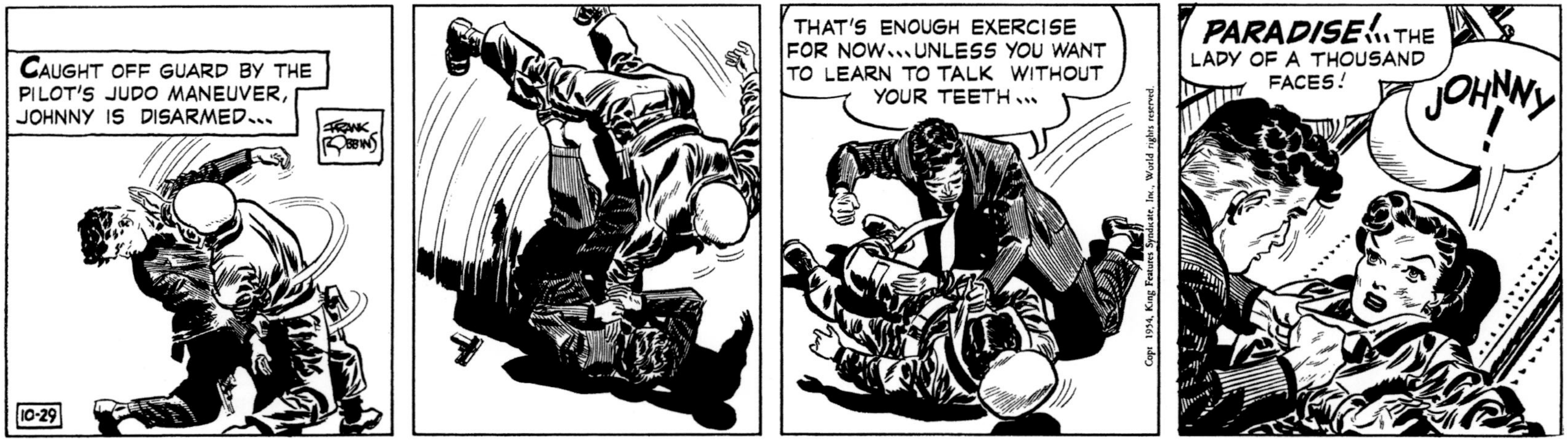

CAUGHT OFF GUARD BY THE PILOT'S JUDO MANEUVER, JOHNNY IS DISARMED...
FRANK ROBBINS
10-29
THAT'S ENOUGH EXERCISE FOR NOW...UNLESS YOU WANT TO LEARN TO TALK WITHOUT YOUR TEETH...
Copr. 1954, King Features Syndicate, Inc., World rights reserved.
PARADISE!...THE LADY OF A THOUSAND FACES!
JOHNNY!

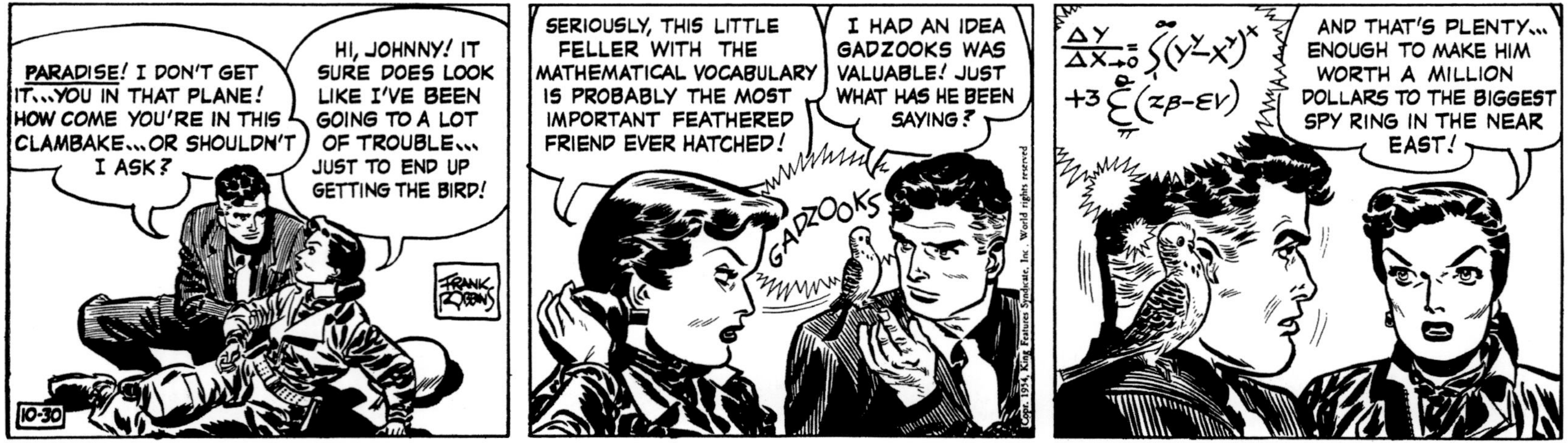

PARADISE! I DON'T GET IT...YOU IN THAT PLANE! HOW COME YOU'RE IN THIS CLAMBAKE...OR SHOULDN'T I ASK?
HI, JOHNNY! IT SURE DOES LOOK LIKE I'VE BEEN GOING TO A LOT OF TROUBLE... JUST TO END UP GETTING THE BIRD!
FRANK ROBBINS
10-30
SERIOUSLY, THIS LITTLE FELLER WITH THE MATHEMATICAL VOCABULARY IS PROBABLY THE MOST IMPORTANT FEATHERED FRIEND EVER HATCHED!
I HAD AN IDEA GADZOOKS WAS VALUABLE! JUST WHAT HAS HE BEEN SAYING?
GADZOOKS
Copr. 1954, King Features Syndicate, Inc. World rights reserved
AND THAT'S PLENTY... ENOUGH TO MAKE HIM WORTH A MILLION DOLLARS TO THE BIGGEST SPY RING IN THE NEAR EAST!

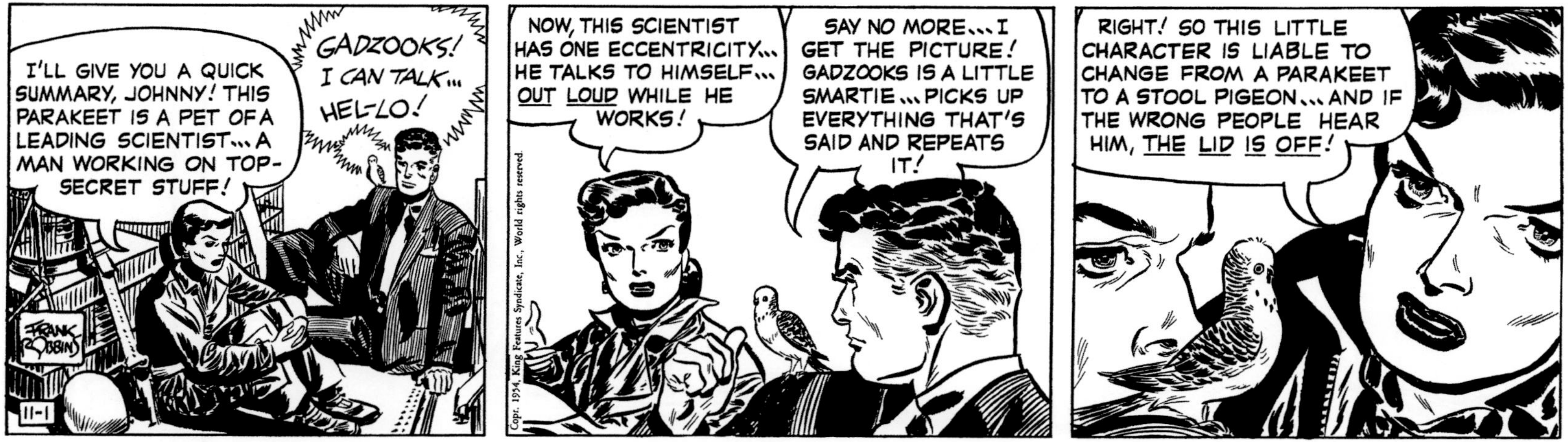
I'LL GIVE YOU A QUICK SUMMARY, JOHNNY! THIS PARAKEET IS A PET OF A LEADING SCIENTIST... A MAN WORKING ON TOP-SECRET STUFF!
GADZOOKS! I CAN TALK... HEL-LO!
FRANK ROBBINS
11-1
NOW, THIS SCIENTIST HAS ONE ECCENTRICITY... HE TALKS TO HIMSELF... OUT LOUD WHILE HE WORKS!
SAY NO MORE... I GET THE PICTURE! GADZOOKS IS A LITTLE SMARTIE... PICKS UP EVERYTHING THAT'S SAID AND REPEATS IT!
Copr. 1954, King Features Syndicate, Inc., World rights reserved.
RIGHT! SO THIS LITTLE CHARACTER IS LIABLE TO CHANGE FROM A PARAKEET TO A STOOL PIGEON... AND IF THE WRONG PEOPLE HEAR HIM, THE LID IS OFF!

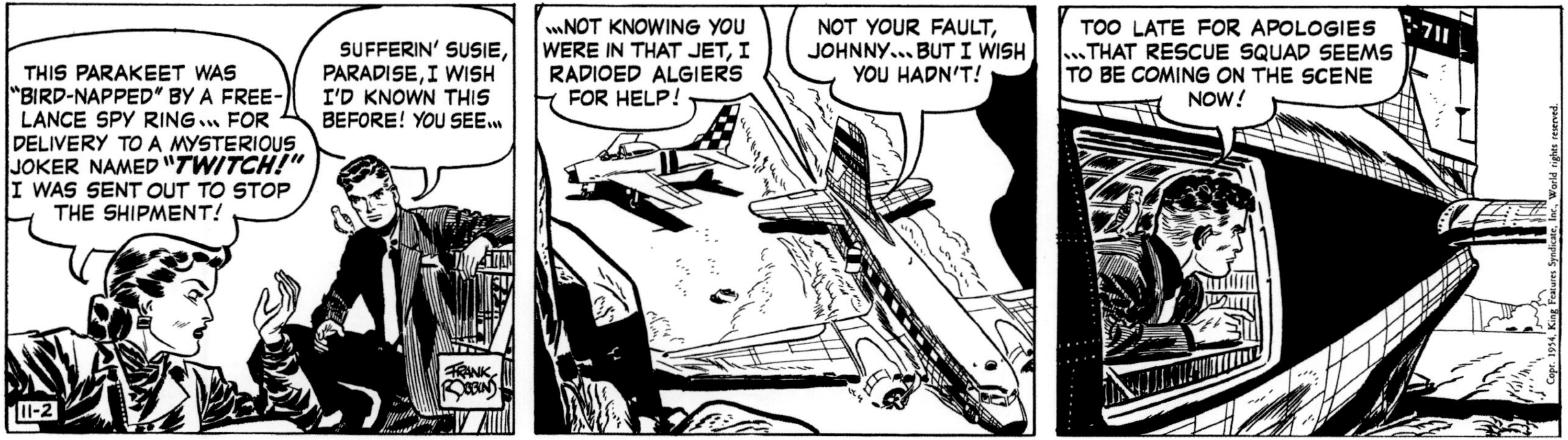
THIS PARAKEET WAS "BIRD-NAPPED" BY A FREE-LANCE SPY RING... FOR DELIVERY TO A MYSTERIOUS JOKER NAMED "TWITCH!" I WAS SENT OUT TO STOP THE SHIPMENT!
SUFFERIN' SUSIE, PARADISE, I WISH I'D KNOWN THIS BEFORE! YOU SEE...
FRANK ROBBINS
11-2
...NOT KNOWING YOU WERE IN THAT JET, I RADIOED ALGIERS FOR HELP!
NOT YOUR FAULT, JOHNNY... BUT I WISH YOU HADN'T!
TOO LATE FOR APOLOGIES ...THAT RESCUE SQUAD SEEMS TO BE COMING ON THE SCENE NOW!
Copr. 1954, King Features Syndicate, Inc., World rights reserved.

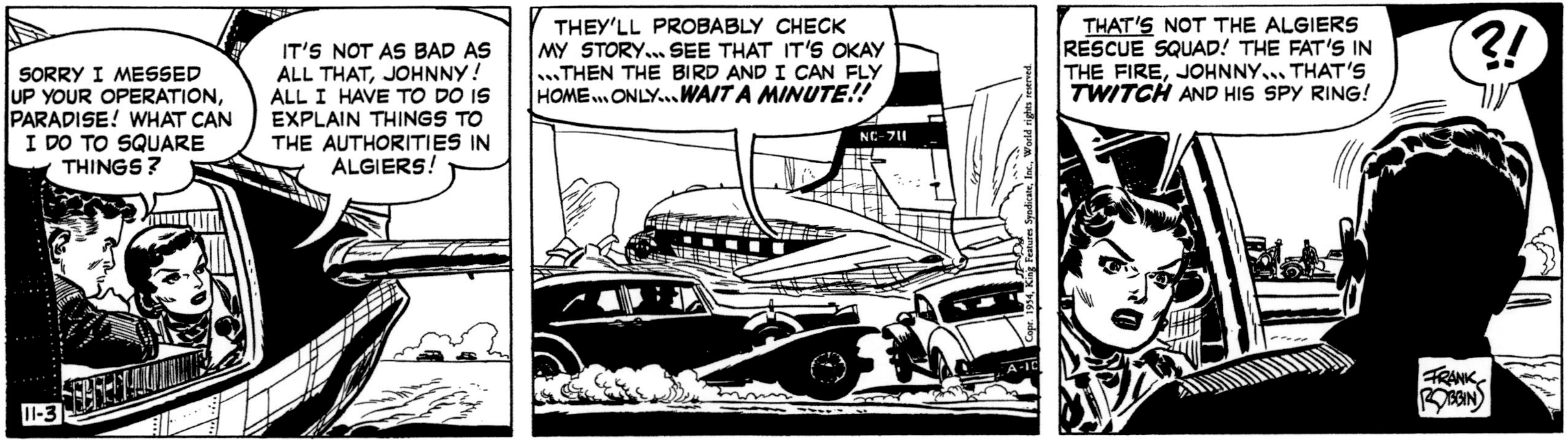
SORRY I MESSED UP YOUR OPERATION, PARADISE! WHAT CAN I DO TO SQUARE THINGS?
IT'S NOT AS BAD AS ALL THAT, JOHNNY! ALL I HAVE TO DO IS EXPLAIN THINGS TO THE AUTHORITIES IN ALGIERS!
11-3
THEY'LL PROBABLY CHECK MY STORY... SEE THAT IT'S OKAY ...THEN THE BIRD AND I CAN FLY HOME... ONLY... WAIT A MINUTE!!
NC-711
Copr. 1954, King Features Syndicate, Inc., World rights reserved.
THAT'S NOT THE ALGIERS RESCUE SQUAD! THE FAT'S IN THE FIRE, JOHNNY... THAT'S TWITCH AND HIS SPY RING!
?!
FRANK ROBBINS

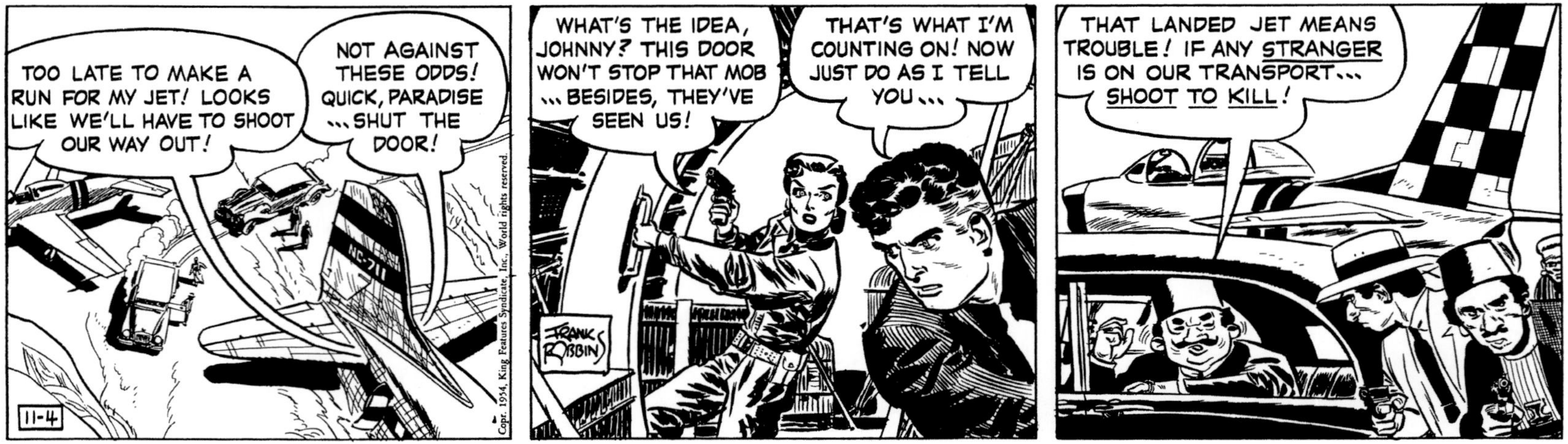
TOO LATE TO MAKE A RUN FOR MY JET! LOOKS LIKE WE'LL HAVE TO SHOOT OUR WAY OUT!
NOT AGAINST THESE ODDS! QUICK, PARADISE ...SHUT THE DOOR!
NC-711
11-4
Copr. 1954, King Features Syndicate, Inc., World rights reserved.
WHAT'S THE IDEA, JOHNNY? THIS DOOR WON'T STOP THAT MOB ... BESIDES, THEY'VE SEEN US!
THAT'S WHAT I'M COUNTING ON! NOW JUST DO AS I TELL YOU...
FRANK ROBBINS
THAT LANDED JET MEANS TROUBLE! IF ANY STRANGER IS ON OUR TRANSPORT... SHOOT TO KILL!

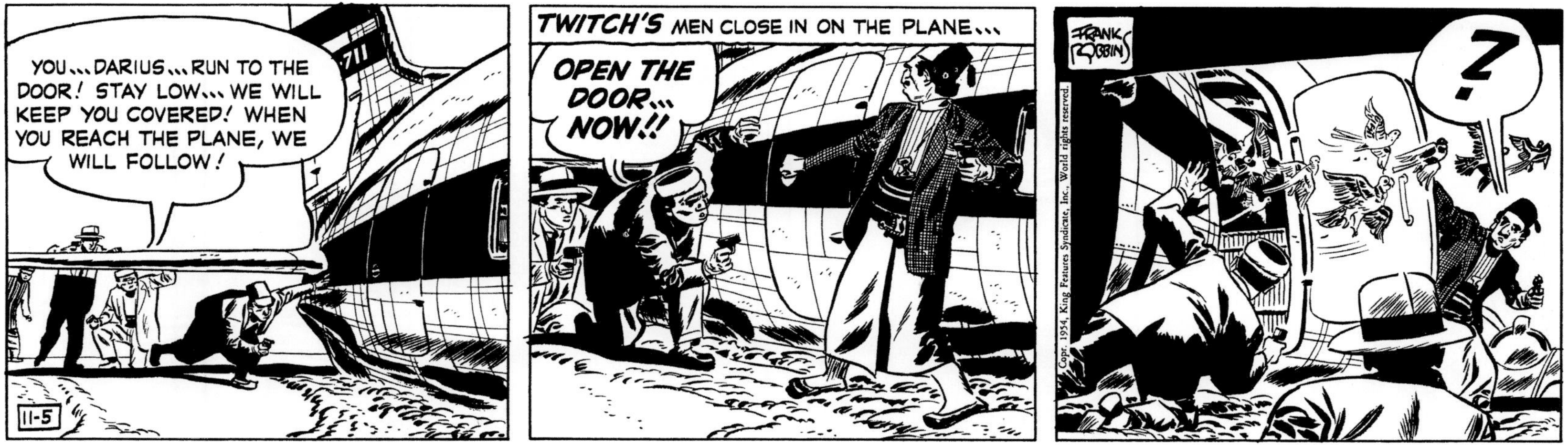
11-5
YOU...DARIUS...RUN TO THE DOOR! STAY LOW... WE WILL KEEP YOU COVERED! WHEN YOU REACH THE PLANE, WE WILL FOLLOW!
TWITCH'S MEN CLOSE IN ON THE PLANE...
OPEN THE DOOR... NOW!!
FRANK ROBBINS
Copr. 1954, King Features Syndicate, Inc., World rights reserved.
?

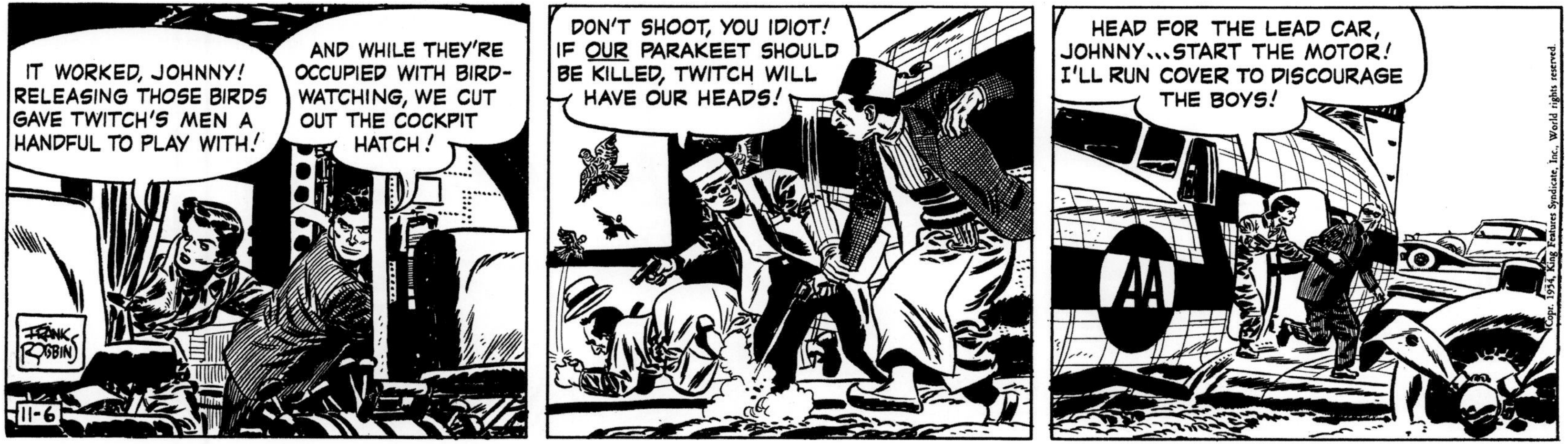
IT WORKED, JOHNNY! RELEASING THOSE BIRDS GAVE TWITCH'S MEN A HANDFUL TO PLAY WITH!
AND WHILE THEY'RE OCCUPIED WITH BIRD-WATCHING, WE CUT OUT THE COCKPIT HATCH!
FRANK ROBBINS
11-6
DON'T SHOOT, YOU IDIOT! IF OUR PARAKEET SHOULD BE KILLED, TWITCH WILL HAVE OUR HEADS!
HEAD FOR THE LEAD CAR, JOHNNY...START THE MOTOR! I'LL RUN COVER TO DISCOURAGE THE BOYS!
AA
Copr. 1954, King Features Syndicate, Inc., World rights reserved.

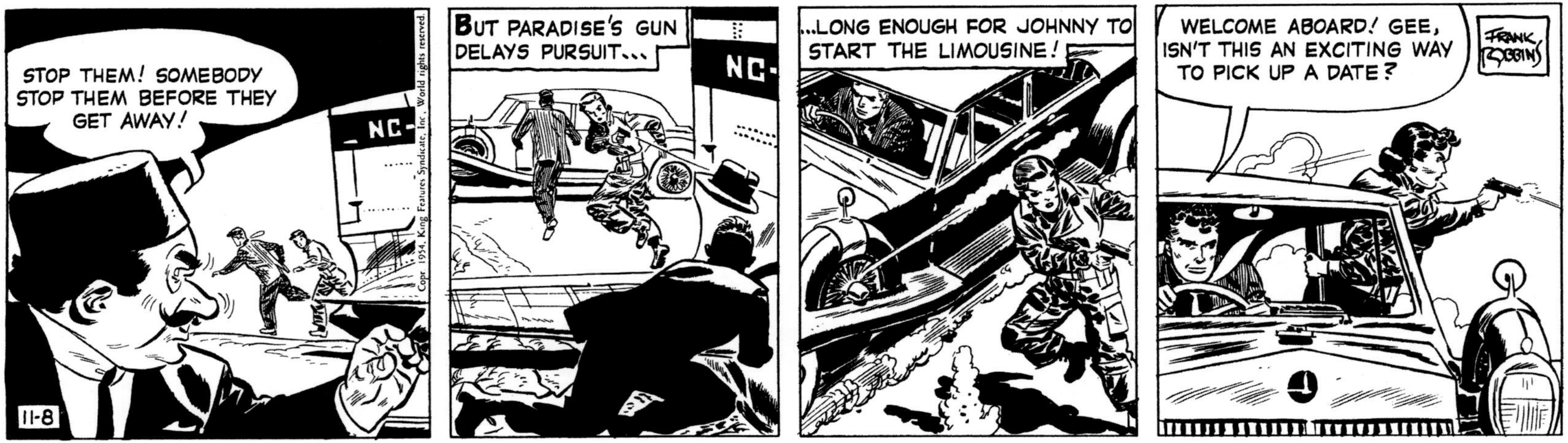
11-8
STOP THEM! SOMEBODY STOP THEM BEFORE THEY GET AWAY!
NC-
Copr 1954, King Features Syndicate, Inc., World rights reserved.
BUT PARADISE'S GUN DELAYS PURSUIT...
NC-
...LONG ENOUGH FOR JOHNNY TO START THE LIMOUSINE!
WELCOME ABOARD! GEE, ISN'T THIS AN EXCITING WAY TO PICK UP A DATE?
FRANK ROBBINS

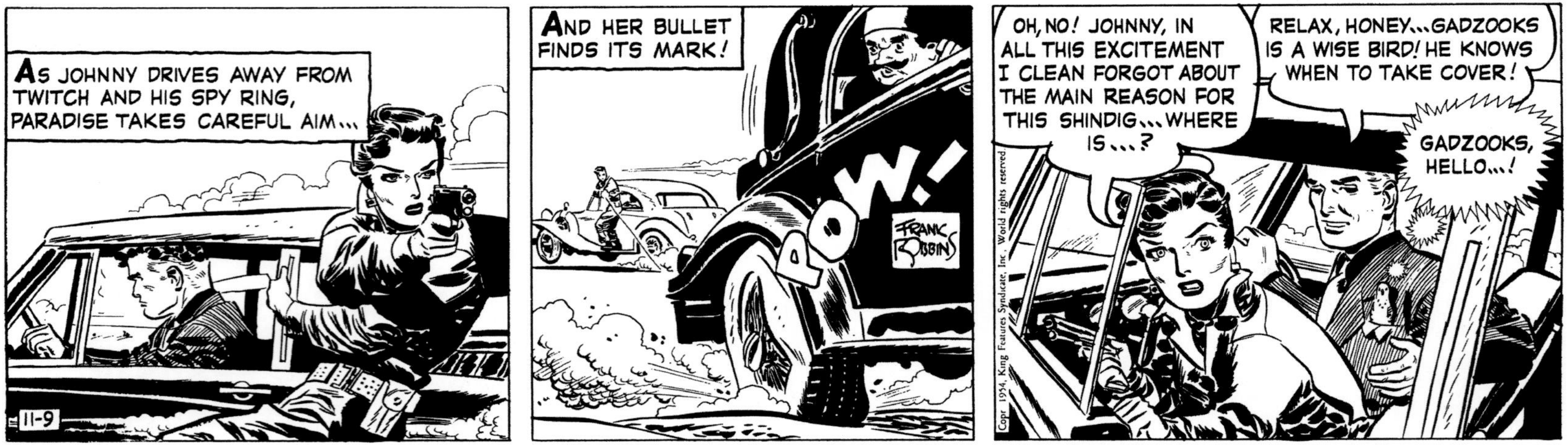
11-9
AS JOHNNY DRIVES AWAY FROM TWITCH AND HIS SPY RING, PARADISE TAKES CAREFUL AIM...
AND HER BULLET FINDS ITS MARK!
POW!
FRANK ROBBINS
Copr 1954, King Features Syndicate, Inc., World rights reserved.
OH, NO! JOHNNY, IN ALL THIS EXCITEMENT I CLEAN FORGOT ABOUT THE MAIN REASON FOR THIS SHINDIG...WHERE IS...?
RELAX, HONEY...GADZOOKS IS A WISE BIRD! HE KNOWS WHEN TO TAKE COVER!
GADZOOKS, HELLO...!

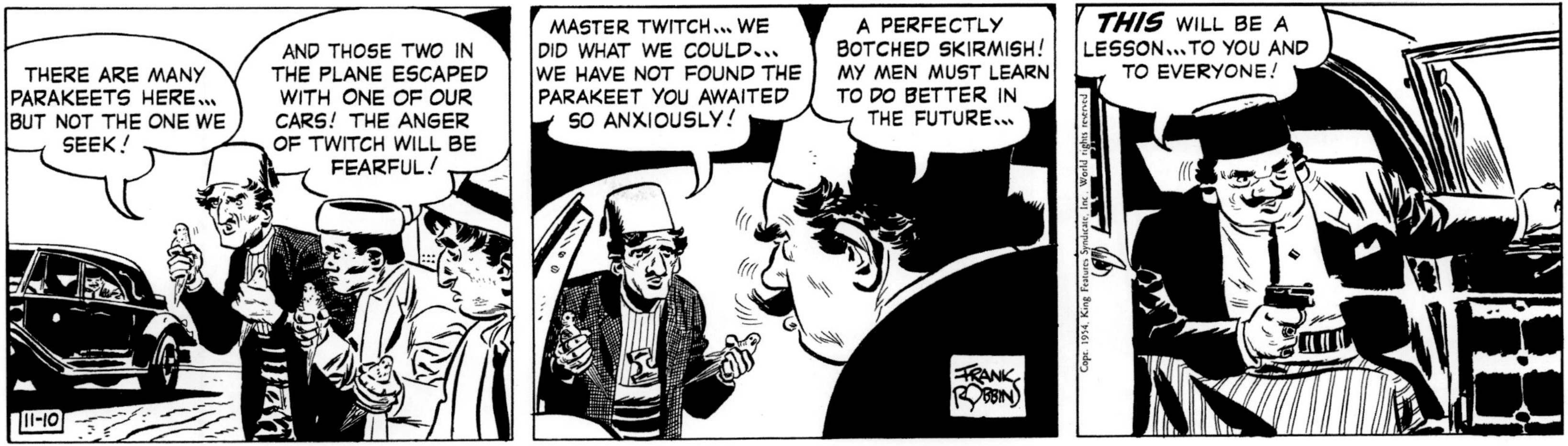
THERE ARE MANY PARAKEETS HERE... BUT NOT THE ONE WE SEEK!
AND THOSE TWO IN THE PLANE ESCAPED WITH ONE OF OUR CARS! THE ANGER OF TWITCH WILL BE FEARFUL!
11-10
MASTER TWITCH... WE DID WHAT WE COULD... WE HAVE NOT FOUND THE PARAKEET YOU AWAITED SO ANXIOUSLY!
A PERFECTLY BOTCHED SKIRMISH! MY MEN MUST LEARN TO DO BETTER IN THE FUTURE...
FRANK ROBBINS
THIS WILL BE A LESSON... TO YOU AND TO EVERYONE!
Copr. 1954, King Features Syndicate, Inc., World rights reserved

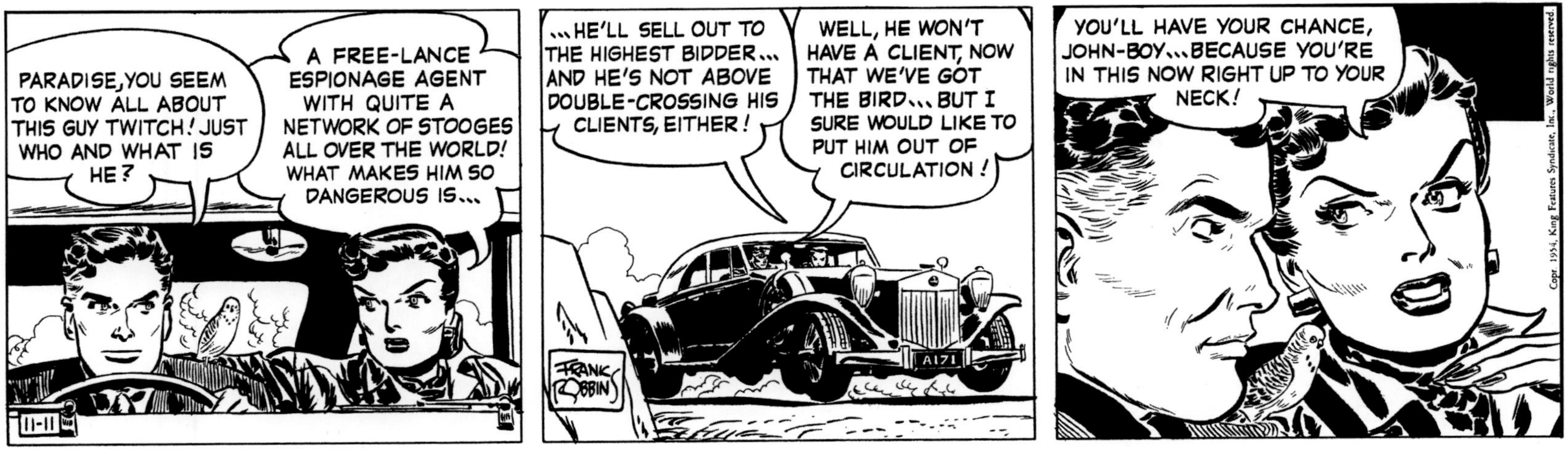
PARADISE, YOU SEEM TO KNOW ALL ABOUT THIS GUY TWITCH! JUST WHO AND WHAT IS HE?
A FREE-LANCE ESPIONAGE AGENT WITH QUITE A NETWORK OF STOOGES ALL OVER THE WORLD! WHAT MAKES HIM SO DANGEROUS IS...
11-11
...HE'LL SELL OUT TO THE HIGHEST BIDDER... AND HE'S NOT ABOVE DOUBLE-CROSSING HIS CLIENTS, EITHER!
WELL, HE WON'T HAVE A CLIENT, NOW THAT WE'VE GOT THE BIRD... BUT I SURE WOULD LIKE TO PUT HIM OUT OF CIRCULATION!
FRANK ROBBINS
A171
YOU'LL HAVE YOUR CHANCE, JOHN-BOY... BECAUSE YOU'RE IN THIS NOW RIGHT UP TO YOUR NECK!
Copr. 1954, King Features Syndicate, Inc., World rights reserved.

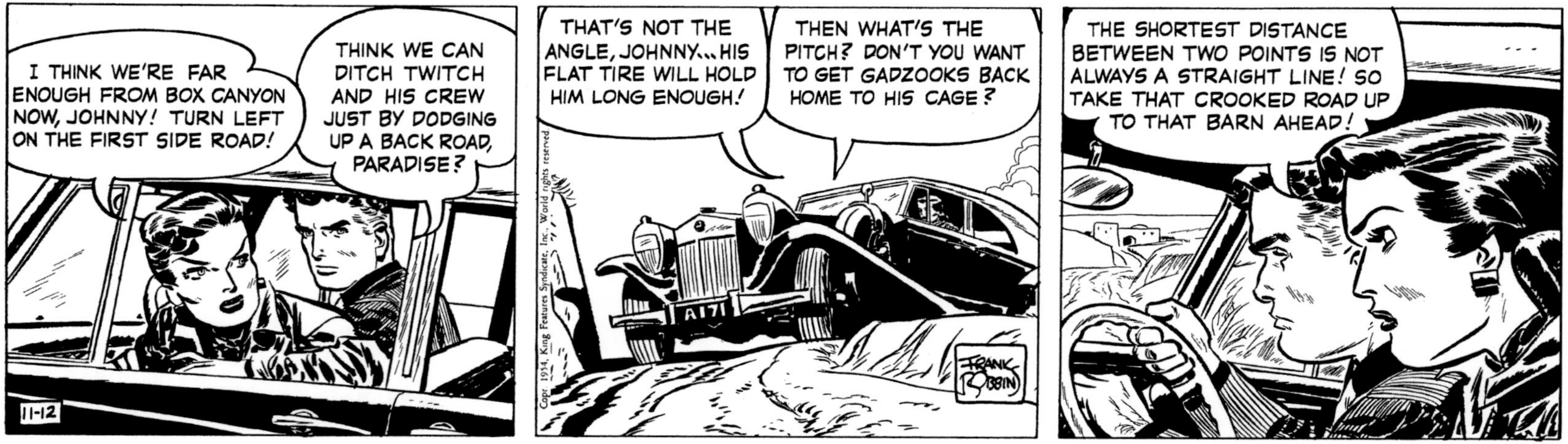
I THINK WE'RE FAR ENOUGH FROM BOX CANYON NOW, JOHNNY! TURN LEFT ON THE FIRST SIDE ROAD!
THINK WE CAN DITCH TWITCH AND HIS CREW JUST BY DODGING UP A BACK ROAD, PARADISE?
11-12
THAT'S NOT THE ANGLE, JOHNNY... HIS FLAT TIRE WILL HOLD HIM LONG ENOUGH!
THEN WHAT'S THE PITCH? DON'T YOU WANT TO GET GADZOOKS BACK HOME TO HIS CAGE?
Copr. 1954, King Features Syndicate, Inc., World rights reserved
A 171
FRANK ROBBINS
THE SHORTEST DISTANCE BETWEEN TWO POINTS IS NOT ALWAYS A STRAIGHT LINE! SO TAKE THAT CROOKED ROAD UP TO THAT BARN AHEAD!

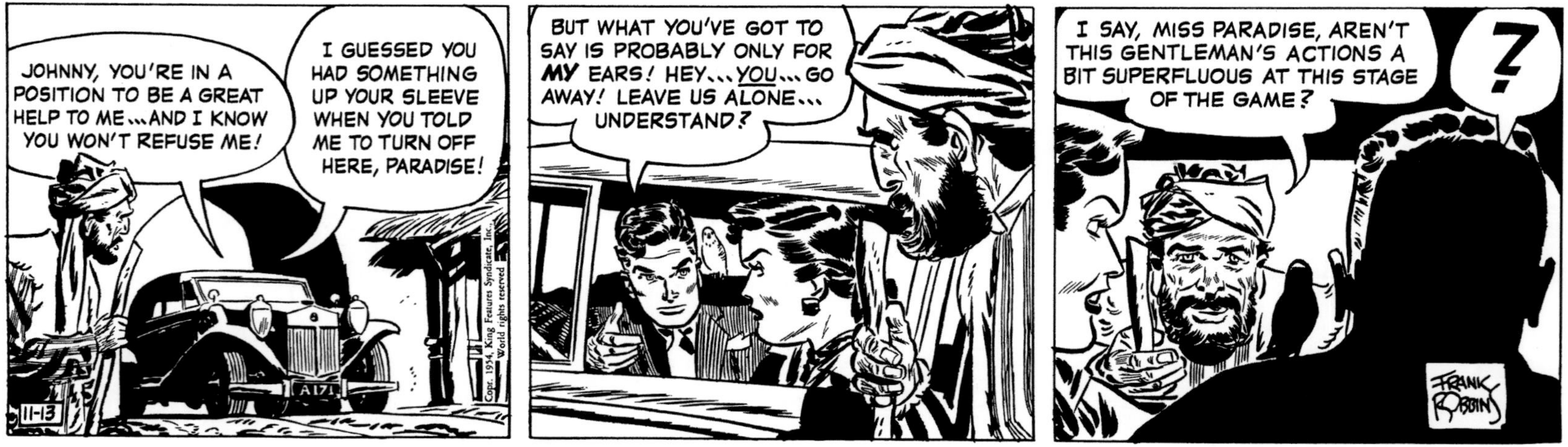
JOHNNY, YOU'RE IN A POSITION TO BE A GREAT HELP TO ME...AND I KNOW YOU WON'T REFUSE ME!
I GUESSED YOU HAD SOMETHING UP YOUR SLEEVE WHEN YOU TOLD ME TO TURN OFF HERE, PARADISE!
Copr. 1954, King Features Syndicate, Inc., World rights reserved
A 171
11-13
BUT WHAT YOU'VE GOT TO SAY IS PROBABLY ONLY FOR MY EARS! HEY... YOU... GO AWAY! LEAVE US ALONE... UNDERSTAND?
I SAY, MISS PARADISE, AREN'T THIS GENTLEMAN'S ACTIONS A BIT SUPERFLUOUS AT THIS STAGE OF THE GAME?
?
FRANK ROBBINS

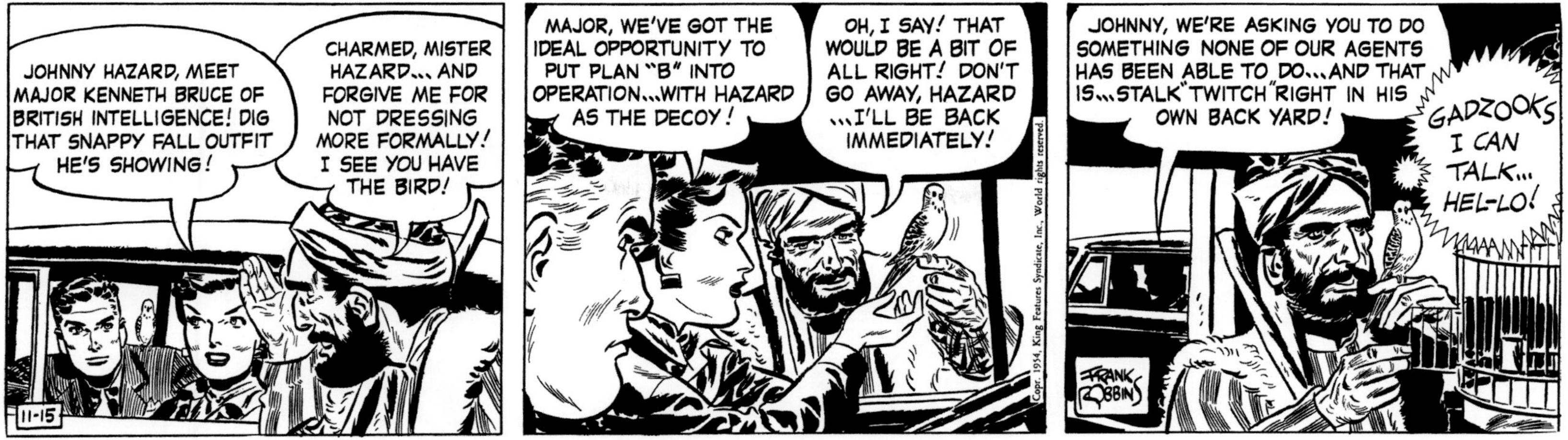
JOHNNY HAZARD, MEET MAJOR KENNETH BRUCE OF BRITISH INTELLIGENCE! DIG THAT SNAPPY FALL OUTFIT HE'S SHOWING!
CHARMED, MISTER HAZARD... AND FORGIVE ME FOR NOT DRESSING MORE FORMALLY! I SEE YOU HAVE THE BIRD!
11-15
MAJOR, WE'VE GOT THE IDEAL OPPORTUNITY TO PUT PLAN "B" INTO OPERATION...WITH HAZARD AS THE DECOY!
OH, I SAY! THAT WOULD BE A BIT OF ALL RIGHT! DON'T GO AWAY, HAZARD ...I'LL BE BACK IMMEDIATELY!
Copr. 1954, King Features Syndicate, Inc., World rights reserved.
JOHNNY, WE'RE ASKING YOU TO DO SOMETHING NONE OF OUR AGENTS HAS BEEN ABLE TO DO...AND THAT IS...STALK "TWITCH" RIGHT IN HIS OWN BACK YARD!
GADZOOKS I CAN TALK... HEL-LO!
FRANK ROBBINS

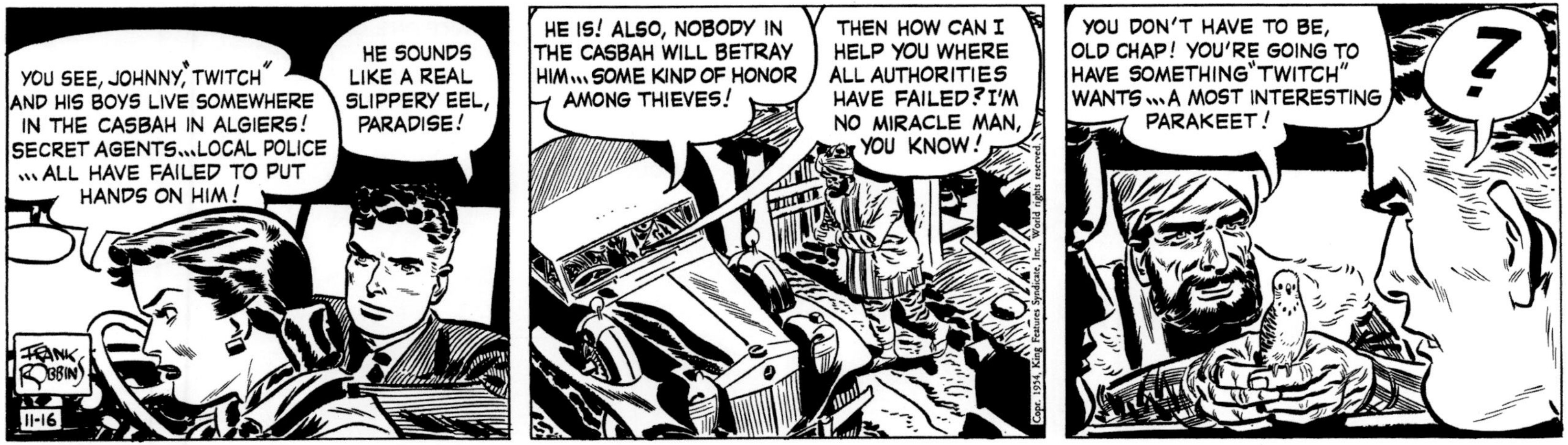
YOU SEE, JOHNNY, "TWITCH" AND HIS BOYS LIVE SOMEWHERE IN THE CASBAH IN ALGIERS! SECRET AGENTS...LOCAL POLICE ...ALL HAVE FAILED TO PUT HANDS ON HIM!
HE SOUNDS LIKE A REAL SLIPPERY EEL, PARADISE!
FRANK ROBBINS
11-16
HE IS! ALSO, NOBODY IN THE CASBAH WILL BETRAY HIM... SOME KIND OF HONOR AMONG THIEVES!
THEN HOW CAN I HELP YOU WHERE ALL AUTHORITIES HAVE FAILED? I'M NO MIRACLE MAN, YOU KNOW!
Copr. 1954, King Features Syndicate, Inc., World rights reserved.
YOU DON'T HAVE TO BE, OLD CHAP! YOU'RE GOING TO HAVE SOMETHING "TWITCH" WANTS... A MOST INTERESTING PARAKEET!
?

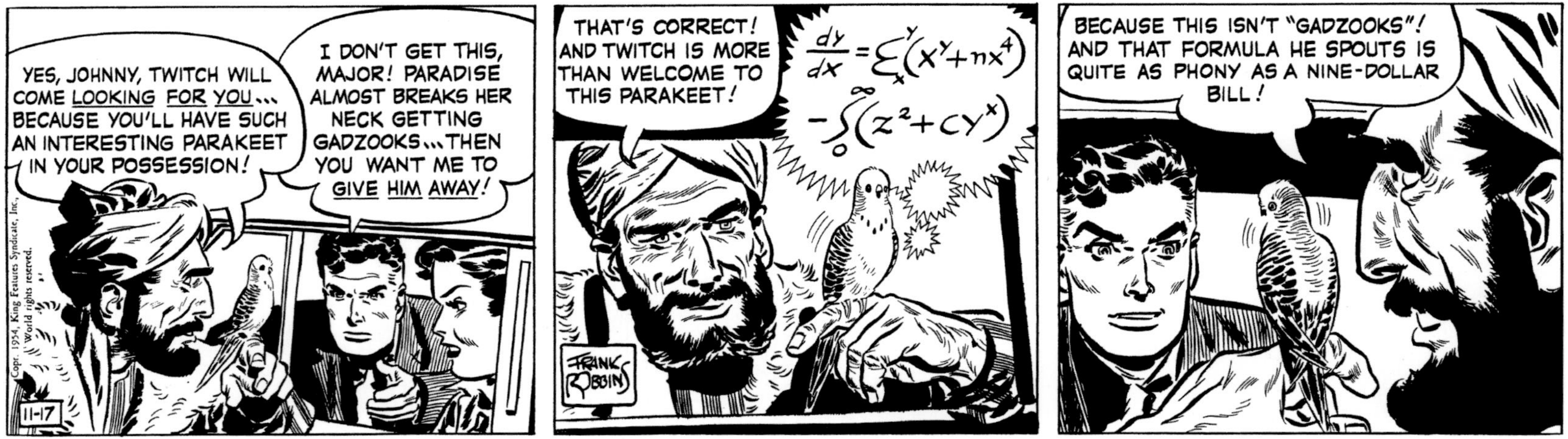
YES, JOHNNY, TWITCH WILL COME LOOKING FOR YOU... BECAUSE YOU'LL HAVE SUCH AN INTERESTING PARAKEET IN YOUR POSSESSION!
I DON'T GET THIS, MAJOR! PARADISE ALMOST BREAKS HER NECK GETTING GADZOOKS... THEN YOU WANT ME TO GIVE HIM AWAY!
Copr. 1954, King Features Syndicate, Inc., World rights reserved.
11-17
THAT'S CORRECT! AND TWITCH IS MORE THAN WELCOME TO THIS PARAKEET!
$\frac{dy}{dx} = \sum_x^y (x^y + nx^4) - \int_0^\infty (z^2 + cy^x)$
FRANK ROBBINS
BECAUSE THIS ISN'T "GADZOOKS"! AND THAT FORMULA HE SPOUTS IS QUITE AS PHONY AS A NINE-DOLLAR BILL!

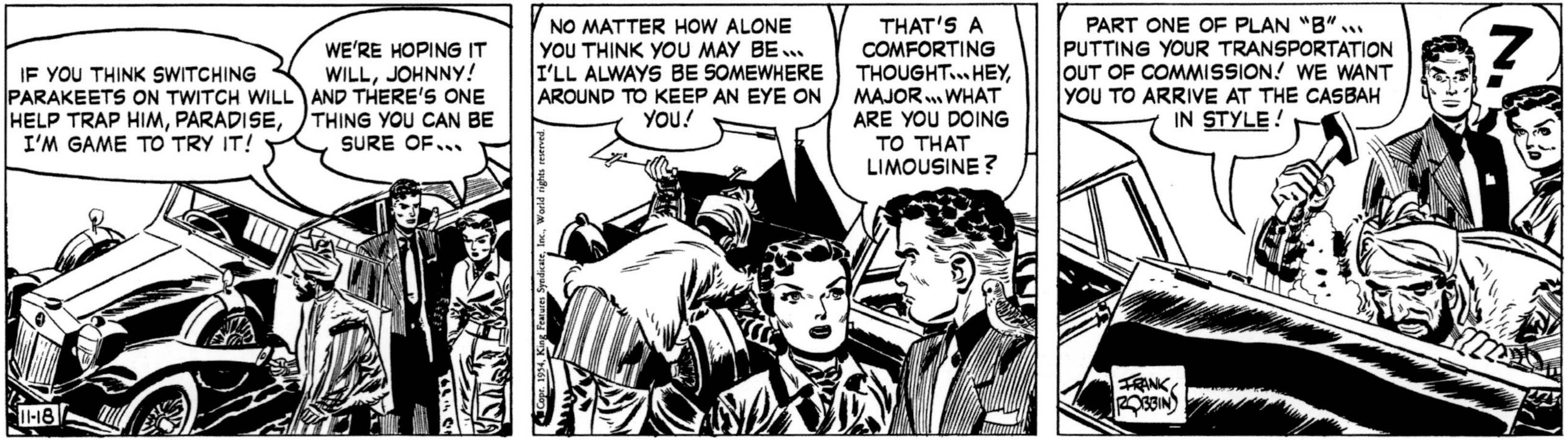
IF YOU THINK SWITCHING PARAKEETS ON TWITCH WILL HELP TRAP HIM, PARADISE, I'M GAME TO TRY IT!
WE'RE HOPING IT WILL, JOHNNY! AND THERE'S ONE THING YOU CAN BE SURE OF...
11-18
NO MATTER HOW ALONE YOU THINK YOU MAY BE... I'LL ALWAYS BE SOMEWHERE AROUND TO KEEP AN EYE ON YOU!
THAT'S A COMFORTING THOUGHT... HEY, MAJOR... WHAT ARE YOU DOING TO THAT LIMOUSINE?
Copr. 1954, King Features Syndicate, Inc., World rights reserved.
PART ONE OF PLAN "B"... PUTTING YOUR TRANSPORTATION OUT OF COMMISSION! WE WANT YOU TO ARRIVE AT THE CASBAH IN STYLE!
?
FRANK ROBBINS

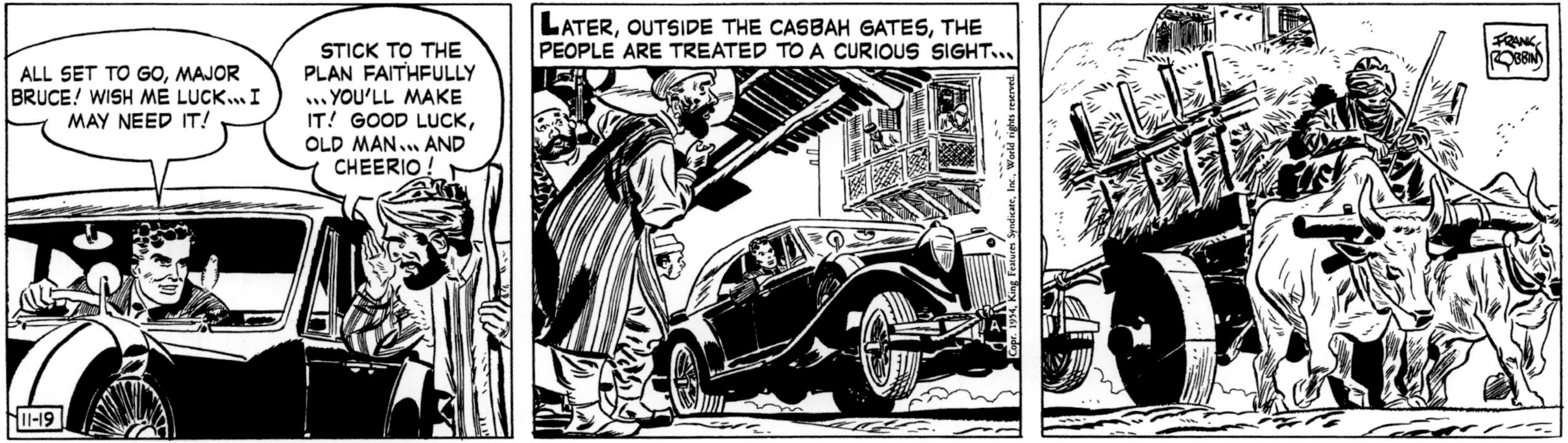
ALL SET TO GO, MAJOR BRUCE! WISH ME LUCK... I MAY NEED IT!
STICK TO THE PLAN FAITHFULLY ...YOU'LL MAKE IT! GOOD LUCK, OLD MAN... AND CHEERIO!
11-19
LATER, OUTSIDE THE CASBAH GATES, THE PEOPLE ARE TREATED TO A CURIOUS SIGHT...
Copr. 1954, King Features Syndicate, Inc., World rights reserved.
FRANK ROBBINS

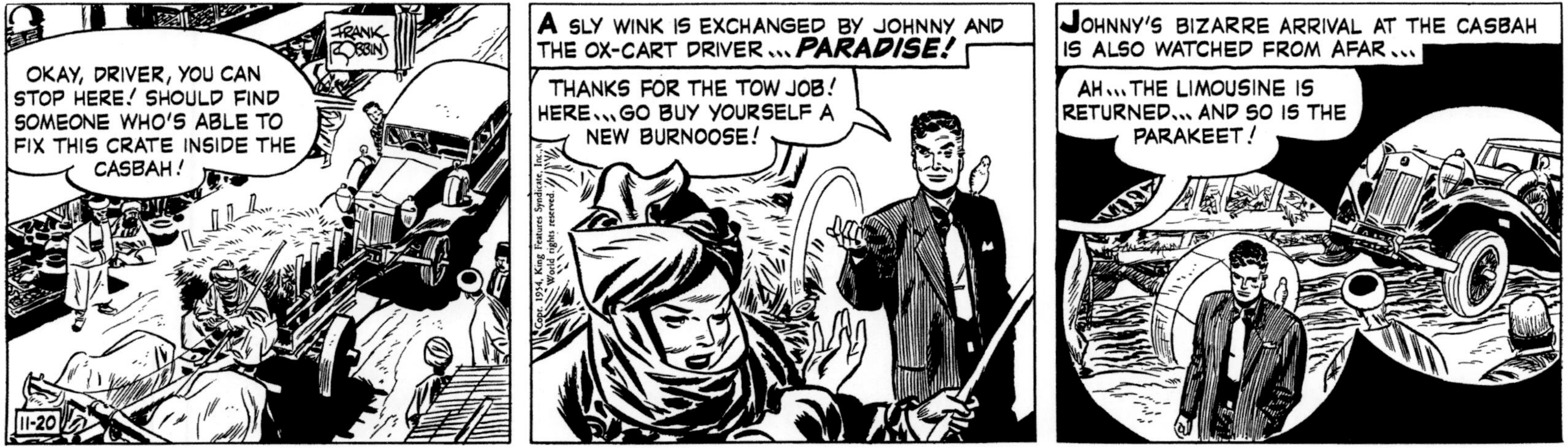
FRANK ROBBINS
OKAY, DRIVER, YOU CAN STOP HERE! SHOULD FIND SOMEONE WHO'S ABLE TO FIX THIS CRATE INSIDE THE CASBAH!
11-20
A SLY WINK IS EXCHANGED BY JOHNNY AND THE OX-CART DRIVER... PARADISE!
THANKS FOR THE TOW JOB! HERE... GO BUY YOURSELF A NEW BURNOOSE!
Copr. 1954, King Features Syndicate, Inc., World rights reserved.
JOHNNY'S BIZARRE ARRIVAL AT THE CASBAH IS ALSO WATCHED FROM AFAR...
AH... THE LIMOUSINE IS RETURNED... AND SO IS THE PARAKEET!

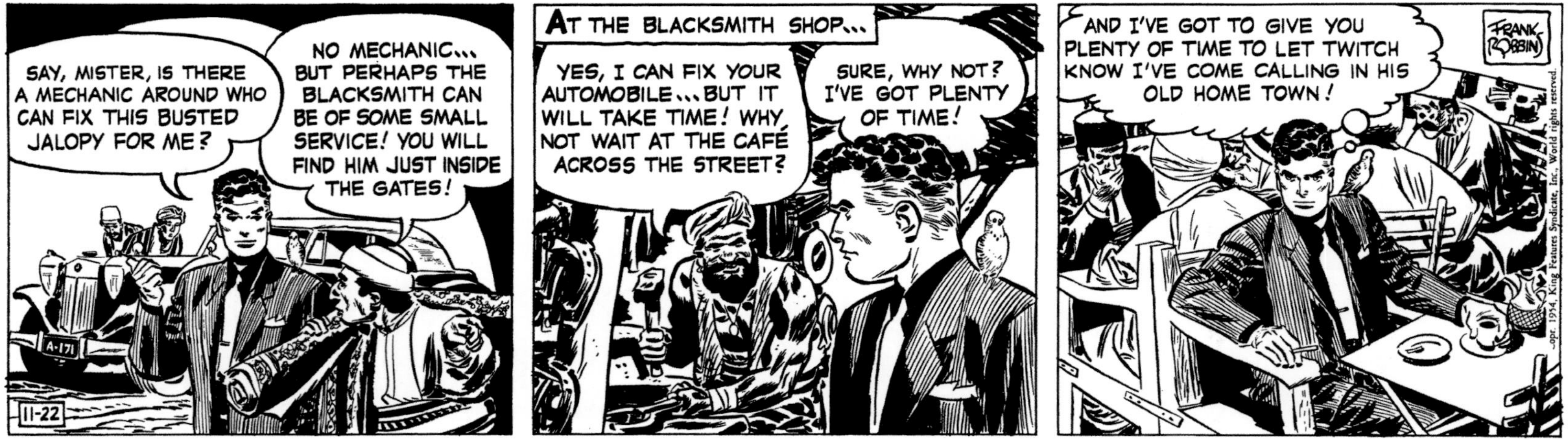
SAY, MISTER, IS THERE A MECHANIC AROUND WHO CAN FIX THIS BUSTED JALOPY FOR ME?
NO MECHANIC... BUT PERHAPS THE BLACKSMITH CAN BE OF SOME SMALL SERVICE! YOU WILL FIND HIM JUST INSIDE THE GATES!
A-171
11-22
AT THE BLACKSMITH SHOP...
YES, I CAN FIX YOUR AUTOMOBILE... BUT IT WILL TAKE TIME! WHY NOT WAIT AT THE CAFÉ ACROSS THE STREET?
SURE, WHY NOT? I'VE GOT PLENTY OF TIME!
AND I'VE GOT TO GIVE YOU PLENTY OF TIME TO LET TWITCH KNOW I'VE COME CALLING IN HIS OLD HOME TOWN!
FRANK ROBBIN
opr. 1954, King Features Syndicate, Inc., World rights reserved.

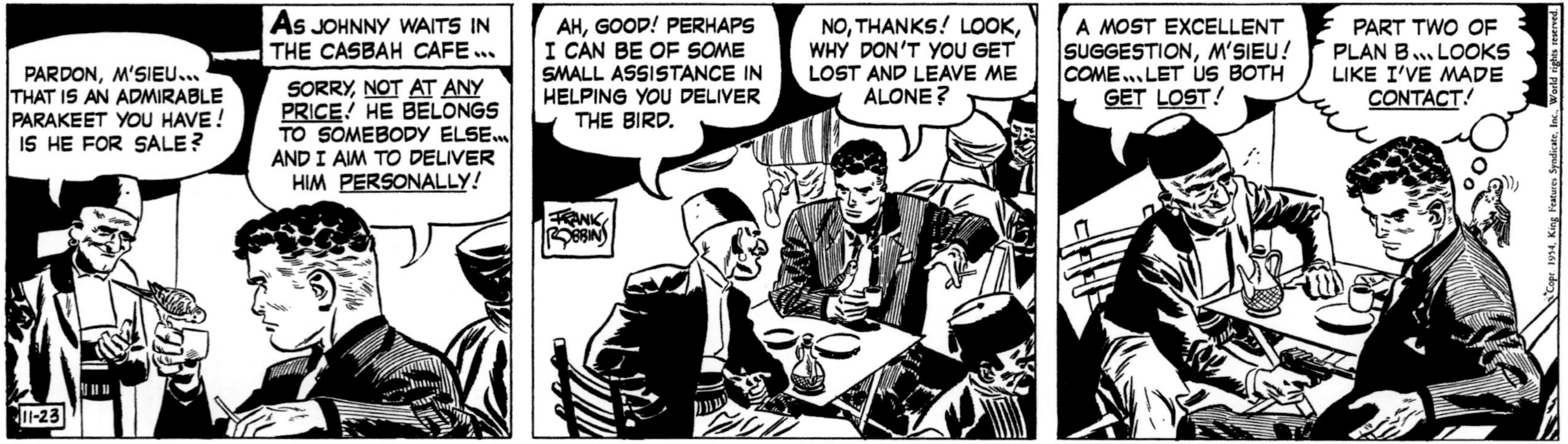
AS JOHNNY WAITS IN THE CASBAH CAFE...
PARDON, M'SIEU... THAT IS AN ADMIRABLE PARAKEET YOU HAVE! IS HE FOR SALE?
SORRY, NOT AT ANY PRICE! HE BELONGS TO SOMEBODY ELSE... AND I AIM TO DELIVER HIM PERSONALLY!
11-23
AH, GOOD! PERHAPS I CAN BE OF SOME SMALL ASSISTANCE IN HELPING YOU DELIVER THE BIRD.
NO, THANKS! LOOK, WHY DON'T YOU GET LOST AND LEAVE ME ALONE?
FRANK ROBBIN
A MOST EXCELLENT SUGGESTION, M'SIEU! COME... LET US BOTH GET LOST!
PART TWO OF PLAN B... LOOKS LIKE I'VE MADE CONTACT!
Copr. 1954, King Features Syndicate, Inc., World rights reserved.

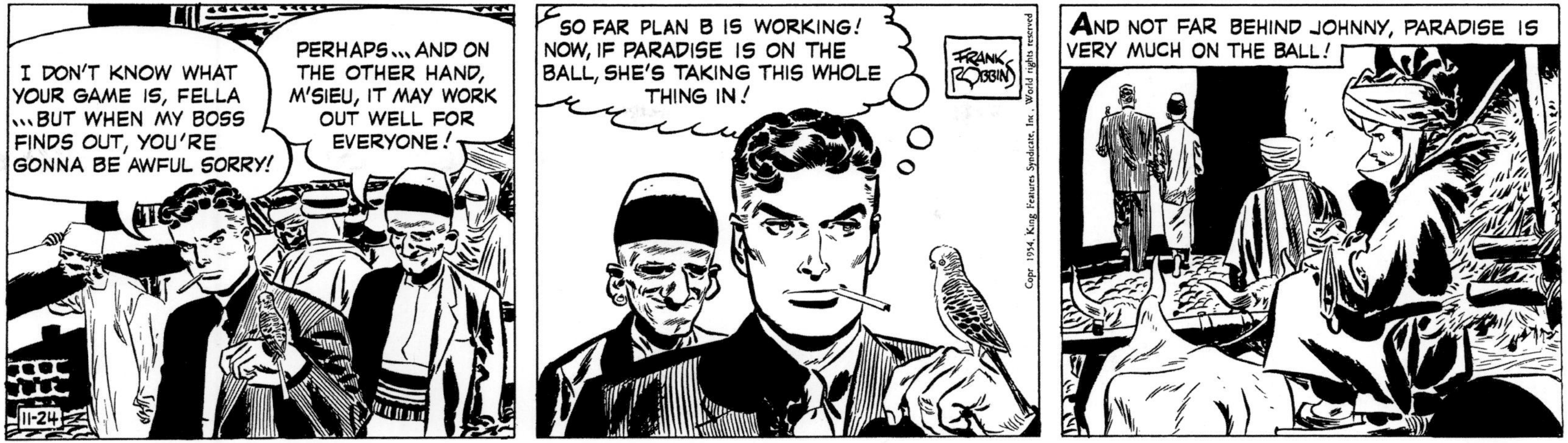
11-24
I DON'T KNOW WHAT YOUR GAME IS, FELLA ...BUT WHEN MY BOSS FINDS OUT, YOU'RE GONNA BE AWFUL SORRY!
PERHAPS ... AND ON THE OTHER HAND, M'SIEU, IT MAY WORK OUT WELL FOR EVERYONE!
SO FAR PLAN B IS WORKING! NOW, IF PARADISE IS ON THE BALL, SHE'S TAKING THIS WHOLE THING IN!
FRANK ROBBINS
Copr 1954, King Features Syndicate, Inc., World rights reserved
AND NOT FAR BEHIND JOHNNY, PARADISE IS VERY MUCH ON THE BALL!

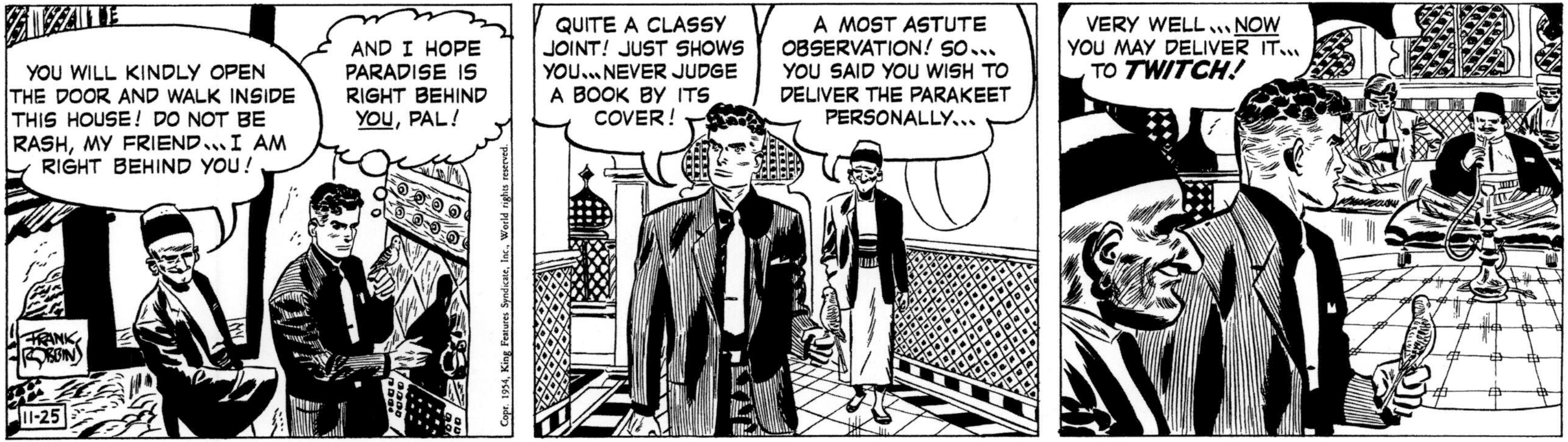
YOU WILL KINDLY OPEN THE DOOR AND WALK INSIDE THIS HOUSE! DO NOT BE RASH, MY FRIEND ... I AM RIGHT BEHIND YOU!
AND I HOPE PARADISE IS RIGHT BEHIND YOU, PAL!
FRANK ROBBINS
11-25
Copr. 1954, King Features Syndicate, Inc., World rights reserved.
QUITE A CLASSY JOINT! JUST SHOWS YOU ... NEVER JUDGE A BOOK BY ITS COVER!
A MOST ASTUTE OBSERVATION! SO ... YOU SAID YOU WISH TO DELIVER THE PARAKEET PERSONALLY...
VERY WELL ... NOW YOU MAY DELIVER IT ... TO TWITCH!

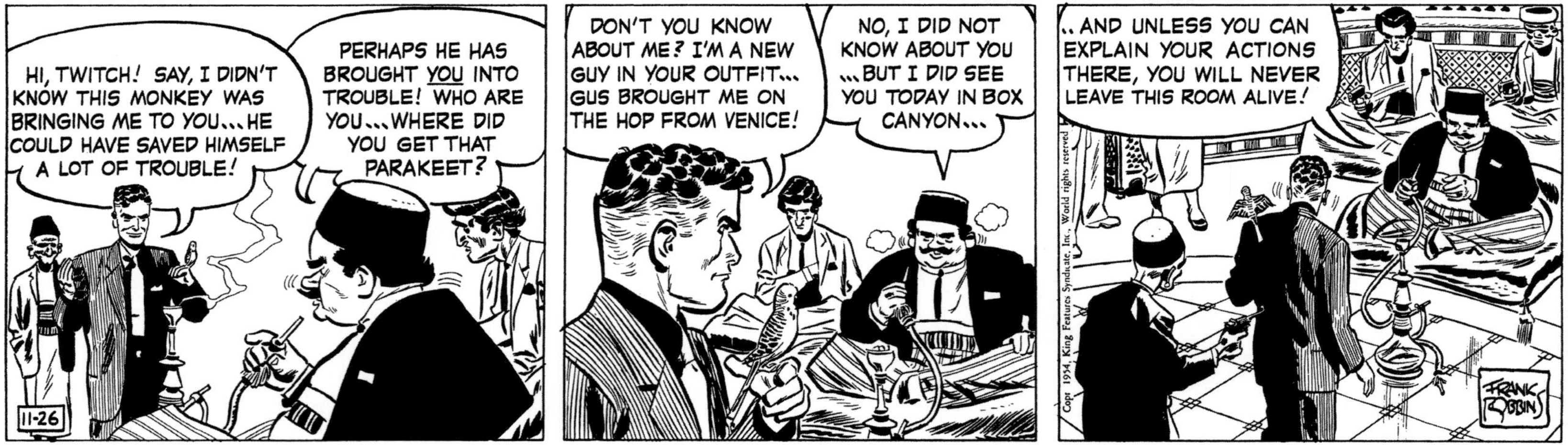
11-26
HI, TWITCH! SAY, I DIDN'T KNOW THIS MONKEY WAS BRINGING ME TO YOU... HE COULD HAVE SAVED HIMSELF A LOT OF TROUBLE!
PERHAPS HE HAS BROUGHT YOU INTO TROUBLE! WHO ARE YOU... WHERE DID YOU GET THAT PARAKEET?
DON'T YOU KNOW ABOUT ME? I'M A NEW GUY IN YOUR OUTFIT... GUS BROUGHT ME ON THE HOP FROM VENICE!
NO, I DID NOT KNOW ABOUT YOU ...BUT I DID SEE YOU TODAY IN BOX CANYON...
..AND UNLESS YOU CAN EXPLAIN YOUR ACTIONS THERE, YOU WILL NEVER LEAVE THIS ROOM ALIVE!
FRANK ROBBINS
Copr. 1954, King Features Syndicate, Inc., World rights reserved

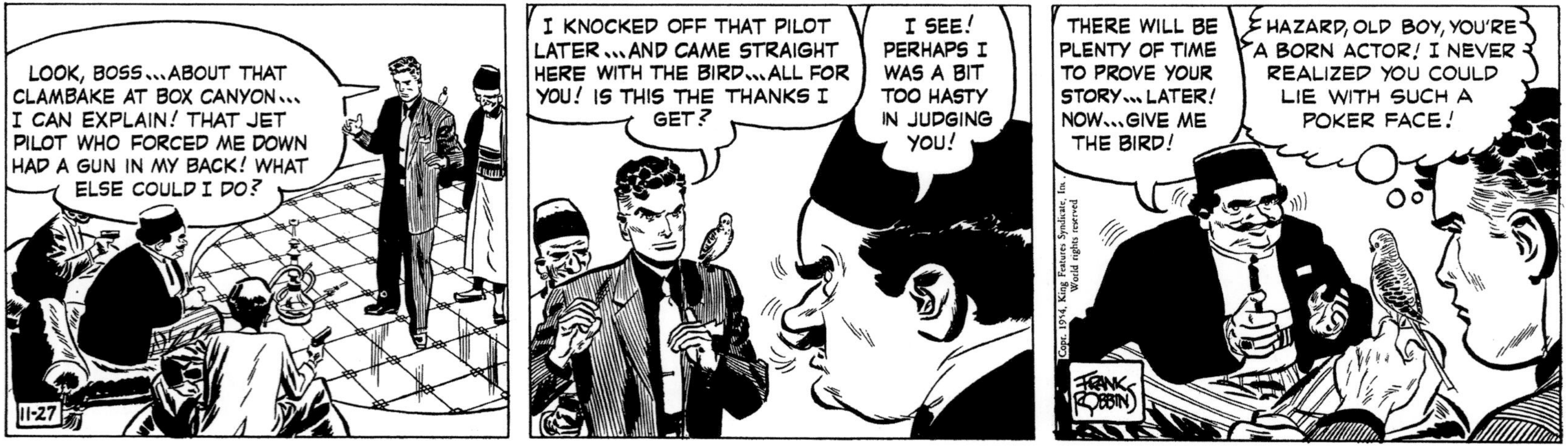
11-27
LOOK, BOSS... ABOUT THAT CLAMBAKE AT BOX CANYON... I CAN EXPLAIN! THAT JET PILOT WHO FORCED ME DOWN HAD A GUN IN MY BACK! WHAT ELSE COULD I DO?
I KNOCKED OFF THAT PILOT LATER... AND CAME STRAIGHT HERE WITH THE BIRD... ALL FOR YOU! IS THIS THE THANKS I GET?
I SEE! PERHAPS I WAS A BIT TOO HASTY IN JUDGING YOU!
THERE WILL BE PLENTY OF TIME TO PROVE YOUR STORY... LATER! NOW... GIVE ME THE BIRD!
HAZARD, OLD BOY, YOU'RE A BORN ACTOR! I NEVER REALIZED YOU COULD LIE WITH SUCH A POKER FACE!
FRANK ROBBINS
Copr. 1954, King Features Syndicate, Inc. World rights reserved

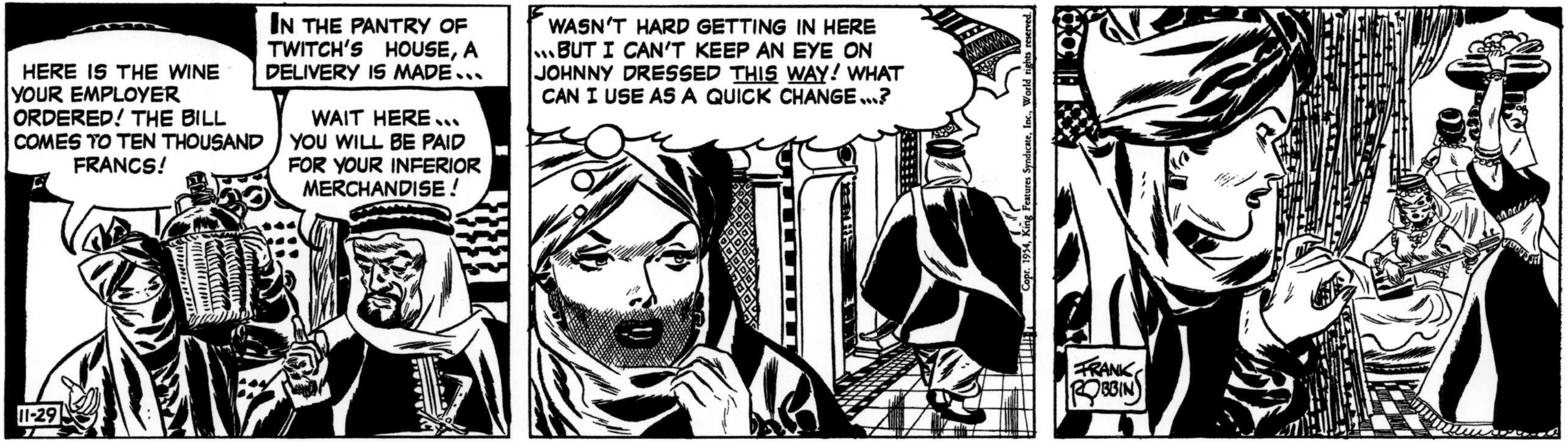
IN THE PANTRY OF TWITCH'S HOUSE, A DELIVERY IS MADE...
HERE IS THE WINE YOUR EMPLOYER ORDERED! THE BILL COMES TO TEN THOUSAND FRANCS!
WAIT HERE... YOU WILL BE PAID FOR YOUR INFERIOR MERCHANDISE!
11-29
WASN'T HARD GETTING IN HERE ...BUT I CAN'T KEEP AN EYE ON JOHNNY DRESSED THIS WAY! WHAT CAN I USE AS A QUICK CHANGE...?
Copr. 1954, King Features Syndicate, Inc., World rights reserved.
FRANK ROBBINS

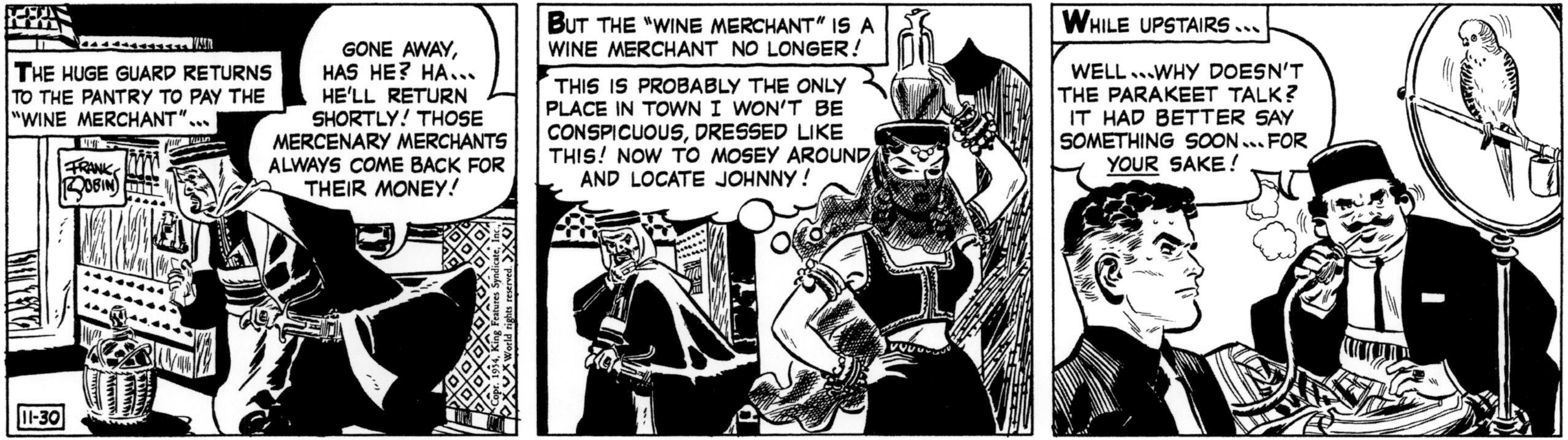
THE HUGE GUARD RETURNS TO THE PANTRY TO PAY THE "WINE MERCHANT"...
GONE AWAY, HAS HE? HA... HE'LL RETURN SHORTLY! THOSE MERCENARY MERCHANTS ALWAYS COME BACK FOR THEIR MONEY!
FRANK ROBBINS
Copr. 1954, King Features Syndicate, Inc., World rights reserved.
11-30
BUT THE "WINE MERCHANT" IS A WINE MERCHANT NO LONGER!
THIS IS PROBABLY THE ONLY PLACE IN TOWN I WON'T BE CONSPICUOUS, DRESSED LIKE THIS! NOW TO MOSEY AROUND AND LOCATE JOHNNY!
WHILE UPSTAIRS...
WELL...WHY DOESN'T THE PARAKEET TALK? IT HAD BETTER SAY SOMETHING SOON...FOR YOUR SAKE!

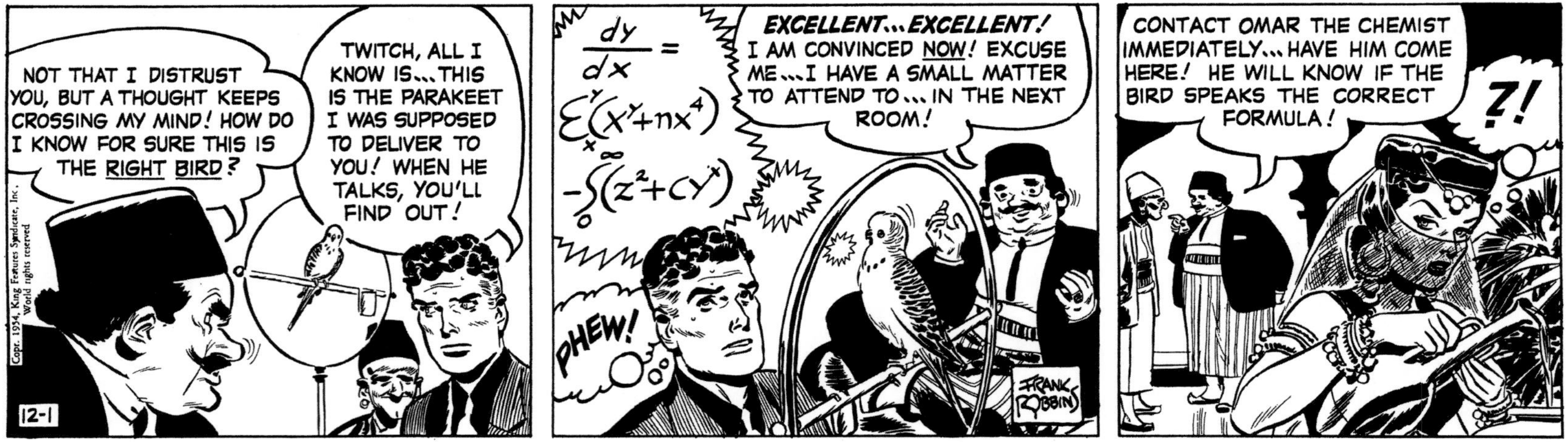
NOT THAT I DISTRUST YOU, BUT A THOUGHT KEEPS CROSSING MY MIND! HOW DO I KNOW FOR SURE THIS IS THE RIGHT BIRD?
TWITCH, ALL I KNOW IS... THIS IS THE PARAKEET I WAS SUPPOSED TO DELIVER TO YOU! WHEN HE TALKS, YOU'LL FIND OUT!
Copr. 1954, King Features Syndicate, Inc., World rights reserved
12-1
$\frac{dy}{dx} = \sum_{+}^{y}(x^{y}+nx^{4}) - \int_{0}^{\infty}(z^{2}+cy^{+})$
PHEW!
EXCELLENT... EXCELLENT! I AM CONVINCED NOW! EXCUSE ME... I HAVE A SMALL MATTER TO ATTEND TO... IN THE NEXT ROOM!
FRANK ROBBINS
CONTACT OMAR THE CHEMIST IMMEDIATELY... HAVE HIM COME HERE! HE WILL KNOW IF THE BIRD SPEAKS THE CORRECT FORMULA!
?!

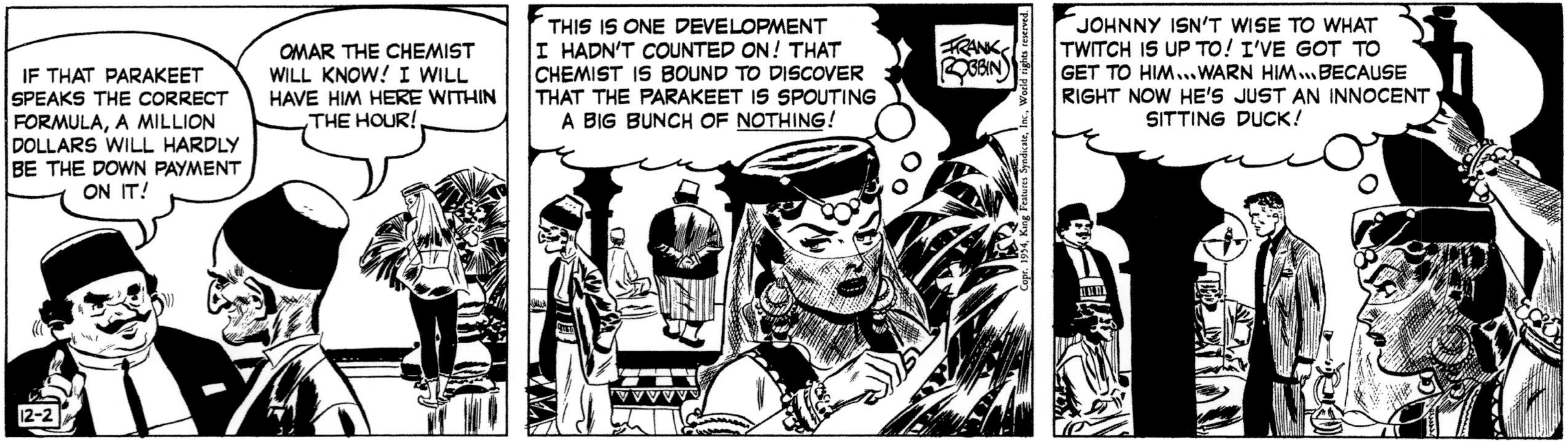
IF THAT PARAKEET SPEAKS THE CORRECT FORMULA, A MILLION DOLLARS WILL HARDLY BE THE DOWN PAYMENT ON IT!
OMAR THE CHEMIST WILL KNOW! I WILL HAVE HIM HERE WITHIN THE HOUR!
12-2
THIS IS ONE DEVELOPMENT I HADN'T COUNTED ON! THAT CHEMIST IS BOUND TO DISCOVER THAT THE PARAKEET IS SPOUTING A BIG BUNCH OF NOTHING!
FRANK ROBBINS
Copr. 1954, King Features Syndicate, Inc., World rights reserved.
JOHNNY ISN'T WISE TO WHAT TWITCH IS UP TO! I'VE GOT TO GET TO HIM... WARN HIM... BECAUSE RIGHT NOW HE'S JUST AN INNOCENT SITTING DUCK!

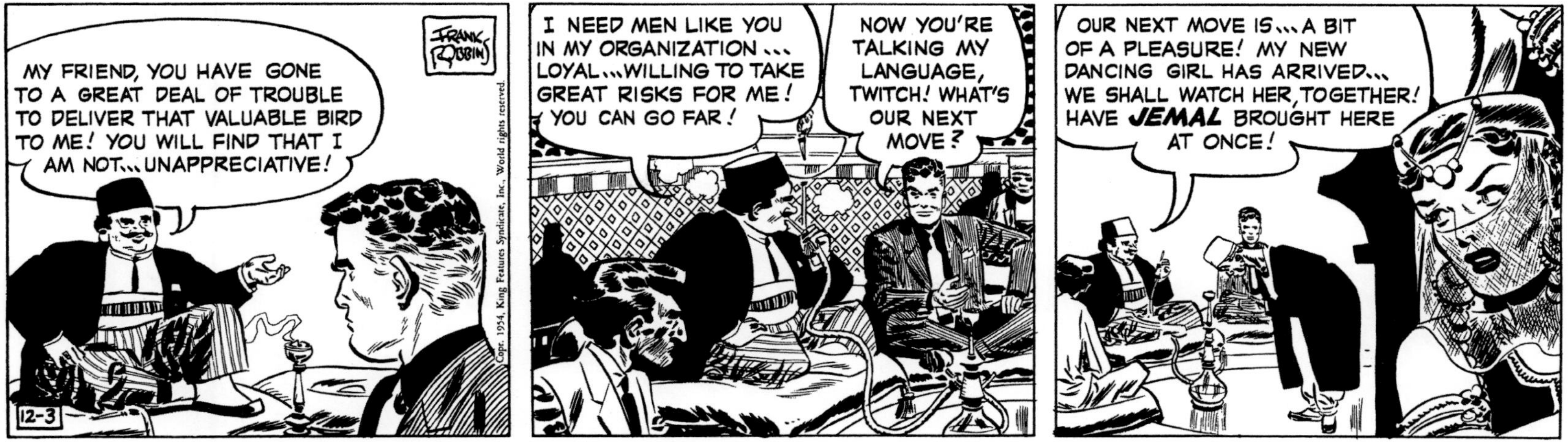
FRANK ROBBINS
Copr. 1954, King Features Syndicate, Inc., World rights reserved.
MY FRIEND, YOU HAVE GONE TO A GREAT DEAL OF TROUBLE TO DELIVER THAT VALUABLE BIRD TO ME! YOU WILL FIND THAT I AM NOT... UNAPPRECIATIVE!
12-3
I NEED MEN LIKE YOU IN MY ORGANIZATION... LOYAL... WILLING TO TAKE GREAT RISKS FOR ME! YOU CAN GO FAR!
NOW YOU'RE TALKING MY LANGUAGE, TWITCH! WHAT'S OUR NEXT MOVE?
OUR NEXT MOVE IS... A BIT OF A PLEASURE! MY NEW DANCING GIRL HAS ARRIVED... WE SHALL WATCH HER, TOGETHER! HAVE JEMAL BROUGHT HERE AT ONCE!

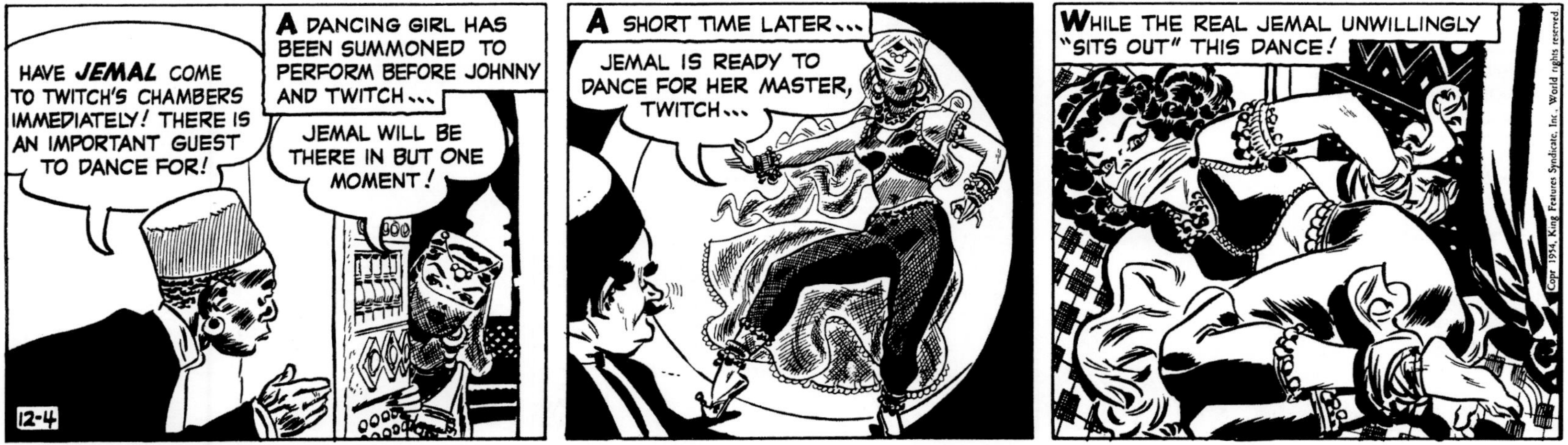
HAVE JEMAL COME TO TWITCH'S CHAMBERS IMMEDIATELY! THERE IS AN IMPORTANT GUEST TO DANCE FOR!
A DANCING GIRL HAS BEEN SUMMONED TO PERFORM BEFORE JOHNNY AND TWITCH...
JEMAL WILL BE THERE IN BUT ONE MOMENT!
12-4
A SHORT TIME LATER...
JEMAL IS READY TO DANCE FOR HER MASTER, TWITCH...
WHILE THE REAL JEMAL UNWILLINGLY "SITS OUT" THIS DANCE!
Copr 1954, King Features Syndicate, Inc., World rights reserved.

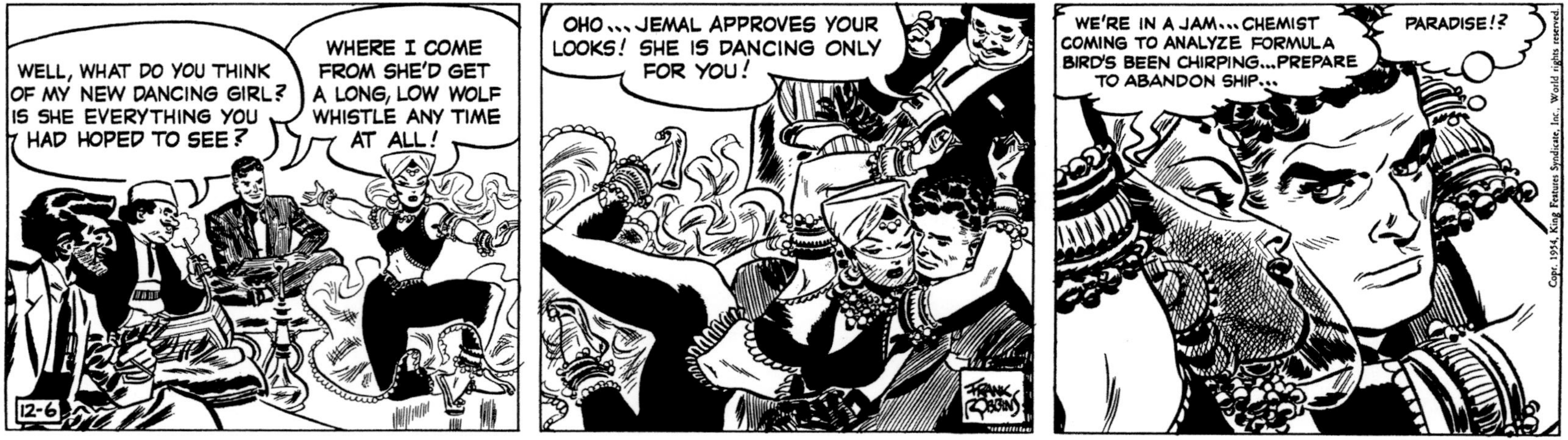
WELL, WHAT DO YOU THINK OF MY NEW DANCING GIRL? IS SHE EVERYTHING YOU HAD HOPED TO SEE?
WHERE I COME FROM SHE'D GET A LONG, LOW WOLF WHISTLE ANY TIME AT ALL!
12-6
OHO... JEMAL APPROVES YOUR LOOKS! SHE IS DANCING ONLY FOR YOU!
FRANK ROBBINS
WE'RE IN A JAM... CHEMIST COMING TO ANALYZE FORMULA BIRD'S BEEN CHIRPING... PREPARE TO ABANDON SHIP...
PARADISE!?
Copr. 1954, King Features Syndicate, Inc., World rights reserved.

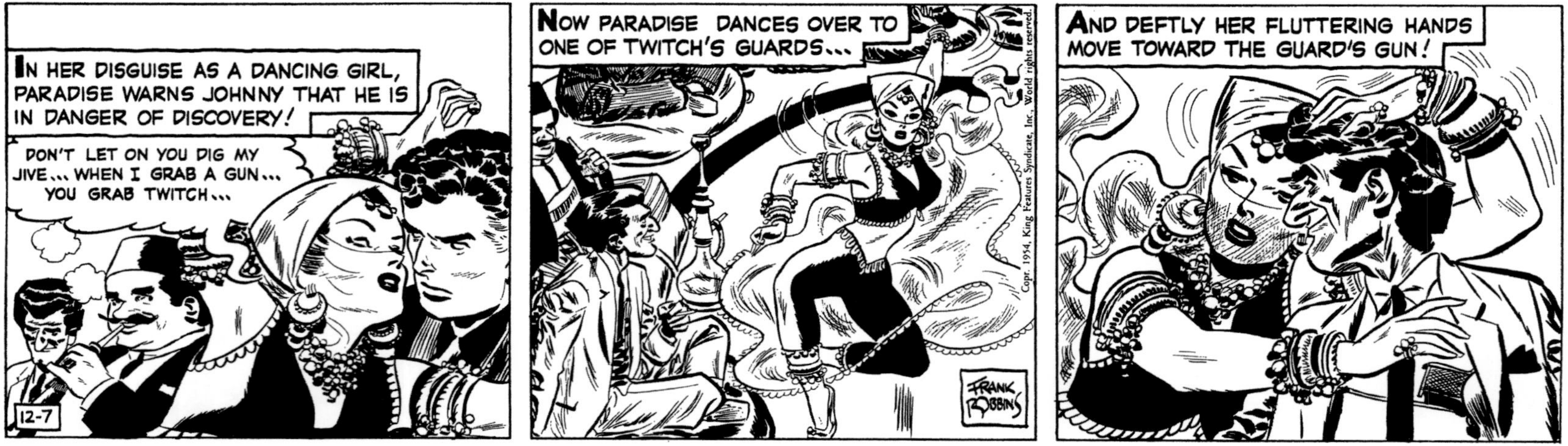
IN HER DISGUISE AS A DANCING GIRL, PARADISE WARNS JOHNNY THAT HE IS IN DANGER OF DISCOVERY!
DON'T LET ON YOU DIG MY JIVE... WHEN I GRAB A GUN... YOU GRAB TWITCH...
12-7
NOW PARADISE DANCES OVER TO ONE OF TWITCH'S GUARDS...
Copr. 1954, King Features Syndicate, Inc., World rights reserved.
FRANK ROBBINS
AND DEFTLY HER FLUTTERING HANDS MOVE TOWARD THE GUARD'S GUN!

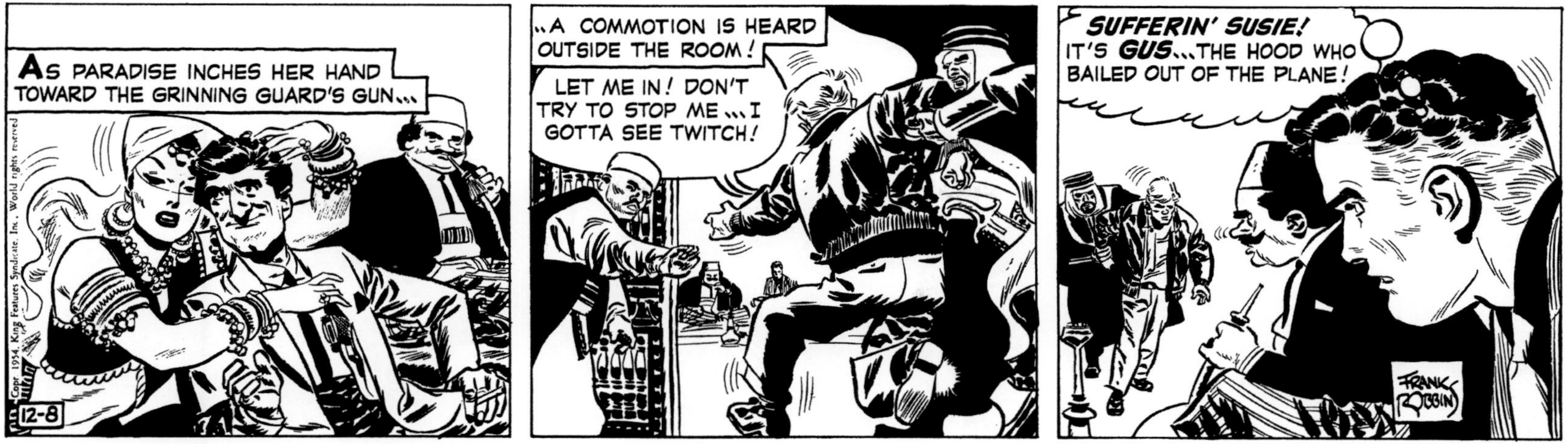
AS PARADISE INCHES HER HAND TOWARD THE GRINNING GUARD'S GUN...
Copr. 1954, King Features Syndicate, Inc., World rights reserved
12-8
..A COMMOTION IS HEARD OUTSIDE THE ROOM!
LET ME IN! DON'T TRY TO STOP ME ... I GOTTA SEE TWITCH!
SUFFERIN' SUSIE! IT'S GUS...THE HOOD WHO BAILED OUT OF THE PLANE!
FRANK ROBBINS

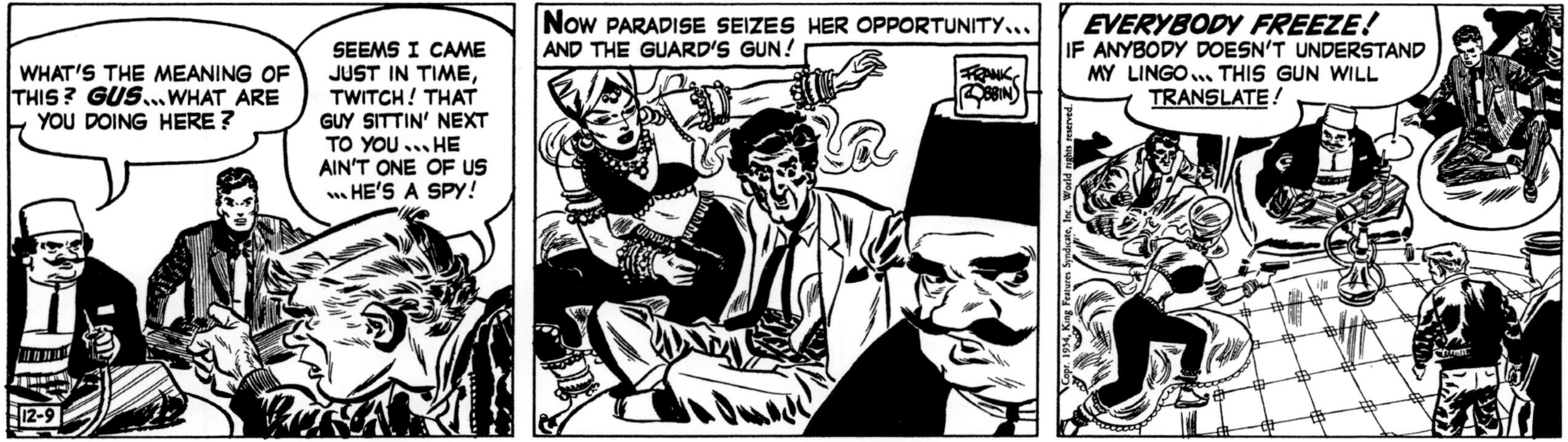
WHAT'S THE MEANING OF THIS? GUS...WHAT ARE YOU DOING HERE?
SEEMS I CAME JUST IN TIME, TWITCH! THAT GUY SITTIN' NEXT TO YOU ... HE AIN'T ONE OF US ...HE'S A SPY!
12-9
NOW PARADISE SEIZES HER OPPORTUNITY... AND THE GUARD'S GUN!
FRANK ROBBINS
EVERYBODY FREEZE! IF ANYBODY DOESN'T UNDERSTAND MY LINGO ... THIS GUN WILL TRANSLATE!
Copr. 1954, King Features Syndicate, Inc., World rights reserved.

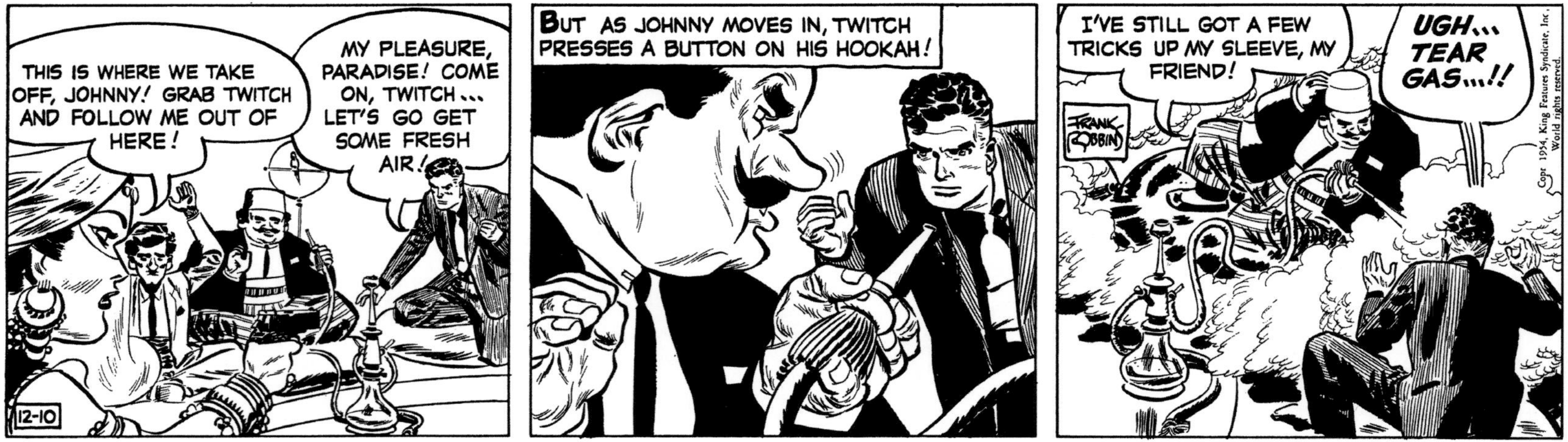
THIS IS WHERE WE TAKE OFF, JOHNNY! GRAB TWITCH AND FOLLOW ME OUT OF HERE!
MY PLEASURE, PARADISE! COME ON, TWITCH... LET'S GO GET SOME FRESH AIR!
12-10
BUT AS JOHNNY MOVES IN, TWITCH PRESSES A BUTTON ON HIS HOOKAH!
I'VE STILL GOT A FEW TRICKS UP MY SLEEVE, MY FRIEND!
UGH... TEAR GAS...!!
FRANK ROBBINS
Copr 1954, King Features Syndicate, Inc., World rights reserved.

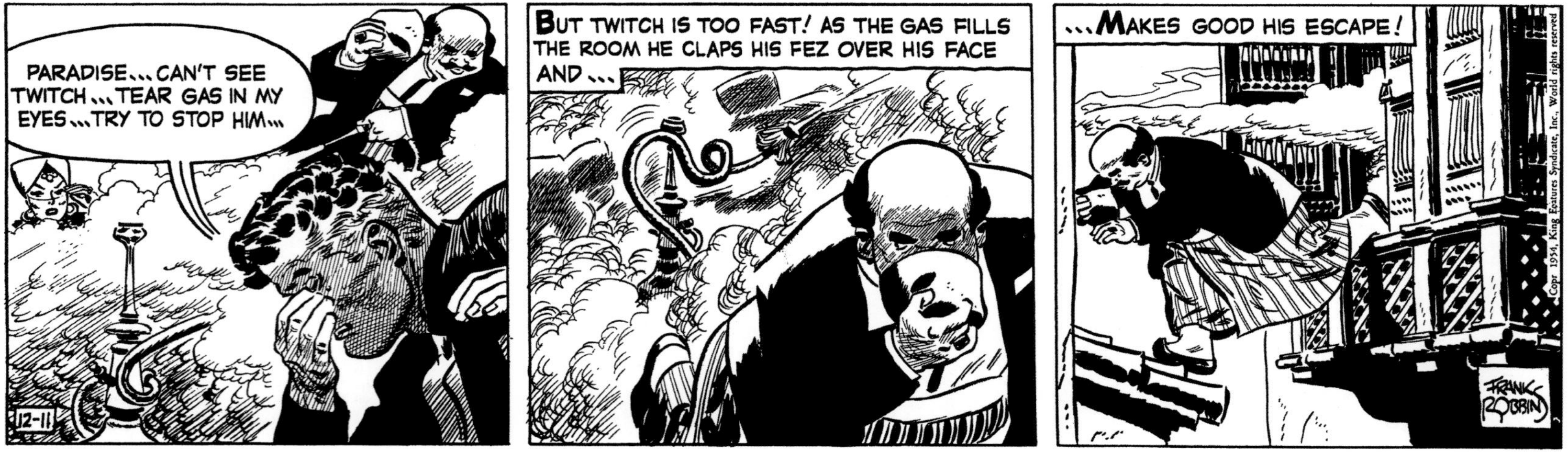
PARADISE... CAN'T SEE TWITCH... TEAR GAS IN MY EYES... TRY TO STOP HIM...
12-11
BUT TWITCH IS TOO FAST! AS THE GAS FILLS THE ROOM HE CLAPS HIS FEZ OVER HIS FACE AND...
...MAKES GOOD HIS ESCAPE!
Copr 1954, King Features Syndicate, Inc., World rights reserved
FRANK ROBBINS

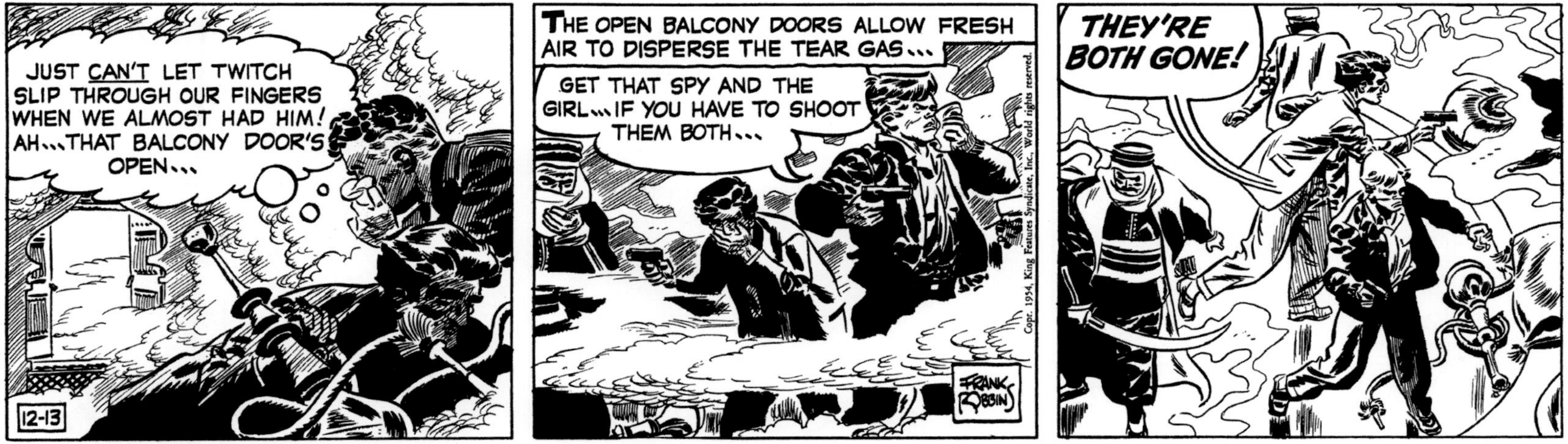
JUST CAN'T LET TWITCH SLIP THROUGH OUR FINGERS WHEN WE ALMOST HAD HIM! AH...THAT BALCONY DOOR'S OPEN...
12-13
THE OPEN BALCONY DOORS ALLOW FRESH AIR TO DISPERSE THE TEAR GAS...
GET THAT SPY AND THE GIRL...IF YOU HAVE TO SHOOT THEM BOTH...
Copr. 1954, King Features Syndicate, Inc., World rights reserved.
FRANK ROBBINS
THEY'RE BOTH GONE!

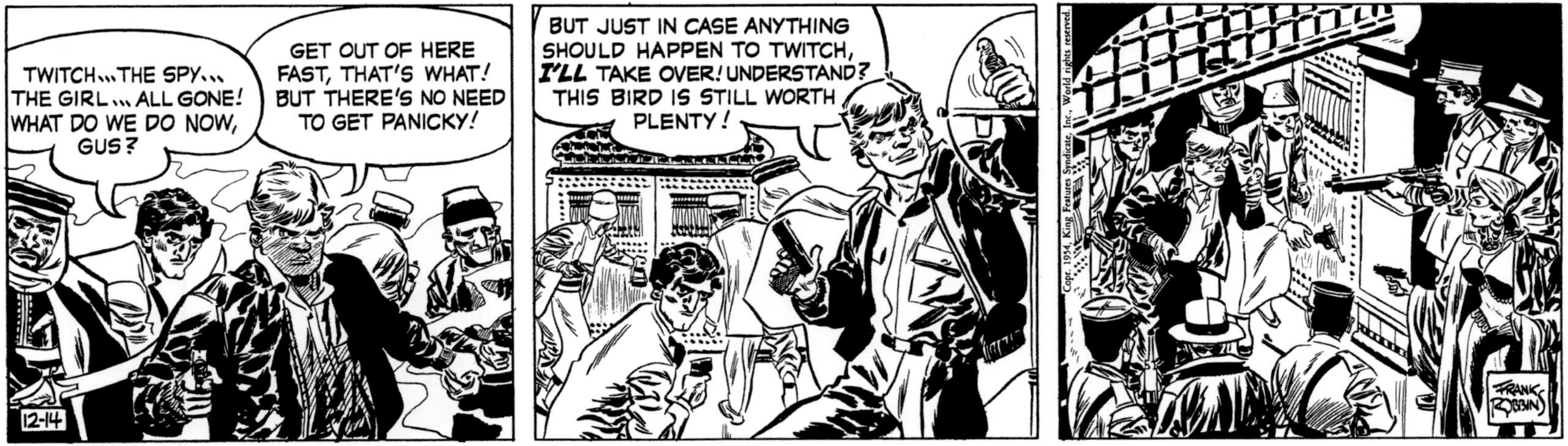
TWITCH...THE SPY... THE GIRL... ALL GONE! WHAT DO WE DO NOW, GUS?
GET OUT OF HERE FAST, THAT'S WHAT! BUT THERE'S NO NEED TO GET PANICKY!
12-14
BUT JUST IN CASE ANYTHING SHOULD HAPPEN TO TWITCH, I'LL TAKE OVER! UNDERSTAND? THIS BIRD IS STILL WORTH PLENTY!
Copr. 1954, King Features Syndicate, Inc., World rights reserved.
FRANK ROBBINS

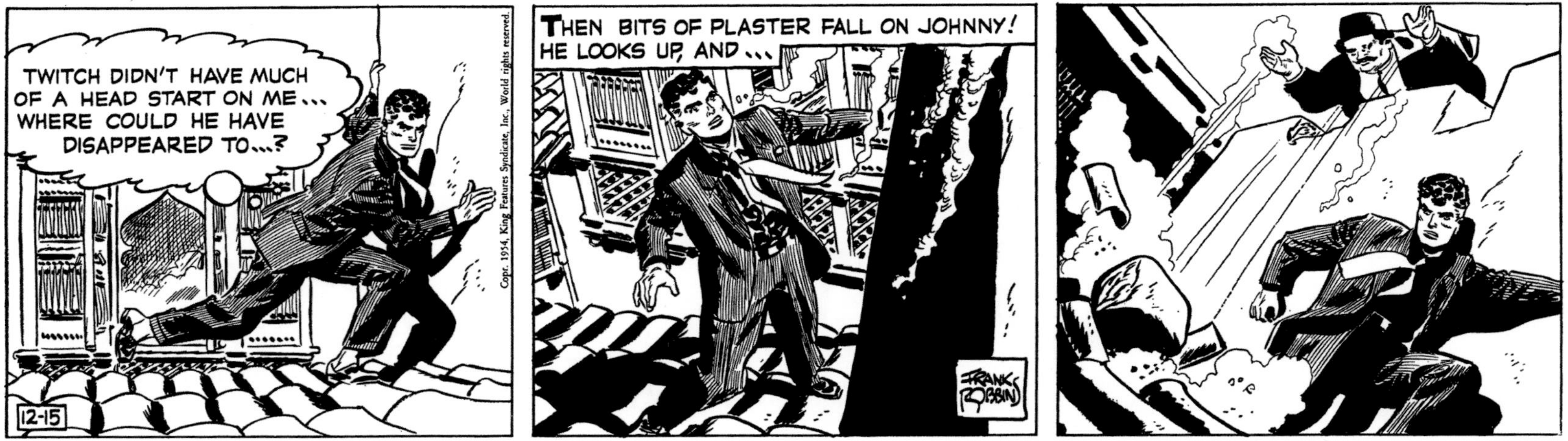
TWITCH DIDN'T HAVE MUCH OF A HEAD START ON ME... WHERE COULD HE HAVE DISAPPEARED TO...?
Copr. 1954, King Features Syndicate, Inc., World rights reserved.
12-15
THEN BITS OF PLASTER FALL ON JOHNNY! HE LOOKS UP, AND...
FRANK ROBBINS

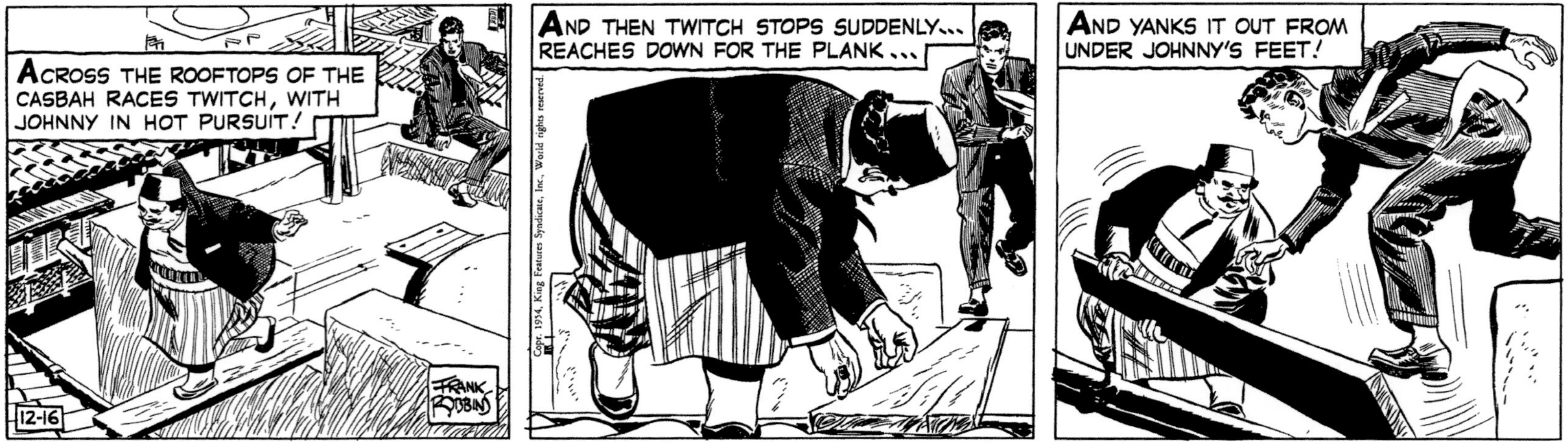
ACROSS THE ROOFTOPS OF THE CASBAH RACES TWITCH, WITH JOHNNY IN HOT PURSUIT!
12-16
FRANK ROBBINS
AND THEN TWITCH STOPS SUDDENLY... REACHES DOWN FOR THE PLANK...
Copr. 1954, King Features Syndicate, Inc., World rights reserved.
AND YANKS IT OUT FROM UNDER JOHNNY'S FEET!

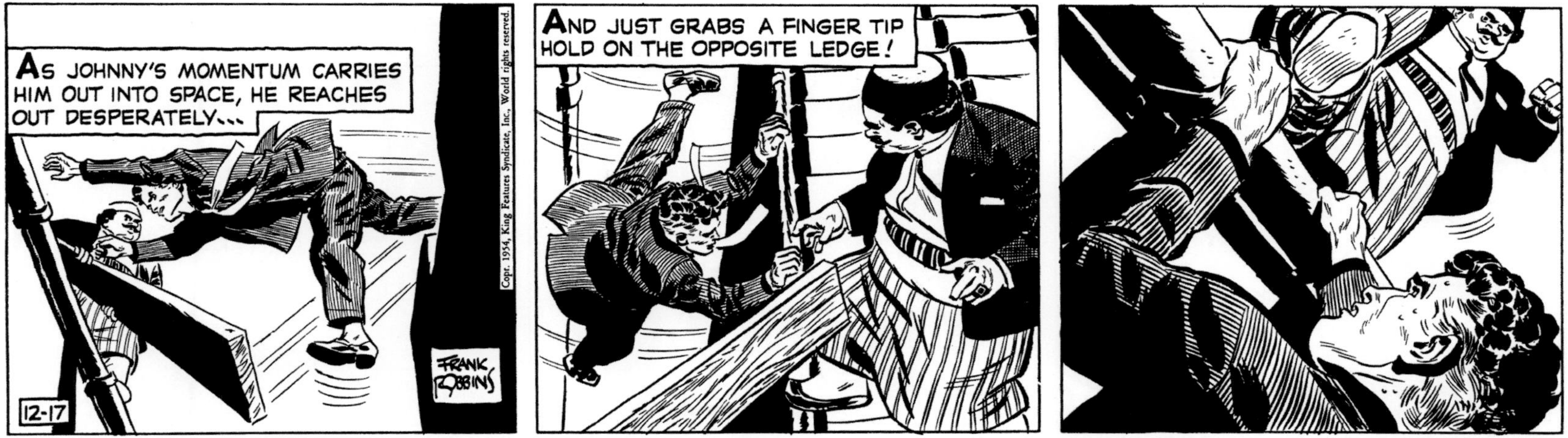
AS JOHNNY'S MOMENTUM CARRIES HIM OUT INTO SPACE, HE REACHES OUT DESPERATELY...
12-17
FRANK ROBBINS
Copr. 1954, King Features Syndicate, Inc., World rights reserved.
AND JUST GRABS A FINGER TIP HOLD ON THE OPPOSITE LEDGE!

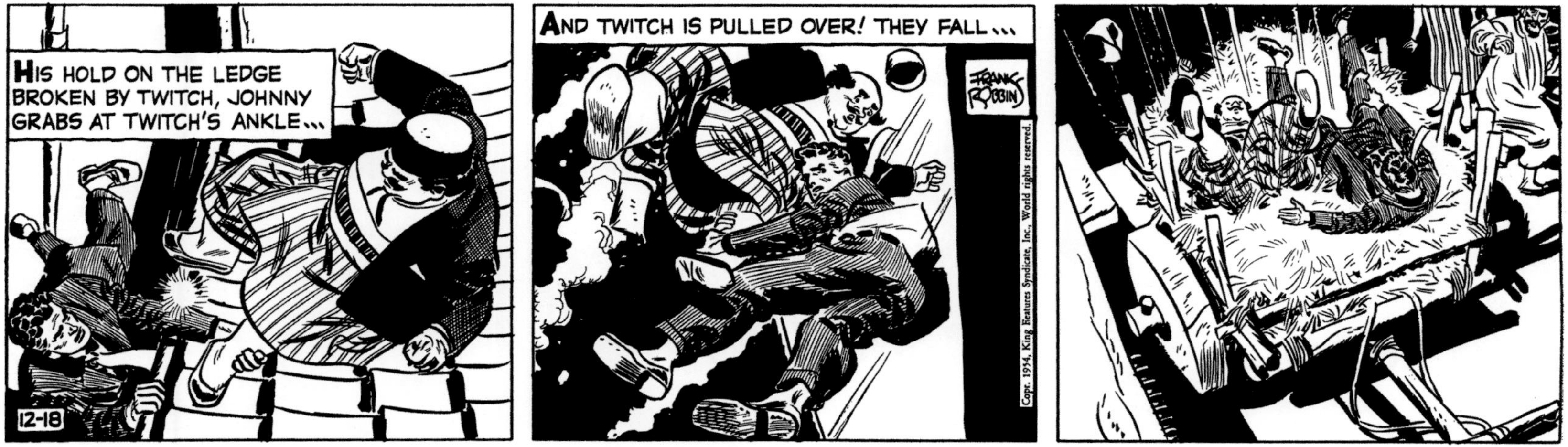
HIS HOLD ON THE LEDGE BROKEN BY TWITCH, JOHNNY GRABS AT TWITCH'S ANKLE...
12-18
AND TWITCH IS PULLED OVER! THEY FALL...
FRANK ROBBINS
Copr. 1954, King Features Syndicate, Inc., World rights reserved.

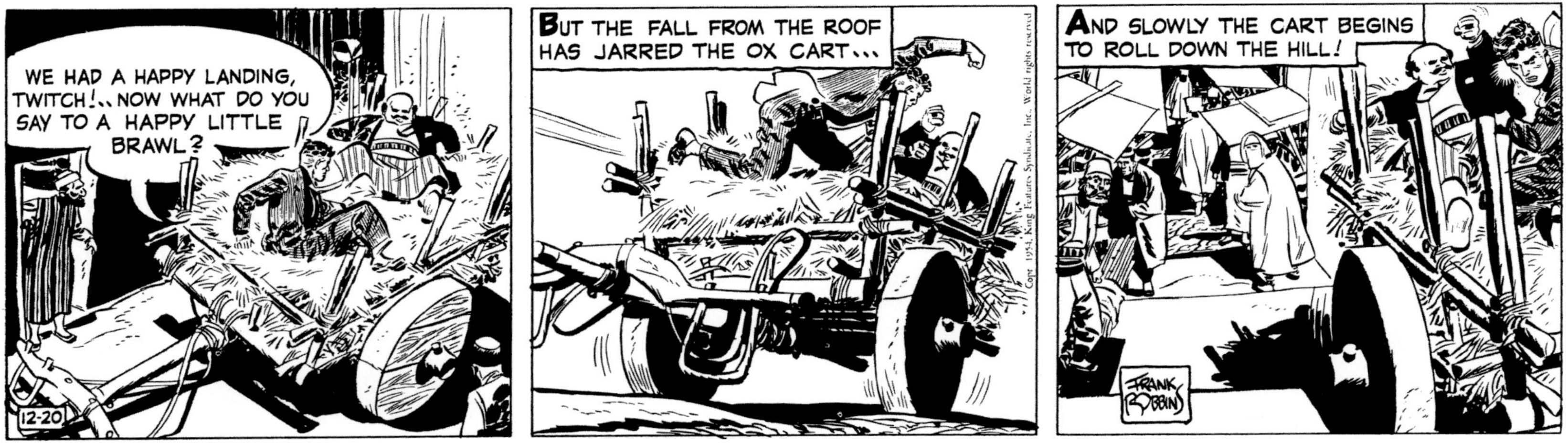
WE HAD A HAPPY LANDING, TWITCH!.. NOW WHAT DO YOU SAY TO A HAPPY LITTLE BRAWL?
12-20
BUT THE FALL FROM THE ROOF HAS JARRED THE OX CART...
Copr 1954, King Features Syndicate, Inc., World rights reserved
AND SLOWLY THE CART BEGINS TO ROLL DOWN THE HILL!
FRANK ROBBINS

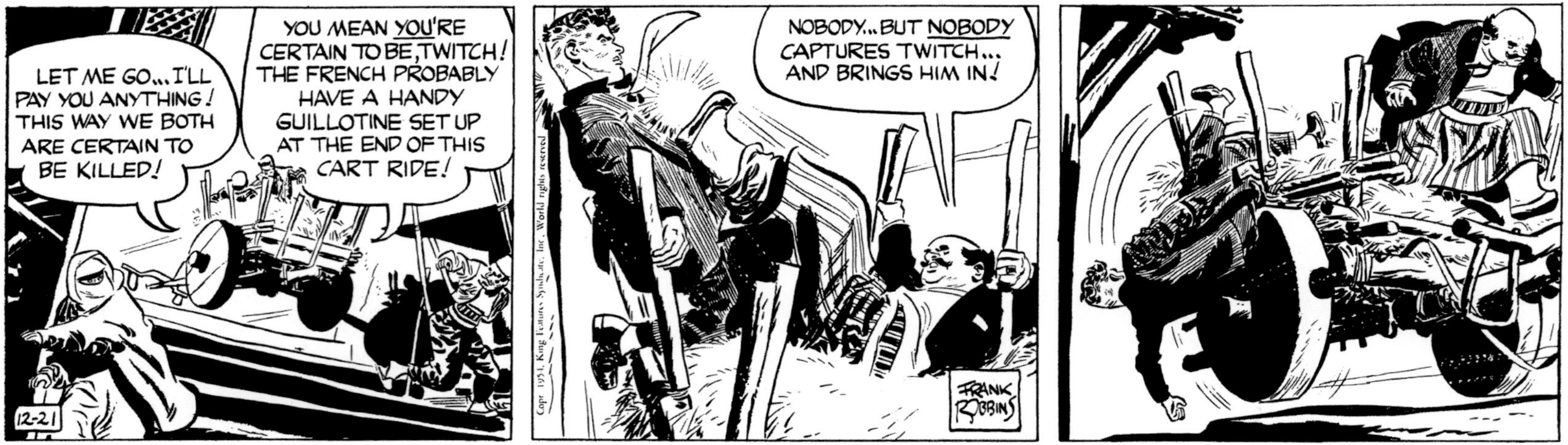
LET ME GO... I'LL PAY YOU ANYTHING! THIS WAY WE BOTH ARE CERTAIN TO BE KILLED!
YOU MEAN YOU'RE CERTAIN TO BE, TWITCH! THE FRENCH PROBABLY HAVE A HANDY GUILLOTINE SET UP AT THE END OF THIS CART RIDE!
12-21
Copr 1954, King Features Syndicate, Inc., World rights reserved
NOBODY... BUT NOBODY CAPTURES TWITCH... AND BRINGS HIM IN!
FRANK ROBBINS

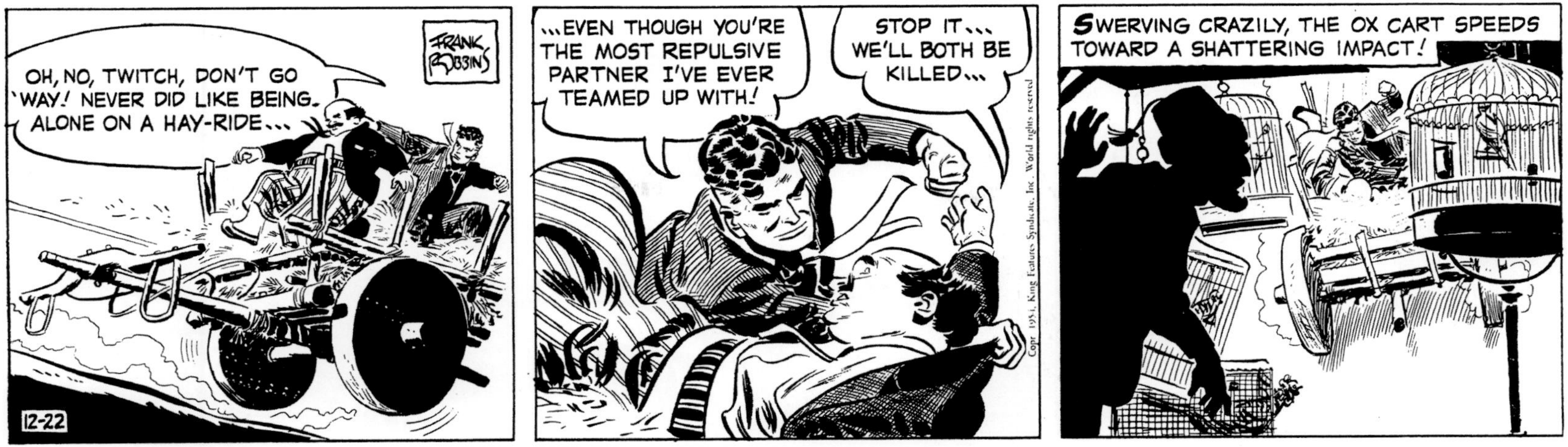
FRANK ROBBINS
OH, NO, TWITCH, DON'T GO 'WAY! NEVER DID LIKE BEING ALONE ON A HAY-RIDE...
12-22
...EVEN THOUGH YOU'RE THE MOST REPULSIVE PARTNER I'VE EVER TEAMED UP WITH!
STOP IT... WE'LL BOTH BE KILLED...
Copr 1954, King Features Syndicate, Inc., World rights reserved
SWERVING CRAZILY, THE OX CART SPEEDS TOWARD A SHATTERING IMPACT!

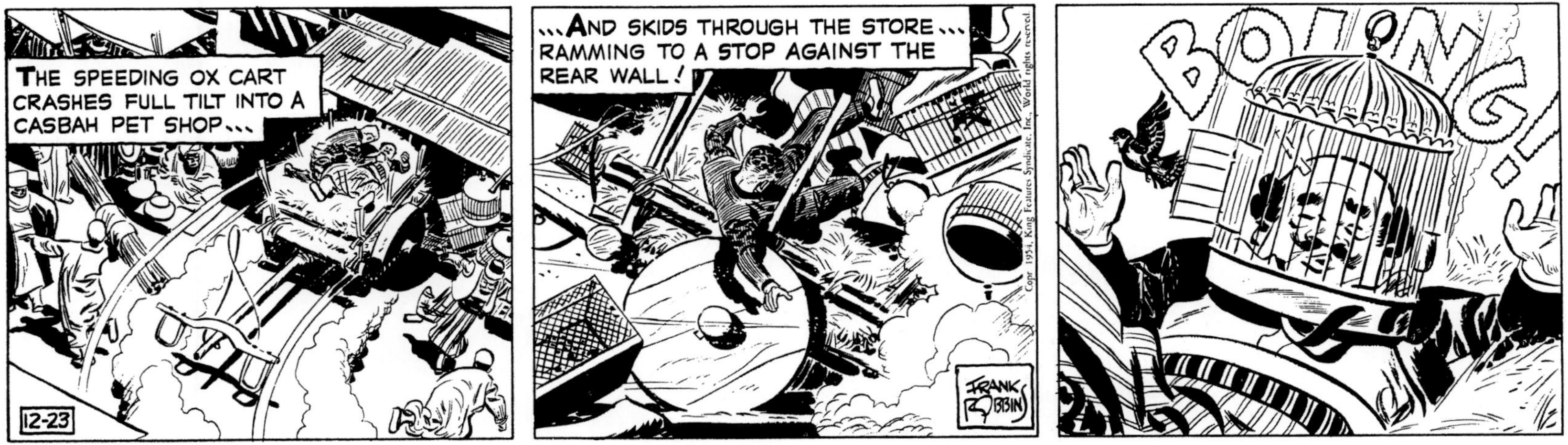
THE SPEEDING OX CART CRASHES FULL TILT INTO A CASBAH PET SHOP...
12-23
...AND SKIDS THROUGH THE STORE... RAMMING TO A STOP AGAINST THE REAR WALL!
Copr 1954, King Features Syndicate, Inc., World rights reserved
FRANK ROBBINS
BOING!!

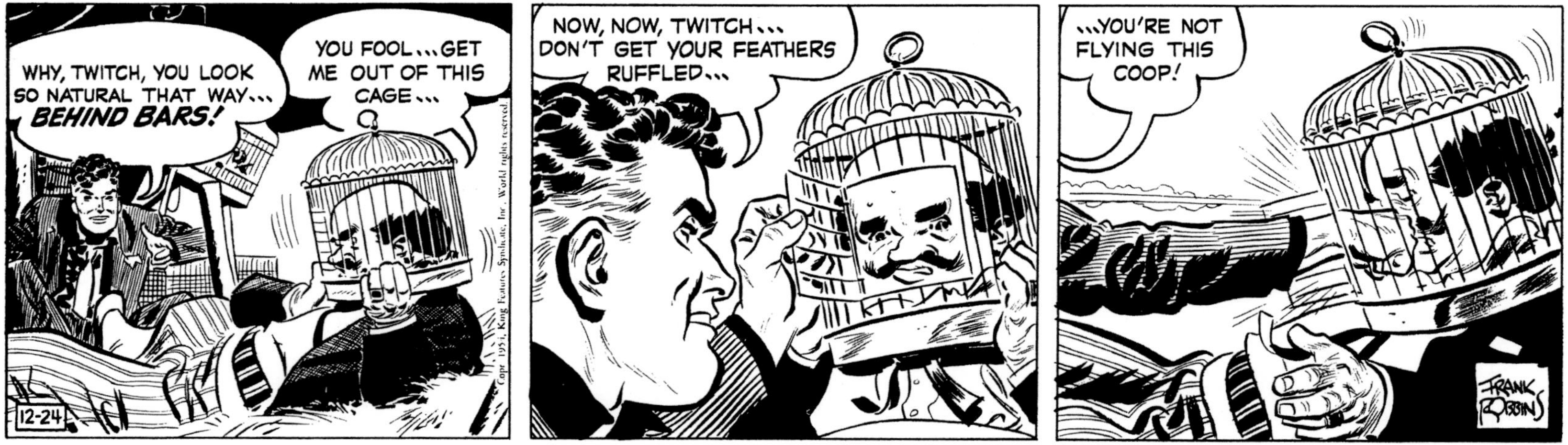
12-24
WHY, TWITCH, YOU LOOK SO NATURAL THAT WAY... BEHIND BARS!
YOU FOOL...GET ME OUT OF THIS CAGE...
Copr. 1951, King Features Syndicate, Inc., World rights reserved
NOW, NOW, TWITCH... DON'T GET YOUR FEATHERS RUFFLED...
...YOU'RE NOT FLYING THIS COOP!
FRANK ROBBINS

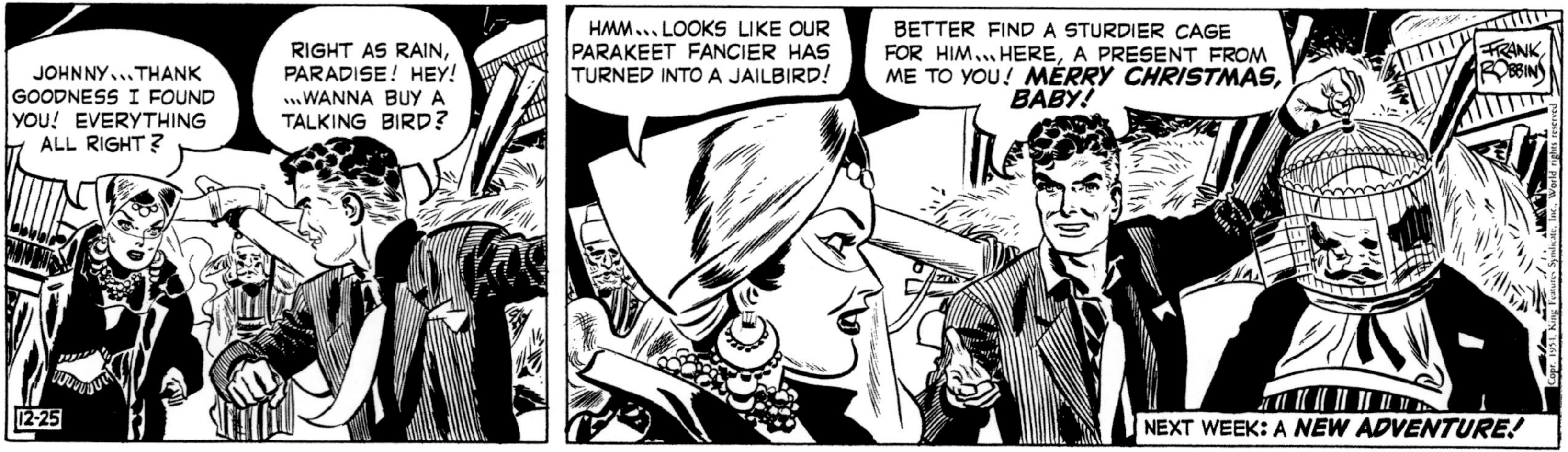
12-25
JOHNNY...THANK GOODNESS I FOUND YOU! EVERYTHING ALL RIGHT?
RIGHT AS RAIN, PARADISE! HEY! ...WANNA BUY A TALKING BIRD?
HMM...LOOKS LIKE OUR PARAKEET FANCIER HAS TURNED INTO A JAILBIRD!
BETTER FIND A STURDIER CAGE FOR HIM...HERE, A PRESENT FROM ME TO YOU! MERRY CHRISTMAS, BABY!
FRANK ROBBINS
Copr. 1951, King Features Syndicate, Inc., World rights reserved
NEXT WEEK: A NEW ADVENTURE!

THAT'S CORRECT! AND TWITCH IS MORE THAN WELCOME TO THIS PARAKEET!
$\frac{dy}{dx} = \sum_{x}^{y}(x^{y} + nx^{4}) - \int_{0}^{\infty}(z^{2} + cy^{x})$
FRANK ROBBINS

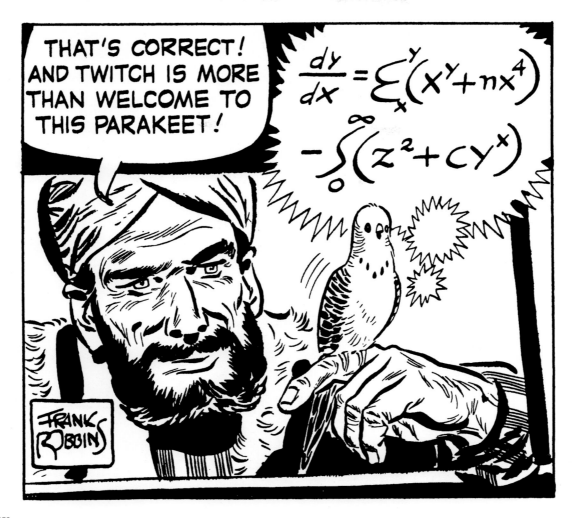

JOHNNY HAZARD

Chapter Three: It's a Snap

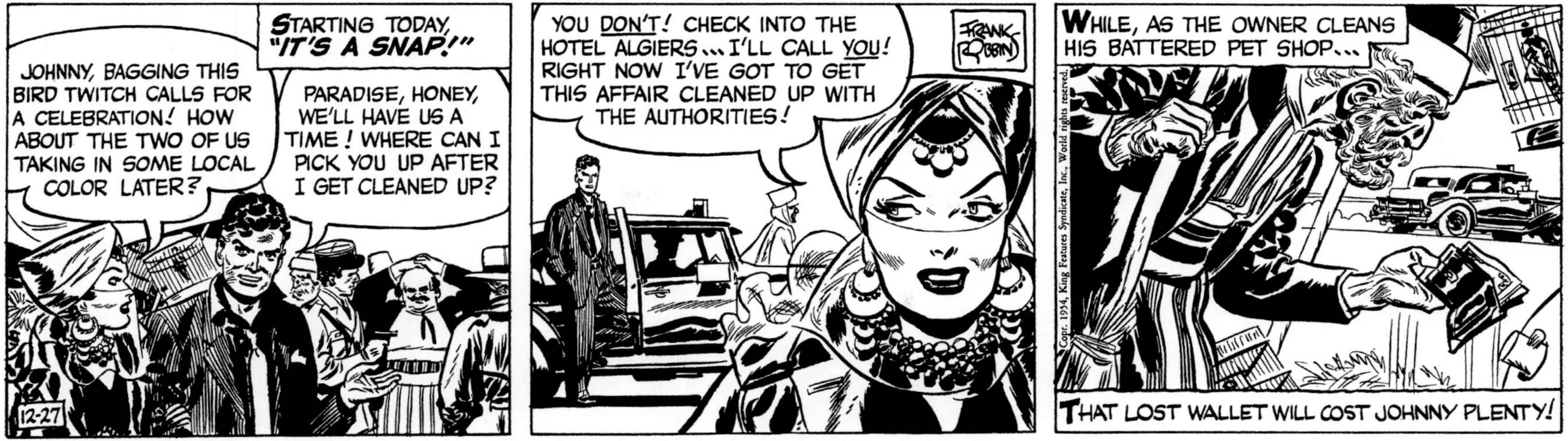

STARTING TODAY, "IT'S A SNAP!"
JOHNNY, BAGGING THIS BIRD TWITCH CALLS FOR A CELEBRATION! HOW ABOUT THE TWO OF US TAKING IN SOME LOCAL COLOR LATER?
PARADISE, HONEY, WE'LL HAVE US A TIME! WHERE CAN I PICK YOU UP AFTER I GET CLEANED UP?
12-27
YOU DON'T! CHECK INTO THE HOTEL ALGIERS ... I'LL CALL YOU! RIGHT NOW I'VE GOT TO GET THIS AFFAIR CLEANED UP WITH THE AUTHORITIES!
FRANK ROBBINS
WHILE, AS THE OWNER CLEANS HIS BATTERED PET SHOP ...
Copr. 1954, King Features Syndicate, Inc., World rights reserved.
THAT LOST WALLET WILL COST JOHNNY PLENTY!

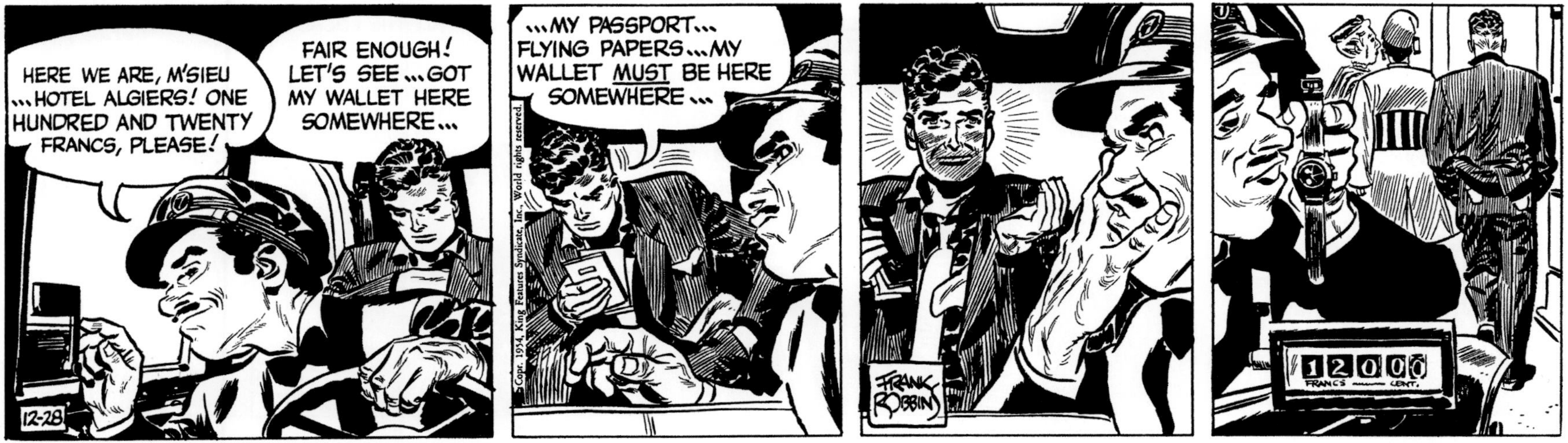

HERE WE ARE, M'SIEU ... HOTEL ALGIERS! ONE HUNDRED AND TWENTY FRANCS, PLEASE!
FAIR ENOUGH! LET'S SEE ... GOT MY WALLET HERE SOMEWHERE ...
12-28
... MY PASSPORT ... FLYING PAPERS ... MY WALLET MUST BE HERE SOMEWHERE ...
Copr. 1954, King Features Syndicate, Inc., World rights reserved.
FRANK ROBBINS
12000
FRANCS CENT.

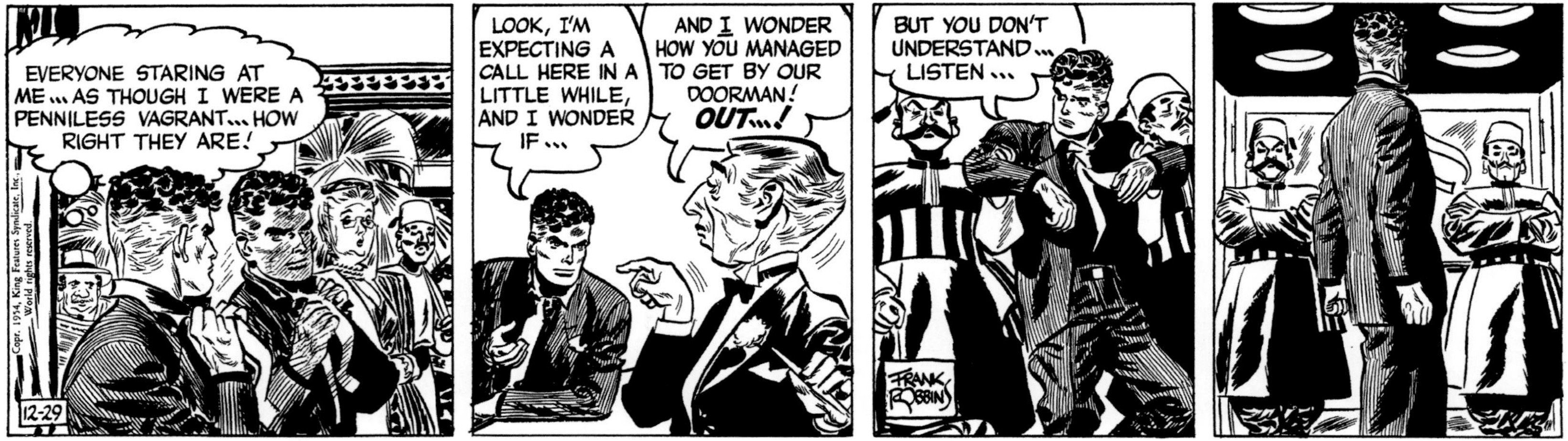
12-29
Copr. 1954, King Features Syndicate, Inc., World rights reserved.
EVERYONE STARING AT ME... AS THOUGH I WERE A PENNILESS VAGRANT... HOW RIGHT THEY ARE!
LOOK, I'M EXPECTING A CALL HERE IN A LITTLE WHILE, AND I WONDER IF ...
AND I WONDER HOW YOU MANAGED TO GET BY OUR DOORMAN! OUT...!
BUT YOU DON'T UNDERSTAND... LISTEN ...
FRANK ROBBINS

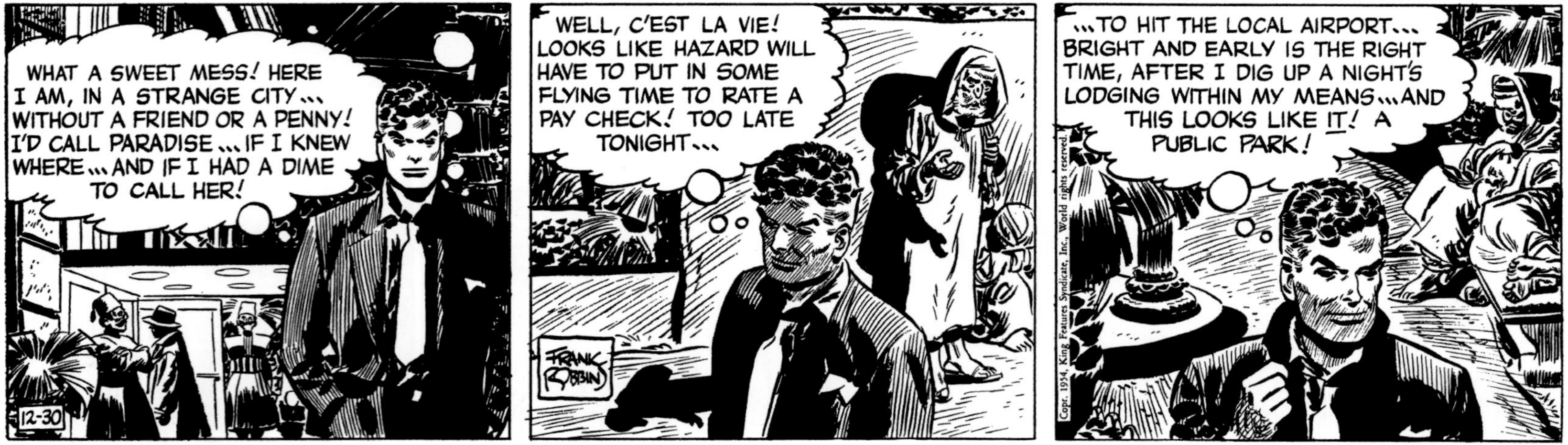
12-30
WHAT A SWEET MESS! HERE I AM, IN A STRANGE CITY... WITHOUT A FRIEND OR A PENNY! I'D CALL PARADISE... IF I KNEW WHERE... AND IF I HAD A DIME TO CALL HER!
WELL, C'EST LA VIE! LOOKS LIKE HAZARD WILL HAVE TO PUT IN SOME FLYING TIME TO RATE A PAY CHECK! TOO LATE TONIGHT...
FRANK ROBBINS
...TO HIT THE LOCAL AIRPORT... BRIGHT AND EARLY IS THE RIGHT TIME, AFTER I DIG UP A NIGHT'S LODGING WITHIN MY MEANS... AND THIS LOOKS LIKE IT! A PUBLIC PARK!
Copr. 1954, King Features Syndicate, Inc., World rights reserved.

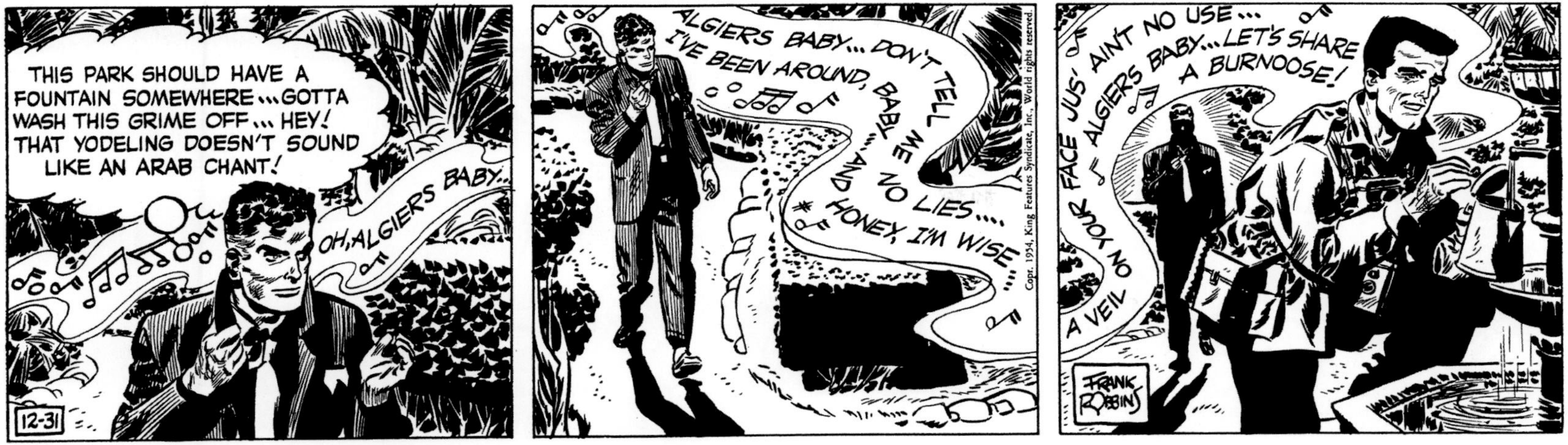
THIS PARK SHOULD HAVE A FOUNTAIN SOMEWHERE...GOTTA WASH THIS GRIME OFF... HEY! THAT YODELING DOESN'T SOUND LIKE AN ARAB CHANT!
OH, ALGIERS BABY...
12-31
ALGIERS BABY... DON'T TELL ME NO LIES.... I'VE BEEN AROUND, BABY... AND HONEY, I'M WISE....
Copr. 1954, King Features Syndicate, Inc., World rights reserved.
A VEIL ON YOUR FACE JUS' AIN'T NO USE... ALGIERS BABY... LET'S SHARE A BURNOOSE!
FRANK ROBBINS

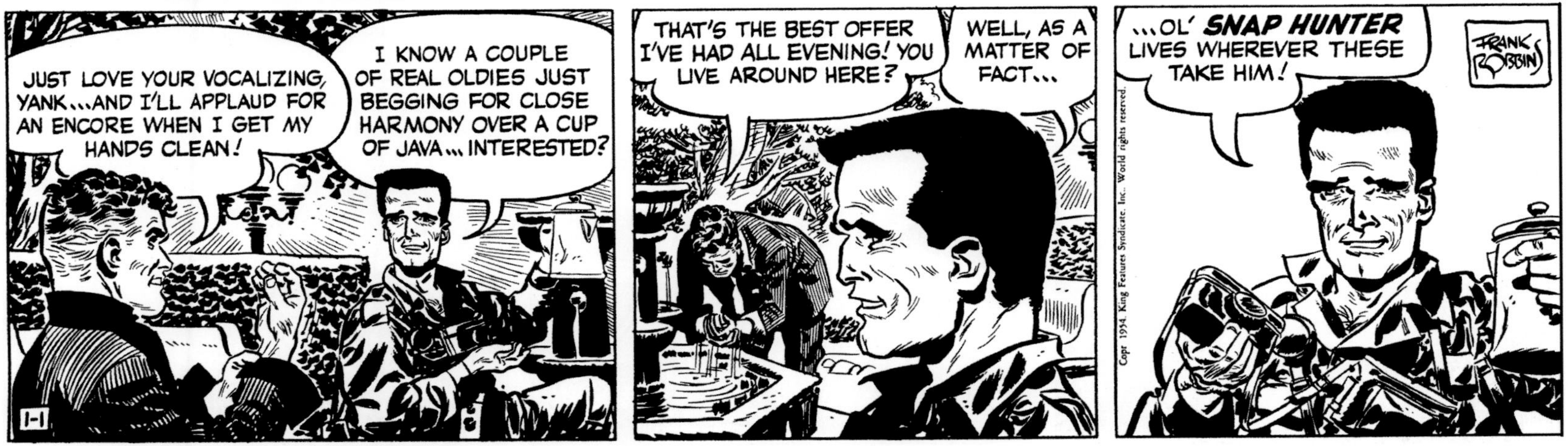
JUST LOVE YOUR VOCALIZING, YANK...AND I'LL APPLAUD FOR AN ENCORE WHEN I GET MY HANDS CLEAN!
I KNOW A COUPLE OF REAL OLDIES JUST BEGGING FOR CLOSE HARMONY OVER A CUP OF JAVA... INTERESTED?
1-1
THAT'S THE BEST OFFER I'VE HAD ALL EVENING! YOU LIVE AROUND HERE?
WELL, AS A MATTER OF FACT...
...OL' SNAP HUNTER LIVES WHEREVER THESE TAKE HIM!
FRANK ROBBINS
Copr 1954, King Features Syndicate, Inc. World rights reserved.

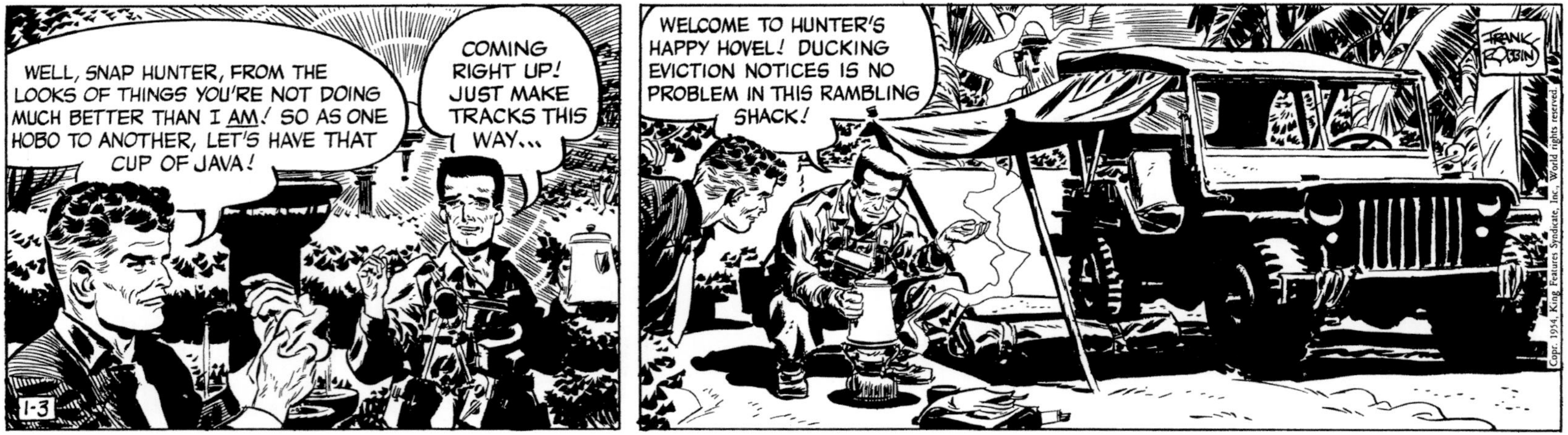
1-3
WELL, SNAP HUNTER, FROM THE LOOKS OF THINGS YOU'RE NOT DOING MUCH BETTER THAN I AM! SO AS ONE HOBO TO ANOTHER, LET'S HAVE THAT CUP OF JAVA!
COMING RIGHT UP! JUST MAKE TRACKS THIS WAY...
WELCOME TO HUNTER'S HAPPY HOVEL! DUCKING EVICTION NOTICES IS NO PROBLEM IN THIS RAMBLING SHACK!
FRANK ROBBINS
Copr. 1954, King Features Syndicate, Inc., World rights reserved.

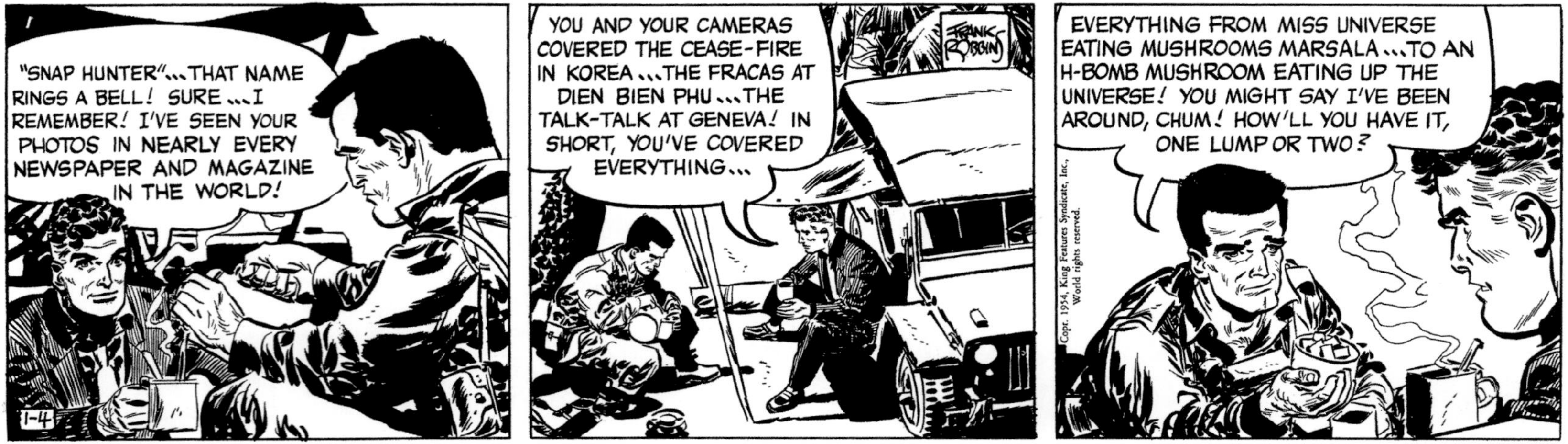
1-4
"SNAP HUNTER"...THAT NAME RINGS A BELL! SURE...I REMEMBER! I'VE SEEN YOUR PHOTOS IN NEARLY EVERY NEWSPAPER AND MAGAZINE IN THE WORLD!
YOU AND YOUR CAMERAS COVERED THE CEASE-FIRE IN KOREA...THE FRACAS AT DIEN BIEN PHU...THE TALK-TALK AT GENEVA! IN SHORT, YOU'VE COVERED EVERYTHING...
FRANK ROBBINS
Copr. 1954, King Features Syndicate, Inc., World rights reserved.
EVERYTHING FROM MISS UNIVERSE EATING MUSHROOMS MARSALA...TO AN H-BOMB MUSHROOM EATING UP THE UNIVERSE! YOU MIGHT SAY I'VE BEEN AROUND, CHUM! HOW'LL YOU HAVE IT, ONE LUMP OR TWO?

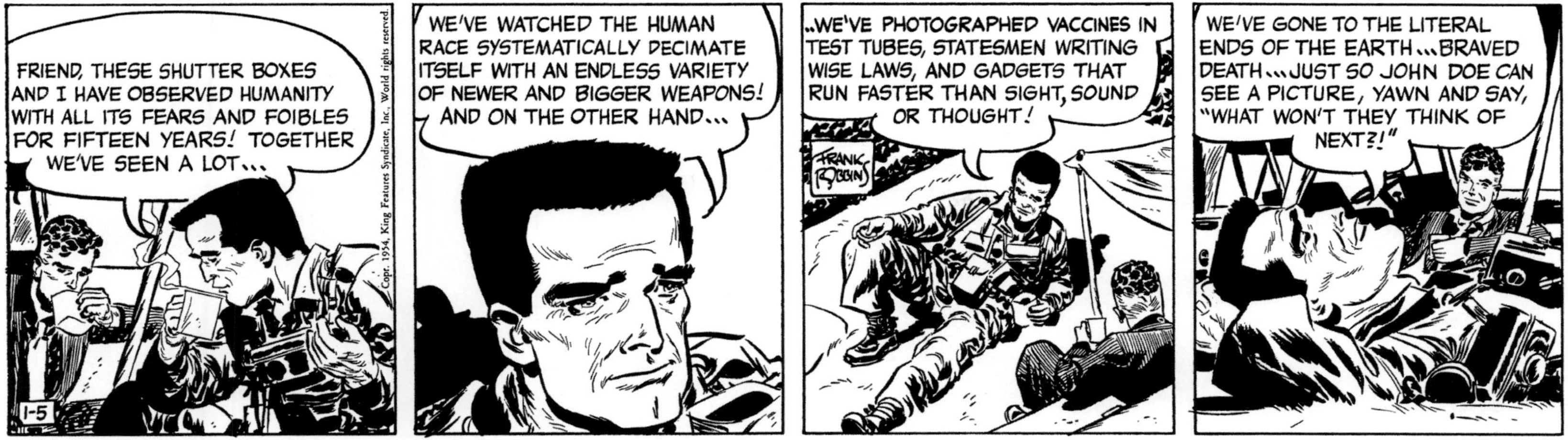
FRIEND, THESE SHUTTER BOXES AND I HAVE OBSERVED HUMANITY WITH ALL ITS FEARS AND FOIBLES FOR FIFTEEN YEARS! TOGETHER WE'VE SEEN A LOT...
Copr. 1954, King Features Syndicate, Inc., World rights reserved.
1-5
WE'VE WATCHED THE HUMAN RACE SYSTEMATICALLY DECIMATE ITSELF WITH AN ENDLESS VARIETY OF NEWER AND BIGGER WEAPONS! AND ON THE OTHER HAND...
..WE'VE PHOTOGRAPHED VACCINES IN TEST TUBES, STATESMEN WRITING WISE LAWS, AND GADGETS THAT RUN FASTER THAN SIGHT, SOUND OR THOUGHT!
FRANK ROBBINS
WE'VE GONE TO THE LITERAL ENDS OF THE EARTH...BRAVED DEATH...JUST SO JOHN DOE CAN SEE A PICTURE, YAWN AND SAY, "WHAT WON'T THEY THINK OF NEXT?!"

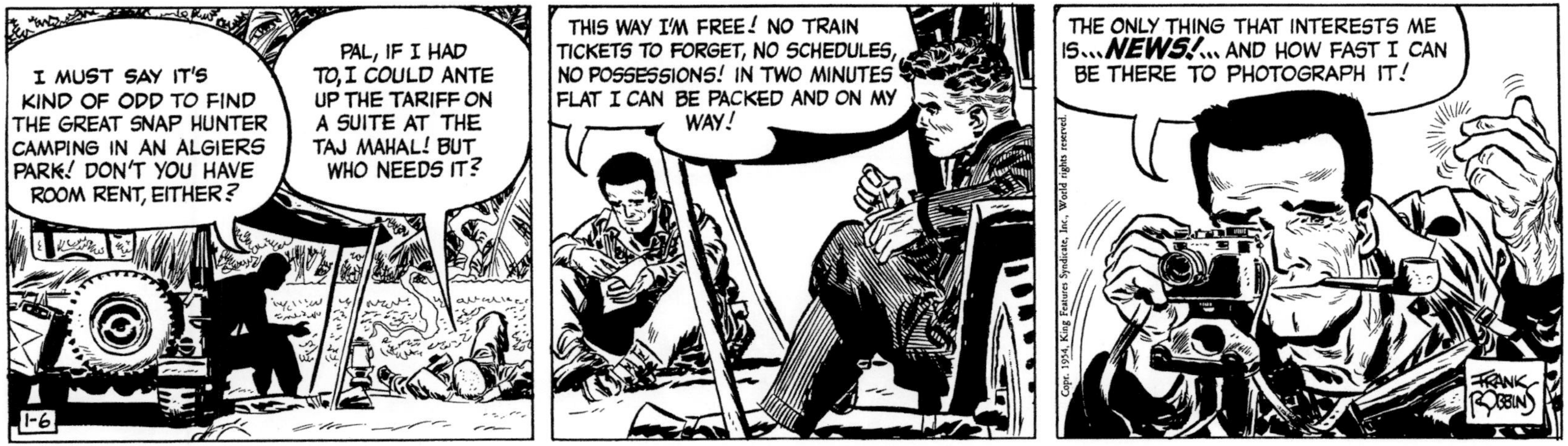
I MUST SAY IT'S KIND OF ODD TO FIND THE GREAT SNAP HUNTER CAMPING IN AN ALGIERS PARK! DON'T YOU HAVE ROOM RENT, EITHER?
PAL, IF I HAD TO, I COULD ANTE UP THE TARIFF ON A SUITE AT THE TAJ MAHAL! BUT WHO NEEDS IT?
1-6
THIS WAY I'M FREE! NO TRAIN TICKETS TO FORGET, NO SCHEDULES, NO POSSESSIONS! IN TWO MINUTES FLAT I CAN BE PACKED AND ON MY WAY!
THE ONLY THING THAT INTERESTS ME IS...**NEWS!**... AND HOW FAST I CAN BE THERE TO PHOTOGRAPH IT!
Copr. 1954, King Features Syndicate, Inc., World rights reserved.
FRANK ROBBINS

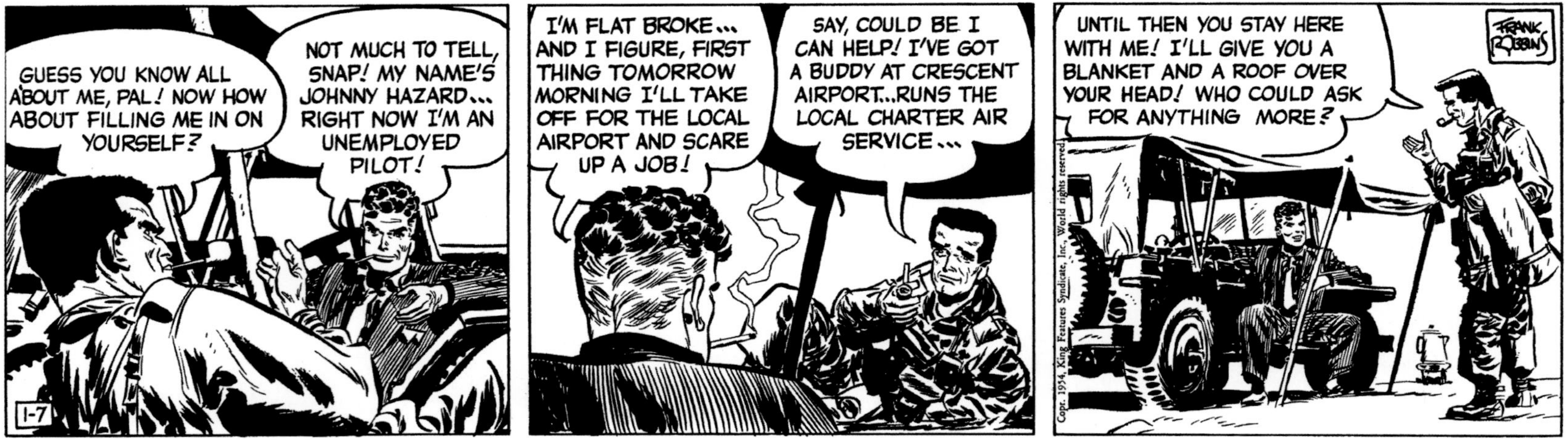
1-7
GUESS YOU KNOW ALL ABOUT ME, PAL! NOW HOW ABOUT FILLING ME IN ON YOURSELF?
NOT MUCH TO TELL, SNAP! MY NAME'S JOHNNY HAZARD... RIGHT NOW I'M AN UNEMPLOYED PILOT!
I'M FLAT BROKE... AND I FIGURE, FIRST THING TOMORROW MORNING I'LL TAKE OFF FOR THE LOCAL AIRPORT AND SCARE UP A JOB!
SAY, COULD BE I CAN HELP! I'VE GOT A BUDDY AT CRESCENT AIRPORT...RUNS THE LOCAL CHARTER AIR SERVICE...
UNTIL THEN YOU STAY HERE WITH ME! I'LL GIVE YOU A BLANKET AND A ROOF OVER YOUR HEAD! WHO COULD ASK FOR ANYTHING MORE?
FRANK ROBBINS
Copr. 1954, King Features Syndicate, Inc., World rights reserved.

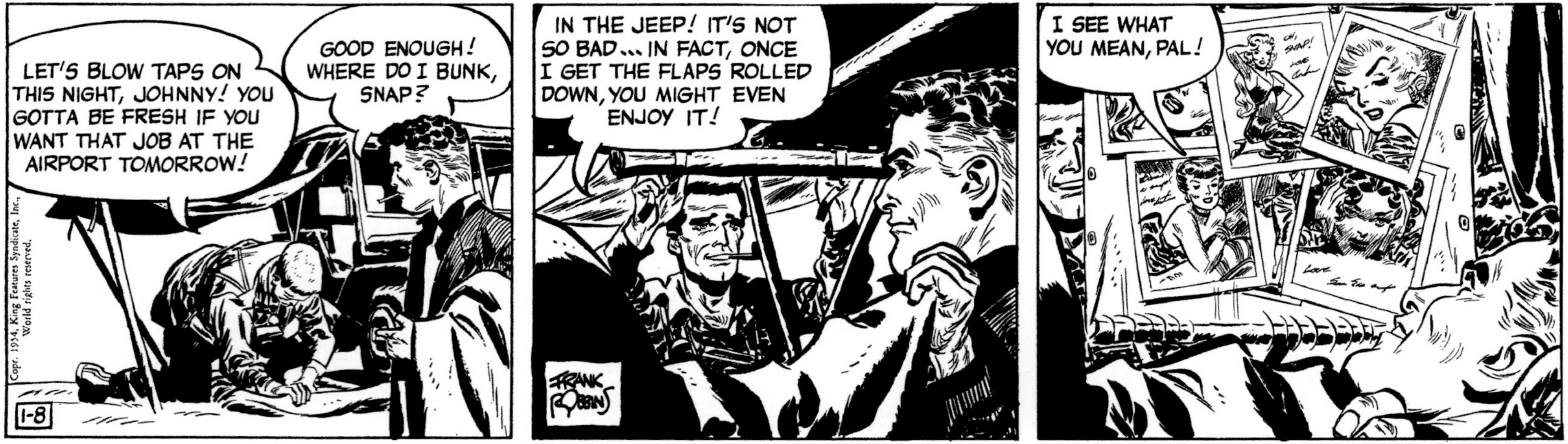
1-8
LET'S BLOW TAPS ON THIS NIGHT, JOHNNY! YOU GOTTA BE FRESH IF YOU WANT THAT JOB AT THE AIRPORT TOMORROW!
GOOD ENOUGH! WHERE DO I BUNK, SNAP?
Copr. 1954, King Features Syndicate, Inc., World rights reserved.
IN THE JEEP! IT'S NOT SO BAD... IN FACT, ONCE I GET THE FLAPS ROLLED DOWN, YOU MIGHT EVEN ENJOY IT!
FRANK ROBBINS
I SEE WHAT YOU MEAN, PAL!

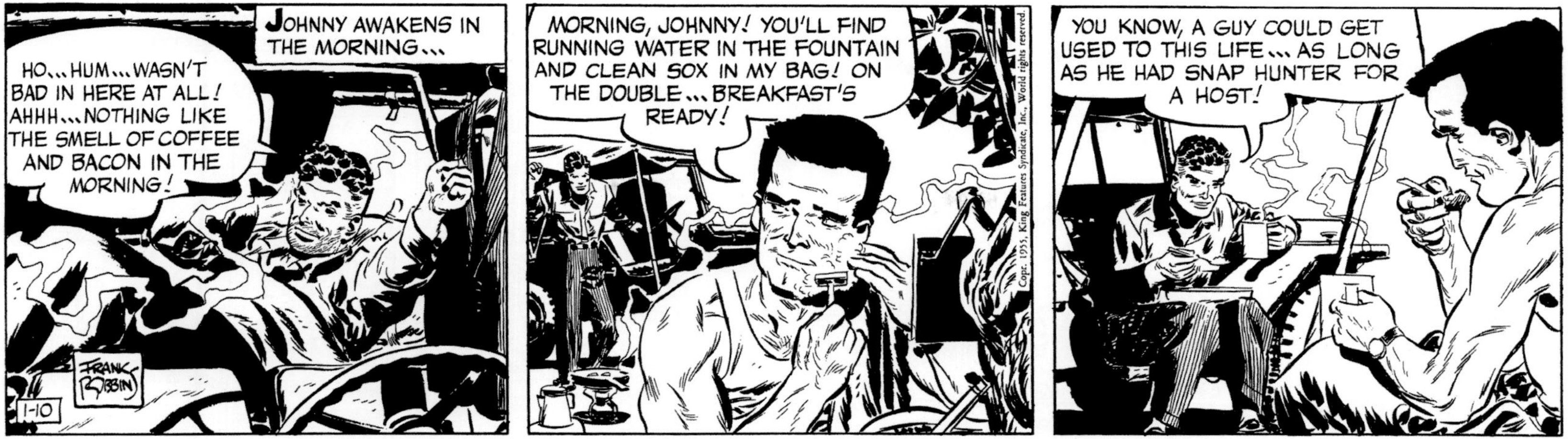

JOHNNY AWAKENS IN THE MORNING...
HO... HUM... WASN'T BAD IN HERE AT ALL! AHHH... NOTHING LIKE THE SMELL OF COFFEE AND BACON IN THE MORNING!
FRANK ROBBINS
1-10
MORNING, JOHNNY! YOU'LL FIND RUNNING WATER IN THE FOUNTAIN AND CLEAN SOX IN MY BAG! ON THE DOUBLE... BREAKFAST'S READY!
Copr. 1955, King Features Syndicate, Inc., World rights reserved.
YOU KNOW, A GUY COULD GET USED TO THIS LIFE... AS LONG AS HE HAD SNAP HUNTER FOR A HOST!

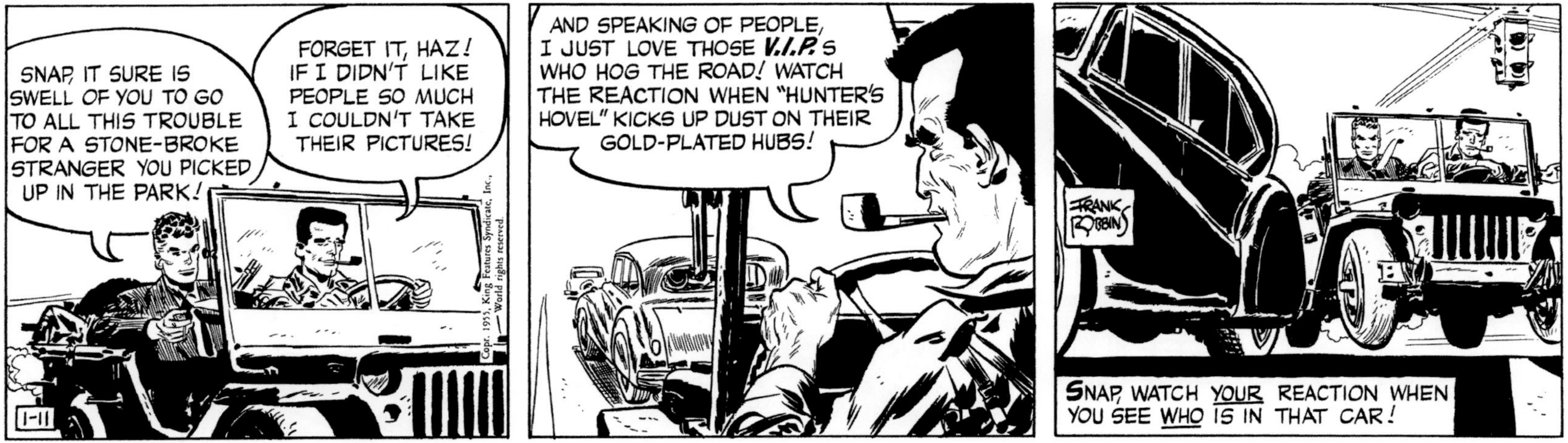

SNAP, IT SURE IS SWELL OF YOU TO GO TO ALL THIS TROUBLE FOR A STONE-BROKE STRANGER YOU PICKED UP IN THE PARK!
FORGET IT, HAZ! IF I DIDN'T LIKE PEOPLE SO MUCH I COULDN'T TAKE THEIR PICTURES!
Copr. 1955, King Features Syndicate, Inc., World rights reserved.
1-11
AND SPEAKING OF PEOPLE, I JUST LOVE THOSE V.I.P.'S WHO HOG THE ROAD! WATCH THE REACTION WHEN "HUNTER'S HOVEL" KICKS UP DUST ON THEIR GOLD-PLATED HUBS!
FRANK ROBBINS
SNAP, WATCH YOUR REACTION WHEN YOU SEE WHO IS IN THAT CAR!

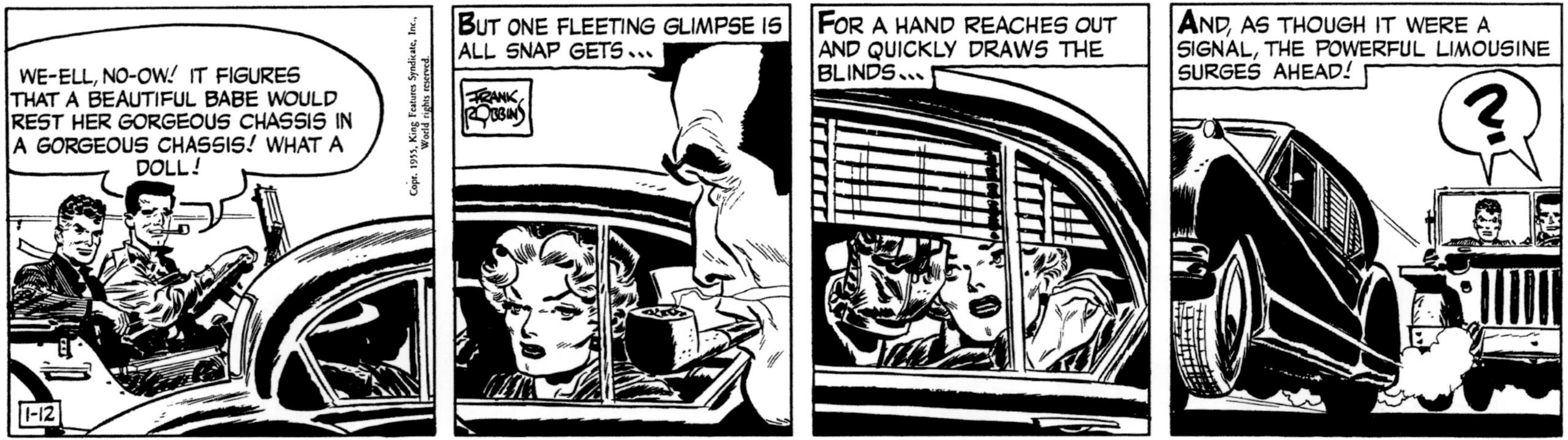
WE-ELL, NO-OW! IT FIGURES THAT A BEAUTIFUL BABE WOULD REST HER GORGEOUS CHASSIS IN A GORGEOUS CHASSIS! WHAT A DOLL!
Copr. 1955, King Features Syndicate, Inc., World rights reserved.
1-12
BUT ONE FLEETING GLIMPSE IS ALL SNAP GETS...
FRANK ROBBINS
FOR A HAND REACHES OUT AND QUICKLY DRAWS THE BLINDS...
AND, AS THOUGH IT WERE A SIGNAL, THE POWERFUL LIMOUSINE SURGES AHEAD!
?

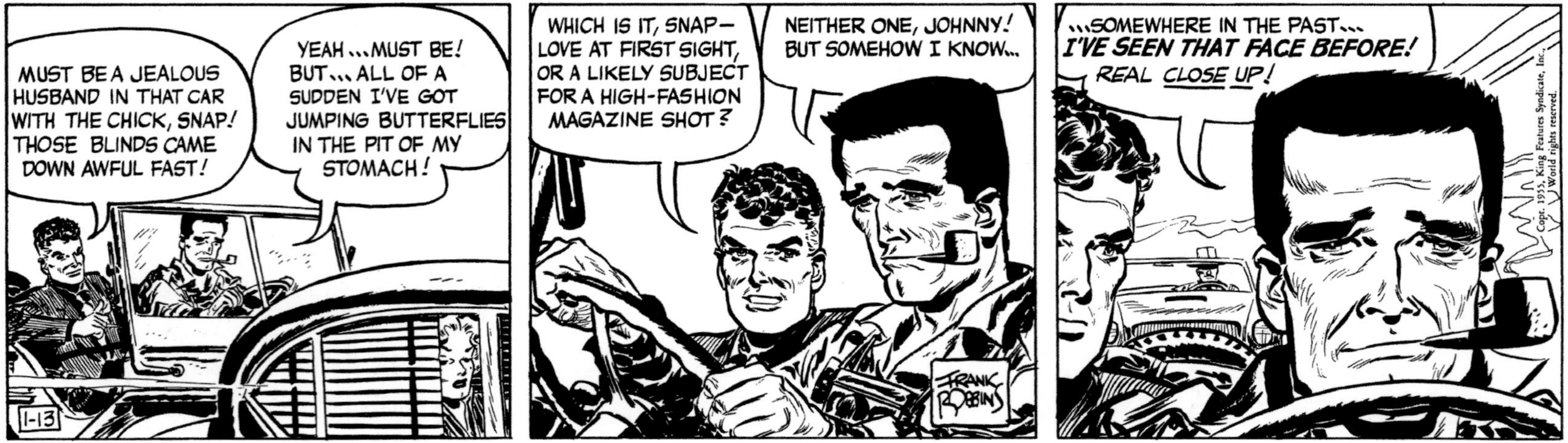
MUST BE A JEALOUS HUSBAND IN THAT CAR WITH THE CHICK, SNAP! THOSE BLINDS CAME DOWN AWFUL FAST!
YEAH ... MUST BE! BUT ... ALL OF A SUDDEN I'VE GOT JUMPING BUTTERFLIES IN THE PIT OF MY STOMACH!
1-13
WHICH IS IT, SNAP— LOVE AT FIRST SIGHT, OR A LIKELY SUBJECT FOR A HIGH-FASHION MAGAZINE SHOT?
NEITHER ONE, JOHNNY! BUT SOMEHOW I KNOW...
FRANK ROBBINS
...SOMEWHERE IN THE PAST... *I'VE SEEN THAT FACE BEFORE!* REAL CLOSE UP!
Copr. 1955, King Features Syndicate, Inc., World rights reserved.

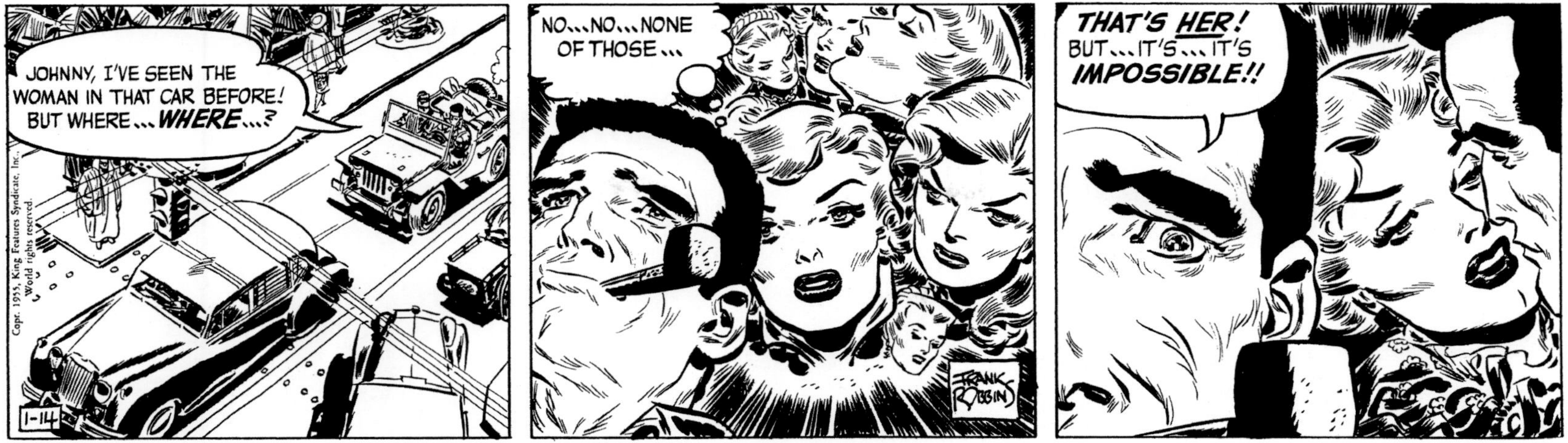
JOHNNY, I'VE SEEN THE WOMAN IN THAT CAR BEFORE! BUT WHERE... WHERE...?
Copr. 1955, King Features Syndicate, Inc., World rights reserved.
1-14
NO... NO... NONE OF THOSE...
THAT'S HER! BUT... IT'S... IT'S IMPOSSIBLE!!

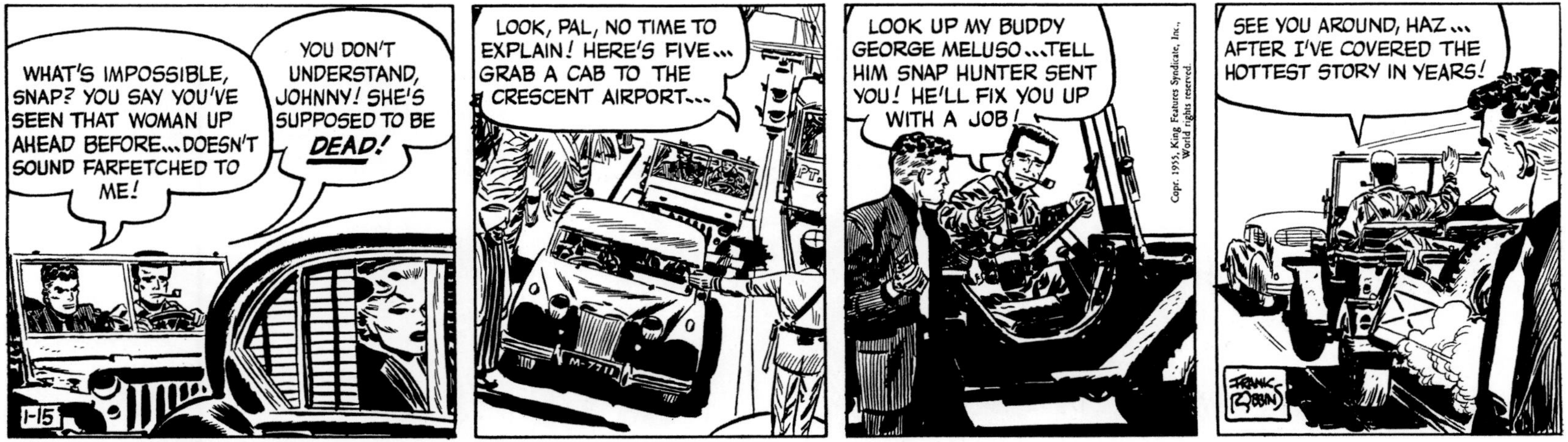
WHAT'S IMPOSSIBLE, SNAP? YOU SAY YOU'VE SEEN THAT WOMAN UP AHEAD BEFORE... DOESN'T SOUND FARFETCHED TO ME!
YOU DON'T UNDERSTAND, JOHNNY! SHE'S SUPPOSED TO BE DEAD!
1-15
LOOK, PAL, NO TIME TO EXPLAIN! HERE'S FIVE... GRAB A CAB TO THE CRESCENT AIRPORT...
M-771
LOOK UP MY BUDDY GEORGE MELUSO... TELL HIM SNAP HUNTER SENT YOU! HE'LL FIX YOU UP WITH A JOB!
Copr. 1955, King Features Syndicate, Inc., World rights reserved.
SEE YOU AROUND, HAZ... AFTER I'VE COVERED THE HOTTEST STORY IN YEARS!

THROUGH THE STREETS OF ALGIERS 'SNAP' FOLLOWS THE LIMOUSINE UNTIL IT STOPS AT A SWANK HOTEL ON THE OUTSKIRTS OF THE CITY!

1-17

IT *LOOKS* LIKE 'SHARI'... BUT... HOW CAN I BE SURE AFTER ALL THESE YEARS?... ONLY ONE WAY TO FIND OUT!

FRANK ROBBIN

Copr. 1959, King Features Syndicate, Inc. World rights reserved

HOLD IT, *SHARI*, HONEY!

I WAS RIGHT! IT IS *SHARI*... AFTER ALL THESE YEARS!

1-18

FRANK ROBBIN

Copr. 1959, King Features Syndicate, Inc. World rights reserved

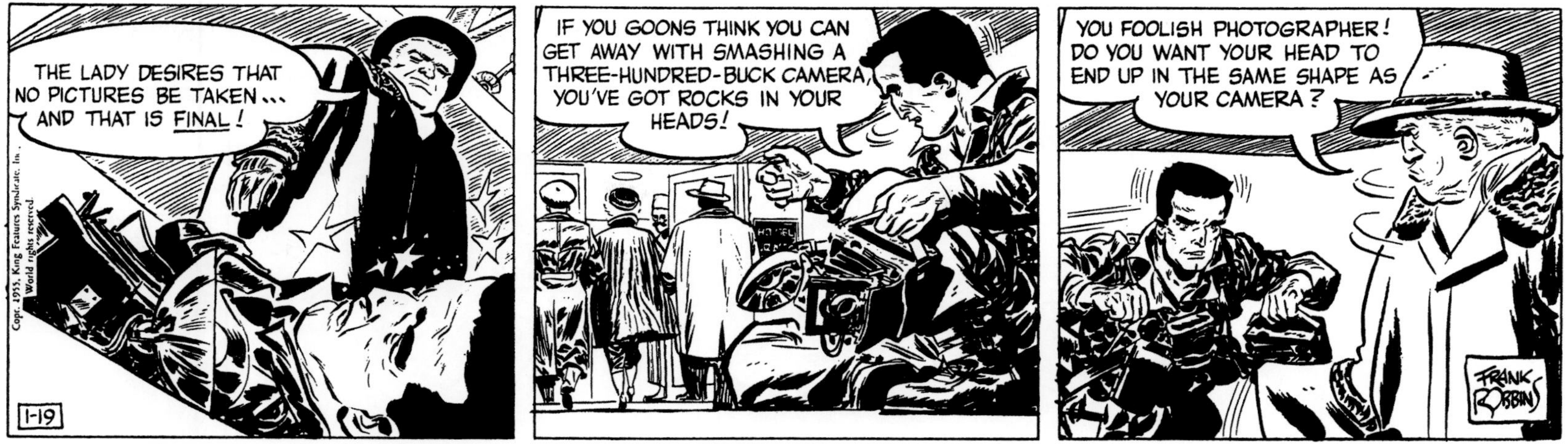
THE LADY DESIRES THAT NO PICTURES BE TAKEN... AND THAT IS FINAL!
Copr. 1955, King Features Syndicate, Inc. World rights reserved.
1-19
IF YOU GOONS THINK YOU CAN GET AWAY WITH SMASHING A THREE-HUNDRED-BUCK CAMERA, YOU'VE GOT ROCKS IN YOUR HEADS!
YOU FOOLISH PHOTOGRAPHER! DO YOU WANT YOUR HEAD TO END UP IN THE SAME SHAPE AS YOUR CAMERA?
FRANK ROBBINS

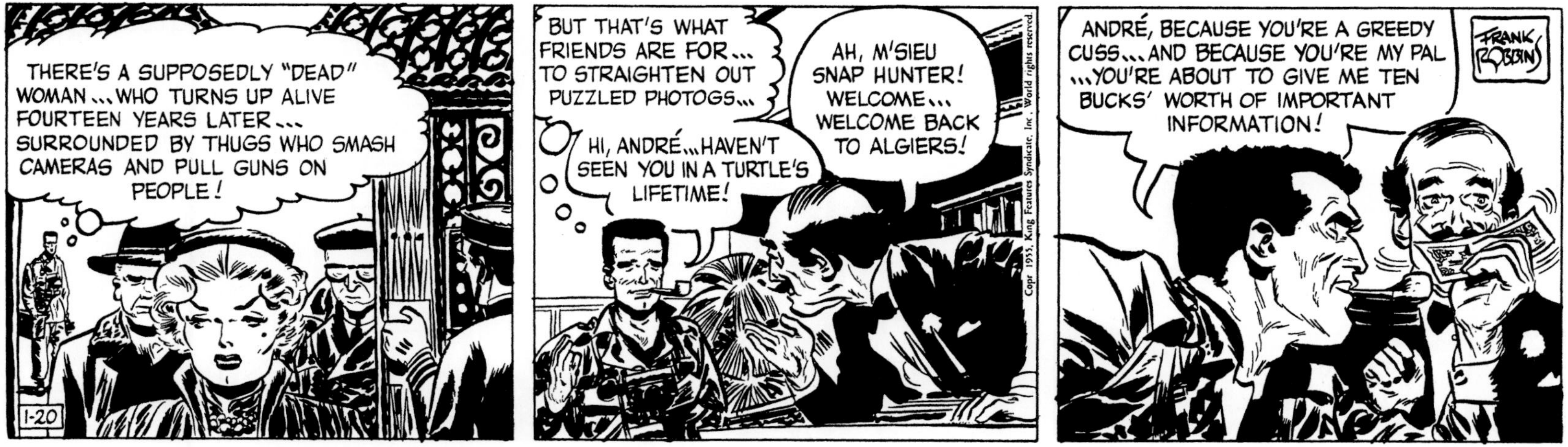
THERE'S A SUPPOSEDLY "DEAD" WOMAN... WHO TURNS UP ALIVE FOURTEEN YEARS LATER... SURROUNDED BY THUGS WHO SMASH CAMERAS AND PULL GUNS ON PEOPLE!
1-20
BUT THAT'S WHAT FRIENDS ARE FOR... TO STRAIGHTEN OUT PUZZLED PHOTOGS...
HI, ANDRÉ... HAVEN'T SEEN YOU IN A TURTLE'S LIFETIME!
AH, M'SIEU SNAP HUNTER! WELCOME... WELCOME BACK TO ALGIERS!
Copr. 1955, King Features Syndicate, Inc. World rights reserved.
ANDRÉ, BECAUSE YOU'RE A GREEDY CUSS... AND BECAUSE YOU'RE MY PAL ...YOU'RE ABOUT TO GIVE ME TEN BUCKS' WORTH OF IMPORTANT INFORMATION!
FRANK ROBBINS

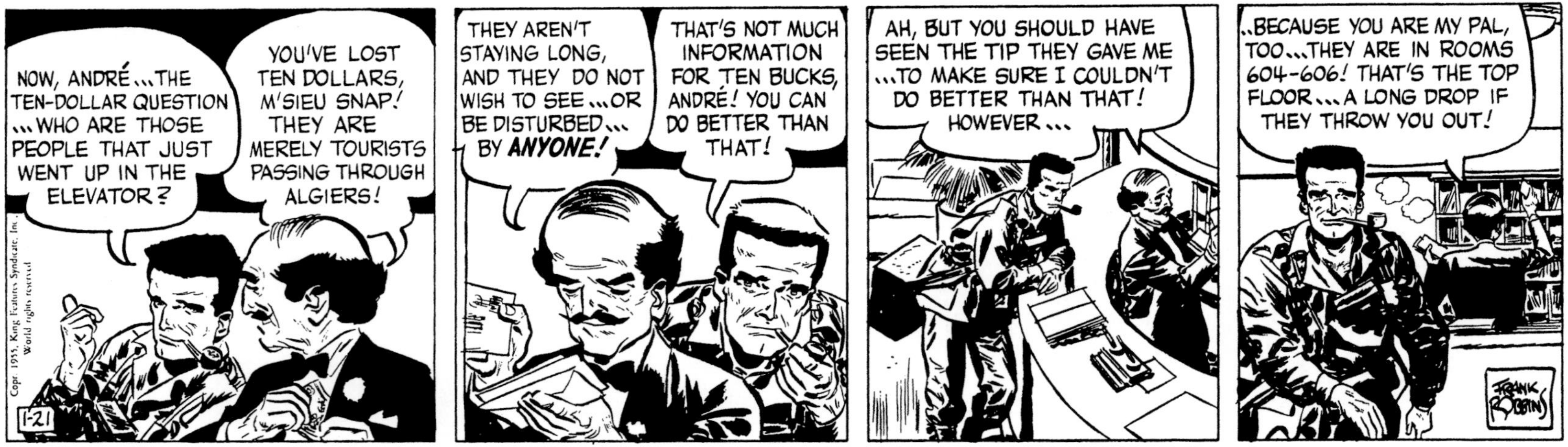
NOW, ANDRÉ ... THE TEN-DOLLAR QUESTION ... WHO ARE THOSE PEOPLE THAT JUST WENT UP IN THE ELEVATOR?
YOU'VE LOST TEN DOLLARS, M'SIEU SNAP! THEY ARE MERELY TOURISTS PASSING THROUGH ALGIERS!
Copr. 1955, King Features Syndicate, Inc. World rights reserved
1-21
THEY AREN'T STAYING LONG, AND THEY DO NOT WISH TO SEE ... OR BE DISTURBED ... BY ***ANYONE!***
THAT'S NOT MUCH INFORMATION FOR TEN BUCKS, ANDRÉ! YOU CAN DO BETTER THAN THAT!
AH, BUT YOU SHOULD HAVE SEEN THE TIP THEY GAVE ME ... TO MAKE SURE I COULDN'T DO BETTER THAN THAT! HOWEVER ...
.. BECAUSE YOU ARE MY PAL, TOO ... THEY ARE IN ROOMS 604-606! THAT'S THE TOP FLOOR ... A LONG DROP IF THEY THROW YOU OUT!
FRANK ROBBINS

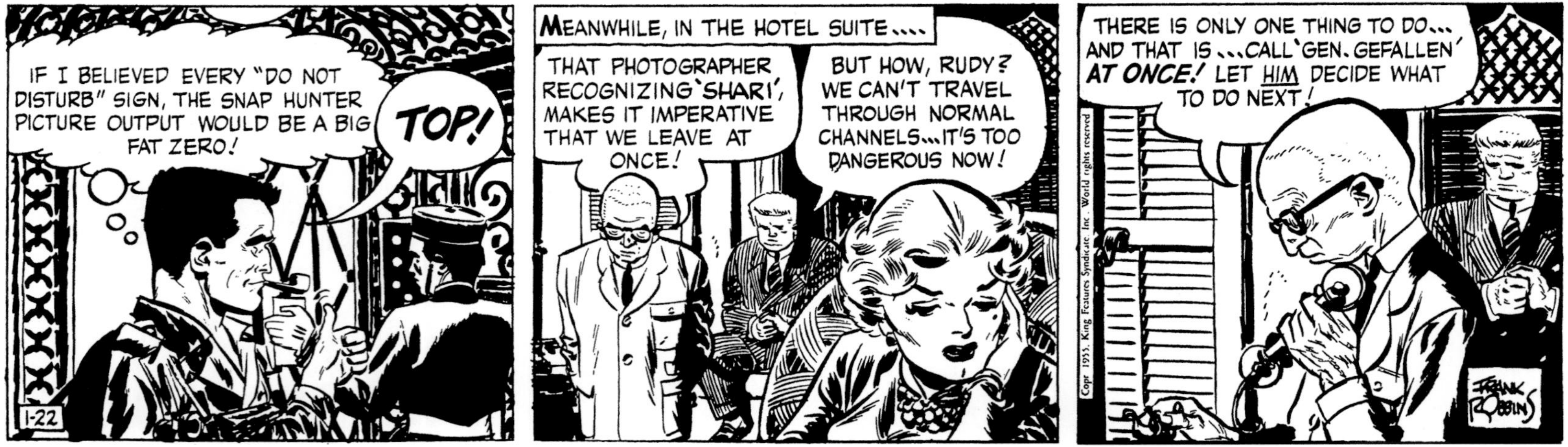
IF I BELIEVED EVERY "DO NOT DISTURB" SIGN, THE SNAP HUNTER PICTURE OUTPUT WOULD BE A BIG FAT ZERO!
TOP!
1-22
MEANWHILE, IN THE HOTEL SUITE ....
THAT PHOTOGRAPHER RECOGNIZING 'SHARI', MAKES IT IMPERATIVE THAT WE LEAVE AT ONCE!
BUT HOW, RUDY? WE CAN'T TRAVEL THROUGH NORMAL CHANNELS ... IT'S TOO DANGEROUS NOW!
THERE IS ONLY ONE THING TO DO ... AND THAT IS ... CALL 'GEN. GEFALLEN' ***AT ONCE!*** LET HIM DECIDE WHAT TO DO NEXT!
Copr. 1955, King Features Syndicate, Inc. World rights reserved
FRANK ROBBINS

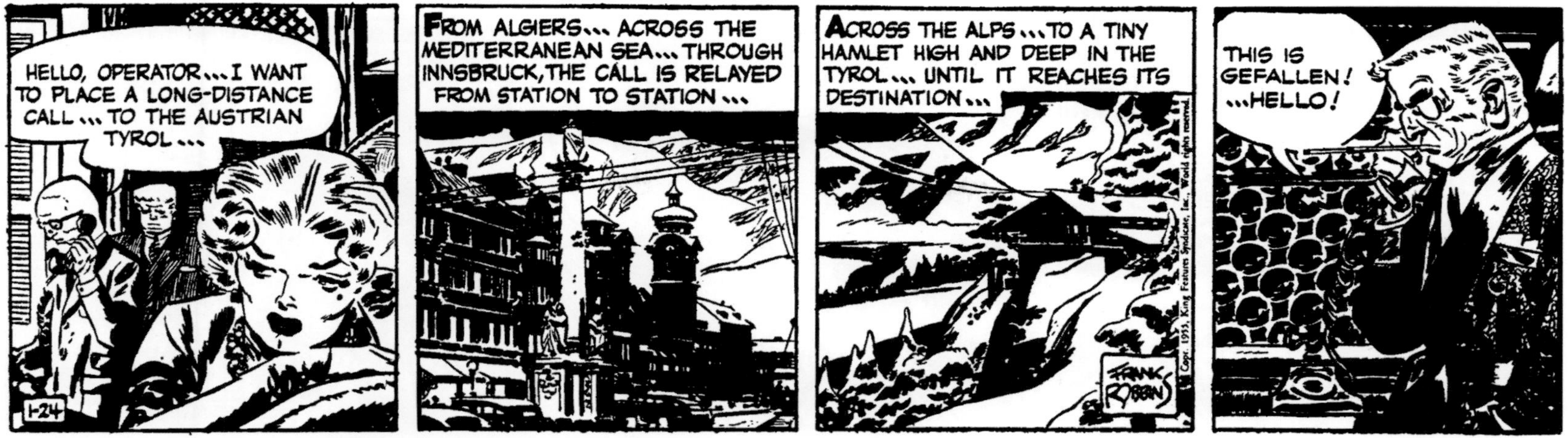
1-24
HELLO, OPERATOR... I WANT TO PLACE A LONG-DISTANCE CALL... TO THE AUSTRIAN TYROL...
FROM ALGIERS... ACROSS THE MEDITERRANEAN SEA... THROUGH INNSBRUCK, THE CALL IS RELAYED FROM STATION TO STATION...
ACROSS THE ALPS... TO A TINY HAMLET HIGH AND DEEP IN THE TYROL... UNTIL IT REACHES ITS DESTINATION...
FRANK ROBBINS
Copr. 1955, King Features Syndicate, Inc., World rights reserved.
THIS IS GEFALLEN! ...HELLO!

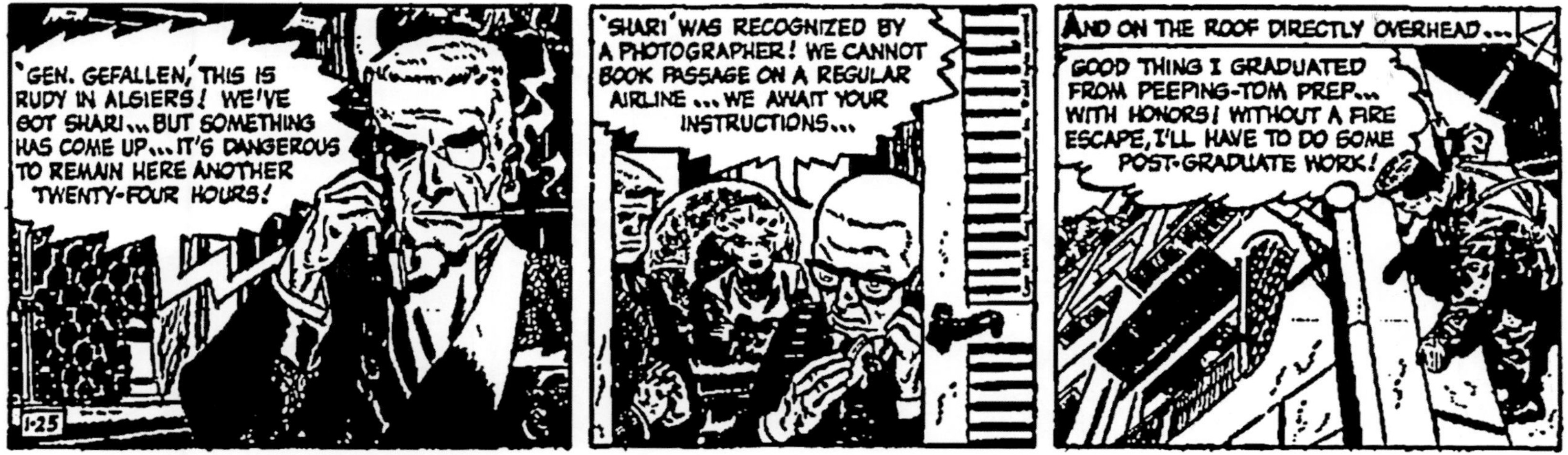
1-25
'GEN. GEFALLEN,' THIS IS RUDY IN ALGIERS! WE'VE GOT SHARI... BUT SOMETHING HAS COME UP... IT'S DANGEROUS TO REMAIN HERE ANOTHER TWENTY-FOUR HOURS!
'SHARI' WAS RECOGNIZED BY A PHOTOGRAPHER! WE CANNOT BOOK PASSAGE ON A REGULAR AIRLINE... WE AWAIT YOUR INSTRUCTIONS...
AND ON THE ROOF DIRECTLY OVERHEAD...
GOOD THING I GRADUATED FROM PEEPING-TOM PREP... WITH HONORS! WITHOUT A FIRE ESCAPE, I'LL HAVE TO DO SOME POST-GRADUATE WORK!

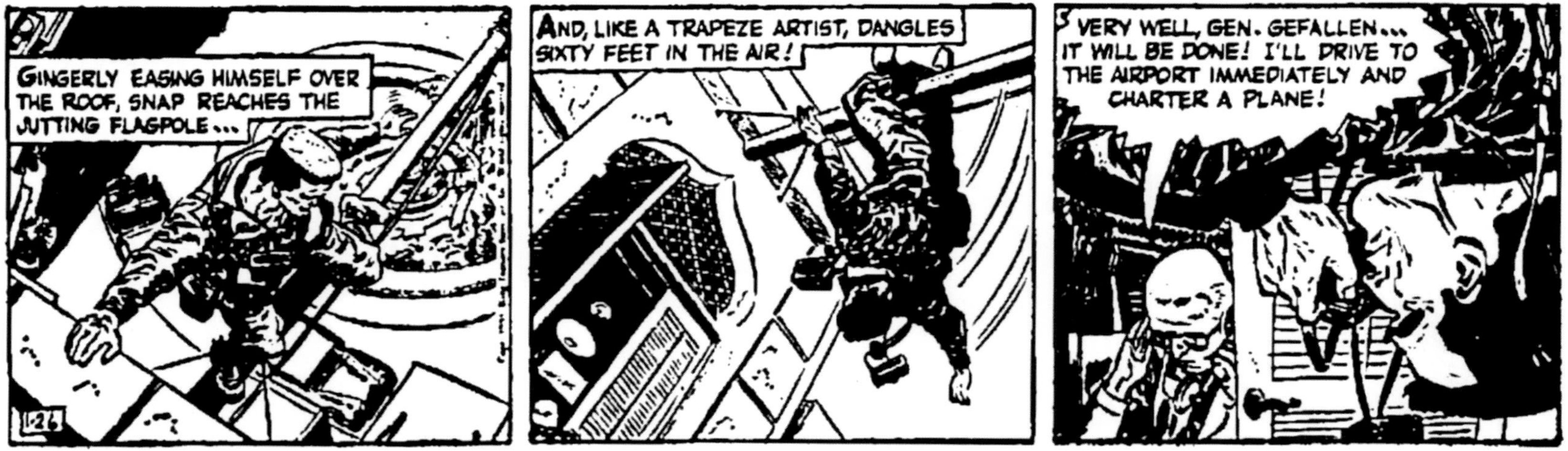
GINGERLY EASING HIMSELF OVER THE ROOF, SNAP REACHES THE JUTTING FLAGPOLE...
AND, LIKE A TRAPEZE ARTIST, DANGLES SIXTY FEET IN THE AIR!
VERY WELL, GEN. GEFALLEN... IT WILL BE DONE! I'LL DRIVE TO THE AIRPORT IMMEDIATELY AND CHARTER A PLANE!

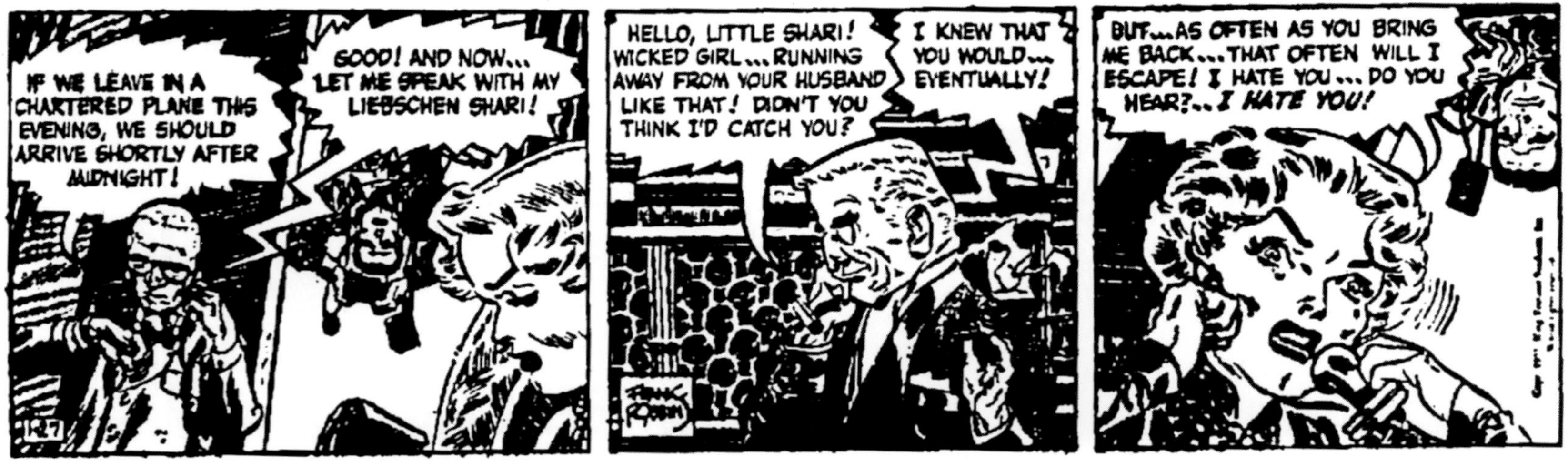
IF WE LEAVE IN A CHARTERED PLANE THIS EVENING, WE SHOULD ARRIVE SHORTLY AFTER MIDNIGHT!
GOOD! AND NOW... LET ME SPEAK WITH MY LIEBSCHEN SHARI!
HELLO, LITTLE SHARI! WICKED GIRL... RUNNING AWAY FROM YOUR HUSBAND LIKE THAT! DIDN'T YOU THINK I'D CATCH YOU?
I KNEW THAT YOU WOULD... EVENTUALLY!
BUT...AS OFTEN AS YOU BRING ME BACK...THAT OFTEN WILL I ESCAPE! I HATE YOU... DO YOU HEAR?..I HATE YOU!
FRANK ROBBINS

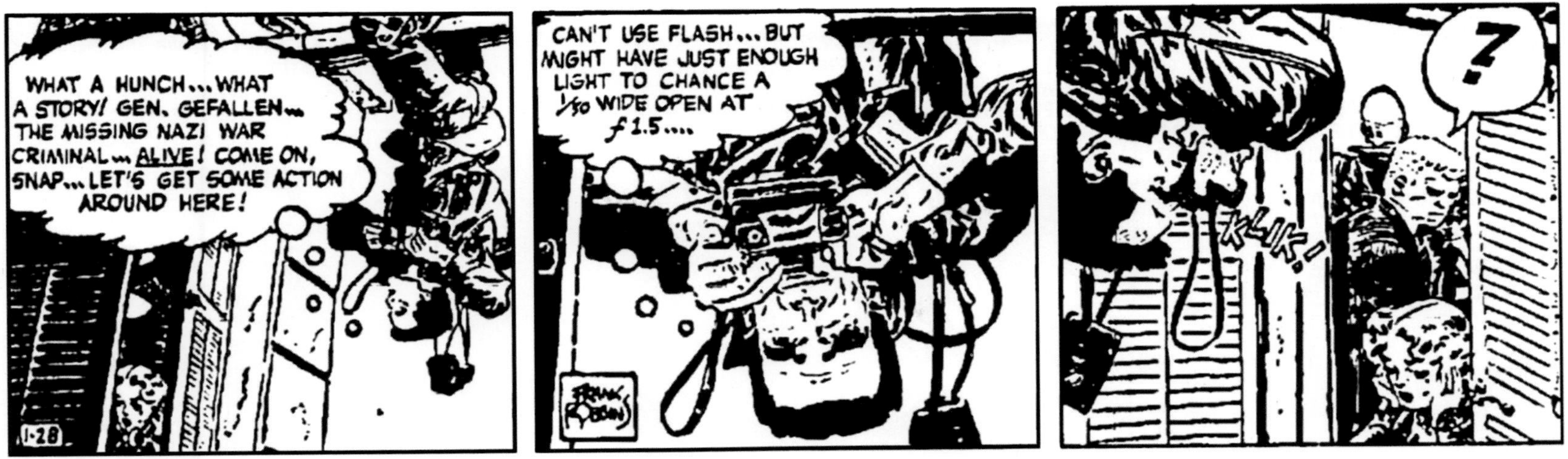
WHAT A HUNCH... WHAT A STORY! GEN. GEFALLEN... THE MISSING NAZI WAR CRIMINAL... ALIVE! COME ON, SNAP... LET'S GET SOME ACTION AROUND HERE!
1-28
CAN'T USE FLASH... BUT MIGHT HAVE JUST ENOUGH LIGHT TO CHANCE A 1/50 WIDE OPEN AT f 1.5....
?
KLIK!

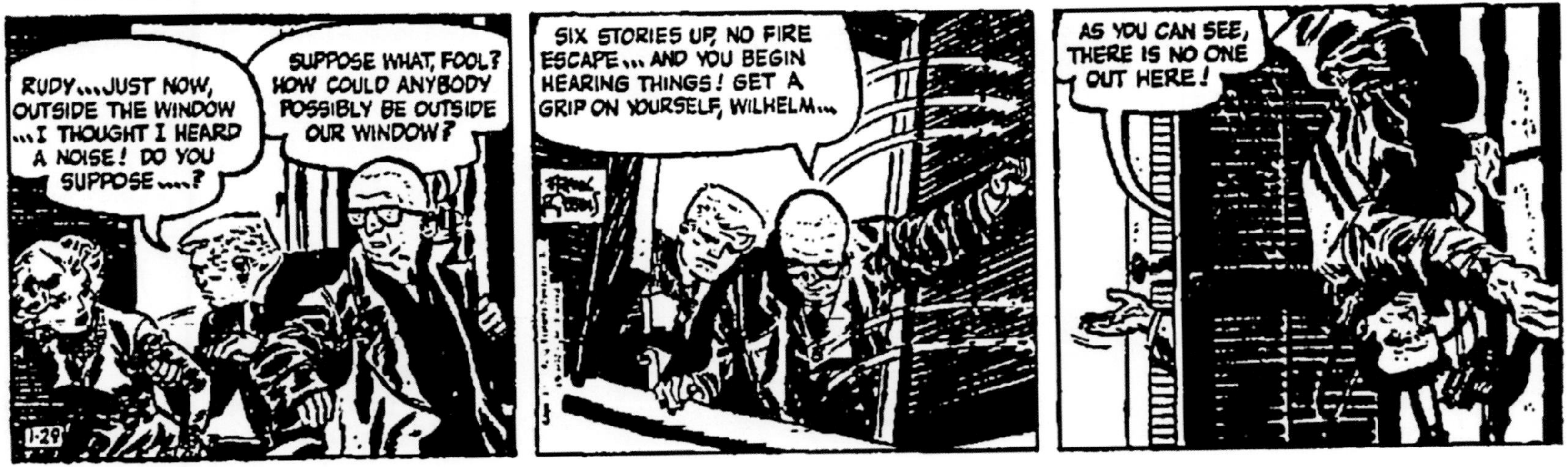
RUDY... JUST NOW, OUTSIDE THE WINDOW ...I THOUGHT I HEARD A NOISE! DO YOU SUPPOSE....?
SUPPOSE WHAT, FOOL? HOW COULD ANYBODY POSSIBLY BE OUTSIDE OUR WINDOW?
1-29
SIX STORIES UP, NO FIRE ESCAPE... AND YOU BEGIN HEARING THINGS! GET A GRIP ON YOURSELF, WILHELM...
AS YOU CAN SEE, THERE IS NO ONE OUT HERE!

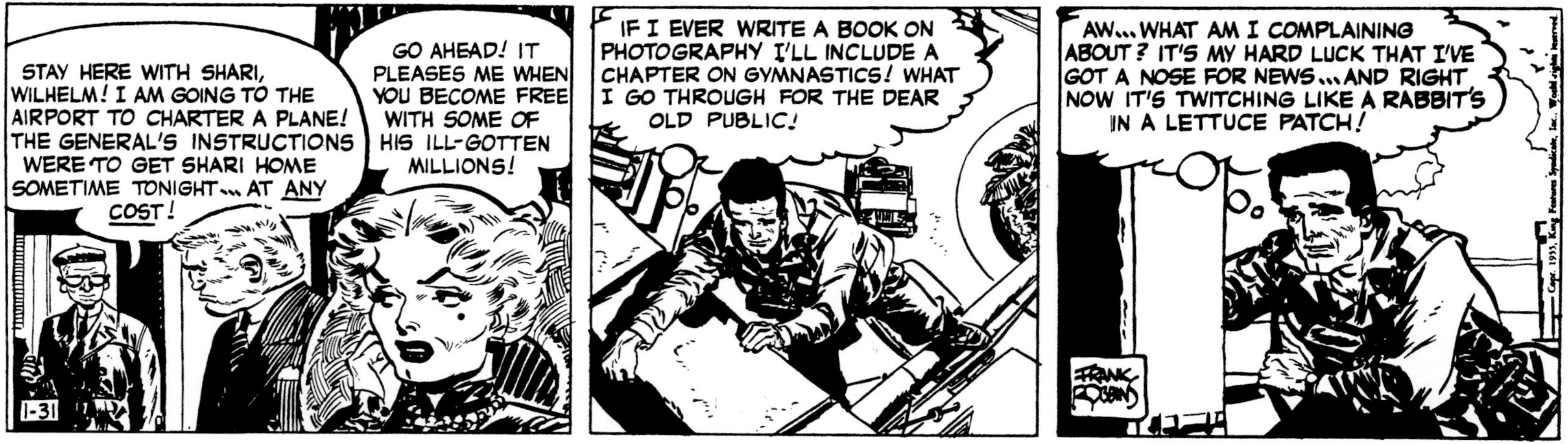
1-31
STAY HERE WITH SHARI, WILHELM! I AM GOING TO THE AIRPORT TO CHARTER A PLANE! THE GENERAL'S INSTRUCTIONS WERE TO GET SHARI HOME SOMETIME TONIGHT... AT ANY COST!
GO AHEAD! IT PLEASES ME WHEN YOU BECOME FREE WITH SOME OF HIS ILL-GOTTEN MILLIONS!
IF I EVER WRITE A BOOK ON PHOTOGRAPHY I'LL INCLUDE A CHAPTER ON GYMNASTICS! WHAT I GO THROUGH FOR THE DEAR OLD PUBLIC!
AW... WHAT AM I COMPLAINING ABOUT? IT'S MY HARD LUCK THAT I'VE GOT A NOSE FOR NEWS... AND RIGHT NOW IT'S TWITCHING LIKE A RABBIT'S IN A LETTUCE PATCH!
FRANK ROBBINS
Copr. 1955, King Features Syndicate, Inc., World rights reserved.

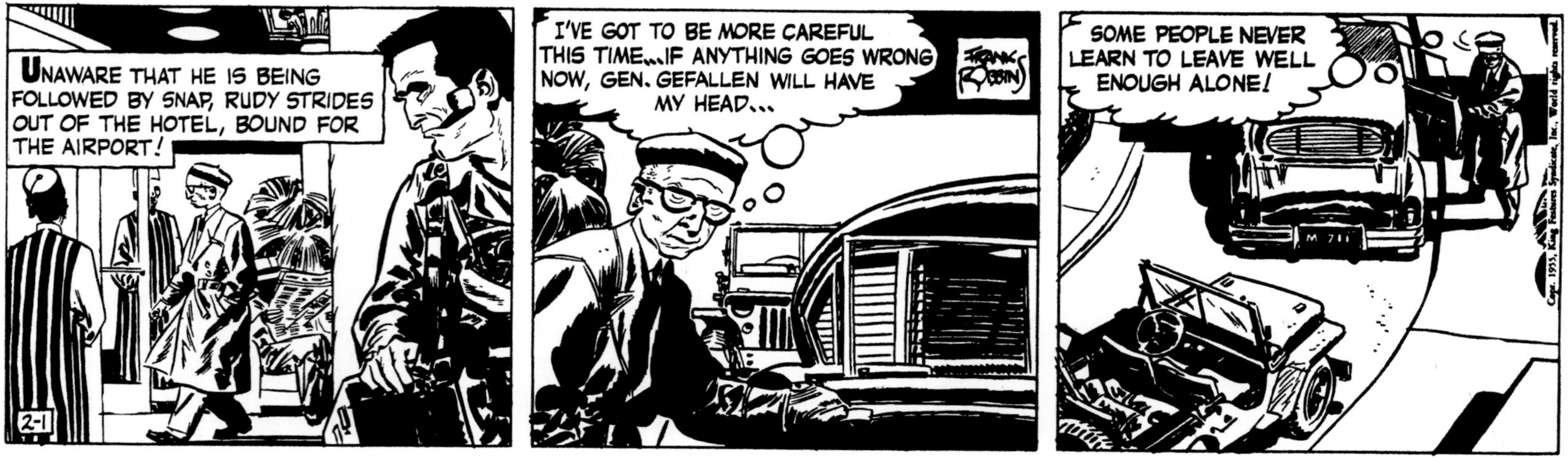
2-1
UNAWARE THAT HE IS BEING FOLLOWED BY SNAP, RUDY STRIDES OUT OF THE HOTEL, BOUND FOR THE AIRPORT!
I'VE GOT TO BE MORE CAREFUL THIS TIME... IF ANYTHING GOES WRONG NOW, GEN. GEFALLEN WILL HAVE MY HEAD...
FRANK ROBBINS
SOME PEOPLE NEVER LEARN TO LEAVE WELL ENOUGH ALONE!
Copr. 1955, King Features Syndicate, Inc., World rights reserved.

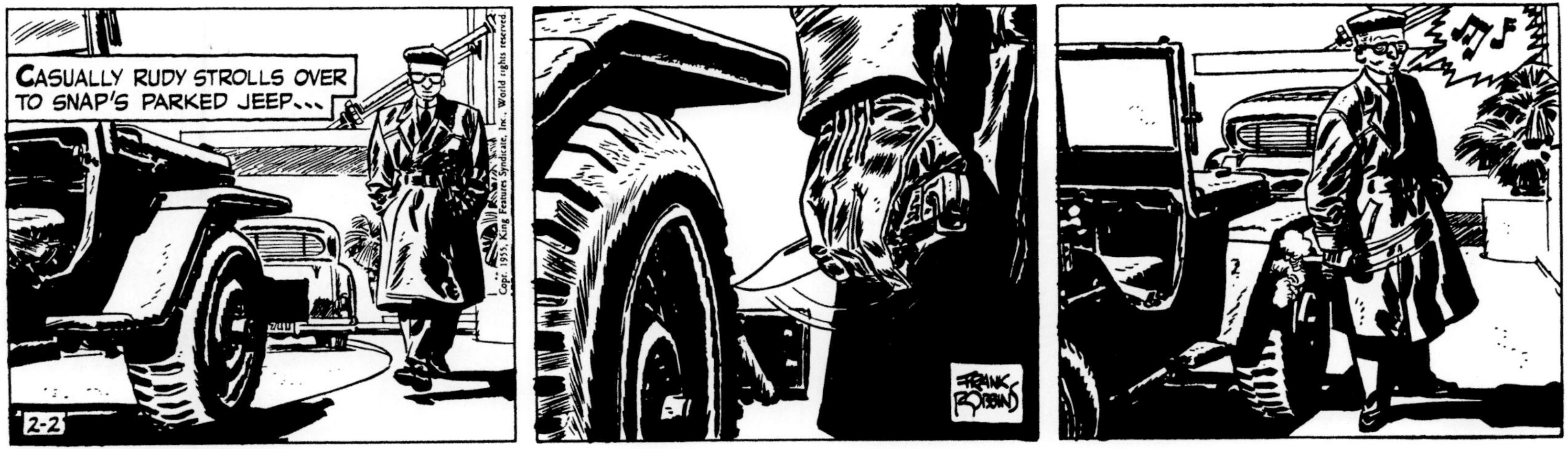
CASUALLY RUDY STROLLS OVER TO SNAP'S PARKED JEEP...
2-2
Copr. 1955, King Features Syndicate, Inc., World rights reserved.
FRANK ROBBINS

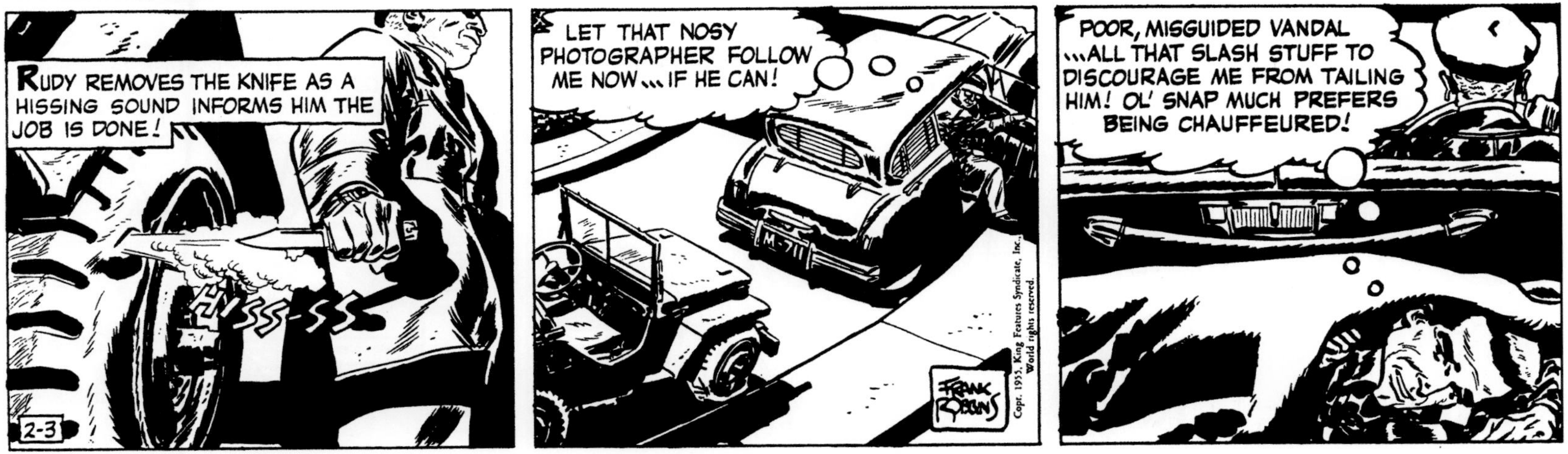
RUDY REMOVES THE KNIFE AS A HISSING SOUND INFORMS HIM THE JOB IS DONE!
HISS-SS
2-3
LET THAT NOSY PHOTOGRAPHER FOLLOW ME NOW... IF HE CAN!
M-711
Copr. 1955, King Features Syndicate, Inc., World rights reserved.
FRANK ROBBINS
POOR, MISGUIDED VANDAL ...ALL THAT SLASH STUFF TO DISCOURAGE ME FROM TAILING HIM! OL' SNAP MUCH PREFERS BEING CHAUFFEURED!

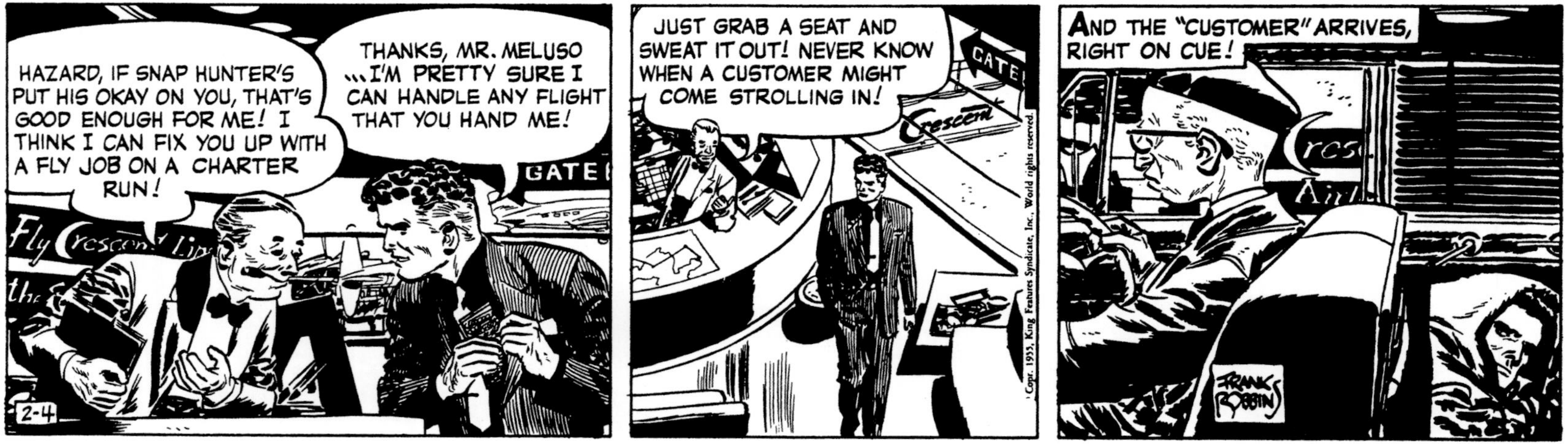
2-4
HAZARD, IF SNAP HUNTER'S PUT HIS OKAY ON YOU, THAT'S GOOD ENOUGH FOR ME! I THINK I CAN FIX YOU UP WITH A FLY JOB ON A CHARTER RUN!
THANKS, MR. MELUSO ...I'M PRETTY SURE I CAN HANDLE ANY FLIGHT THAT YOU HAND ME!
JUST GRAB A SEAT AND SWEAT IT OUT! NEVER KNOW WHEN A CUSTOMER MIGHT COME STROLLING IN!
Copr. 1955, King Features Syndicate, Inc., World rights reserved.
AND THE "CUSTOMER" ARRIVES, RIGHT ON CUE!
FRANK ROBBINS

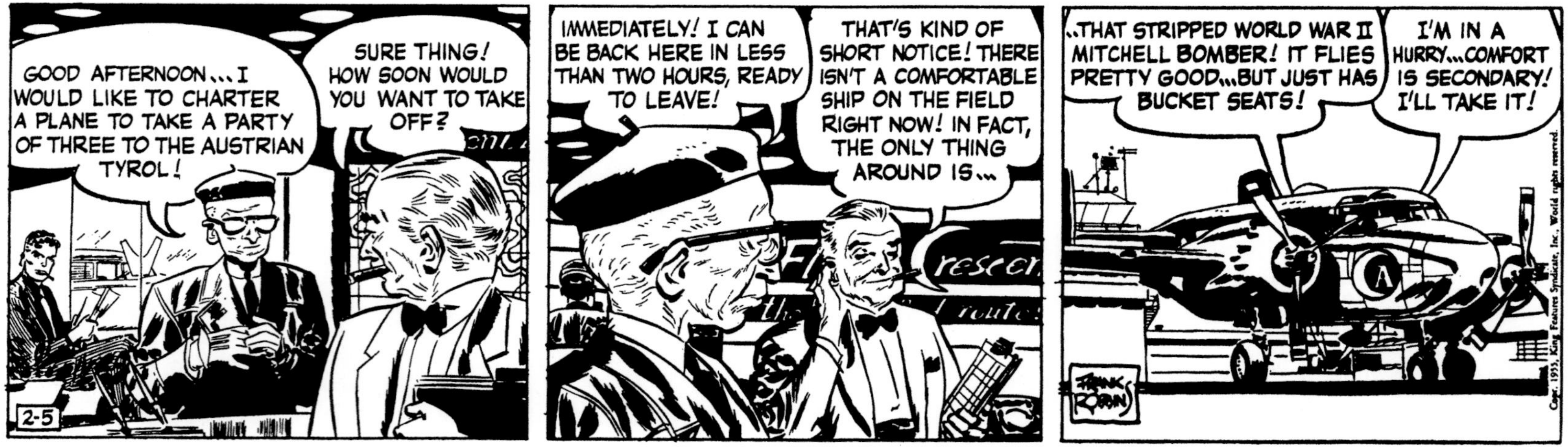
2-5
GOOD AFTERNOON... I WOULD LIKE TO CHARTER A PLANE TO TAKE A PARTY OF THREE TO THE AUSTRIAN TYROL!
SURE THING! HOW SOON WOULD YOU WANT TO TAKE OFF?
IMMEDIATELY! I CAN BE BACK HERE IN LESS THAN TWO HOURS, READY TO LEAVE!
THAT'S KIND OF SHORT NOTICE! THERE ISN'T A COMFORTABLE SHIP ON THE FIELD RIGHT NOW! IN FACT, THE ONLY THING AROUND IS...
..THAT STRIPPED WORLD WAR II MITCHELL BOMBER! IT FLIES PRETTY GOOD...BUT JUST HAS BUCKET SEATS!
I'M IN A HURRY...COMFORT IS SECONDARY! I'LL TAKE IT!
Copr. 1955, King Features Syndicate, Inc., World rights reserved.
FRANK ROBBINS

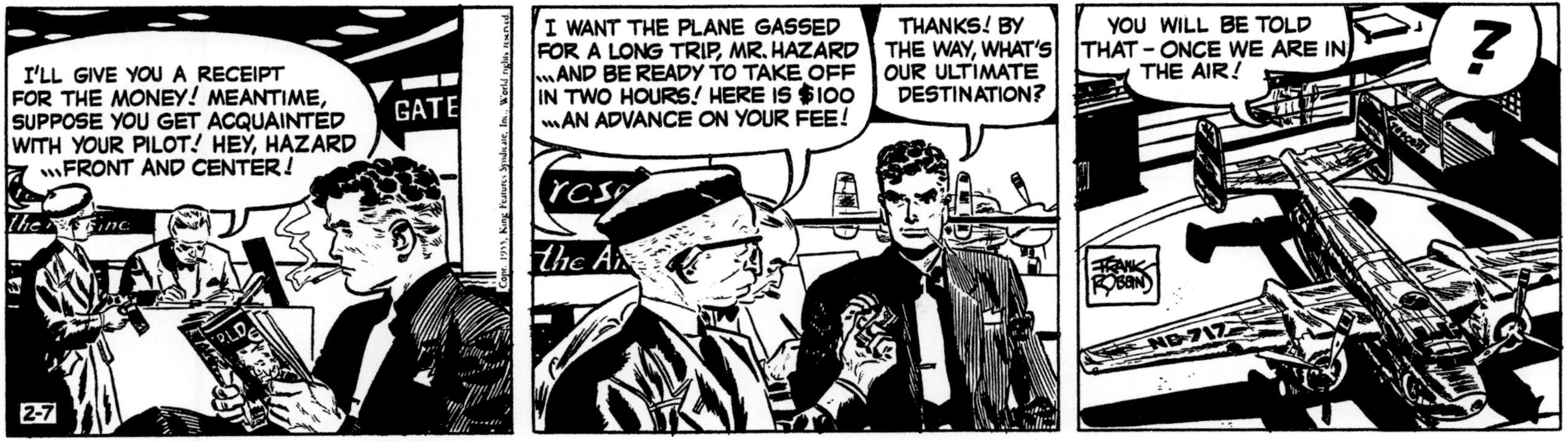
2-7
I'LL GIVE YOU A RECEIPT FOR THE MONEY! MEANTIME, SUPPOSE YOU GET ACQUAINTED WITH YOUR PILOT! HEY, HAZARD ...FRONT AND CENTER!
GATE
Copr. 1955, King Features Syndicate, Inc., World rights reserved.
I WANT THE PLANE GASSED FOR A LONG TRIP, MR. HAZARD ...AND BE READY TO TAKE OFF IN TWO HOURS! HERE IS $100 ...AN ADVANCE ON YOUR FEE!
THANKS! BY THE WAY, WHAT'S OUR ULTIMATE DESTINATION?
YOU WILL BE TOLD THAT - ONCE WE ARE IN THE AIR!
?
FRANK ROBBINS
NB-717

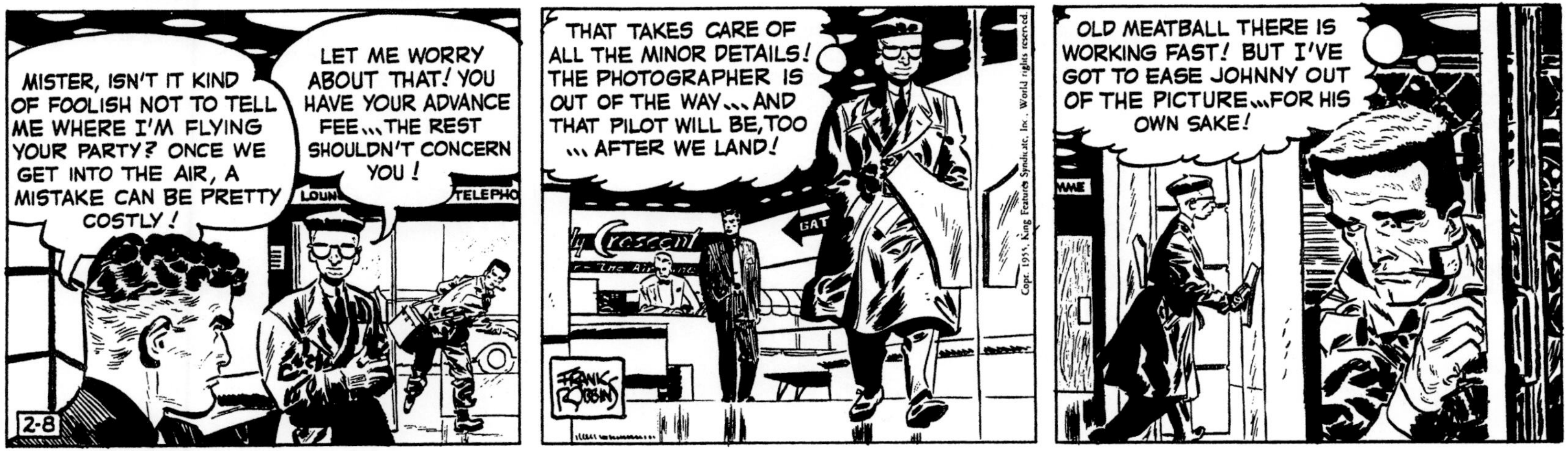
2-8
MISTER, ISN'T IT KIND OF FOOLISH NOT TO TELL ME WHERE I'M FLYING YOUR PARTY? ONCE WE GET INTO THE AIR, A MISTAKE CAN BE PRETTY COSTLY!
LET ME WORRY ABOUT THAT! YOU HAVE YOUR ADVANCE FEE ... THE REST SHOULDN'T CONCERN YOU!
THAT TAKES CARE OF ALL THE MINOR DETAILS! THE PHOTOGRAPHER IS OUT OF THE WAY ... AND THAT PILOT WILL BE, TOO ... AFTER WE LAND!
Copr. 1955, King Features Syndicate, Inc. World rights reserved.
FRANK ROBBINS
OLD MEATBALL THERE IS WORKING FAST! BUT I'VE GOT TO EASE JOHNNY OUT OF THE PICTURE ... FOR HIS OWN SAKE!

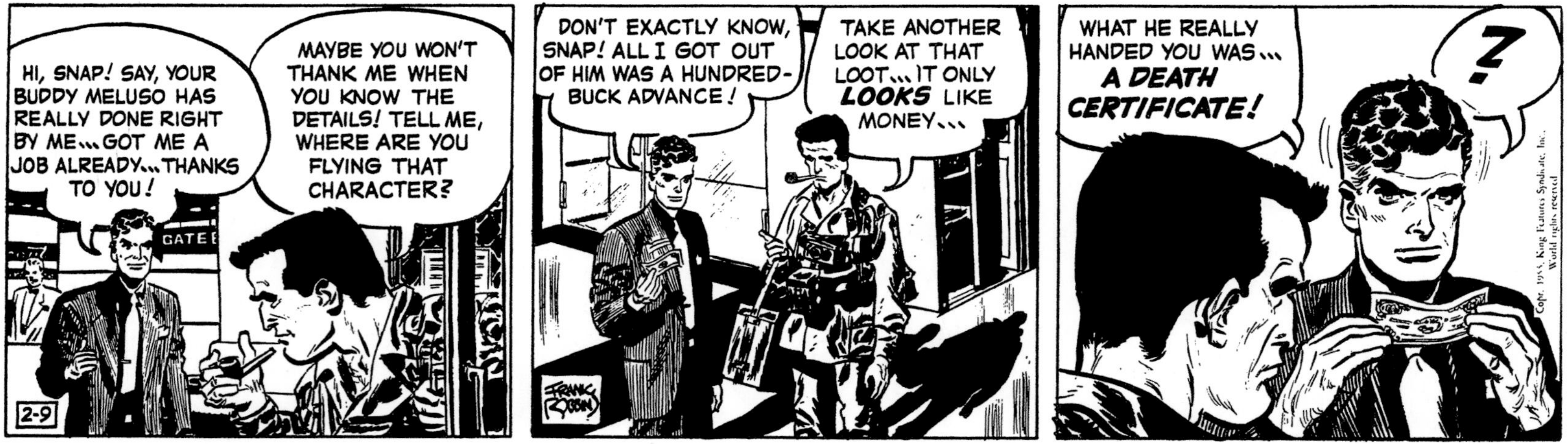
2-9
HI, SNAP! SAY, YOUR BUDDY MELUSO HAS REALLY DONE RIGHT BY ME... GOT ME A JOB ALREADY... THANKS TO YOU!
MAYBE YOU WON'T THANK ME WHEN YOU KNOW THE DETAILS! TELL ME, WHERE ARE YOU FLYING THAT CHARACTER?
GATE
DON'T EXACTLY KNOW, SNAP! ALL I GOT OUT OF HIM WAS A HUNDRED-BUCK ADVANCE!
TAKE ANOTHER LOOK AT THAT LOOT... IT ONLY **LOOKS** LIKE MONEY...
FRANK ROBBINS
WHAT HE REALLY HANDED YOU WAS... **A DEATH CERTIFICATE!**
?
Copr. 1955, King Features Syndicate, Inc. World rights reserved.

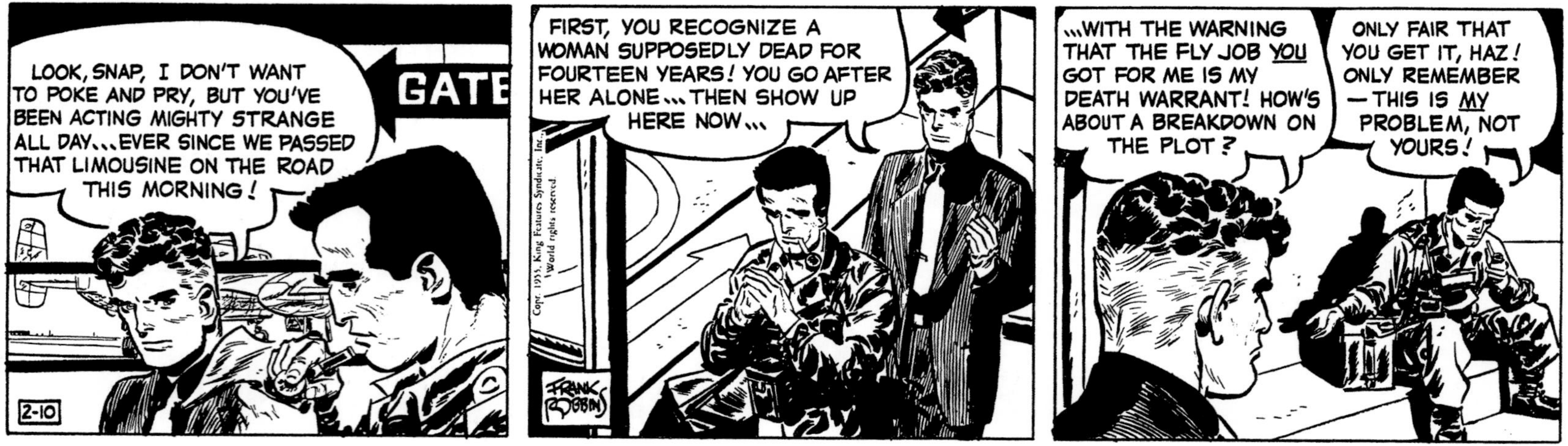
2-10
LOOK, SNAP, I DON'T WANT TO POKE AND PRY, BUT YOU'VE BEEN ACTING MIGHTY STRANGE ALL DAY... EVER SINCE WE PASSED THAT LIMOUSINE ON THE ROAD THIS MORNING!
GATE
FIRST, YOU RECOGNIZE A WOMAN SUPPOSEDLY DEAD FOR FOURTEEN YEARS! YOU GO AFTER HER ALONE... THEN SHOW UP HERE NOW...
Copr. 1955, King Features Syndicate, Inc. World rights reserved.
FRANK ROBBINS
...WITH THE WARNING THAT THE FLY JOB YOU GOT FOR ME IS MY DEATH WARRANT! HOW'S ABOUT A BREAKDOWN ON THE PLOT?
ONLY FAIR THAT YOU GET IT, HAZ! ONLY REMEMBER —THIS IS MY PROBLEM, NOT YOURS!

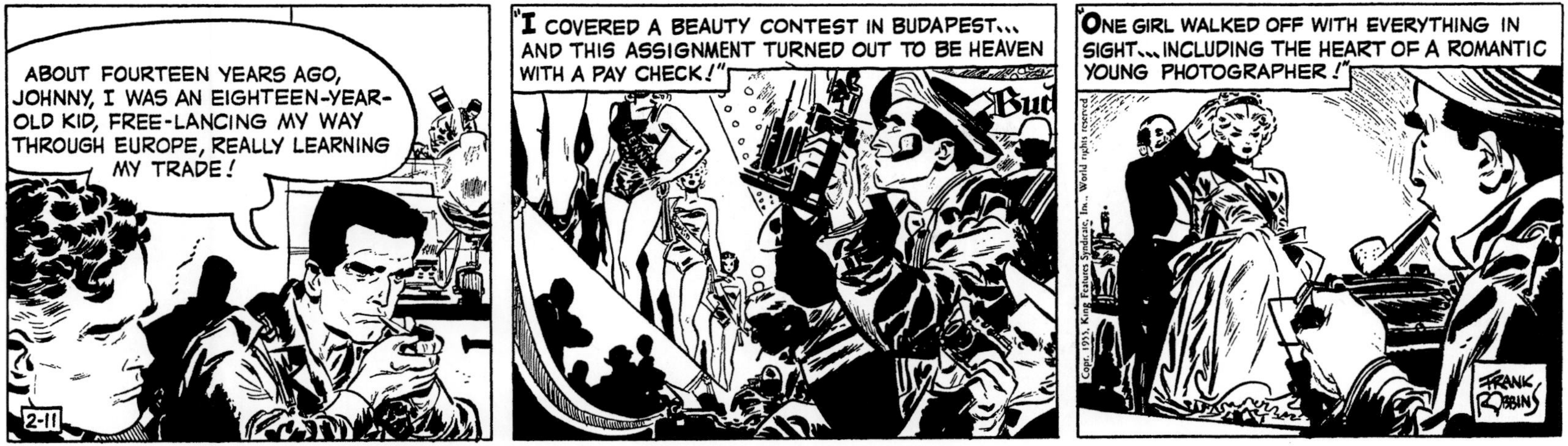
ABOUT FOURTEEN YEARS AGO, JOHNNY, I WAS AN EIGHTEEN-YEAR-OLD KID, FREE-LANCING MY WAY THROUGH EUROPE, REALLY LEARNING MY TRADE!
2-11
"I COVERED A BEAUTY CONTEST IN BUDAPEST... AND THIS ASSIGNMENT TURNED OUT TO BE HEAVEN WITH A PAY CHECK!"
"ONE GIRL WALKED OFF WITH EVERYTHING IN SIGHT... INCLUDING THE HEART OF A ROMANTIC YOUNG PHOTOGRAPHER!"
Copr. 1955, King Features Syndicate, Inc., World rights reserved
FRANK ROBBINS

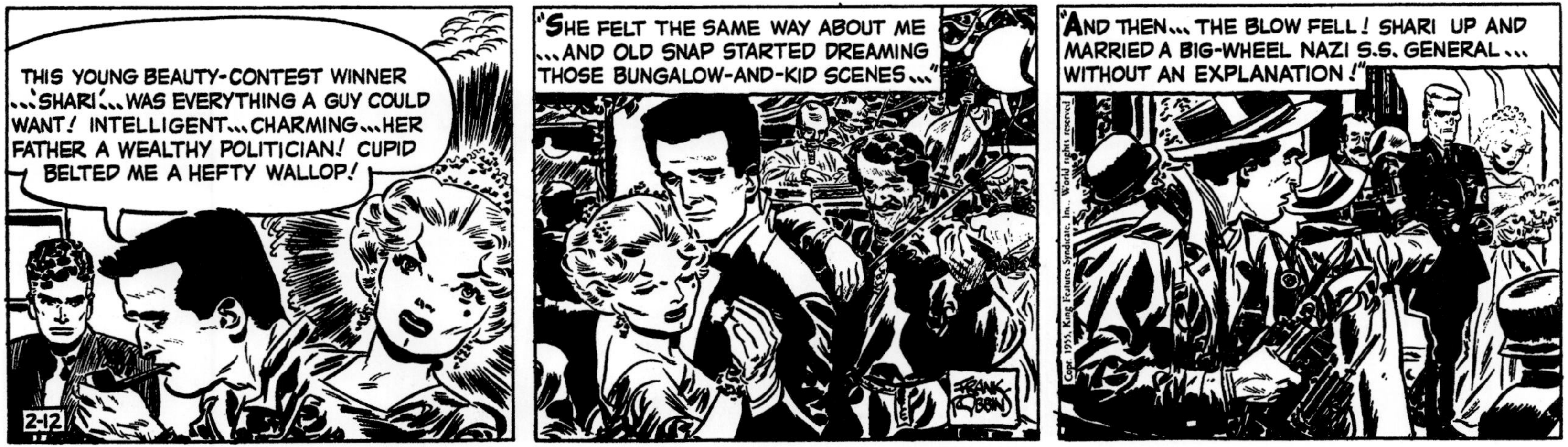
THIS YOUNG BEAUTY-CONTEST WINNER ...'SHARI'... WAS EVERYTHING A GUY COULD WANT! INTELLIGENT... CHARMING... HER FATHER A WEALTHY POLITICIAN! CUPID BELTED ME A HEFTY WALLOP!
2-12
"SHE FELT THE SAME WAY ABOUT ME ...AND OLD SNAP STARTED DREAMING THOSE BUNGALOW-AND-KID SCENES..."
FRANK ROBBINS
"AND THEN... THE BLOW FELL! SHARI UP AND MARRIED A BIG-WHEEL NAZI S.S. GENERAL... WITHOUT AN EXPLANATION!"
Copr. 1955, King Features Syndicate, Inc., World rights reserved

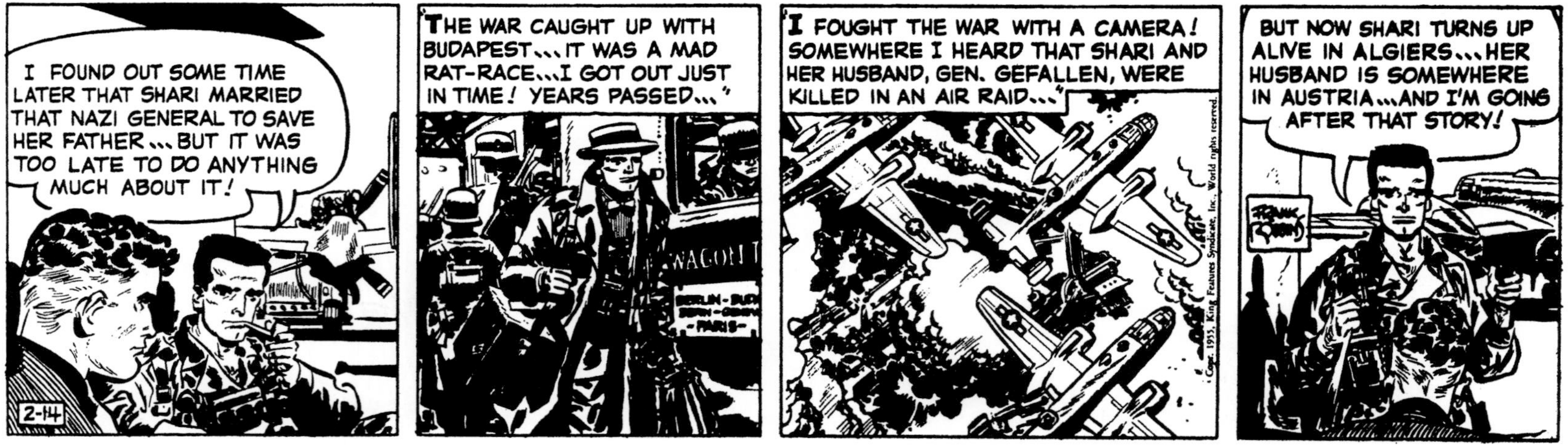
I FOUND OUT SOME TIME LATER THAT SHARI MARRIED THAT NAZI GENERAL TO SAVE HER FATHER... BUT IT WAS TOO LATE TO DO ANYTHING MUCH ABOUT IT!
2-14
"THE WAR CAUGHT UP WITH BUDAPEST... IT WAS A MAD RAT-RACE... I GOT OUT JUST IN TIME! YEARS PASSED..."
WAGON
BERLIN
PARIS
"I FOUGHT THE WAR WITH A CAMERA! SOMEWHERE I HEARD THAT SHARI AND HER HUSBAND, GEN. GEFALLEN, WERE KILLED IN AN AIR RAID..."
Copr. 1955, King Features Syndicate, Inc., World rights reserved.
BUT NOW SHARI TURNS UP ALIVE IN ALGIERS... HER HUSBAND IS SOMEWHERE IN AUSTRIA... AND I'M GOING AFTER THAT STORY!
FRANK ROBBINS

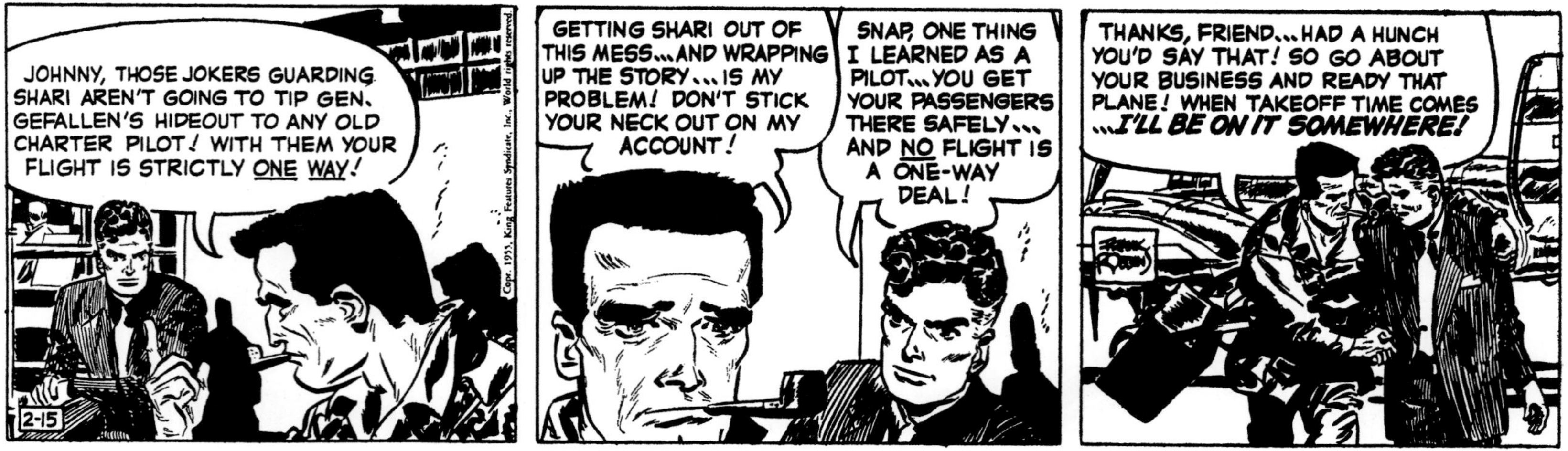
JOHNNY, THOSE JOKERS GUARDING SHARI AREN'T GOING TO TIP GEN. GEFALLEN'S HIDEOUT TO ANY OLD CHARTER PILOT! WITH THEM YOUR FLIGHT IS STRICTLY ONE WAY!
Copr. 1955, King Features Syndicate, Inc., World rights reserved.
2-15
GETTING SHARI OUT OF THIS MESS... AND WRAPPING UP THE STORY... IS MY PROBLEM! DON'T STICK YOUR NECK OUT ON MY ACCOUNT!
SNAP, ONE THING I LEARNED AS A PILOT... YOU GET YOUR PASSENGERS THERE SAFELY... AND NO FLIGHT IS A ONE-WAY DEAL!
THANKS, FRIEND... HAD A HUNCH YOU'D SAY THAT! SO GO ABOUT YOUR BUSINESS AND READY THAT PLANE! WHEN TAKEOFF TIME COMES ...I'LL BE ON IT SOMEWHERE!
FRANK ROBBINS

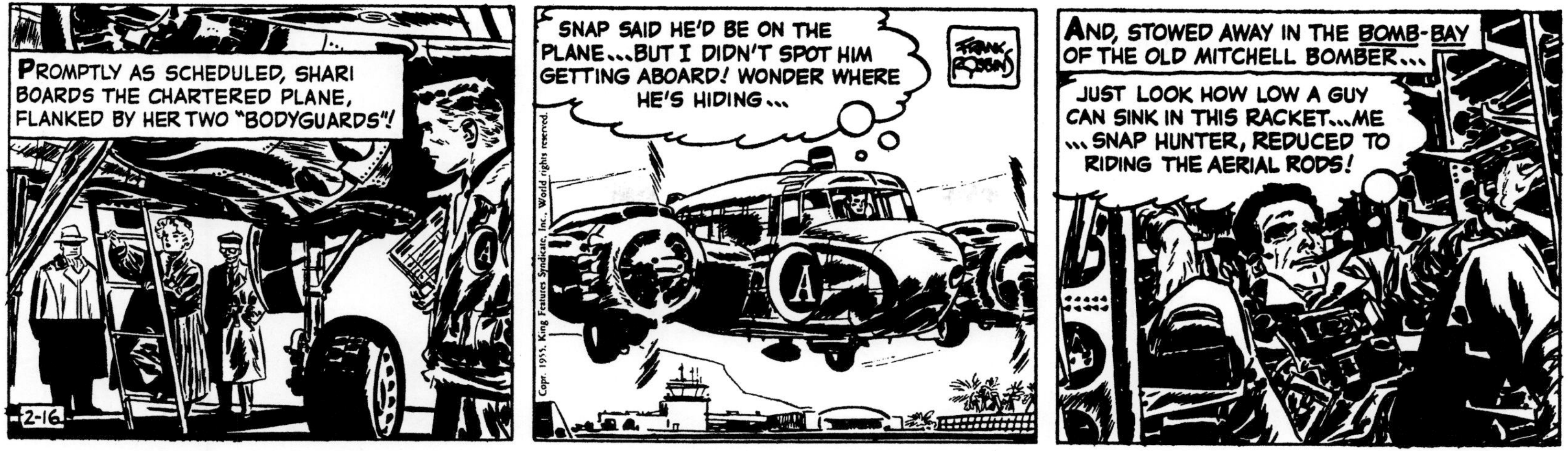
PROMPTLY AS SCHEDULED, SHARI BOARDS THE CHARTERED PLANE, FLANKED BY HER TWO "BODYGUARDS"!
2-16
SNAP SAID HE'D BE ON THE PLANE...BUT I DIDN'T SPOT HIM GETTING ABOARD! WONDER WHERE HE'S HIDING...
FRANK ROBBINS
Copr. 1955, King Features Syndicate, Inc., World rights reserved.
AND, STOWED AWAY IN THE BOMB-BAY OF THE OLD MITCHELL BOMBER...
JUST LOOK HOW LOW A GUY CAN SINK IN THIS RACKET...ME ...SNAP HUNTER, REDUCED TO RIDING THE AERIAL RODS!

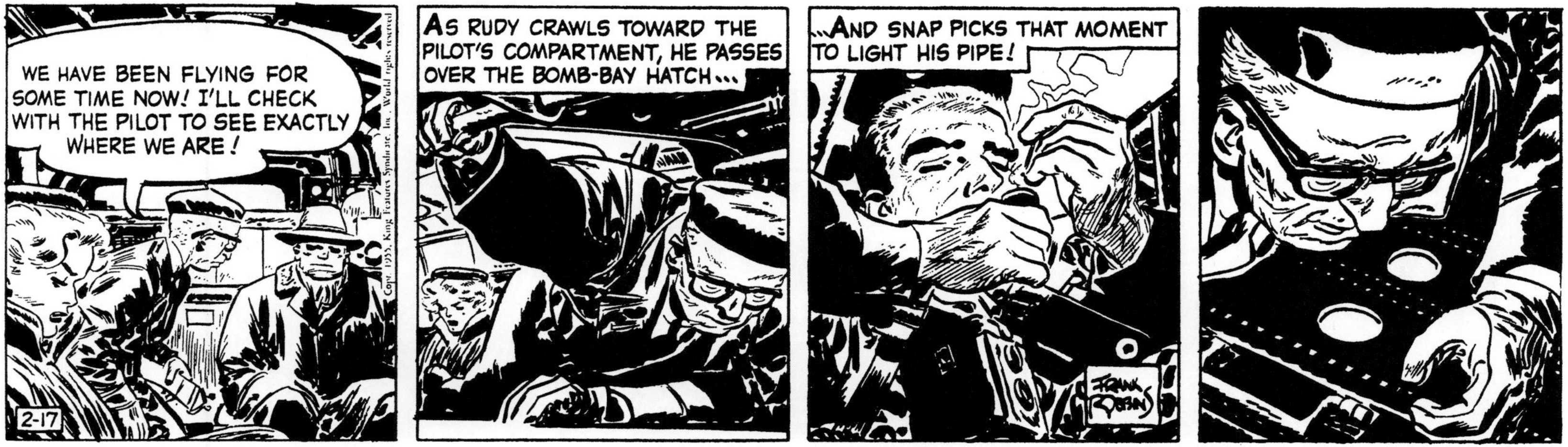
WE HAVE BEEN FLYING FOR SOME TIME NOW! I'LL CHECK WITH THE PILOT TO SEE EXACTLY WHERE WE ARE!
2-17
Copr. 1955, King Features Syndicate, Inc., World rights reserved
AS RUDY CRAWLS TOWARD THE PILOT'S COMPARTMENT, HE PASSES OVER THE BOMB-BAY HATCH...
...AND SNAP PICKS THAT MOMENT TO LIGHT HIS PIPE!
FRANK ROBBINS

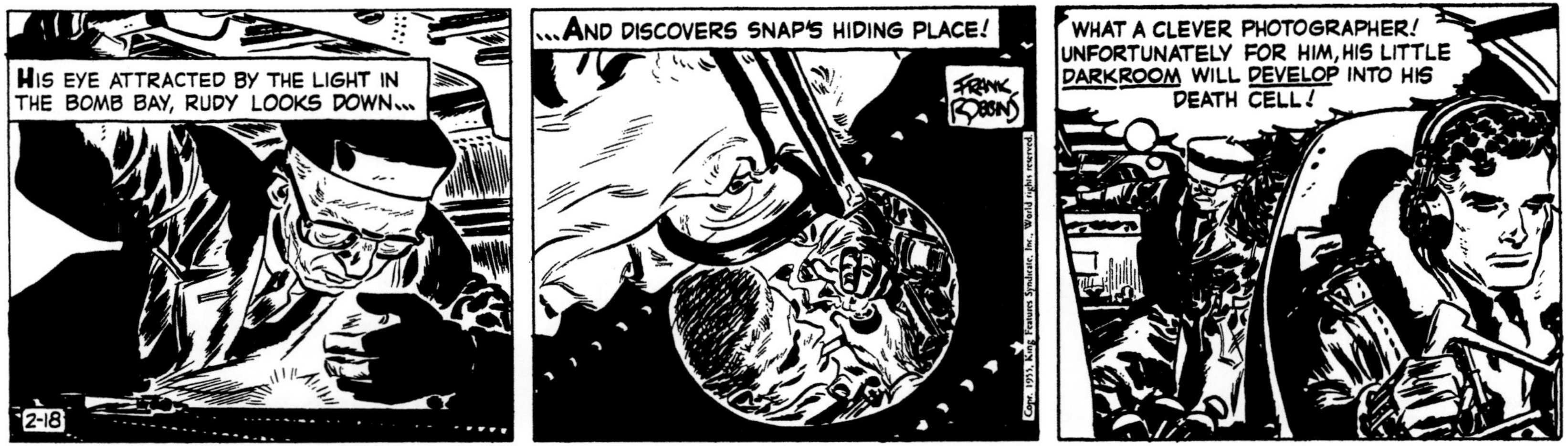
HIS EYE ATTRACTED BY THE LIGHT IN THE BOMB BAY, RUDY LOOKS DOWN...
2-18
...AND DISCOVERS SNAP'S HIDING PLACE!
FRANK ROBBINS
WHAT A CLEVER PHOTOGRAPHER! UNFORTUNATELY FOR HIM, HIS LITTLE DARKROOM WILL DEVELOP INTO HIS DEATH CELL!

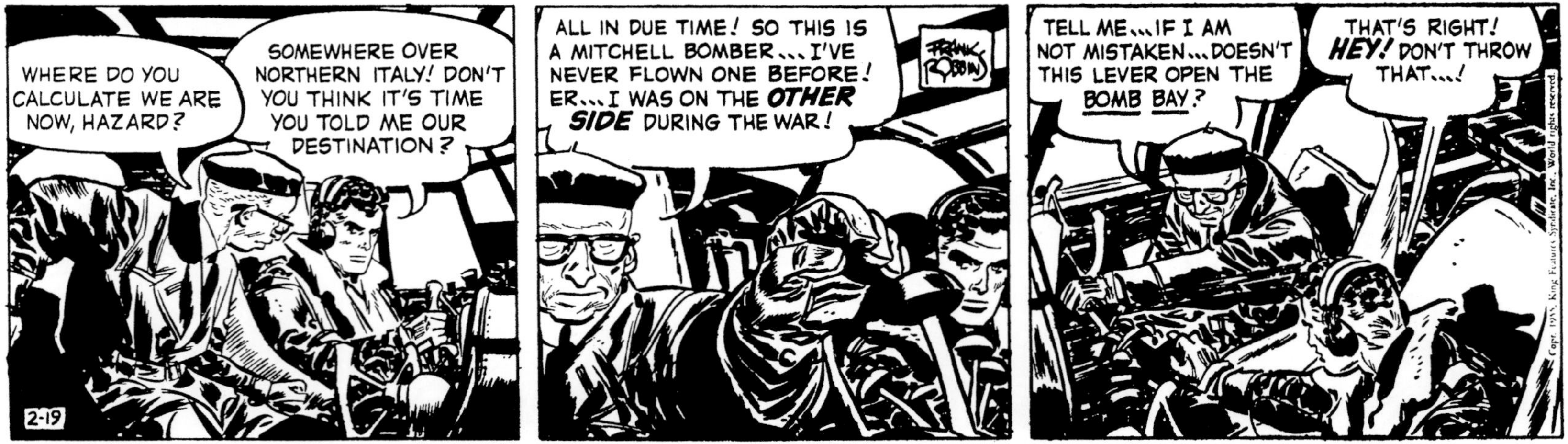
WHERE DO YOU CALCULATE WE ARE NOW, HAZARD?
SOMEWHERE OVER NORTHERN ITALY! DON'T YOU THINK IT'S TIME YOU TOLD ME OUR DESTINATION?
2-19
ALL IN DUE TIME! SO THIS IS A MITCHELL BOMBER... I'VE NEVER FLOWN ONE BEFORE! ER... I WAS ON THE OTHER SIDE DURING THE WAR!
FRANK ROBBINS
TELL ME... IF I AM NOT MISTAKEN... DOESN'T THIS LEVER OPEN THE BOMB BAY?
THAT'S RIGHT! HEY! DON'T THROW THAT...!

2-21
HEY, YOU STUPID FOOL! LEAVE THAT BOMB-BAY SWITCH ALONE! WHAT DO YOU THINK YOU'RE DOING...?
BUT THE DAMAGE IS DONE! THE BOMB-BAY DOORS SWING OPEN...
Copr. 1955, King Features Syndicate, Inc., World rights reserved.
FRANK ROBBINS
...AND "SNAP" HUNTER LITERALLY FINDS THE FLOOR PULLED OUT FROM UNDER HIM!

2-22
LOOK, MISTER, THIS IS A CHARTERED TRANSPORT FLIGHT, NOT A BOMBING DRY-RUN! PUSH THAT SWITCH BACK TO...OFF!
ONLY WHEN I'M READY TO, MR. HAZARD ...LET'S GIVE YOUR PHOTOGRAPHER FRIEND TIME TO DROP CLEAR FROM THE BOMB BAY!
WHILE IN THE BOMB BAY...
OH, MO-THER... SING US A FAST CHORUS OF "I DIDN'T RAISE MY BOY TO BE A BOMB!"
YOU MEAN..."SNAP" WAS STOWED THERE? WHY, YOU MURDERING DEVIL...!!
SOFTLY, MY FRIEND! I'M CLOSING THE BOMB BAY NOW! IT DOES CREATE QUITE A DRAFT, AND I WOULDN'T WANT YOU TO DIE OF A CHILL!
FRANK ROBBINS
Copr. 1955, King Features Syndicate, Inc., World rights reserved

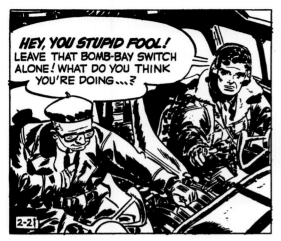

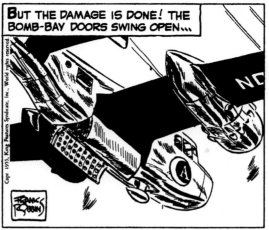

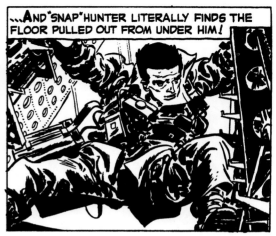

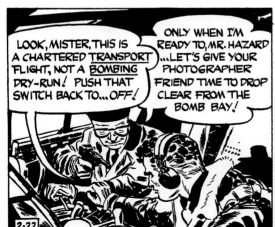

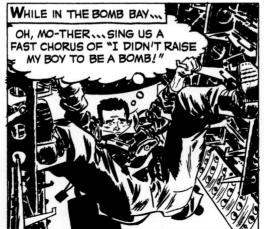

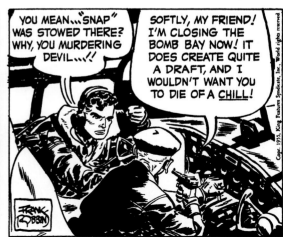

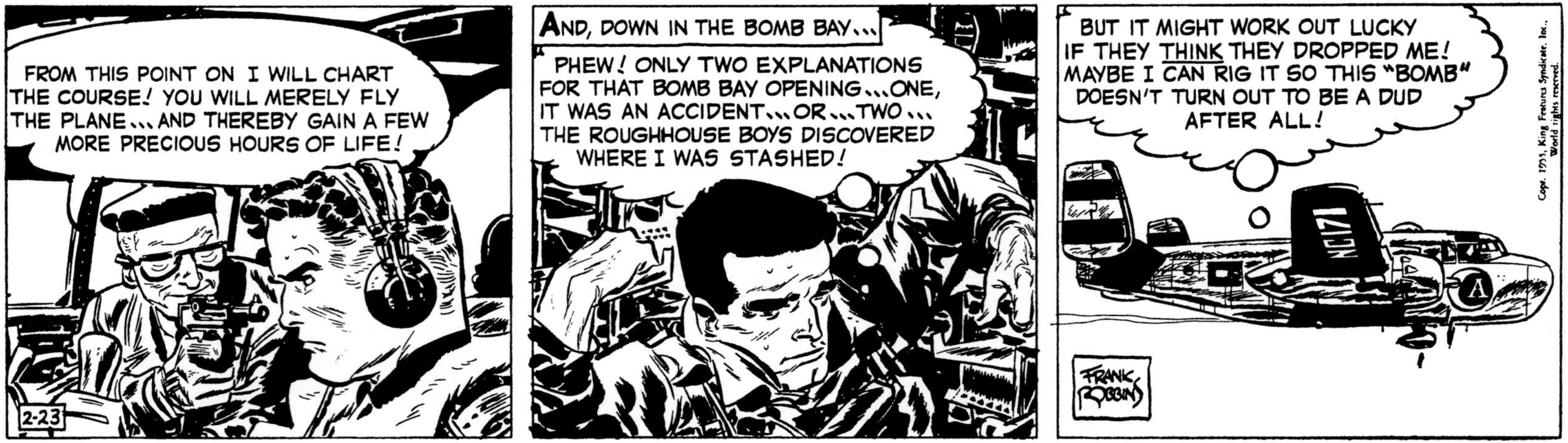
2-23
FROM THIS POINT ON I WILL CHART THE COURSE! YOU WILL MERELY FLY THE PLANE... AND THEREBY GAIN A FEW MORE PRECIOUS HOURS OF LIFE!
AND, DOWN IN THE BOMB BAY...
PHEW! ONLY TWO EXPLANATIONS FOR THAT BOMB BAY OPENING... ONE, IT WAS AN ACCIDENT... OR... TWO... THE ROUGHHOUSE BOYS DISCOVERED WHERE I WAS STASHED!
BUT IT MIGHT WORK OUT LUCKY IF THEY THINK THEY DROPPED ME! MAYBE I CAN RIG IT SO THIS "BOMB" DOESN'T TURN OUT TO BE A DUD AFTER ALL!
FRANK ROBBINS
Copr. 1955, King Features Syndicate, Inc., World rights reserved.

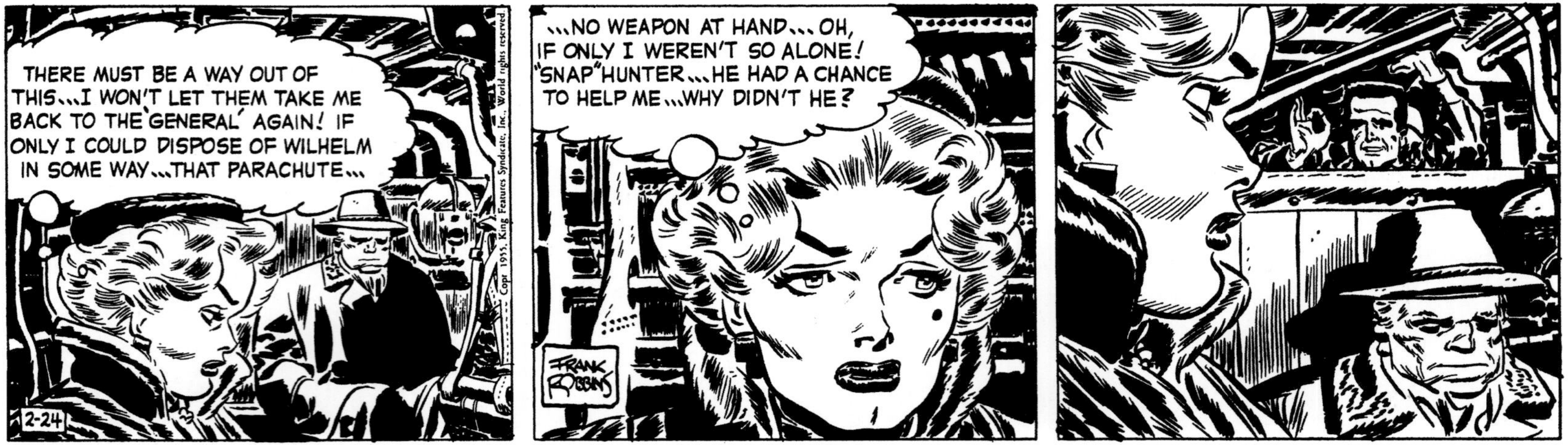
2-24
THERE MUST BE A WAY OUT OF THIS... I WON'T LET THEM TAKE ME BACK TO THE 'GENERAL' AGAIN! IF ONLY I COULD DISPOSE OF WILHELM IN SOME WAY... THAT PARACHUTE...
Copr. 1955, King Features Syndicate, Inc., World rights reserved
...NO WEAPON AT HAND... OH, IF ONLY I WEREN'T SO ALONE! "SNAP" HUNTER... HE HAD A CHANCE TO HELP ME... WHY DIDN'T HE?
FRANK ROBBINS

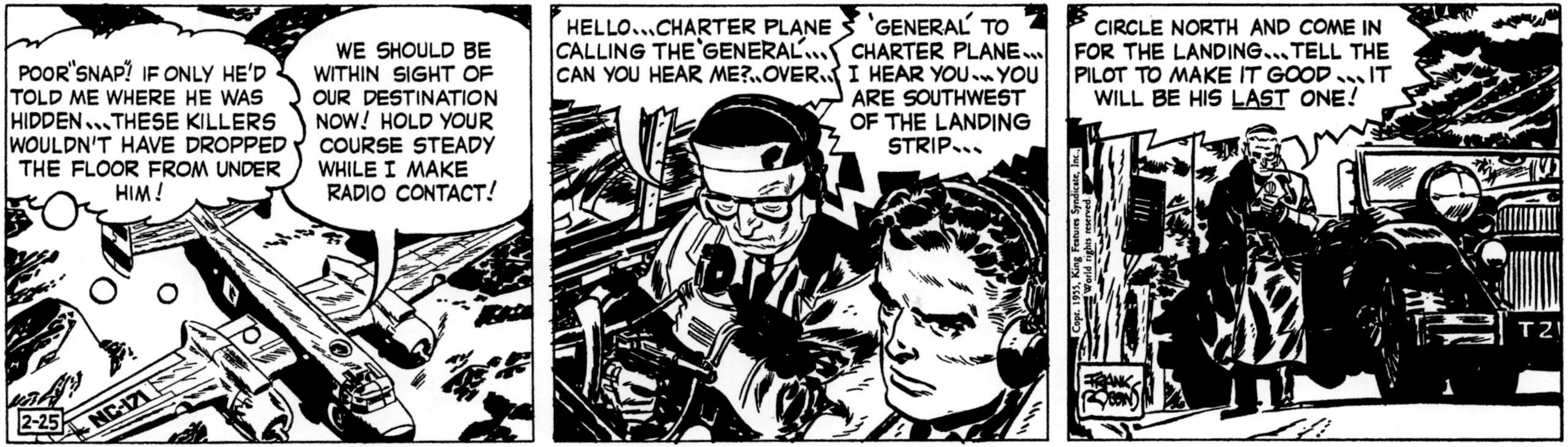
2-25
POOR "SNAP"! IF ONLY HE'D TOLD ME WHERE HE WAS HIDDEN... THESE KILLERS WOULDN'T HAVE DROPPED THE FLOOR FROM UNDER HIM!
WE SHOULD BE WITHIN SIGHT OF OUR DESTINATION NOW! HOLD YOUR COURSE STEADY WHILE I MAKE RADIO CONTACT!
NC-171
HELLO... CHARTER PLANE CALLING THE 'GENERAL'... CAN YOU HEAR ME?.. OVER...
'GENERAL' TO CHARTER PLANE... I HEAR YOU... YOU ARE SOUTHWEST OF THE LANDING STRIP...
CIRCLE NORTH AND COME IN FOR THE LANDING... TELL THE PILOT TO MAKE IT GOOD... IT WILL BE HIS LAST ONE!
Copr. 1955, King Features Syndicate, Inc., World rights reserved
FRANK ROBBINS

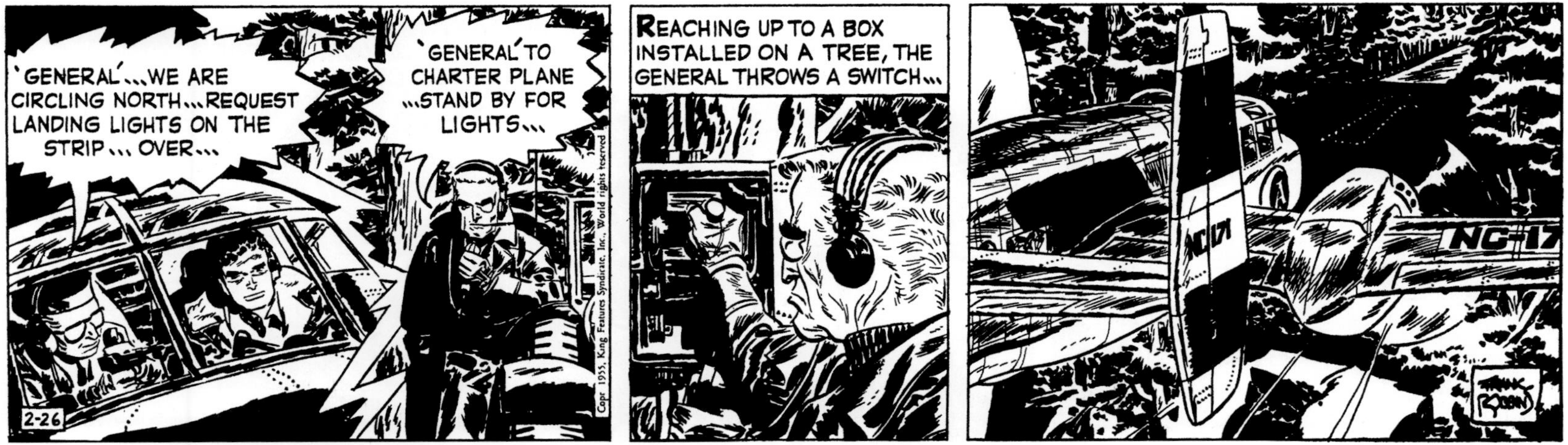
2-26
'GENERAL'... WE ARE CIRCLING NORTH... REQUEST LANDING LIGHTS ON THE STRIP... OVER...
'GENERAL' TO CHARTER PLANE ...STAND BY FOR LIGHTS...
Copr. 1955, King Features Syndicate, Inc., World rights reserved
REACHING UP TO A BOX INSTALLED ON A TREE, THE GENERAL THROWS A SWITCH...
NC-171
NC-17
FRANK ROBBINS

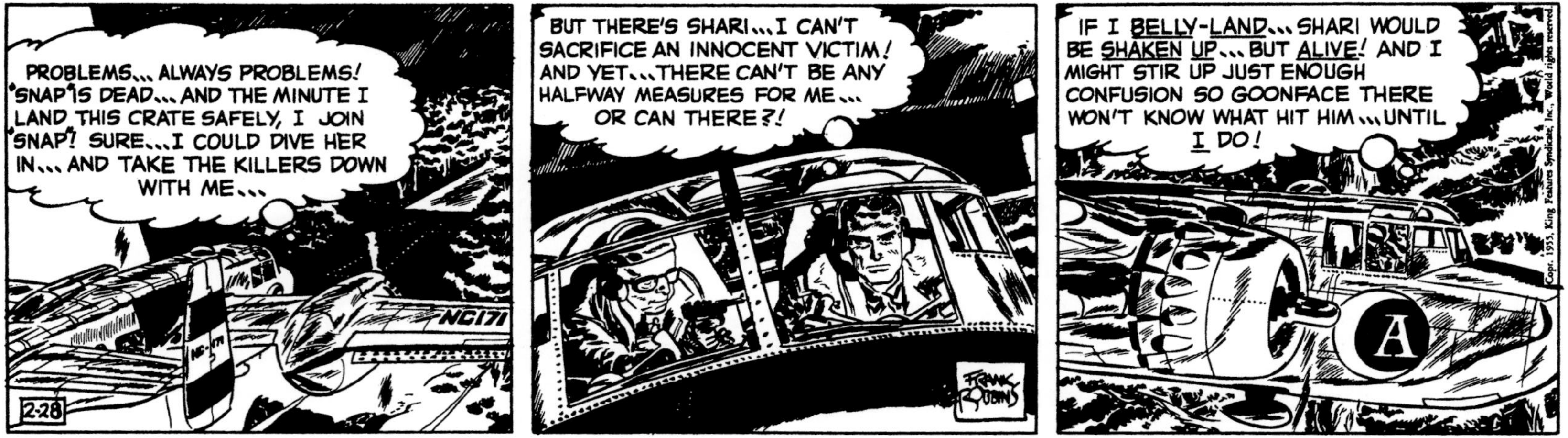
PROBLEMS... ALWAYS PROBLEMS! "SNAP" IS DEAD... AND THE MINUTE I LAND THIS CRATE SAFELY, I JOIN "SNAP"! SURE...I COULD DIVE HER IN... AND TAKE THE KILLERS DOWN WITH ME...
NC171
2-28
BUT THERE'S SHARI...I CAN'T SACRIFICE AN INNOCENT VICTIM! AND YET...THERE CAN'T BE ANY HALFWAY MEASURES FOR ME... OR CAN THERE?!
FRANK ROBBINS
IF I BELLY-LAND... SHARI WOULD BE SHAKEN UP... BUT ALIVE! AND I MIGHT STIR UP JUST ENOUGH CONFUSION SO GOONFACE THERE WON'T KNOW WHAT HIT HIM... UNTIL I DO!
A
Copr. 1955, King Features Syndicate, Inc., World rights reserved.

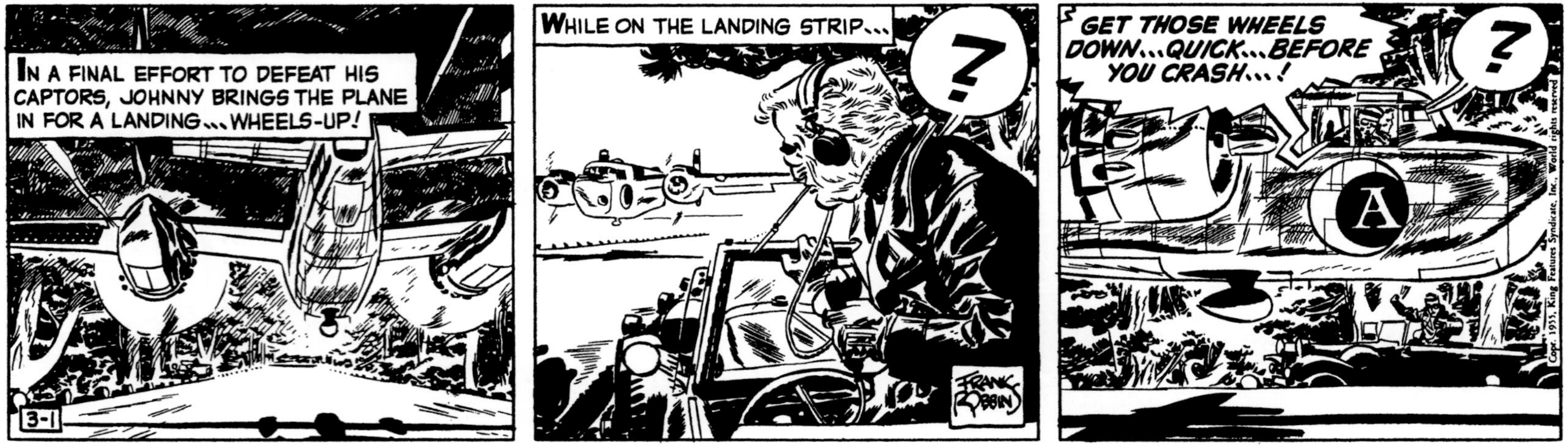
IN A FINAL EFFORT TO DEFEAT HIS CAPTORS, JOHNNY BRINGS THE PLANE IN FOR A LANDING... WHEELS-UP!
3-1
WHILE ON THE LANDING STRIP...
?
FRANK ROBBINS
GET THOSE WHEELS DOWN...QUICK...BEFORE YOU CRASH...!
?
A
Copr. 1955, King Features Syndicate, Inc., World rights reserved.

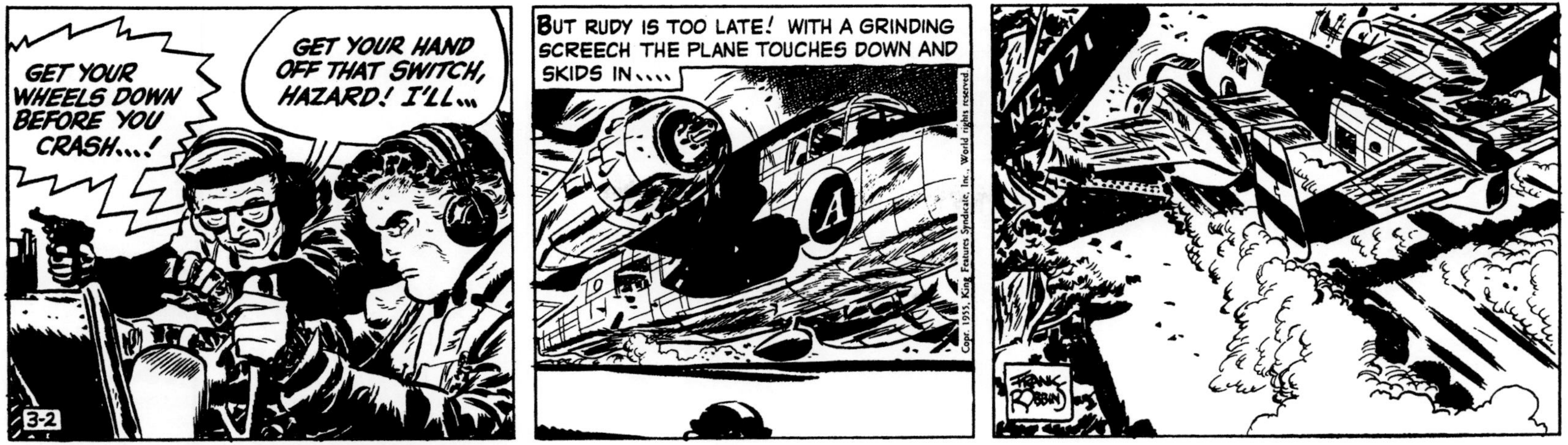
GET YOUR WHEELS DOWN BEFORE YOU CRASH...!
GET YOUR HAND OFF THAT SWITCH, HAZARD! I'LL...
3-2
BUT RUDY IS TOO LATE! WITH A GRINDING SCREECH THE PLANE TOUCHES DOWN AND SKIDS IN....
Copr. 1955, King Features Syndicate, Inc., World rights reserved.
NC 171
FRANK ROBBINS

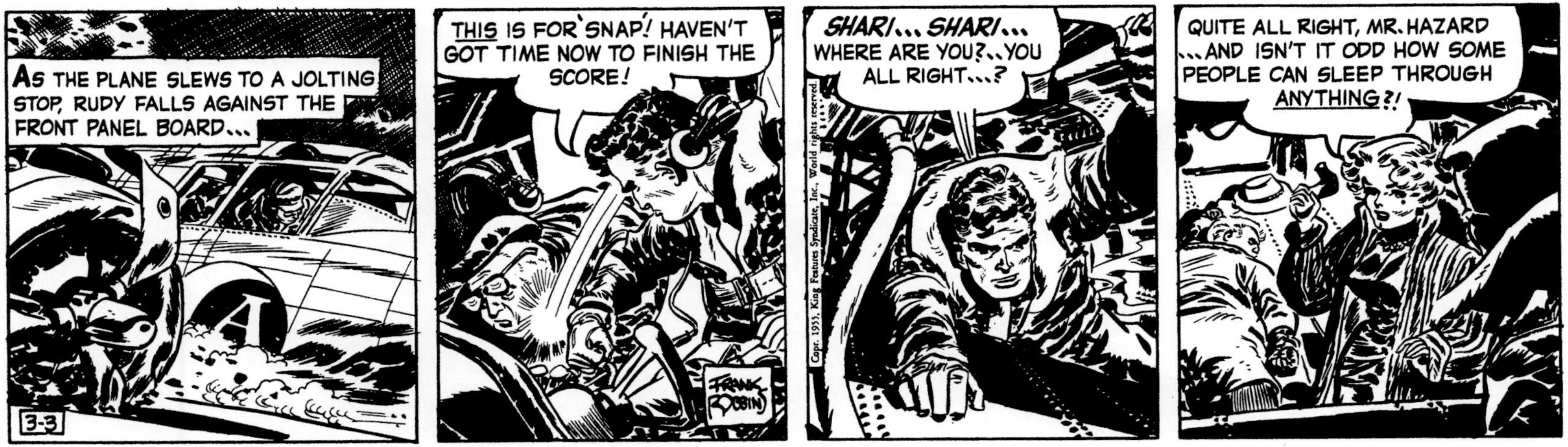
AS THE PLANE SLEWS TO A JOLTING STOP, RUDY FALLS AGAINST THE FRONT PANEL BOARD...
3-3
THIS IS FOR 'SNAP'! HAVEN'T GOT TIME NOW TO FINISH THE SCORE!
FRANK ROBBINS
Copr. 1955, King Features Syndicate, Inc., World rights reserved.
SHARI... SHARI... WHERE ARE YOU?..YOU ALL RIGHT...?
QUITE ALL RIGHT, MR. HAZARD ...AND ISN'T IT ODD HOW SOME PEOPLE CAN SLEEP THROUGH ANYTHING?!

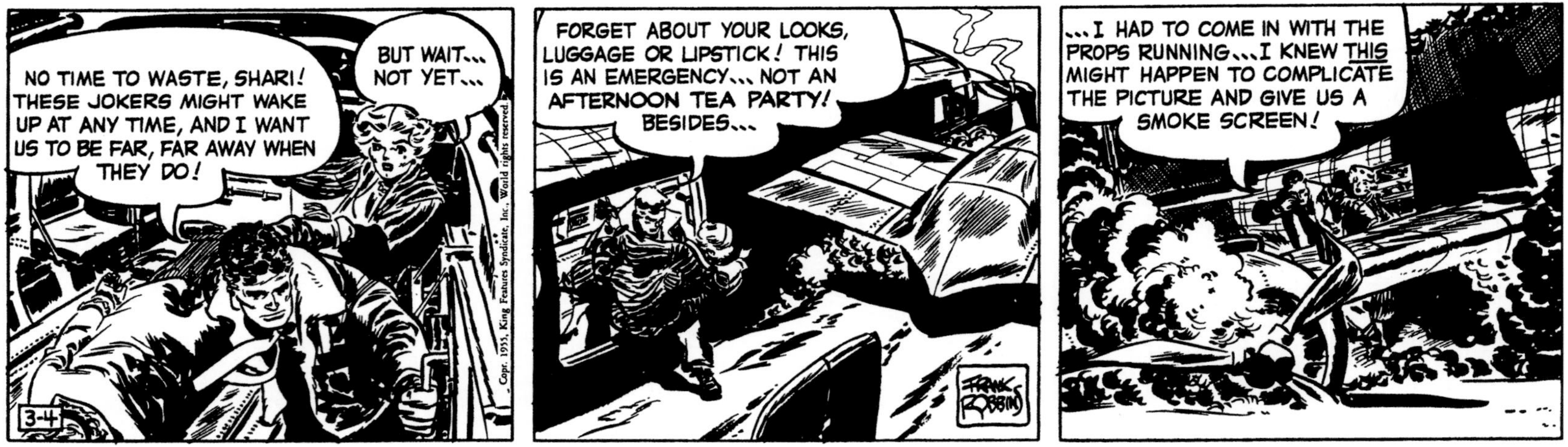
NO TIME TO WASTE, SHARI! THESE JOKERS MIGHT WAKE UP AT ANY TIME, AND I WANT US TO BE FAR, FAR AWAY WHEN THEY DO!
BUT WAIT... NOT YET...
Copr. 1955, King Features Syndicate, Inc., World rights reserved.
3-4
FORGET ABOUT YOUR LOOKS, LUGGAGE OR LIPSTICK! THIS IS AN EMERGENCY... NOT AN AFTERNOON TEA PARTY! BESIDES...
FRANK ROBBINS
...I HAD TO COME IN WITH THE PROPS RUNNING...I KNEW THIS MIGHT HAPPEN TO COMPLICATE THE PICTURE AND GIVE US A SMOKE SCREEN!

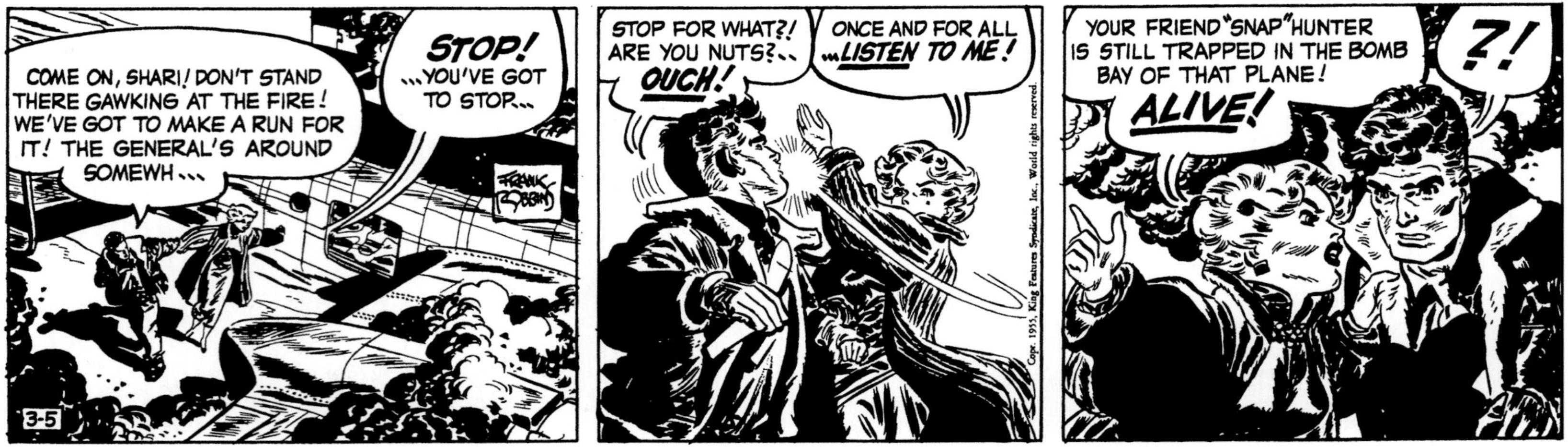
COME ON, SHARI! DON'T STAND THERE GAWKING AT THE FIRE! WE'VE GOT TO MAKE A RUN FOR IT! THE GENERAL'S AROUND SOMEWH...
STOP! ...YOU'VE GOT TO STOP...
FRANK ROBBINS
3-5
STOP FOR WHAT?! ARE YOU NUTS?.. OUCH!
ONCE AND FOR ALL ...LISTEN TO ME!
Copr. 1955, King Features Syndicate, Inc., World rights reserved.
YOUR FRIEND "SNAP" HUNTER IS STILL TRAPPED IN THE BOMB BAY OF THAT PLANE! ALIVE!
?!

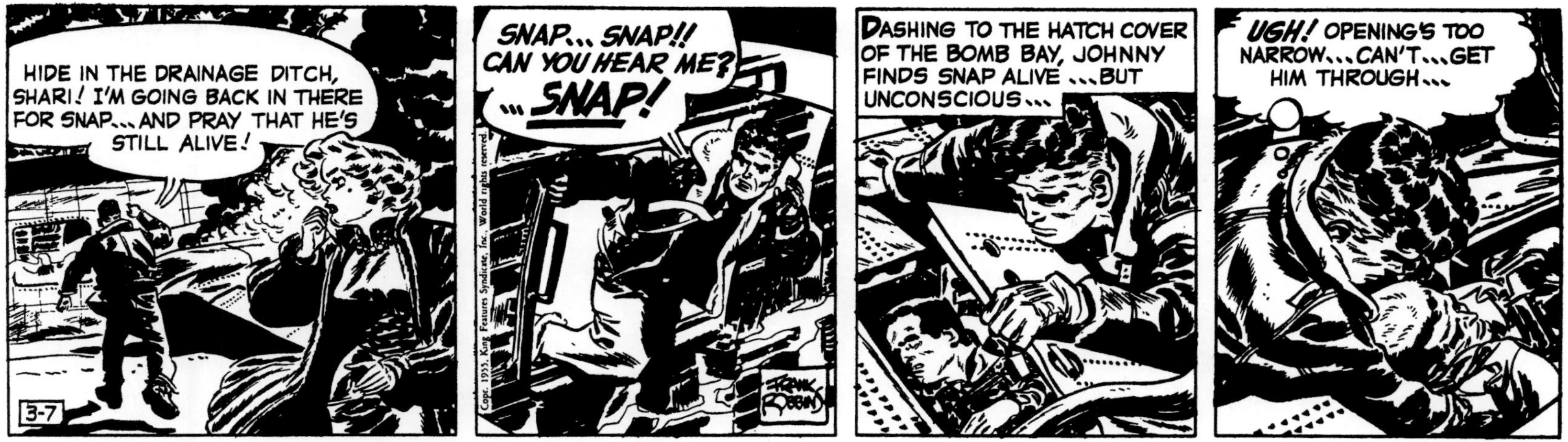

3-7
HIDE IN THE DRAINAGE DITCH, SHARI! I'M GOING BACK IN THERE FOR SNAP... AND PRAY THAT HE'S STILL ALIVE!
SNAP... SNAP!! CAN YOU HEAR ME? ... SNAP!
Copr. 1955, King Features Syndicate, Inc., World rights reserved.
FRANK ROBBINS
DASHING TO THE HATCH COVER OF THE BOMB BAY, JOHNNY FINDS SNAP ALIVE ...BUT UNCONSCIOUS...
UGH! OPENING'S TOO NARROW...CAN'T...GET HIM THROUGH...

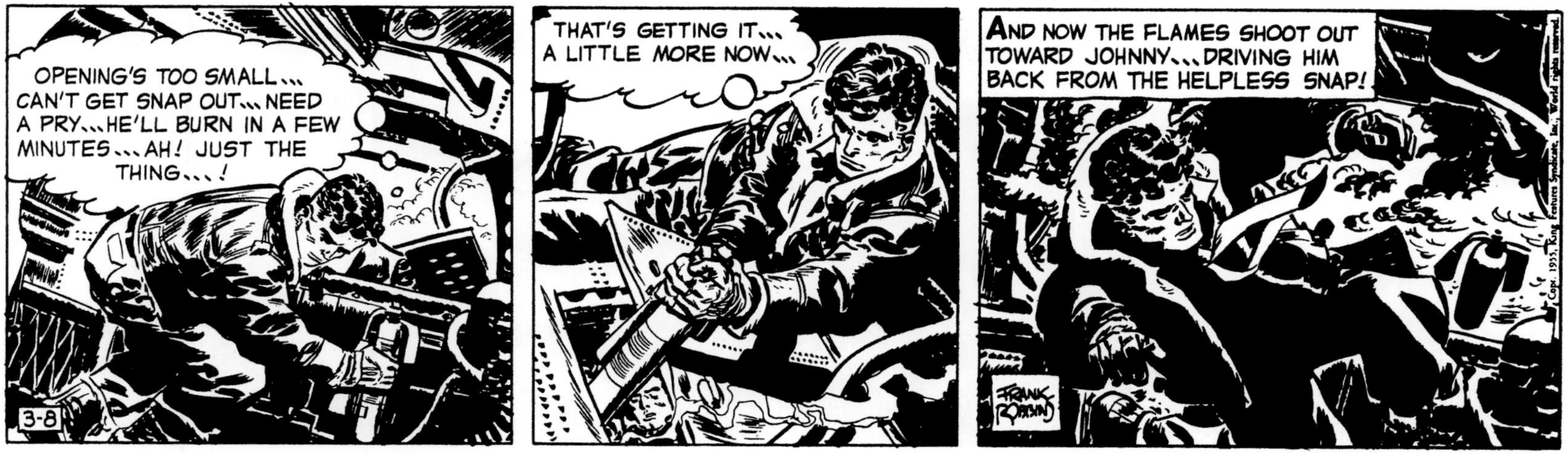

OPENING'S TOO SMALL... CAN'T GET SNAP OUT... NEED A PRY...HE'LL BURN IN A FEW MINUTES...AH! JUST THE THING...!
3-8
THAT'S GETTING IT... A LITTLE MORE NOW...
FRANK ROBBINS
AND NOW THE FLAMES SHOOT OUT TOWARD JOHNNY...DRIVING HIM BACK FROM THE HELPLESS SNAP!
Copr. 1955, King Features Syndicate, Inc., World rights reserved.

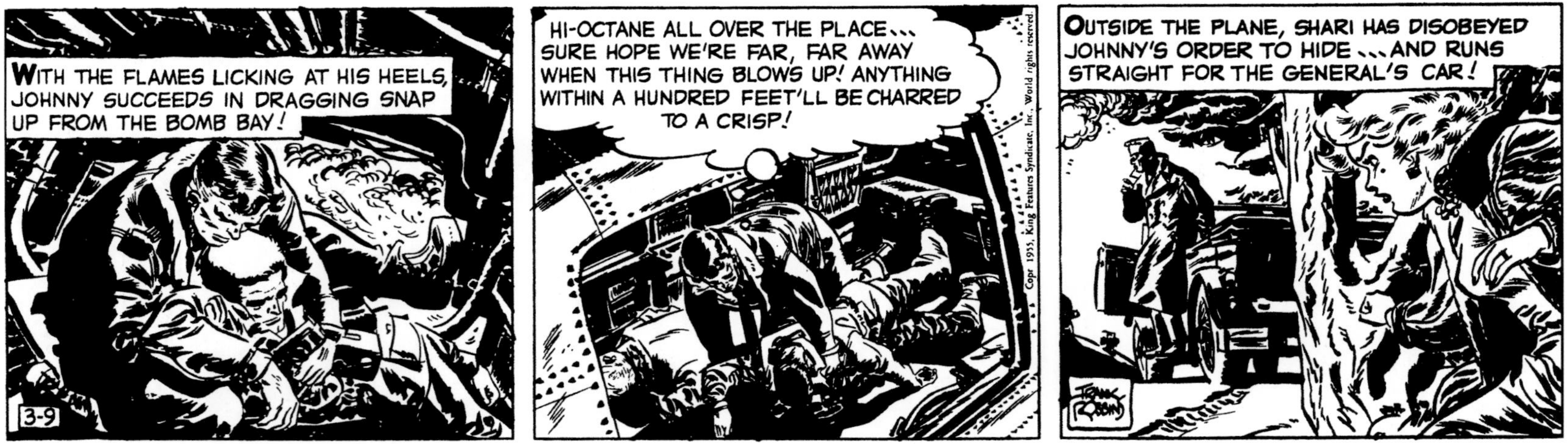
3-9
WITH THE FLAMES LICKING AT HIS HEELS, JOHNNY SUCCEEDS IN DRAGGING SNAP UP FROM THE BOMB BAY!
HI-OCTANE ALL OVER THE PLACE... SURE HOPE WE'RE FAR, FAR AWAY WHEN THIS THING BLOWS UP! ANYTHING WITHIN A HUNDRED FEET'LL BE CHARRED TO A CRISP!
Copr. 1955, King Features Syndicate, Inc., World rights reserved.
OUTSIDE THE PLANE, SHARI HAS DISOBEYED JOHNNY'S ORDER TO HIDE... AND RUNS STRAIGHT FOR THE GENERAL'S CAR!

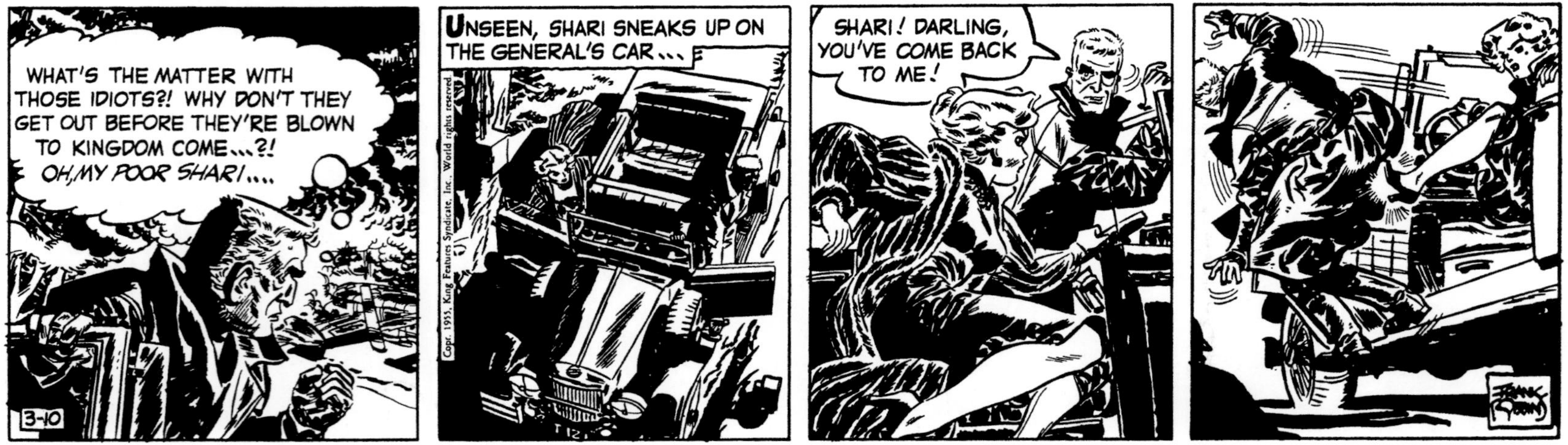
3-10
WHAT'S THE MATTER WITH THOSE IDIOTS?! WHY DON'T THEY GET OUT BEFORE THEY'RE BLOWN TO KINGDOM COME...?! OH, MY POOR SHARI....
UNSEEN, SHARI SNEAKS UP ON THE GENERAL'S CAR...
Copr. 1955, King Features Syndicate, Inc., World rights reserved.
SHARI! DARLING, YOU'VE COME BACK TO ME!

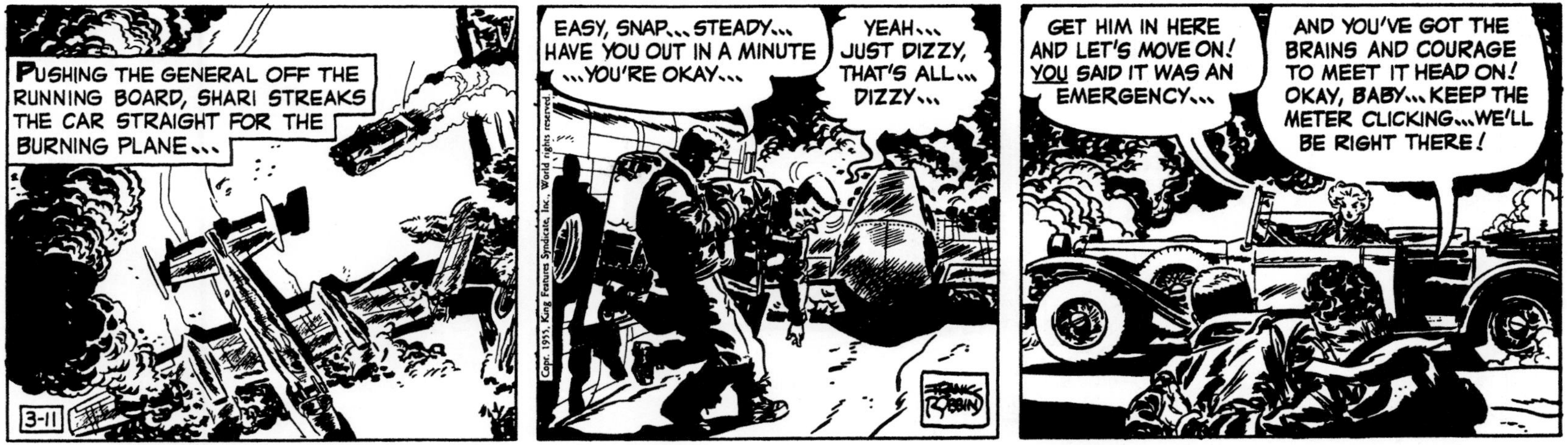
PUSHING THE GENERAL OFF THE RUNNING BOARD, SHARI STREAKS THE CAR STRAIGHT FOR THE BURNING PLANE...
3-11
EASY, SNAP... STEADY... HAVE YOU OUT IN A MINUTE ...YOU'RE OKAY...
YEAH... JUST DIZZY, THAT'S ALL... DIZZY...
Copr. 1955, King Features Syndicate, Inc., World rights reserved.
FRANK ROBBINS
GET HIM IN HERE AND LET'S MOVE ON! YOU SAID IT WAS AN EMERGENCY...
AND YOU'VE GOT THE BRAINS AND COURAGE TO MEET IT HEAD ON! OKAY, BABY... KEEP THE METER CLICKING... WE'LL BE RIGHT THERE!

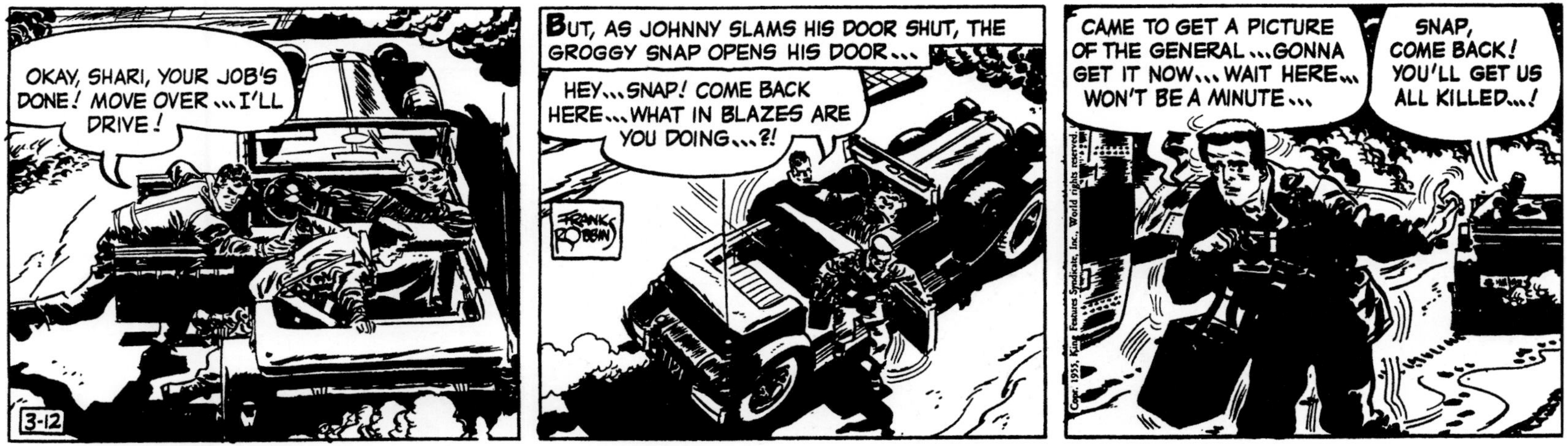
OKAY, SHARI, YOUR JOB'S DONE! MOVE OVER ... I'LL DRIVE!
3-12
BUT, AS JOHNNY SLAMS HIS DOOR SHUT, THE GROGGY SNAP OPENS HIS DOOR...
HEY... SNAP! COME BACK HERE... WHAT IN BLAZES ARE YOU DOING...?!
FRANK ROBBINS
CAME TO GET A PICTURE OF THE GENERAL ...GONNA GET IT NOW... WAIT HERE... WON'T BE A MINUTE...
SNAP, COME BACK! YOU'LL GET US ALL KILLED...!
Copr. 1955, King Features Syndicate, Inc., World rights reserved.

JOHNNY...WHAT IS SNAP DOING?...DOESN'T HE REALIZE THE DANGER TO US ALL...?

HE COULDN'T, SHARI! HE'S PROBABLY STILL GROGGY FROM THE CRACK-UP! HANG ON...HERE WE GO!

3-14

ABOUT TIME YOU GOT YOURSELVES OUT OF THAT INFERNO! COME ON! SHARI IS SOMEWHERE OUT ON THE FIELD!

FRANK ROBBINS

Copr. 1953, King Features Syndicate, Inc. World rights reserved

JUST ONE SHOT, GENERAL ...HOLD THAT POSE!

!?!

SNAP GETS HIS PICTURE... BUT THE GENERAL AND HIS HENCHMEN REACT QUICKLY...

FRANK ROBBINS

3-15

AS THE GENERAL SIGHTS AT SNAP, JOHNNY COMES RACING AROUND THE PLANE...

Copr. 1953, King Features Syndicate, Inc. World rights reserved

...AND THE BULLETPROOF CAR TAKES THE BULLETS MEANT FOR SNAP!

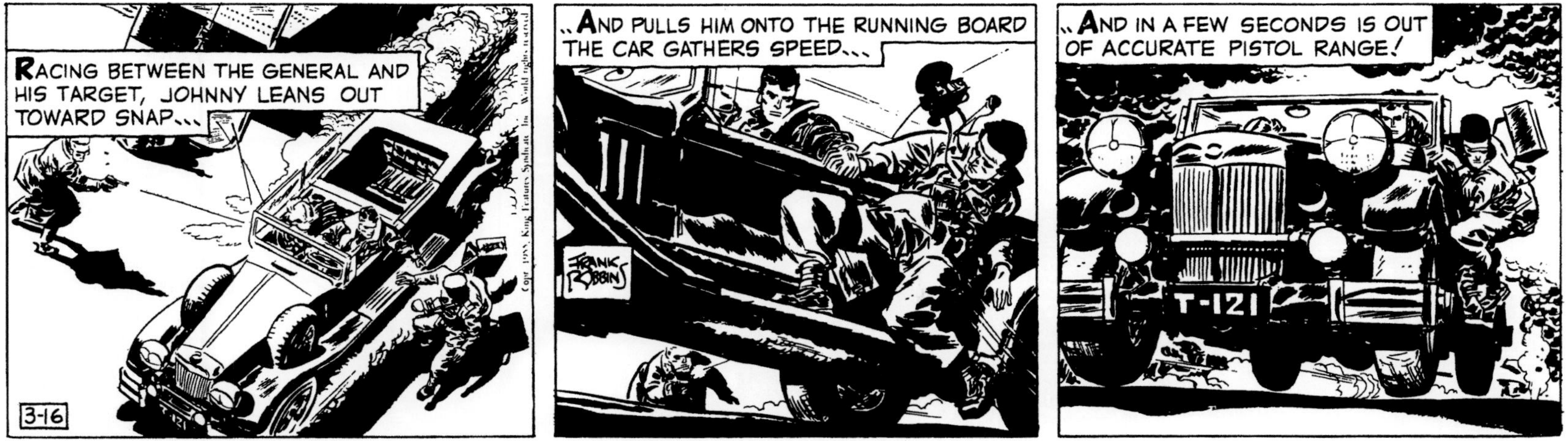

RACING BETWEEN THE GENERAL AND HIS TARGET, JOHNNY LEANS OUT TOWARD SNAP...
3-16
..AND PULLS HIM ONTO THE RUNNING BOARD THE CAR GATHERS SPEED...
FRANK ROBBINS
..AND IN A FEW SECONDS IS OUT OF ACCURATE PISTOL RANGE!
T-121

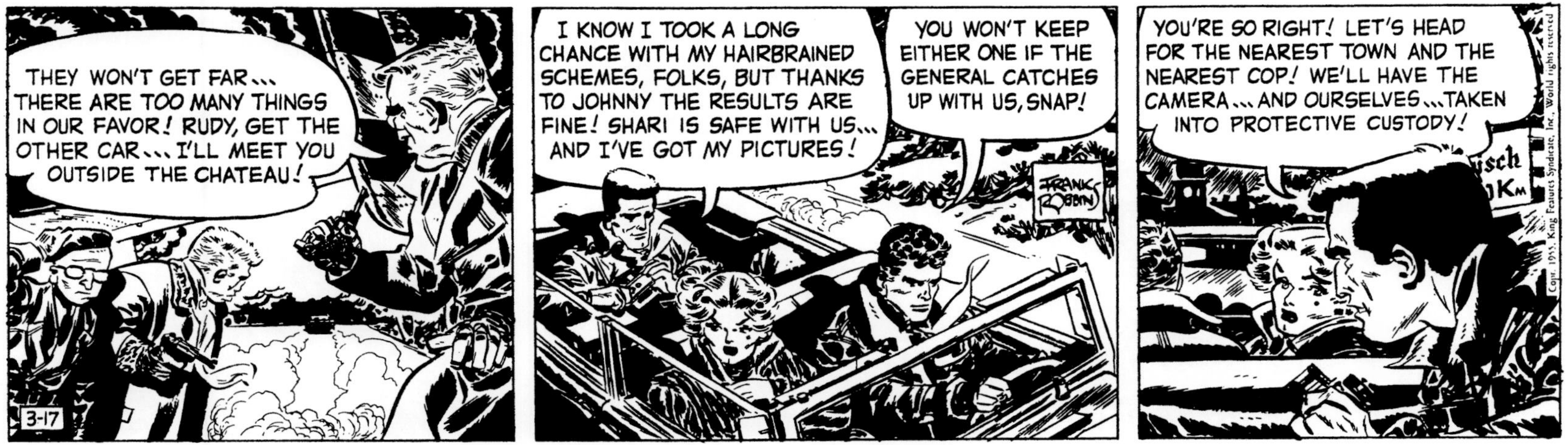

THEY WON'T GET FAR... THERE ARE TOO MANY THINGS IN OUR FAVOR! RUDY, GET THE OTHER CAR... I'LL MEET YOU OUTSIDE THE CHATEAU!
3-17
I KNOW I TOOK A LONG CHANCE WITH MY HAIRBRAINED SCHEMES, FOLKS, BUT THANKS TO JOHNNY THE RESULTS ARE FINE! SHARI IS SAFE WITH US... AND I'VE GOT MY PICTURES!
YOU WON'T KEEP EITHER ONE IF THE GENERAL CATCHES UP WITH US, SNAP!
FRANK ROBBINS
YOU'RE SO RIGHT! LET'S HEAD FOR THE NEAREST TOWN AND THE NEAREST COP! WE'LL HAVE THE CAMERA... AND OURSELVES... TAKEN INTO PROTECTIVE CUSTODY!

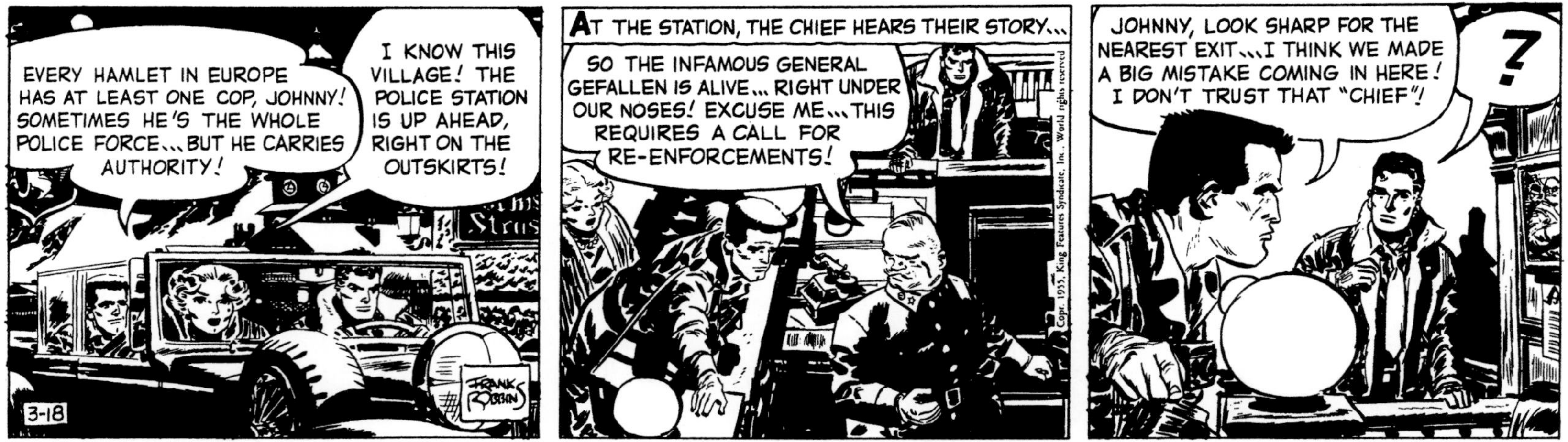
EVERY HAMLET IN EUROPE HAS AT LEAST ONE COP, JOHNNY! SOMETIMES HE'S THE WHOLE POLICE FORCE... BUT HE CARRIES AUTHORITY!
I KNOW THIS VILLAGE! THE POLICE STATION IS UP AHEAD, RIGHT ON THE OUTSKIRTS!
FRANK ROBBINS
3-18
AT THE STATION, THE CHIEF HEARS THEIR STORY...
SO THE INFAMOUS GENERAL GEFALLEN IS ALIVE... RIGHT UNDER OUR NOSES! EXCUSE ME... THIS REQUIRES A CALL FOR RE-ENFORCEMENTS!
Copr. 1955, King Features Syndicate, Inc., World rights reserved
JOHNNY, LOOK SHARP FOR THE NEAREST EXIT... I THINK WE MADE A BIG MISTAKE COMING IN HERE! I DON'T TRUST THAT "CHIEF"!
?

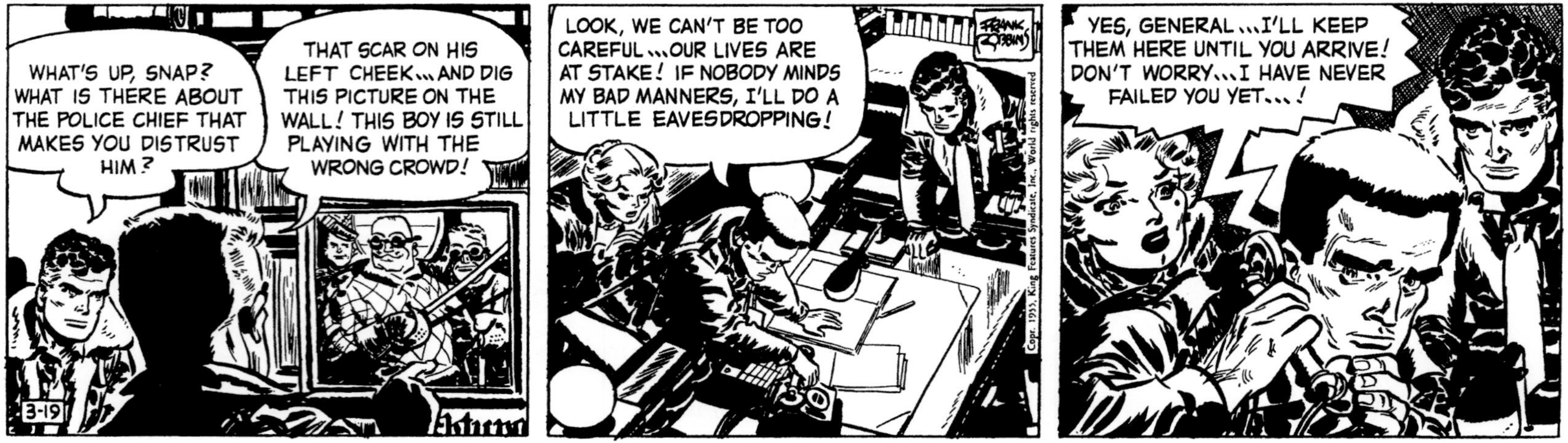
WHAT'S UP, SNAP? WHAT IS THERE ABOUT THE POLICE CHIEF THAT MAKES YOU DISTRUST HIM?
THAT SCAR ON HIS LEFT CHEEK... AND DIG THIS PICTURE ON THE WALL! THIS BOY IS STILL PLAYING WITH THE WRONG CROWD!
3-19
LOOK, WE CAN'T BE TOO CAREFUL... OUR LIVES ARE AT STAKE! IF NOBODY MINDS MY BAD MANNERS, I'LL DO A LITTLE EAVESDROPPING!
FRANK ROBBINS
Copr. 1955, King Features Syndicate, Inc., World rights reserved
YES, GENERAL... I'LL KEEP THEM HERE UNTIL YOU ARRIVE! DON'T WORRY... I HAVE NEVER FAILED YOU YET...!

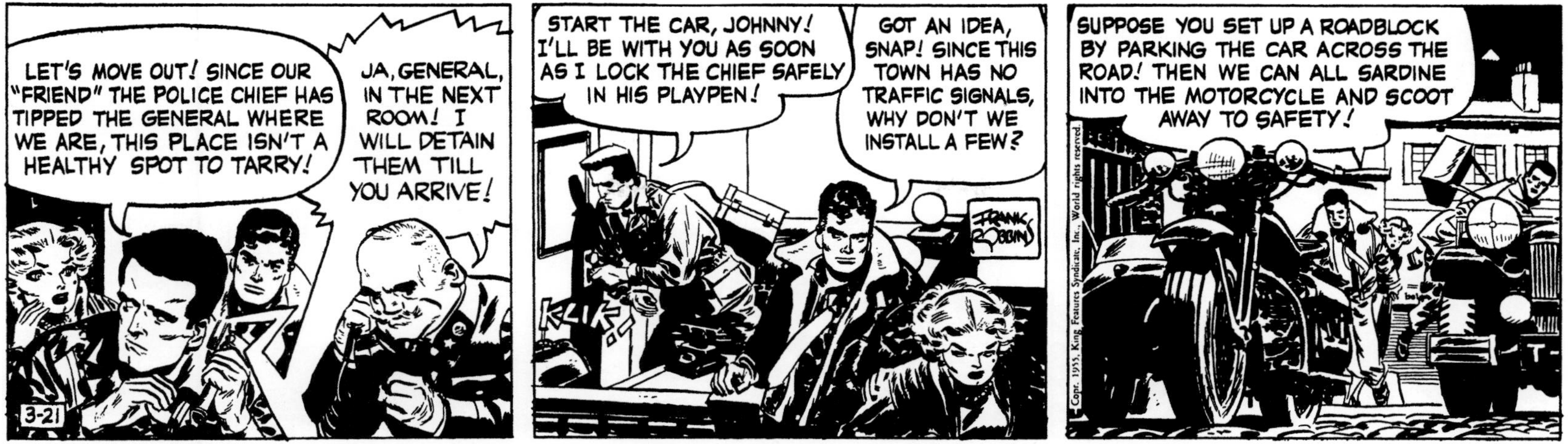
3-21
LET'S MOVE OUT! SINCE OUR "FRIEND" THE POLICE CHIEF HAS TIPPED THE GENERAL WHERE WE ARE, THIS PLACE ISN'T A HEALTHY SPOT TO TARRY!
JA, GENERAL, IN THE NEXT ROOM! I WILL DETAIN THEM TILL YOU ARRIVE!
START THE CAR, JOHNNY! I'LL BE WITH YOU AS SOON AS I LOCK THE CHIEF SAFELY IN HIS PLAYPEN!
KLIK
GOT AN IDEA, SNAP! SINCE THIS TOWN HAS NO TRAFFIC SIGNALS, WHY DON'T WE INSTALL A FEW?
FRANK ROBBINS
SUPPOSE YOU SET UP A ROADBLOCK BY PARKING THE CAR ACROSS THE ROAD! THEN WE CAN ALL SARDINE INTO THE MOTORCYCLE AND SCOOT AWAY TO SAFETY!
Copr. 1955, King Features Syndicate, Inc., World rights reserved.

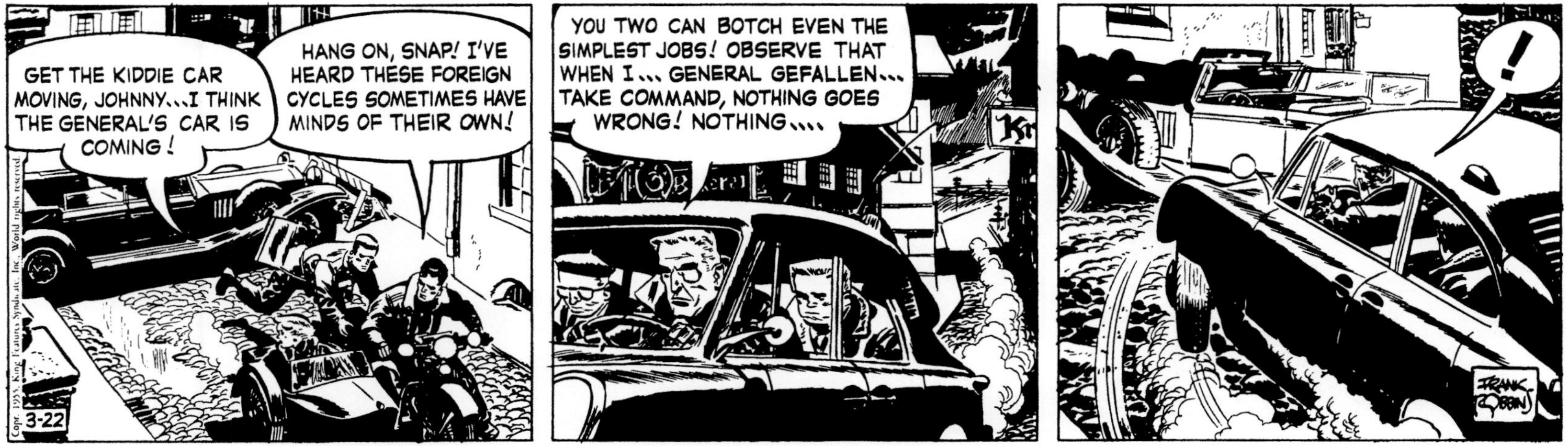
3-22
GET THE KIDDIE CAR MOVING, JOHNNY...I THINK THE GENERAL'S CAR IS COMING!
HANG ON, SNAP! I'VE HEARD THESE FOREIGN CYCLES SOMETIMES HAVE MINDS OF THEIR OWN!
Copr. 1955, King Features Syndicate, Inc., World rights reserved.
YOU TWO CAN BOTCH EVEN THE SIMPLEST JOBS! OBSERVE THAT WHEN I... GENERAL GEFALLEN... TAKE COMMAND, NOTHING GOES WRONG! NOTHING....
!
FRANK ROBBINS

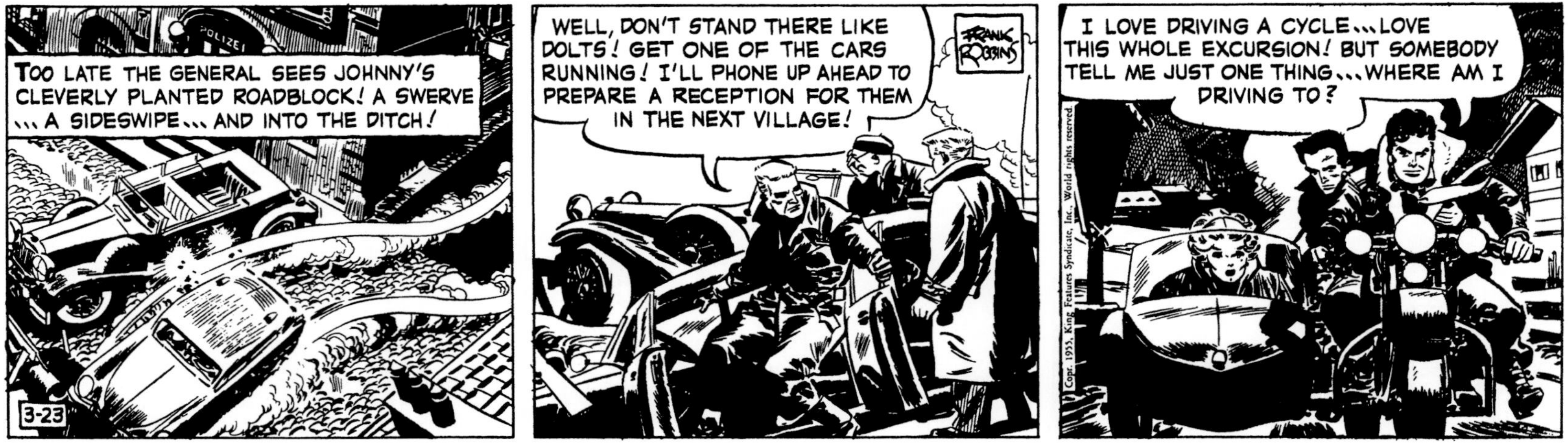
TOO LATE THE GENERAL SEES JOHNNY'S CLEVERLY PLANTED ROADBLOCK! A SWERVE ... A SIDESWIPE ... AND INTO THE DITCH!
POLIZEI
3-23
WELL, DON'T STAND THERE LIKE DOLTS! GET ONE OF THE CARS RUNNING! I'LL PHONE UP AHEAD TO PREPARE A RECEPTION FOR THEM IN THE NEXT VILLAGE!
FRANK ROBBINS
Copr. 1955, King Features Syndicate, Inc., World rights reserved.
I LOVE DRIVING A CYCLE ... LOVE THIS WHOLE EXCURSION! BUT SOMEBODY TELL ME JUST ONE THING ... WHERE AM I DRIVING TO?

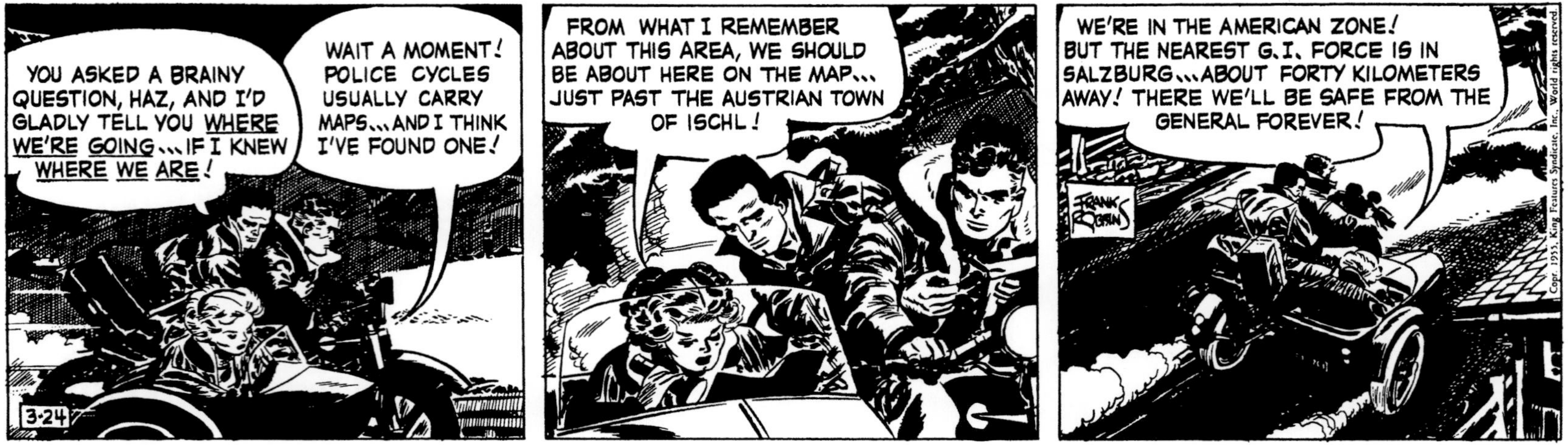
YOU ASKED A BRAINY QUESTION, HAZ, AND I'D GLADLY TELL YOU WHERE WE'RE GOING ... IF I KNEW WHERE WE ARE!
WAIT A MOMENT! POLICE CYCLES USUALLY CARRY MAPS ... AND I THINK I'VE FOUND ONE!
3-24
FROM WHAT I REMEMBER ABOUT THIS AREA, WE SHOULD BE ABOUT HERE ON THE MAP ... JUST PAST THE AUSTRIAN TOWN OF ISCHL!
WE'RE IN THE AMERICAN ZONE! BUT THE NEAREST G.I. FORCE IS IN SALZBURG ... ABOUT FORTY KILOMETERS AWAY! THERE WE'LL BE SAFE FROM THE GENERAL FOREVER!
FRANK ROBBINS
Copr. 1955, King Features Syndicate, Inc., World rights reserved.

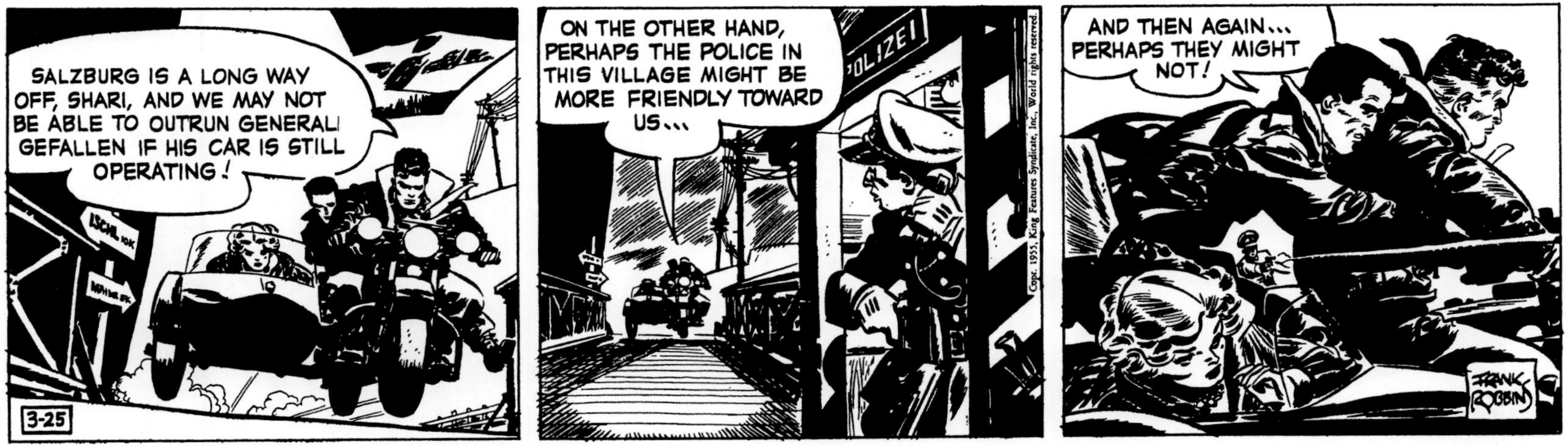
SALZBURG IS A LONG WAY OFF, SHARI, AND WE MAY NOT BE ABLE TO OUTRUN GENERAL GEFALLEN IF HIS CAR IS STILL OPERATING!
3-25
ON THE OTHER HAND, PERHAPS THE POLICE IN THIS VILLAGE MIGHT BE MORE FRIENDLY TOWARD US...
OLIZEI
Copr. 1955, King Features Syndicate, Inc., World rights reserved.
AND THEN AGAIN... PERHAPS THEY MIGHT NOT!
FRANK ROBBINS

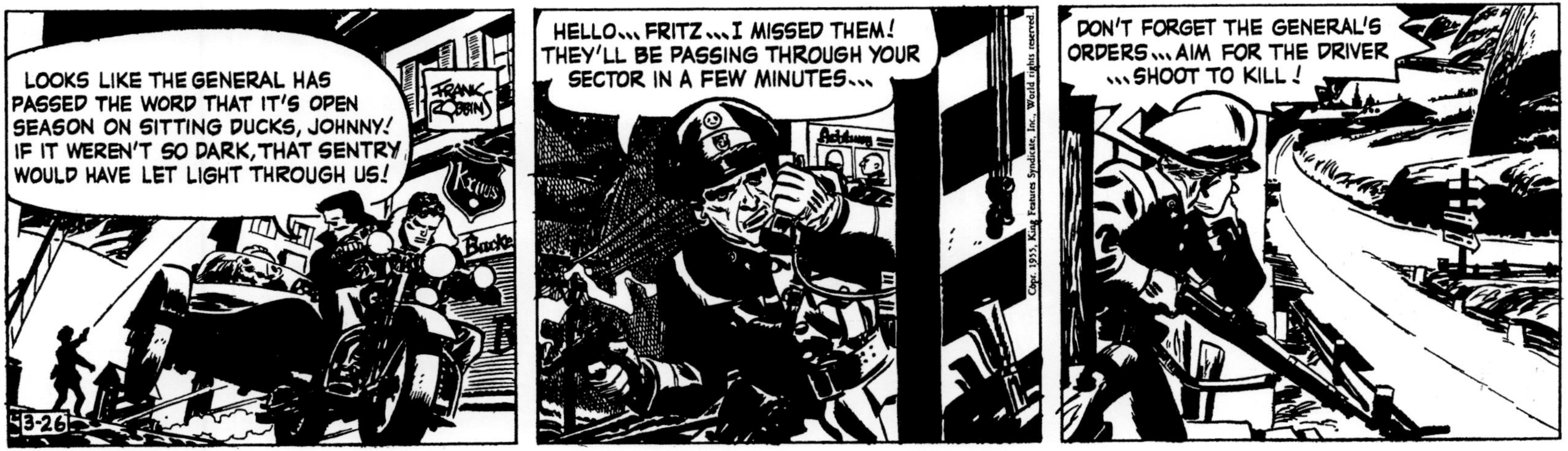
LOOKS LIKE THE GENERAL HAS PASSED THE WORD THAT IT'S OPEN SEASON ON SITTING DUCKS, JOHNNY! IF IT WEREN'T SO DARK, THAT SENTRY WOULD HAVE LET LIGHT THROUGH US!
FRANK ROBBINS
3-26
HELLO... FRITZ... I MISSED THEM! THEY'LL BE PASSING THROUGH YOUR SECTOR IN A FEW MINUTES...
Copr. 1955, King Features Syndicate, Inc., World rights reserved.
DON'T FORGET THE GENERAL'S ORDERS... AIM FOR THE DRIVER ...SHOOT TO KILL!

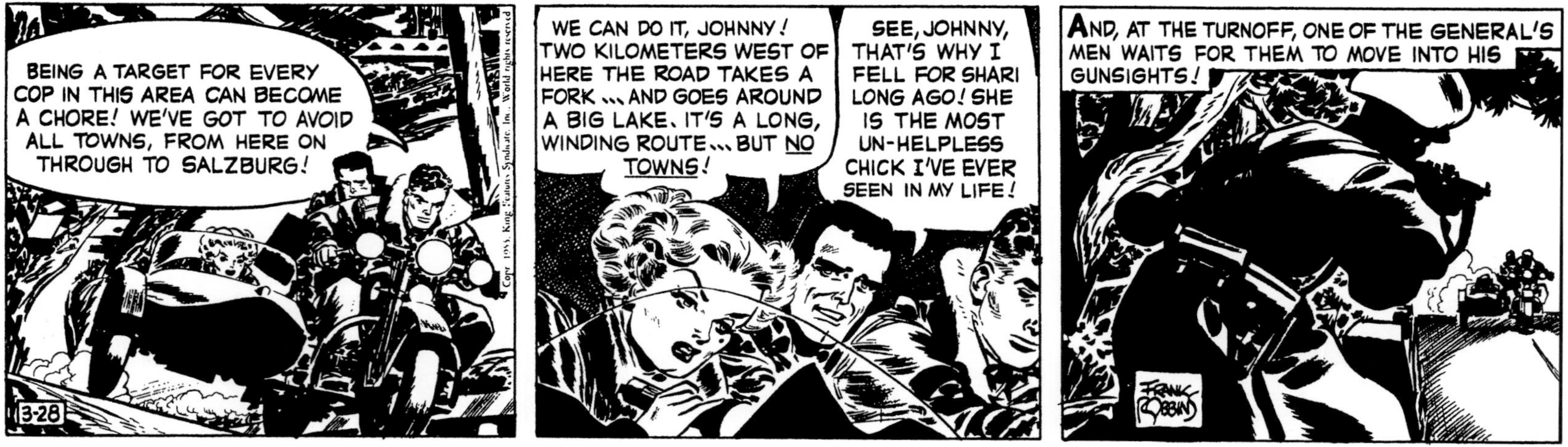
BEING A TARGET FOR EVERY COP IN THIS AREA CAN BECOME A CHORE! WE'VE GOT TO AVOID ALL TOWNS, FROM HERE ON THROUGH TO SALZBURG!
Copr 1955, King Features Syndicate, Inc. World rights reserved
3-28
WE CAN DO IT, JOHNNY! TWO KILOMETERS WEST OF HERE THE ROAD TAKES A FORK ... AND GOES AROUND A BIG LAKE. IT'S A LONG, WINDING ROUTE ... BUT NO TOWNS!
SEE, JOHNNY, THAT'S WHY I FELL FOR SHARI LONG AGO! SHE IS THE MOST UN-HELPLESS CHICK I'VE EVER SEEN IN MY LIFE!
AND, AT THE TURNOFF, ONE OF THE GENERAL'S MEN WAITS FOR THEM TO MOVE INTO HIS GUNSIGHTS!
FRANK ROBBINS

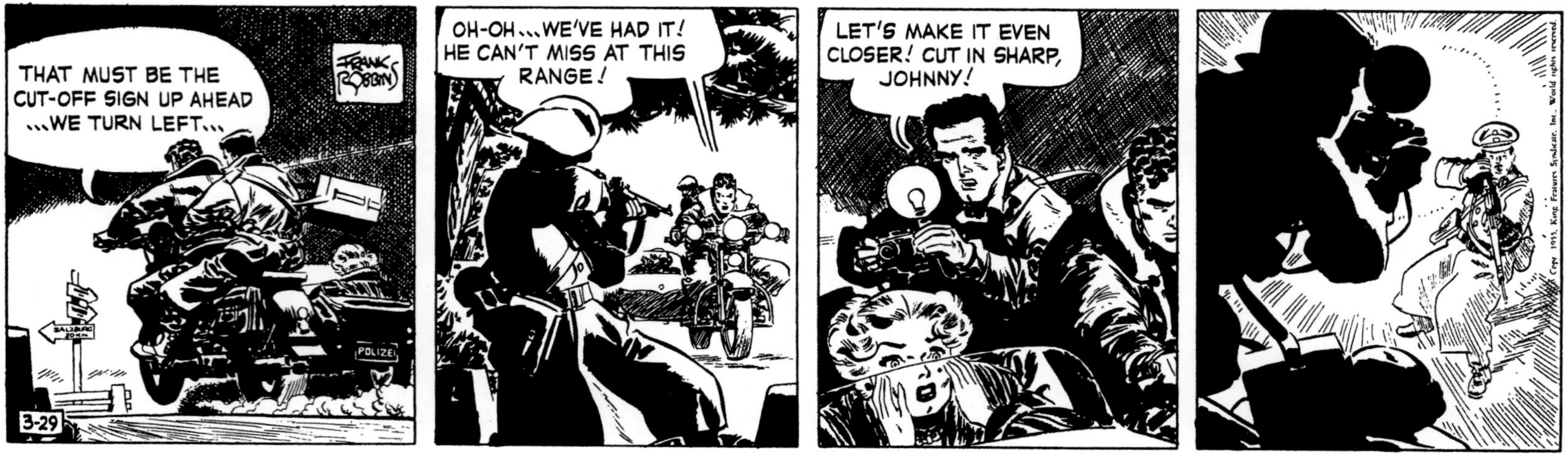
THAT MUST BE THE CUT-OFF SIGN UP AHEAD ...WE TURN LEFT...
FRANK ROBBINS
POLIZEI
3-29
OH-OH ... WE'VE HAD IT! HE CAN'T MISS AT THIS RANGE!
LET'S MAKE IT EVEN CLOSER! CUT IN SHARP, JOHNNY!
Copr 1955, King Features Syndicate, Inc. World rights reserved

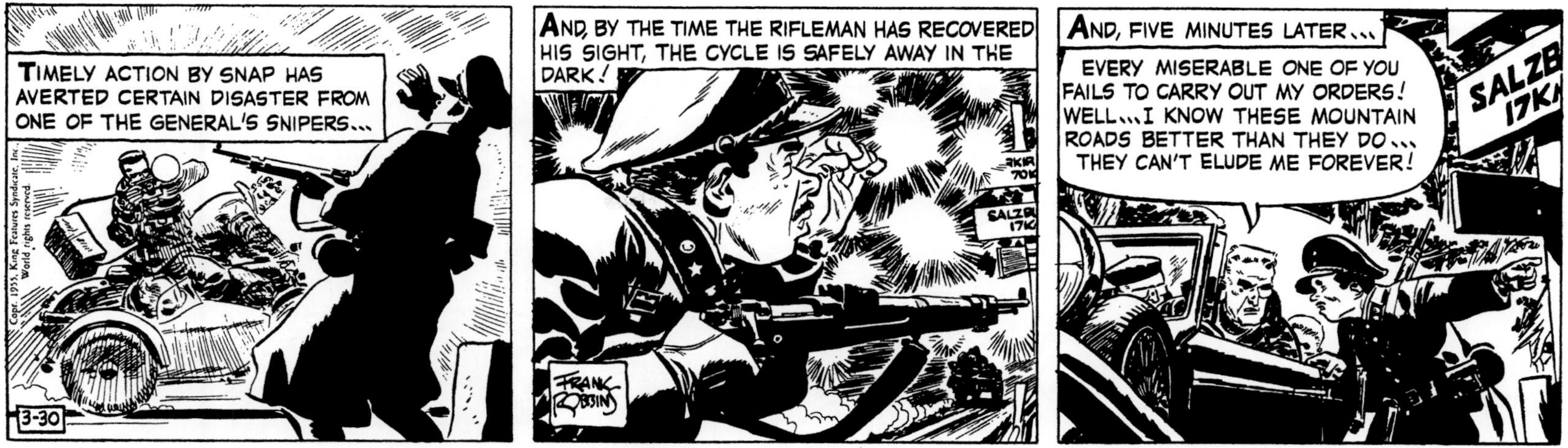
TIMELY ACTION BY SNAP HAS AVERTED CERTAIN DISASTER FROM ONE OF THE GENERAL'S SNIPERS...
Copr. 1955, King Features Syndicate, Inc., World rights reserved.
3-30
AND, BY THE TIME THE RIFLEMAN HAS RECOVERED HIS SIGHT, THE CYCLE IS SAFELY AWAY IN THE DARK!
FRANK ROBBINS
AND, FIVE MINUTES LATER...
EVERY MISERABLE ONE OF YOU FAILS TO CARRY OUT MY ORDERS! WELL...I KNOW THESE MOUNTAIN ROADS BETTER THAN THEY DO... THEY CAN'T ELUDE ME FOREVER!

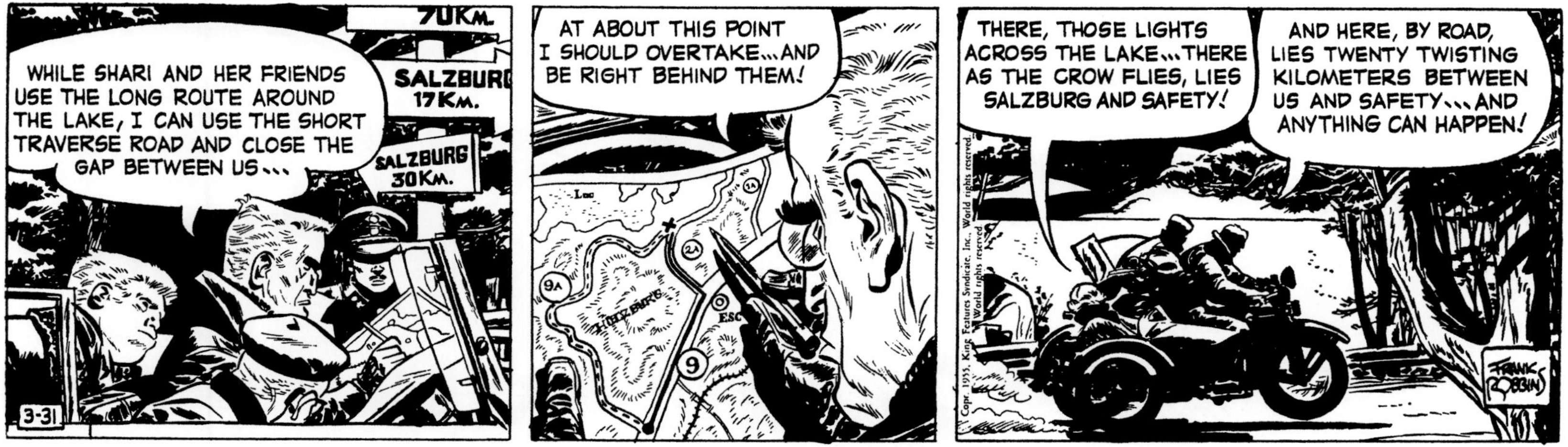
70KM.
SALZBURG 17KM.
WHILE SHARI AND HER FRIENDS USE THE LONG ROUTE AROUND THE LAKE, I CAN USE THE SHORT TRAVERSE ROAD AND CLOSE THE GAP BETWEEN US...
SALZBURG 30KM.
3-31
AT ABOUT THIS POINT I SHOULD OVERTAKE...AND BE RIGHT BEHIND THEM!
THERE, THOSE LIGHTS ACROSS THE LAKE...THERE AS THE CROW FLIES, LIES SALZBURG AND SAFETY!
AND HERE, BY ROAD, LIES TWENTY TWISTING KILOMETERS BETWEEN US AND SAFETY...AND ANYTHING CAN HAPPEN!
Copr. 1955, King Features Syndicate, Inc., World rights reserved.
FRANK ROBBINS

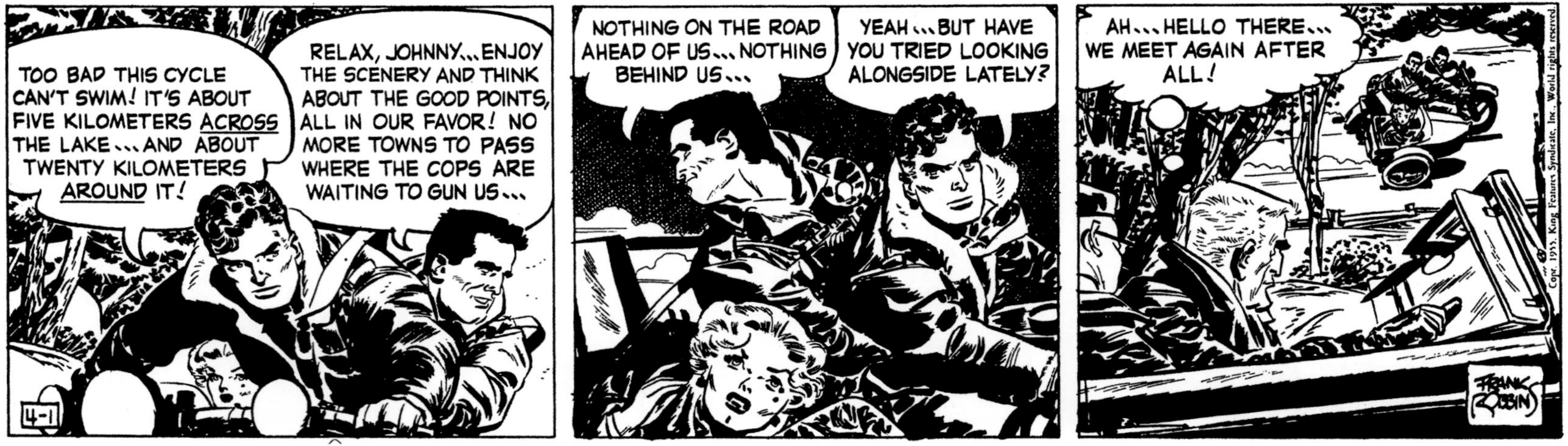
4-1
TOO BAD THIS CYCLE CAN'T SWIM! IT'S ABOUT FIVE KILOMETERS ACROSS THE LAKE... AND ABOUT TWENTY KILOMETERS AROUND IT!
RELAX, JOHNNY... ENJOY THE SCENERY AND THINK ABOUT THE GOOD POINTS, ALL IN OUR FAVOR! NO MORE TOWNS TO PASS WHERE THE COPS ARE WAITING TO GUN US...
NOTHING ON THE ROAD AHEAD OF US... NOTHING BEHIND US...
YEAH... BUT HAVE YOU TRIED LOOKING ALONGSIDE LATELY?
AH... HELLO THERE... WE MEET AGAIN AFTER ALL!
FRANK ROBBINS
Copr. 1955, King Features Syndicate, Inc., World rights reserved.

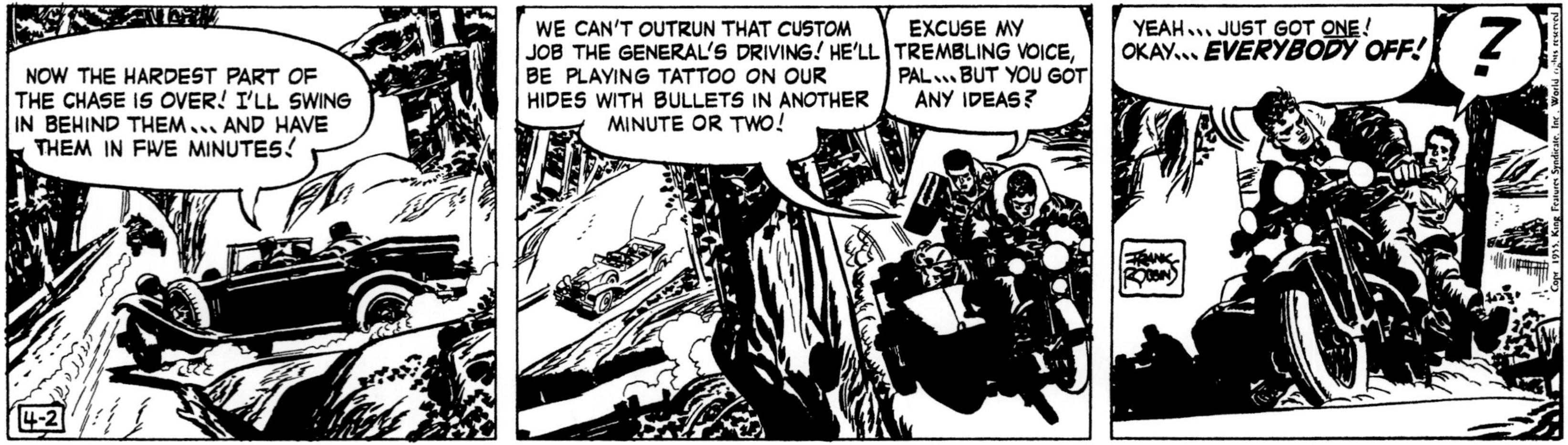
4-2
NOW THE HARDEST PART OF THE CHASE IS OVER! I'LL SWING IN BEHIND THEM... AND HAVE THEM IN FIVE MINUTES!
WE CAN'T OUTRUN THAT CUSTOM JOB THE GENERAL'S DRIVING! HE'LL BE PLAYING TATTOO ON OUR HIDES WITH BULLETS IN ANOTHER MINUTE OR TWO!
EXCUSE MY TREMBLING VOICE, PAL... BUT YOU GOT ANY IDEAS?
YEAH... JUST GOT ONE! OKAY... EVERYBODY OFF!
?
FRANK ROBBINS

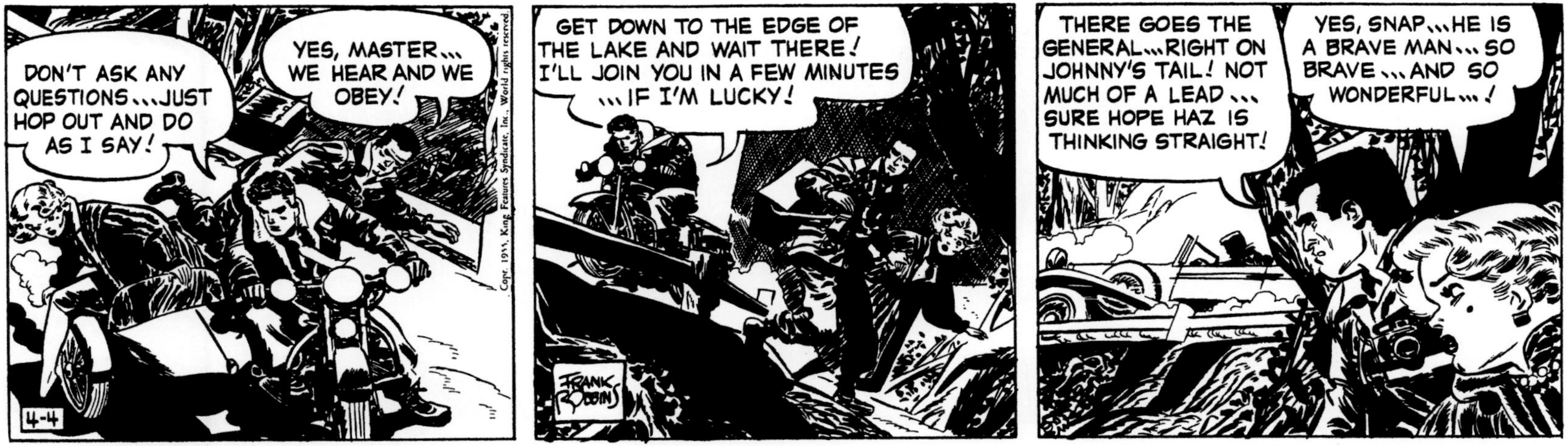
DON'T ASK ANY QUESTIONS...JUST HOP OUT AND DO AS I SAY!
YES, MASTER... WE HEAR AND WE OBEY!
Copr. 1955, King Features Syndicate, Inc., World rights reserved.
4-4
GET DOWN TO THE EDGE OF THE LAKE AND WAIT THERE! I'LL JOIN YOU IN A FEW MINUTES ...IF I'M LUCKY!
FRANK ROBBINS
THERE GOES THE GENERAL...RIGHT ON JOHNNY'S TAIL! NOT MUCH OF A LEAD... SURE HOPE HAZ IS THINKING STRAIGHT!
YES, SNAP...HE IS A BRAVE MAN... SO BRAVE... AND SO WONDERFUL...!

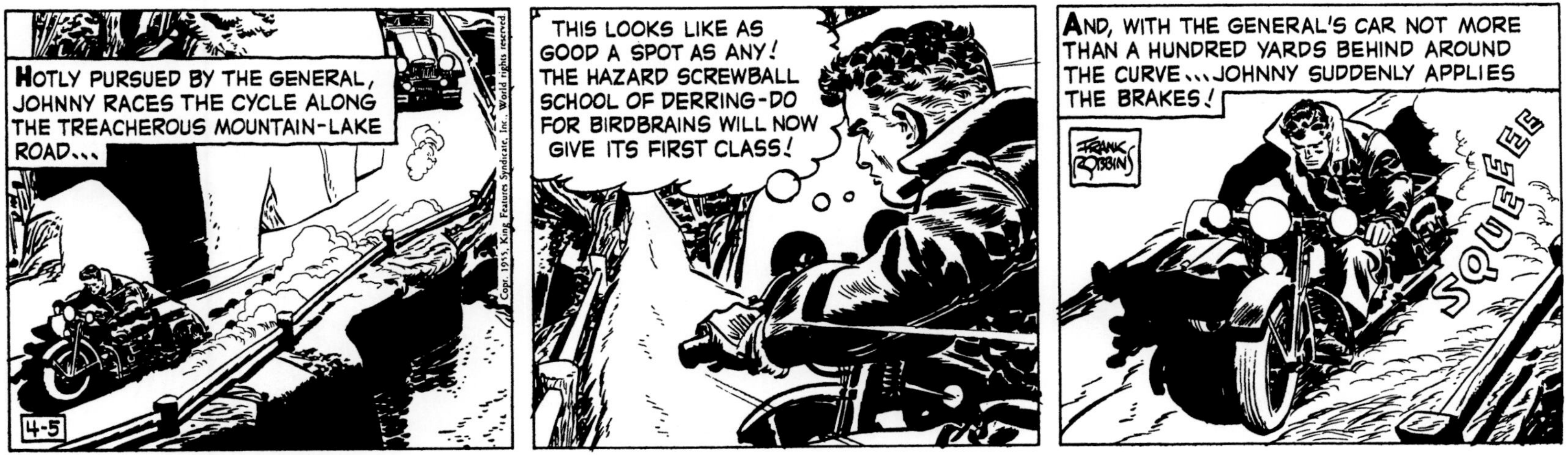
HOTLY PURSUED BY THE GENERAL, JOHNNY RACES THE CYCLE ALONG THE TREACHEROUS MOUNTAIN-LAKE ROAD...
Copr. 1955, King Features Syndicate, Inc., World rights reserved.
4-5
THIS LOOKS LIKE AS GOOD A SPOT AS ANY! THE HAZARD SCREWBALL SCHOOL OF DERRING-DO FOR BIRDBRAINS WILL NOW GIVE ITS FIRST CLASS!
AND, WITH THE GENERAL'S CAR NOT MORE THAN A HUNDRED YARDS BEHIND AROUND THE CURVE...JOHNNY SUDDENLY APPLIES THE BRAKES!
FRANK ROBBINS
SQUEEE

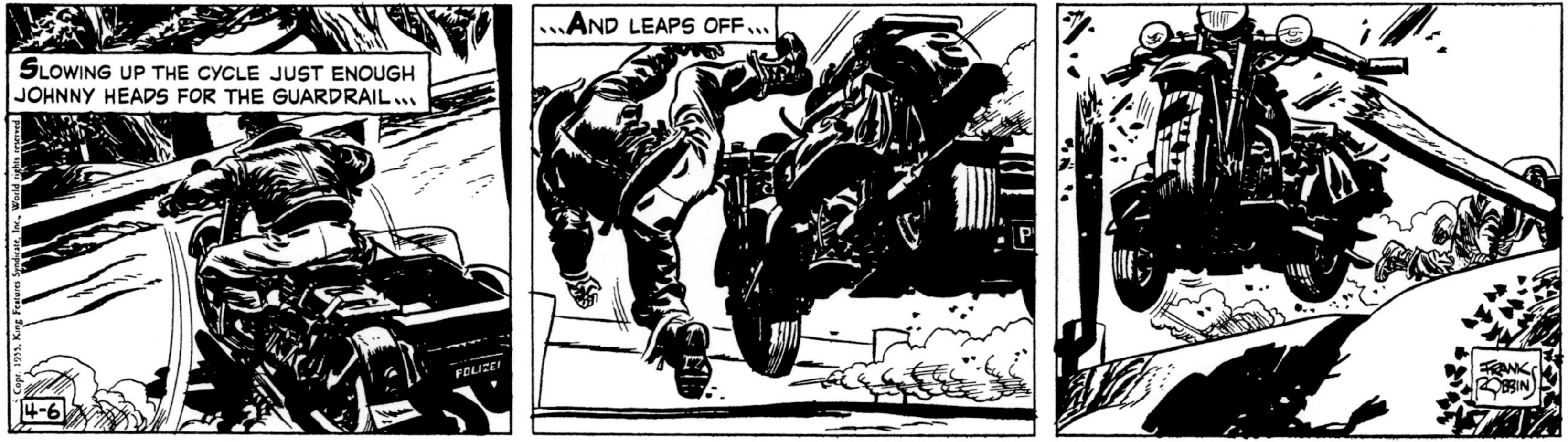
SLOWING UP THE CYCLE JUST ENOUGH JOHNNY HEADS FOR THE GUARDRAIL...
Copr. 1955, King Features Syndicate, Inc., World rights reserved
4-6
POLIZEI
...AND LEAPS OFF...
FRANK ROBBINS

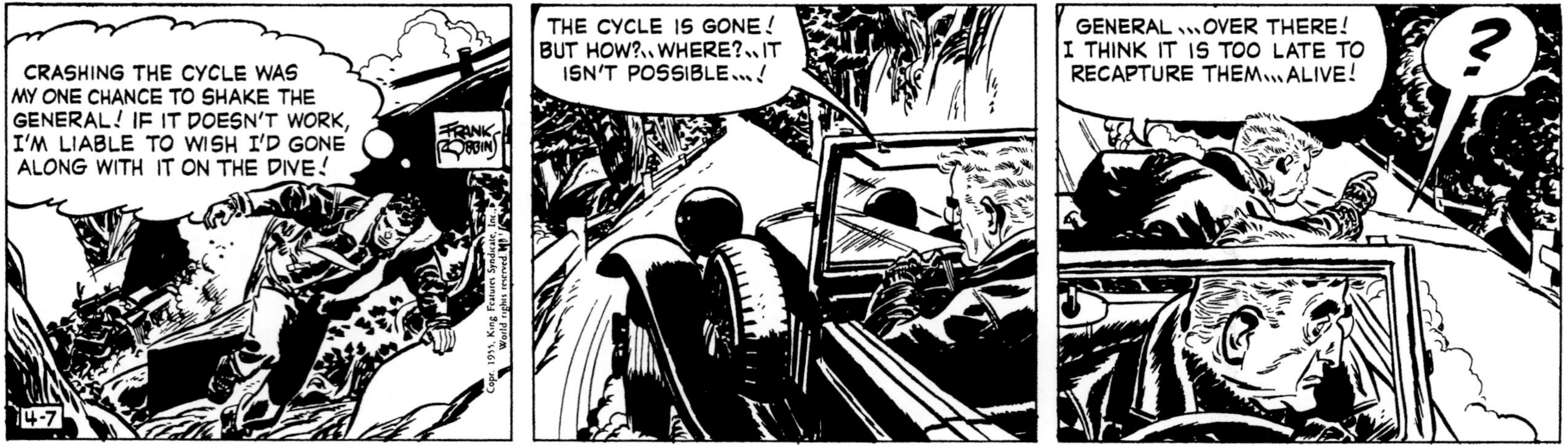
CRASHING THE CYCLE WAS MY ONE CHANCE TO SHAKE THE GENERAL! IF IT DOESN'T WORK, I'M LIABLE TO WISH I'D GONE ALONG WITH IT ON THE DIVE!
FRANK ROBBINS
Copr. 1955, King Features Syndicate, Inc., World rights reserved
4-7
THE CYCLE IS GONE! BUT HOW?.. WHERE?.. IT ISN'T POSSIBLE...!
GENERAL...OVER THERE! I THINK IT IS TOO LATE TO RECAPTURE THEM...ALIVE!
?

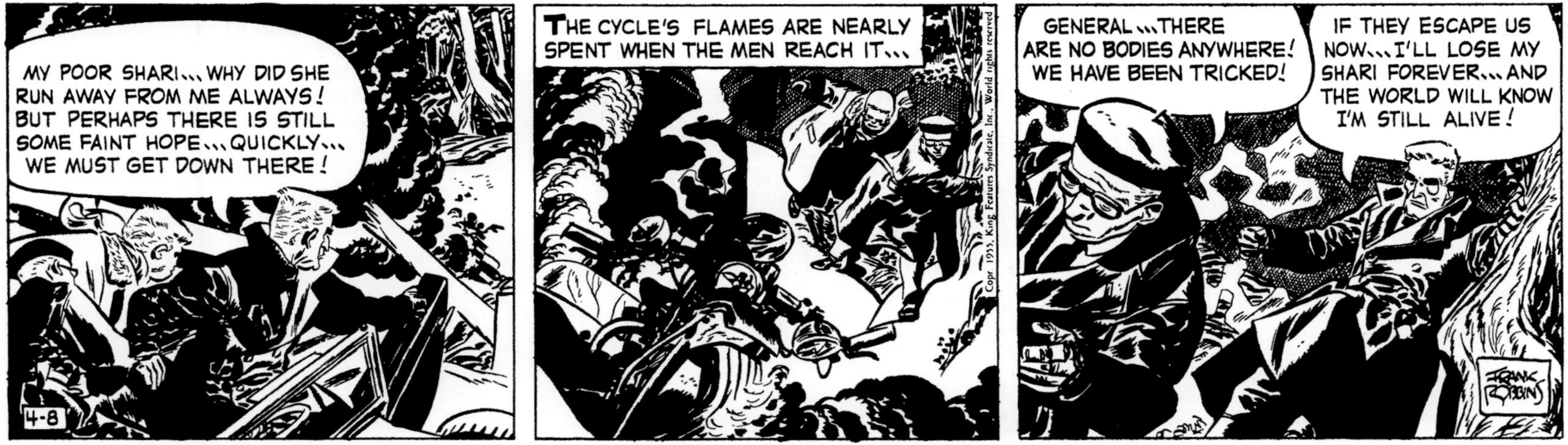
4-8
MY POOR SHARI... WHY DID SHE RUN AWAY FROM ME ALWAYS! BUT PERHAPS THERE IS STILL SOME FAINT HOPE... QUICKLY... WE MUST GET DOWN THERE!
THE CYCLE'S FLAMES ARE NEARLY SPENT WHEN THE MEN REACH IT...
Copr. 1955, King Features Syndicate, Inc., World rights reserved
GENERAL... THERE ARE NO BODIES ANYWHERE! WE HAVE BEEN TRICKED!
IF THEY ESCAPE US NOW... I'LL LOSE MY SHARI FOREVER... AND THE WORLD WILL KNOW I'M STILL ALIVE!
FRANK ROBBINS

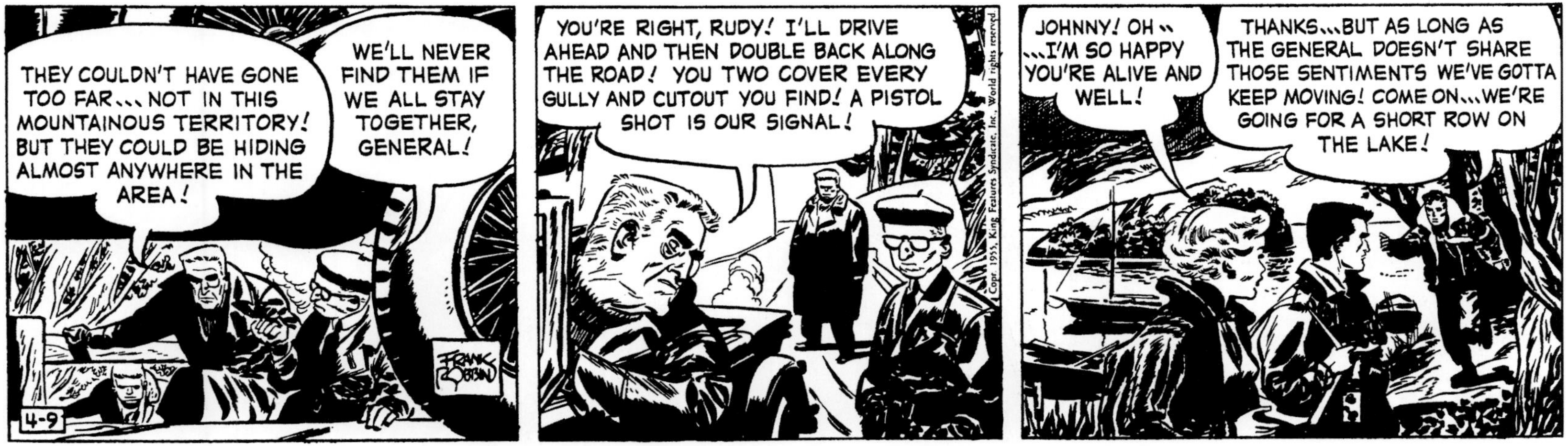
4-9
THEY COULDN'T HAVE GONE TOO FAR... NOT IN THIS MOUNTAINOUS TERRITORY! BUT THEY COULD BE HIDING ALMOST ANYWHERE IN THE AREA!
WE'LL NEVER FIND THEM IF WE ALL STAY TOGETHER, GENERAL!
FRANK ROBBINS
YOU'RE RIGHT, RUDY! I'LL DRIVE AHEAD AND THEN DOUBLE BACK ALONG THE ROAD! YOU TWO COVER EVERY GULLY AND CUTOUT YOU FIND! A PISTOL SHOT IS OUR SIGNAL!
Copr. 1955, King Features Syndicate, Inc., World rights reserved.
JOHNNY! OH... ...I'M SO HAPPY YOU'RE ALIVE AND WELL!
THANKS... BUT AS LONG AS THE GENERAL DOESN'T SHARE THOSE SENTIMENTS WE'VE GOTTA KEEP MOVING! COME ON... WE'RE GOING FOR A SHORT ROW ON THE LAKE!

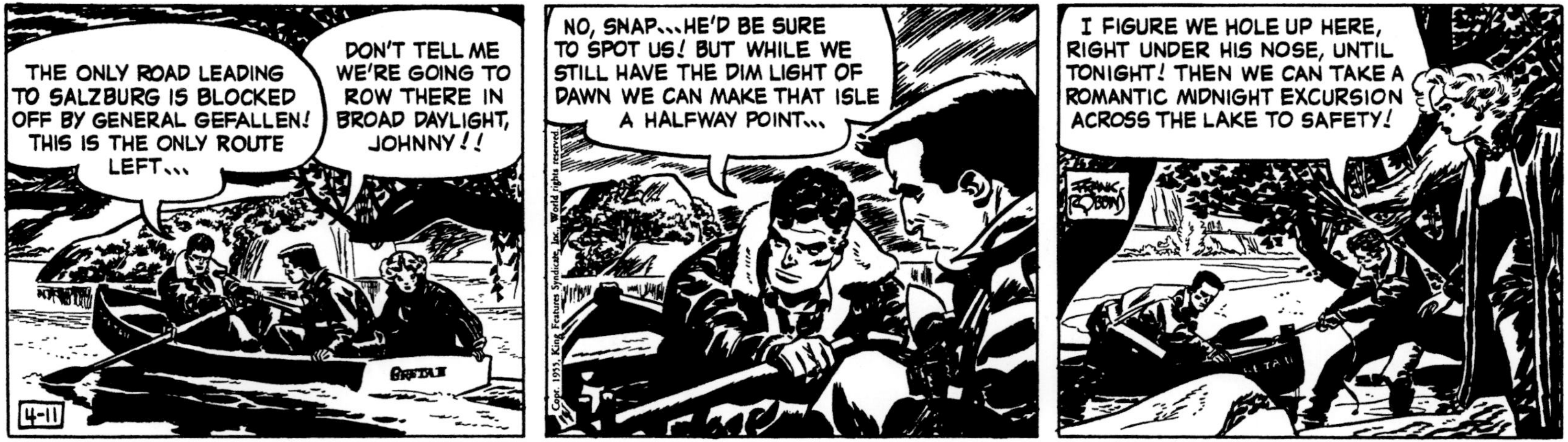

THE ONLY ROAD LEADING TO SALZBURG IS BLOCKED OFF BY GENERAL GEFALLEN! THIS IS THE ONLY ROUTE LEFT...
DON'T TELL ME WE'RE GOING TO ROW THERE IN BROAD DAYLIGHT, JOHNNY!!
4-11
NO, SNAP...HE'D BE SURE TO SPOT US! BUT WHILE WE STILL HAVE THE DIM LIGHT OF DAWN WE CAN MAKE THAT ISLE A HALFWAY POINT...
Copr. 1955, King Features Syndicate, Inc., World rights reserved.
I FIGURE WE HOLE UP HERE, RIGHT UNDER HIS NOSE, UNTIL TONIGHT! THEN WE CAN TAKE A ROMANTIC MIDNIGHT EXCURSION ACROSS THE LAKE TO SAFETY!
FRANK ROBBINS

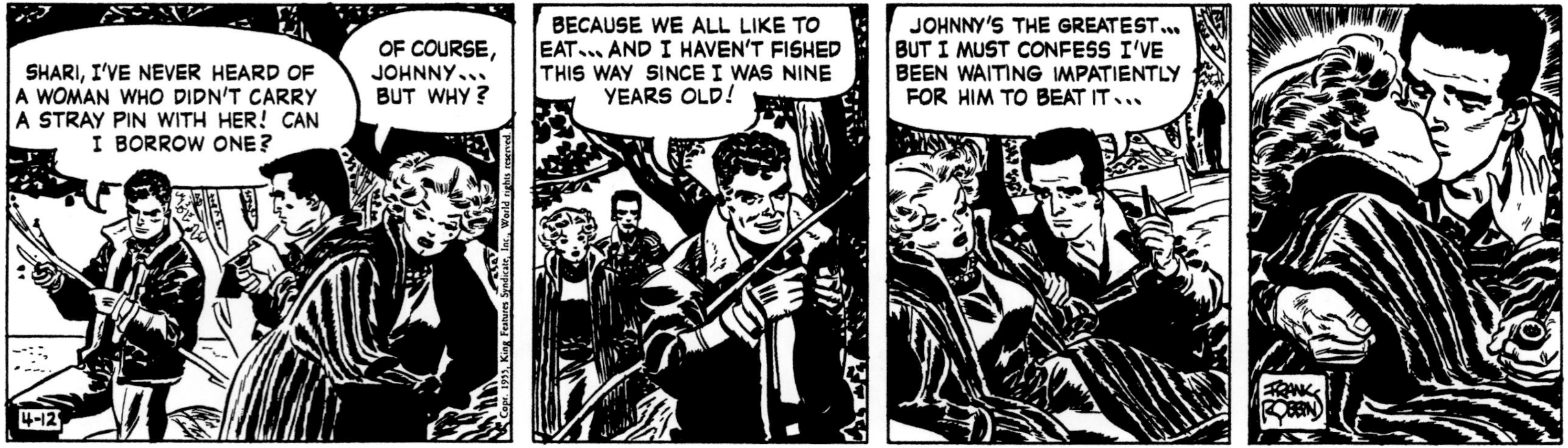

SHARI, I'VE NEVER HEARD OF A WOMAN WHO DIDN'T CARRY A STRAY PIN WITH HER! CAN I BORROW ONE?
OF COURSE, JOHNNY... BUT WHY?
4-12
Copr. 1955, King Features Syndicate, Inc., World rights reserved.
BECAUSE WE ALL LIKE TO EAT... AND I HAVEN'T FISHED THIS WAY SINCE I WAS NINE YEARS OLD!
JOHNNY'S THE GREATEST... BUT I MUST CONFESS I'VE BEEN WAITING IMPATIENTLY FOR HIM TO BEAT IT...
FRANK ROBBINS

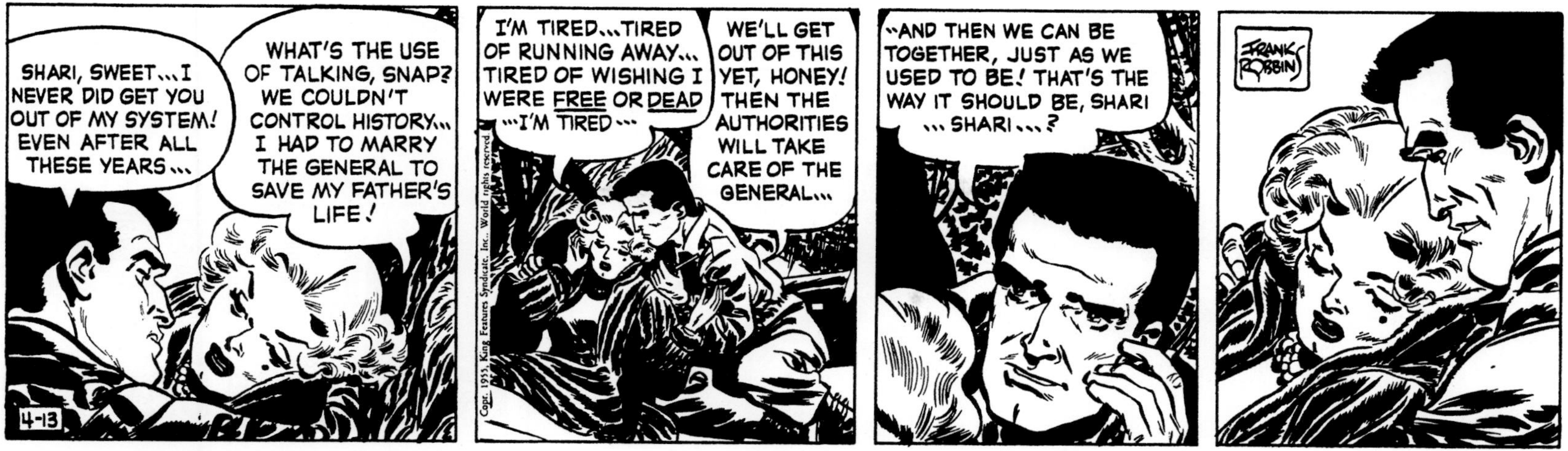
SHARI, SWEET... I NEVER DID GET YOU OUT OF MY SYSTEM! EVEN AFTER ALL THESE YEARS...
WHAT'S THE USE OF TALKING, SNAP? WE COULDN'T CONTROL HISTORY... I HAD TO MARRY THE GENERAL TO SAVE MY FATHER'S LIFE!
4-13
I'M TIRED... TIRED OF RUNNING AWAY... TIRED OF WISHING I WERE FREE OR DEAD ...I'M TIRED...
WE'LL GET OUT OF THIS YET, HONEY! THEN THE AUTHORITIES WILL TAKE CARE OF THE GENERAL...
Copr. 1955, King Features Syndicate, Inc., World rights reserved.
...AND THEN WE CAN BE TOGETHER, JUST AS WE USED TO BE! THAT'S THE WAY IT SHOULD BE, SHARI ... SHARI ... ?
FRANK ROBBINS

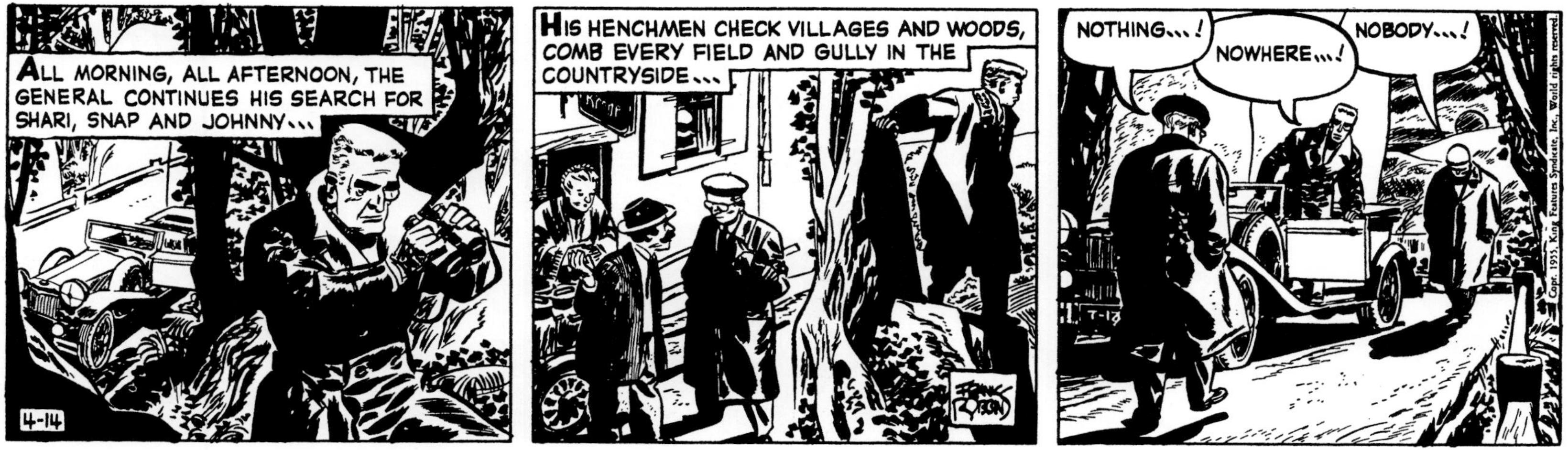
ALL MORNING, ALL AFTERNOON, THE GENERAL CONTINUES HIS SEARCH FOR SHARI, SNAP AND JOHNNY...
4-14
HIS HENCHMEN CHECK VILLAGES AND WOODS, COMB EVERY FIELD AND GULLY IN THE COUNTRYSIDE...
FRANK ROBBINS
NOTHING...!
NOWHERE...!
NOBODY...!
Copr. 1955, King Features Syndicate, Inc., World rights reserved.

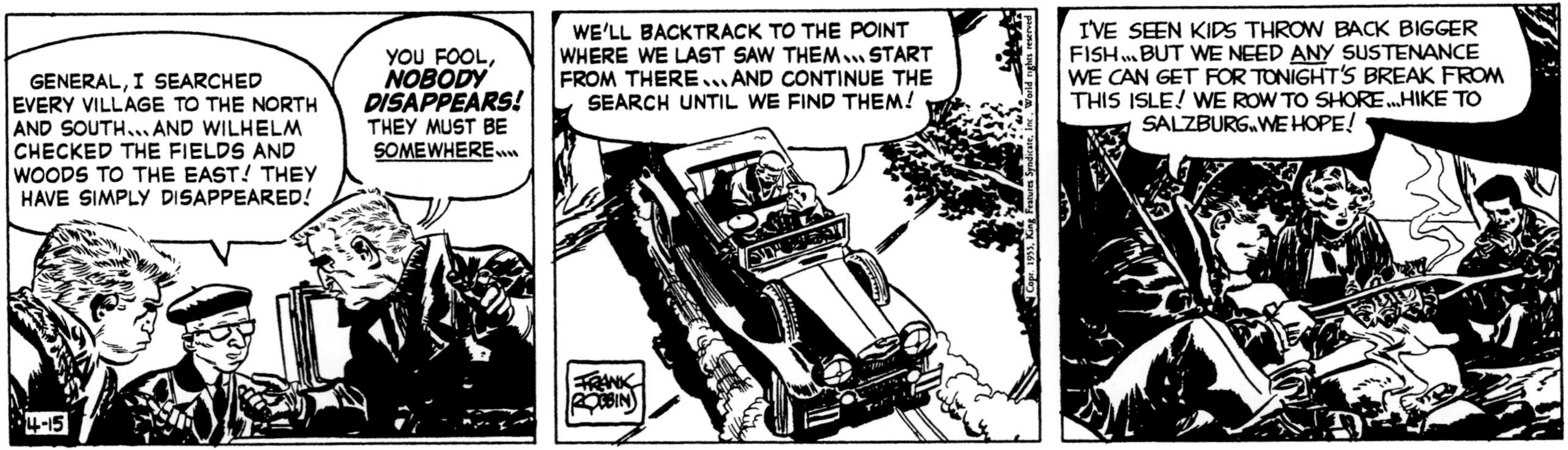
4-15
GENERAL, I SEARCHED EVERY VILLAGE TO THE NORTH AND SOUTH... AND WILHELM CHECKED THE FIELDS AND WOODS TO THE EAST! THEY HAVE SIMPLY DISAPPEARED!
YOU FOOL, NOBODY DISAPPEARS! THEY MUST BE SOMEWHERE....
WE'LL BACKTRACK TO THE POINT WHERE WE LAST SAW THEM... START FROM THERE... AND CONTINUE THE SEARCH UNTIL WE FIND THEM!
FRANK ROBBINS
Copr. 1955, King Features Syndicate, Inc., World rights reserved
I'VE SEEN KIDS THROW BACK BIGGER FISH... BUT WE NEED ANY SUSTENANCE WE CAN GET FOR TONIGHT'S BREAK FROM THIS ISLE! WE ROW TO SHORE...HIKE TO SALZBURG..WE HOPE!

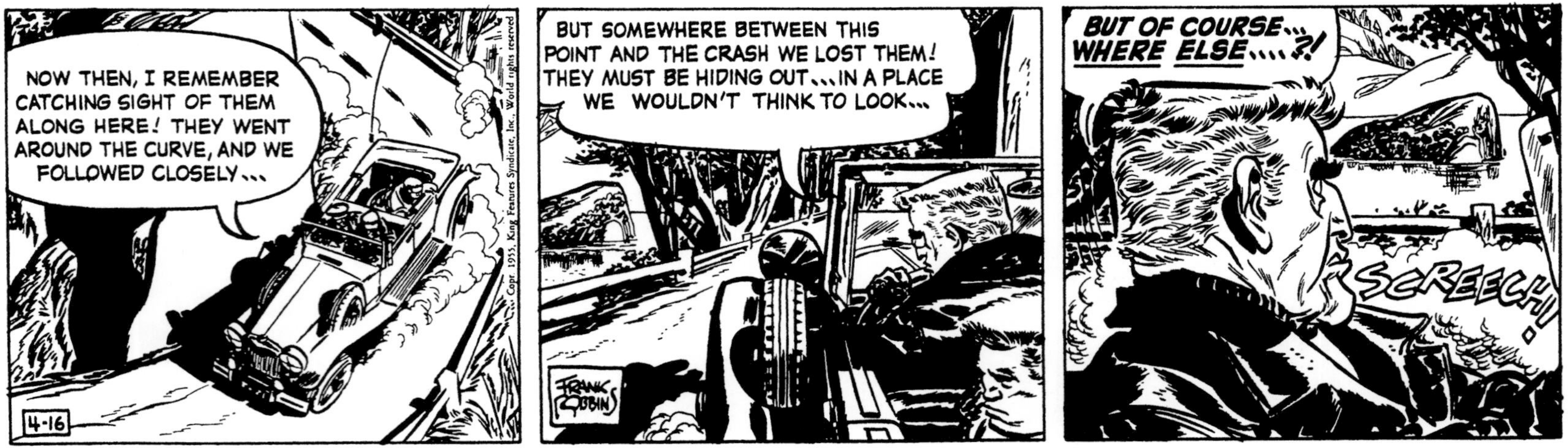
4-16
NOW THEN, I REMEMBER CATCHING SIGHT OF THEM ALONG HERE! THEY WENT AROUND THE CURVE, AND WE FOLLOWED CLOSELY...
Copr. 1955, King Features Syndicate, Inc., World rights reserved
BUT SOMEWHERE BETWEEN THIS POINT AND THE CRASH WE LOST THEM! THEY MUST BE HIDING OUT... IN A PLACE WE WOULDN'T THINK TO LOOK...
FRANK ROBBINS
BUT OF COURSE... WHERE ELSE....?!
SCREECH!

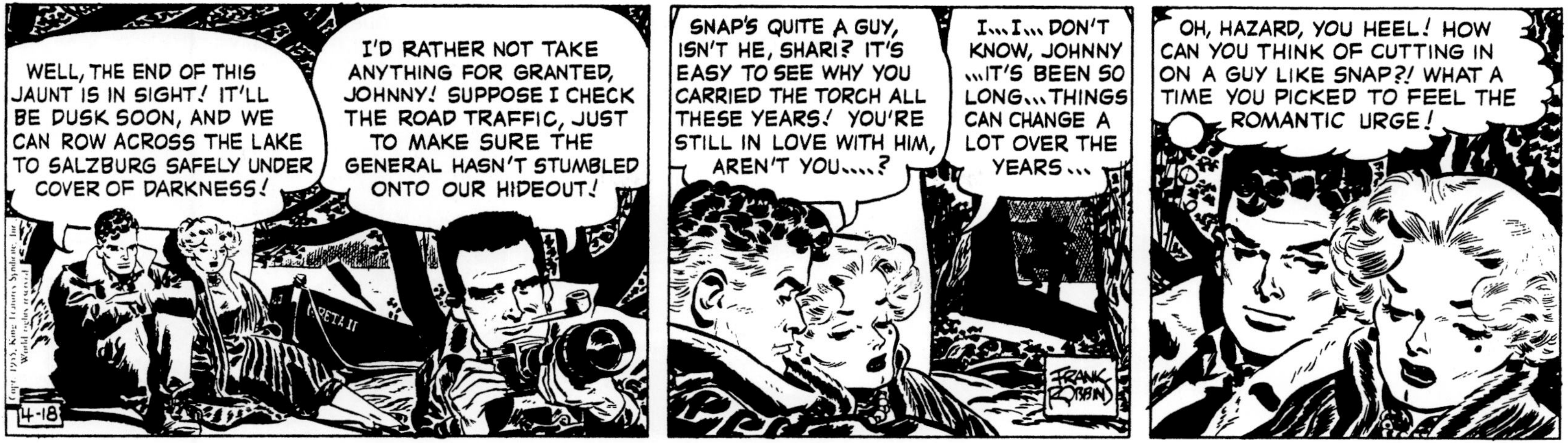
WELL, THE END OF THIS JAUNT IS IN SIGHT! IT'LL BE DUSK SOON, AND WE CAN ROW ACROSS THE LAKE TO SALZBURG SAFELY UNDER COVER OF DARKNESS!
I'D RATHER NOT TAKE ANYTHING FOR GRANTED, JOHNNY! SUPPOSE I CHECK THE ROAD TRAFFIC, JUST TO MAKE SURE THE GENERAL HASN'T STUMBLED ONTO OUR HIDEOUT!
4-18
GRETA II
SNAP'S QUITE A GUY, ISN'T HE, SHARI? IT'S EASY TO SEE WHY YOU CARRIED THE TORCH ALL THESE YEARS! YOU'RE STILL IN LOVE WITH HIM, AREN'T YOU....?
I...I... DON'T KNOW, JOHNNY ...IT'S BEEN SO LONG...THINGS CAN CHANGE A LOT OVER THE YEARS...
FRANK ROBBINS
OH, HAZARD, YOU HEEL! HOW CAN YOU THINK OF CUTTING IN ON A GUY LIKE SNAP?! WHAT A TIME YOU PICKED TO FEEL THE ROMANTIC URGE!

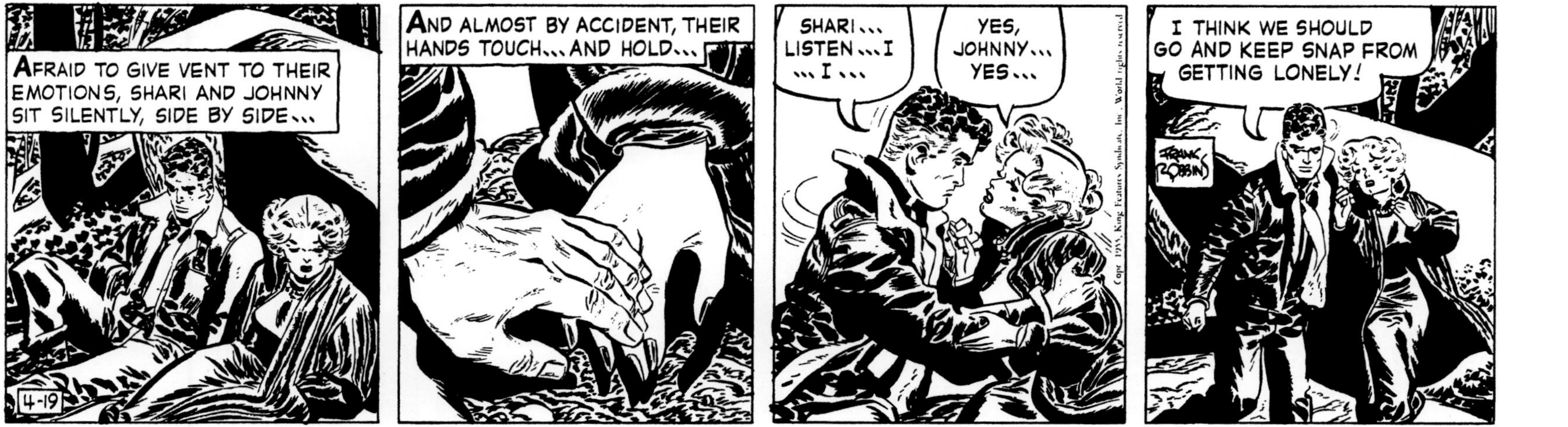
AFRAID TO GIVE VENT TO THEIR EMOTIONS, SHARI AND JOHNNY SIT SILENTLY, SIDE BY SIDE...
4-19
AND ALMOST BY ACCIDENT, THEIR HANDS TOUCH...AND HOLD...
SHARI... LISTEN...I ...I ...
YES, JOHNNY... YES...
I THINK WE SHOULD GO AND KEEP SNAP FROM GETTING LONELY!
FRANK ROBBINS

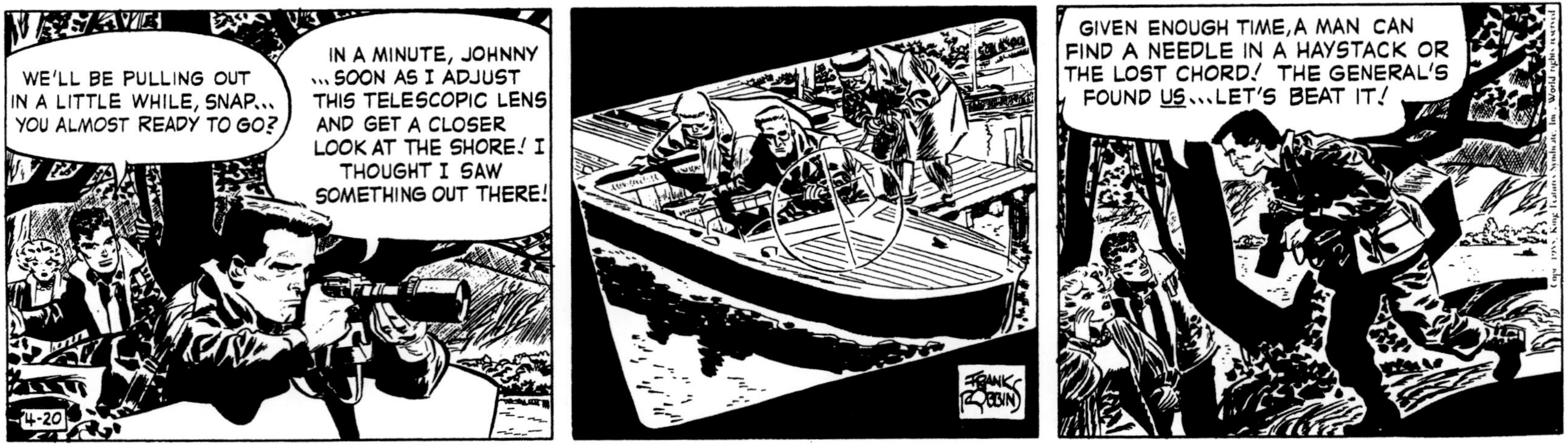
4-20
WE'LL BE PULLING OUT IN A LITTLE WHILE, SNAP... YOU ALMOST READY TO GO?
IN A MINUTE, JOHNNY ... SOON AS I ADJUST THIS TELESCOPIC LENS AND GET A CLOSER LOOK AT THE SHORE! I THOUGHT I SAW SOMETHING OUT THERE!
FRANK ROBBINS
GIVEN ENOUGH TIME, A MAN CAN FIND A NEEDLE IN A HAYSTACK OR THE LOST CHORD! THE GENERAL'S FOUND US ... LET'S BEAT IT!

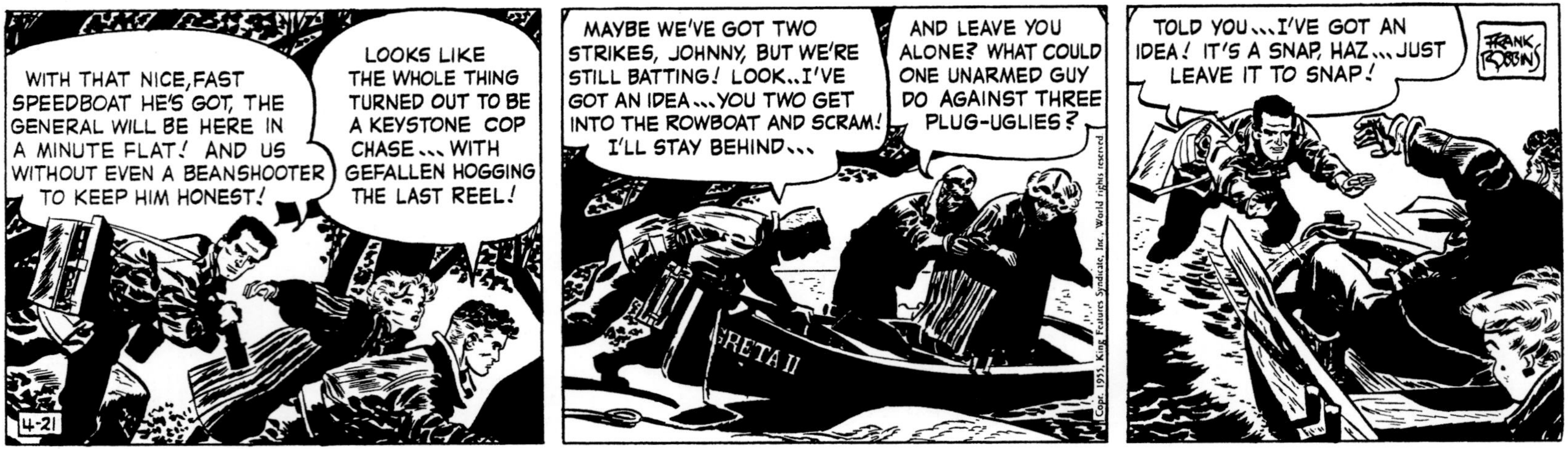
4-21
WITH THAT NICE, FAST SPEEDBOAT HE'S GOT, THE GENERAL WILL BE HERE IN A MINUTE FLAT! AND US WITHOUT EVEN A BEANSHOOTER TO KEEP HIM HONEST!
LOOKS LIKE THE WHOLE THING TURNED OUT TO BE A KEYSTONE COP CHASE ... WITH GEFALLEN HOGGING THE LAST REEL!
MAYBE WE'VE GOT TWO STRIKES, JOHNNY, BUT WE'RE STILL BATTING! LOOK.. I'VE GOT AN IDEA ... YOU TWO GET INTO THE ROWBOAT AND SCRAM! I'LL STAY BEHIND ...
AND LEAVE YOU ALONE? WHAT COULD ONE UNARMED GUY DO AGAINST THREE PLUG-UGLIES?
GRETA II
Copr. 1955, King Features Syndicate, Inc., World rights reserved
TOLD YOU ... I'VE GOT AN IDEA! IT'S A SNAP, HAZ ... JUST LEAVE IT TO SNAP!
FRANK ROBBINS

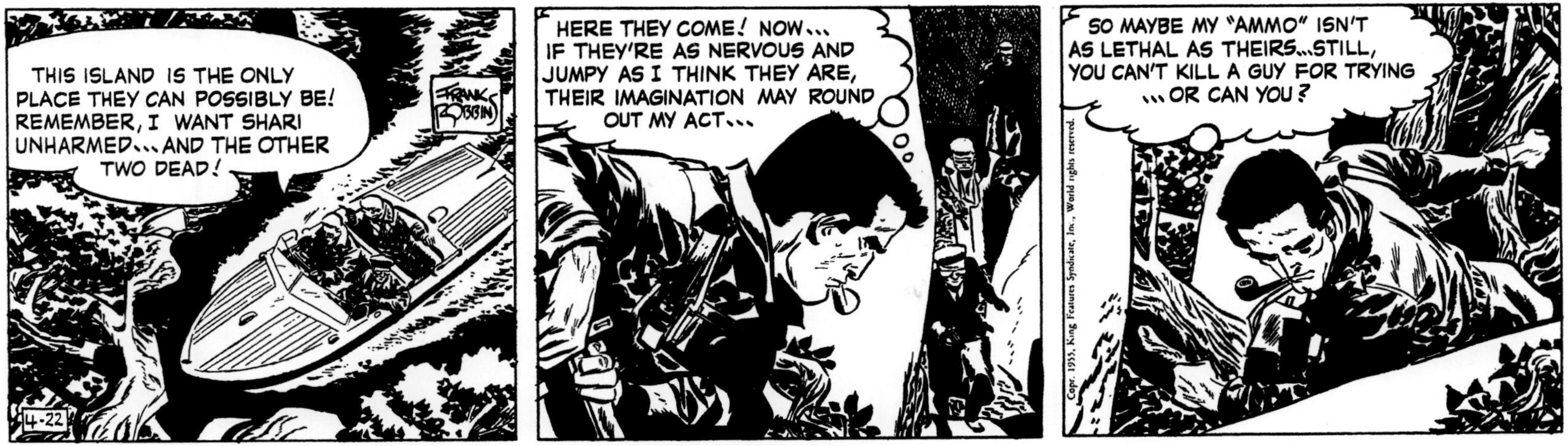
THIS ISLAND IS THE ONLY PLACE THEY CAN POSSIBLY BE! REMEMBER, I WANT SHARI UNHARMED... AND THE OTHER TWO DEAD!
FRANK ROBBINS
4-22
HERE THEY COME! NOW... IF THEY'RE AS NERVOUS AND JUMPY AS I THINK THEY ARE, THEIR IMAGINATION MAY ROUND OUT MY ACT...
SO MAYBE MY "AMMO" ISN'T AS LETHAL AS THEIRS...STILL, YOU CAN'T KILL A GUY FOR TRYING ...OR CAN YOU?
Copr. 1955, King Features Syndicate, Inc., World rights reserved.

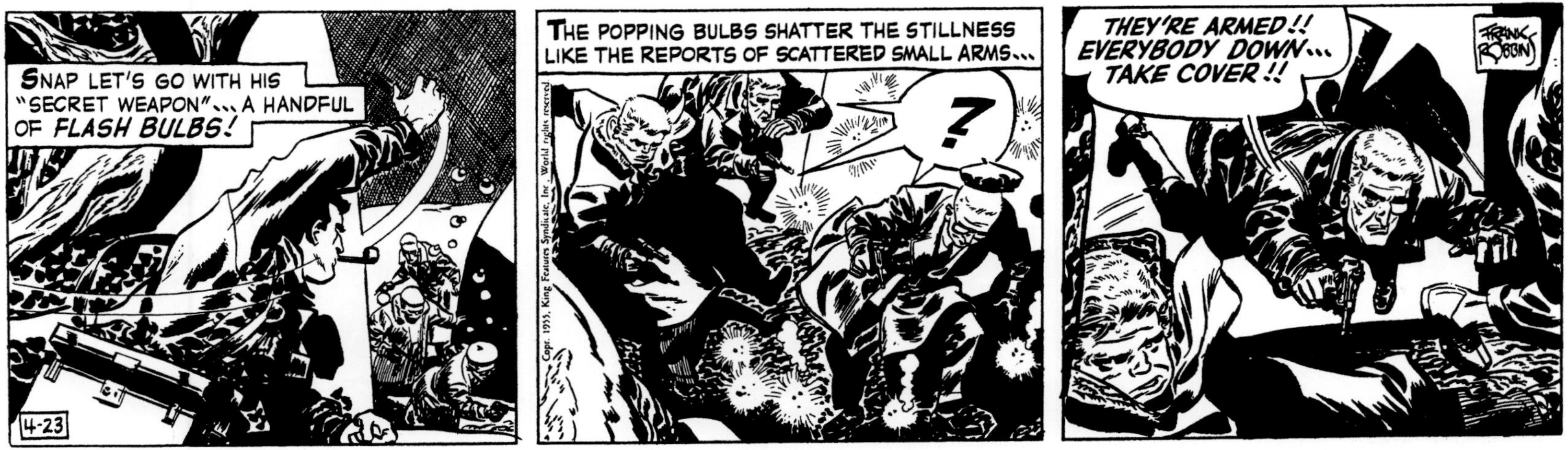
SNAP LET'S GO WITH HIS "SECRET WEAPON"... A HANDFUL OF FLASH BULBS!
4-23
THE POPPING BULBS SHATTER THE STILLNESS LIKE THE REPORTS OF SCATTERED SMALL ARMS...
?
Copr. 1955, King Features Syndicate, Inc., World rights reserved.
THEY'RE ARMED!! EVERYBODY DOWN... TAKE COVER!!
FRANK ROBBINS

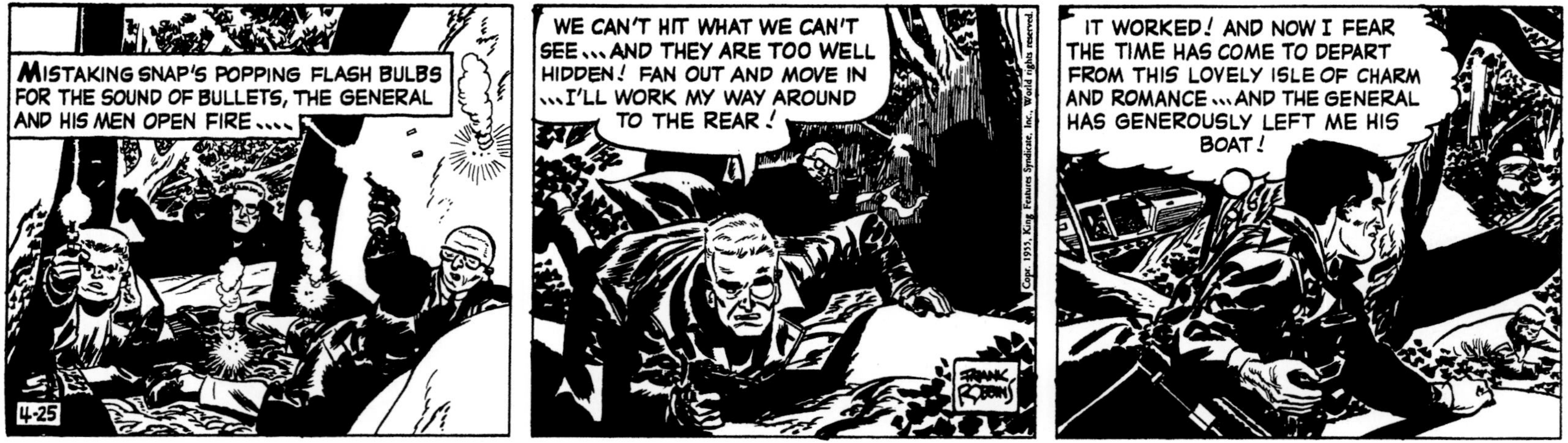
4-25
MISTAKING SNAP'S POPPING FLASH BULBS FOR THE SOUND OF BULLETS, THE GENERAL AND HIS MEN OPEN FIRE....
WE CAN'T HIT WHAT WE CAN'T SEE...AND THEY ARE TOO WELL HIDDEN! FAN OUT AND MOVE IN ...I'LL WORK MY WAY AROUND TO THE REAR!
Copr. 1955, King Features Syndicate, Inc., World rights reserved.
FRANK ROBBINS
IT WORKED! AND NOW I FEAR THE TIME HAS COME TO DEPART FROM THIS LOVELY ISLE OF CHARM AND ROMANCE...AND THE GENERAL HAS GENEROUSLY LEFT ME HIS BOAT!

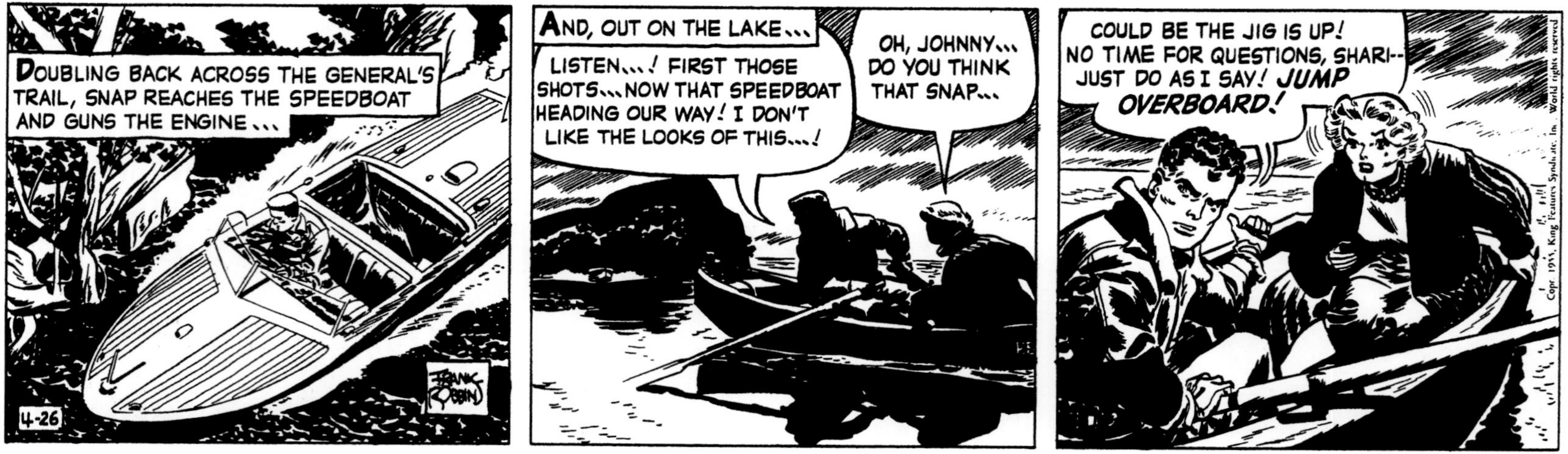
DOUBLING BACK ACROSS THE GENERAL'S TRAIL, SNAP REACHES THE SPEEDBOAT AND GUNS THE ENGINE...
FRANK ROBBINS
4-26
AND, OUT ON THE LAKE...
LISTEN...! FIRST THOSE SHOTS...NOW THAT SPEEDBOAT HEADING OUR WAY! I DON'T LIKE THE LOOKS OF THIS...!
OH, JOHNNY... DO YOU THINK THAT SNAP...
COULD BE THE JIG IS UP! NO TIME FOR QUESTIONS, SHARI-- JUST DO AS I SAY! JUMP OVERBOARD!
Copr. 1955, King Features Syndicate, Inc. World rights reserved

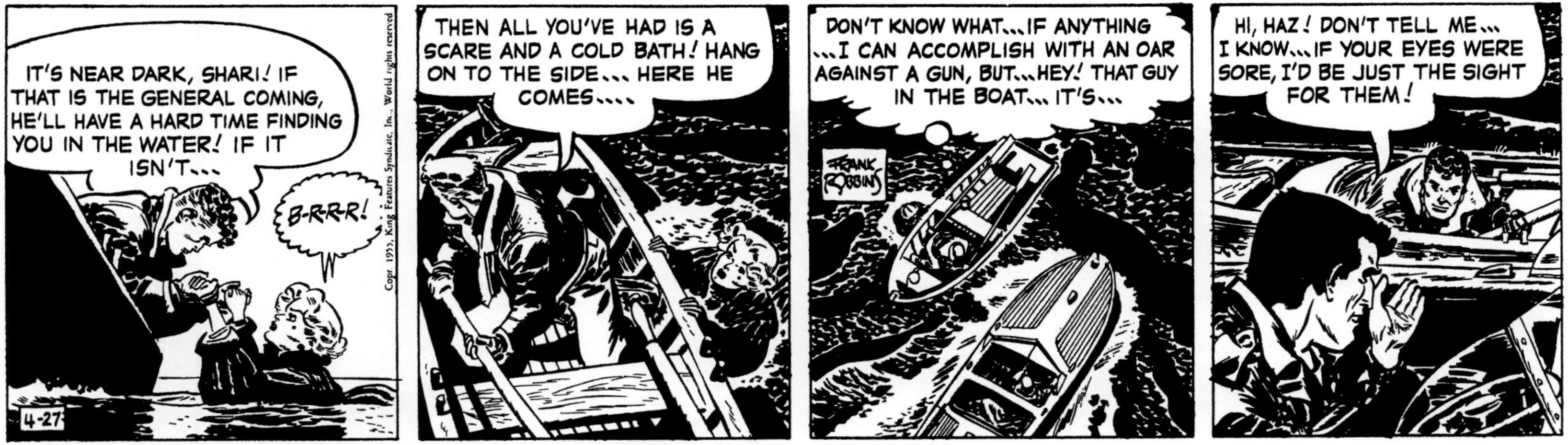
IT'S NEAR DARK, SHARI! IF THAT IS THE GENERAL COMING, HE'LL HAVE A HARD TIME FINDING YOU IN THE WATER! IF IT ISN'T...
B-R-R-R!
4-27
Copr. 1955, King Features Syndicate, Inc., World rights reserved
THEN ALL YOU'VE HAD IS A SCARE AND A COLD BATH! HANG ON TO THE SIDE... HERE HE COMES....
DON'T KNOW WHAT...IF ANYTHING ...I CAN ACCOMPLISH WITH AN OAR AGAINST A GUN, BUT...HEY! THAT GUY IN THE BOAT... IT'S...
FRANK ROBBINS
HI, HAZ! DON'T TELL ME... I KNOW...IF YOUR EYES WERE SORE, I'D BE JUST THE SIGHT FOR THEM!

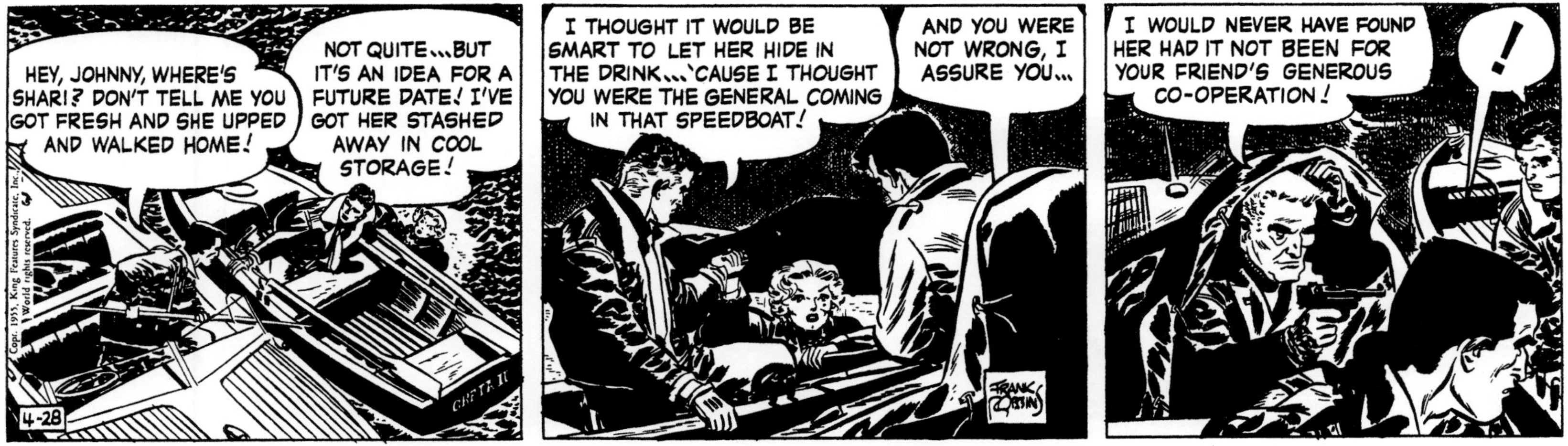
HEY, JOHNNY, WHERE'S SHARI? DON'T TELL ME YOU GOT FRESH AND SHE UPPED AND WALKED HOME!
NOT QUITE...BUT IT'S AN IDEA FOR A FUTURE DATE! I'VE GOT HER STASHED AWAY IN COOL STORAGE!
Copr. 1955, King Features Syndicate, Inc., World rights reserved.
4-28
I THOUGHT IT WOULD BE SMART TO LET HER HIDE IN THE DRINK...'CAUSE I THOUGHT YOU WERE THE GENERAL COMING IN THAT SPEEDBOAT!
AND YOU WERE NOT WRONG, I ASSURE YOU...
FRANK ROBBINS
I WOULD NEVER HAVE FOUND HER HAD IT NOT BEEN FOR YOUR FRIEND'S GENEROUS CO-OPERATION!
!

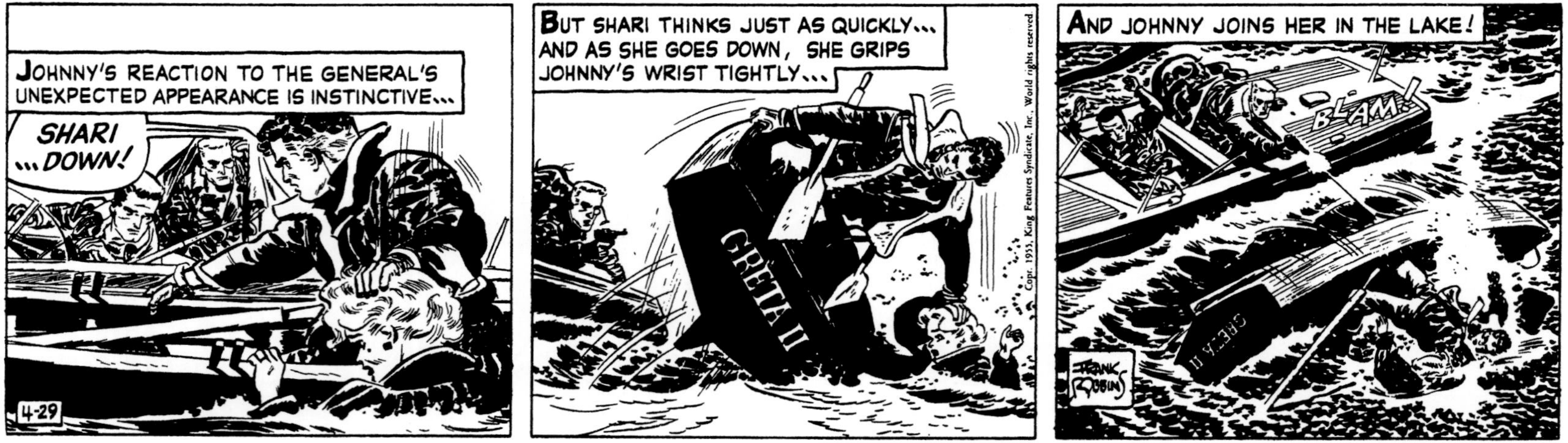
JOHNNY'S REACTION TO THE GENERAL'S UNEXPECTED APPEARANCE IS INSTINCTIVE...
SHARI ...DOWN!
4-29
BUT SHARI THINKS JUST AS QUICKLY... AND AS SHE GOES DOWN, SHE GRIPS JOHNNY'S WRIST TIGHTLY...
GRETA II
Copr. 1955, King Features Syndicate, Inc., World rights reserved.
AND JOHNNY JOINS HER IN THE LAKE!
BLAM!
FRANK ROBBINS

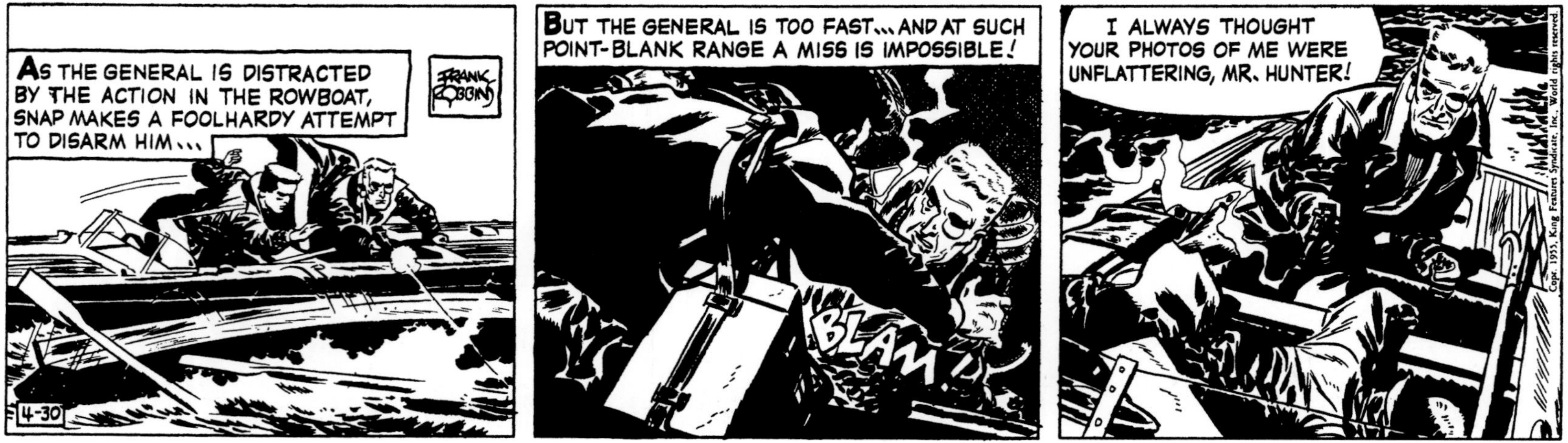
AS THE GENERAL IS DISTRACTED BY THE ACTION IN THE ROWBOAT, SNAP MAKES A FOOLHARDY ATTEMPT TO DISARM HIM...
FRANK ROBBINS
4-30
BUT THE GENERAL IS TOO FAST... AND AT SUCH POINT-BLANK RANGE A MISS IS IMPOSSIBLE!
BLAM!
I ALWAYS THOUGHT YOUR PHOTOS OF ME WERE UNFLATTERING, MR. HUNTER!
Copr. 1955, King Features Syndicate, Inc., World rights reserved.

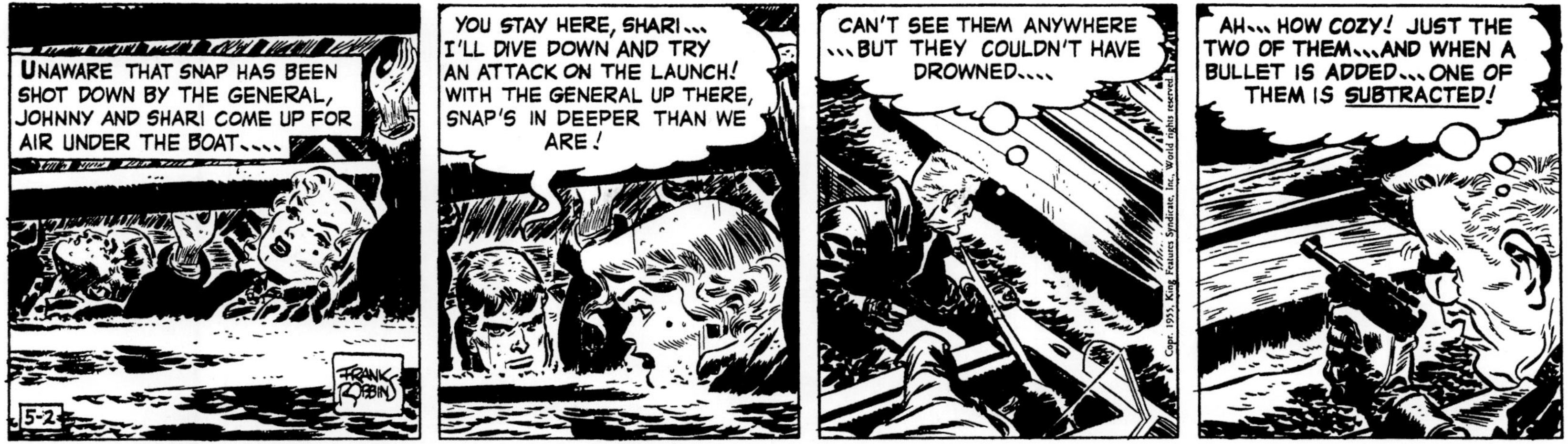

UNAWARE THAT SNAP HAS BEEN SHOT DOWN BY THE GENERAL, JOHNNY AND SHARI COME UP FOR AIR UNDER THE BOAT....
FRANK ROBBIN
5-2
YOU STAY HERE, SHARI... I'LL DIVE DOWN AND TRY AN ATTACK ON THE LAUNCH! WITH THE GENERAL UP THERE, SNAP'S IN DEEPER THAN WE ARE!
CAN'T SEE THEM ANYWHERE ...BUT THEY COULDN'T HAVE DROWNED....
Copr. 1955, King Features Syndicate, Inc., World rights reserved.
AH... HOW COZY! JUST THE TWO OF THEM...AND WHEN A BULLET IS ADDED... ONE OF THEM IS SUBTRACTED!

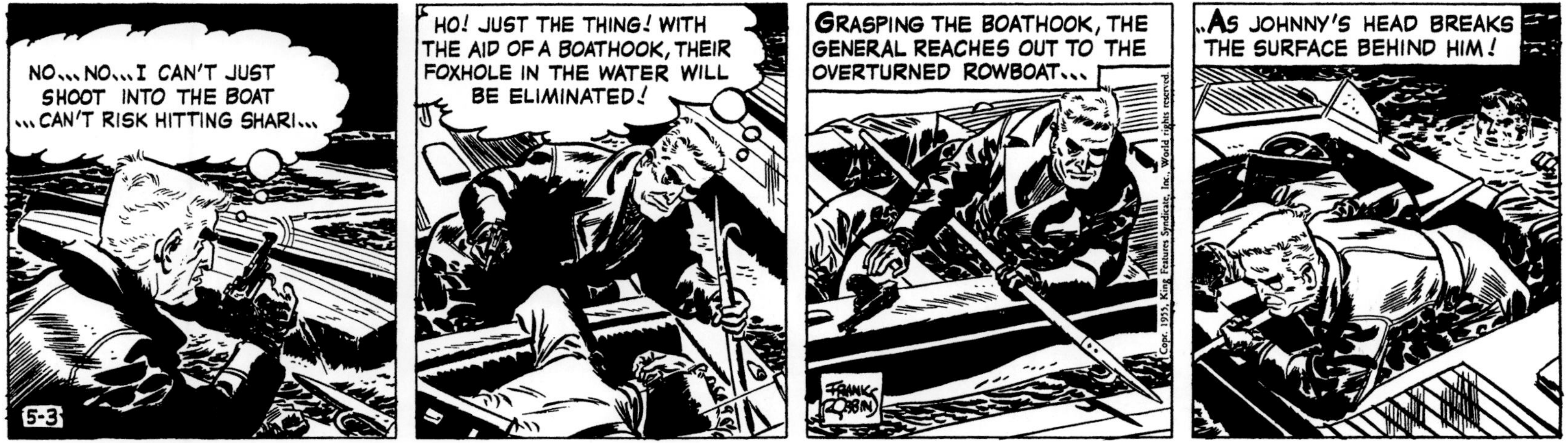

NO... NO... I CAN'T JUST SHOOT INTO THE BOAT ...CAN'T RISK HITTING SHARI...
5-3
HO! JUST THE THING! WITH THE AID OF A BOATHOOK, THEIR FOXHOLE IN THE WATER WILL BE ELIMINATED!
GRASPING THE BOATHOOK, THE GENERAL REACHES OUT TO THE OVERTURNED ROWBOAT...
Copr. 1955, King Features Syndicate, Inc., World rights reserved.
FRANK ROBBIN
..AS JOHNNY'S HEAD BREAKS THE SURFACE BEHIND HIM!

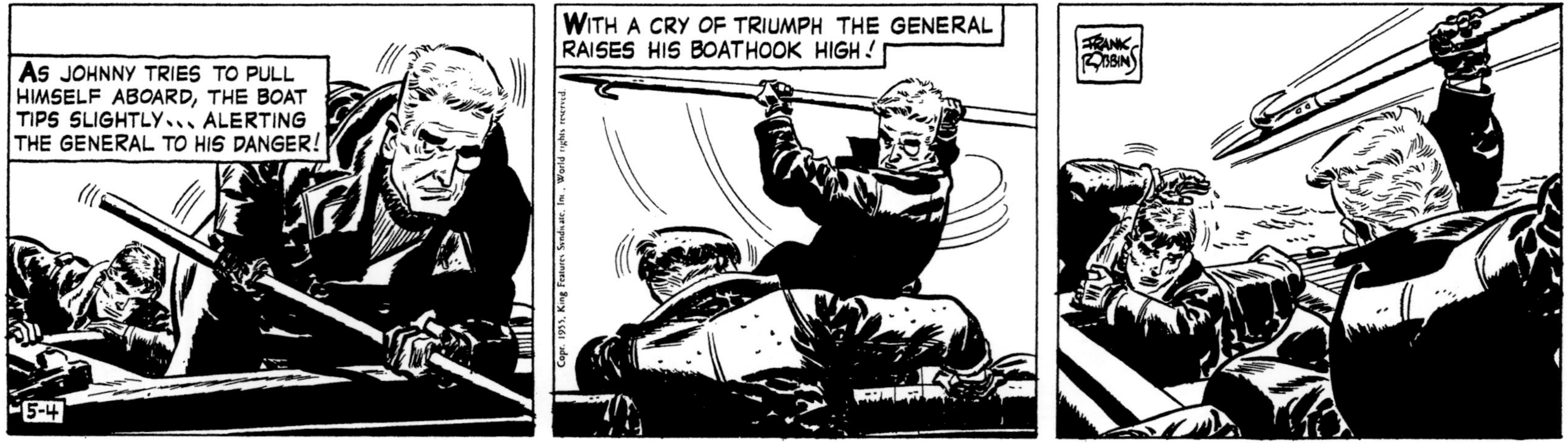
AS JOHNNY TRIES TO PULL HIMSELF ABOARD, THE BOAT TIPS SLIGHTLY... ALERTING THE GENERAL TO HIS DANGER!
5-4
WITH A CRY OF TRIUMPH THE GENERAL RAISES HIS BOATHOOK HIGH!
Copr. 1955, King Features Syndicate, Inc., World rights reserved.
FRANK ROBBINS

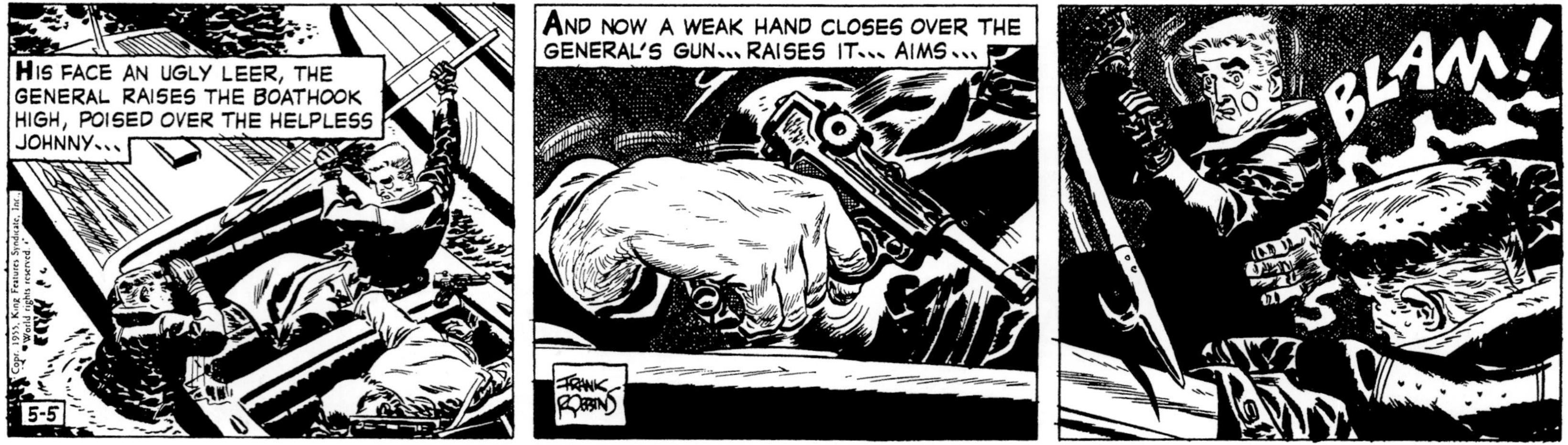
HIS FACE AN UGLY LEER, THE GENERAL RAISES THE BOATHOOK HIGH, POISED OVER THE HELPLESS JOHNNY...
Copr. 1955, King Features Syndicate, Inc. World rights reserved.
5-5
AND NOW A WEAK HAND CLOSES OVER THE GENERAL'S GUN... RAISES IT... AIMS...
FRANK ROBBINS
BLAM!

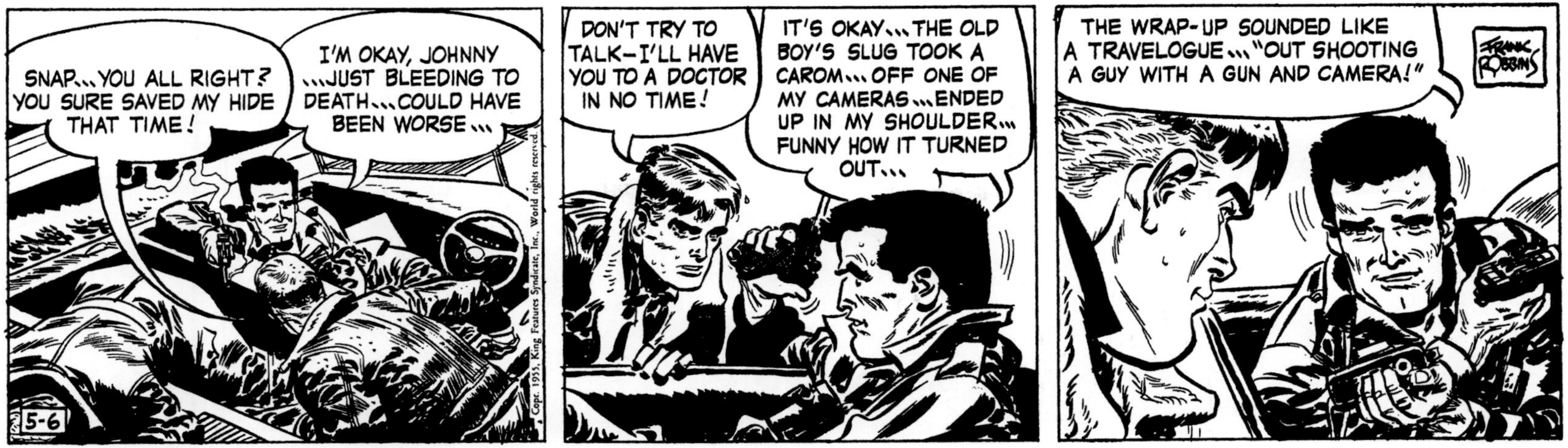
5-6
SNAP... YOU ALL RIGHT? YOU SURE SAVED MY HIDE THAT TIME!
I'M OKAY, JOHNNY ...JUST BLEEDING TO DEATH... COULD HAVE BEEN WORSE...
Copr. 1955, King Features Syndicate, Inc., World rights reserved.
DON'T TRY TO TALK—I'LL HAVE YOU TO A DOCTOR IN NO TIME!
IT'S OKAY... THE OLD BOY'S SLUG TOOK A CAROM... OFF ONE OF MY CAMERAS... ENDED UP IN MY SHOULDER... FUNNY HOW IT TURNED OUT...
THE WRAP-UP SOUNDED LIKE A TRAVELOGUE... "OUT SHOOTING A GUY WITH A GUN AND CAMERA!"
FRANK ROBBINS

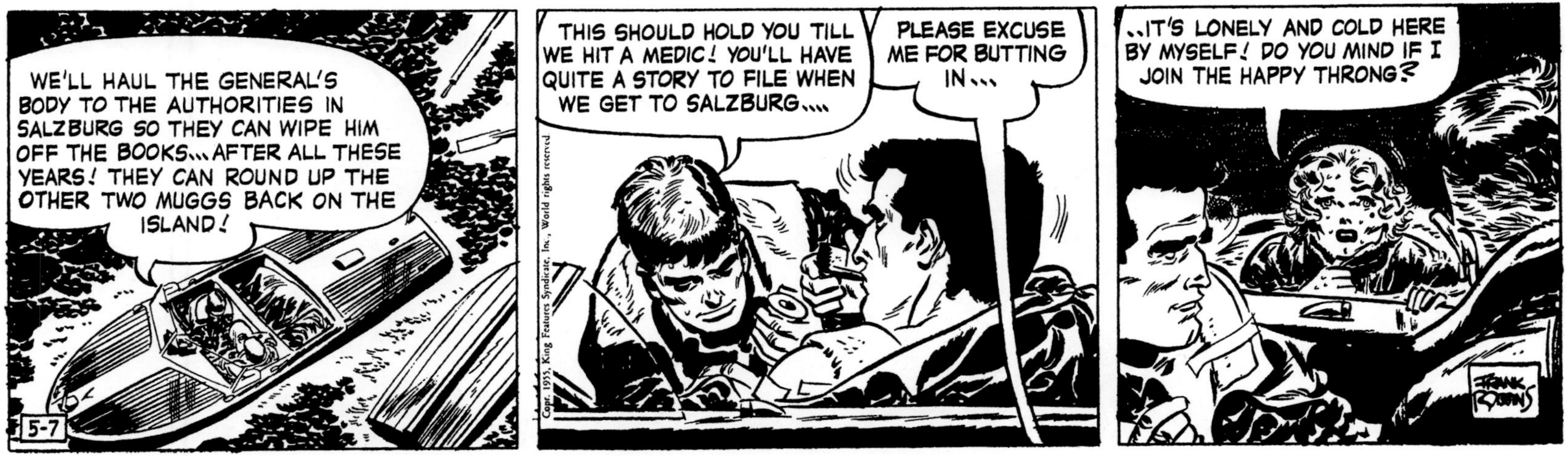
WE'LL HAUL THE GENERAL'S BODY TO THE AUTHORITIES IN SALZBURG SO THEY CAN WIPE HIM OFF THE BOOKS... AFTER ALL THESE YEARS! THEY CAN ROUND UP THE OTHER TWO MUGGS BACK ON THE ISLAND!
5-7
Copr. 1955, King Features Syndicate, Inc., World rights reserved.
THIS SHOULD HOLD YOU TILL WE HIT A MEDIC! YOU'LL HAVE QUITE A STORY TO FILE WHEN WE GET TO SALZBURG....
PLEASE EXCUSE ME FOR BUTTING IN...
..IT'S LONELY AND COLD HERE BY MYSELF! DO YOU MIND IF I JOIN THE HAPPY THRONG?
FRANK ROBBINS

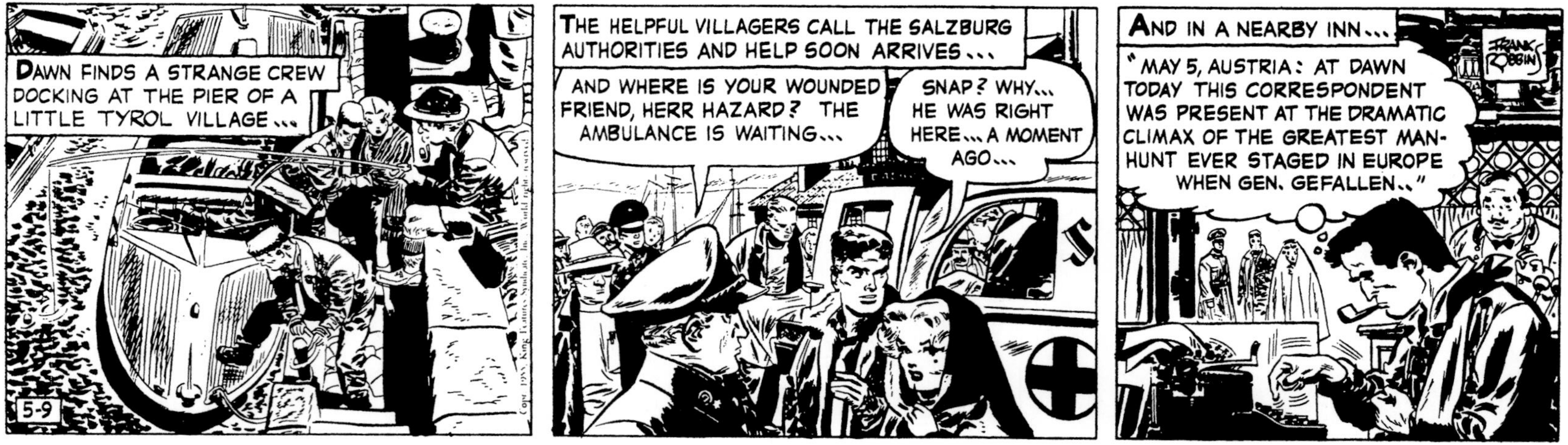
DAWN FINDS A STRANGE CREW DOCKING AT THE PIER OF A LITTLE TYROL VILLAGE...
5-9
THE HELPFUL VILLAGERS CALL THE SALZBURG AUTHORITIES AND HELP SOON ARRIVES...
AND WHERE IS YOUR WOUNDED FRIEND, HERR HAZARD? THE AMBULANCE IS WAITING...
SNAP? WHY... HE WAS RIGHT HERE... A MOMENT AGO...
AND IN A NEARBY INN...
FRANK ROBBINS
"MAY 5, AUSTRIA: AT DAWN TODAY THIS CORRESPONDENT WAS PRESENT AT THE DRAMATIC CLIMAX OF THE GREATEST MAN-HUNT EVER STAGED IN EUROPE WHEN GEN. GEFALLEN.."

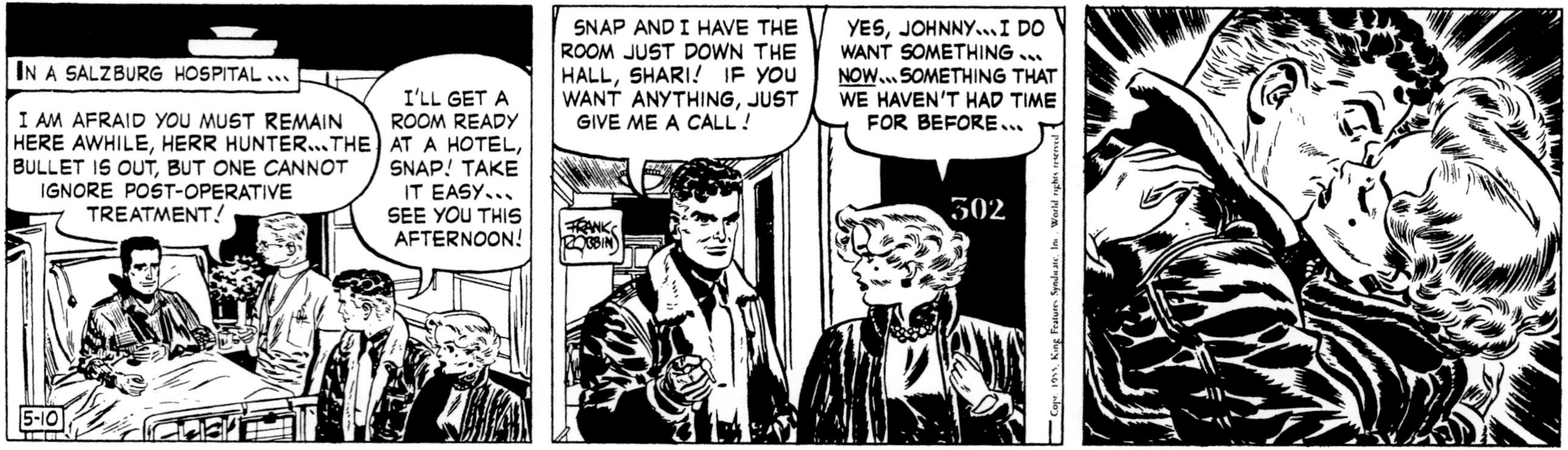
IN A SALZBURG HOSPITAL...
I AM AFRAID YOU MUST REMAIN HERE AWHILE, HERR HUNTER...THE BULLET IS OUT, BUT ONE CANNOT IGNORE POST-OPERATIVE TREATMENT!
I'LL GET A ROOM READY AT A HOTEL, SNAP! TAKE IT EASY... SEE YOU THIS AFTERNOON!
5-10
SNAP AND I HAVE THE ROOM JUST DOWN THE HALL, SHARI! IF YOU WANT ANYTHING, JUST GIVE ME A CALL!
YES, JOHNNY...I DO WANT SOMETHING... NOW...SOMETHING THAT WE HAVEN'T HAD TIME FOR BEFORE...
FRANK ROBBINS
302
Copr. 1955, King Features Syndicate, Inc. World rights reserved

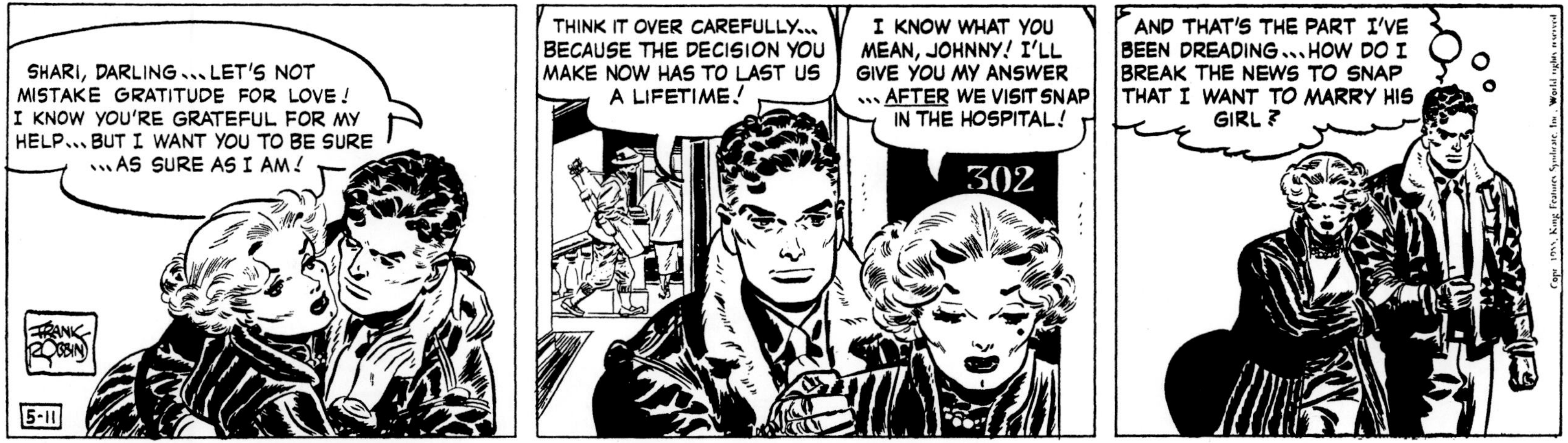
SHARI, DARLING ... LET'S NOT MISTAKE GRATITUDE FOR LOVE! I KNOW YOU'RE GRATEFUL FOR MY HELP... BUT I WANT YOU TO BE SURE ...AS SURE AS I AM!
FRANK ROBBINS
5-11
THINK IT OVER CAREFULLY... BECAUSE THE DECISION YOU MAKE NOW HAS TO LAST US A LIFETIME!
I KNOW WHAT YOU MEAN, JOHNNY! I'LL GIVE YOU MY ANSWER ... AFTER WE VISIT SNAP IN THE HOSPITAL!
302
AND THAT'S THE PART I'VE BEEN DREADING... HOW DO I BREAK THE NEWS TO SNAP THAT I WANT TO MARRY HIS GIRL?

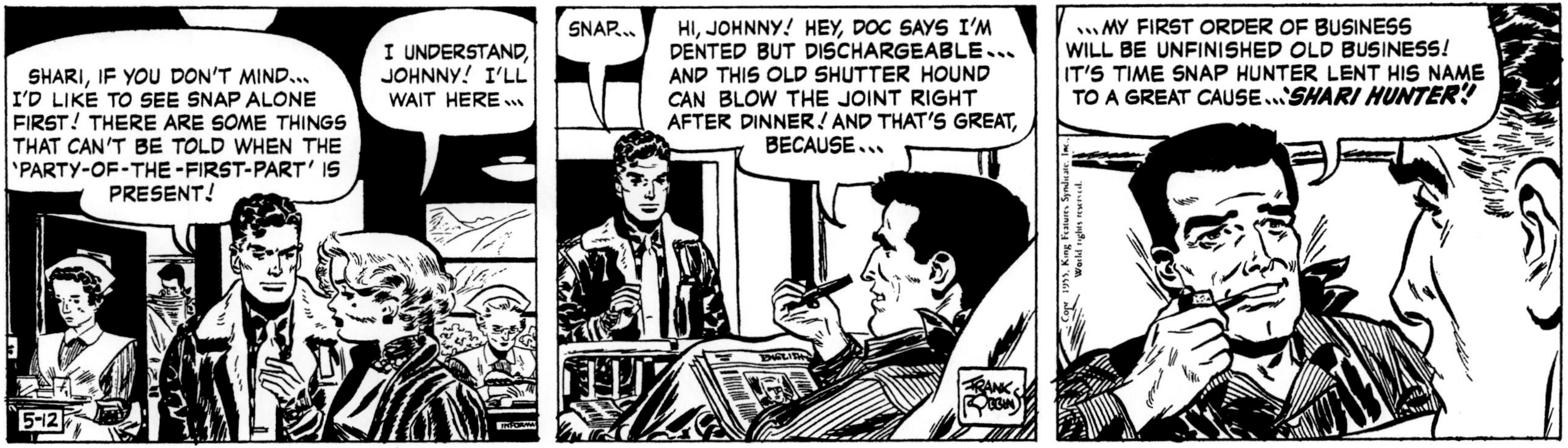
SHARI, IF YOU DON'T MIND... I'D LIKE TO SEE SNAP ALONE FIRST! THERE ARE SOME THINGS THAT CAN'T BE TOLD WHEN THE 'PARTY-OF-THE-FIRST-PART' IS PRESENT!
I UNDERSTAND, JOHNNY! I'LL WAIT HERE...
5-12
SNAP...
HI, JOHNNY! HEY, DOC SAYS I'M DENTED BUT DISCHARGEABLE... AND THIS OLD SHUTTER HOUND CAN BLOW THE JOINT RIGHT AFTER DINNER! AND THAT'S GREAT, BECAUSE...
FRANK ROBBINS
...MY FIRST ORDER OF BUSINESS WILL BE UNFINISHED OLD BUSINESS! IT'S TIME SNAP HUNTER LENT HIS NAME TO A GREAT CAUSE...'SHARI HUNTER'!

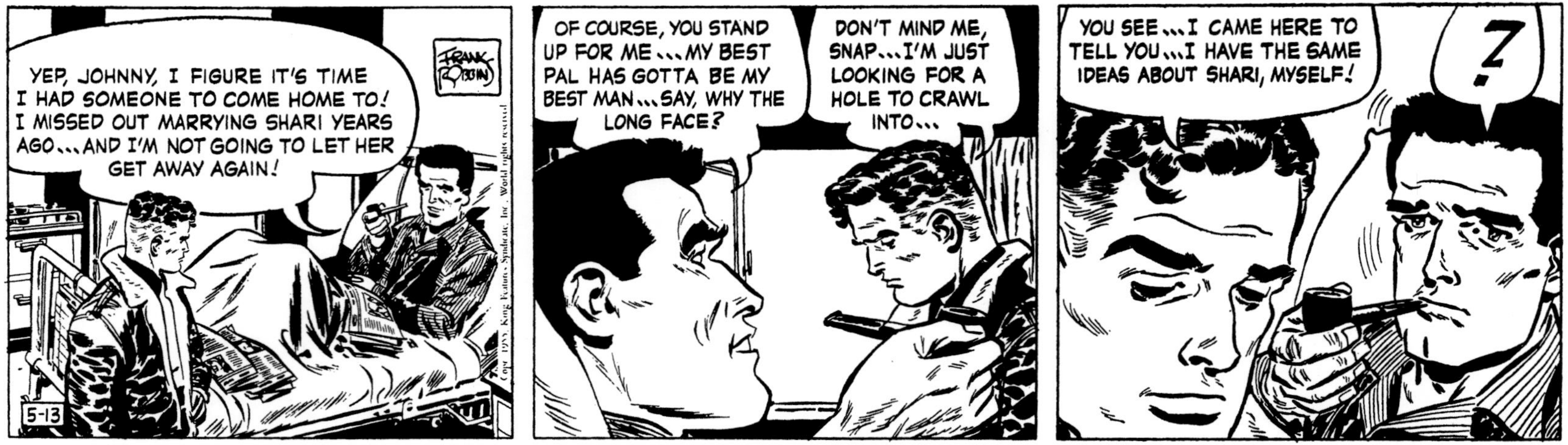
FRANK ROBBINS
5-13
YEP, JOHNNY, I FIGURE IT'S TIME I HAD SOMEONE TO COME HOME TO! I MISSED OUT MARRYING SHARI YEARS AGO... AND I'M NOT GOING TO LET HER GET AWAY AGAIN!
OF COURSE, YOU STAND UP FOR ME... MY BEST PAL HAS GOTTA BE MY BEST MAN... SAY, WHY THE LONG FACE?
DON'T MIND ME, SNAP... I'M JUST LOOKING FOR A HOLE TO CRAWL INTO...
YOU SEE... I CAME HERE TO TELL YOU... I HAVE THE SAME IDEAS ABOUT SHARI, MYSELF!
?

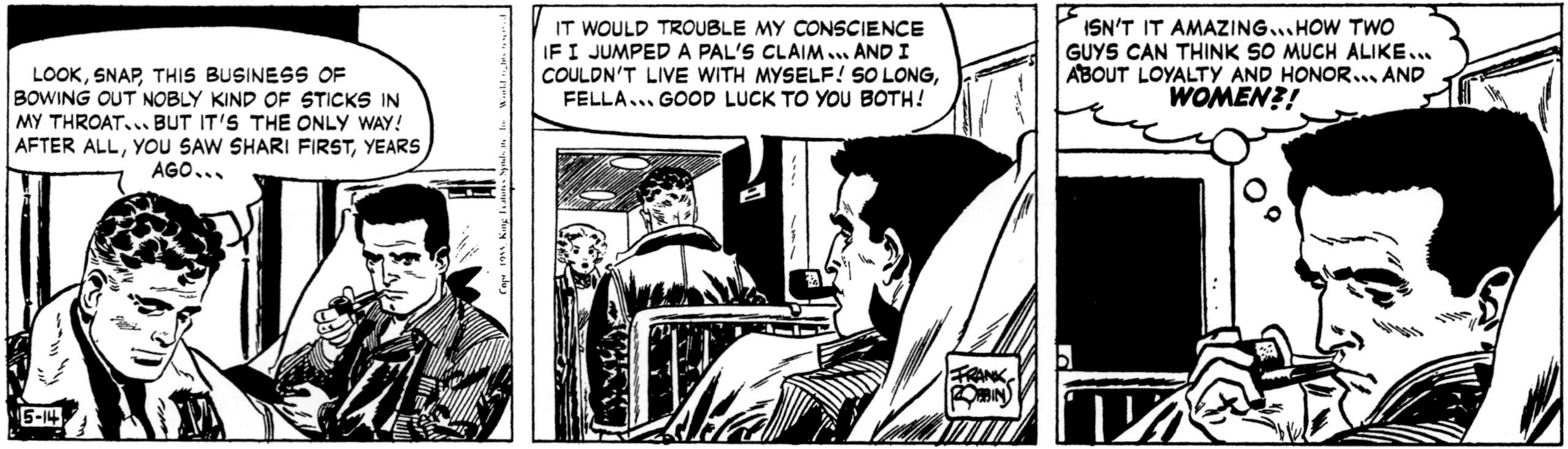
5-14
LOOK, SNAP, THIS BUSINESS OF BOWING OUT NOBLY KIND OF STICKS IN MY THROAT... BUT IT'S THE ONLY WAY! AFTER ALL, YOU SAW SHARI FIRST, YEARS AGO...
IT WOULD TROUBLE MY CONSCIENCE IF I JUMPED A PAL'S CLAIM... AND I COULDN'T LIVE WITH MYSELF! SO LONG, FELLA... GOOD LUCK TO YOU BOTH!
FRANK ROBBINS
ISN'T IT AMAZING... HOW TWO GUYS CAN THINK SO MUCH ALIKE... ABOUT LOYALTY AND HONOR... AND WOMEN?!

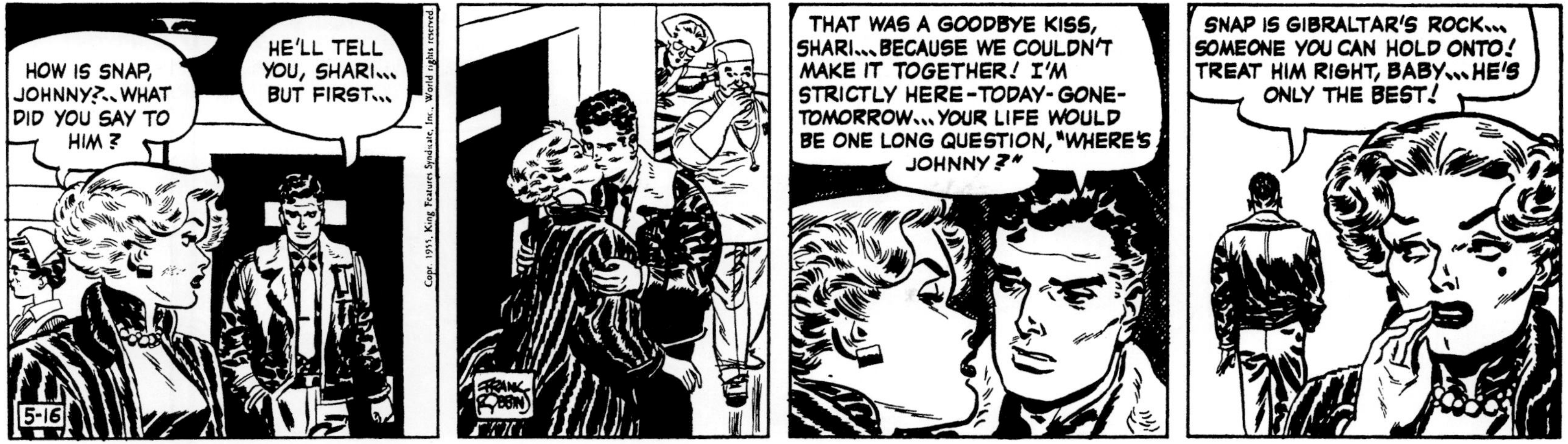
5-16
HOW IS SNAP, JOHNNY?.. WHAT DID YOU SAY TO HIM?
HE'LL TELL YOU, SHARI... BUT FIRST...
Copr. 1955, King Features Syndicate, Inc., World rights reserved
FRANK ROBBINS
THAT WAS A GOODBYE KISS, SHARI... BECAUSE WE COULDN'T MAKE IT TOGETHER! I'M STRICTLY HERE-TODAY-GONE-TOMORROW... YOUR LIFE WOULD BE ONE LONG QUESTION, "WHERE'S JOHNNY?"
SNAP IS GIBRALTAR'S ROCK... SOMEONE YOU CAN HOLD ONTO! TREAT HIM RIGHT, BABY... HE'S ONLY THE BEST!

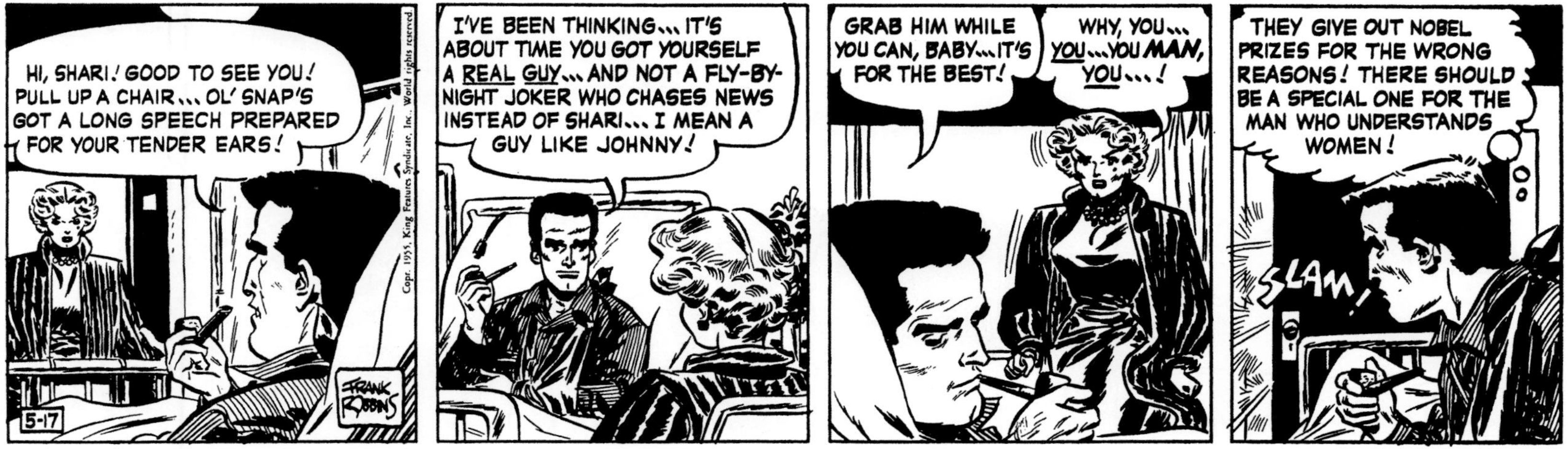
HI, SHARI! GOOD TO SEE YOU! PULL UP A CHAIR... OL' SNAP'S GOT A LONG SPEECH PREPARED FOR YOUR TENDER EARS!
Copr. 1955, King Features Syndicate, Inc., World rights reserved
FRANK ROBBINS
5-17
I'VE BEEN THINKING... IT'S ABOUT TIME YOU GOT YOURSELF A REAL GUY... AND NOT A FLY-BY-NIGHT JOKER WHO CHASES NEWS INSTEAD OF SHARI... I MEAN A GUY LIKE JOHNNY!
GRAB HIM WHILE YOU CAN, BABY... IT'S FOR THE BEST!
WHY, YOU... YOU... YOU MAN, YOU...!
THEY GIVE OUT NOBEL PRIZES FOR THE WRONG REASONS! THERE SHOULD BE A SPECIAL ONE FOR THE MAN WHO UNDERSTANDS WOMEN!
SLAM!

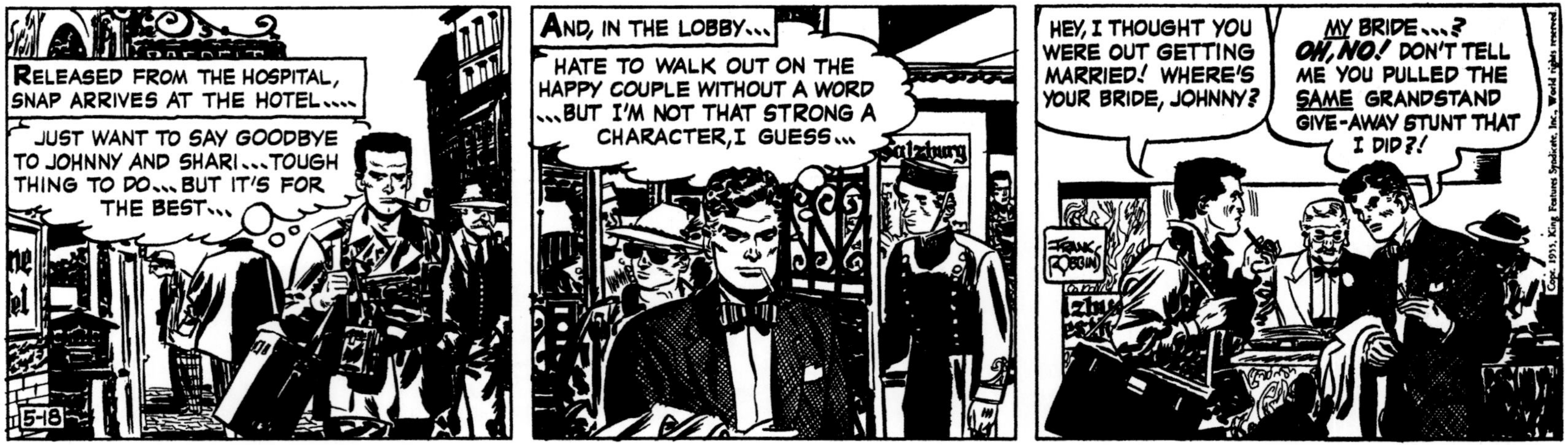
5-18
RELEASED FROM THE HOSPITAL, SNAP ARRIVES AT THE HOTEL....
JUST WANT TO SAY GOODBYE TO JOHNNY AND SHARI...TOUGH THING TO DO...BUT IT'S FOR THE BEST...
AND, IN THE LOBBY...
HATE TO WALK OUT ON THE HAPPY COUPLE WITHOUT A WORD ...BUT I'M NOT THAT STRONG A CHARACTER, I GUESS...
HEY, I THOUGHT YOU WERE OUT GETTING MARRIED! WHERE'S YOUR BRIDE, JOHNNY?
MY BRIDE...? OH, NO! DON'T TELL ME YOU PULLED THE SAME GRANDSTAND GIVE-AWAY STUNT THAT I DID?!
FRANK ROBBINS
Copr. 1955, King Features Syndicate, Inc., World rights reserved.

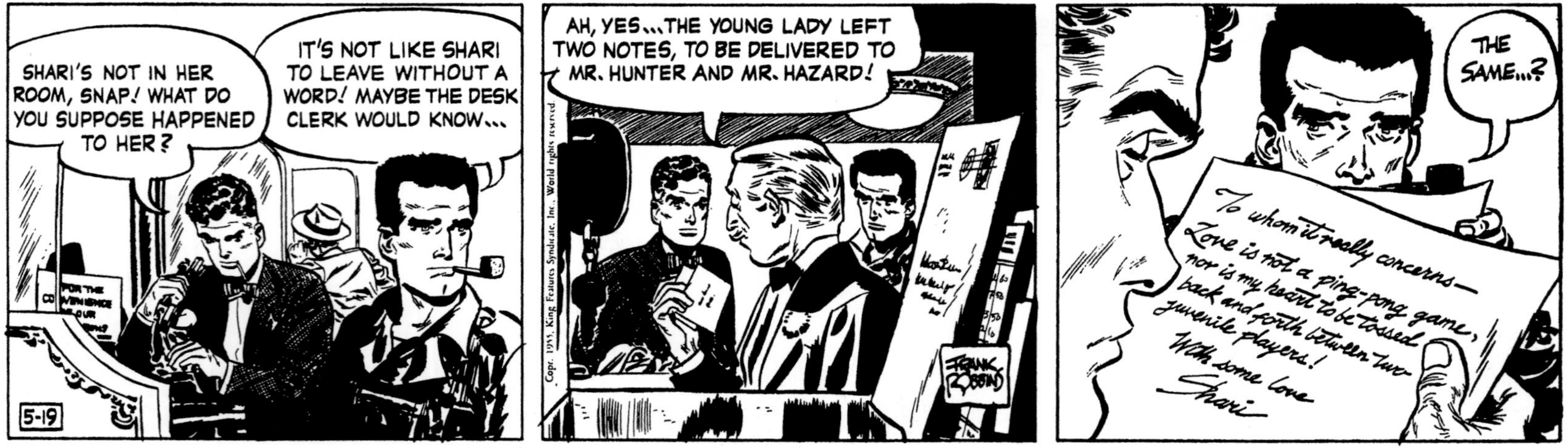
5-19
SHARI'S NOT IN HER ROOM, SNAP! WHAT DO YOU SUPPOSE HAPPENED TO HER?
IT'S NOT LIKE SHARI TO LEAVE WITHOUT A WORD! MAYBE THE DESK CLERK WOULD KNOW...
Copr. 1955, King Features Syndicate, Inc., World rights reserved.
AH, YES...THE YOUNG LADY LEFT TWO NOTES, TO BE DELIVERED TO MR. HUNTER AND MR. HAZARD!
FRANK ROBBINS
THE SAME...?
To whom it really concerns—
Love is not a ping-pong game,
nor is my heart to be tossed
back and forth between two
juvenile players!
With some love
Shari

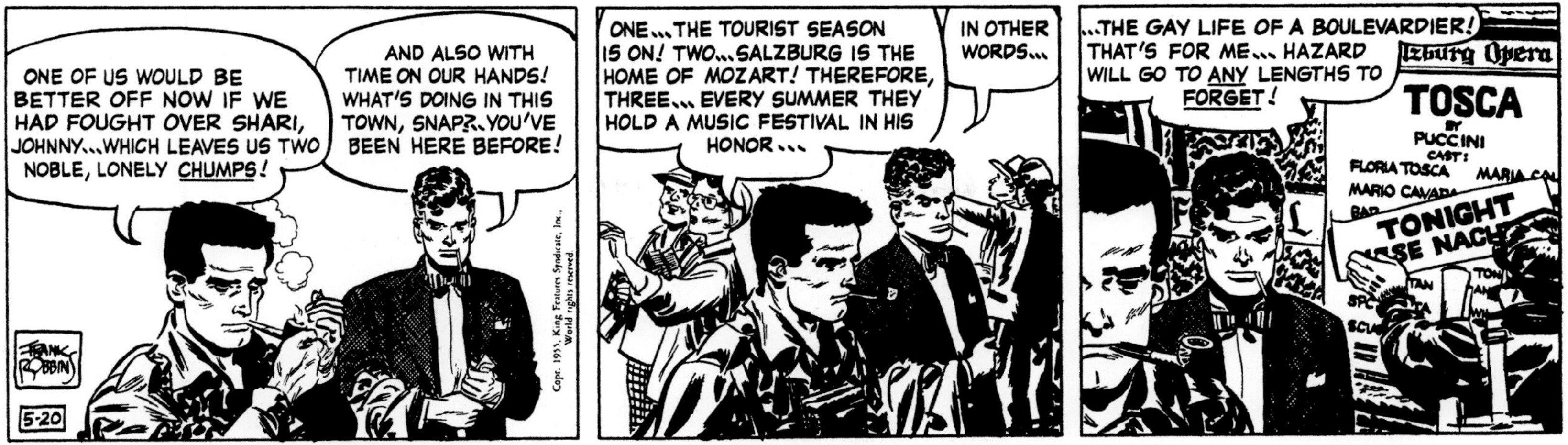
5-20
FRANK ROBBINS
ONE OF US WOULD BE BETTER OFF NOW IF WE HAD FOUGHT OVER SHARI, JOHNNY...WHICH LEAVES US TWO NOBLE, LONELY CHUMPS!
AND ALSO WITH TIME ON OUR HANDS! WHAT'S DOING IN THIS TOWN, SNAP?..YOU'VE BEEN HERE BEFORE!
Copr. 1955, King Features Syndicate, Inc., World rights reserved.
ONE...THE TOURIST SEASON IS ON! TWO...SALZBURG IS THE HOME OF MOZART! THEREFORE, THREE... EVERY SUMMER THEY HOLD A MUSIC FESTIVAL IN HIS HONOR...
IN OTHER WORDS...
...THE GAY LIFE OF A BOULEVARDIER! THAT'S FOR ME... HAZARD WILL GO TO ANY LENGTHS TO FORGET!
TOSCA
BY
PUCCINI
CAST:
FLORIA TOSCA
TONIGHT

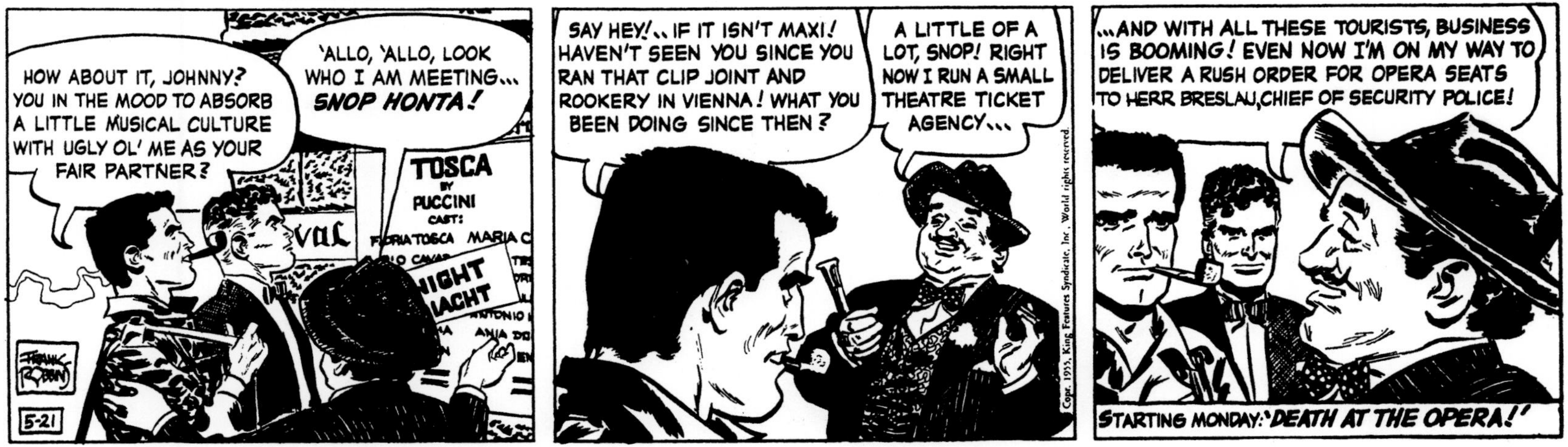
5-21
FRANK ROBBINS
HOW ABOUT IT, JOHNNY? YOU IN THE MOOD TO ABSORB A LITTLE MUSICAL CULTURE WITH UGLY OL' ME AS YOUR FAIR PARTNER?
'ALLO, 'ALLO, LOOK WHO I AM MEETING... SNOP HONTA!
TOSCA
BY
PUCCINI
CAST:
FLORIA TOSCA
SAY HEY!.. IF IT ISN'T MAXI! HAVEN'T SEEN YOU SINCE YOU RAN THAT CLIP JOINT AND ROOKERY IN VIENNA! WHAT YOU BEEN DOING SINCE THEN?
A LITTLE OF A LOT, SNOP! RIGHT NOW I RUN A SMALL THEATRE TICKET AGENCY...
Copr. 1955, King Features Syndicate, Inc. World rights reserved.
...AND WITH ALL THESE TOURISTS, BUSINESS IS BOOMING! EVEN NOW I'M ON MY WAY TO DELIVER A RUSH ORDER FOR OPERA SEATS TO HERR BRESLAU, CHIEF OF SECURITY POLICE!
STARTING MONDAY: 'DEATH AT THE OPERA!'

JOHNNY HAZARD

Chapter Four: Death at the Opera

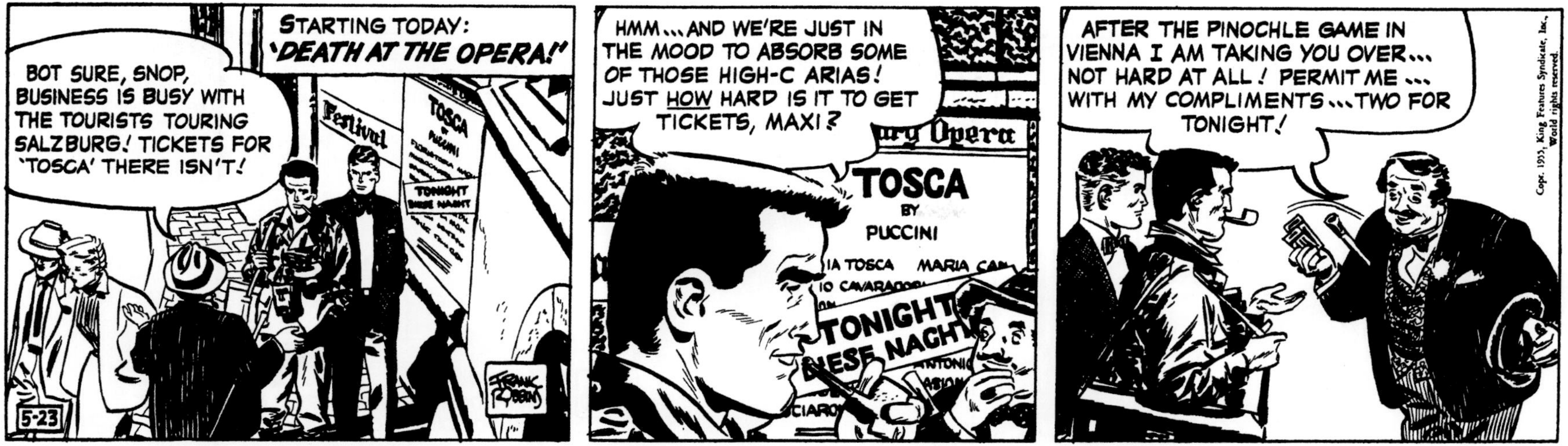
STARTING TODAY: 'DEATH AT THE OPERA!'
BOT SURE, SNOP, BUSINESS IS BUSY WITH THE TOURISTS TOURING SALZBURG! TICKETS FOR 'TOSCA' THERE ISN'T!
Festival
TOSCA
TONIGHT DIESE NACHT
FRANK ROBBINS
5-23
HMM... AND WE'RE JUST IN THE MOOD TO ABSORB SOME OF THOSE HIGH-C ARIAS! JUST HOW HARD IS IT TO GET TICKETS, MAXI?
Opera
TOSCA BY PUCCINI
TONIGHT DIESE NACHT
AFTER THE PINOCHLE GAME IN VIENNA I AM TAKING YOU OVER... NOT HARD AT ALL! PERMIT ME... WITH MY COMPLIMENTS... TWO FOR TONIGHT!
Copr. 1955, King Features Syndicate, Inc., World rights reserved.

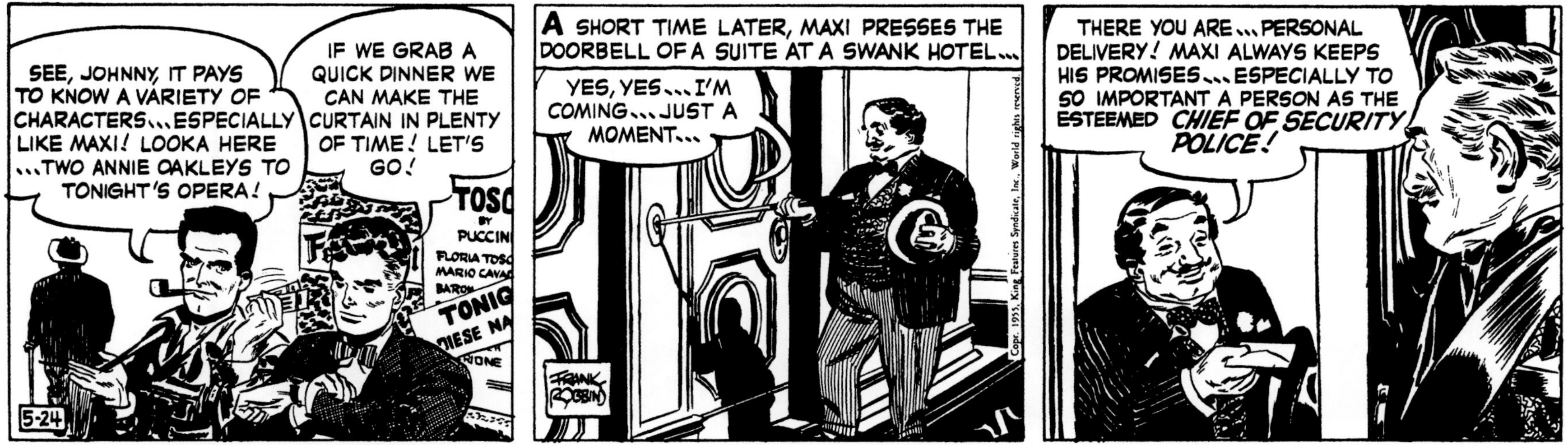
SEE, JOHNNY, IT PAYS TO KNOW A VARIETY OF CHARACTERS... ESPECIALLY LIKE MAXI! LOOKA HERE ...TWO ANNIE OAKLEYS TO TONIGHT'S OPERA!
IF WE GRAB A QUICK DINNER WE CAN MAKE THE CURTAIN IN PLENTY OF TIME! LET'S GO!
TOSC BY PUCCINI
5-24
A SHORT TIME LATER, MAXI PRESSES THE DOORBELL OF A SUITE AT A SWANK HOTEL...
YES, YES... I'M COMING... JUST A MOMENT...
FRANK ROBBINS
Copr. 1955, King Features Syndicate, Inc., World rights reserved.
THERE YOU ARE... PERSONAL DELIVERY! MAXI ALWAYS KEEPS HIS PROMISES... ESPECIALLY TO SO IMPORTANT A PERSON AS THE ESTEEMED CHIEF OF SECURITY POLICE!

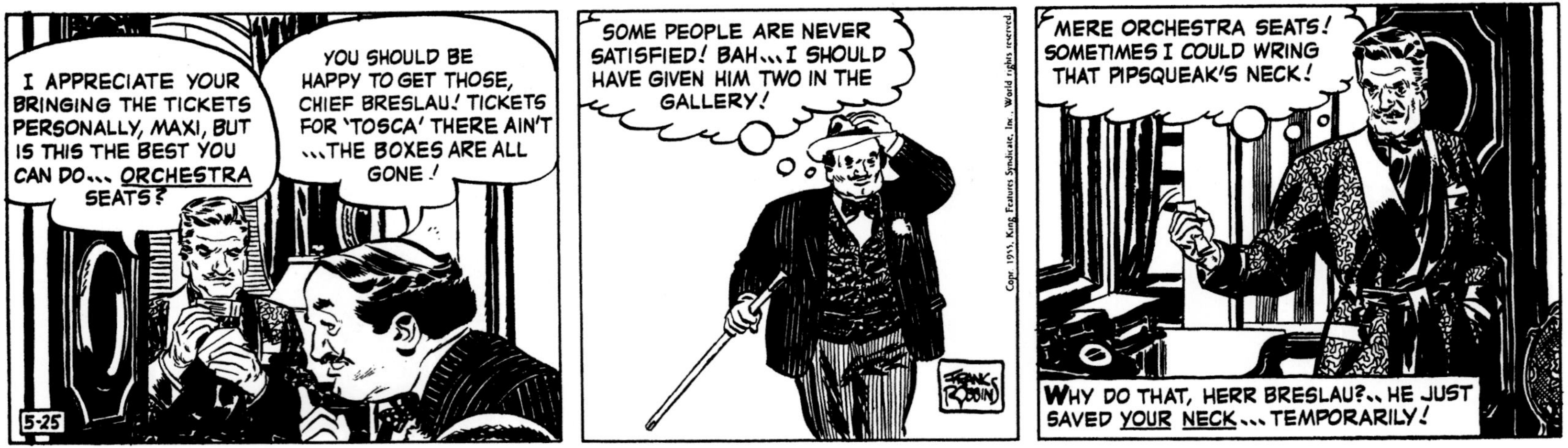
I APPRECIATE YOUR BRINGING THE TICKETS PERSONALLY, MAXI, BUT IS THIS THE BEST YOU CAN DO... ORCHESTRA SEATS?
YOU SHOULD BE HAPPY TO GET THOSE, CHIEF BRESLAU! TICKETS FOR 'TOSCA' THERE AIN'T ...THE BOXES ARE ALL GONE!
5-25
SOME PEOPLE ARE NEVER SATISFIED! BAH...I SHOULD HAVE GIVEN HIM TWO IN THE GALLERY!
FRANK ROBBINS
Copr. 1955, King Features Syndicate, Inc., World rights reserved.
MERE ORCHESTRA SEATS! SOMETIMES I COULD WRING THAT PIPSQUEAK'S NECK!
WHY DO THAT, HERR BRESLAU?.. HE JUST SAVED YOUR NECK... TEMPORARILY!

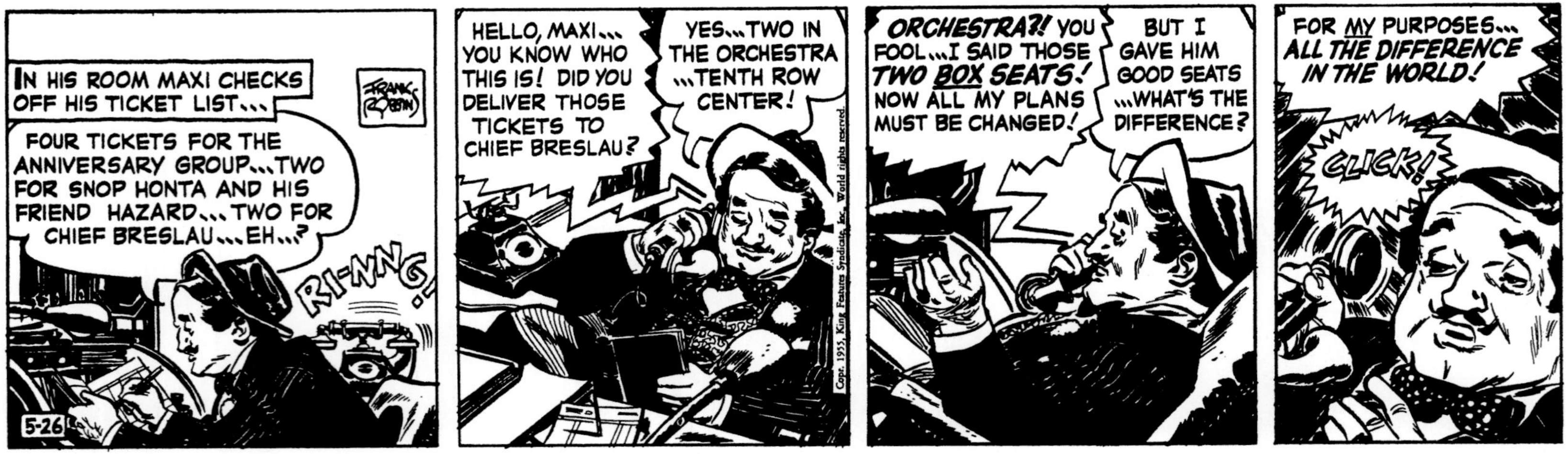
IN HIS ROOM MAXI CHECKS OFF HIS TICKET LIST...
FRANK ROBBINS
FOUR TICKETS FOR THE ANNIVERSARY GROUP...TWO FOR SNOP HONTA AND HIS FRIEND HAZARD... TWO FOR CHIEF BRESLAU...EH..?
RI-NNG!
5-26
HELLO, MAXI... YOU KNOW WHO THIS IS! DID YOU DELIVER THOSE TICKETS TO CHIEF BRESLAU?
YES...TWO IN THE ORCHESTRA ...TENTH ROW CENTER!
Copr. 1955, King Features Syndicate, Inc., World rights reserved.
ORCHESTRA?! YOU FOOL...I SAID THOSE TWO BOX SEATS! NOW ALL MY PLANS MUST BE CHANGED!
BUT I GAVE HIM GOOD SEATS ...WHAT'S THE DIFFERENCE?
FOR MY PURPOSES... ALL THE DIFFERENCE IN THE WORLD!
CLICK!

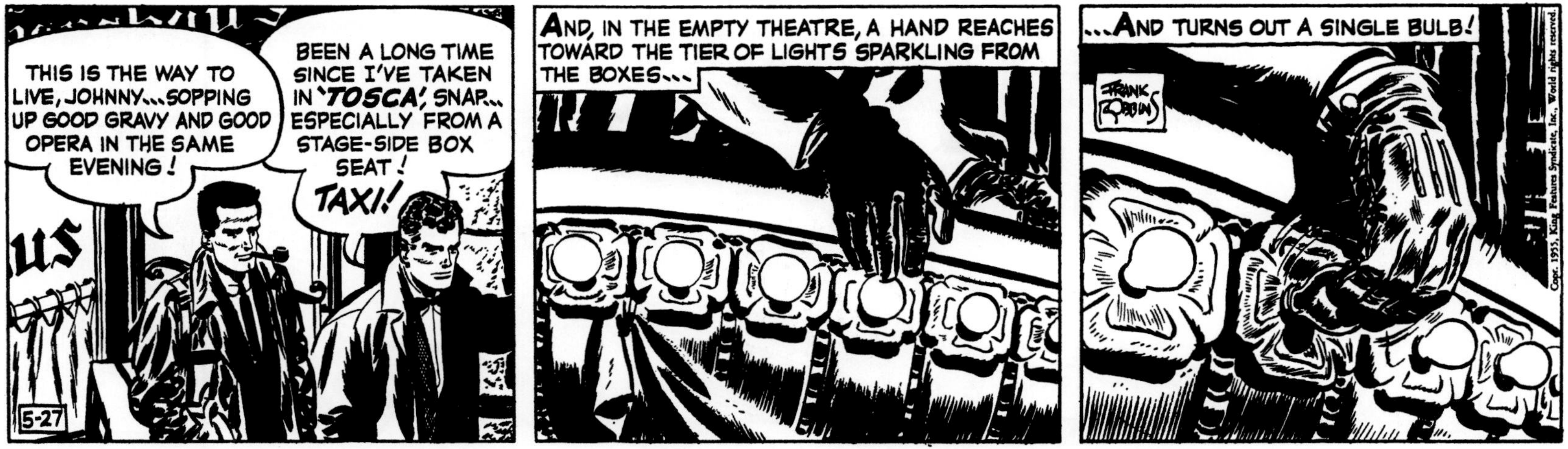
THIS IS THE WAY TO LIVE, JOHNNY... SOPPING UP GOOD GRAVY AND GOOD OPERA IN THE SAME EVENING!
BEEN A LONG TIME SINCE I'VE TAKEN IN 'TOSCA,' SNAP... ESPECIALLY FROM A STAGE-SIDE BOX SEAT!
TAXI!
5-27
AND, IN THE EMPTY THEATRE, A HAND REACHES TOWARD THE TIER OF LIGHTS SPARKLING FROM THE BOXES...
...AND TURNS OUT A SINGLE BULB!
FRANK ROBBINS
Copr. 1955, King Features Syndicate, Inc., World rights reserved.

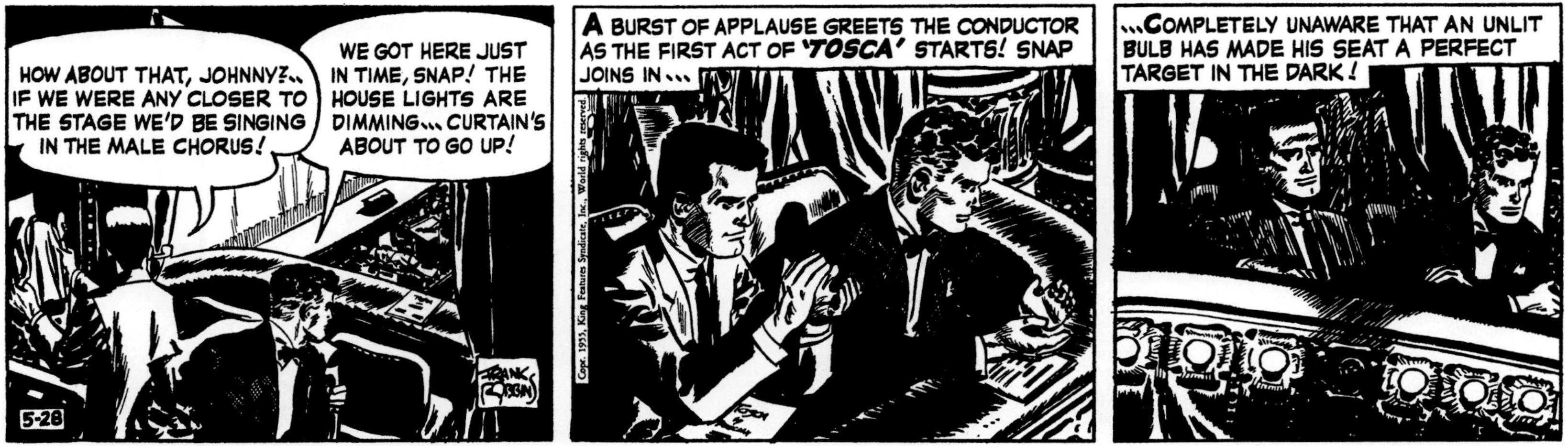
HOW ABOUT THAT, JOHNNY?... IF WE WERE ANY CLOSER TO THE STAGE WE'D BE SINGING IN THE MALE CHORUS!
WE GOT HERE JUST IN TIME, SNAP! THE HOUSE LIGHTS ARE DIMMING... CURTAIN'S ABOUT TO GO UP!
FRANK ROBBINS
5-28
A BURST OF APPLAUSE GREETS THE CONDUCTOR AS THE FIRST ACT OF 'TOSCA' STARTS! SNAP JOINS IN...
Copr. 1955, King Features Syndicate, Inc., World rights reserved.
...COMPLETELY UNAWARE THAT AN UNLIT BULB HAS MADE HIS SEAT A PERFECT TARGET IN THE DARK!

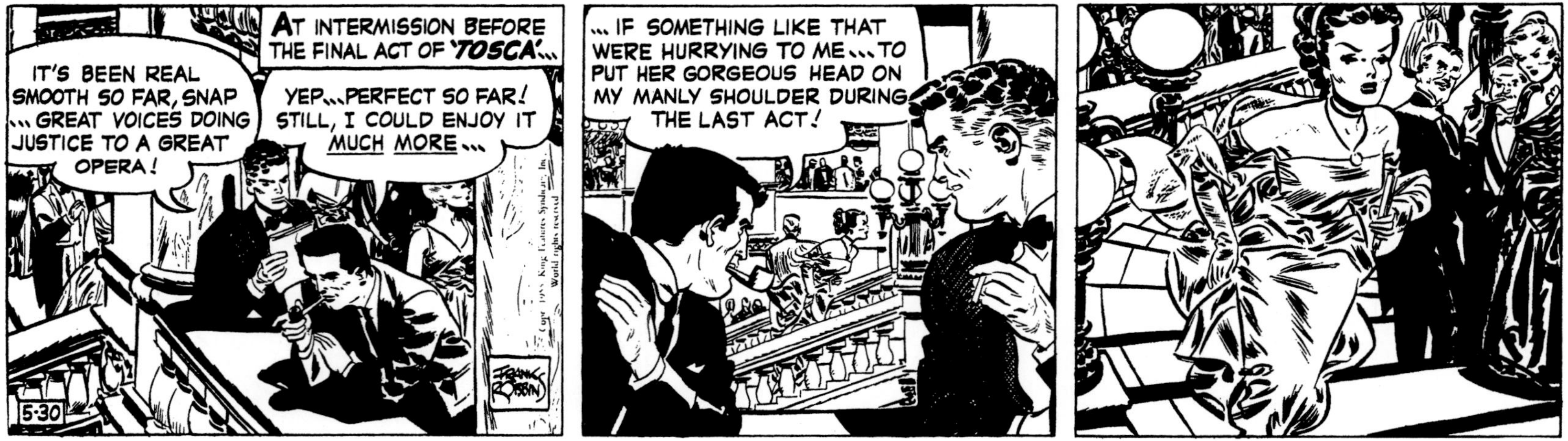
AT INTERMISSION BEFORE THE FINAL ACT OF 'TOSCA'...
IT'S BEEN REAL SMOOTH SO FAR, SNAP ... GREAT VOICES DOING JUSTICE TO A GREAT OPERA!
YEP... PERFECT SO FAR! STILL, I COULD ENJOY IT MUCH MORE...
FRANK ROBBINS
5-30
... IF SOMETHING LIKE THAT WERE HURRYING TO ME ... TO PUT HER GORGEOUS HEAD ON MY MANLY SHOULDER DURING THE LAST ACT!

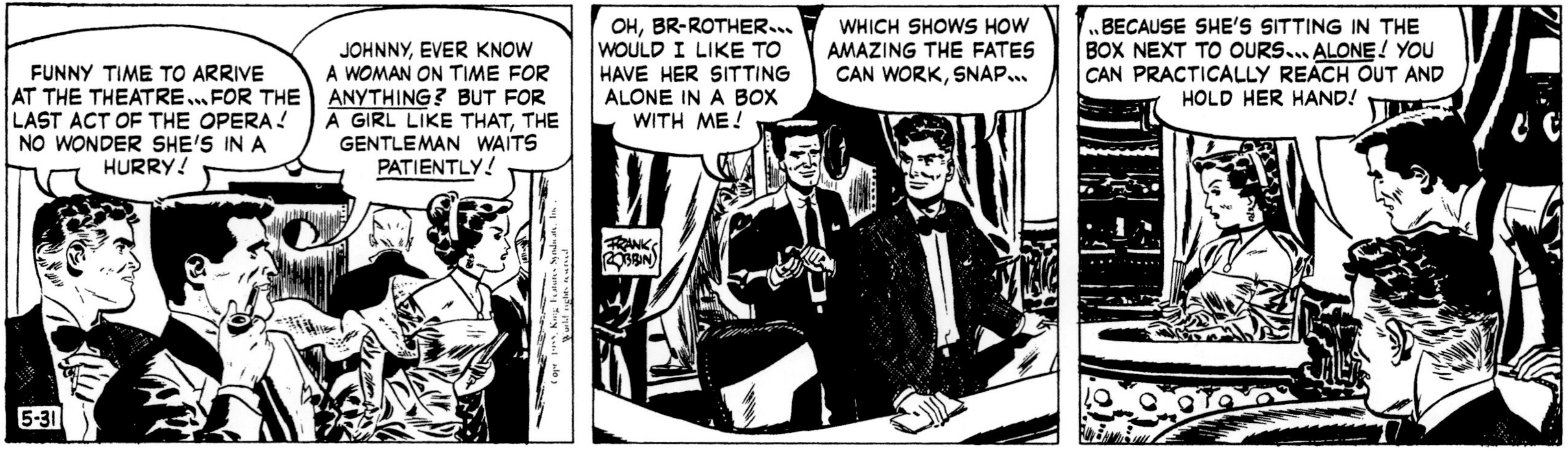
FUNNY TIME TO ARRIVE AT THE THEATRE... FOR THE LAST ACT OF THE OPERA! NO WONDER SHE'S IN A HURRY!
JOHNNY, EVER KNOW A WOMAN ON TIME FOR ANYTHING? BUT FOR A GIRL LIKE THAT, THE GENTLEMAN WAITS PATIENTLY!
5-31
OH, BR-ROTHER... WOULD I LIKE TO HAVE HER SITTING ALONE IN A BOX WITH ME!
WHICH SHOWS HOW AMAZING THE FATES CAN WORK, SNAP...
FRANK ROBBINS
..BECAUSE SHE'S SITTING IN THE BOX NEXT TO OURS... ALONE! YOU CAN PRACTICALLY REACH OUT AND HOLD HER HAND!

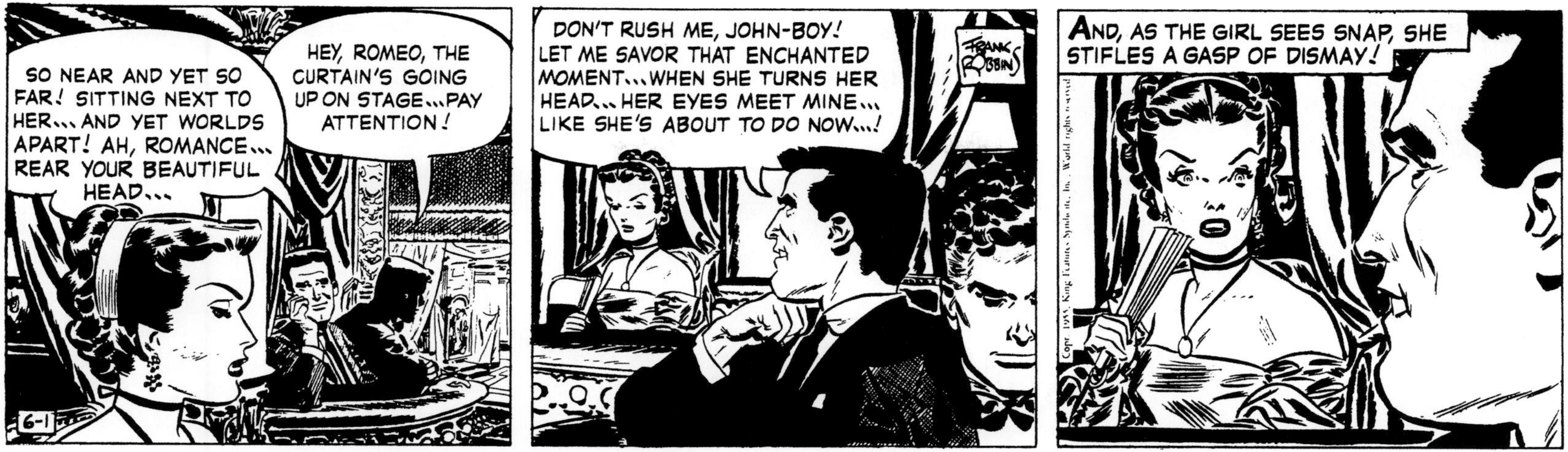
SO NEAR AND YET SO FAR! SITTING NEXT TO HER... AND YET WORLDS APART! AH, ROMANCE... REAR YOUR BEAUTIFUL HEAD...
HEY, ROMEO, THE CURTAIN'S GOING UP ON STAGE...PAY ATTENTION!
6-1
DON'T RUSH ME, JOHN-BOY! LET ME SAVOR THAT ENCHANTED MOMENT... WHEN SHE TURNS HER HEAD... HER EYES MEET MINE... LIKE SHE'S ABOUT TO DO NOW...!
FRANK ROBBINS
AND, AS THE GIRL SEES SNAP, SHE STIFLES A GASP OF DISMAY!
Copr. 1955, King Features Syndicate, Inc., World rights reserved

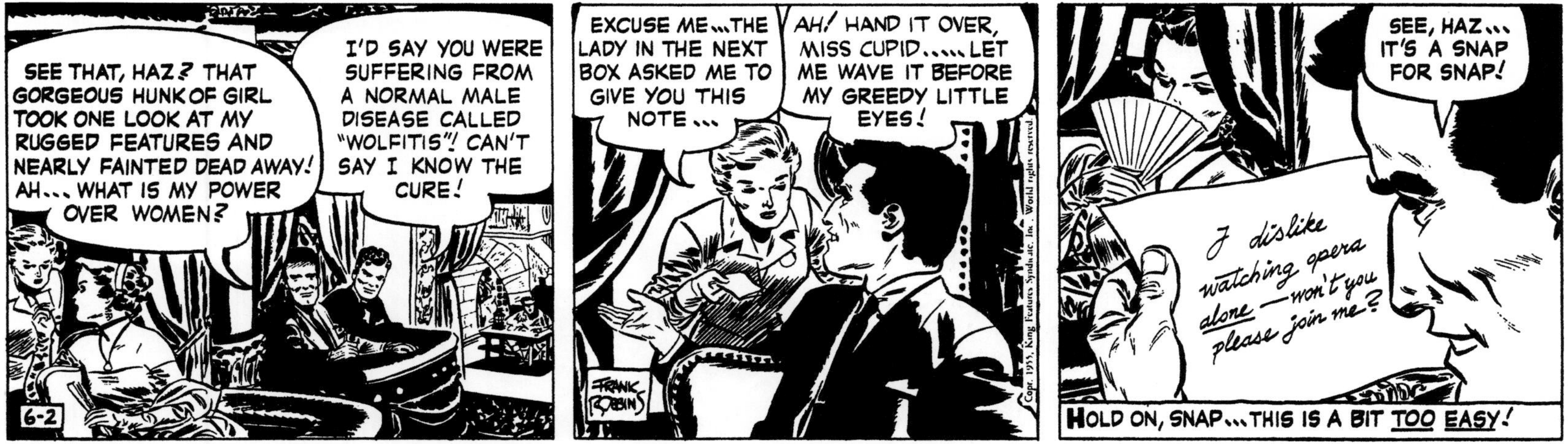
SEE THAT, HAZ? THAT GORGEOUS HUNK OF GIRL TOOK ONE LOOK AT MY RUGGED FEATURES AND NEARLY FAINTED DEAD AWAY! AH... WHAT IS MY POWER OVER WOMEN?
I'D SAY YOU WERE SUFFERING FROM A NORMAL MALE DISEASE CALLED "WOLFITIS"! CAN'T SAY I KNOW THE CURE!
6-2
EXCUSE ME...THE LADY IN THE NEXT BOX ASKED ME TO GIVE YOU THIS NOTE...
AH! HAND IT OVER, MISS CUPID...... LET ME WAVE IT BEFORE MY GREEDY LITTLE EYES!
FRANK ROBBINS
Copr. 1955, King Features Syndicate, Inc., World rights reserved
SEE, HAZ... IT'S A SNAP FOR SNAP!
I dislike watching opera alone — won't you please join me?
HOLD ON, SNAP... THIS IS A BIT TOO EASY!

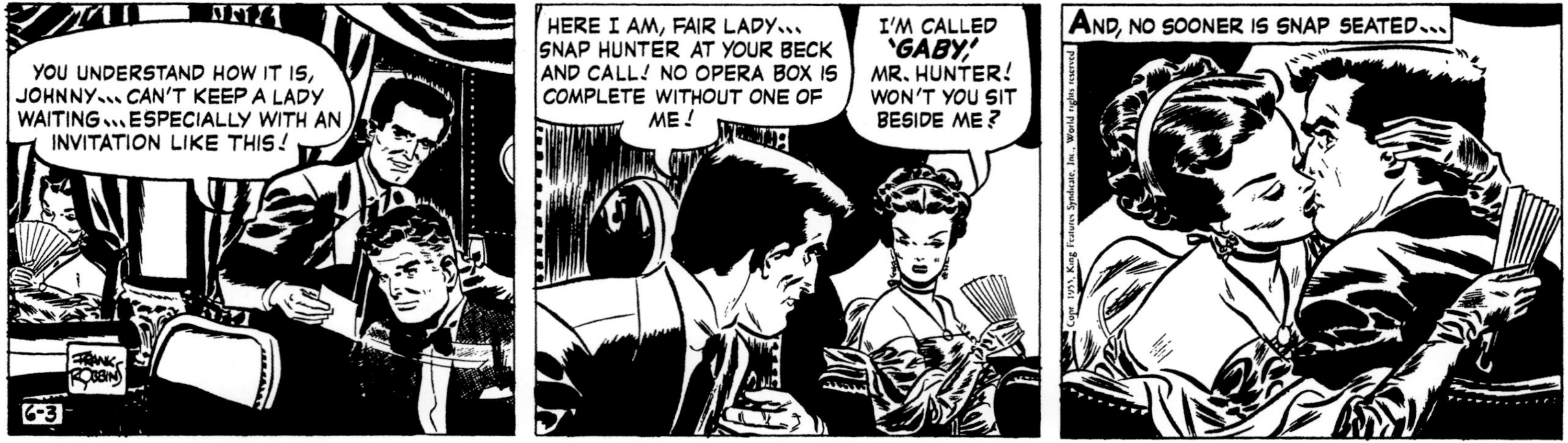
YOU UNDERSTAND HOW IT IS, JOHNNY... CAN'T KEEP A LADY WAITING... ESPECIALLY WITH AN INVITATION LIKE THIS!
FRANK ROBBINS
6-3
HERE I AM, FAIR LADY... SNAP HUNTER AT YOUR BECK AND CALL! NO OPERA BOX IS COMPLETE WITHOUT ONE OF ME!
I'M CALLED 'GABY,' MR. HUNTER! WON'T YOU SIT BESIDE ME?
AND, NO SOONER IS SNAP SEATED...
Copr. 1955, King Features Syndicate, Inc., World rights reserved

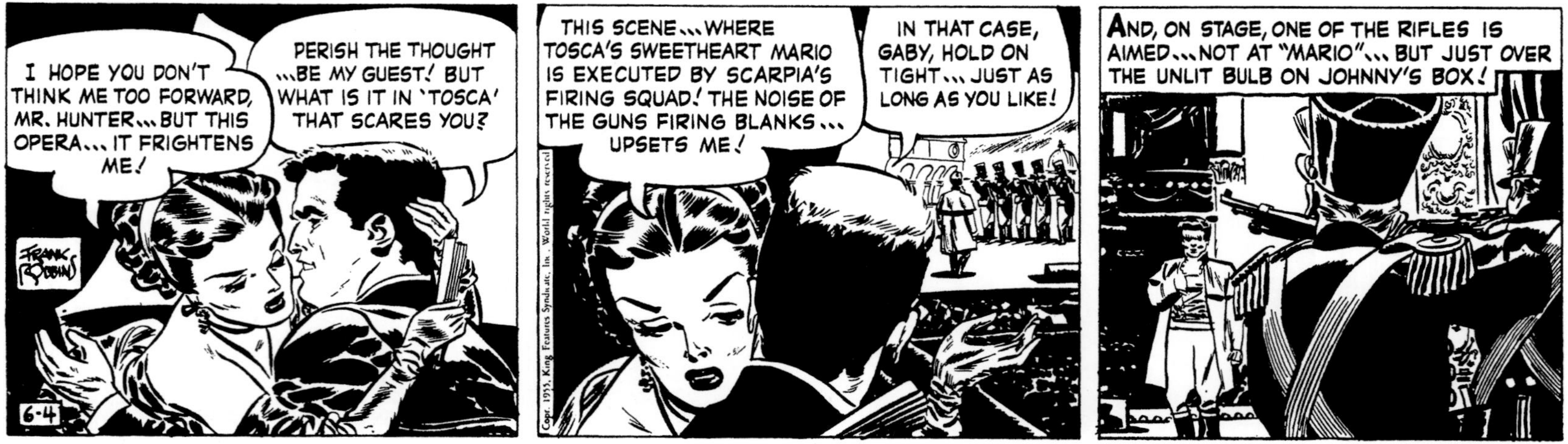
I HOPE YOU DON'T THINK ME TOO FORWARD, MR. HUNTER... BUT THIS OPERA... IT FRIGHTENS ME!
PERISH THE THOUGHT ...BE MY GUEST! BUT WHAT IS IT IN 'TOSCA' THAT SCARES YOU?
FRANK ROBBINS
6-4
THIS SCENE... WHERE TOSCA'S SWEETHEART MARIO IS EXECUTED BY SCARPIA'S FIRING SQUAD! THE NOISE OF THE GUNS FIRING BLANKS... UPSETS ME!
IN THAT CASE, GABY, HOLD ON TIGHT... JUST AS LONG AS YOU LIKE!
Copr. 1955, King Features Syndicate, Inc., World rights reserved
AND, ON STAGE, ONE OF THE RIFLES IS AIMED... NOT AT "MARIO"... BUT JUST OVER THE UNLIT BULB ON JOHNNY'S BOX!

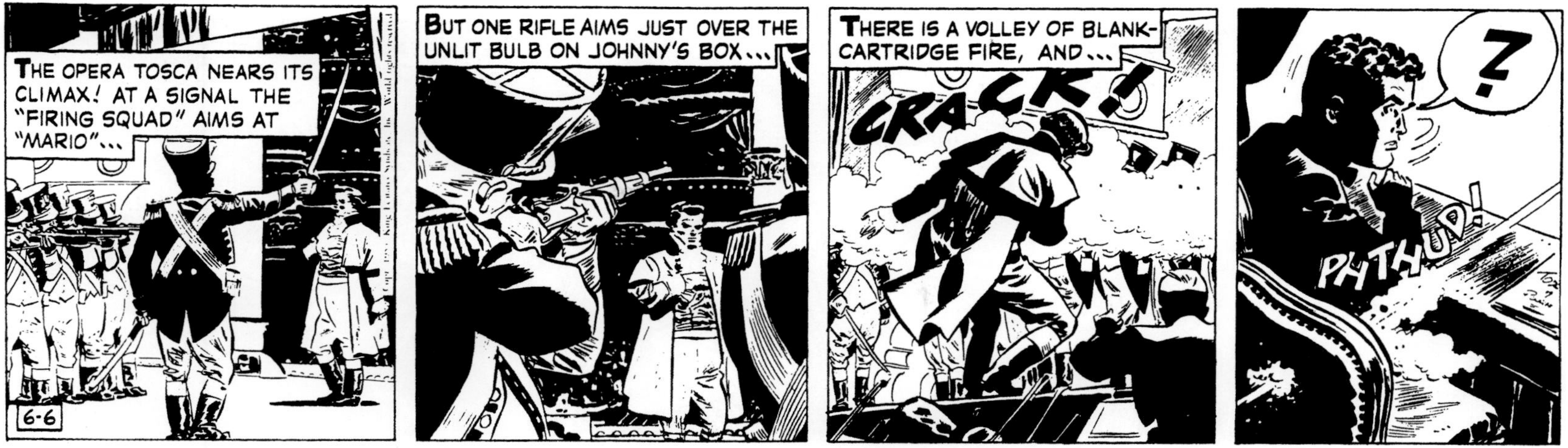
THE OPERA TOSCA NEARS ITS CLIMAX! AT A SIGNAL THE "FIRING SQUAD" AIMS AT "MARIO"...
6-6
BUT ONE RIFLE AIMS JUST OVER THE UNLIT BULB ON JOHNNY'S BOX...
THERE IS A VOLLEY OF BLANK-CARTRIDGE FIRE, AND...
CRACK!
?
PHTHUD!

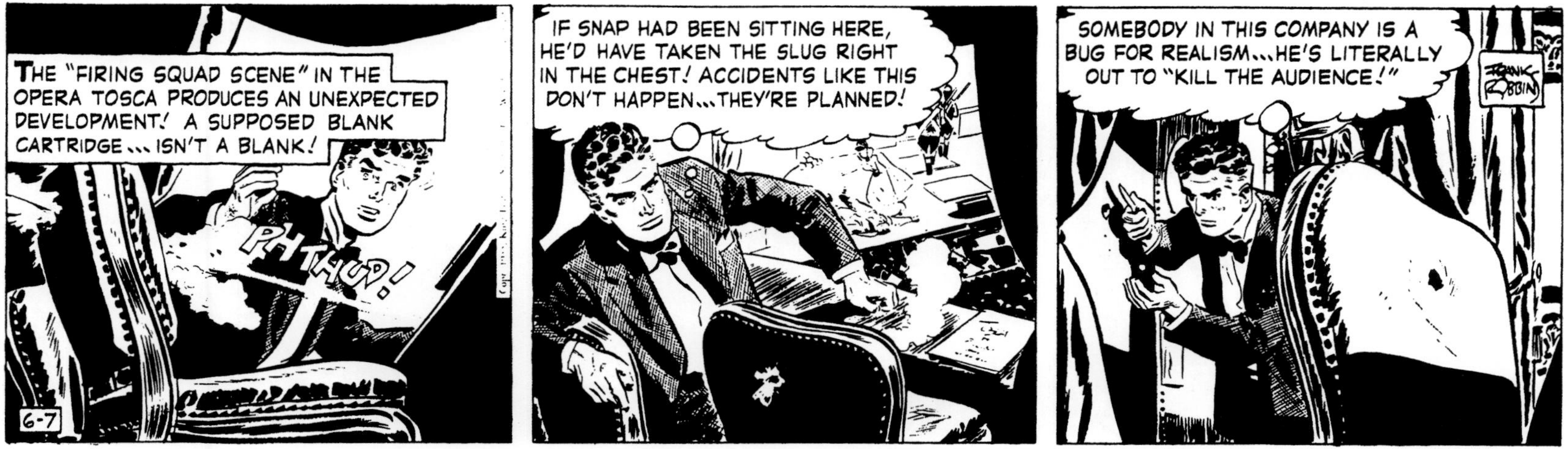
THE "FIRING SQUAD SCENE" IN THE OPERA TOSCA PRODUCES AN UNEXPECTED DEVELOPMENT! A SUPPOSED BLANK CARTRIDGE... ISN'T A BLANK!
PHTHUD!
6-7
IF SNAP HAD BEEN SITTING HERE, HE'D HAVE TAKEN THE SLUG RIGHT IN THE CHEST! ACCIDENTS LIKE THIS DON'T HAPPEN...THEY'RE PLANNED!
SOMEBODY IN THIS COMPANY IS A BUG FOR REALISM...HE'S LITERALLY OUT TO "KILL THE AUDIENCE!"

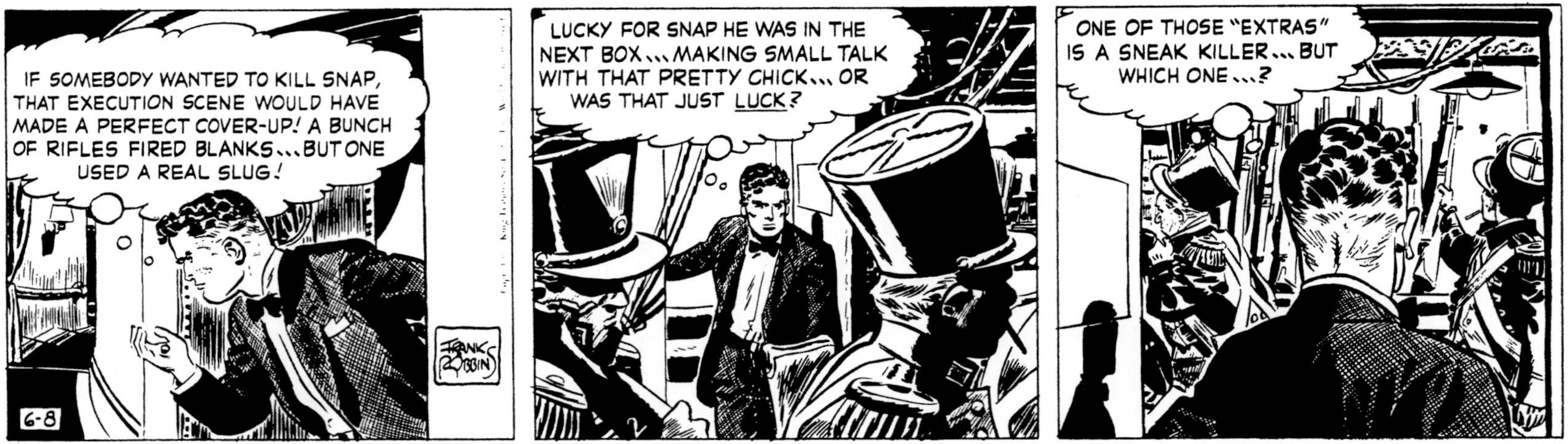
IF SOMEBODY WANTED TO KILL SNAP, THAT EXECUTION SCENE WOULD HAVE MADE A PERFECT COVER-UP! A BUNCH OF RIFLES FIRED BLANKS...BUT ONE USED A REAL SLUG!
FRANK ROBBINS
6-8
LUCKY FOR SNAP HE WAS IN THE NEXT BOX...MAKING SMALL TALK WITH THAT PRETTY CHICK...OR WAS THAT JUST LUCK?
ONE OF THOSE "EXTRAS" IS A SNEAK KILLER...BUT WHICH ONE...?

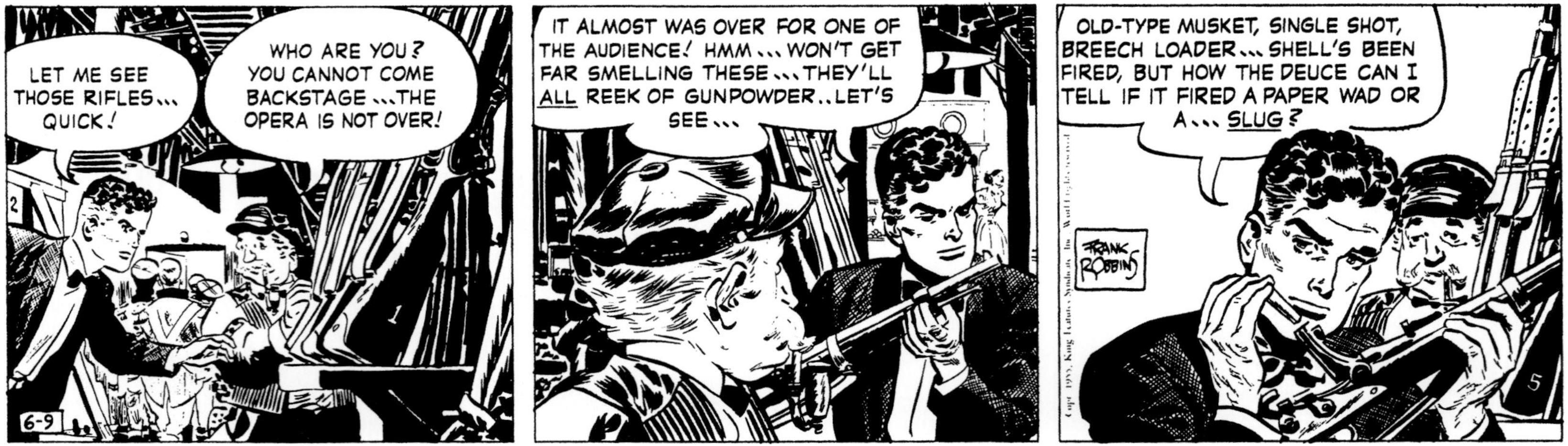
LET ME SEE THOSE RIFLES... QUICK!
WHO ARE YOU? YOU CANNOT COME BACKSTAGE...THE OPERA IS NOT OVER!
6-9
IT ALMOST WAS OVER FOR ONE OF THE AUDIENCE! HMM... WON'T GET FAR SMELLING THESE...THEY'LL ALL REEK OF GUNPOWDER..LET'S SEE...
OLD-TYPE MUSKET, SINGLE SHOT, BREECH LOADER...SHELL'S BEEN FIRED, BUT HOW THE DEUCE CAN I TELL IF IT FIRED A PAPER WAD OR A... SLUG?
FRANK ROBBINS

ONE OF THESE RIFLES FIRED THE REAL SLUG....THE OTHERS BLANKS! NOW IF I CAN ONLY FIND ONE <u>DIFFERENT</u> SHELL....

6-10

TWO MINUTES LATER....

ALL <u>ALIKE</u>! ALL FIRED....BUT NO INDICATION THAT ONE WAS A LIVE CARTRIDGE! MUST BE SOME WAY OF PINNING IT ON THE "EXTRA" WHO MADE THE MURDER TRY!

FRANK ROBBINS

MMM....LIVE SHELL....BLANK SHELL ISSUED BY PROPMAN....OF <u>COURSE</u>! THERE MUST BE AN <u>UNFIRED</u> BLANK AROUND SOMEWHERE!

WHERE'S THE DRESSING ROOM? I MUST CATCH THOSE EXTRAS BEFORE THEY LEAVE!

WHERE IS EVERYBODY?

ACH, THESE EXTRAS....THEY LEAVE AS SOON AS THEY CAN DISCARD THEIR COSTUMES!

6-11

DO YOU HAVE A RECORD OF WHO WORE WHICH UNIFORMS....IF I SHOULD FIND SOMETHING?

CERTAINLY, MEIN HERR ....RIGHT HERE I HAVE THE LIST! EACH UNIFORM'S NUMBERED....EACH NUMBER HAS A NAME!

SUCCESS! HERE IS THE ORIGINAL ISSUED <u>BLANK</u> CARTRIDGE....<u>UNFIRED</u>! WHOEVER WORE THIS OUTFIT PUT HIS OWN <u>LIVE</u> SHELL IN THE MUSKET!

AH-H, No. 6....THAT WAS ISSUED TO.... *ERIC KOLN*....ADDRESS 181 BURGSTRASSE, SALZBURG!

FRANK ROBBINS

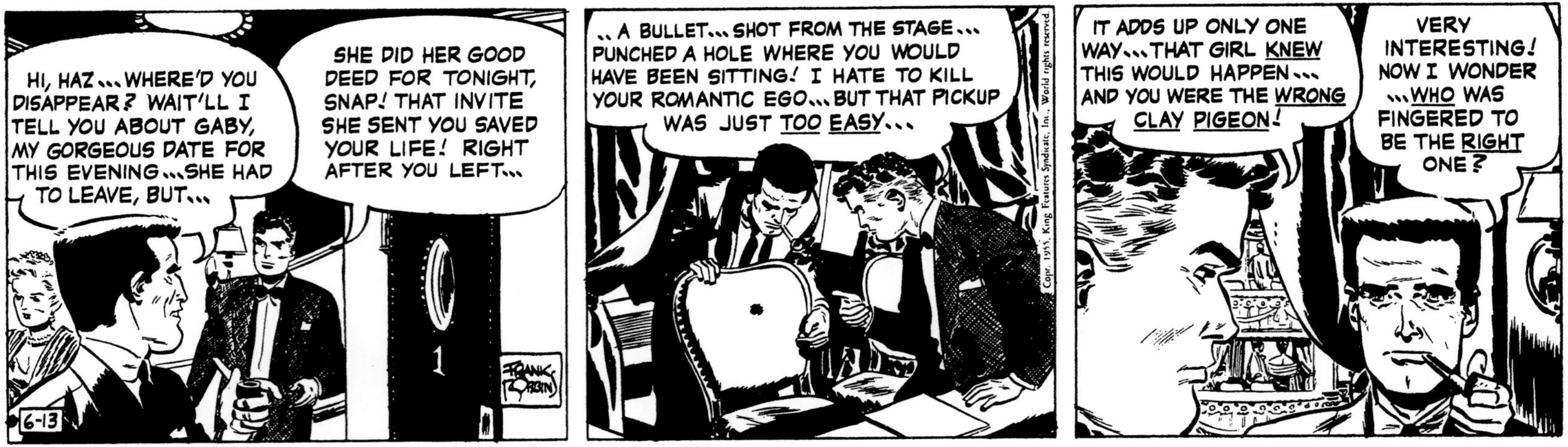
6-13
HI, HAZ... WHERE'D YOU DISAPPEAR? WAIT'LL I TELL YOU ABOUT GABY, MY GORGEOUS DATE FOR THIS EVENING... SHE HAD TO LEAVE, BUT...
SHE DID HER GOOD DEED FOR TONIGHT, SNAP! THAT INVITE SHE SENT YOU SAVED YOUR LIFE! RIGHT AFTER YOU LEFT...
FRANK ROBBINS
.. A BULLET... SHOT FROM THE STAGE... PUNCHED A HOLE WHERE YOU WOULD HAVE BEEN SITTING! I HATE TO KILL YOUR ROMANTIC EGO... BUT THAT PICKUP WAS JUST TOO EASY...
Copr. 1955, King Features Syndicate, Inc., World rights reserved.
IT ADDS UP ONLY ONE WAY... THAT GIRL KNEW THIS WOULD HAPPEN... AND YOU WERE THE WRONG CLAY PIGEON!
VERY INTERESTING! NOW I WONDER ...WHO WAS FINGERED TO BE THE RIGHT ONE?

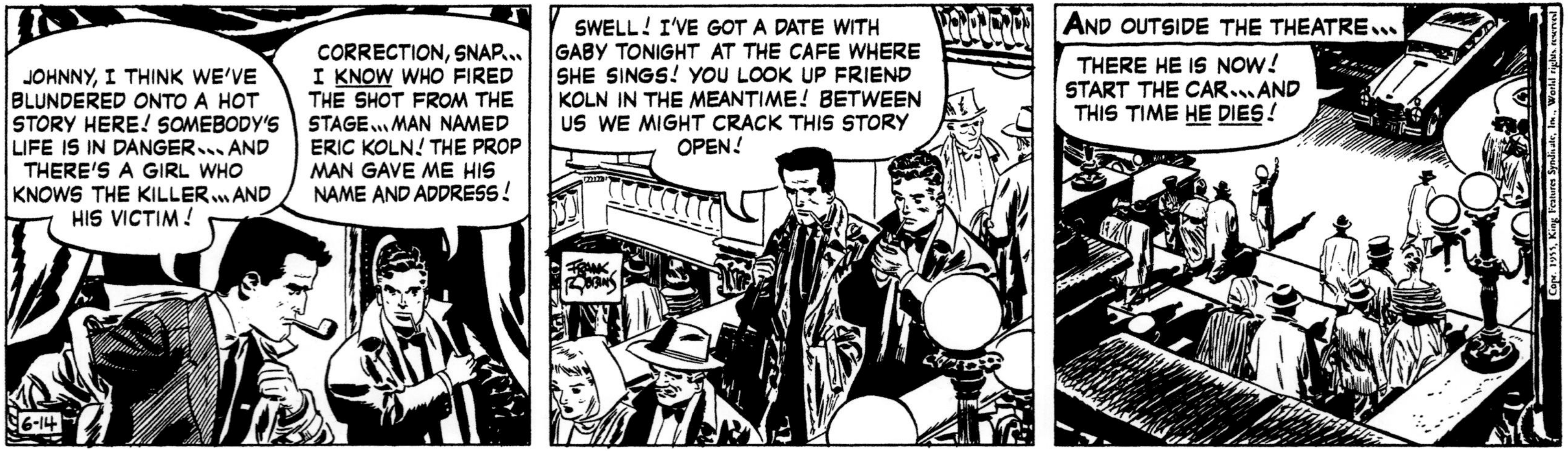
6-14
JOHNNY, I THINK WE'VE BLUNDERED ONTO A HOT STORY HERE! SOMEBODY'S LIFE IS IN DANGER... AND THERE'S A GIRL WHO KNOWS THE KILLER... AND HIS VICTIM!
CORRECTION, SNAP... I KNOW WHO FIRED THE SHOT FROM THE STAGE... MAN NAMED ERIC KOLN! THE PROP MAN GAVE ME HIS NAME AND ADDRESS!
SWELL! I'VE GOT A DATE WITH GABY TONIGHT AT THE CAFE WHERE SHE SINGS! YOU LOOK UP FRIEND KOLN IN THE MEANTIME! BETWEEN US WE MIGHT CRACK THIS STORY OPEN!
FRANK ROBBINS
AND OUTSIDE THE THEATRE...
THERE HE IS NOW! START THE CAR... AND THIS TIME HE DIES!
Copr. 1955, King Features Syndicate, Inc., World rights reserved.

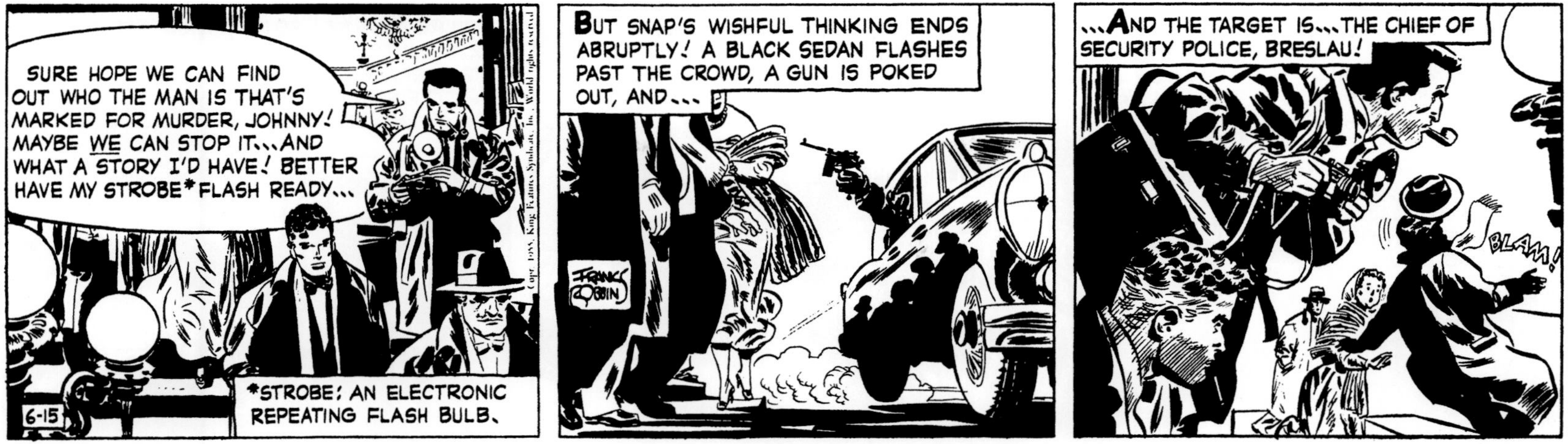
SURE HOPE WE CAN FIND OUT WHO THE MAN IS THAT'S MARKED FOR MURDER, JOHNNY! MAYBE WE CAN STOP IT... AND WHAT A STORY I'D HAVE! BETTER HAVE MY STROBE* FLASH READY...
*STROBE: AN ELECTRONIC REPEATING FLASH BULB.
6-15
BUT SNAP'S WISHFUL THINKING ENDS ABRUPTLY! A BLACK SEDAN FLASHES PAST THE CROWD, A GUN IS POKED OUT, AND...
FRANK ROBBINS
...AND THE TARGET IS... THE CHIEF OF SECURITY POLICE, BRESLAU!
BLAM!

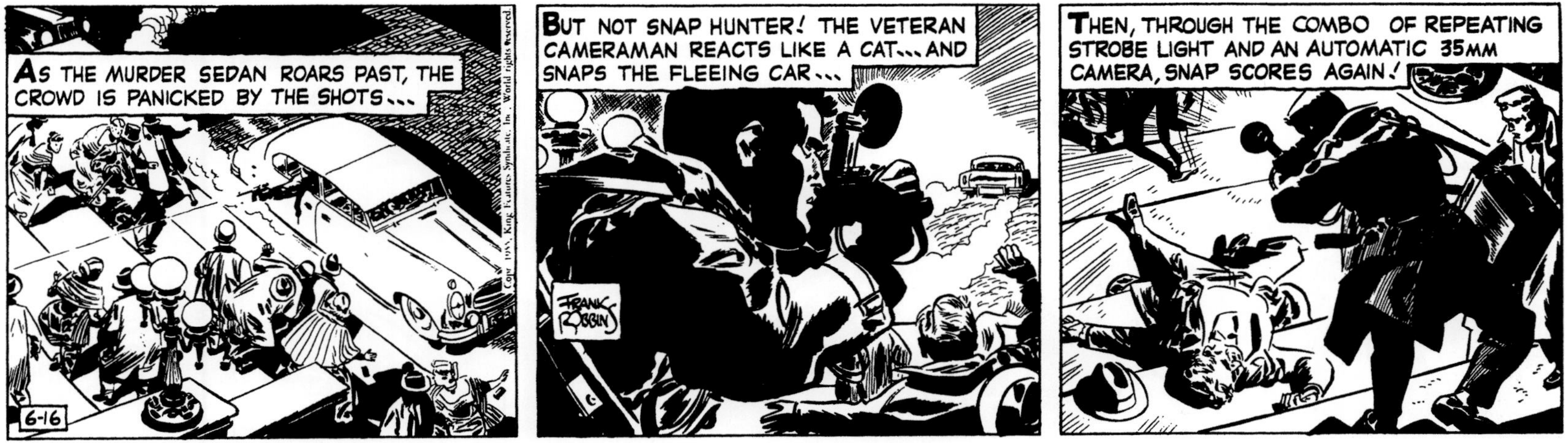
AS THE MURDER SEDAN ROARS PAST, THE CROWD IS PANICKED BY THE SHOTS...
6-16
BUT NOT SNAP HUNTER! THE VETERAN CAMERAMAN REACTS LIKE A CAT... AND SNAPS THE FLEEING CAR...
FRANK ROBBINS
THEN, THROUGH THE COMBO OF REPEATING STROBE LIGHT AND AN AUTOMATIC 35MM CAMERA, SNAP SCORES AGAIN!

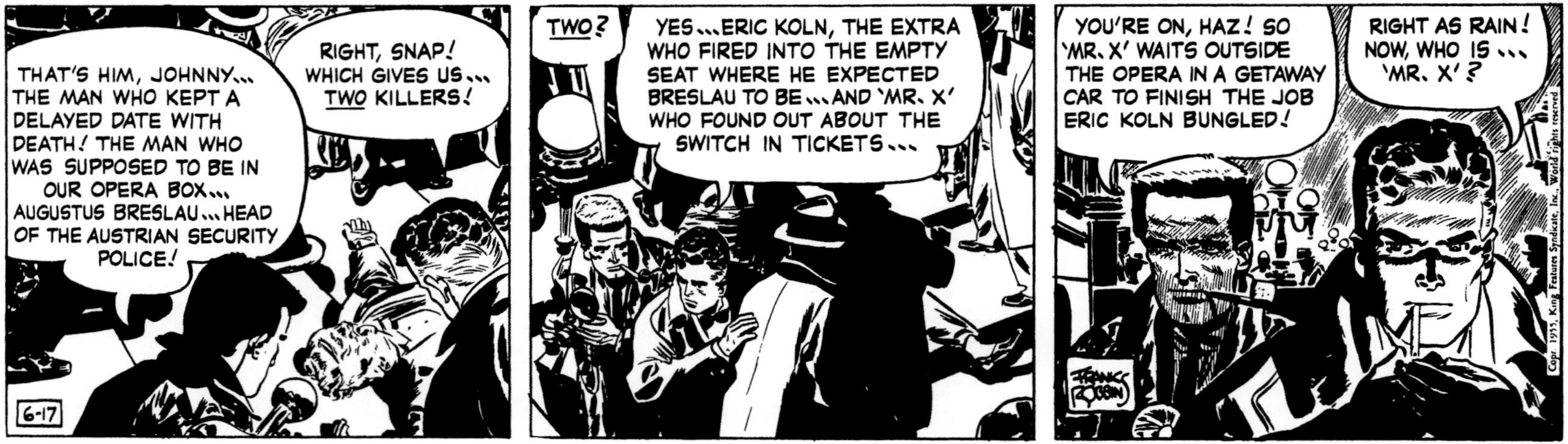
THAT'S HIM, JOHNNY... THE MAN WHO KEPT A DELAYED DATE WITH DEATH! THE MAN WHO WAS SUPPOSED TO BE IN OUR OPERA BOX... AUGUSTUS BRESLAU... HEAD OF THE AUSTRIAN SECURITY POLICE!
RIGHT, SNAP! WHICH GIVES US... TWO KILLERS!
6-17
TWO?
YES... ERIC KOLN, THE EXTRA WHO FIRED INTO THE EMPTY SEAT WHERE HE EXPECTED BRESLAU TO BE... AND 'MR. X' WHO FOUND OUT ABOUT THE SWITCH IN TICKETS...
YOU'RE ON, HAZ! SO 'MR. X' WAITS OUTSIDE THE OPERA IN A GETAWAY CAR TO FINISH THE JOB ERIC KOLN BUNGLED!
RIGHT AS RAIN! NOW, WHO IS... 'MR. X'?
FRANK ROBBINS
Copr. 1955, King Features Syndicate, Inc., World rights reserved

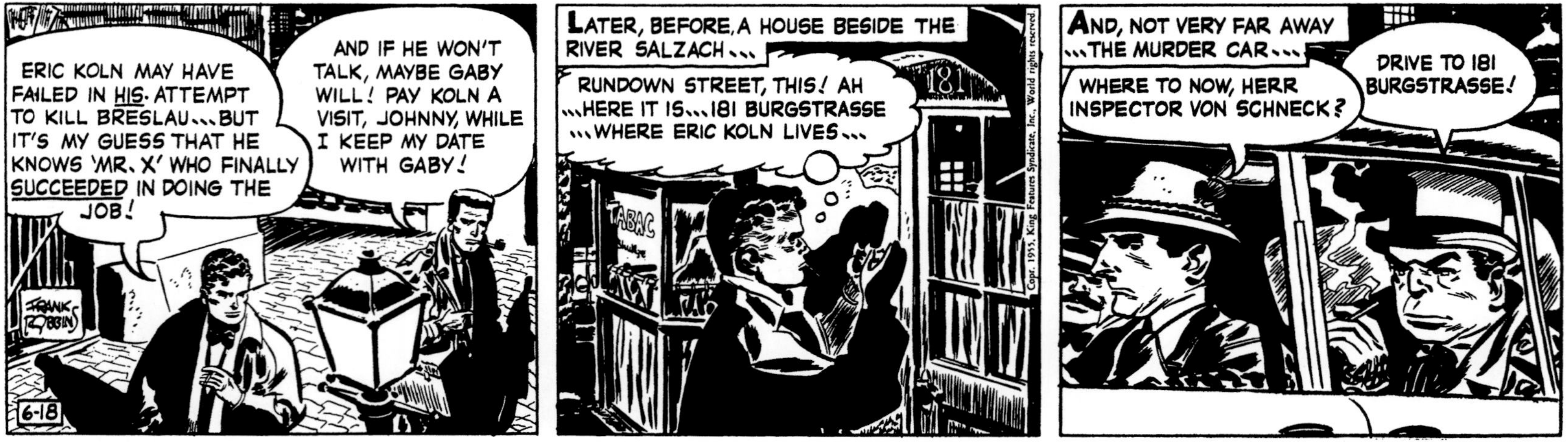
ERIC KOLN MAY HAVE FAILED IN HIS ATTEMPT TO KILL BRESLAU... BUT IT'S MY GUESS THAT HE KNOWS 'MR. X' WHO FINALLY SUCCEEDED IN DOING THE JOB!
AND IF HE WON'T TALK, MAYBE GABY WILL! PAY KOLN A VISIT, JOHNNY, WHILE I KEEP MY DATE WITH GABY!
FRANK ROBBINS
6-18
LATER, BEFORE A HOUSE BESIDE THE RIVER SALZACH...
RUNDOWN STREET, THIS! AH ...HERE IT IS... 181 BURGSTRASSE ...WHERE ERIC KOLN LIVES...
181
TABAC
Copr. 1955, King Features Syndicate, Inc., World rights reserved
AND, NOT VERY FAR AWAY ...THE MURDER CAR...
WHERE TO NOW, HERR INSPECTOR VON SCHNECK?
DRIVE TO 181 BURGSTRASSE!

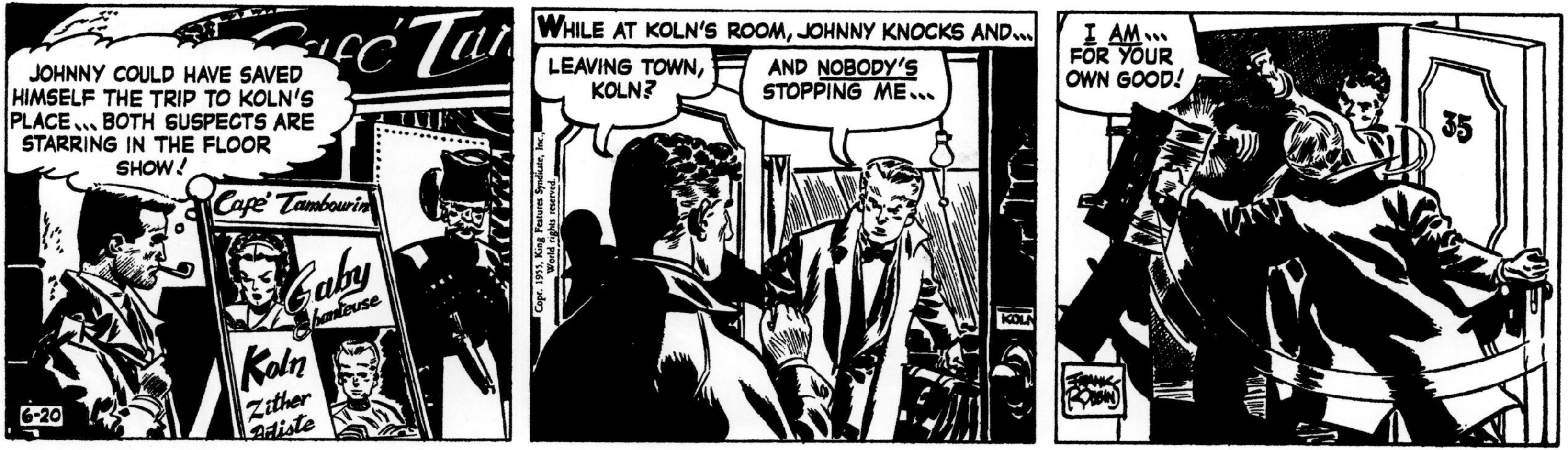

JOHNNY COULD HAVE SAVED HIMSELF THE TRIP TO KOLN'S PLACE... BOTH SUSPECTS ARE STARRING IN THE FLOOR SHOW!
Cafe' Tambourin
Gaby Chanteuse
Koln Zither
6-20
WHILE AT KOLN'S ROOM, JOHNNY KNOCKS AND...
LEAVING TOWN, KOLN?
AND NOBODY'S STOPPING ME...
Copr. 1955, King Features Syndicate, Inc., World rights reserved.
KOLN
I AM... FOR YOUR OWN GOOD!
35
FRANK ROBBINS

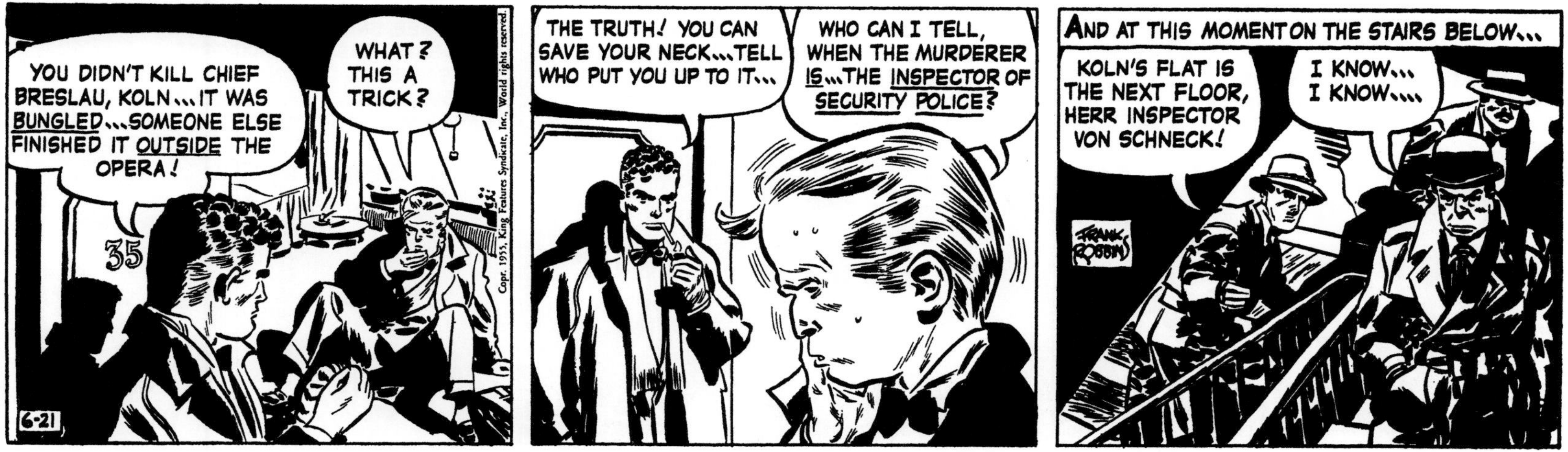

YOU DIDN'T KILL CHIEF BRESLAU, KOLN... IT WAS BUNGLED... SOMEONE ELSE FINISHED IT OUTSIDE THE OPERA!
WHAT? THIS A TRICK?
35
6-21
Copr. 1955, King Features Syndicate, Inc., World rights reserved.
THE TRUTH! YOU CAN SAVE YOUR NECK... TELL WHO PUT YOU UP TO IT...
WHO CAN I TELL, WHEN THE MURDERER IS... THE INSPECTOR OF SECURITY POLICE?
AND AT THIS MOMENT ON THE STAIRS BELOW...
KOLN'S FLAT IS THE NEXT FLOOR, HERR INSPECTOR VON SCHNECK!
I KNOW... I KNOW....
FRANK ROBBINS

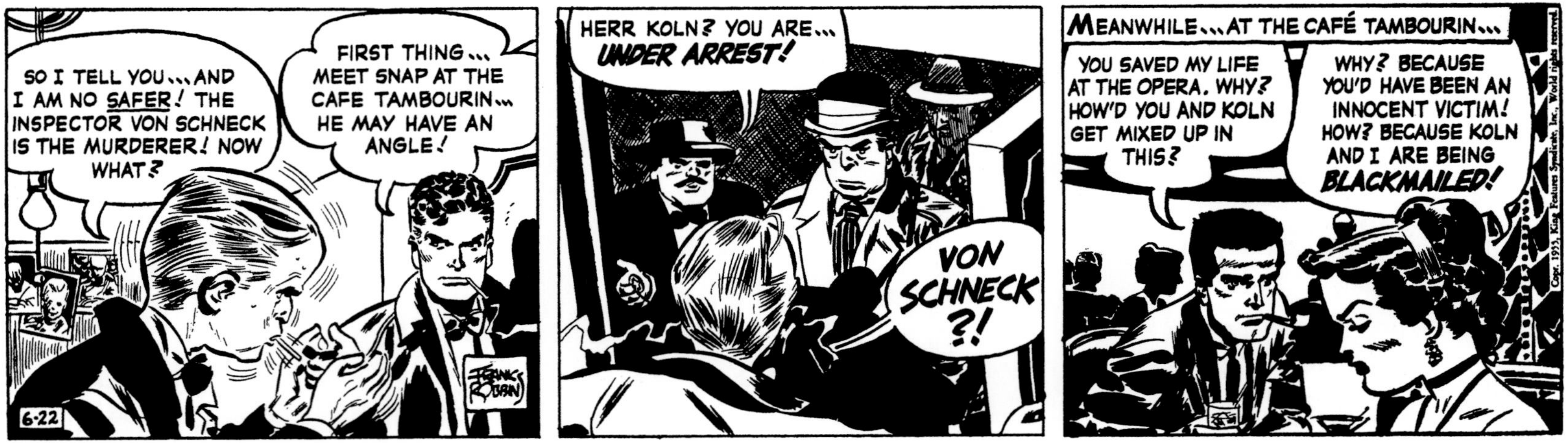
SO I TELL YOU... AND I AM NO SAFER! THE INSPECTOR VON SCHNECK IS THE MURDERER! NOW WHAT?
FIRST THING... MEET SNAP AT THE CAFE TAMBOURIN... HE MAY HAVE AN ANGLE!
FRANK ROBBINS
6-22
HERR KOLN? YOU ARE... UNDER ARREST!
VON SCHNECK?!
MEANWHILE... AT THE CAFÉ TAMBOURIN...
YOU SAVED MY LIFE AT THE OPERA. WHY? HOW'D YOU AND KOLN GET MIXED UP IN THIS?
WHY? BECAUSE YOU'D HAVE BEEN AN INNOCENT VICTIM! HOW? BECAUSE KOLN AND I ARE BEING BLACKMAILED!
Copr. 1955, King Features Syndicate, Inc., World rights reserved.

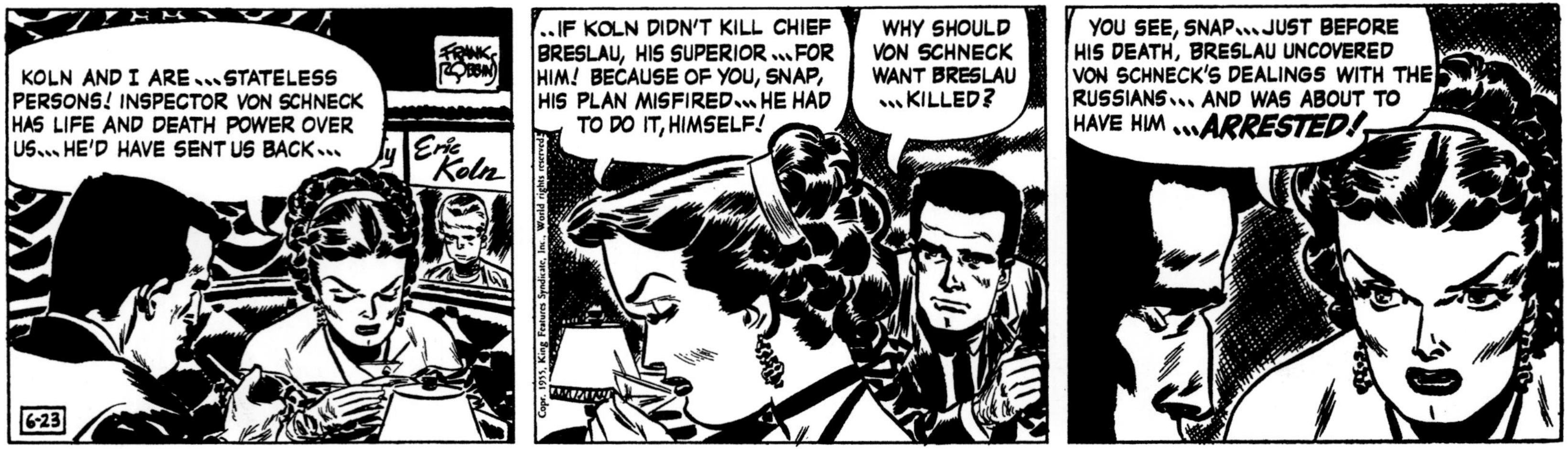
FRANK ROBBINS
KOLN AND I ARE... STATELESS PERSONS! INSPECTOR VON SCHNECK HAS LIFE AND DEATH POWER OVER US... HE'D HAVE SENT US BACK...
Eric Koln
6-23
..IF KOLN DIDN'T KILL CHIEF BRESLAU, HIS SUPERIOR... FOR HIM! BECAUSE OF YOU, SNAP, HIS PLAN MISFIRED... HE HAD TO DO IT, HIMSELF!
WHY SHOULD VON SCHNECK WANT BRESLAU ...KILLED?
Copr. 1955, King Features Syndicate, Inc., World rights reserved.
YOU SEE, SNAP... JUST BEFORE HIS DEATH, BRESLAU UNCOVERED VON SCHNECK'S DEALINGS WITH THE RUSSIANS... AND WAS ABOUT TO HAVE HIM ...ARRESTED!

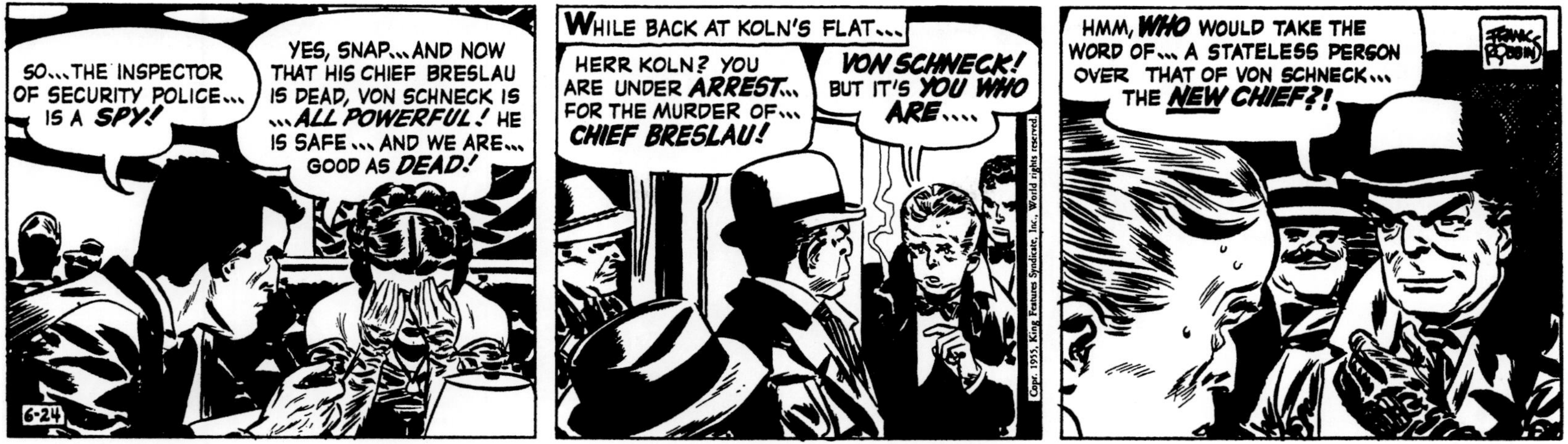
SO...THE INSPECTOR OF SECURITY POLICE... IS A SPY!
YES, SNAP...AND NOW THAT HIS CHIEF BRESLAU IS DEAD, VON SCHNECK IS ...ALL POWERFUL! HE IS SAFE ... AND WE ARE... GOOD AS DEAD!
6-24
WHILE BACK AT KOLN'S FLAT...
HERR KOLN? YOU ARE UNDER ARREST... FOR THE MURDER OF... CHIEF BRESLAU!
VON SCHNECK! BUT IT'S YOU WHO ARE....
Copr. 1955, King Features Syndicate, Inc., World rights reserved.
HMM, WHO WOULD TAKE THE WORD OF... A STATELESS PERSON OVER THAT OF VON SCHNECK... THE NEW CHIEF?!
FRANK ROBBINS

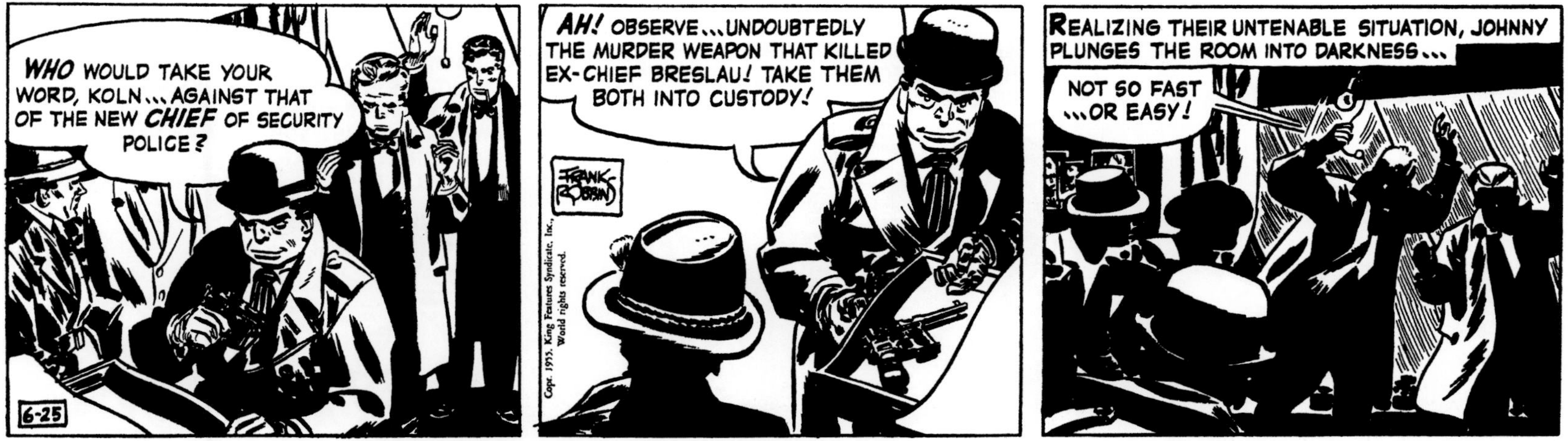
WHO WOULD TAKE YOUR WORD, KOLN...AGAINST THAT OF THE NEW CHIEF OF SECURITY POLICE?
6-25
AH! OBSERVE...UNDOUBTEDLY THE MURDER WEAPON THAT KILLED EX-CHIEF BRESLAU! TAKE THEM BOTH INTO CUSTODY!
FRANK ROBBINS
Copr. 1955, King Features Syndicate, Inc., World rights reserved.
REALIZING THEIR UNTENABLE SITUATION, JOHNNY PLUNGES THE ROOM INTO DARKNESS...
NOT SO FAST ...OR EASY!

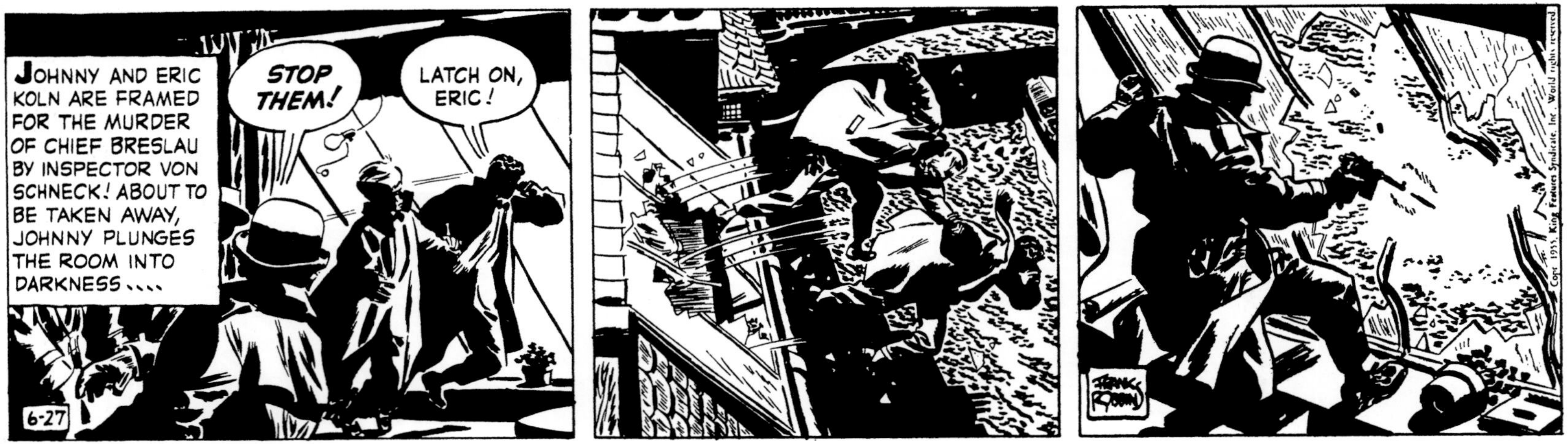

JOHNNY AND ERIC KOLN ARE FRAMED FOR THE MURDER OF CHIEF BRESLAU BY INSPECTOR VON SCHNECK! ABOUT TO BE TAKEN AWAY, JOHNNY PLUNGES THE ROOM INTO DARKNESS....
STOP THEM!
LATCH ON, ERIC!
6-27
FRANK ROBBINS

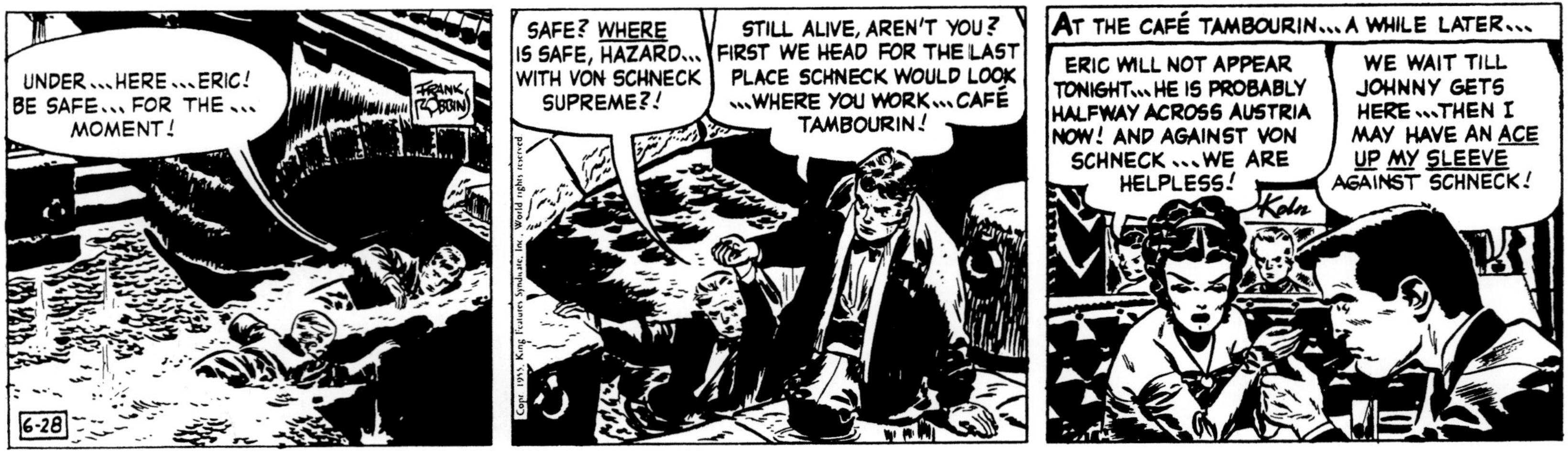

UNDER...HERE...ERIC! BE SAFE... FOR THE... MOMENT!
FRANK ROBBINS
6-28
SAFE? WHERE IS SAFE, HAZARD... WITH VON SCHNECK SUPREME?!
STILL ALIVE, AREN'T YOU? FIRST WE HEAD FOR THE LAST PLACE SCHNECK WOULD LOOK ...WHERE YOU WORK... CAFÉ TAMBOURIN!
AT THE CAFÉ TAMBOURIN... A WHILE LATER...
ERIC WILL NOT APPEAR TONIGHT... HE IS PROBABLY HALFWAY ACROSS AUSTRIA NOW! AND AGAINST VON SCHNECK ...WE ARE HELPLESS!
Koln
WE WAIT TILL JOHNNY GETS HERE...THEN I MAY HAVE AN ACE UP MY SLEEVE AGAINST SCHNECK!

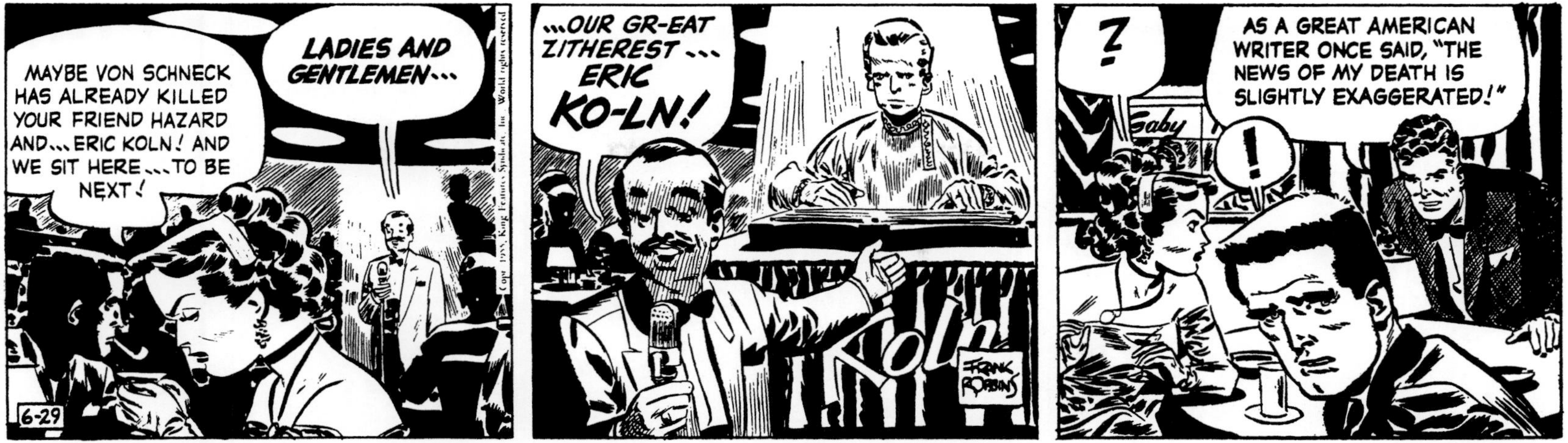
MAYBE VON SCHNECK HAS ALREADY KILLED YOUR FRIEND HAZARD AND... ERIC KOLN! AND WE SIT HERE... TO BE NEXT!
LADIES AND GENTLEMEN...
6-29
...OUR GR-EAT ZITHEREST... ERIC KO-LN!
KOLN
FRANK ROBBINS
?
AS A GREAT AMERICAN WRITER ONCE SAID, "THE NEWS OF MY DEATH IS SLIGHTLY EXAGGERATED!"
!

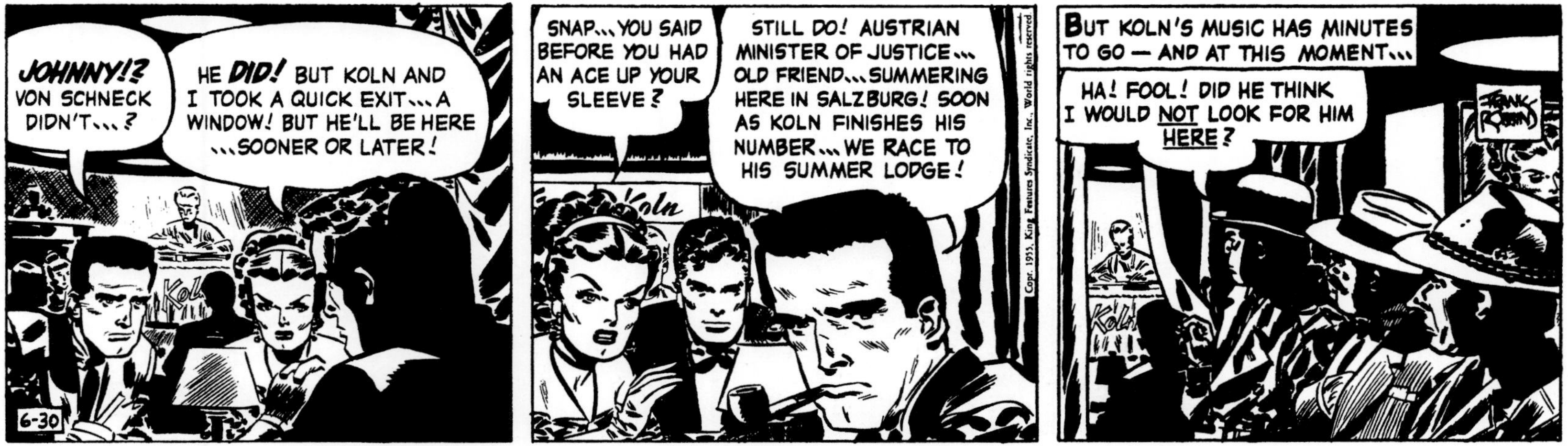
JOHNNY!? VON SCHNECK DIDN'T...?
HE DID! BUT KOLN AND I TOOK A QUICK EXIT... A WINDOW! BUT HE'LL BE HERE ...SOONER OR LATER!
6-30
SNAP... YOU SAID BEFORE YOU HAD AN ACE UP YOUR SLEEVE?
STILL DO! AUSTRIAN MINISTER OF JUSTICE... OLD FRIEND... SUMMERING HERE IN SALZBURG! SOON AS KOLN FINISHES HIS NUMBER... WE RACE TO HIS SUMMER LODGE!
Copr. 1955, King Features Syndicate, Inc., World rights reserved
BUT KOLN'S MUSIC HAS MINUTES TO GO — AND AT THIS MOMENT...
HA! FOOL! DID HE THINK I WOULD NOT LOOK FOR HIM HERE?
FRANK ROBBINS

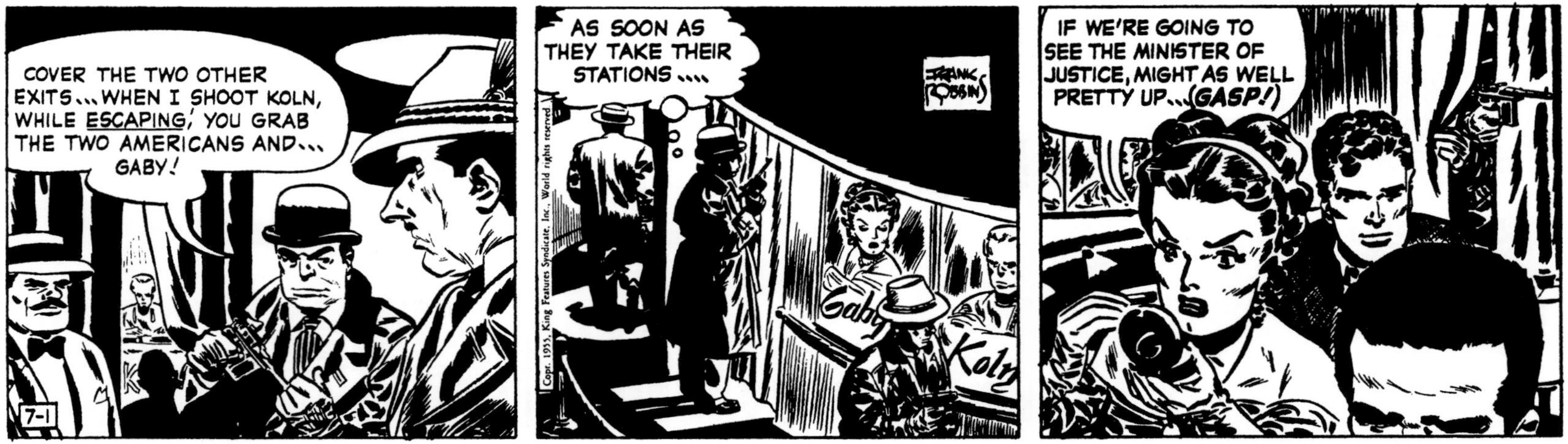
7-1
COVER THE TWO OTHER EXITS...WHEN I SHOOT KOLN, WHILE ESCAPING, YOU GRAB THE TWO AMERICANS AND... GABY!
AS SOON AS THEY TAKE THEIR STATIONS....
Copr. 1955, King Features Syndicate, Inc., World rights reserved
FRANK ROBBINS
IF WE'RE GOING TO SEE THE MINISTER OF JUSTICE, MIGHT AS WELL PRETTY UP...(GASP!)

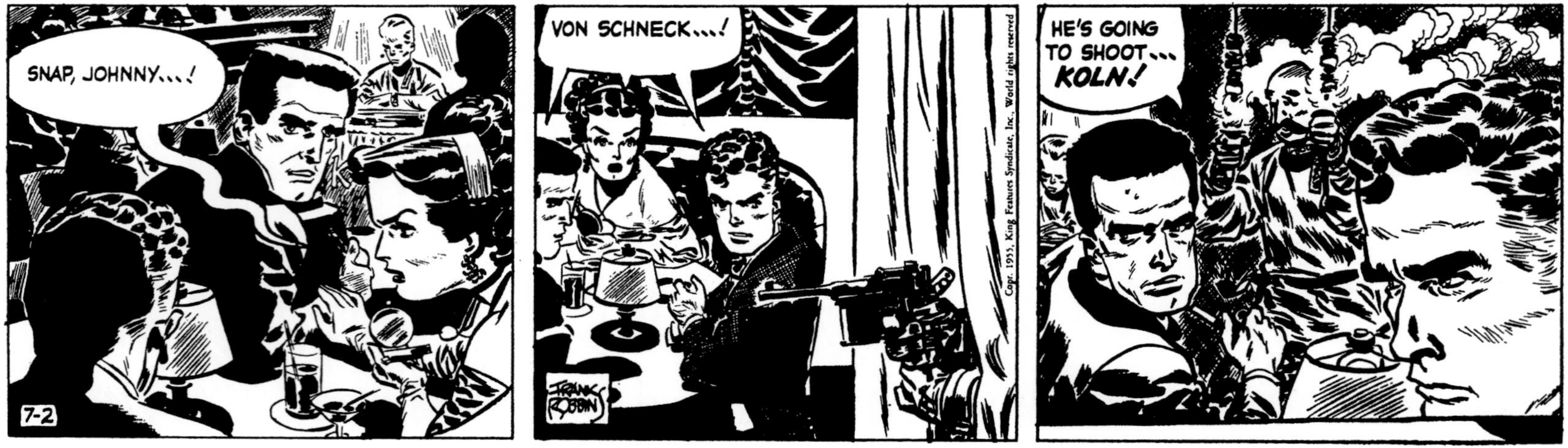
7-2
SNAP, JOHNNY...!
VON SCHNECK...!
FRANK ROBBINS
Copr. 1955, King Features Syndicate, Inc., World rights reserved
HE'S GOING TO SHOOT... KOLN!

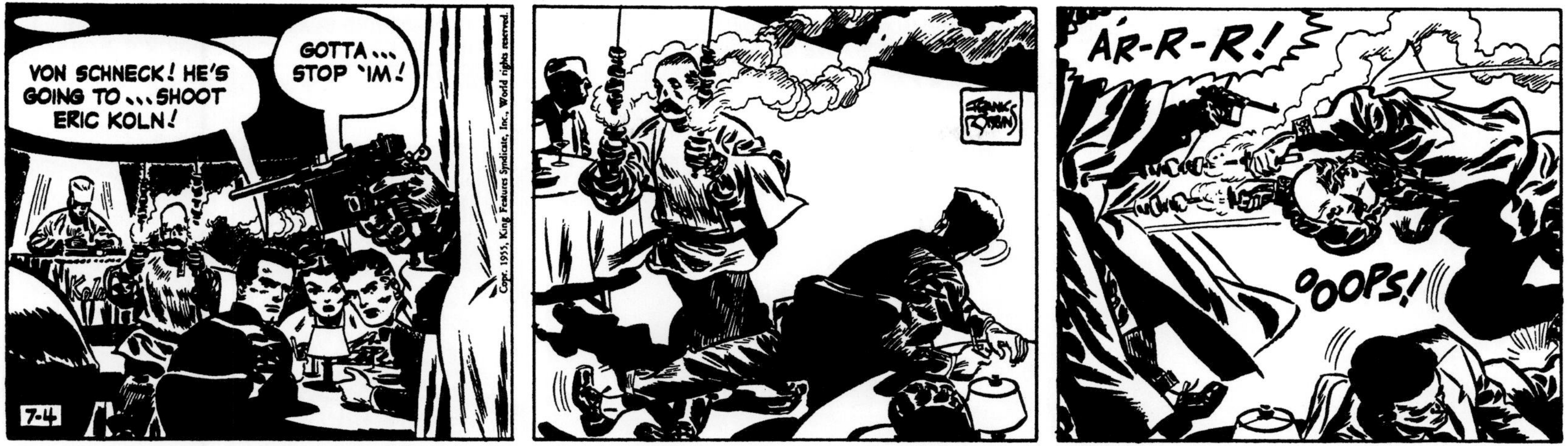
VON SCHNECK! HE'S GOING TO ... SHOOT ERIC KOLN!
GOTTA ... STOP 'IM!
Copr. 1955, King Features Syndicate, Inc., World rights reserved.
7-4
FRANK ROBBINS
AR-R-R!
OOOPS!

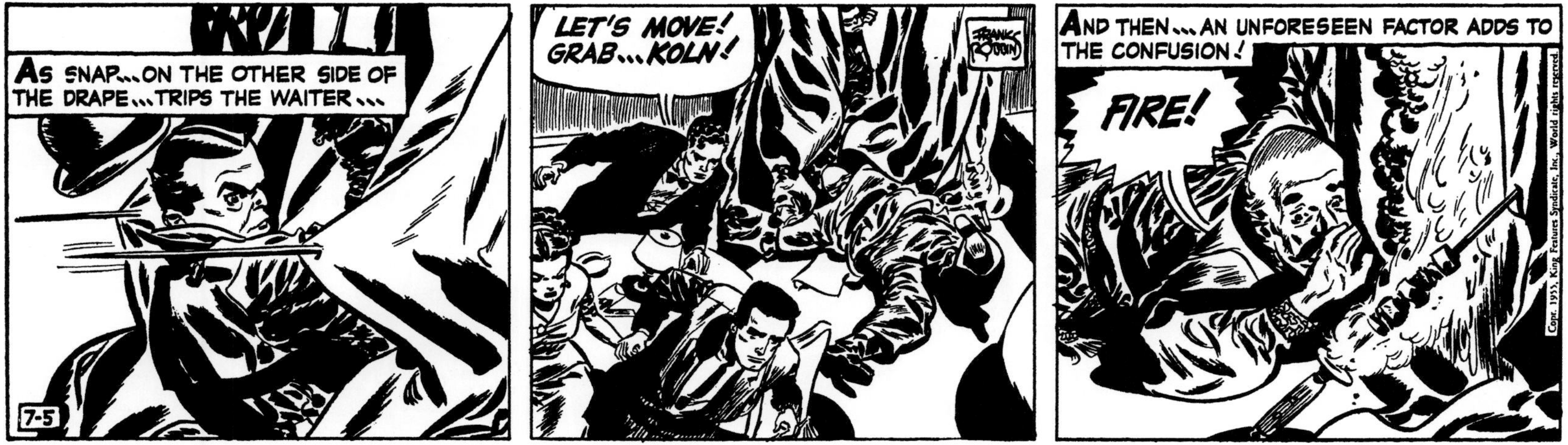
AS SNAP... ON THE OTHER SIDE OF THE DRAPE... TRIPS THE WAITER...
7-5
LET'S MOVE! GRAB... KOLN!
FRANK ROBBINS
AND THEN... AN UNFORESEEN FACTOR ADDS TO THE CONFUSION!
FIRE!
Copr. 1955, King Features Syndicate, Inc., World rights reserved.

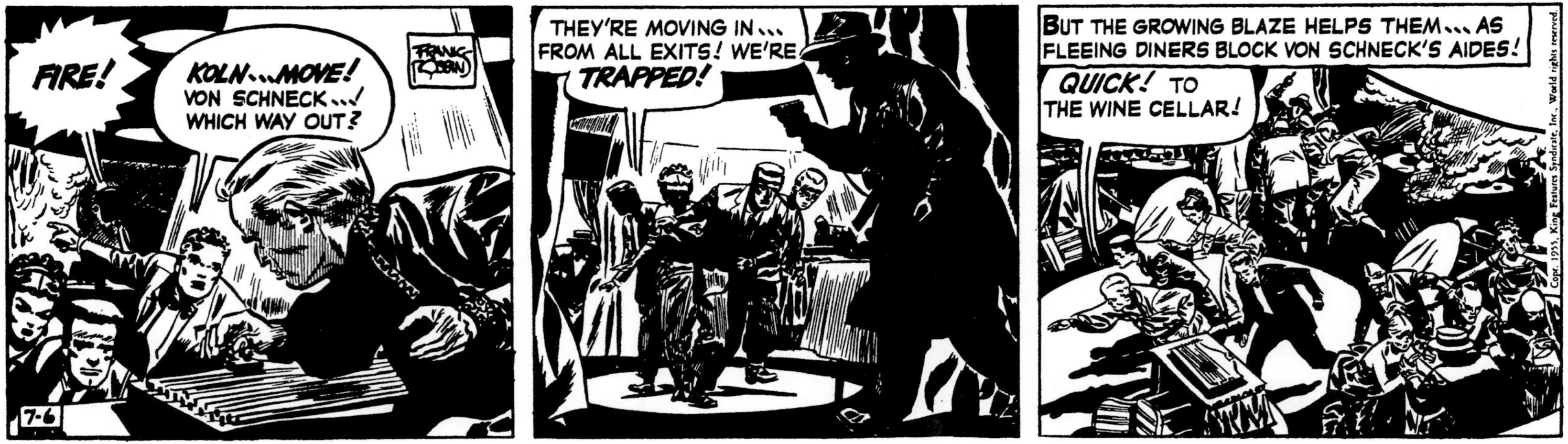
7-6
FIRE!
KOLN...MOVE! VON SCHNECK...! WHICH WAY OUT?
THEY'RE MOVING IN... FROM ALL EXITS! WE'RE TRAPPED!
BUT THE GROWING BLAZE HELPS THEM... AS FLEEING DINERS BLOCK VON SCHNECK'S AIDES!
QUICK! TO THE WINE CELLAR!
Copr. 1955, King Features Syndicate, Inc., World rights reserved.

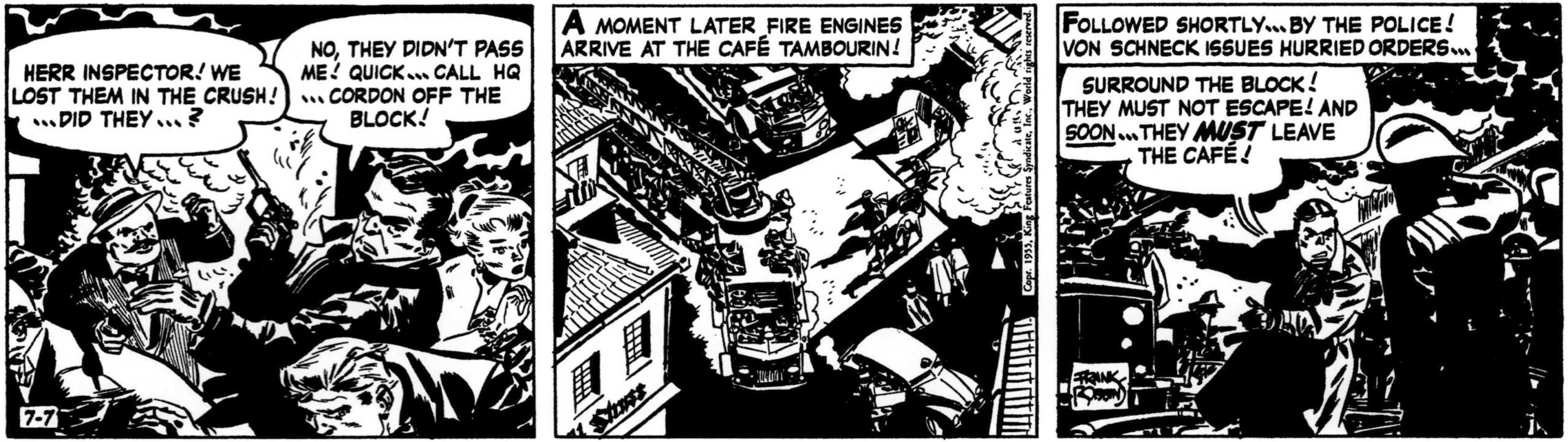
7-7
HERR INSPECTOR! WE LOST THEM IN THE CRUSH! ...DID THEY...?
NO, THEY DIDN'T PASS ME! QUICK... CALL HQ ...CORDON OFF THE BLOCK!
A MOMENT LATER FIRE ENGINES ARRIVE AT THE CAFÉ TAMBOURIN!
Copr. 1955, King Features Syndicate, Inc., World rights reserved.
FOLLOWED SHORTLY... BY THE POLICE! VON SCHNECK ISSUES HURRIED ORDERS...
SURROUND THE BLOCK! THEY MUST NOT ESCAPE! AND SOON... THEY MUST LEAVE THE CAFÉ!

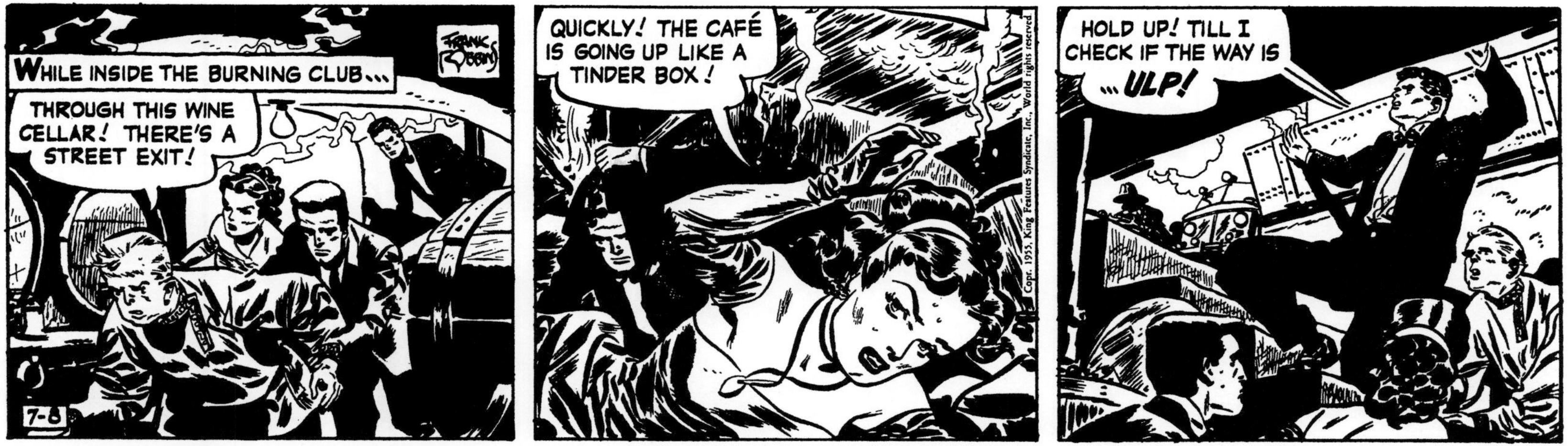
FRANK ROBBINS
WHILE INSIDE THE BURNING CLUB...
THROUGH THIS WINE CELLAR! THERE'S A STREET EXIT!
7-8
QUICKLY! THE CAFÉ IS GOING UP LIKE A TINDER BOX!
Copr. 1955, King Features Syndicate, Inc., World rights reserved
HOLD UP! TILL I CHECK IF THE WAY IS ...ULP!

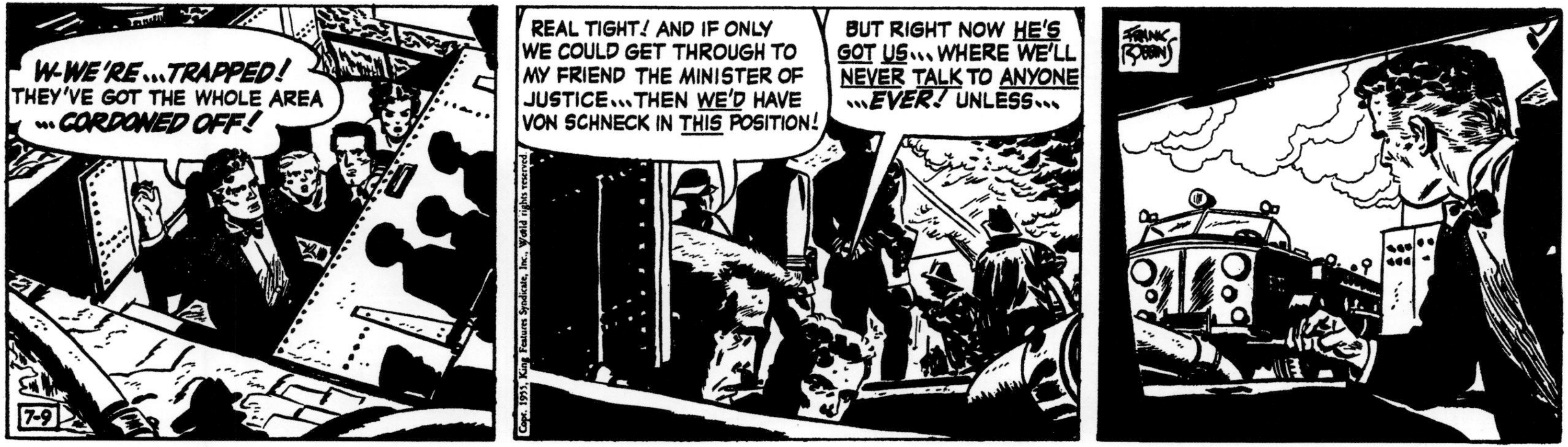
W-WE'RE...TRAPPED! THEY'VE GOT THE WHOLE AREA ...CORDONED OFF!
7-9
REAL TIGHT! AND IF ONLY WE COULD GET THROUGH TO MY FRIEND THE MINISTER OF JUSTICE...THEN WE'D HAVE VON SCHNECK IN THIS POSITION!
BUT RIGHT NOW HE'S GOT US...WHERE WE'LL NEVER TALK TO ANYONE ...EVER! UNLESS...
Copr. 1955, King Features Syndicate, Inc., World rights reserved.
FRANK ROBBINS

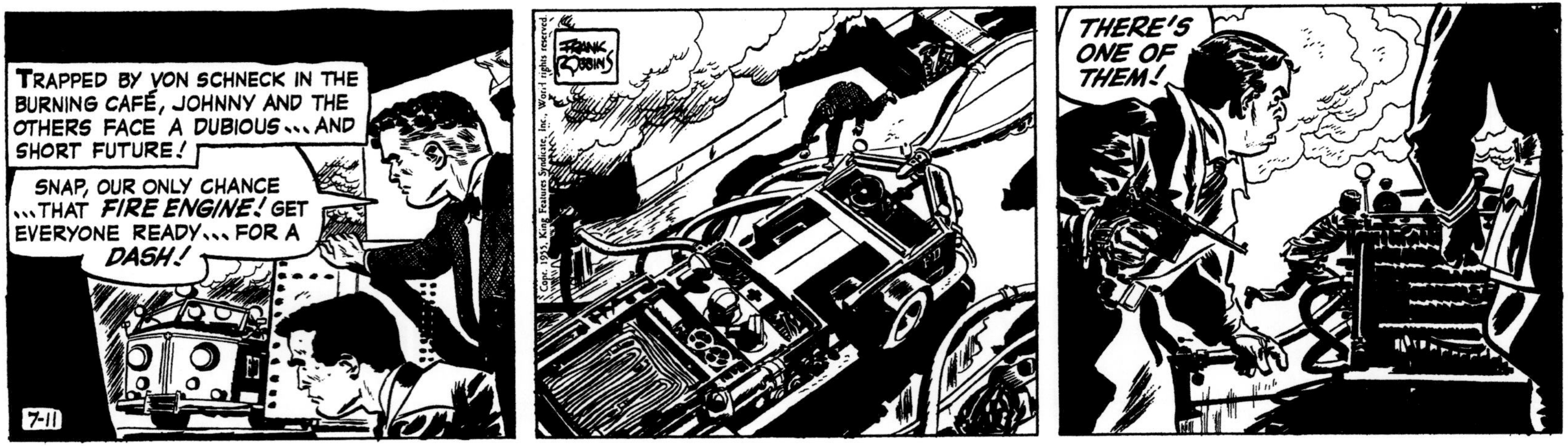
TRAPPED BY VON SCHNECK IN THE BURNING CAFÉ, JOHNNY AND THE OTHERS FACE A DUBIOUS ... AND SHORT FUTURE!
SNAP, OUR ONLY CHANCE ... THAT FIRE ENGINE! GET EVERYONE READY ... FOR A DASH!
7-11
FRANK ROBBINS
Copr. 1955, King Features Syndicate, Inc., World rights reserved.
THERE'S ONE OF THEM!

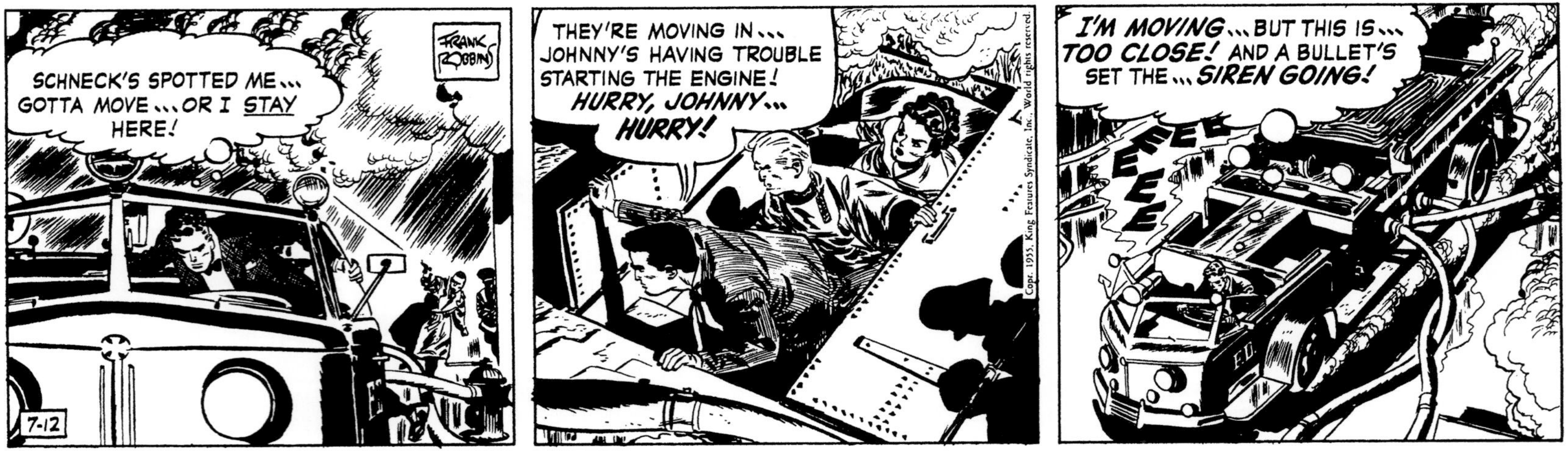
FRANK ROBBINS
SCHNECK'S SPOTTED ME ... GOTTA MOVE ... OR I STAY HERE!
7-12
THEY'RE MOVING IN ... JOHNNY'S HAVING TROUBLE STARTING THE ENGINE! HURRY, JOHNNY ... HURRY!
Copr. 1955, King Features Syndicate, Inc., World rights reserved.
I'M MOVING ... BUT THIS IS ... TOO CLOSE! AND A BULLET'S SET THE ... SIREN GOING!

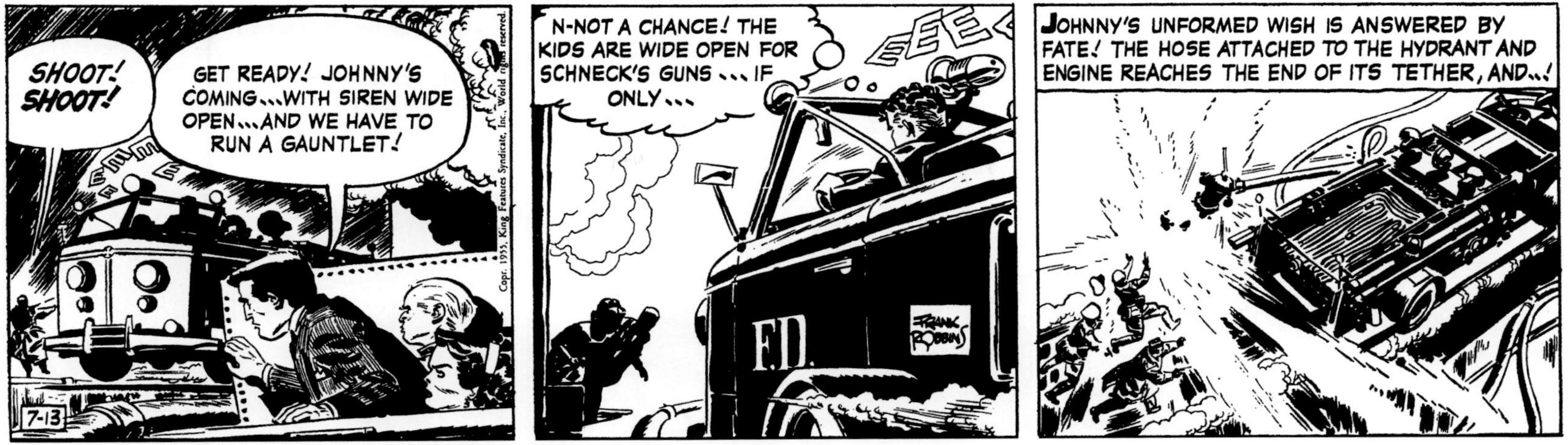
SHOOT! SHOOT!
GET READY! JOHNNY'S COMING...WITH SIREN WIDE OPEN...AND WE HAVE TO RUN A GAUNTLET!
Copr. 1955, King Features Syndicate, Inc., World rights reserved.
7-13
N-NOT A CHANCE! THE KIDS ARE WIDE OPEN FOR SCHNECK'S GUNS... IF ONLY...
EEEE
F.D.
FRANK ROBBINS
JOHNNY'S UNFORMED WISH IS ANSWERED BY FATE! THE HOSE ATTACHED TO THE HYDRANT AND ENGINE REACHES THE END OF ITS TETHER, AND...!

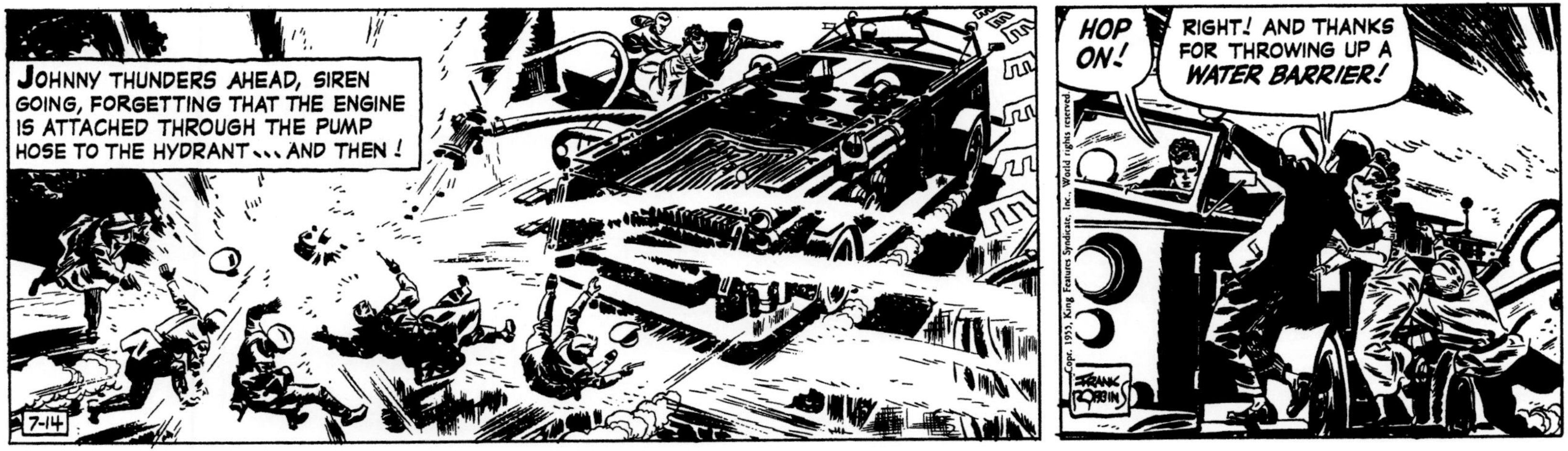
JOHNNY THUNDERS AHEAD, SIREN GOING, FORGETTING THAT THE ENGINE IS ATTACHED THROUGH THE PUMP HOSE TO THE HYDRANT... AND THEN!
7-14
HOP ON!
RIGHT! AND THANKS FOR THROWING UP A *WATER BARRIER!*
Copr. 1955, King Features Syndicate, Inc., World rights reserved.
FRANK ROBBINS

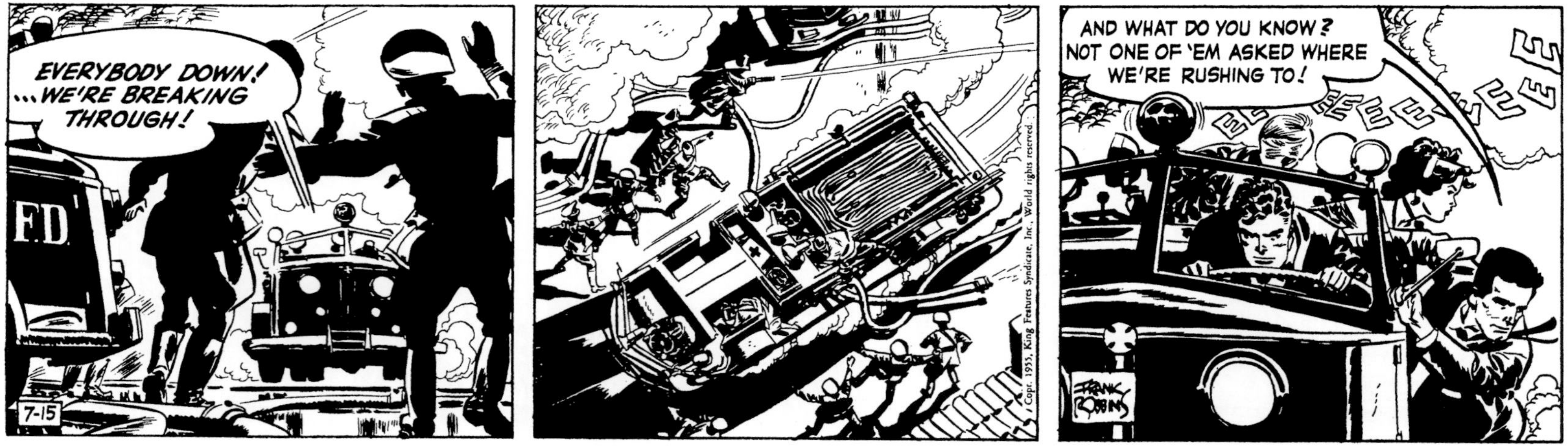
EVERYBODY DOWN! ...WE'RE BREAKING THROUGH!
7-15
Copr. 1955, King Features Syndicate, Inc., World rights reserved.
AND WHAT DO YOU KNOW? NOT ONE OF 'EM ASKED WHERE WE'RE RUSHING TO!
FRANK ROBBINS

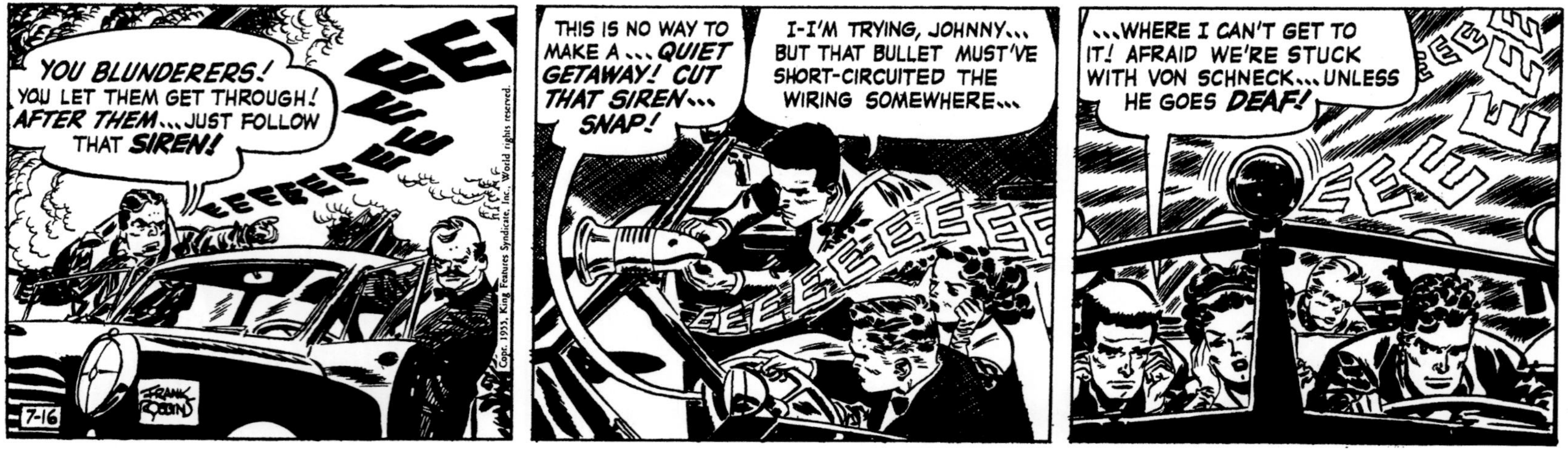
YOU BLUNDERERS! YOU LET THEM GET THROUGH! AFTER THEM...JUST FOLLOW THAT SIREN!
7-16
FRANK ROBBINS
Copr. 1955, King Features Syndicate, Inc., World rights reserved.
THIS IS NO WAY TO MAKE A... QUIET GETAWAY! CUT THAT SIREN... SNAP!
I-I'M TRYING, JOHNNY... BUT THAT BULLET MUST'VE SHORT-CIRCUITED THE WIRING SOMEWHERE...
...WHERE I CAN'T GET TO IT! AFRAID WE'RE STUCK WITH VON SCHNECK...UNLESS HE GOES DEAF!

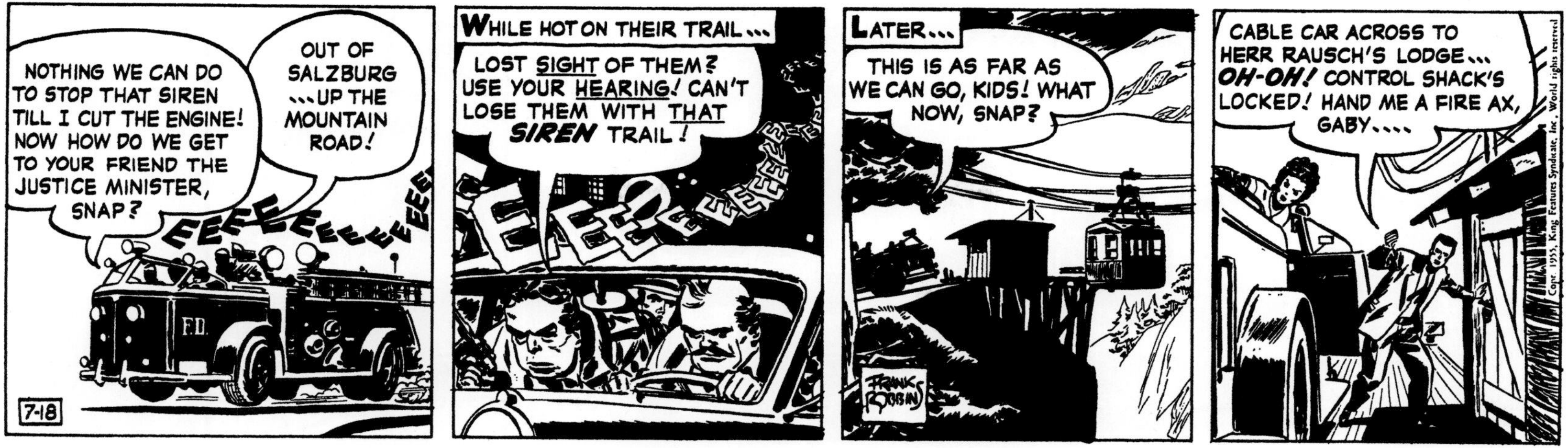
NOTHING WE CAN DO TO STOP THAT SIREN TILL I CUT THE ENGINE! NOW HOW DO WE GET TO YOUR FRIEND THE JUSTICE MINISTER, SNAP?
OUT OF SALZBURG ...UP THE MOUNTAIN ROAD!
EEEEEEEEEEEE
F.D.
7-18
WHILE HOT ON THEIR TRAIL...
LOST SIGHT OF THEM? USE YOUR HEARING! CAN'T LOSE THEM WITH THAT SIREN TRAIL!
LATER...
THIS IS AS FAR AS WE CAN GO, KIDS! WHAT NOW, SNAP?
FRANK ROBBINS
CABLE CAR ACROSS TO HERR RAUSCH'S LODGE... OH-OH! CONTROL SHACK'S LOCKED! HAND ME A FIRE AX, GABY....
Copr. 1955, King Features Syndicate, Inc., World rights reserved

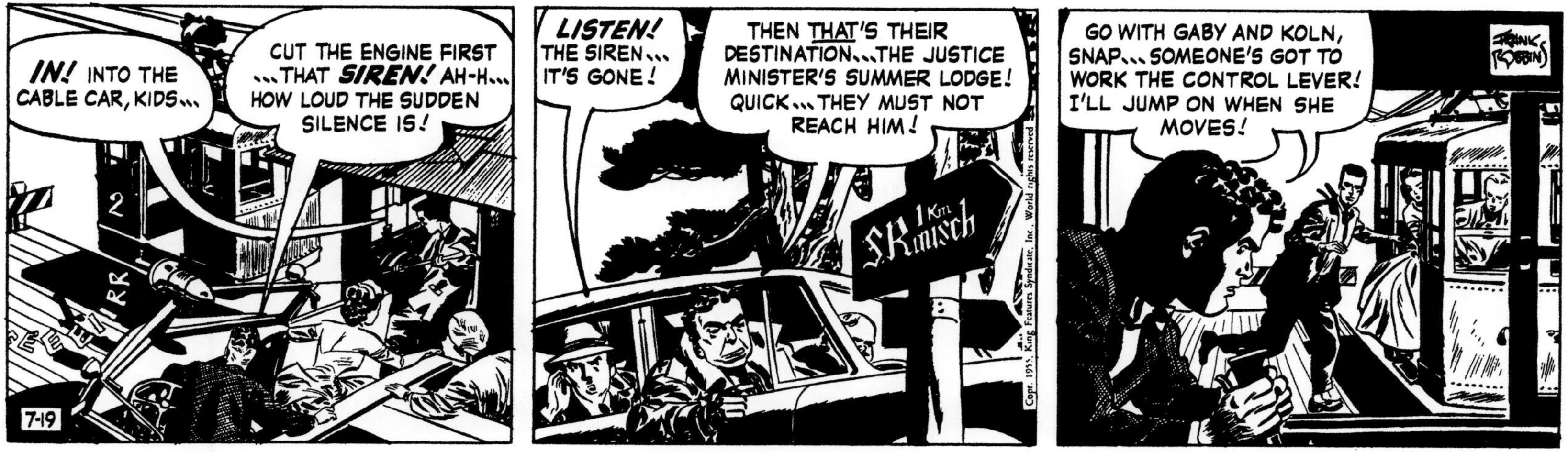
IN! INTO THE CABLE CAR, KIDS...
CUT THE ENGINE FIRST ...THAT SIREN! AH-H... HOW LOUD THE SUDDEN SILENCE IS!
2
7-19
LISTEN! THE SIREN... IT'S GONE!
THEN THAT'S THEIR DESTINATION...THE JUSTICE MINISTER'S SUMMER LODGE! QUICK...THEY MUST NOT REACH HIM!
1 Km
Rausch
Copr. 1955, King Features Syndicate, Inc., World rights reserved
GO WITH GABY AND KOLN, SNAP... SOMEONE'S GOT TO WORK THE CONTROL LEVER! I'LL JUMP ON WHEN SHE MOVES!
FRANK ROBBINS

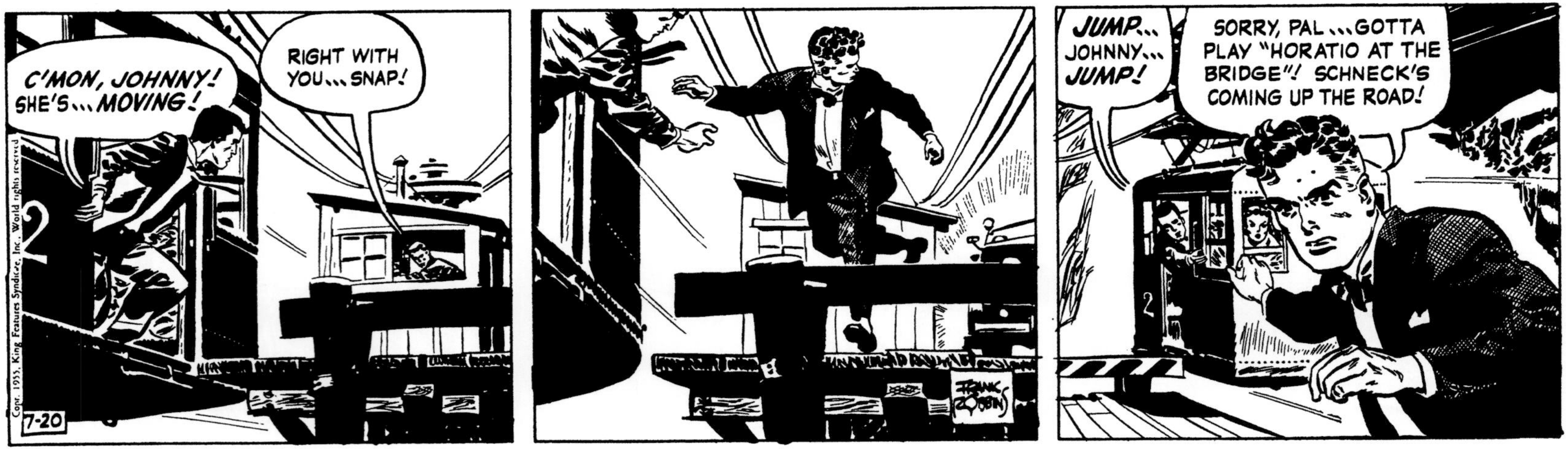

7-20
Copr. 1955, King Features Syndicate, Inc., World rights reserved
C'MON, JOHNNY! SHE'S... MOVING!
RIGHT WITH YOU... SNAP!
FRANK ROBBINS
JUMP... JOHNNY... JUMP!
SORRY, PAL... GOTTA PLAY "HORATIO AT THE BRIDGE"! SCHNECK'S COMING UP THE ROAD!

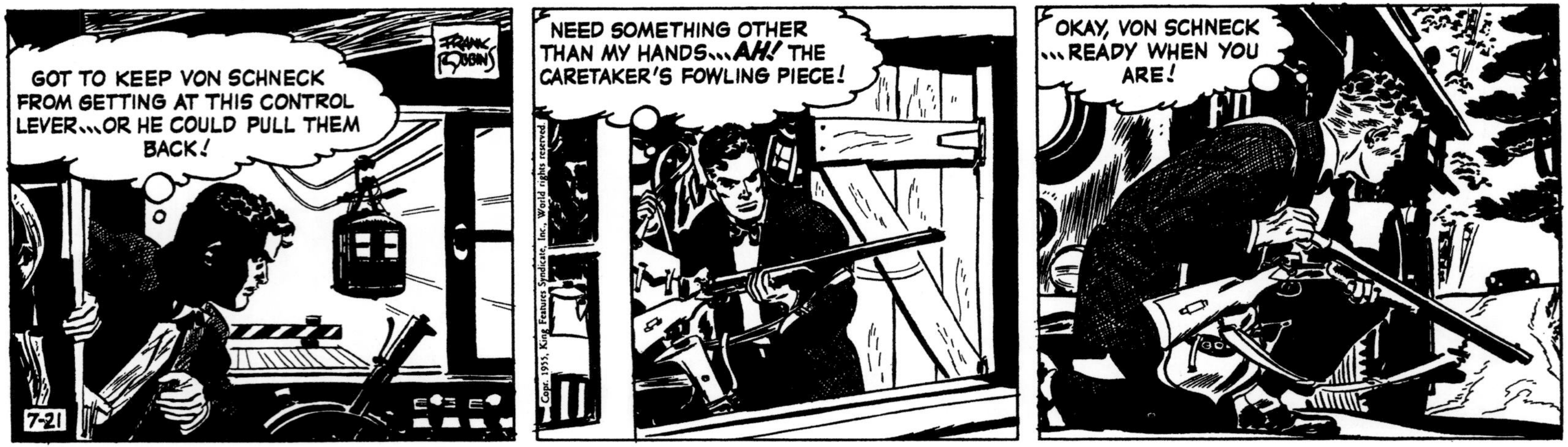

7-21
FRANK ROBBINS
GOT TO KEEP VON SCHNECK FROM GETTING AT THIS CONTROL LEVER... OR HE COULD PULL THEM BACK!
Copr. 1955, King Features Syndicate, Inc., World rights reserved.
NEED SOMETHING OTHER THAN MY HANDS... AH! THE CARETAKER'S FOWLING PIECE!
OKAY, VON SCHNECK ...READY WHEN YOU ARE!

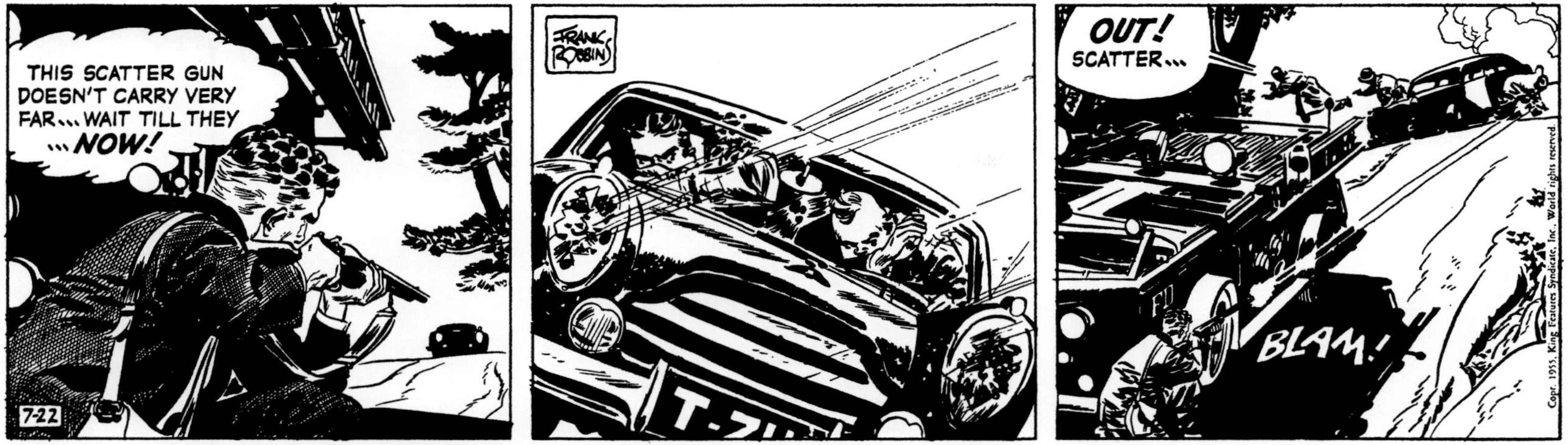
THIS SCATTER GUN DOESN'T CARRY VERY FAR... WAIT TILL THEY ...NOW!
7-22
FRANK ROBBINS
OUT! SCATTER...
BLAM!
Copr. 1955, King Features Syndicate, Inc., World rights reserved.

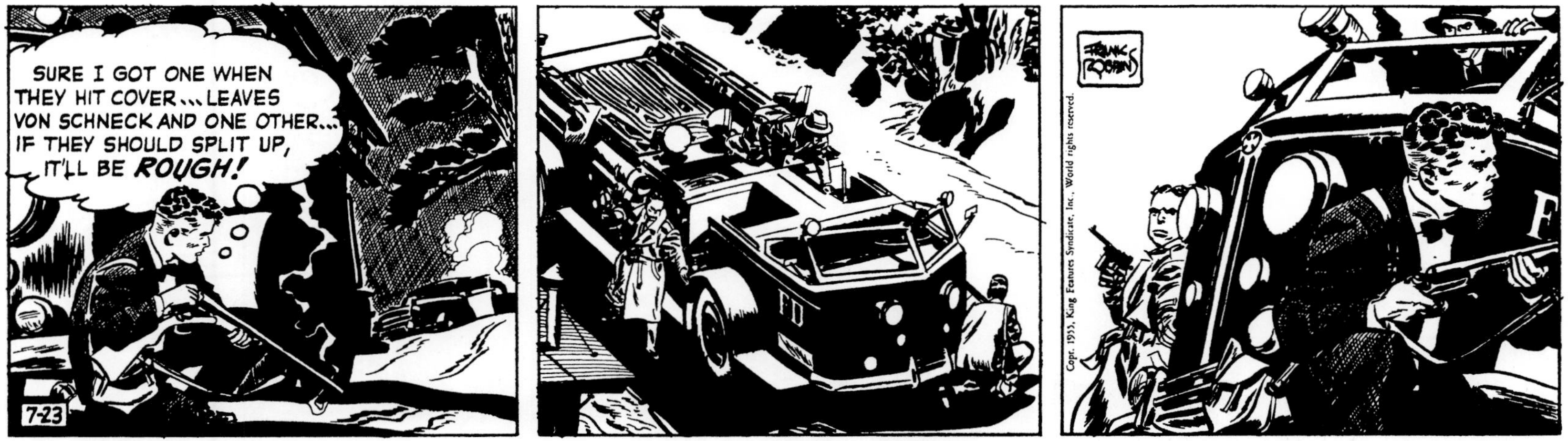
SURE I GOT ONE WHEN THEY HIT COVER... LEAVES VON SCHNECK AND ONE OTHER... IF THEY SHOULD SPLIT UP, IT'LL BE ROUGH!
7-23
FD
Copr. 1955, King Features Syndicate, Inc., World rights reserved.
FRANK ROBBINS

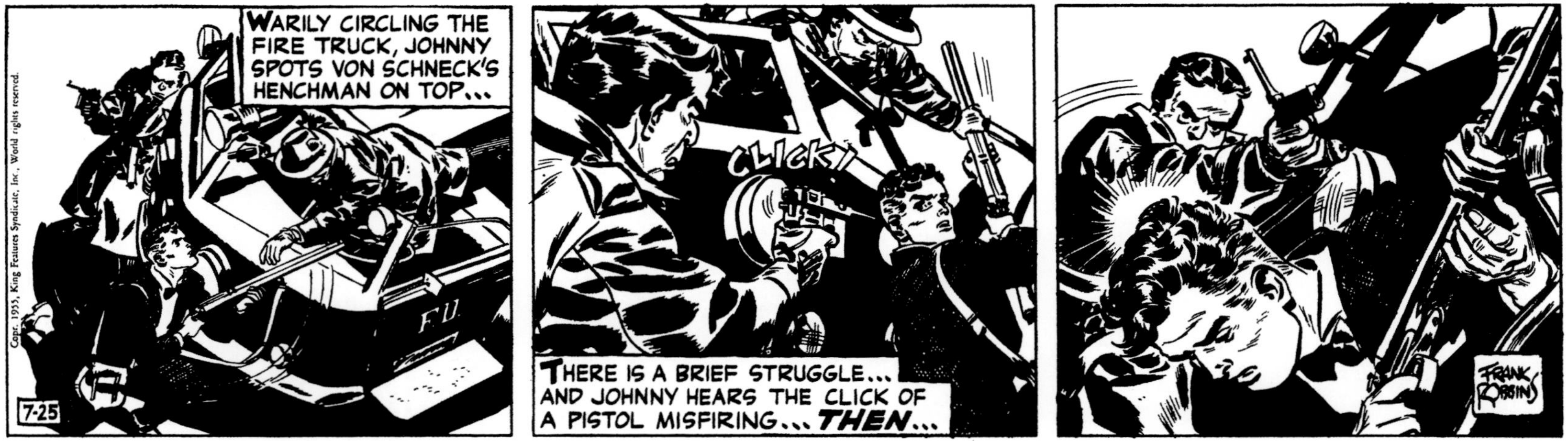
WARILY CIRCLING THE FIRE TRUCK, JOHNNY SPOTS VON SCHNECK'S HENCHMAN ON TOP...
Copr. 1955, King Features Syndicate, Inc., World rights reserved.
7-25
CLICK!
THERE IS A BRIEF STRUGGLE... AND JOHNNY HEARS THE CLICK OF A PISTOL MISFIRING... THEN...
FRANK ROBBINS

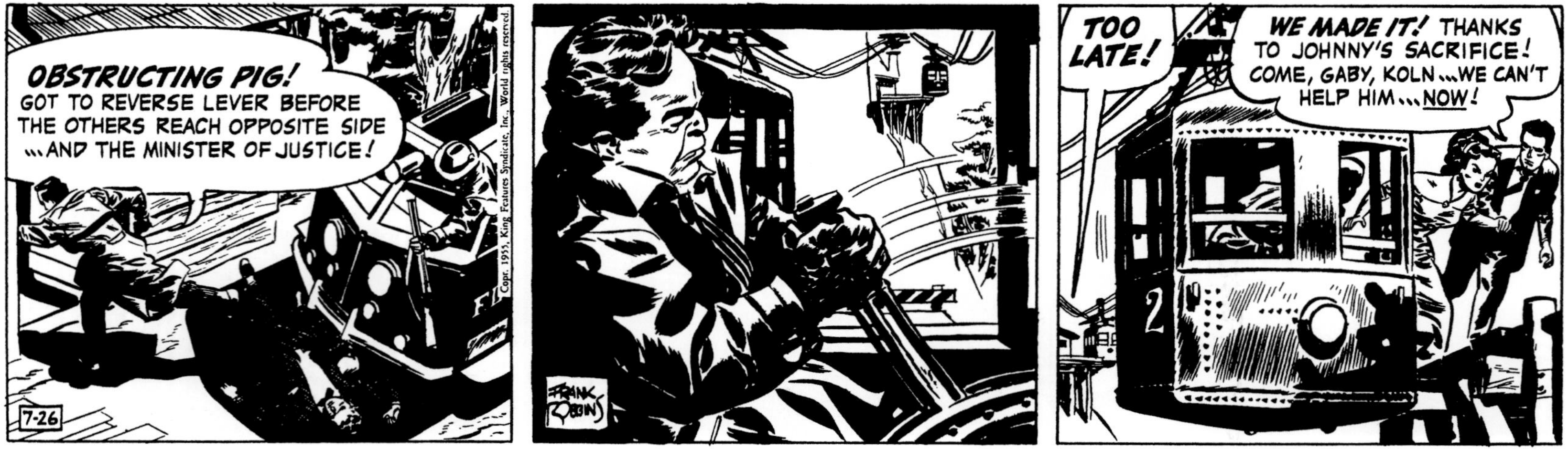
OBSTRUCTING PIG! GOT TO REVERSE LEVER BEFORE THE OTHERS REACH OPPOSITE SIDE ...AND THE MINISTER OF JUSTICE!
Copr. 1955, King Features Syndicate, Inc., World rights reserved.
7-26
FRANK ROBBINS
TOO LATE!
WE MADE IT! THANKS TO JOHNNY'S SACRIFICE! COME, GABY, KOLN...WE CAN'T HELP HIM...NOW!

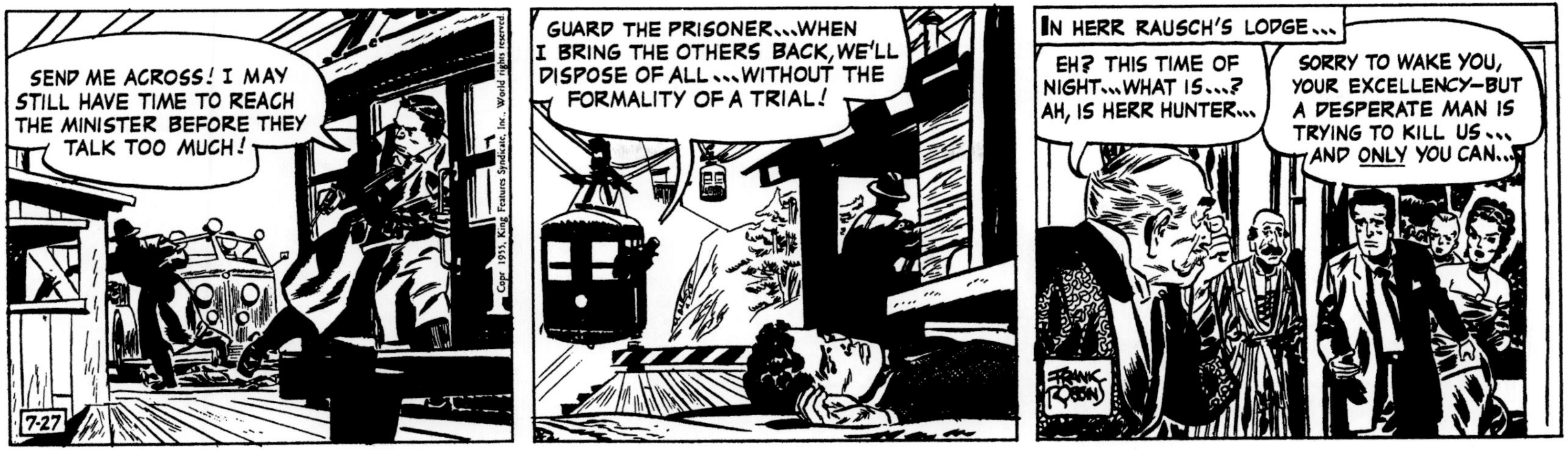
SEND ME ACROSS! I MAY STILL HAVE TIME TO REACH THE MINISTER BEFORE THEY TALK TOO MUCH!
Copr 1955, King Features Syndicate, Inc., World rights reserved.
7-27
GUARD THE PRISONER...WHEN I BRING THE OTHERS BACK, WE'LL DISPOSE OF ALL...WITHOUT THE FORMALITY OF A TRIAL!
IN HERR RAUSCH'S LODGE...
EH? THIS TIME OF NIGHT...WHAT IS...? AH, IS HERR HUNTER...
SORRY TO WAKE YOU, YOUR EXCELLENCY—BUT A DESPERATE MAN IS TRYING TO KILL US... AND ONLY YOU CAN...
FRANK ROBBINS

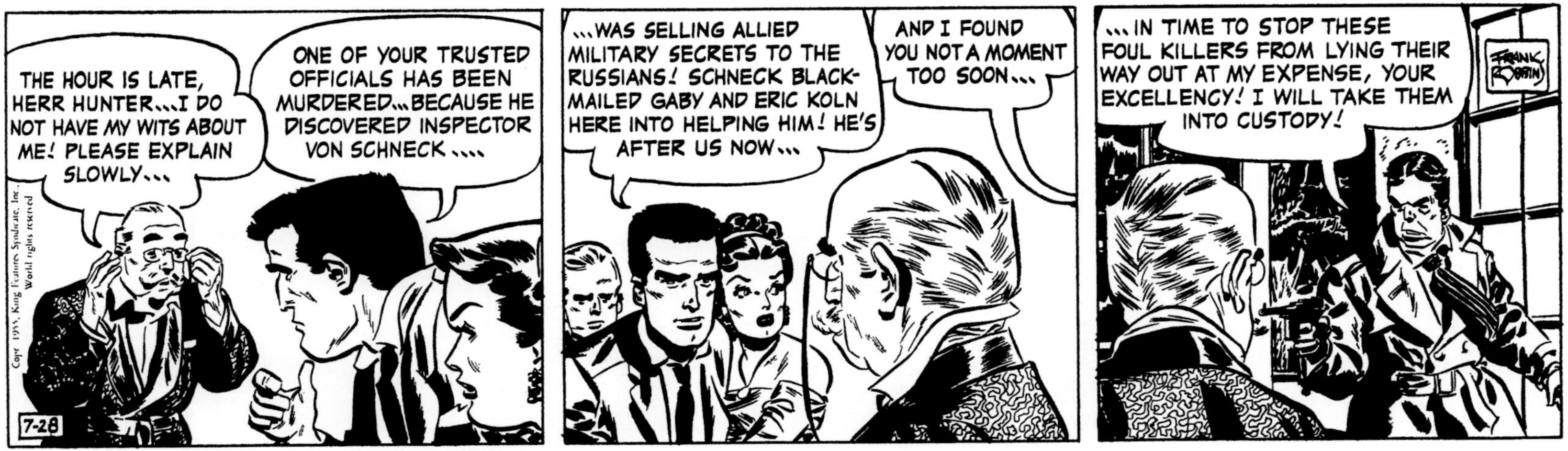
THE HOUR IS LATE, HERR HUNTER...I DO NOT HAVE MY WITS ABOUT ME! PLEASE EXPLAIN SLOWLY...
ONE OF YOUR TRUSTED OFFICIALS HAS BEEN MURDERED...BECAUSE HE DISCOVERED INSPECTOR VON SCHNECK....
Copr 1955, King Features Syndicate, Inc., World rights reserved
7-28
...WAS SELLING ALLIED MILITARY SECRETS TO THE RUSSIANS! SCHNECK BLACK-MAILED GABY AND ERIC KOLN HERE INTO HELPING HIM! HE'S AFTER US NOW...
AND I FOUND YOU NOT A MOMENT TOO SOON...
...IN TIME TO STOP THESE FOUL KILLERS FROM LYING THEIR WAY OUT AT MY EXPENSE, YOUR EXCELLENCY! I WILL TAKE THEM INTO CUSTODY!
FRANK ROBBINS

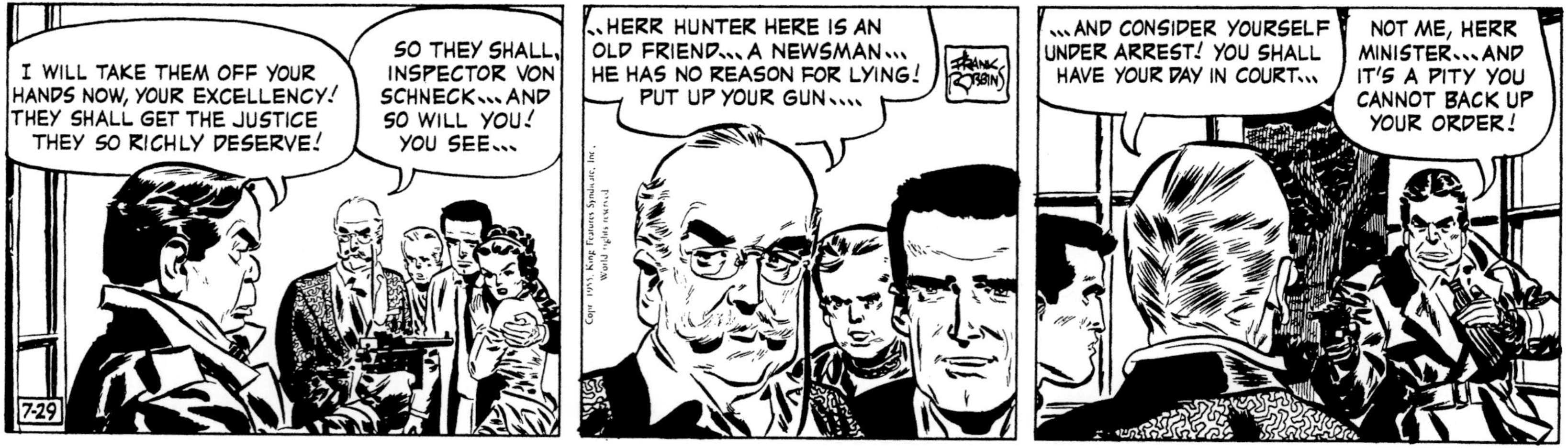
7-29
I WILL TAKE THEM OFF YOUR HANDS NOW, YOUR EXCELLENCY! THEY SHALL GET THE JUSTICE THEY SO RICHLY DESERVE!
SO THEY SHALL, INSPECTOR VON SCHNECK...AND SO WILL YOU! YOU SEE...
..HERR HUNTER HERE IS AN OLD FRIEND...A NEWSMAN... HE HAS NO REASON FOR LYING! PUT UP YOUR GUN....
FRANK ROBBINS
...AND CONSIDER YOURSELF UNDER ARREST! YOU SHALL HAVE YOUR DAY IN COURT...
NOT ME, HERR MINISTER...AND IT'S A PITY YOU CANNOT BACK UP YOUR ORDER!

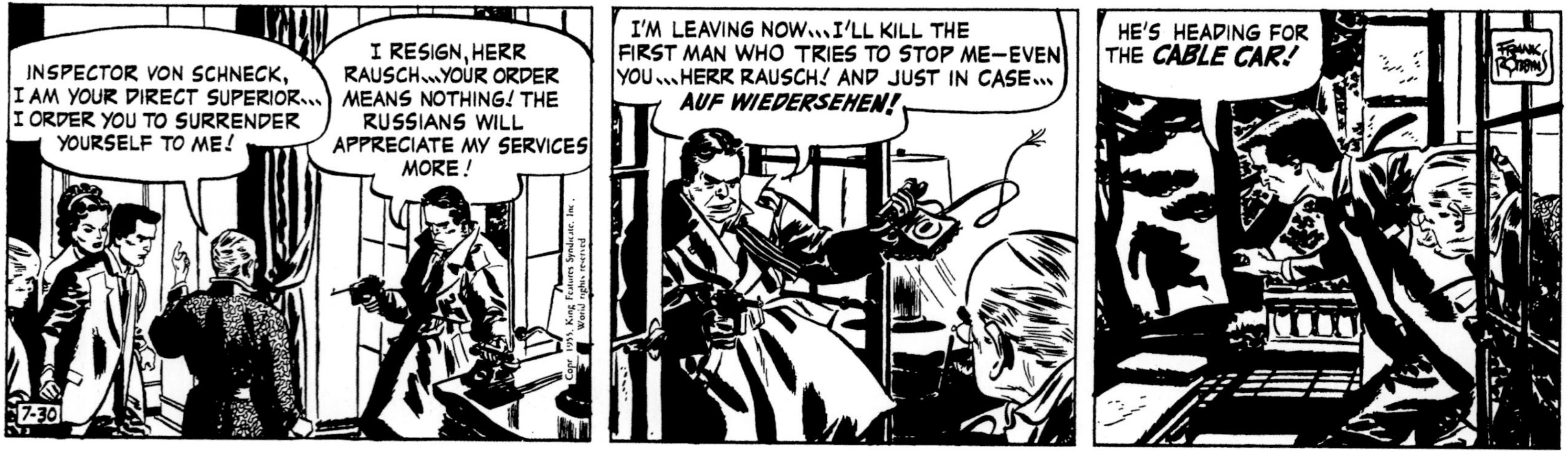
7-30
INSPECTOR VON SCHNECK, I AM YOUR DIRECT SUPERIOR... I ORDER YOU TO SURRENDER YOURSELF TO ME!
I RESIGN, HERR RAUSCH...YOUR ORDER MEANS NOTHING! THE RUSSIANS WILL APPRECIATE MY SERVICES MORE!
I'M LEAVING NOW...I'LL KILL THE FIRST MAN WHO TRIES TO STOP ME—EVEN YOU...HERR RAUSCH! AND JUST IN CASE... AUF WIEDERSEHEN!
HE'S HEADING FOR THE CABLE CAR!
FRANK ROBBINS

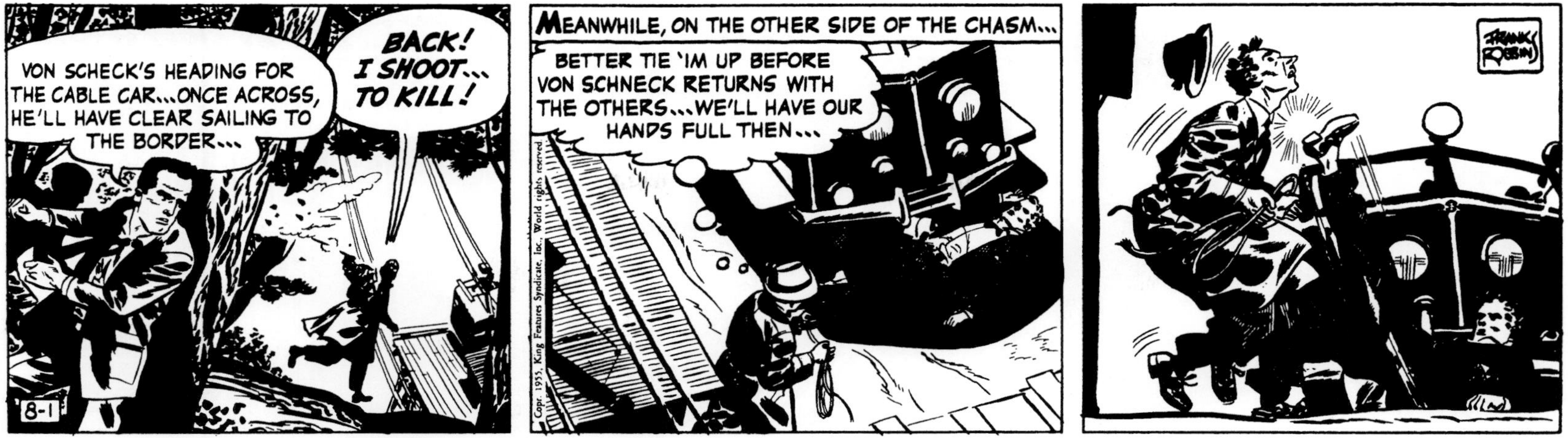
VON SCHECK'S HEADING FOR THE CABLE CAR...ONCE ACROSS, HE'LL HAVE CLEAR SAILING TO THE BORDER...
BACK! I SHOOT... TO KILL!
8-1
MEANWHILE, ON THE OTHER SIDE OF THE CHASM...
BETTER TIE 'IM UP BEFORE VON SCHNECK RETURNS WITH THE OTHERS...WE'LL HAVE OUR HANDS FULL THEN...
Copr. 1955, King Features Syndicate, Inc., World rights reserved
FRANK ROBBINS

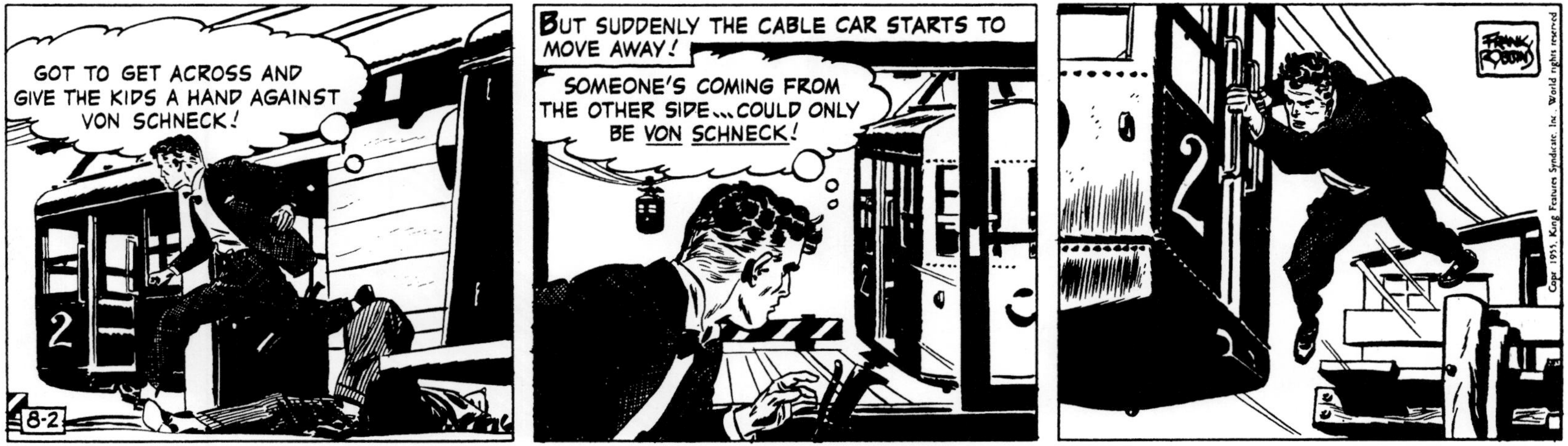
GOT TO GET ACROSS AND GIVE THE KIDS A HAND AGAINST VON SCHNECK!
8-2
BUT SUDDENLY THE CABLE CAR STARTS TO MOVE AWAY!
SOMEONE'S COMING FROM THE OTHER SIDE...COULD ONLY BE VON SCHNECK!
FRANK ROBBINS
Copr. 1955, King Features Syndicate, Inc., World rights reserved

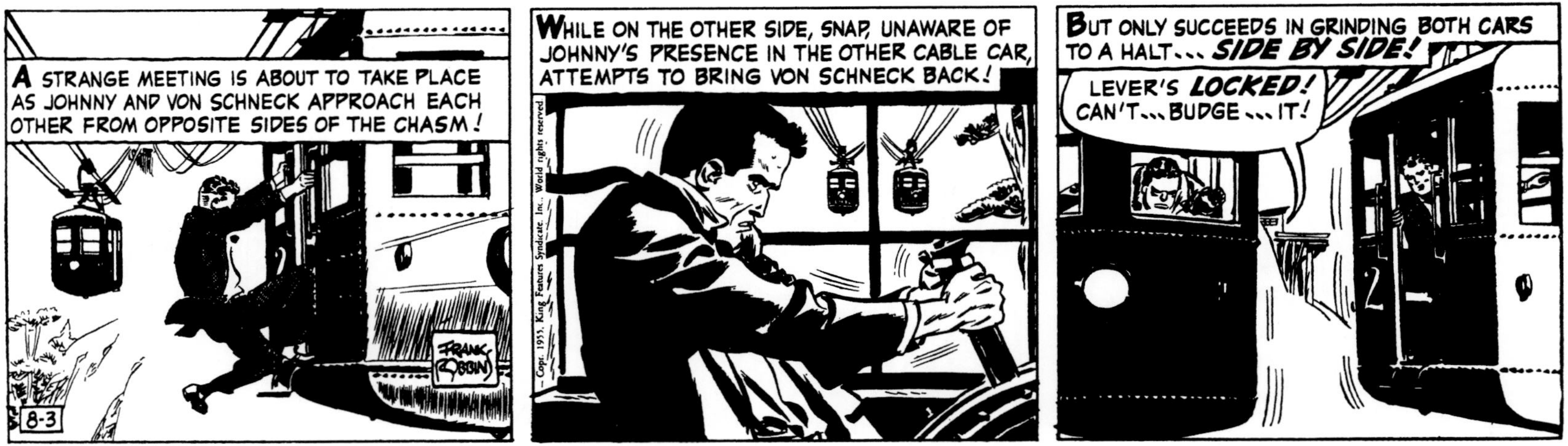
A STRANGE MEETING IS ABOUT TO TAKE PLACE AS JOHNNY AND VON SCHNECK APPROACH EACH OTHER FROM OPPOSITE SIDES OF THE CHASM!
FRANK ROBBIN
8-3
WHILE ON THE OTHER SIDE, SNAP, UNAWARE OF JOHNNY'S PRESENCE IN THE OTHER CABLE CAR, ATTEMPTS TO BRING VON SCHNECK BACK!
Copr. 1955, King Features Syndicate, Inc., World rights reserved
BUT ONLY SUCCEEDS IN GRINDING BOTH CARS TO A HALT... SIDE BY SIDE!
LEVER'S LOCKED! CAN'T... BUDGE... IT!

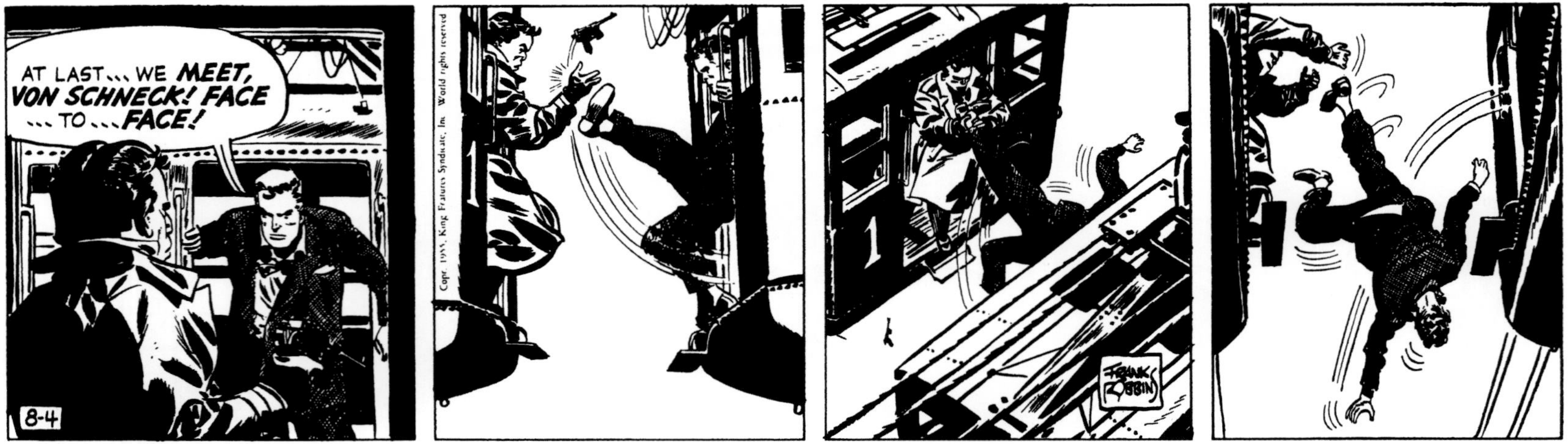
AT LAST... WE MEET, VON SCHNECK! FACE ... TO ... FACE!
8-4
Copr. 1955, King Features Syndicate, Inc. World rights reserved
FRANK ROBBIN

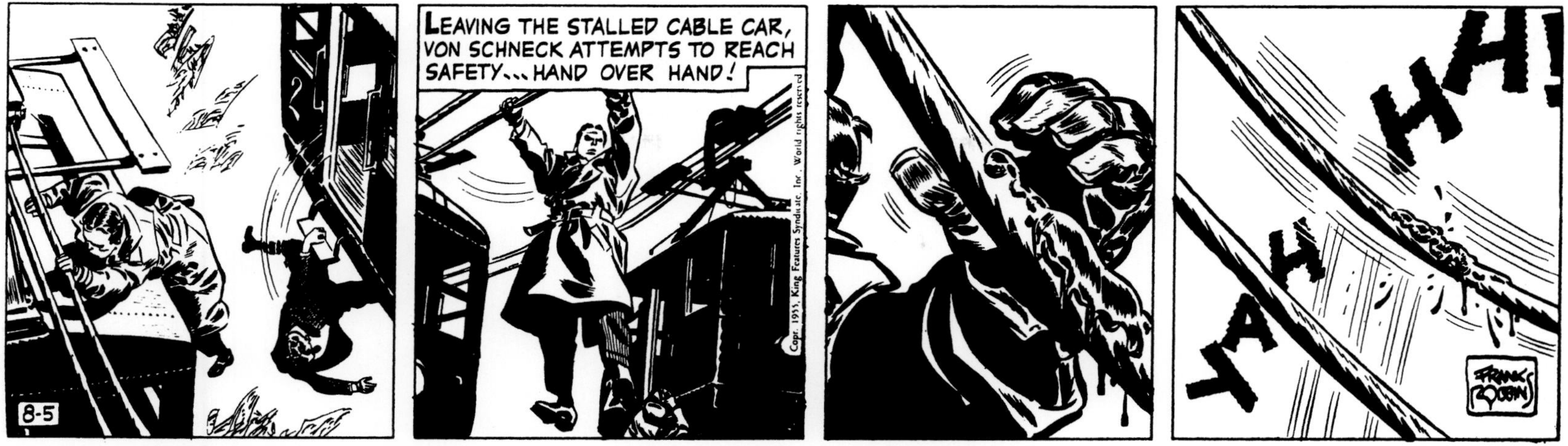
8-5
LEAVING THE STALLED CABLE CAR, VON SCHNECK ATTEMPTS TO REACH SAFETY... HAND OVER HAND!
Copr. 1955, King Features Syndicate, Inc. World rights reserved
YAHHH!
FRANK ROBBINS

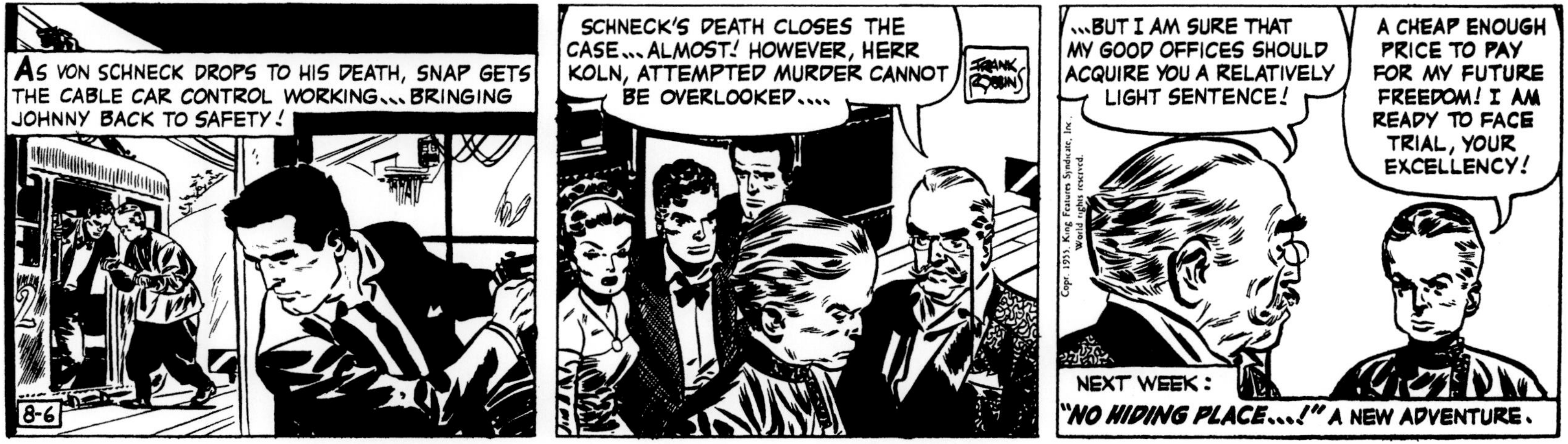
AS VON SCHNECK DROPS TO HIS DEATH, SNAP GETS THE CABLE CAR CONTROL WORKING... BRINGING JOHNNY BACK TO SAFETY!
8-6
SCHNECK'S DEATH CLOSES THE CASE... ALMOST! HOWEVER, HERR KOLN, ATTEMPTED MURDER CANNOT BE OVERLOOKED....
FRANK ROBBINS
...BUT I AM SURE THAT MY GOOD OFFICES SHOULD ACQUIRE YOU A RELATIVELY LIGHT SENTENCE!
A CHEAP ENOUGH PRICE TO PAY FOR MY FUTURE FREEDOM! I AM READY TO FACE TRIAL, YOUR EXCELLENCY!
Copr. 1955, King Features Syndicate, Inc. World rights reserved.
NEXT WEEK: "NO HIDING PLACE...!" A NEW ADVENTURE.

JOHNNY HAZARD

Chapter Five: There's No Hidding Place

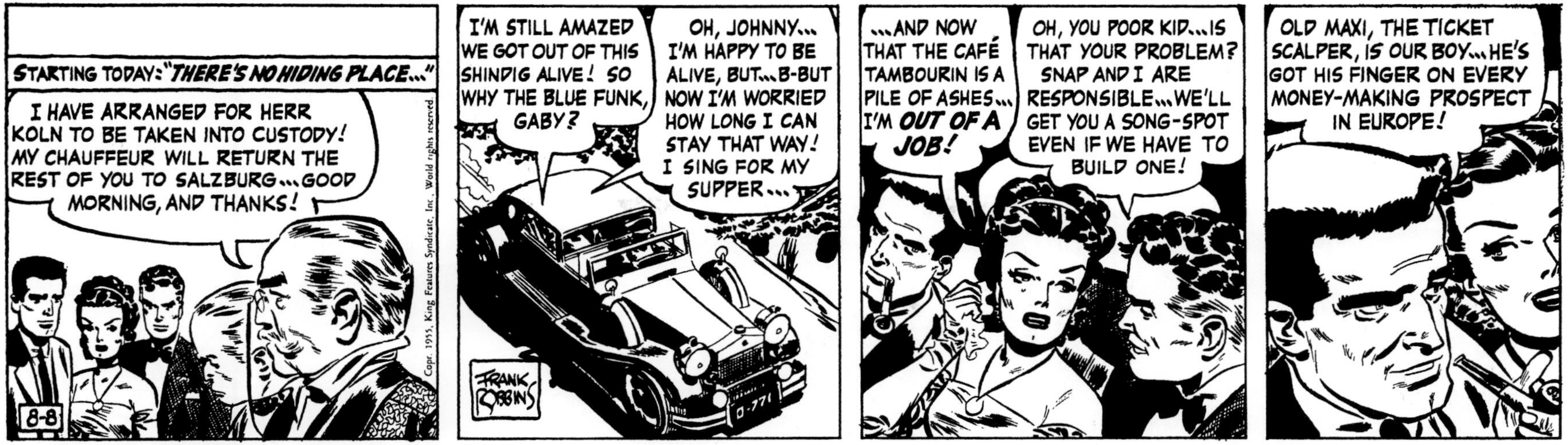
8-8
STARTING TODAY: "THERE'S NO HIDING PLACE..."
I HAVE ARRANGED FOR HERR KOLN TO BE TAKEN INTO CUSTODY! MY CHAUFFEUR WILL RETURN THE REST OF YOU TO SALZBURG...GOOD MORNING, AND THANKS!
Copr. 1955, King Features Syndicate, Inc., World rights reserved.
I'M STILL AMAZED WE GOT OUT OF THIS SHINDIG ALIVE! SO WHY THE BLUE FUNK, GABY?
OH, JOHNNY... I'M HAPPY TO BE ALIVE, BUT...B-BUT NOW I'M WORRIED HOW LONG I CAN STAY THAT WAY! I SING FOR MY SUPPER...
FRANK ROBBINS
...AND NOW THAT THE CAFÉ TAMBOURIN IS A PILE OF ASHES... I'M OUT OF A JOB!
OH, YOU POOR KID...IS THAT YOUR PROBLEM? SNAP AND I ARE RESPONSIBLE...WE'LL GET YOU A SONG-SPOT EVEN IF WE HAVE TO BUILD ONE!
OLD MAXI, THE TICKET SCALPER, IS OUR BOY...HE'S GOT HIS FINGER ON EVERY MONEY-MAKING PROSPECT IN EUROPE!

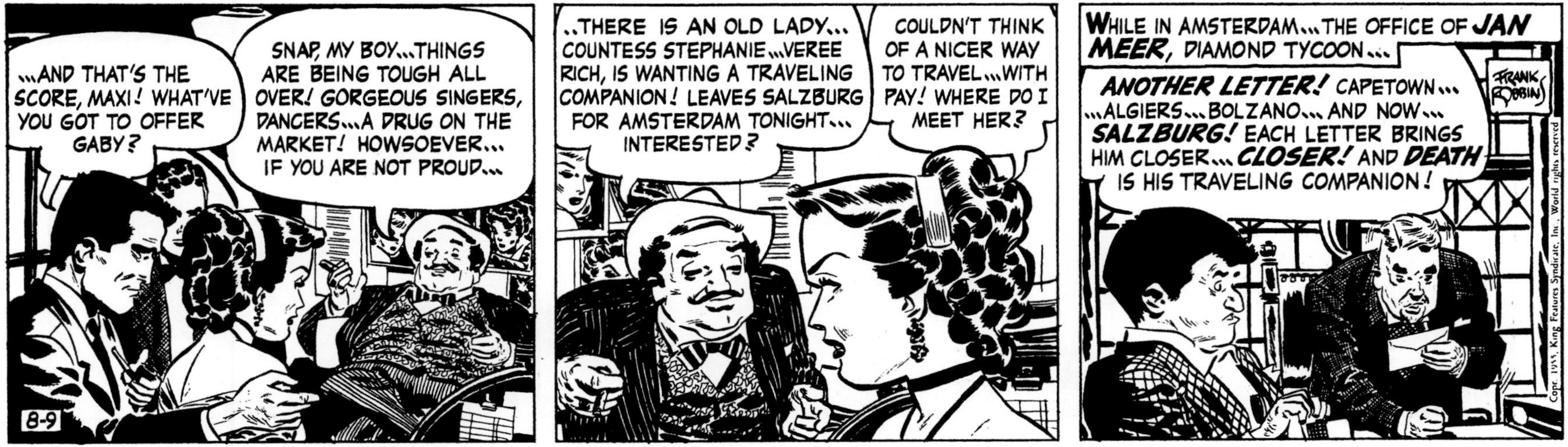
8-9
...AND THAT'S THE SCORE, MAXI! WHAT'VE YOU GOT TO OFFER GABY?
SNAP, MY BOY...THINGS ARE BEING TOUGH ALL OVER! GORGEOUS SINGERS, DANCERS...A DRUG ON THE MARKET! HOWSOEVER... IF YOU ARE NOT PROUD...
..THERE IS AN OLD LADY... COUNTESS STEPHANIE...VEREE RICH, IS WANTING A TRAVELING COMPANION! LEAVES SALZBURG FOR AMSTERDAM TONIGHT... INTERESTED?
COULDN'T THINK OF A NICER WAY TO TRAVEL...WITH PAY! WHERE DO I MEET HER?
WHILE IN AMSTERDAM...THE OFFICE OF JAN MEER, DIAMOND TYCOON...
ANOTHER LETTER! CAPETOWN... ...ALGIERS...BOLZANO... AND NOW... SALZBURG! EACH LETTER BRINGS HIM CLOSER... CLOSER! AND DEATH IS HIS TRAVELING COMPANION!
FRANK ROBBINS
Copr. 1955, King Features Syndicate, Inc., World rights reserved

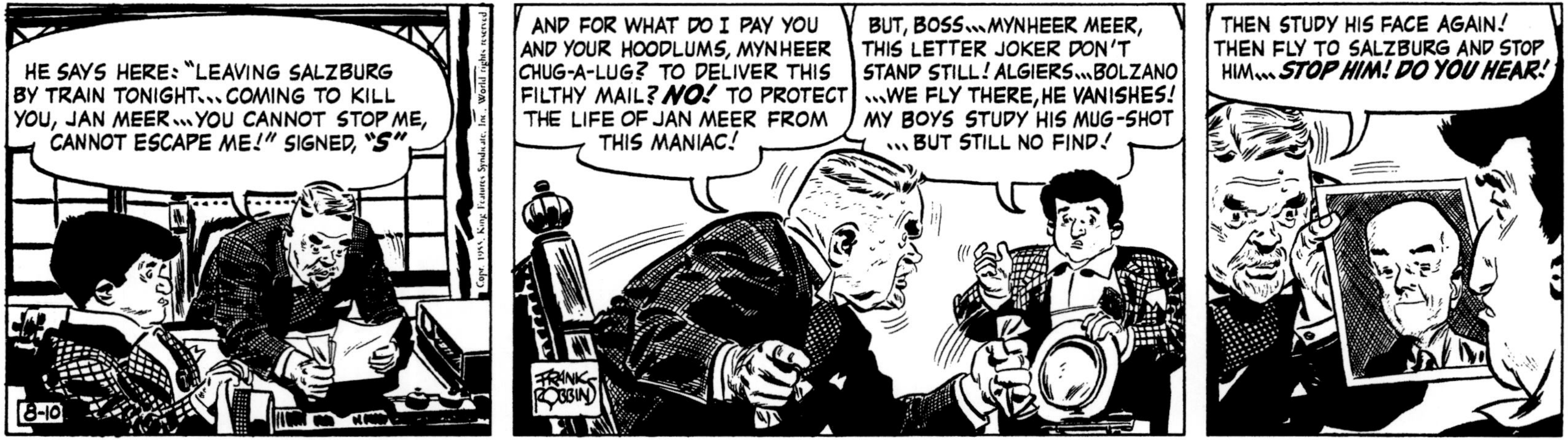
HE SAYS HERE: "LEAVING SALZBURG BY TRAIN TONIGHT... COMING TO KILL YOU, JAN MEER... YOU CANNOT STOP ME, CANNOT ESCAPE ME!" SIGNED, "S"
Copr. 1955, King Features Syndicate, Inc., World rights reserved
8-10
AND FOR WHAT DO I PAY YOU AND YOUR HOODLUMS, MYNHEER CHUG-A-LUG? TO DELIVER THIS FILTHY MAIL? NO! TO PROTECT THE LIFE OF JAN MEER FROM THIS MANIAC!
BUT, BOSS... MYNHEER MEER, THIS LETTER JOKER DON'T STAND STILL! ALGIERS... BOLZANO ...WE FLY THERE, HE VANISHES! MY BOYS STUDY HIS MUG-SHOT ... BUT STILL NO FIND!
FRANK ROBBINS
THEN STUDY HIS FACE AGAIN! THEN FLY TO SALZBURG AND STOP HIM... STOP HIM! DO YOU HEAR!

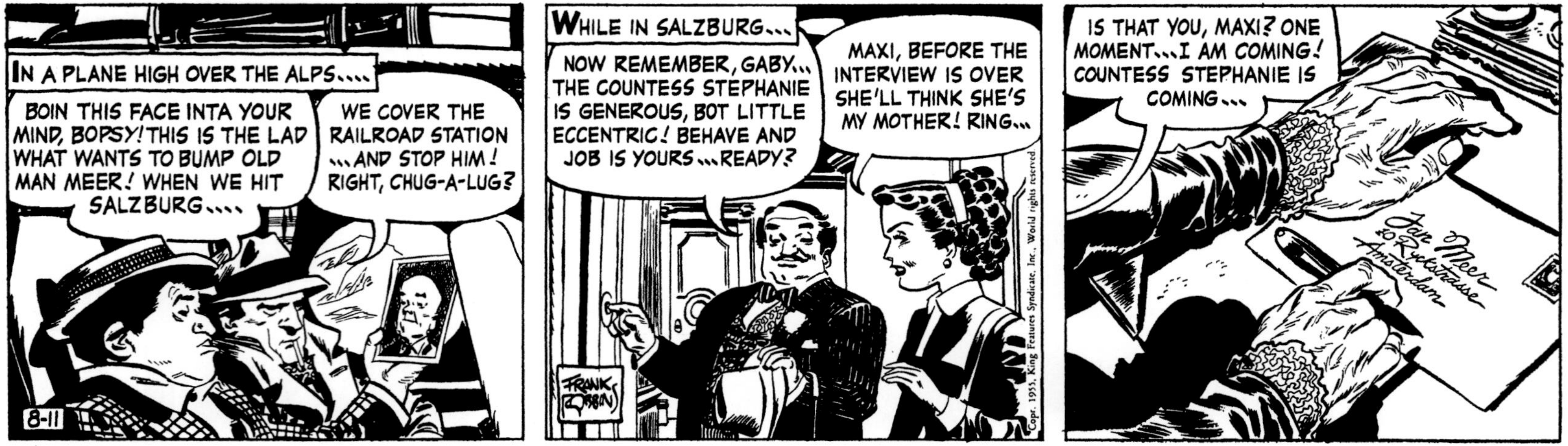
IN A PLANE HIGH OVER THE ALPS....
BOIN THIS FACE INTA YOUR MIND, BOPSY! THIS IS THE LAD WHAT WANTS TO BUMP OLD MAN MEER! WHEN WE HIT SALZBURG....
WE COVER THE RAILROAD STATION ... AND STOP HIM! RIGHT, CHUG-A-LUG?
8-11
WHILE IN SALZBURG...
NOW REMEMBER, GABY... THE COUNTESS STEPHANIE IS GENEROUS, BOT LITTLE ECCENTRIC! BEHAVE AND JOB IS YOURS... READY?
MAXI, BEFORE THE INTERVIEW IS OVER SHE'LL THINK SHE'S MY MOTHER! RING...
FRANK ROBBINS
Copr. 1955, King Features Syndicate, Inc., World rights reserved
IS THAT YOU, MAXI? ONE MOMENT... I AM COMING! COUNTESS STEPHANIE IS COMING...
Jan Meer
Amsterdam

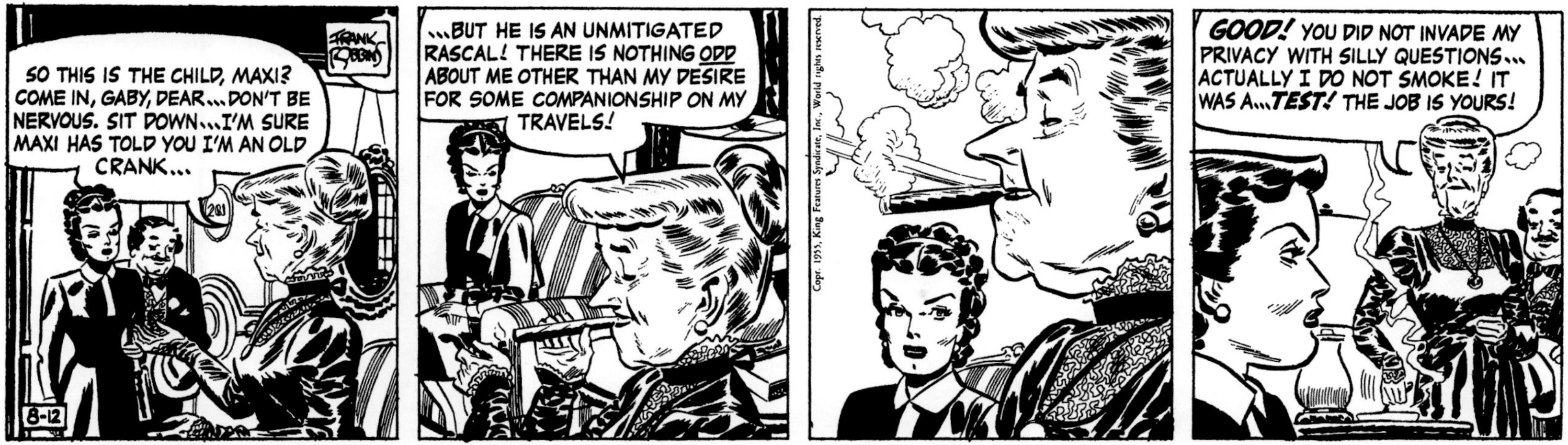
FRANK ROBBINS
SO THIS IS THE CHILD, MAXI? COME IN, GABY, DEAR... DON'T BE NERVOUS. SIT DOWN... I'M SURE MAXI HAS TOLD YOU I'M AN OLD CRANK...
8-12
...BUT HE IS AN UNMITIGATED RASCAL! THERE IS NOTHING ODD ABOUT ME OTHER THAN MY DESIRE FOR SOME COMPANIONSHIP ON MY TRAVELS!
Copr. 1955, King Features Syndicate, Inc., World rights reserved.
GOOD! YOU DID NOT INVADE MY PRIVACY WITH SILLY QUESTIONS... ACTUALLY I DO NOT SMOKE! IT WAS A... TEST! THE JOB IS YOURS!

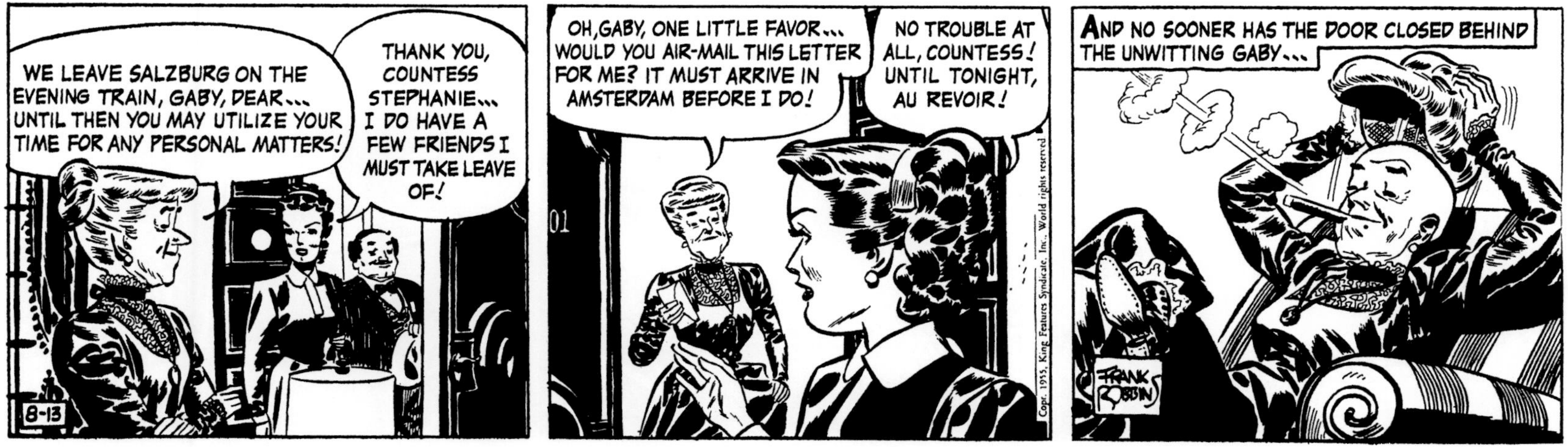
WE LEAVE SALZBURG ON THE EVENING TRAIN, GABY, DEAR... UNTIL THEN YOU MAY UTILIZE YOUR TIME FOR ANY PERSONAL MATTERS!
THANK YOU, COUNTESS STEPHANIE... I DO HAVE A FEW FRIENDS I MUST TAKE LEAVE OF!
8-13
OH, GABY, ONE LITTLE FAVOR... WOULD YOU AIR-MAIL THIS LETTER FOR ME? IT MUST ARRIVE IN AMSTERDAM BEFORE I DO!
NO TROUBLE AT ALL, COUNTESS! UNTIL TONIGHT, AU REVOIR!
Copr. 1955, King Features Syndicate, Inc., World rights reserved.
AND NO SOONER HAS THE DOOR CLOSED BEHIND THE UNWITTING GABY...
FRANK ROBBINS

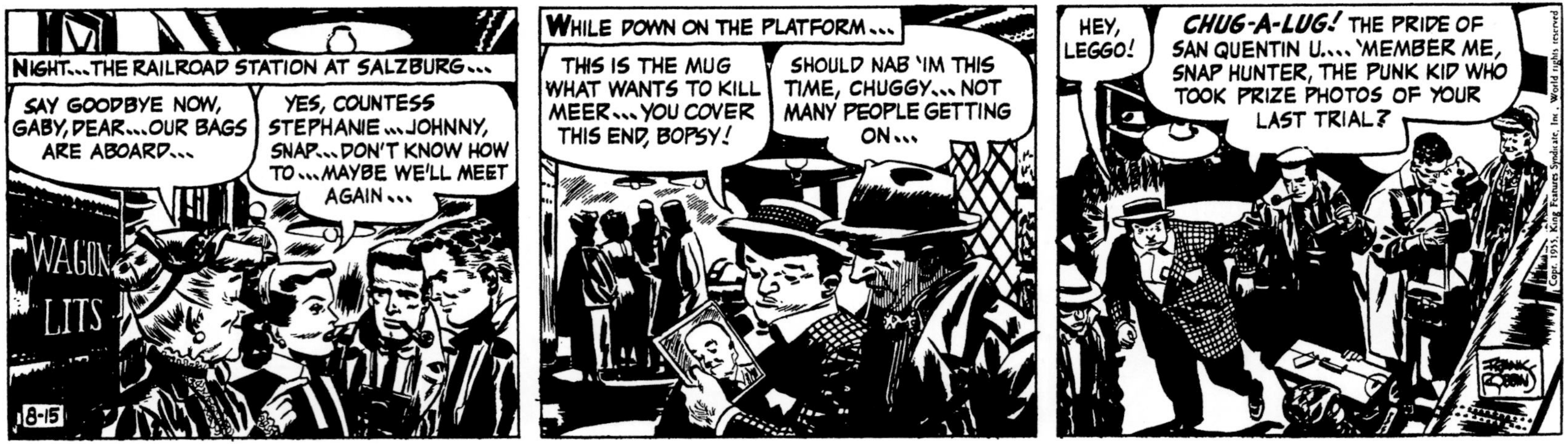
NIGHT...THE RAILROAD STATION AT SALZBURG...
SAY GOODBYE NOW, GABY, DEAR...OUR BAGS ARE ABOARD...
YES, COUNTESS STEPHANIE...JOHNNY, SNAP...DON'T KNOW HOW TO...MAYBE WE'LL MEET AGAIN...
WAGON LITS
8-15
WHILE DOWN ON THE PLATFORM...
THIS IS THE MUG WHAT WANTS TO KILL MEER...YOU COVER THIS END, BOPSY!
SHOULD NAB 'IM THIS TIME, CHUGGY...NOT MANY PEOPLE GETTING ON...
HEY, LEGGO!
CHUG-A-LUG! THE PRIDE OF SAN QUENTIN U....'MEMBER ME, SNAP HUNTER, THE PUNK KID WHO TOOK PRIZE PHOTOS OF YOUR LAST TRIAL?
Copr. 1955, King Features Syndicate, Inc., World rights reserved
FRANK ROBBINS

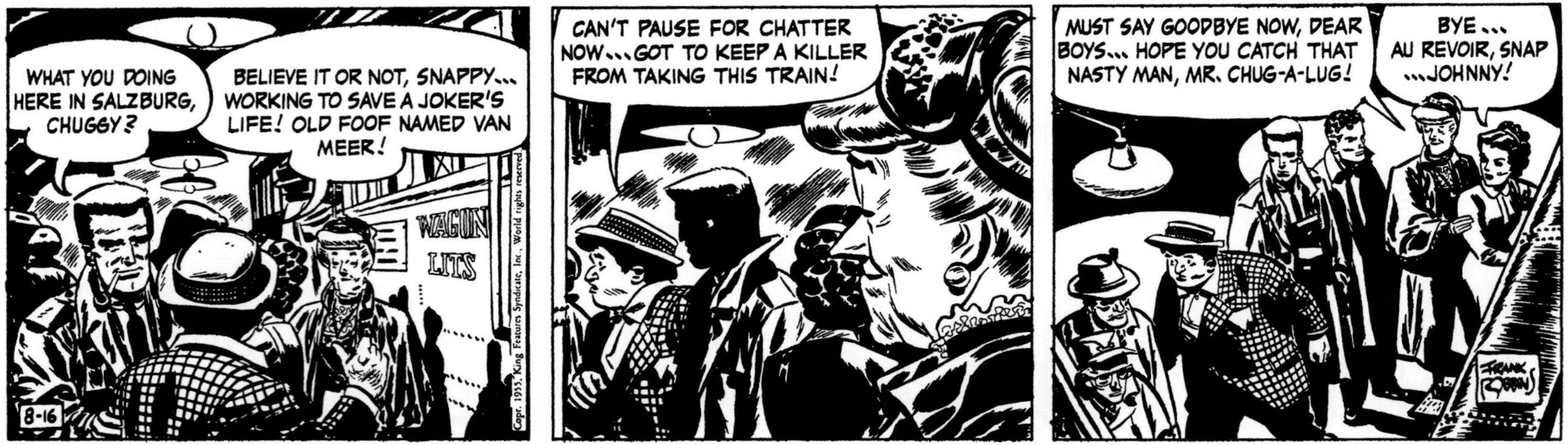
WHAT YOU DOING HERE IN SALZBURG, CHUGGY?
BELIEVE IT OR NOT, SNAPPY...WORKING TO SAVE A JOKER'S LIFE! OLD FOOF NAMED VAN MEER!
WAGON LITS
8-16
Copr. 1955, King Features Syndicate, Inc., World rights reserved
CAN'T PAUSE FOR CHATTER NOW...GOT TO KEEP A KILLER FROM TAKING THIS TRAIN!
MUST SAY GOODBYE NOW, DEAR BOYS...HOPE YOU CATCH THAT NASTY MAN, MR. CHUG-A-LUG!
BYE...AU REVOIR, SNAP...JOHNNY!
FRANK ROBBINS

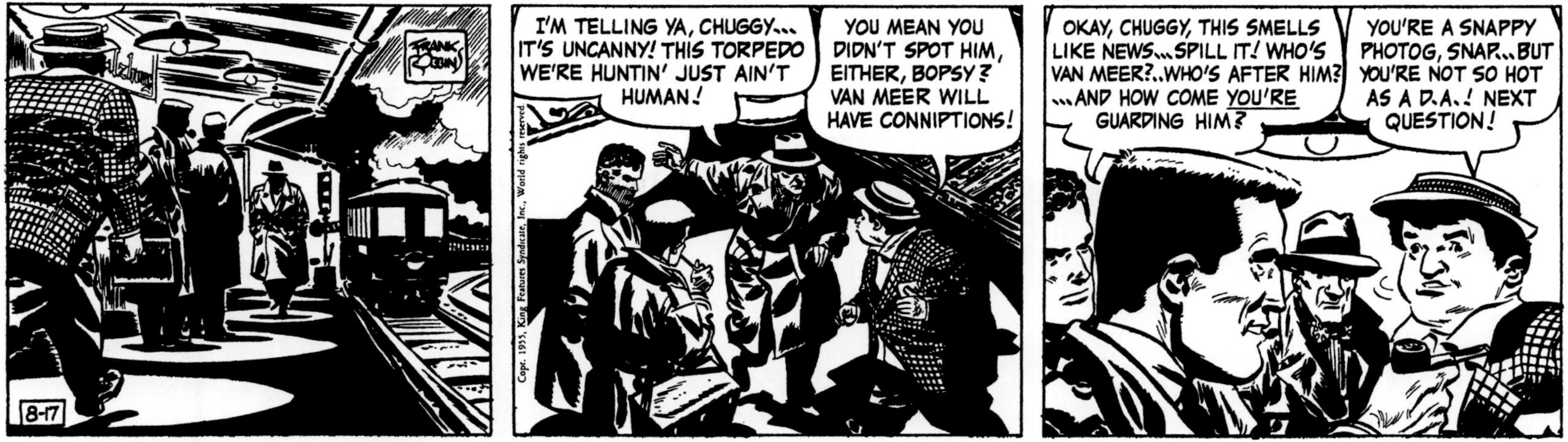
FRANK ROBBINS
8-17
I'M TELLING YA, CHUGGY... IT'S UNCANNY! THIS TORPEDO WE'RE HUNTIN' JUST AIN'T HUMAN!
YOU MEAN YOU DIDN'T SPOT HIM, EITHER, BOPSY? VAN MEER WILL HAVE CONNIPTIONS!
Copr. 1955, King Features Syndicate, Inc., World rights reserved.
OKAY, CHUGGY, THIS SMELLS LIKE NEWS...SPILL IT! WHO'S VAN MEER?..WHO'S AFTER HIM? ...AND HOW COME YOU'RE GUARDING HIM?
YOU'RE A SNAPPY PHOTOG, SNAP...BUT YOU'RE NOT SO HOT AS A D.A.! NEXT QUESTION!

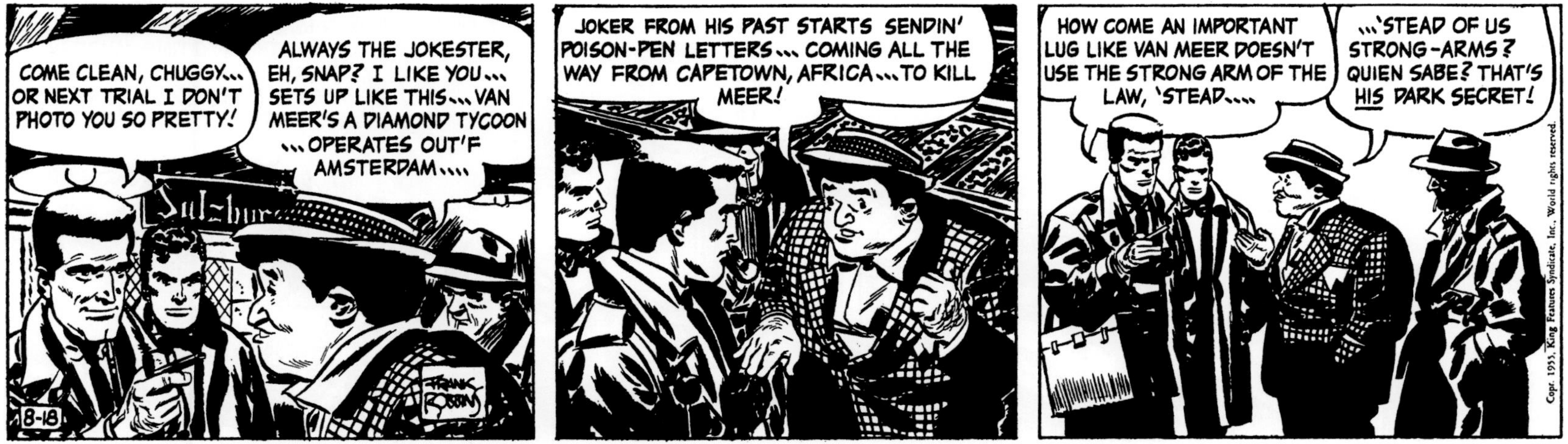
COME CLEAN, CHUGGY... OR NEXT TRIAL I DON'T PHOTO YOU SO PRETTY!
ALWAYS THE JOKESTER, EH, SNAP? I LIKE YOU... SETS UP LIKE THIS...VAN MEER'S A DIAMOND TYCOON ...OPERATES OUT'F AMSTERDAM....
FRANK ROBBINS
8-18
JOKER FROM HIS PAST STARTS SENDIN' POISON-PEN LETTERS... COMING ALL THE WAY FROM CAPETOWN, AFRICA...TO KILL MEER!
HOW COME AN IMPORTANT LUG LIKE VAN MEER DOESN'T USE THE STRONG ARM OF THE LAW, 'STEAD...
...'STEAD OF US STRONG-ARMS? QUIEN SABE? THAT'S HIS DARK SECRET!
Copr. 1955, King Features Syndicate, Inc., World rights reserved.

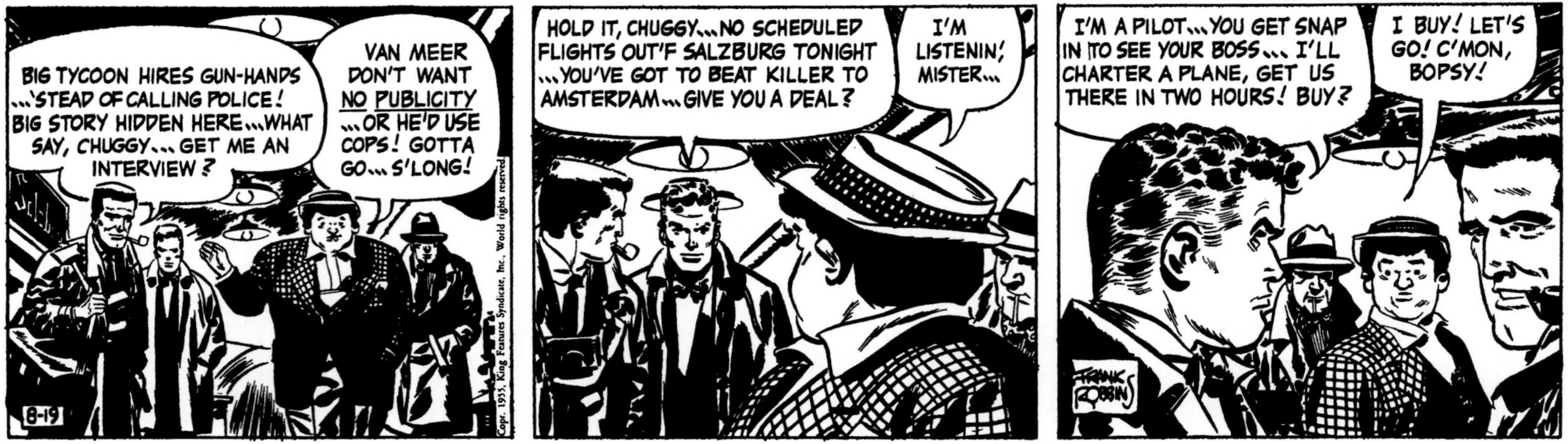
BIG TYCOON HIRES GUN-HANDS ...'STEAD OF CALLING POLICE! BIG STORY HIDDEN HERE...WHAT SAY, CHUGGY... GET ME AN INTERVIEW?
VAN MEER DON'T WANT NO PUBLICITY ...OR HE'D USE COPS! GOTTA GO... S'LONG!
8-19
Copr. 1955, King Features Syndicate, Inc., World rights reserved.
HOLD IT, CHUGGY...NO SCHEDULED FLIGHTS OUT'F SALZBURG TONIGHT ...YOU'VE GOT TO BEAT KILLER TO AMSTERDAM...GIVE YOU A DEAL?
I'M LISTENIN', MISTER...
I'M A PILOT...YOU GET SNAP IN TO SEE YOUR BOSS... I'LL CHARTER A PLANE, GET US THERE IN TWO HOURS! BUY?
I BUY! LET'S GO! C'MON, BOPSY!
FRANK ROBBINS

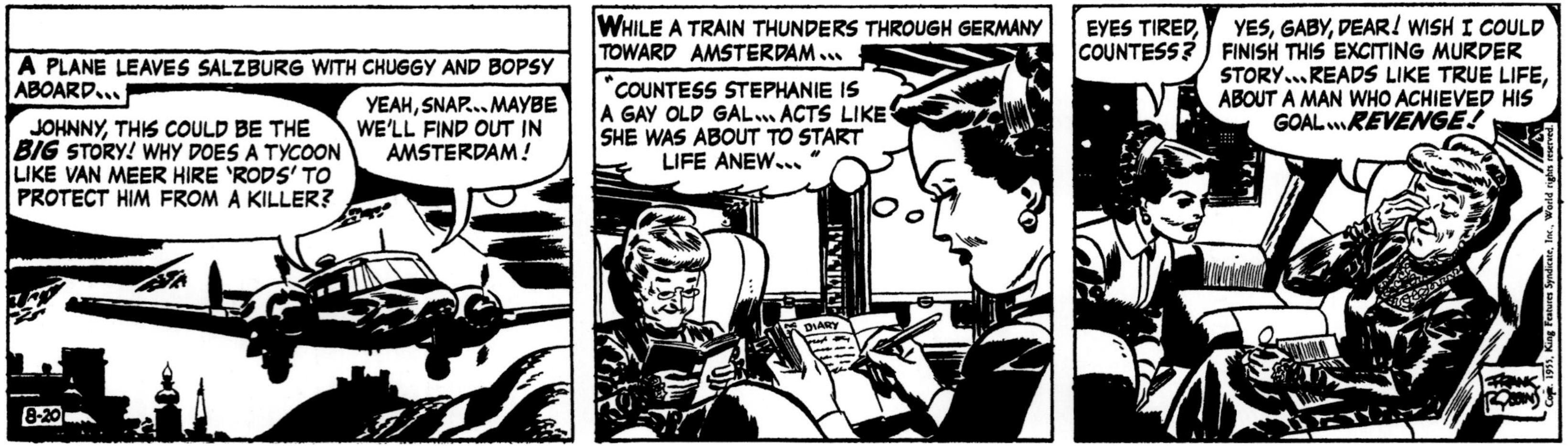
A PLANE LEAVES SALZBURG WITH CHUGGY AND BOPSY ABOARD...
JOHNNY, THIS COULD BE THE BIG STORY! WHY DOES A TYCOON LIKE VAN MEER HIRE 'RODS' TO PROTECT HIM FROM A KILLER?
YEAH, SNAP...MAYBE WE'LL FIND OUT IN AMSTERDAM!
8-20
WHILE A TRAIN THUNDERS THROUGH GERMANY TOWARD AMSTERDAM...
"COUNTESS STEPHANIE IS A GAY OLD GAL...ACTS LIKE SHE WAS ABOUT TO START LIFE ANEW..."
DIARY
EYES TIRED, COUNTESS?
YES, GABY, DEAR! WISH I COULD FINISH THIS EXCITING MURDER STORY...READS LIKE TRUE LIFE, ABOUT A MAN WHO ACHIEVED HIS GOAL...REVENGE!
Copr. 1955, King Features Syndicate, Inc., World rights reserved.
FRANK ROBBINS

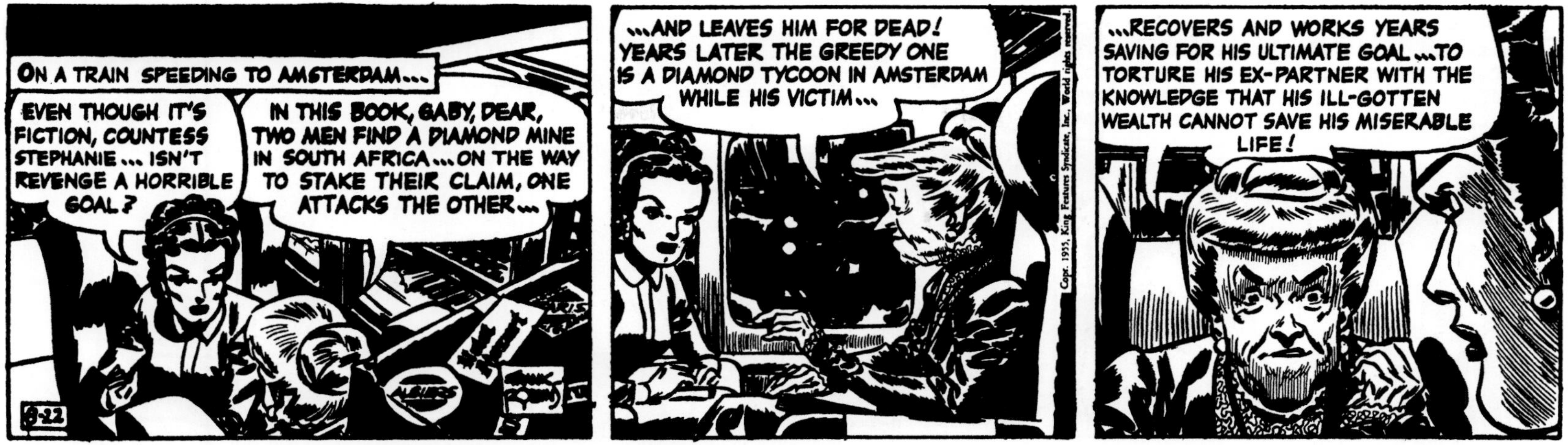
ON A TRAIN SPEEDING TO AMSTERDAM...
EVEN THOUGH IT'S FICTION, COUNTESS STEPHANIE... ISN'T REVENGE A HORRIBLE GOAL?
IN THIS BOOK, GABY, DEAR, TWO MEN FIND A DIAMOND MINE IN SOUTH AFRICA...ON THE WAY TO STAKE THEIR CLAIM, ONE ATTACKS THE OTHER...
8-22
...AND LEAVES HIM FOR DEAD! YEARS LATER THE GREEDY ONE IS A DIAMOND TYCOON IN AMSTERDAM WHILE HIS VICTIM...
Copr. 1955, King Features Syndicate, Inc., World rights reserved.
...RECOVERS AND WORKS YEARS SAVING FOR HIS ULTIMATE GOAL...TO TORTURE HIS EX-PARTNER WITH THE KNOWLEDGE THAT HIS ILL-GOTTEN WEALTH CANNOT SAVE HIS MISERABLE LIFE!

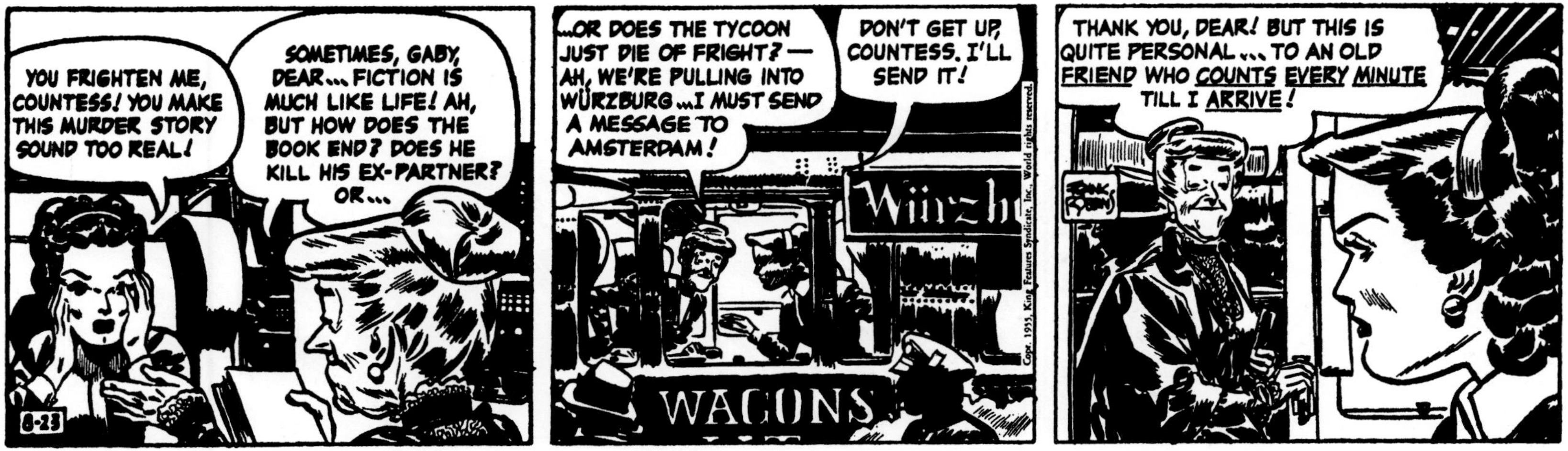
YOU FRIGHTEN ME, COUNTESS! YOU MAKE THIS MURDER STORY SOUND TOO REAL!
SOMETIMES, GABY, DEAR... FICTION IS MUCH LIKE LIFE! AH, BUT HOW DOES THE BOOK END? DOES HE KILL HIS EX-PARTNER? OR...
8-23
...OR DOES THE TYCOON JUST DIE OF FRIGHT? — AH, WE'RE PULLING INTO WÜRZBURG...I MUST SEND A MESSAGE TO AMSTERDAM!
DON'T GET UP, COUNTESS. I'LL SEND IT!
WAGONS
Copr. 1955, King Features Syndicate, Inc., World rights reserved.
THANK YOU, DEAR! BUT THIS IS QUITE PERSONAL... TO AN OLD FRIEND WHO COUNTS EVERY MINUTE TILL I ARRIVE!

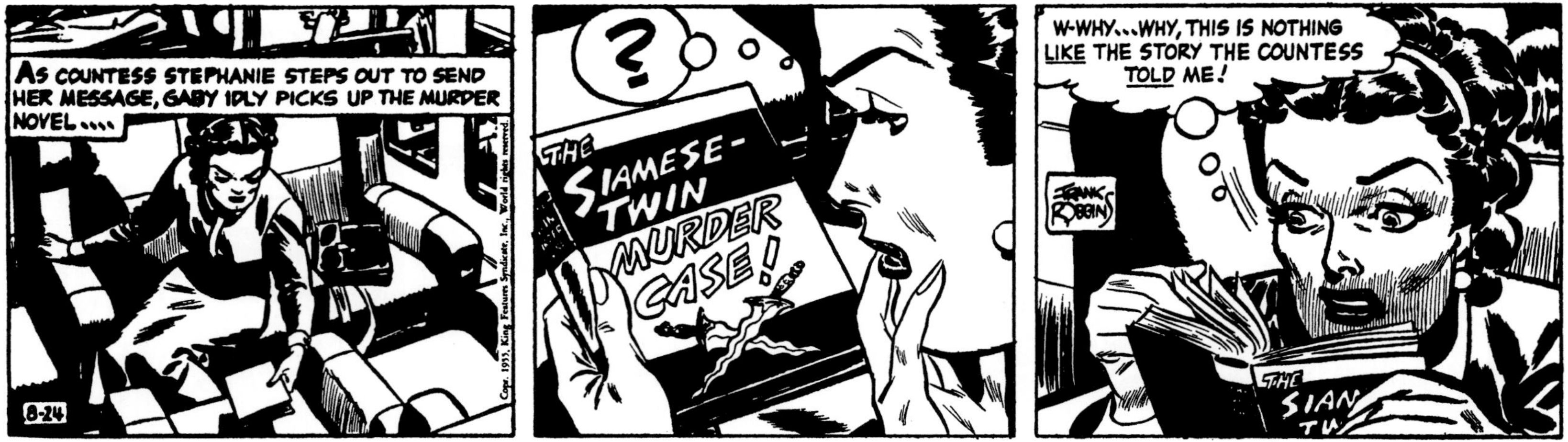
AS COUNTESS STEPHANIE STEPS OUT TO SEND HER MESSAGE, GABY IDLY PICKS UP THE MURDER NOVEL....
8-24
Copr. 1955, King Features Syndicate, Inc., World rights reserved.
?
THE SIAMESE-TWIN MURDER CASE!
W-WHY...WHY, THIS IS NOTHING LIKE THE STORY THE COUNTESS TOLD ME!
FRANK ROBBINS
THE SIAN

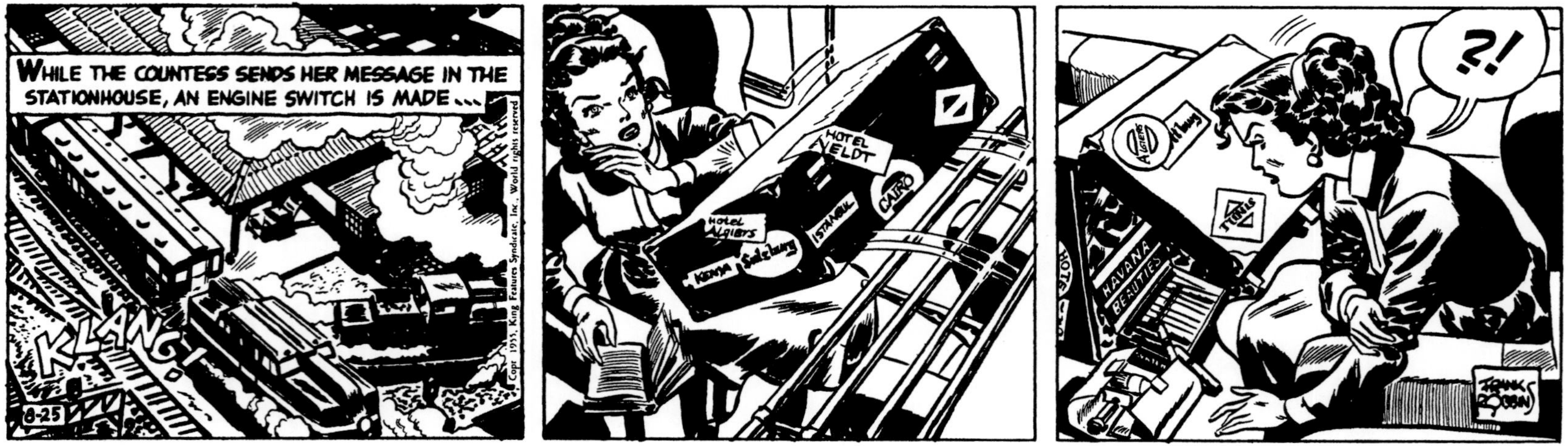
WHILE THE COUNTESS SENDS HER MESSAGE IN THE STATIONHOUSE, AN ENGINE SWITCH IS MADE...
KLANG!
8-25
Copr. 1955, King Features Syndicate, Inc., World rights reserved
HOTEL VELDT
CAIRO
ISTANBUL
HOTEL ALGIERS
KENYA
Salzburg
?!
HAVANA BEAUTIES
FRANK ROBBINS

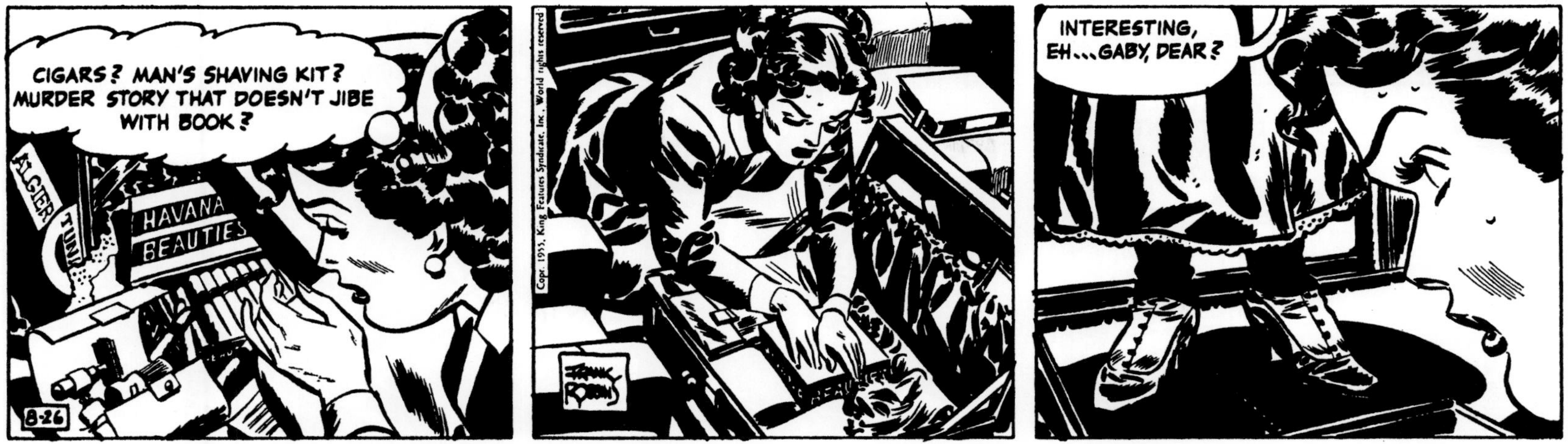
CIGARS? MAN'S SHAVING KIT? MURDER STORY THAT DOESN'T JIBE WITH BOOK?
ALGIER
TUNI
HAVANA BEAUTIES
8-26
Copr. 1955, King Features Syndicate, Inc., World rights reserved
FRANK ROBBINS
INTERESTING, EH...GABY, DEAR?

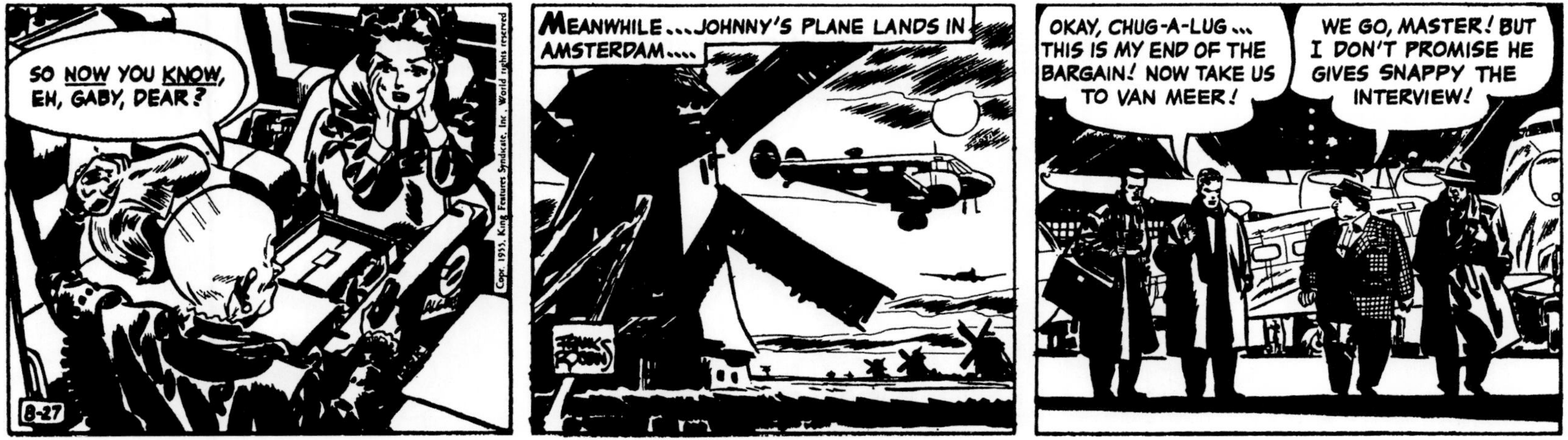
SO NOW YOU KNOW, EH, GABY, DEAR?
8-27
Copr. 1955, King Features Syndicate, Inc., World rights reserved
MEANWHILE...JOHNNY'S PLANE LANDS IN AMSTERDAM....
FRANK ROBBINS
OKAY, CHUG-A-LUG... THIS IS MY END OF THE BARGAIN! NOW TAKE US TO VAN MEER!
WE GO, MASTER! BUT I DON'T PROMISE HE GIVES SNAPPY THE INTERVIEW!

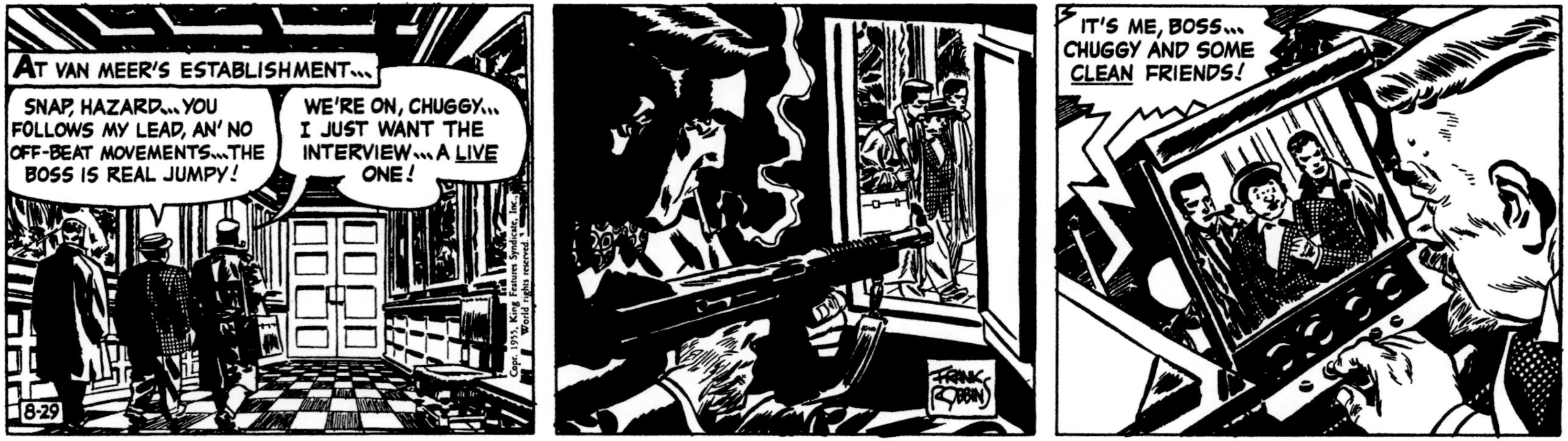
AT VAN MEER'S ESTABLISHMENT...
SNAP, HAZARD... YOU FOLLOWS MY LEAD, AN' NO OFF-BEAT MOVEMENTS... THE BOSS IS REAL JUMPY!
WE'RE ON, CHUGGY... I JUST WANT THE INTERVIEW... A LIVE ONE!
8-29
Copr. 1955, King Features Syndicate, Inc., World rights reserved.
FRANK ROBBIN
IT'S ME, BOSS... CHUGGY AND SOME CLEAN FRIENDS!

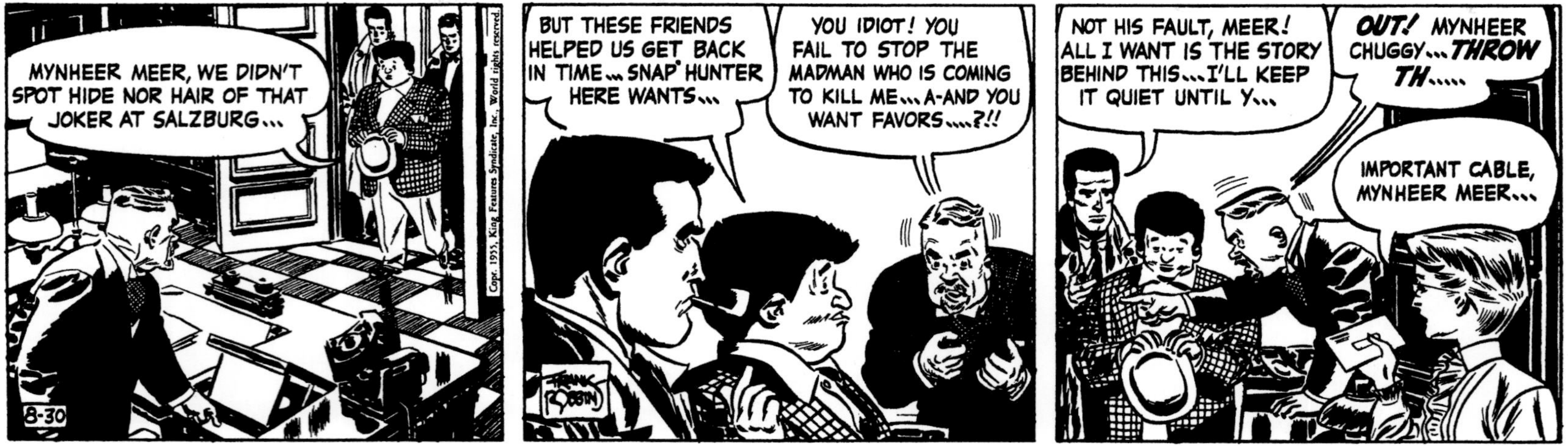
MYNHEER MEER, WE DIDN'T SPOT HIDE NOR HAIR OF THAT JOKER AT SALZBURG...
8-30
Copr. 1955, King Features Syndicate, Inc., World rights reserved.
BUT THESE FRIENDS HELPED US GET BACK IN TIME... SNAP HUNTER HERE WANTS...
YOU IDIOT! YOU FAIL TO STOP THE MADMAN WHO IS COMING TO KILL ME... A-AND YOU WANT FAVORS....?!!
FRANK ROBBIN
NOT HIS FAULT, MEER! ALL I WANT IS THE STORY BEHIND THIS... I'LL KEEP IT QUIET UNTIL Y...
OUT! MYNHEER CHUGGY... THROW TH.....
IMPORTANT CABLE, MYNHEER MEER...

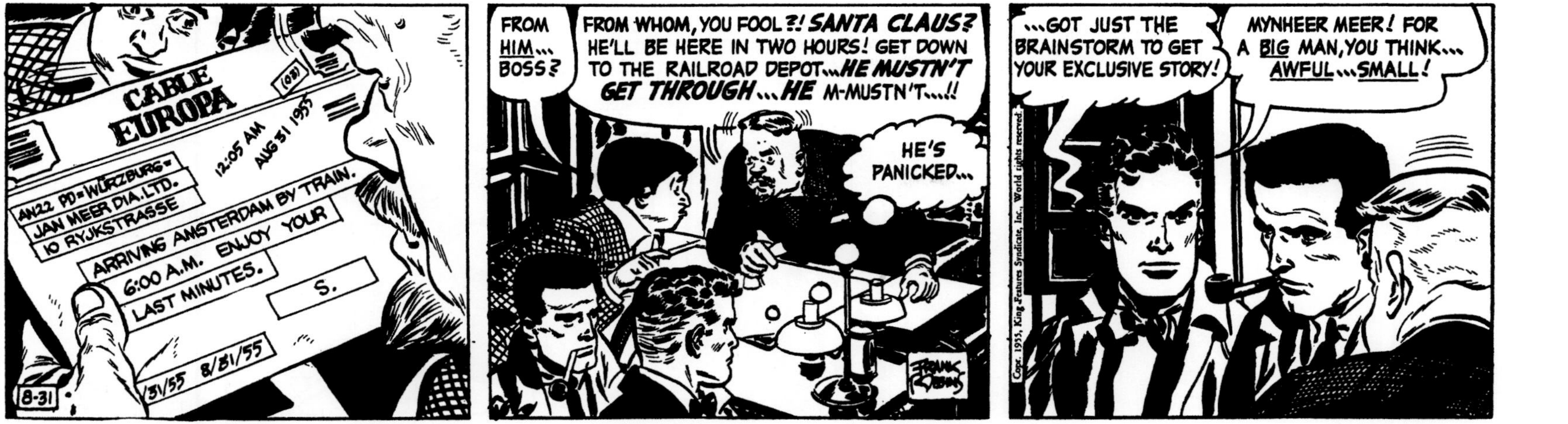

CABLE EUROPA
AN22 PD=WÜRZBURG=
JAN MEER DIA.LTD.
10 RYJKSTRASSE
12:05 AM AUG 31 1955
ARRIVING AMSTERDAM BY TRAIN. 6:00 A.M. ENJOY YOUR LAST MINUTES.
S.
8-31
FROM HIM... BOSS?
FROM WHOM, YOU FOOL?! SANTA CLAUS? HE'LL BE HERE IN TWO HOURS! GET DOWN TO THE RAILROAD DEPOT...HE MUSTN'T GET THROUGH...HE M-MUSTN'T...!!
HE'S PANICKED...
FRANK ROBBINS
...GOT JUST THE BRAINSTORM TO GET YOUR EXCLUSIVE STORY!
MYNHEER MEER! FOR A BIG MAN, YOU THINK... AWFUL...SMALL!
Copr. 1955, King Features Syndicate, Inc., World rights reserved.

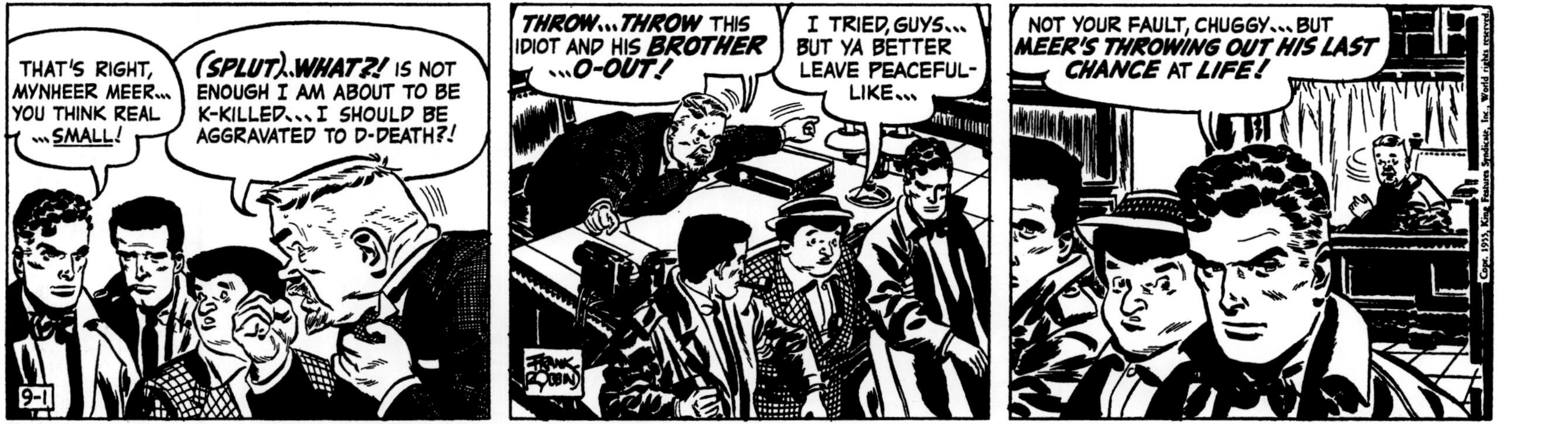

9-1
THAT'S RIGHT, MYNHEER MEER... YOU THINK REAL ...SMALL!
(SPLUT)..WHAT?! IS NOT ENOUGH I AM ABOUT TO BE K-KILLED...I SHOULD BE AGGRAVATED TO D-DEATH?!
THROW...THROW THIS IDIOT AND HIS BROTHER ...O-OUT!
I TRIED, GUYS... BUT YA BETTER LEAVE PEACEFUL-LIKE...
FRANK ROBBINS
NOT YOUR FAULT, CHUGGY...BUT MEER'S THROWING OUT HIS LAST CHANCE AT LIFE!
Copr. 1955, King Features Syndicate, Inc., World rights reserved.

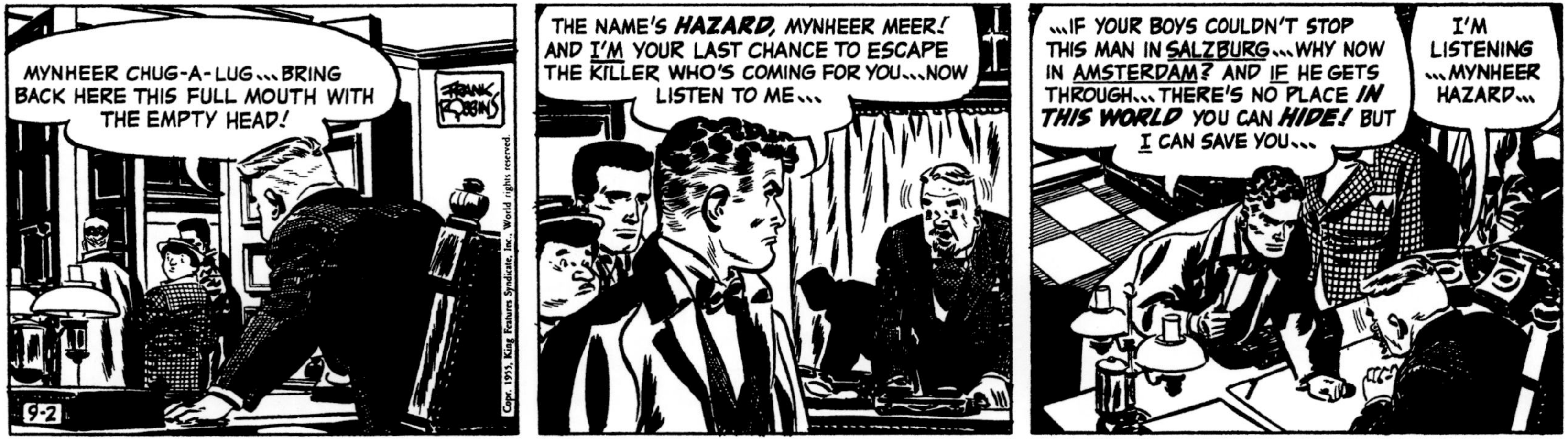
MYNHEER CHUG-A-LUG... BRING BACK HERE THIS FULL MOUTH WITH THE EMPTY HEAD!
FRANK ROBBINS
Copr. 1955, King Features Syndicate, Inc., World rights reserved.
9-2
THE NAME'S HAZARD, MYNHEER MEER! AND I'M YOUR LAST CHANCE TO ESCAPE THE KILLER WHO'S COMING FOR YOU... NOW LISTEN TO ME...
...IF YOUR BOYS COULDN'T STOP THIS MAN IN SALZBURG... WHY NOW IN AMSTERDAM? AND IF HE GETS THROUGH... THERE'S NO PLACE IN THIS WORLD YOU CAN HIDE! BUT I CAN SAVE YOU...
I'M LISTENING ...MYNHEER HAZARD...

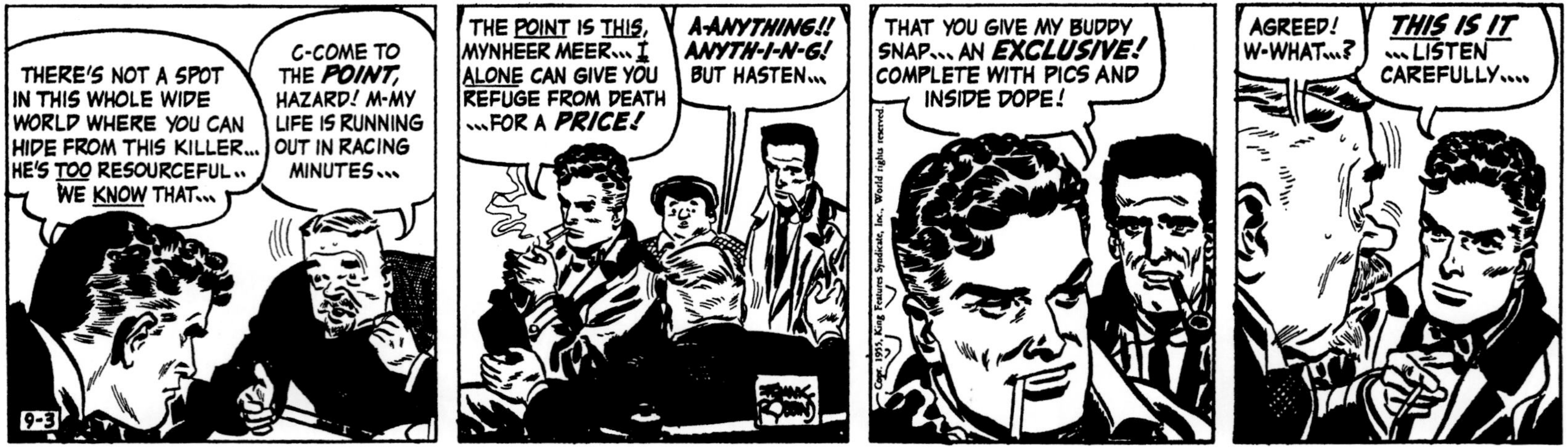
9-3
THERE'S NOT A SPOT IN THIS WHOLE WIDE WORLD WHERE YOU CAN HIDE FROM THIS KILLER... HE'S TOO RESOURCEFUL.. WE KNOW THAT...
C-COME TO THE POINT, HAZARD! M-MY LIFE IS RUNNING OUT IN RACING MINUTES...
THE POINT IS THIS, MYNHEER MEER... I ALONE CAN GIVE YOU REFUGE FROM DEATH ...FOR A PRICE!
A-ANYTHING!! ANYTH-I-N-G! BUT HASTEN...
FRANK ROBBINS
Copr. 1955, King Features Syndicate, Inc., World rights reserved.
THAT YOU GIVE MY BUDDY SNAP... AN EXCLUSIVE! COMPLETE WITH PICS AND INSIDE DOPE!
AGREED! W-WHAT...?
THIS IS IT ...LISTEN CAREFULLY....

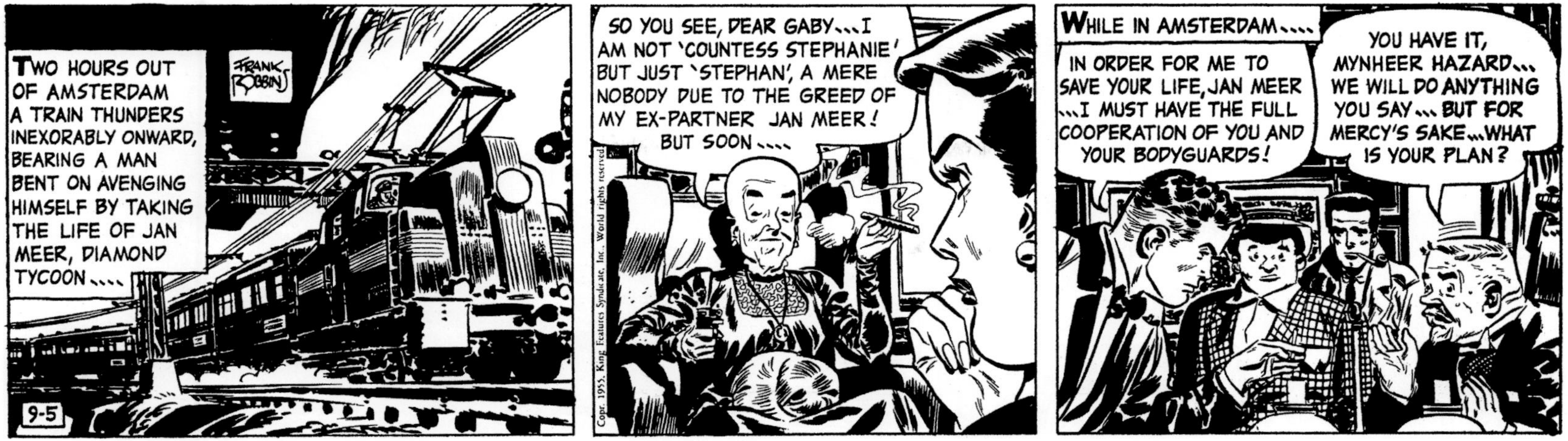
TWO HOURS OUT OF AMSTERDAM A TRAIN THUNDERS INEXORABLY ONWARD, BEARING A MAN BENT ON AVENGING HIMSELF BY TAKING THE LIFE OF JAN MEER, DIAMOND TYCOON....
FRANK ROBBINS
9-5
SO YOU SEE, DEAR GABY...I AM NOT 'COUNTESS STEPHANIE' BUT JUST 'STEPHAN', A MERE NOBODY DUE TO THE GREED OF MY EX-PARTNER JAN MEER! BUT SOON....
Copr. 1955, King Features Syndicate, Inc., World rights reserved
WHILE IN AMSTERDAM....
IN ORDER FOR ME TO SAVE YOUR LIFE, JAN MEER ...I MUST HAVE THE FULL COOPERATION OF YOU AND YOUR BODYGUARDS!
YOU HAVE IT, MYNHEER HAZARD... WE WILL DO ANYTHING YOU SAY... BUT FOR MERCY'S SAKE...WHAT IS YOUR PLAN?

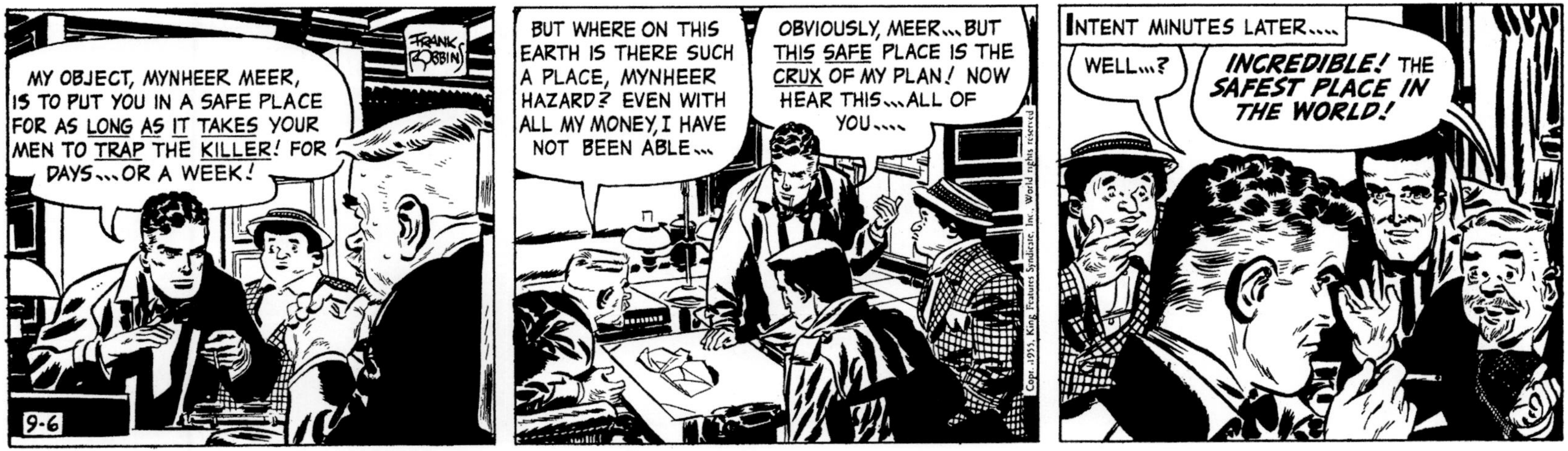
FRANK ROBBINS
MY OBJECT, MYNHEER MEER, IS TO PUT YOU IN A SAFE PLACE FOR AS LONG AS IT TAKES YOUR MEN TO TRAP THE KILLER! FOR DAYS...OR A WEEK!
9-6
BUT WHERE ON THIS EARTH IS THERE SUCH A PLACE, MYNHEER HAZARD? EVEN WITH ALL MY MONEY, I HAVE NOT BEEN ABLE...
OBVIOUSLY, MEER...BUT THIS SAFE PLACE IS THE CRUX OF MY PLAN! NOW HEAR THIS...ALL OF YOU....
Copr. 1955, King Features Syndicate, Inc., World rights reserved
INTENT MINUTES LATER....
WELL...?
INCREDIBLE! THE SAFEST PLACE IN THE WORLD!

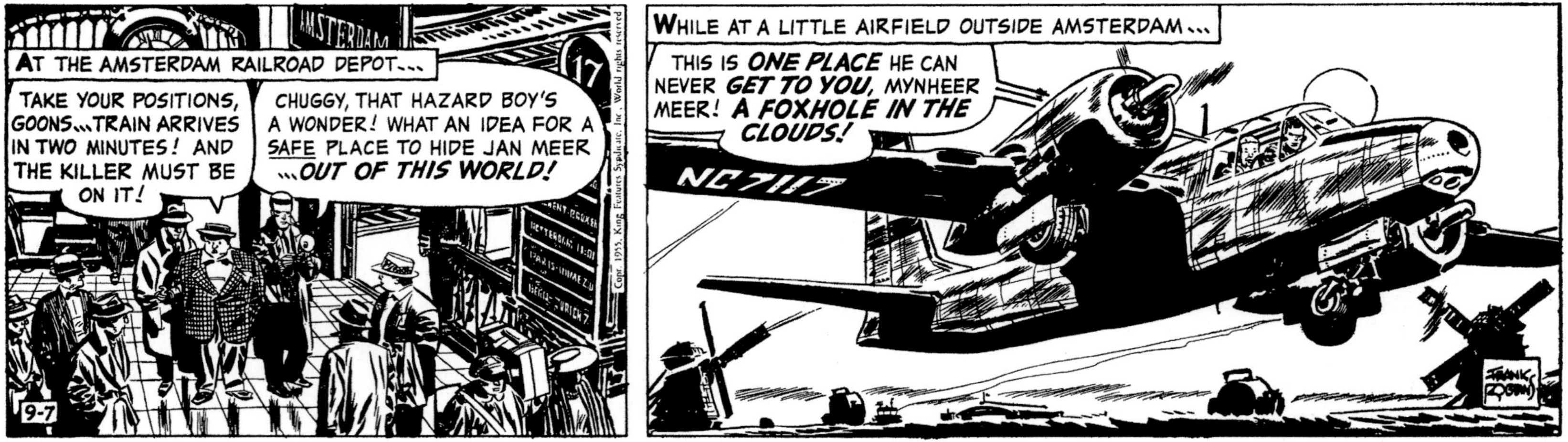
AMSTERDAM
AT THE AMSTERDAM RAILROAD DEPOT...
TAKE YOUR POSITIONS, GOONS...TRAIN ARRIVES IN TWO MINUTES! AND THE KILLER MUST BE ON IT!
CHUGGY, THAT HAZARD BOY'S A WONDER! WHAT AN IDEA FOR A SAFE PLACE TO HIDE JAN MEER ...OUT OF THIS WORLD!
17
Copr. 1955, King Features Syndicate, Inc., World rights reserved
9-7
WHILE AT A LITTLE AIRFIELD OUTSIDE AMSTERDAM...
THIS IS ONE PLACE HE CAN NEVER GET TO YOU, MYNHEER MEER! A FOXHOLE IN THE CLOUDS!
NC7117
FRANK ROBBINS

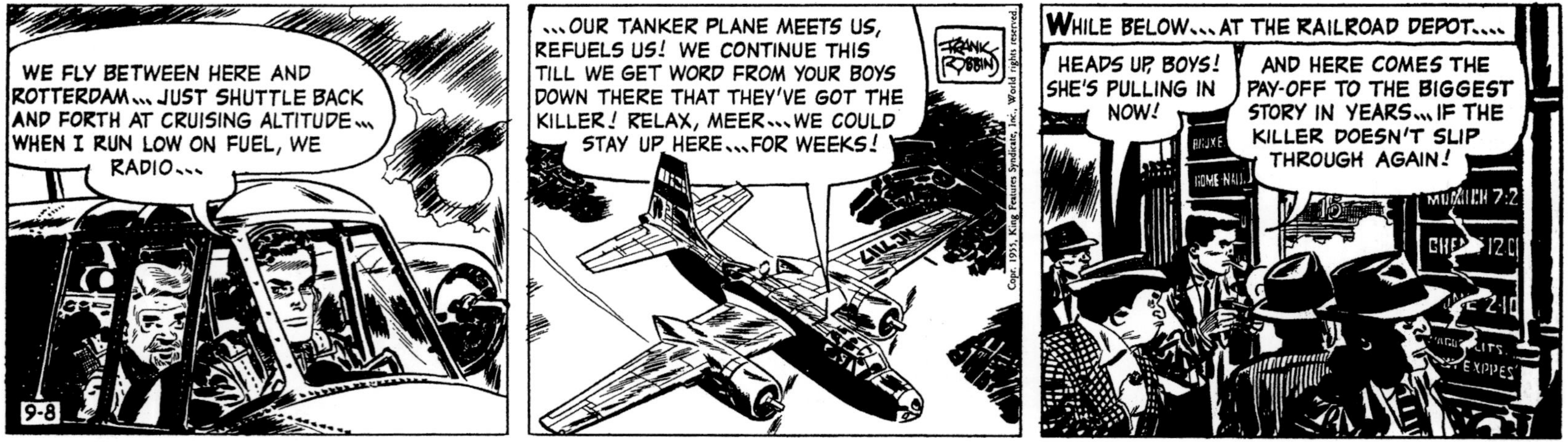
WE FLY BETWEEN HERE AND ROTTERDAM...JUST SHUTTLE BACK AND FORTH AT CRUISING ALTITUDE... WHEN I RUN LOW ON FUEL, WE RADIO...
9-8
...OUR TANKER PLANE MEETS US, REFUELS US! WE CONTINUE THIS TILL WE GET WORD FROM YOUR BOYS DOWN THERE THAT THEY'VE GOT THE KILLER! RELAX, MEER...WE COULD STAY UP HERE...FOR WEEKS!
FRANK ROBBINS
Copr. 1955, King Features Syndicate, Inc., World rights reserved.
WHILE BELOW...AT THE RAILROAD DEPOT....
HEADS UP, BOYS! SHE'S PULLING IN NOW!
AND HERE COMES THE PAY-OFF TO THE BIGGEST STORY IN YEARS...IF THE KILLER DOESN'T SLIP THROUGH AGAIN!

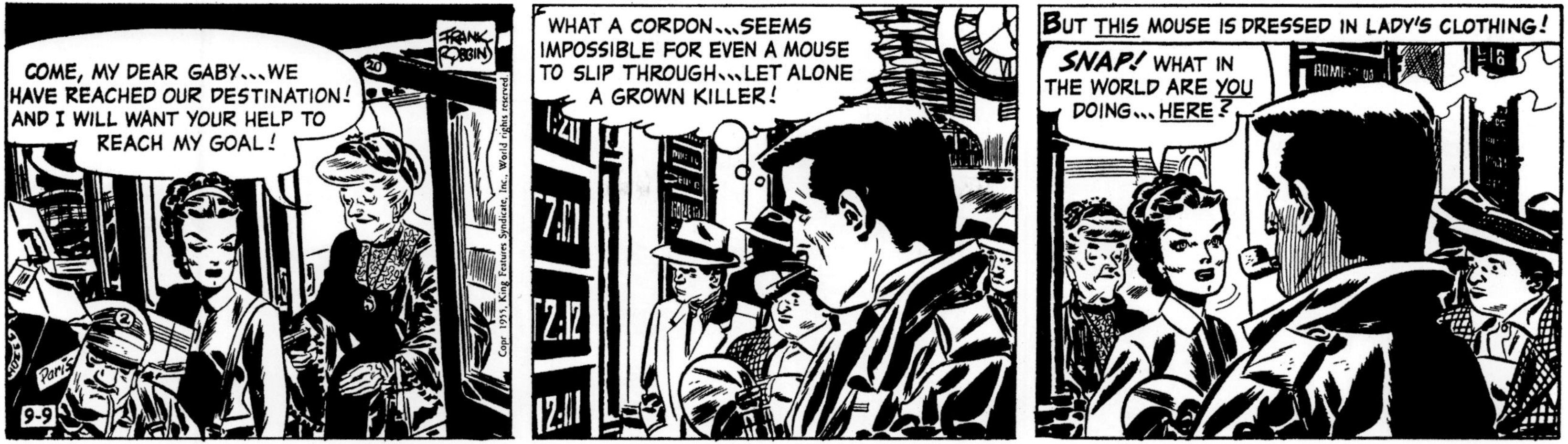
FRANK ROBBINS
COME, MY DEAR GABY... WE HAVE REACHED OUR DESTINATION! AND I WILL WANT YOUR HELP TO REACH MY GOAL!
Copr 1955, King Features Syndicate, Inc., World rights reserved.
9-9
PARIS
WHAT A CORDON... SEEMS IMPOSSIBLE FOR EVEN A MOUSE TO SLIP THROUGH... LET ALONE A GROWN KILLER!
BUT THIS MOUSE IS DRESSED IN LADY'S CLOTHING!
SNAP! WHAT IN THE WORLD ARE YOU DOING... HERE?

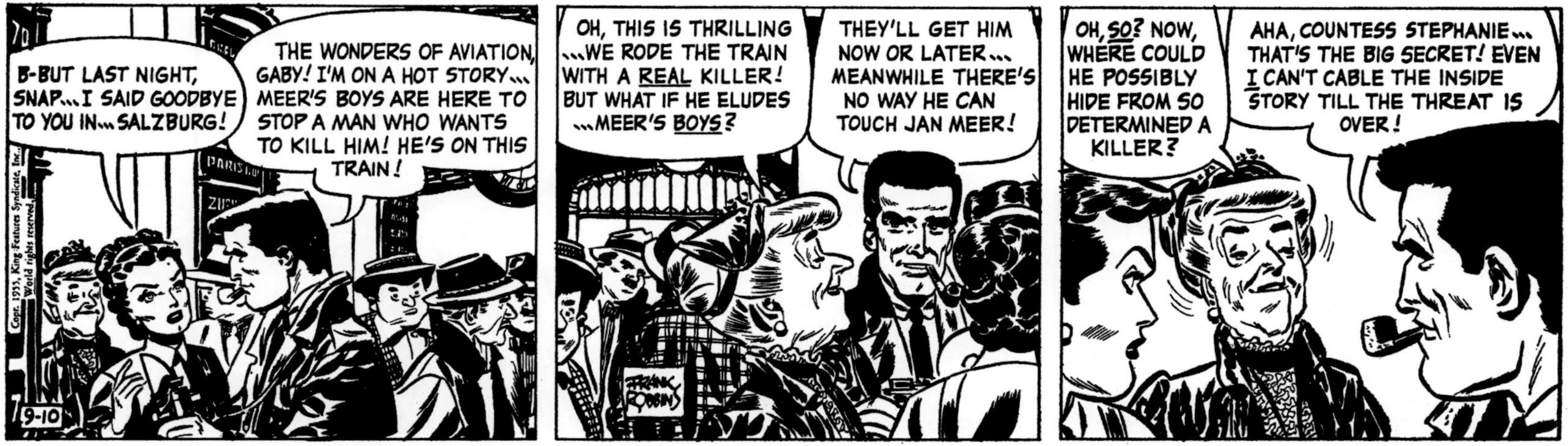
B-BUT LAST NIGHT, SNAP... I SAID GOODBYE TO YOU IN... SALZBURG!
THE WONDERS OF AVIATION, GABY! I'M ON A HOT STORY... MEER'S BOYS ARE HERE TO STOP A MAN WHO WANTS TO KILL HIM! HE'S ON THIS TRAIN!
Copr. 1955, King Features Syndicate, Inc., World rights reserved.
9-10
OH, THIS IS THRILLING ...WE RODE THE TRAIN WITH A REAL KILLER! BUT WHAT IF HE ELUDES ...MEER'S BOYS?
THEY'LL GET HIM NOW OR LATER... MEANWHILE THERE'S NO WAY HE CAN TOUCH JAN MEER!
FRANK ROBBINS
OH, SO? NOW, WHERE COULD HE POSSIBLY HIDE FROM SO DETERMINED A KILLER?
AHA, COUNTESS STEPHANIE... THAT'S THE BIG SECRET! EVEN I CAN'T CABLE THE INSIDE STORY TILL THE THREAT IS OVER!

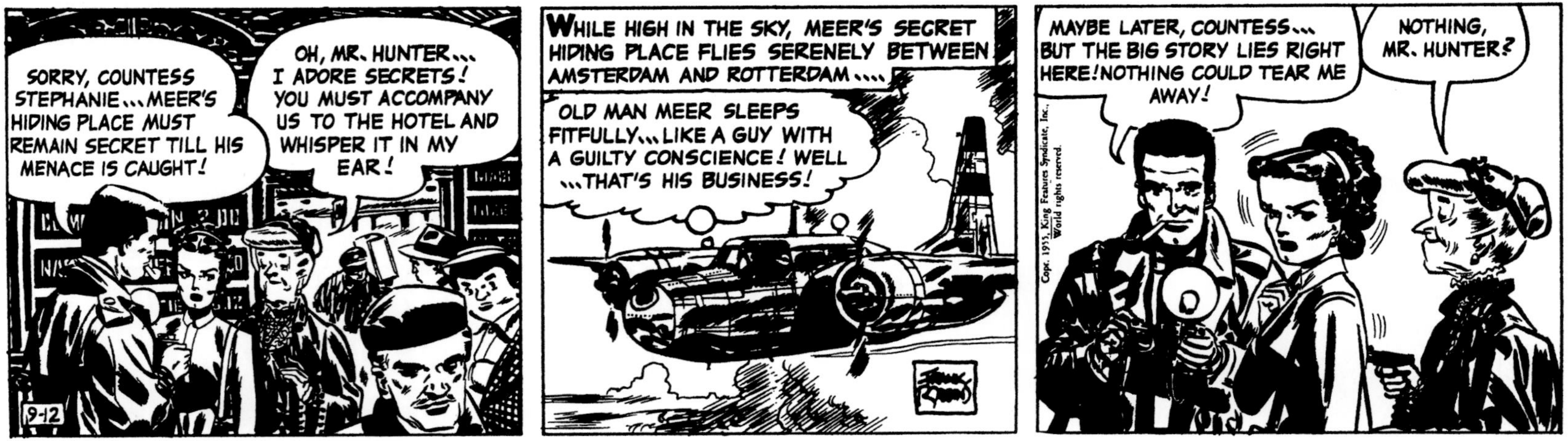
9-12
SORRY, COUNTESS STEPHANIE...MEER'S HIDING PLACE MUST REMAIN SECRET TILL HIS MENACE IS CAUGHT!
OH, MR. HUNTER... I ADORE SECRETS! YOU MUST ACCOMPANY US TO THE HOTEL AND WHISPER IT IN MY EAR!
WHILE HIGH IN THE SKY, MEER'S SECRET HIDING PLACE FLIES SERENELY BETWEEN AMSTERDAM AND ROTTERDAM....
OLD MAN MEER SLEEPS FITFULLY... LIKE A GUY WITH A GUILTY CONSCIENCE! WELL ...THAT'S HIS BUSINESS!
MAYBE LATER, COUNTESS... BUT THE BIG STORY LIES RIGHT HERE! NOTHING COULD TEAR ME AWAY!
NOTHING, MR. HUNTER?
Copr. 1955, King Features Syndicate, Inc. World rights reserved.

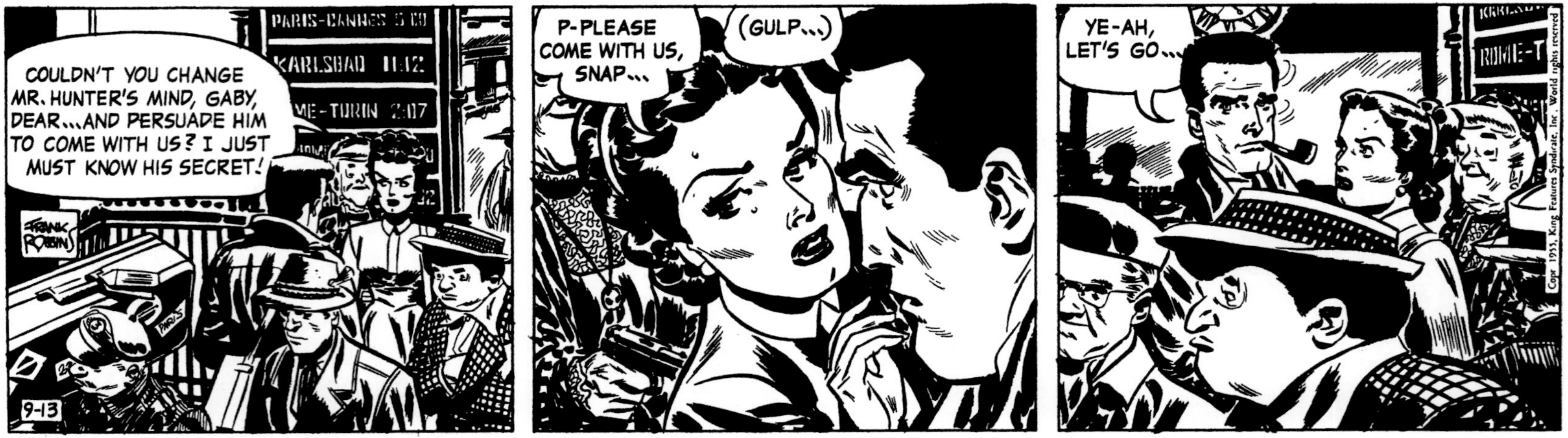
9-13
PARIS-CANNES 5:10
KARLSBAD 11:12
ME-TURIN 2:07
COULDN'T YOU CHANGE MR. HUNTER'S MIND, GABY, DEAR...AND PERSUADE HIM TO COME WITH US? I JUST MUST KNOW HIS SECRET!
FRANK ROBBINS
P-PLEASE COME WITH US, SNAP...
(GULP...)
YE-AH, LET'S GO...
ROME-T
Copr. 1955, King Features Syndicate, Inc. World rights reserved

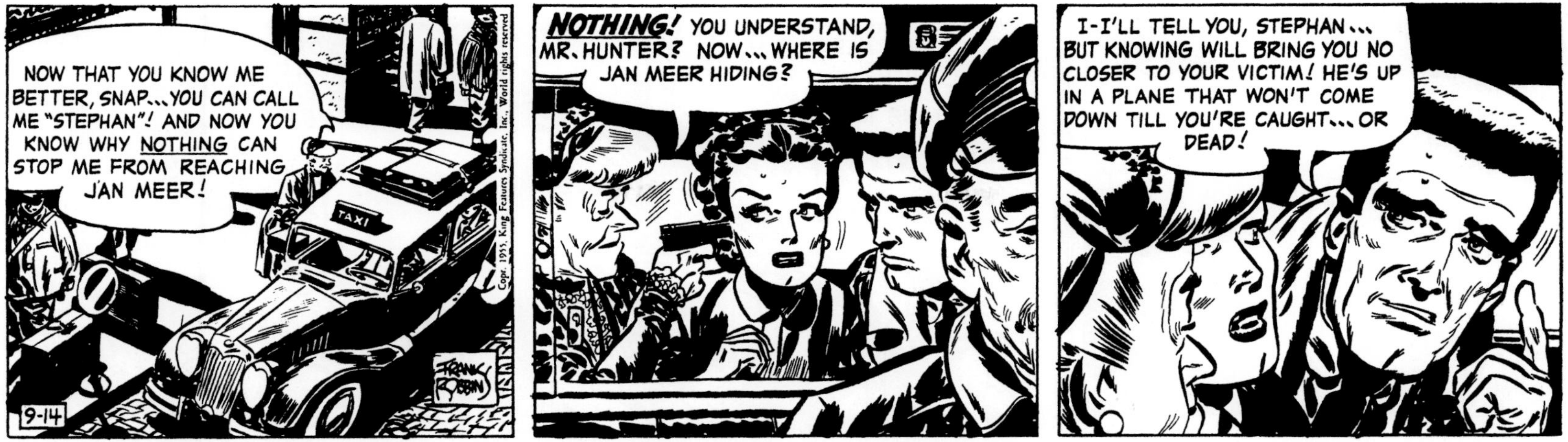
NOW THAT YOU KNOW ME BETTER, SNAP...YOU CAN CALL ME "STEPHAN"! AND NOW YOU KNOW WHY NOTHING CAN STOP ME FROM REACHING JAN MEER!
TAXI
Copr. 1955, King Features Syndicate, Inc., World rights reserved
FRANK ROBBIN
9-14
NOTHING! YOU UNDERSTAND, MR. HUNTER? NOW...WHERE IS JAN MEER HIDING?
I-I'LL TELL YOU, STEPHAN... BUT KNOWING WILL BRING YOU NO CLOSER TO YOUR VICTIM! HE'S UP IN A PLANE THAT WON'T COME DOWN TILL YOU'RE CAUGHT...OR DEAD!

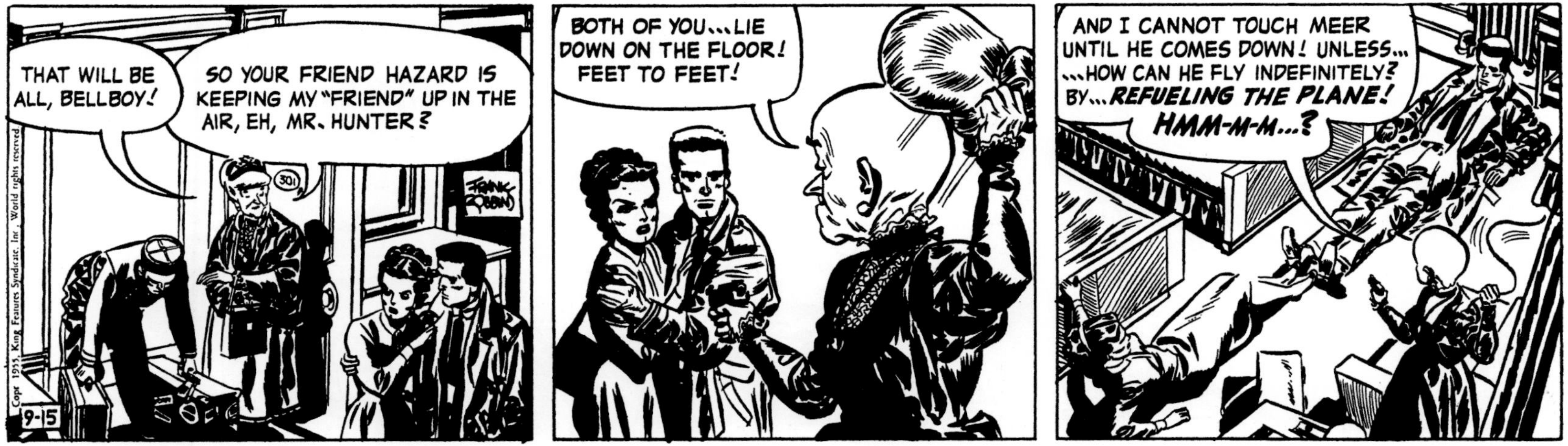
THAT WILL BE ALL, BELLBOY!
SO YOUR FRIEND HAZARD IS KEEPING MY "FRIEND" UP IN THE AIR, EH, MR. HUNTER?
301
FRANK ROBBIN
Copr. 1955, King Features Syndicate, Inc., World rights reserved
9-15
BOTH OF YOU...LIE DOWN ON THE FLOOR! FEET TO FEET!
AND I CANNOT TOUCH MEER UNTIL HE COMES DOWN! UNLESS... ...HOW CAN HE FLY INDEFINITELY? BY...REFUELING THE PLANE!
HMM-M-M...?

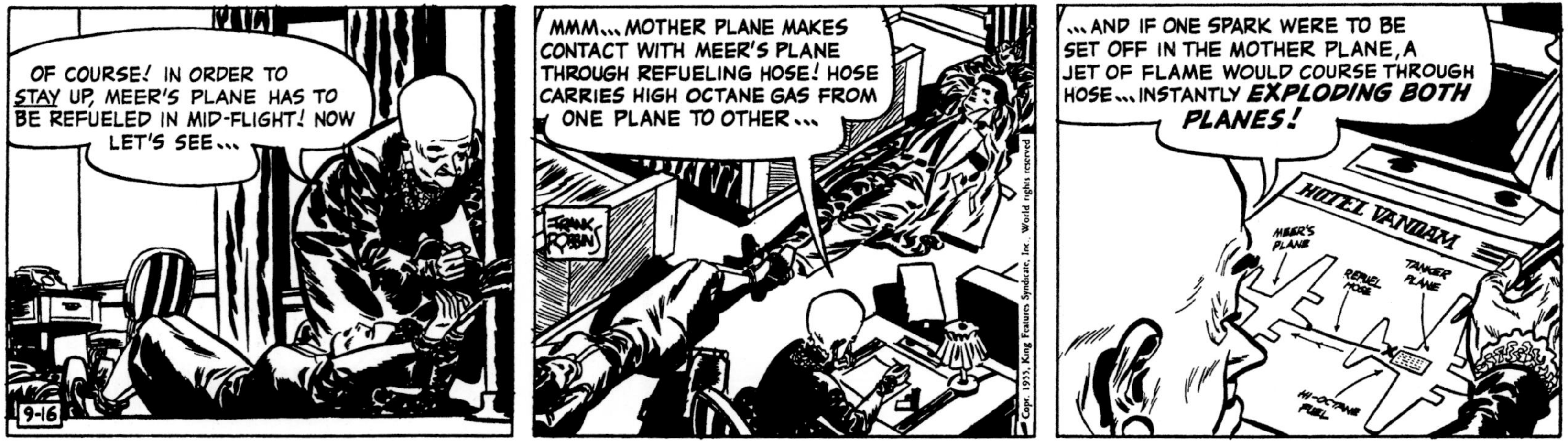
9-16
OF COURSE! IN ORDER TO STAY UP, MEER'S PLANE HAS TO BE REFUELED IN MID-FLIGHT! NOW LET'S SEE...
MMM... MOTHER PLANE MAKES CONTACT WITH MEER'S PLANE THROUGH REFUELING HOSE! HOSE CARRIES HIGH OCTANE GAS FROM ONE PLANE TO OTHER...
FRANK ROBBINS
Copr. 1955, King Features Syndicate, Inc., World rights reserved
...AND IF ONE SPARK WERE TO BE SET OFF IN THE MOTHER PLANE, A JET OF FLAME WOULD COURSE THROUGH HOSE... INSTANTLY EXPLODING BOTH PLANES!
HOTEL VANDAM
MEER'S PLANE
REFUEL HOSE
TANKER PLANE
HI-OCTANE FUEL

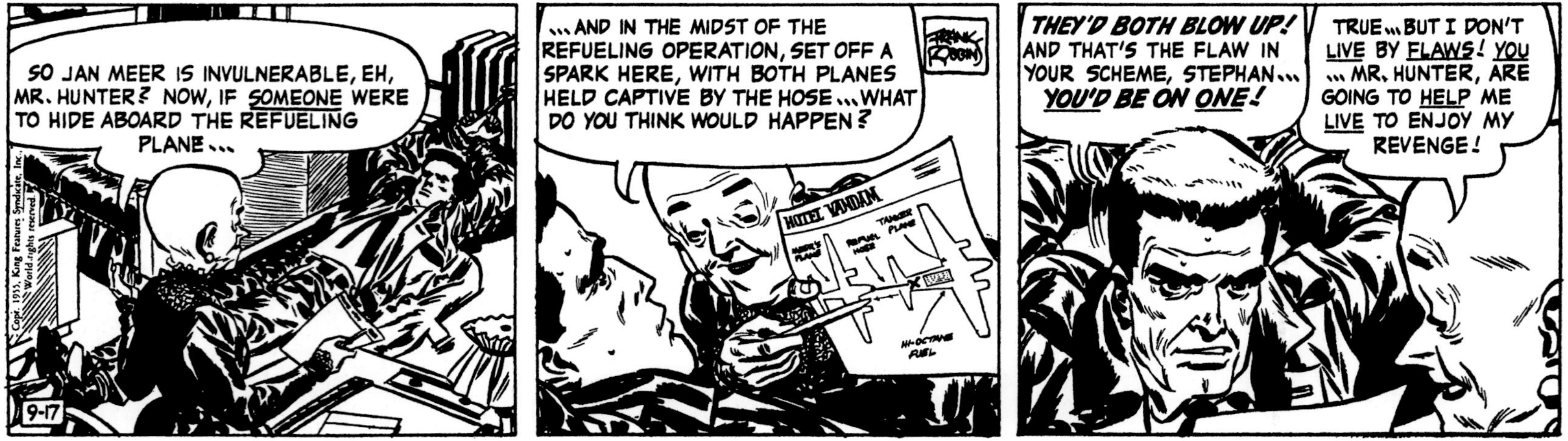
SO JAN MEER IS INVULNERABLE, EH, MR. HUNTER? NOW, IF SOMEONE WERE TO HIDE ABOARD THE REFUELING PLANE...
Copr. 1955, King Features Syndicate, Inc., World rights reserved.
9-17
...AND IN THE MIDST OF THE REFUELING OPERATION, SET OFF A SPARK HERE, WITH BOTH PLANES HELD CAPTIVE BY THE HOSE... WHAT DO YOU THINK WOULD HAPPEN?
FRANK ROBBINS
HOTEL VANDAM
MEER'S PLANE
REFUEL HOSE
TANKER PLANE
HI-OCTANE FUEL
THEY'D BOTH BLOW UP! AND THAT'S THE FLAW IN YOUR SCHEME, STEPHAN... YOU'D BE ON ONE!
TRUE... BUT I DON'T LIVE BY FLAWS! YOU ... MR. HUNTER, ARE GOING TO HELP ME LIVE TO ENJOY MY REVENGE!

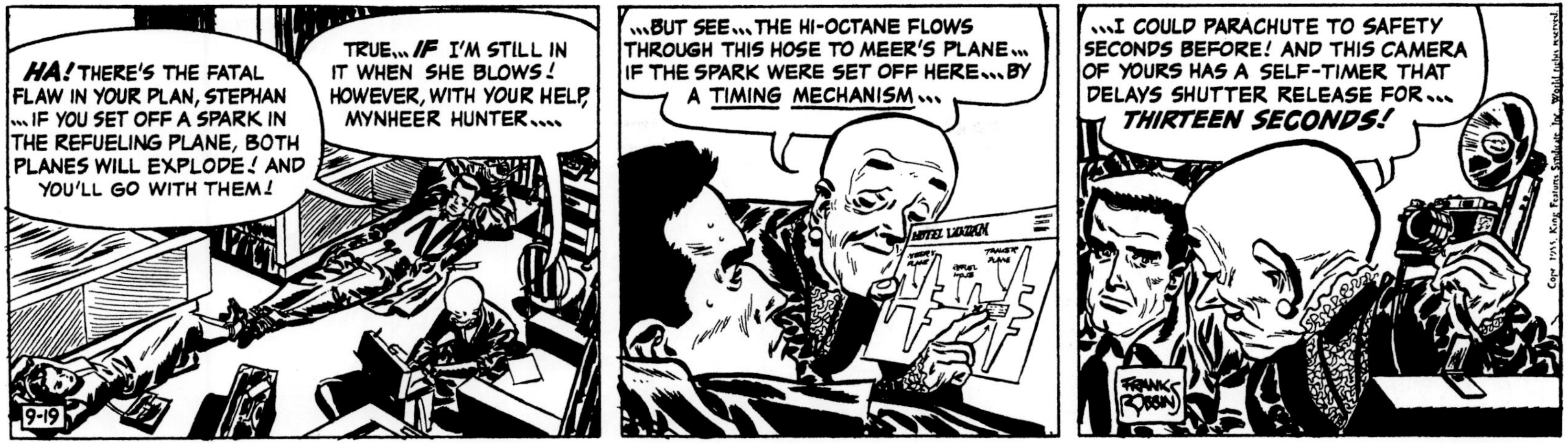

9-19
HA! THERE'S THE FATAL FLAW IN YOUR PLAN, STEPHAN ...IF YOU SET OFF A SPARK IN THE REFUELING PLANE, BOTH PLANES WILL EXPLODE! AND YOU'LL GO WITH THEM!
TRUE... IF I'M STILL IN IT WHEN SHE BLOWS! HOWEVER, WITH YOUR HELP, MYNHEER HUNTER....
...BUT SEE... THE HI-OCTANE FLOWS THROUGH THIS HOSE TO MEER'S PLANE... IF THE SPARK WERE SET OFF HERE... BY A TIMING MECHANISM...
...I COULD PARACHUTE TO SAFETY SECONDS BEFORE! AND THIS CAMERA OF YOURS HAS A SELF-TIMER THAT DELAYS SHUTTER RELEASE FOR... THIRTEEN SECONDS!
Copr 1955, King Features Syndicate, Inc. World rights reserved

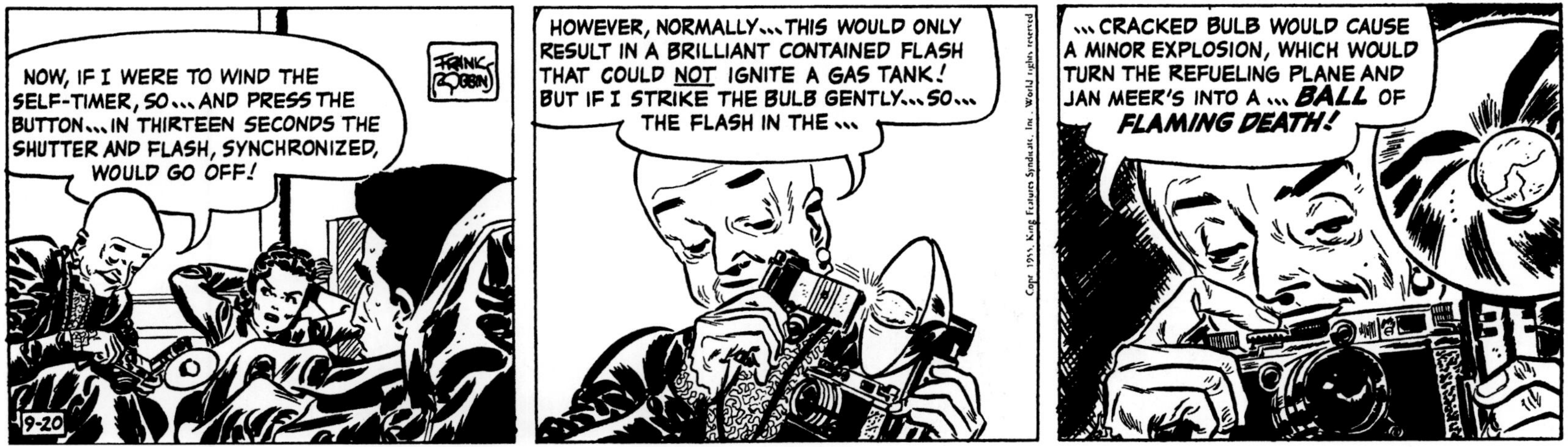

9-20
NOW, IF I WERE TO WIND THE SELF-TIMER, SO... AND PRESS THE BUTTON... IN THIRTEEN SECONDS THE SHUTTER AND FLASH, SYNCHRONIZED, WOULD GO OFF!
HOWEVER, NORMALLY... THIS WOULD ONLY RESULT IN A BRILLIANT CONTAINED FLASH THAT COULD NOT IGNITE A GAS TANK! BUT IF I STRIKE THE BULB GENTLY... SO... THE FLASH IN THE ...
...CRACKED BULB WOULD CAUSE A MINOR EXPLOSION, WHICH WOULD TURN THE REFUELING PLANE AND JAN MEER'S INTO A... BALL OF FLAMING DEATH!
Copr 1955, King Features Syndicate, Inc. World rights reserved

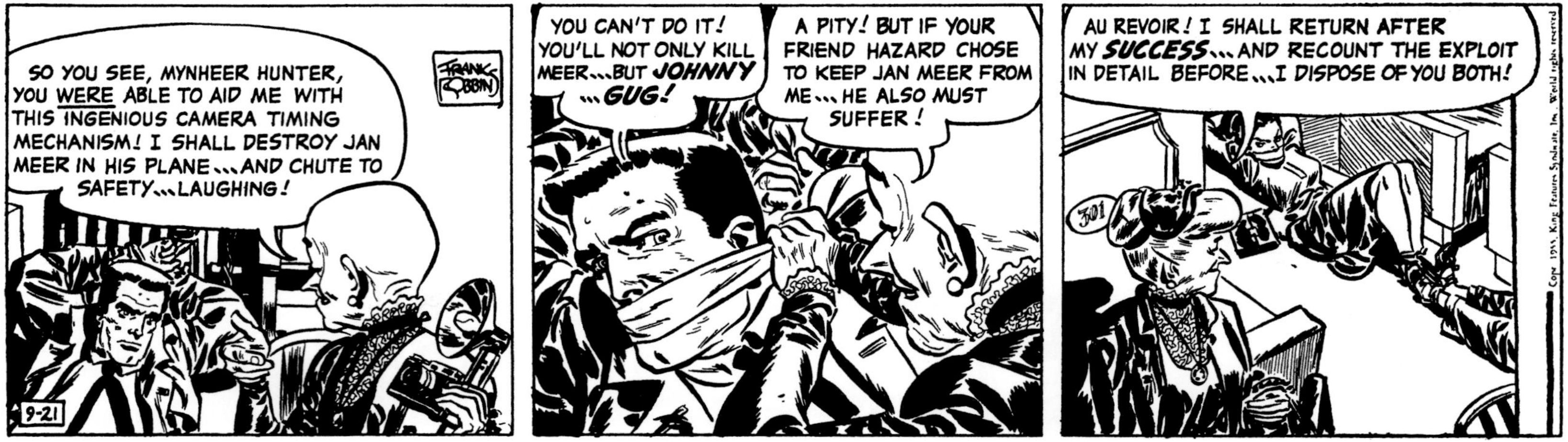
FRANK ROBBINS
9-21
SO YOU SEE, MYNHEER HUNTER, YOU WERE ABLE TO AID ME WITH THIS INGENIOUS CAMERA TIMING MECHANISM! I SHALL DESTROY JAN MEER IN HIS PLANE...AND CHUTE TO SAFETY...LAUGHING!
YOU CAN'T DO IT! YOU'LL NOT ONLY KILL MEER...BUT JOHNNY ...GUG!
A PITY! BUT IF YOUR FRIEND HAZARD CHOSE TO KEEP JAN MEER FROM ME...HE ALSO MUST SUFFER!
AU REVOIR! I SHALL RETURN AFTER MY SUCCESS...AND RECOUNT THE EXPLOIT IN DETAIL BEFORE...I DISPOSE OF YOU BOTH!
301
Copr. 1955, King Features Syndicate, Inc. World rights reserved

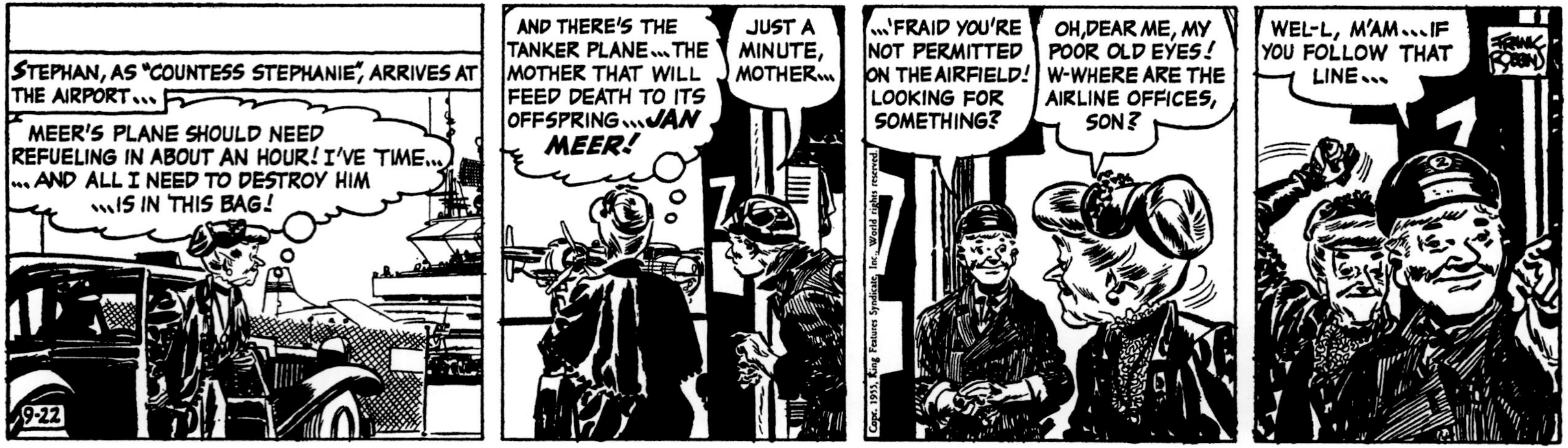
9-22
STEPHAN, AS "COUNTESS STEPHANIE", ARRIVES AT THE AIRPORT...
MEER'S PLANE SHOULD NEED REFUELING IN ABOUT AN HOUR! I'VE TIME... ...AND ALL I NEED TO DESTROY HIM ...IS IN THIS BAG!
AND THERE'S THE TANKER PLANE...THE MOTHER THAT WILL FEED DEATH TO ITS OFFSPRING...JAN MEER!
JUST A MINUTE, MOTHER...
...'FRAID YOU'RE NOT PERMITTED ON THE AIRFIELD! LOOKING FOR SOMETHING?
OH, DEAR ME, MY POOR OLD EYES! W-WHERE ARE THE AIRLINE OFFICES, SON?
Copr. 1955, King Features Syndicate, Inc., World rights reserved.
WEL-L, M'AM...IF YOU FOLLOW THAT LINE...
FRANK ROBBINS

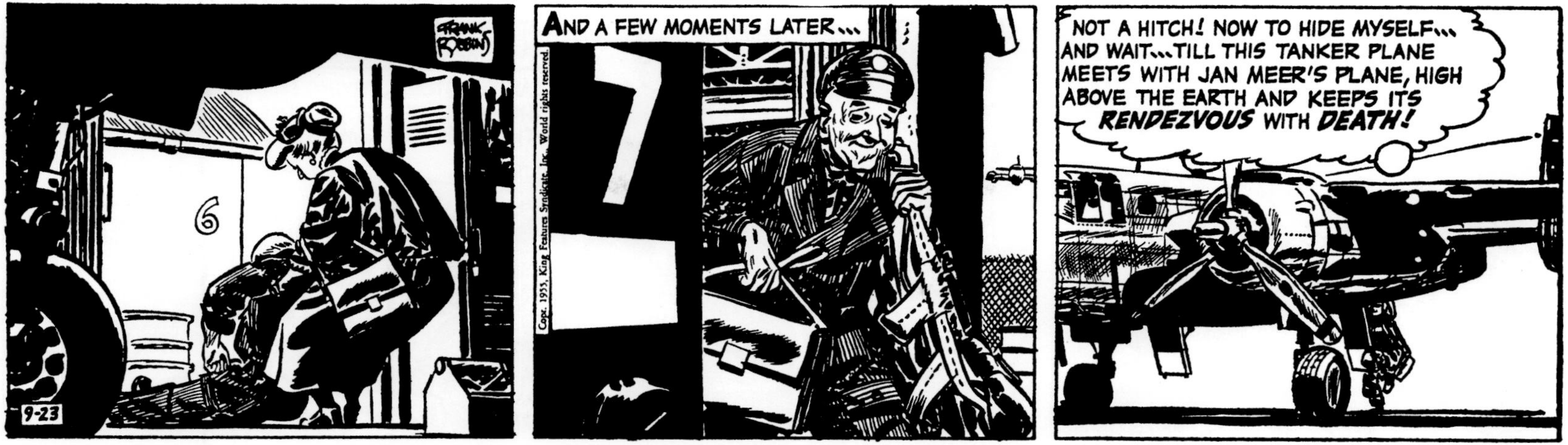
FRANK ROBBINS
9-23
AND A FEW MOMENTS LATER...
Copr. 1955, King Features Syndicate, Inc., World rights reserved.
7
NOT A HITCH! NOW TO HIDE MYSELF... AND WAIT... TILL THIS TANKER PLANE MEETS WITH JAN MEER'S PLANE, HIGH ABOVE THE EARTH AND KEEPS ITS *RENDEZVOUS* WITH *DEATH!*

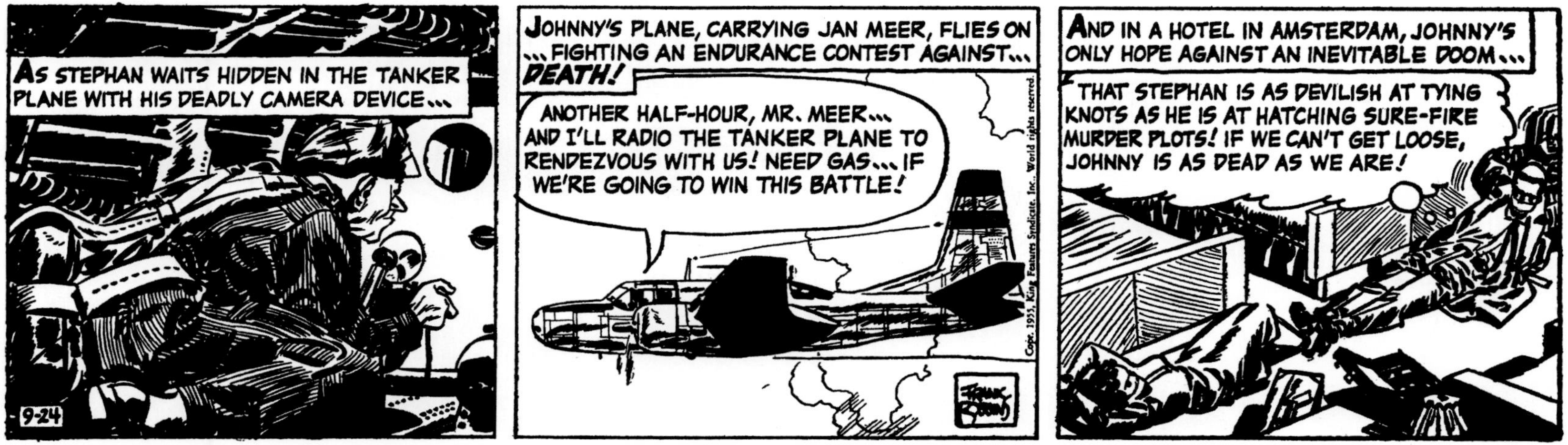
AS STEPHAN WAITS HIDDEN IN THE TANKER PLANE WITH HIS DEADLY CAMERA DEVICE...
9-24
JOHNNY'S PLANE, CARRYING JAN MEER, FLIES ON ... FIGHTING AN ENDURANCE CONTEST AGAINST... *DEATH!*
ANOTHER HALF-HOUR, MR. MEER... AND I'LL RADIO THE TANKER PLANE TO RENDEZVOUS WITH US! NEED GAS... IF WE'RE GOING TO WIN THIS BATTLE!
Copr. 1955, King Features Syndicate, Inc., World rights reserved.
FRANK ROBBINS
AND IN A HOTEL IN AMSTERDAM, JOHNNY'S ONLY HOPE AGAINST AN INEVITABLE DOOM...
THAT STEPHAN IS AS DEVILISH AT TYING KNOTS AS HE IS AT HATCHING SURE-FIRE MURDER PLOTS! IF WE CAN'T GET LOOSE, JOHNNY IS AS DEAD AS WE ARE!

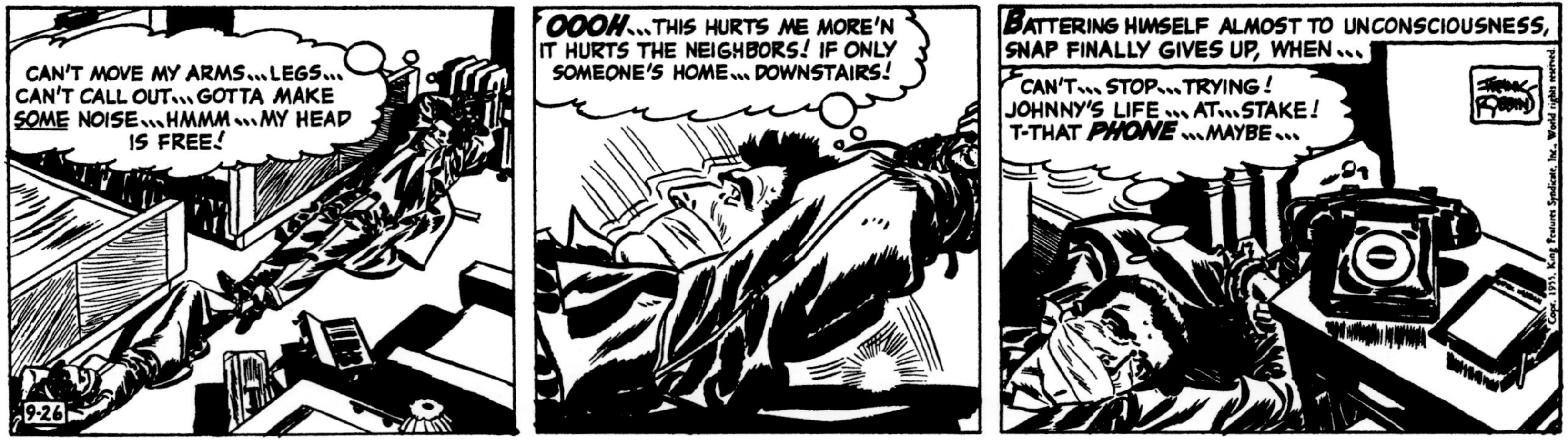
CAN'T MOVE MY ARMS... LEGS... CAN'T CALL OUT... GOTTA MAKE SOME NOISE... HMMM... MY HEAD IS FREE!
9-26
OOOH... THIS HURTS ME MORE'N IT HURTS THE NEIGHBORS! IF ONLY SOMEONE'S HOME... DOWNSTAIRS!
BATTERING HIMSELF ALMOST TO UNCONSCIOUSNESS, SNAP FINALLY GIVES UP, WHEN...
CAN'T... STOP... TRYING! JOHNNY'S LIFE... AT... STAKE! T-THAT PHONE... MAYBE...
FRANK ROBBINS
Copr. 1955, King Features Syndicate, Inc., World rights reserved

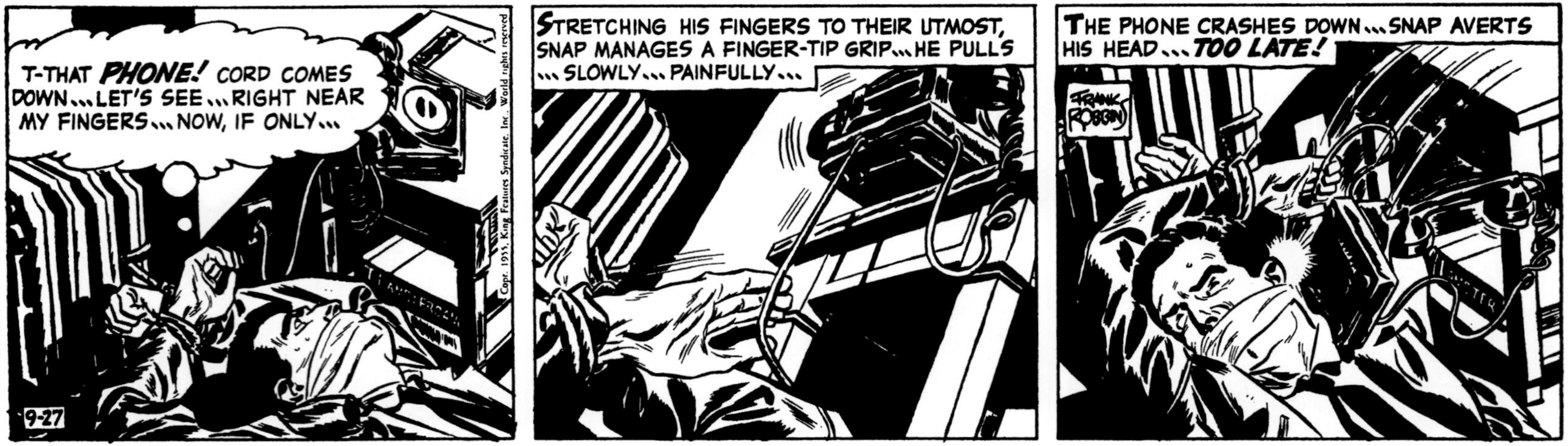
T-THAT PHONE! CORD COMES DOWN... LET'S SEE... RIGHT NEAR MY FINGERS... NOW, IF ONLY...
9-27
Copr. 1955, King Features Syndicate, Inc., World rights reserved
STRETCHING HIS FINGERS TO THEIR UTMOST, SNAP MANAGES A FINGER-TIP GRIP... HE PULLS ... SLOWLY... PAINFULLY...
THE PHONE CRASHES DOWN... SNAP AVERTS HIS HEAD... TOO LATE!
FRANK ROBBINS

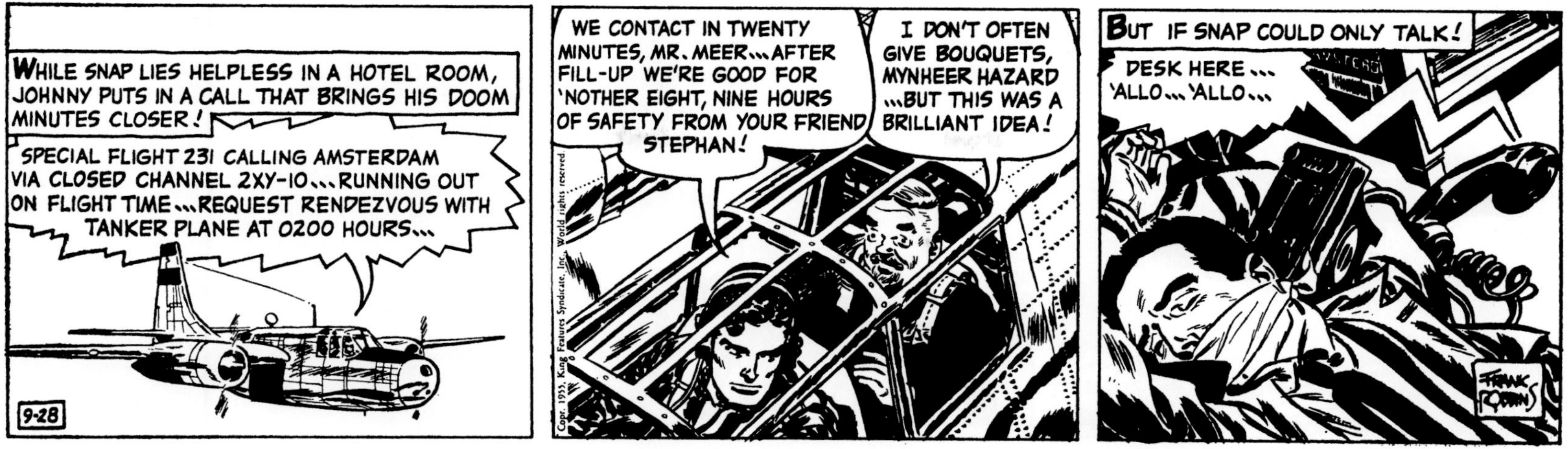
WHILE SNAP LIES HELPLESS IN A HOTEL ROOM, JOHNNY PUTS IN A CALL THAT BRINGS HIS DOOM MINUTES CLOSER!
SPECIAL FLIGHT 231 CALLING AMSTERDAM VIA CLOSED CHANNEL 2XY-10... RUNNING OUT ON FLIGHT TIME... REQUEST RENDEZVOUS WITH TANKER PLANE AT 0200 HOURS...
9-28
WE CONTACT IN TWENTY MINUTES, MR. MEER... AFTER FILL-UP WE'RE GOOD FOR 'NOTHER EIGHT, NINE HOURS OF SAFETY FROM YOUR FRIEND STEPHAN!
I DON'T OFTEN GIVE BOUQUETS, MYNHEER HAZARD ...BUT THIS WAS A BRILLIANT IDEA!
Copr. 1955, King Features Syndicate, Inc., World rights reserved
BUT IF SNAP COULD ONLY TALK!
DESK HERE... 'ALLO... 'ALLO...
FRANK ROBBINS

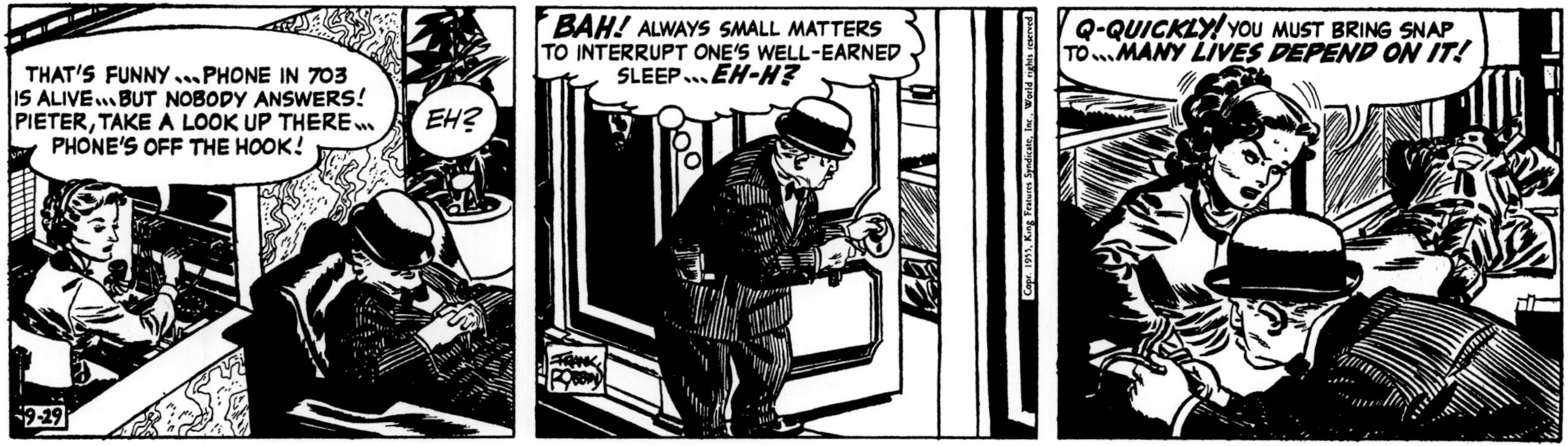
THAT'S FUNNY... PHONE IN 703 IS ALIVE... BUT NOBODY ANSWERS! PIETER, TAKE A LOOK UP THERE... PHONE'S OFF THE HOOK!
EH?
9-29
BAH! ALWAYS SMALL MATTERS TO INTERRUPT ONE'S WELL-EARNED SLEEP... EH-H?
FRANK ROBBINS
Copr. 1955, King Features Syndicate, Inc., World rights reserved
Q-QUICKLY! YOU MUST BRING SNAP TO... MANY LIVES DEPEND ON IT!

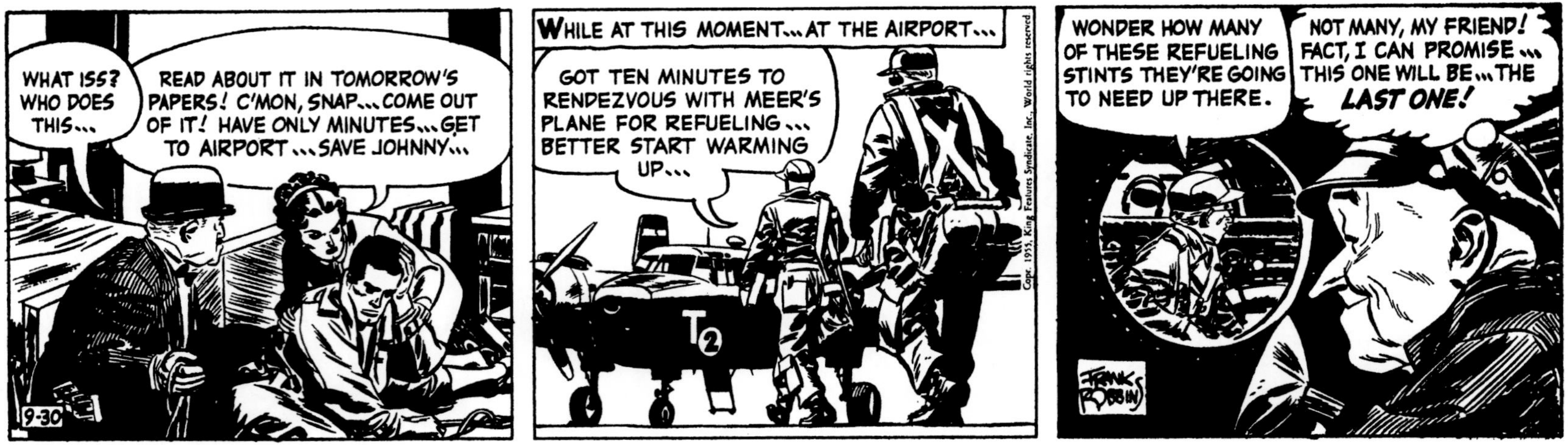
9-30
WHAT ISS? WHO DOES THIS...
READ ABOUT IT IN TOMORROW'S PAPERS! C'MON, SNAP...COME OUT OF IT! HAVE ONLY MINUTES...GET TO AIRPORT...SAVE JOHNNY...
WHILE AT THIS MOMENT...AT THE AIRPORT...
GOT TEN MINUTES TO RENDEZVOUS WITH MEER'S PLANE FOR REFUELING... BETTER START WARMING UP...
T2
Copr. 1955, King Features Syndicate, Inc., World rights reserved
WONDER HOW MANY OF THESE REFUELING STINTS THEY'RE GOING TO NEED UP THERE.
NOT MANY, MY FRIEND! FACT, I CAN PROMISE... THIS ONE WILL BE...THE ***LAST ONE!***
FRANK ROBBINS

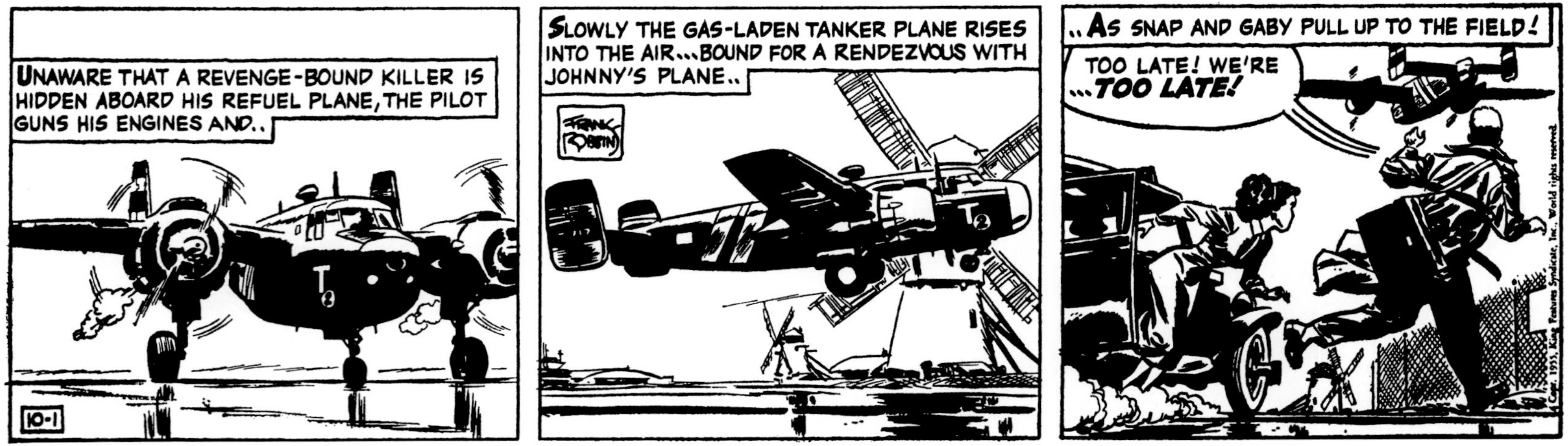
UNAWARE THAT A REVENGE-BOUND KILLER IS HIDDEN ABOARD HIS REFUEL PLANE, THE PILOT GUNS HIS ENGINES AND..
T2
10-1
SLOWLY THE GAS-LADEN TANKER PLANE RISES INTO THE AIR...BOUND FOR A RENDEZVOUS WITH JOHNNY'S PLANE..
FRANK ROBBINS
T2
..AS SNAP AND GABY PULL UP TO THE FIELD!
TOO LATE! WE'RE ...***TOO LATE!***
Copr. 1955, King Features Syndicate, Inc., World rights reserved

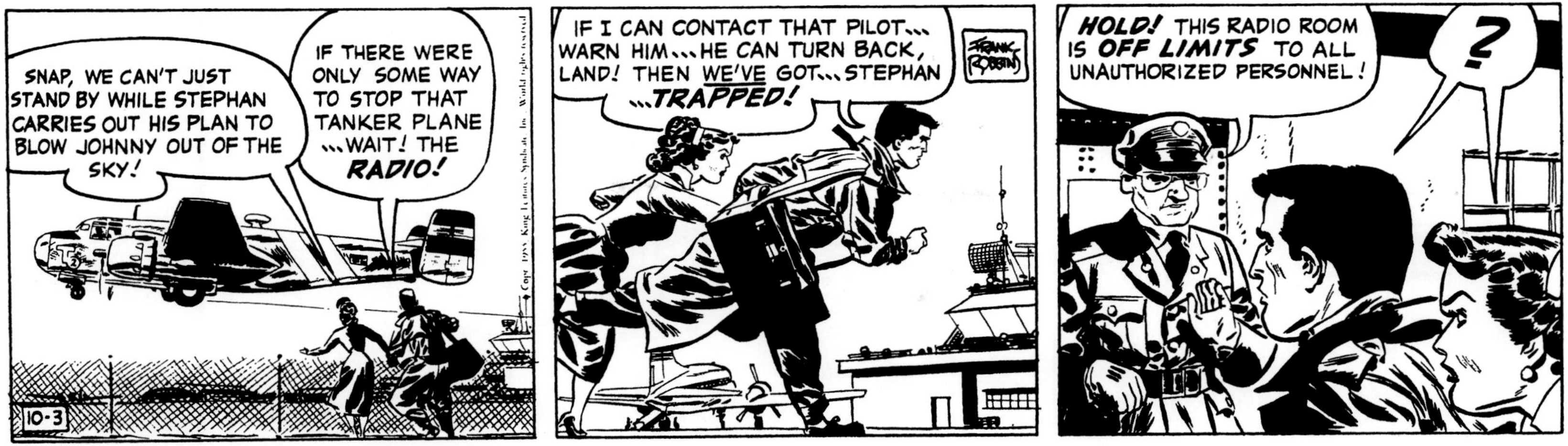
SNAP, WE CAN'T JUST STAND BY WHILE STEPHAN CARRIES OUT HIS PLAN TO BLOW JOHNNY OUT OF THE SKY!
IF THERE WERE ONLY SOME WAY TO STOP THAT TANKER PLANE ...WAIT! THE RADIO!
10-3
IF I CAN CONTACT THAT PILOT... WARN HIM... HE CAN TURN BACK, LAND! THEN WE'VE GOT... STEPHAN ...TRAPPED!
FRANK ROBBINS
HOLD! THIS RADIO ROOM IS OFF LIMITS TO ALL UNAUTHORIZED PERSONNEL!
?

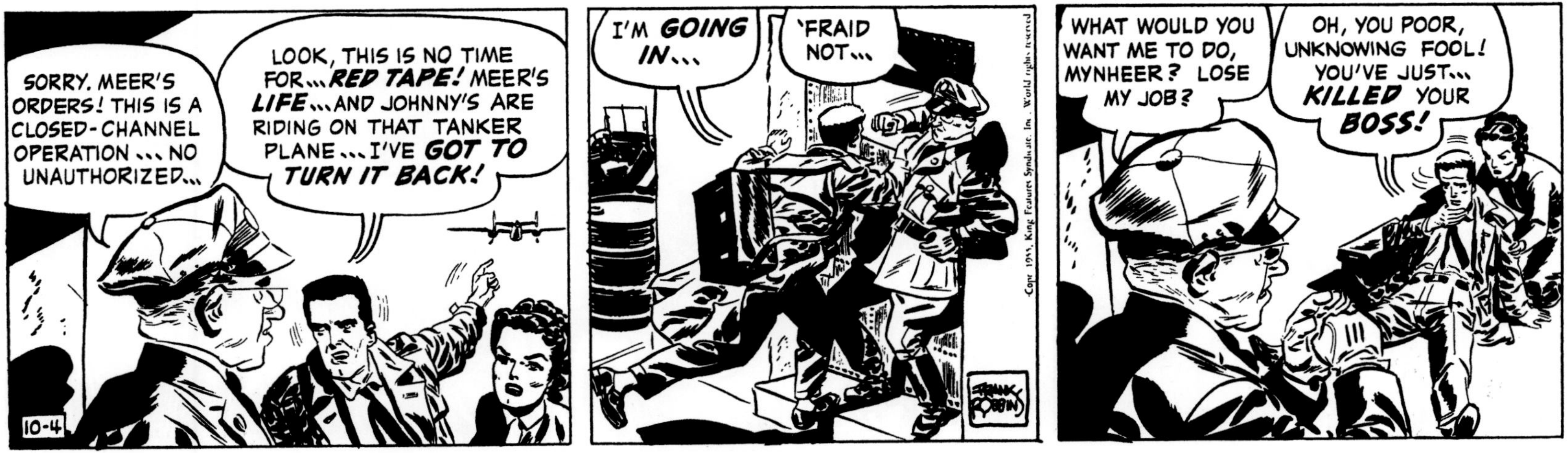
SORRY. MEER'S ORDERS! THIS IS A CLOSED-CHANNEL OPERATION ... NO UNAUTHORIZED...
LOOK, THIS IS NO TIME FOR... RED TAPE! MEER'S LIFE... AND JOHNNY'S ARE RIDING ON THAT TANKER PLANE... I'VE GOT TO TURN IT BACK!
10-4
I'M GOING IN...
'FRAID NOT...
FRANK ROBBINS
WHAT WOULD YOU WANT ME TO DO, MYNHEER? LOSE MY JOB?
OH, YOU POOR, UNKNOWING FOOL! YOU'VE JUST... KILLED YOUR BOSS!

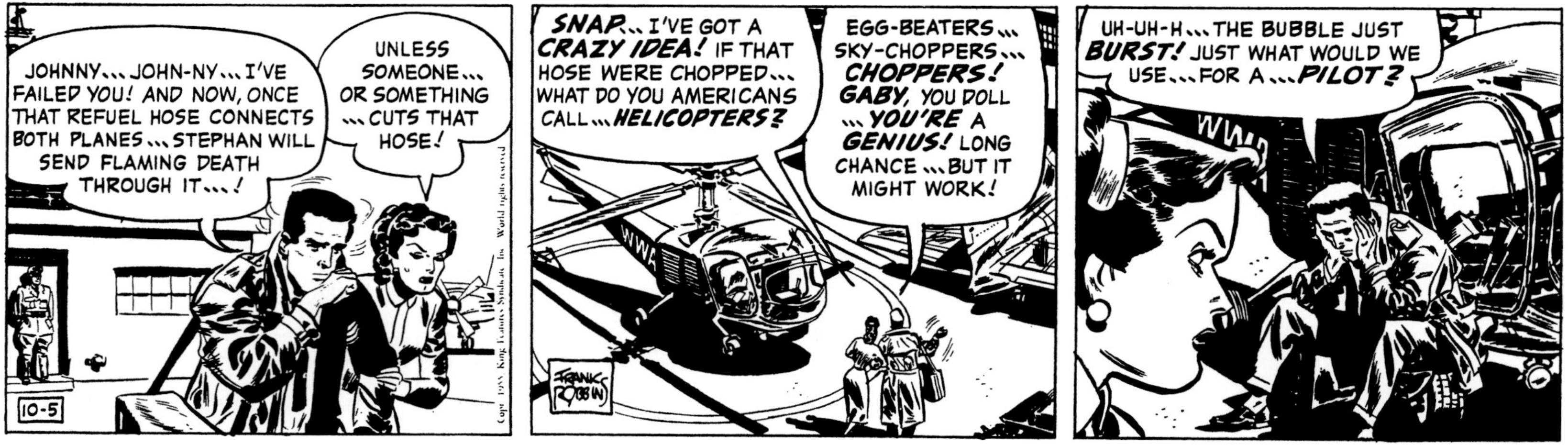
JOHNNY... JOHN-NY... I'VE FAILED YOU! AND NOW, ONCE THAT REFUEL HOSE CONNECTS BOTH PLANES... STEPHAN WILL SEND FLAMING DEATH THROUGH IT...!
UNLESS SOMEONE... OR SOMETHING ...CUTS THAT HOSE!
10-5
SNAP... I'VE GOT A CRAZY IDEA! IF THAT HOSE WERE CHOPPED... WHAT DO YOU AMERICANS CALL... HELICOPTERS?
EGG-BEATERS... SKY-CHOPPERS... CHOPPERS! GABY, YOU DOLL ...YOU'RE A GENIUS! LONG CHANCE ... BUT IT MIGHT WORK!
FRANK ROBBINS
UH-UH-H... THE BUBBLE JUST BURST! JUST WHAT WOULD WE USE... FOR A ...PILOT?

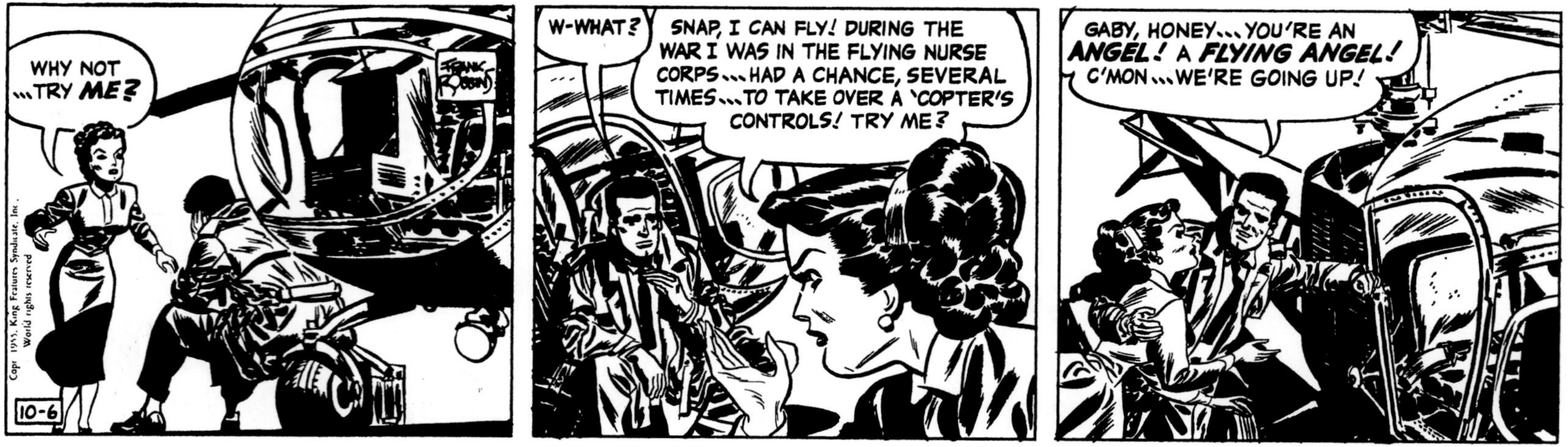
WHY NOT ...TRY ME?
FRANK ROBBINS
10-6
W-WHAT?
SNAP, I CAN FLY! DURING THE WAR I WAS IN THE FLYING NURSE CORPS... HAD A CHANCE, SEVERAL TIMES... TO TAKE OVER A 'COPTER'S CONTROLS! TRY ME?
GABY, HONEY... YOU'RE AN ANGEL! A FLYING ANGEL! C'MON... WE'RE GOING UP!

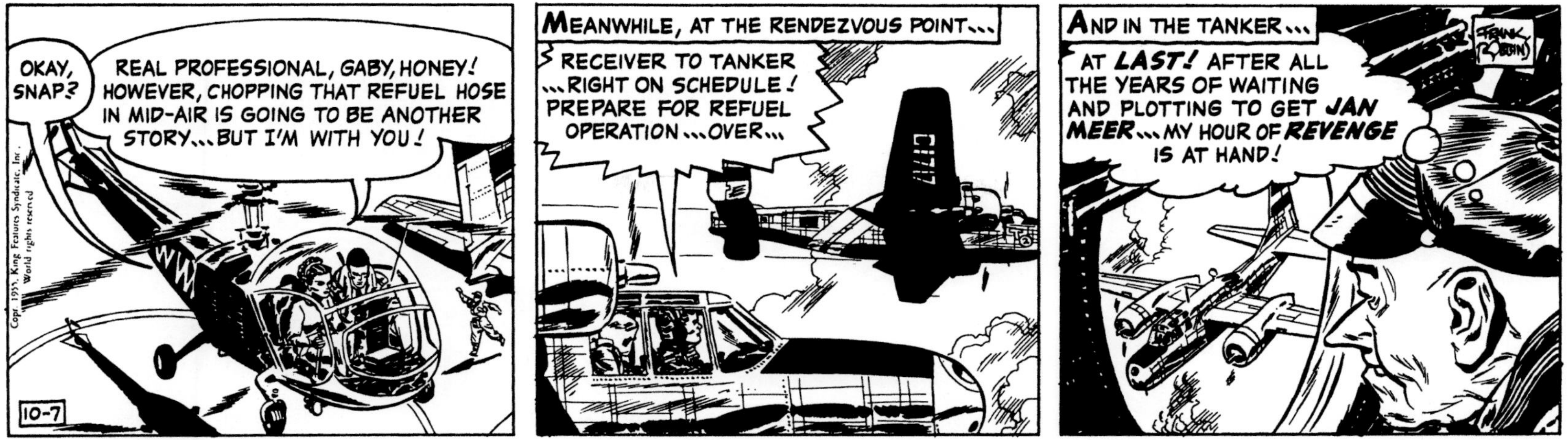
OKAY, SNAP?
REAL PROFESSIONAL, GABY, HONEY! HOWEVER, CHOPPING THAT REFUEL HOSE IN MID-AIR IS GOING TO BE ANOTHER STORY... BUT I'M WITH YOU!
Copr. 1955, King Features Syndicate, Inc. World rights reserved
10-7
MEANWHILE, AT THE RENDEZVOUS POINT...
RECEIVER TO TANKER ...RIGHT ON SCHEDULE! PREPARE FOR REFUEL OPERATION ...OVER...
AND IN THE TANKER...
AT LAST! AFTER ALL THE YEARS OF WAITING AND PLOTTING TO GET JAN MEER... MY HOUR OF REVENGE IS AT HAND!

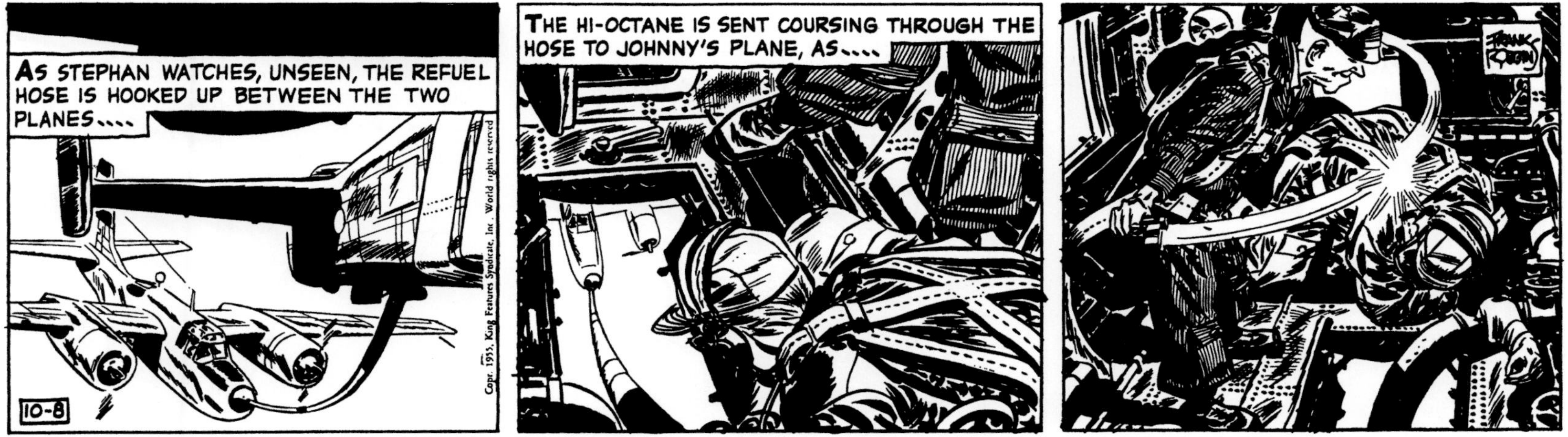
AS STEPHAN WATCHES, UNSEEN, THE REFUEL HOSE IS HOOKED UP BETWEEN THE TWO PLANES....
Copr. 1955, King Features Syndicate, Inc. World rights reserved
10-8
THE HI-OCTANE IS SENT COURSING THROUGH THE HOSE TO JOHNNY'S PLANE, AS....

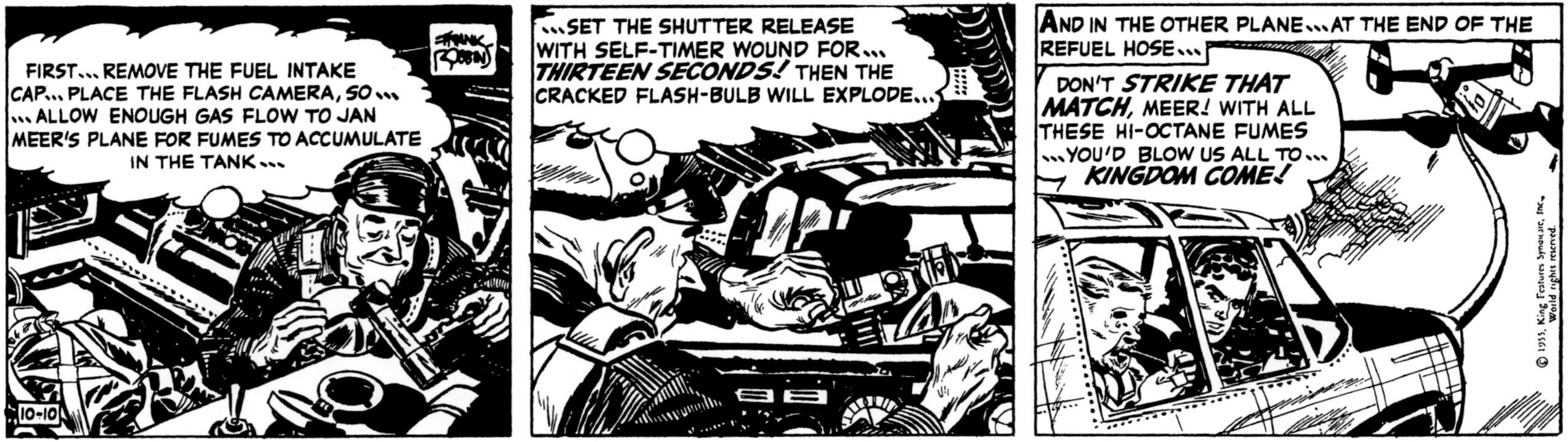
FRANK ROBBINS
FIRST... REMOVE THE FUEL INTAKE CAP... PLACE THE FLASH CAMERA, SO... ...ALLOW ENOUGH GAS FLOW TO JAN MEER'S PLANE FOR FUMES TO ACCUMULATE IN THE TANK...
10-10
...SET THE SHUTTER RELEASE WITH SELF-TIMER WOUND FOR... THIRTEEN SECONDS! THEN THE CRACKED FLASH-BULB WILL EXPLODE...
AND IN THE OTHER PLANE... AT THE END OF THE REFUEL HOSE...
DON'T STRIKE THAT MATCH, MEER! WITH ALL THESE HI-OCTANE FUMES ...YOU'D BLOW US ALL TO... KINGDOM COME!
© 1955, King Features Syndicate, Inc., World rights reserved.

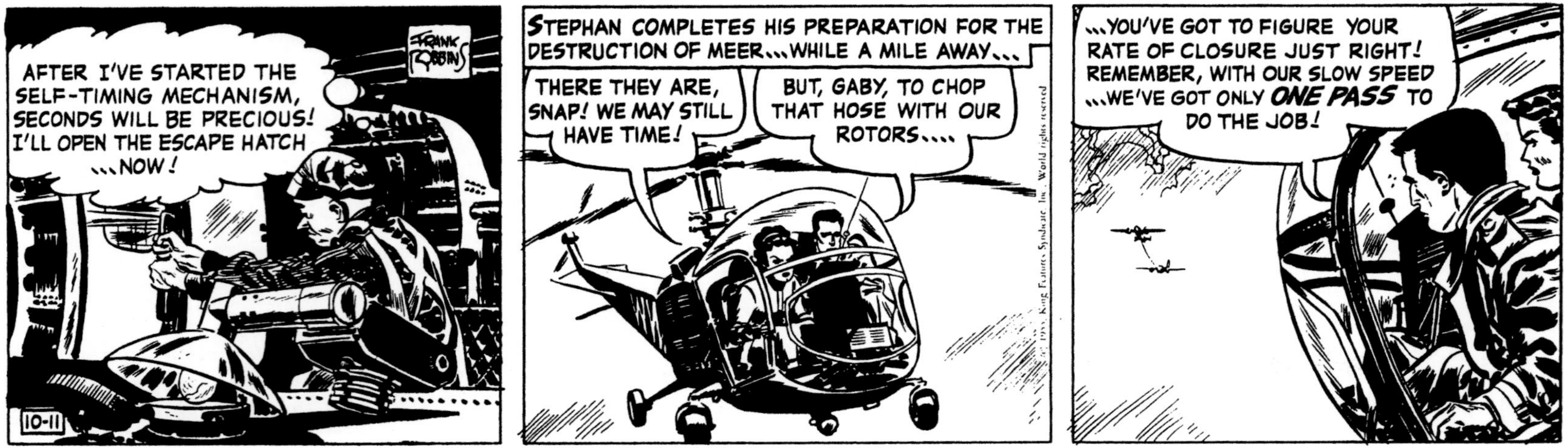
FRANK ROBBINS
AFTER I'VE STARTED THE SELF-TIMING MECHANISM, SECONDS WILL BE PRECIOUS! I'LL OPEN THE ESCAPE HATCH ...NOW!
10-11
STEPHAN COMPLETES HIS PREPARATION FOR THE DESTRUCTION OF MEER... WHILE A MILE AWAY...
THERE THEY ARE, SNAP! WE MAY STILL HAVE TIME!
BUT, GABY, TO CHOP THAT HOSE WITH OUR ROTORS....
...YOU'VE GOT TO FIGURE YOUR RATE OF CLOSURE JUST RIGHT! REMEMBER, WITH OUR SLOW SPEED ...WE'VE GOT ONLY ONE PASS TO DO THE JOB!

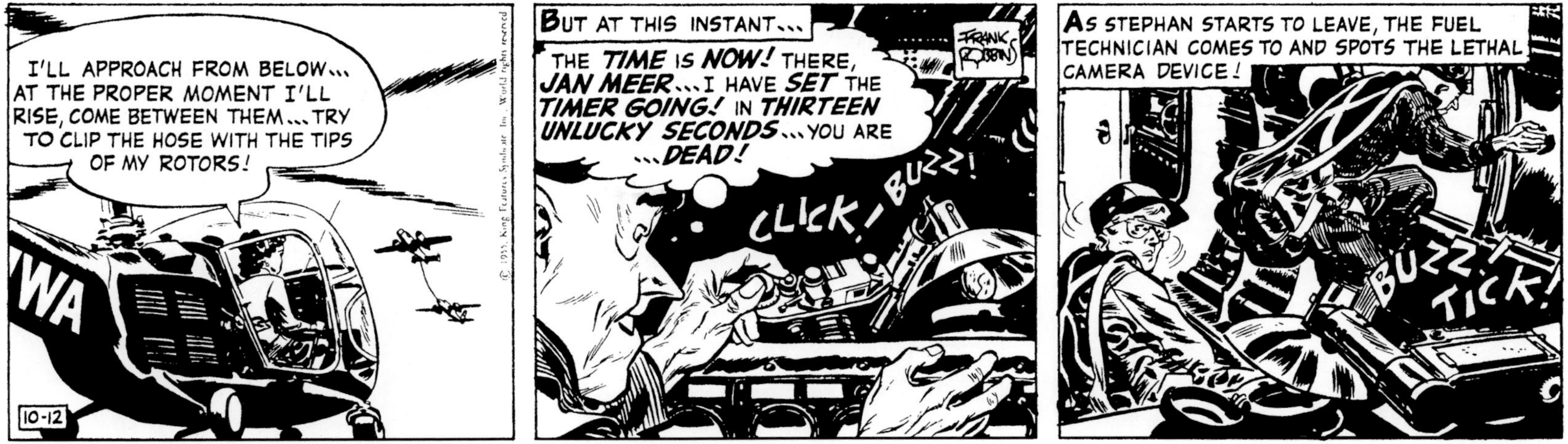
I'LL APPROACH FROM BELOW... AT THE PROPER MOMENT I'LL RISE, COME BETWEEN THEM... TRY TO CLIP THE HOSE WITH THE TIPS OF MY ROTORS!
WA
© 1955, King Features Syndicate, Inc., World rights reserved
10-12
BUT AT THIS INSTANT...
FRANK ROBBINS
THE TIME IS NOW! THERE, JAN MEER... I HAVE SET THE TIMER GOING! IN THIRTEEN UNLUCKY SECONDS... YOU ARE ...DEAD!
CLICK! BUZZ!
AS STEPHAN STARTS TO LEAVE, THE FUEL TECHNICIAN COMES TO AND SPOTS THE LETHAL CAMERA DEVICE!
BUZZ! TICK!

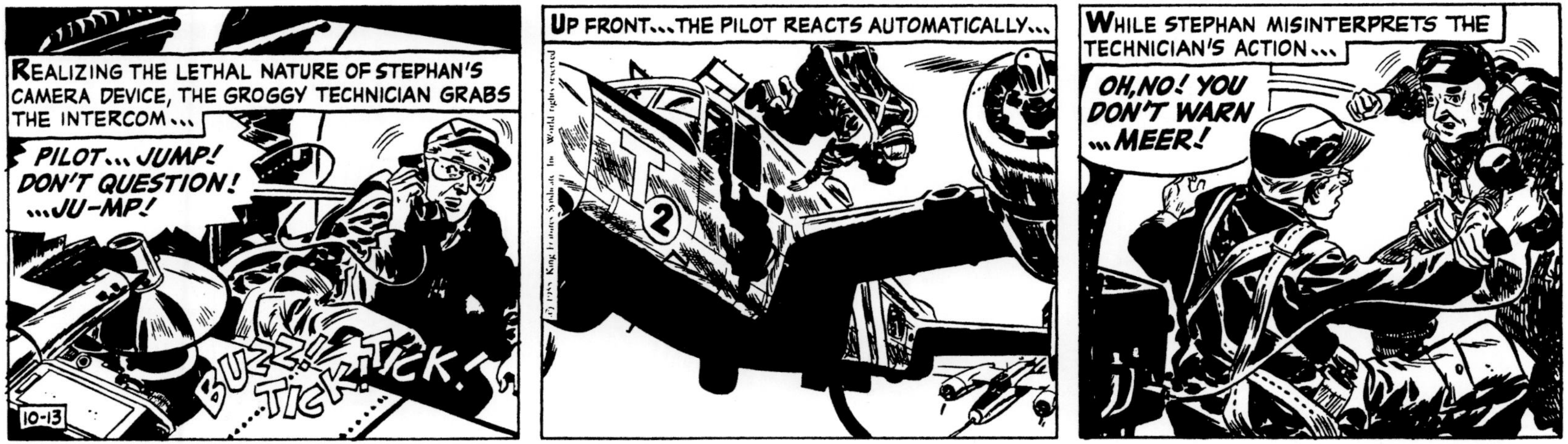
REALIZING THE LETHAL NATURE OF STEPHAN'S CAMERA DEVICE, THE GROGGY TECHNICIAN GRABS THE INTERCOM...
PILOT... JUMP! DON'T QUESTION! ...JU-MP!
BUZZ! TICK! TICK!
10-13
UP FRONT... THE PILOT REACTS AUTOMATICALLY...
© 1955, King Features Syndicate, Inc., World rights reserved
T
2
WHILE STEPHAN MISINTERPRETS THE TECHNICIAN'S ACTION...
OH, NO! YOU DON'T WARN ...MEER!

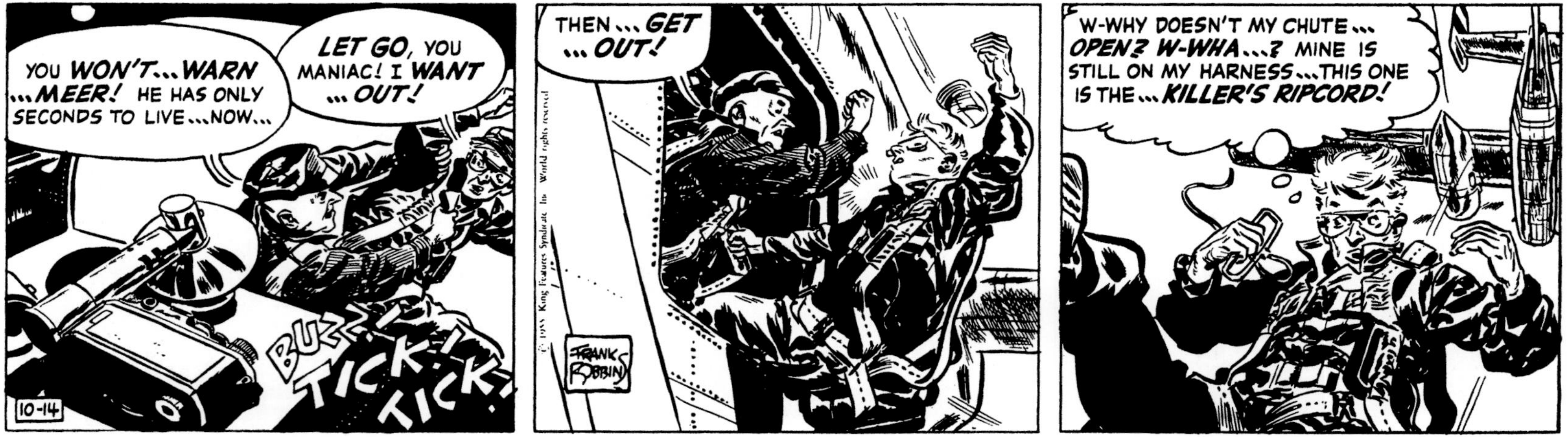
10-14
YOU WON'T...WARN ...MEER! HE HAS ONLY SECONDS TO LIVE...NOW...
LET GO, YOU MANIAC! I WANT ...OUT!
BUZZ! TICK! TICK!
THEN...GET ...OUT!
FRANK ROBBINS
W-WHY DOESN'T MY CHUTE... OPEN? W-WHA...? MINE IS STILL ON MY HARNESS...THIS ONE IS THE...KILLER'S RIPCORD!

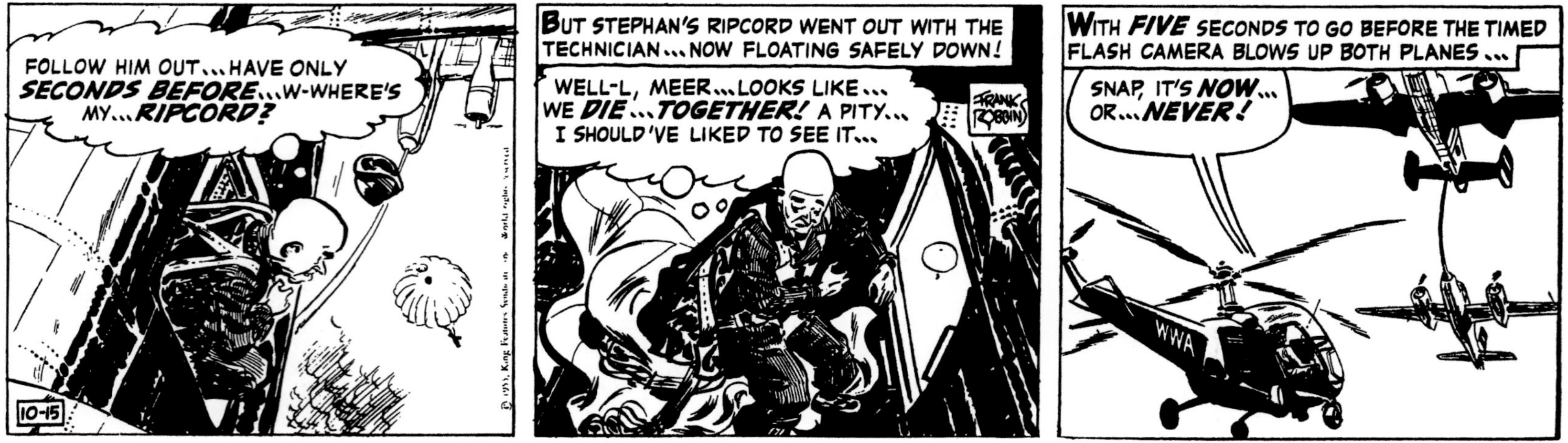
10-15
FOLLOW HIM OUT...HAVE ONLY SECONDS BEFORE...W-WHERE'S MY...RIPCORD?
BUT STEPHAN'S RIPCORD WENT OUT WITH THE TECHNICIAN...NOW FLOATING SAFELY DOWN!
WELL-L, MEER...LOOKS LIKE... WE DIE...TOGETHER! A PITY... I SHOULD'VE LIKED TO SEE IT...
FRANK ROBBINS
WITH FIVE SECONDS TO GO BEFORE THE TIMED FLASH CAMERA BLOWS UP BOTH PLANES...
SNAP, IT'S NOW... OR...NEVER!
WWA

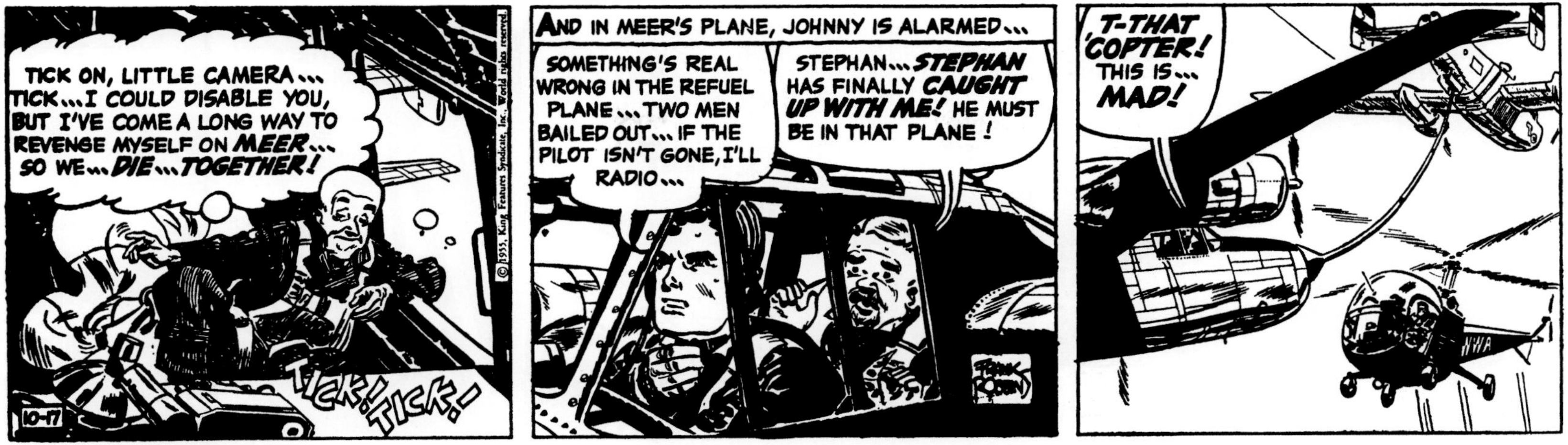
TICK ON, LITTLE CAMERA... TICK... I COULD DISABLE YOU, BUT I'VE COME A LONG WAY TO REVENGE MYSELF ON MEER... SO WE... DIE... TOGETHER!
TICK! TICK!
10-17
© 1955, King Features Syndicate, Inc., World rights reserved.
AND IN MEER'S PLANE, JOHNNY IS ALARMED...
SOMETHING'S REAL WRONG IN THE REFUEL PLANE... TWO MEN BAILED OUT... IF THE PILOT ISN'T GONE, I'LL RADIO...
STEPHAN... STEPHAN HAS FINALLY CAUGHT UP WITH ME! HE MUST BE IN THAT PLANE!
FRANK ROBBINS
T-THAT 'COPTER! THIS IS... MAD!
WWA

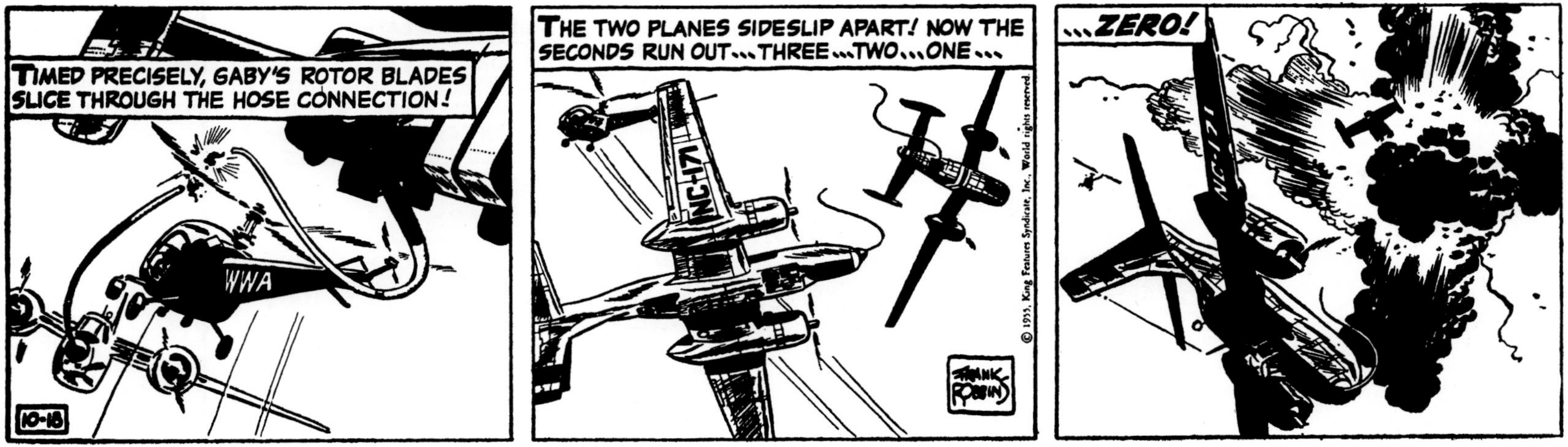
TIMED PRECISELY, GABY'S ROTOR BLADES SLICE THROUGH THE HOSE CONNECTION!
WWA
10-18
THE TWO PLANES SIDESLIP APART! NOW THE SECONDS RUN OUT... THREE... TWO... ONE...
NC-171
© 1955, King Features Syndicate, Inc., World rights reserved.
FRANK ROBBINS
...ZERO!

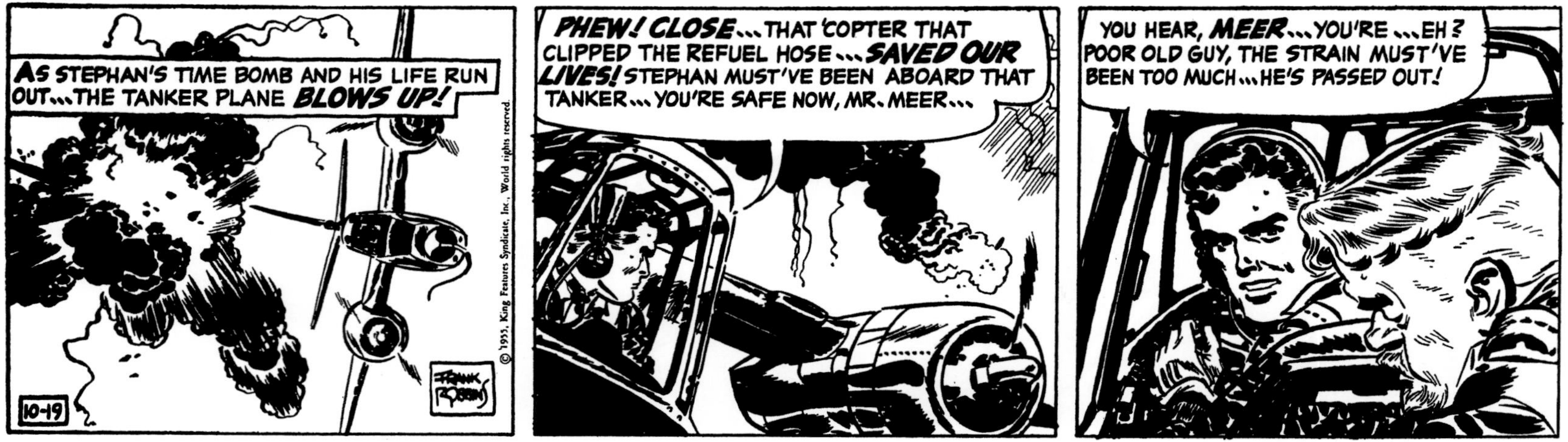
AS STEPHAN'S TIME BOMB AND HIS LIFE RUN OUT... THE TANKER PLANE BLOWS UP!
10-19
FRANK ROBBINS
© 1955, King Features Syndicate, Inc., World rights reserved.
PHEW! CLOSE... THAT 'COPTER THAT CLIPPED THE REFUEL HOSE... SAVED OUR LIVES! STEPHAN MUST'VE BEEN ABOARD THAT TANKER... YOU'RE SAFE NOW, MR. MEER...
YOU HEAR, MEER... YOU'RE ... EH? POOR OLD GUY, THE STRAIN MUST'VE BEEN TOO MUCH... HE'S PASSED OUT!

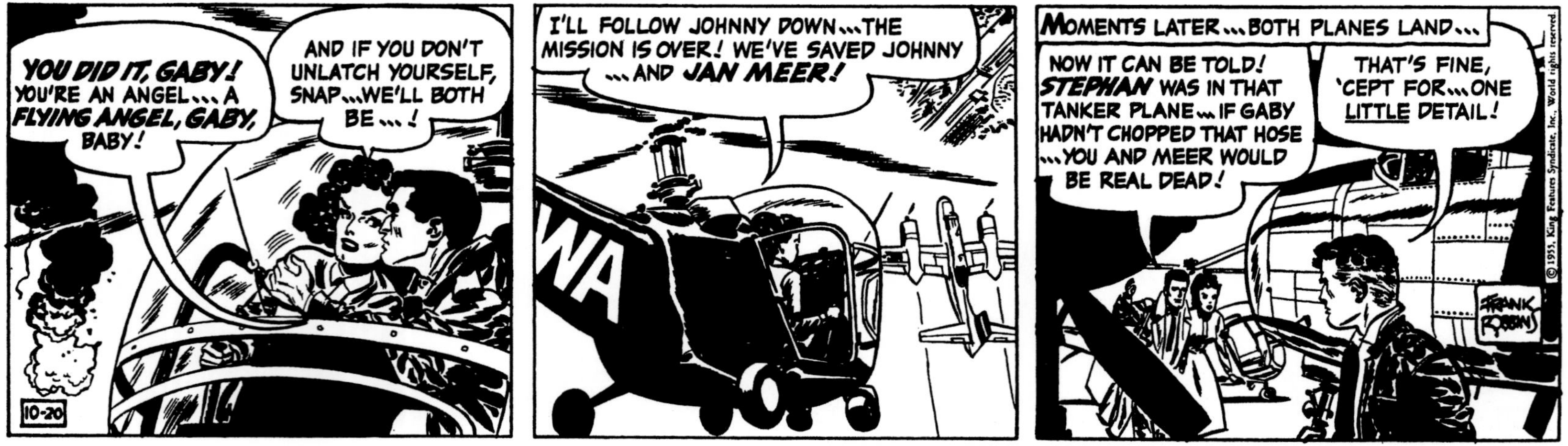
YOU DID IT, GABY! YOU'RE AN ANGEL... A FLYING ANGEL, GABY, BABY!
AND IF YOU DON'T UNLATCH YOURSELF, SNAP... WE'LL BOTH BE...!
10-20
I'LL FOLLOW JOHNNY DOWN... THE MISSION IS OVER! WE'VE SAVED JOHNNY ...AND JAN MEER!
WA
MOMENTS LATER... BOTH PLANES LAND...
NOW IT CAN BE TOLD! STEPHAN WAS IN THAT TANKER PLANE... IF GABY HADN'T CHOPPED THAT HOSE ...YOU AND MEER WOULD BE REAL DEAD!
THAT'S FINE, 'CEPT FOR... ONE LITTLE DETAIL!
FRANK ROBBINS
© 1955, King Features Syndicate, Inc., World rights reserved.

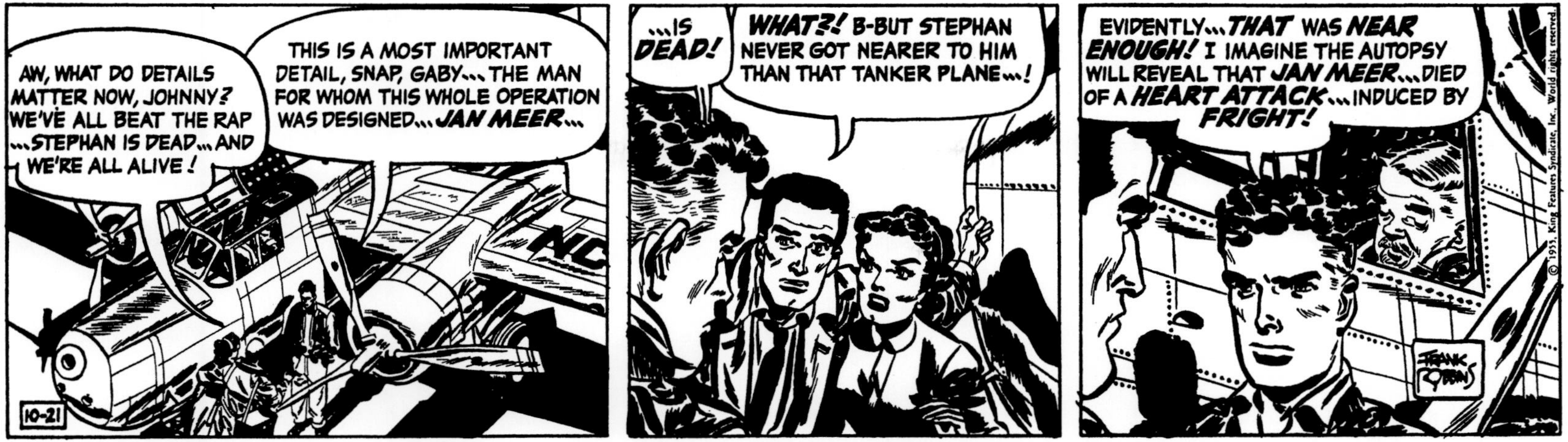
AW, WHAT DO DETAILS MATTER NOW, JOHNNY? WE'VE ALL BEAT THE RAP ...STEPHAN IS DEAD... AND WE'RE ALL ALIVE!
THIS IS A MOST IMPORTANT DETAIL, SNAP, GABY... THE MAN FOR WHOM THIS WHOLE OPERATION WAS DESIGNED... JAN MEER...
10-21
...IS DEAD!
WHAT?! B-BUT STEPHAN NEVER GOT NEARER TO HIM THAN THAT TANKER PLANE...!
EVIDENTLY... THAT WAS NEAR ENOUGH! I IMAGINE THE AUTOPSY WILL REVEAL THAT JAN MEER... DIED OF A HEART ATTACK... INDUCED BY FRIGHT!
FRANK ROBBINS
© 1955, King Features Syndicate, Inc., World rights reserved.

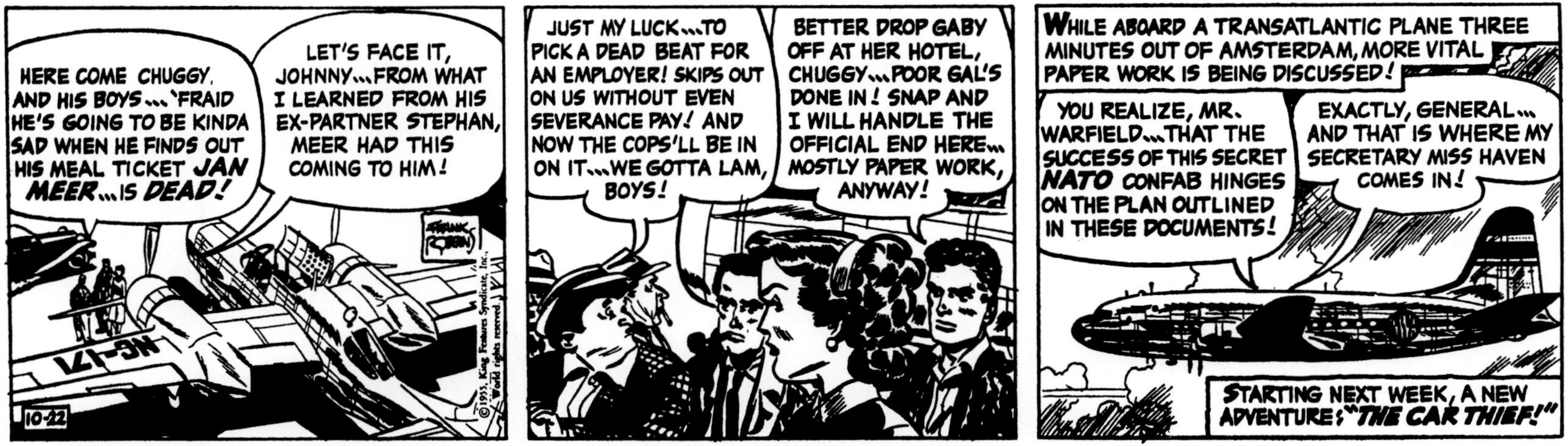
HERE COME CHUGGY AND HIS BOYS... 'FRAID HE'S GOING TO BE KINDA SAD WHEN HE FINDS OUT HIS MEAL TICKET JAN MEER... IS DEAD!
LET'S FACE IT, JOHNNY... FROM WHAT I LEARNED FROM HIS EX-PARTNER STEPHAN, MEER HAD THIS COMING TO HIM!
FRANK ROBBINS
NC-171
10-22
© 1955, King Features Syndicate, Inc., World rights reserved.
JUST MY LUCK...TO PICK A DEAD BEAT FOR AN EMPLOYER! SKIPS OUT ON US WITHOUT EVEN SEVERANCE PAY! AND NOW THE COPS'LL BE IN ON IT... WE GOTTA LAM, BOYS!
BETTER DROP GABY OFF AT HER HOTEL, CHUGGY... POOR GAL'S DONE IN! SNAP AND I WILL HANDLE THE OFFICIAL END HERE... MOSTLY PAPER WORK, ANYWAY!
WHILE ABOARD A TRANSATLANTIC PLANE THREE MINUTES OUT OF AMSTERDAM, MORE VITAL PAPER WORK IS BEING DISCUSSED!
YOU REALIZE, MR. WARFIELD... THAT THE SUCCESS OF THIS SECRET NATO CONFAB HINGES ON THE PLAN OUTLINED IN THESE DOCUMENTS!
EXACTLY, GENERAL... AND THAT IS WHERE MY SECRETARY MISS HAVEN COMES IN!
STARTING NEXT WEEK, A NEW ADVENTURE: "THE CAR THIEF!"

JOHNNY HAZARD

Chapter Six: The Car Thief

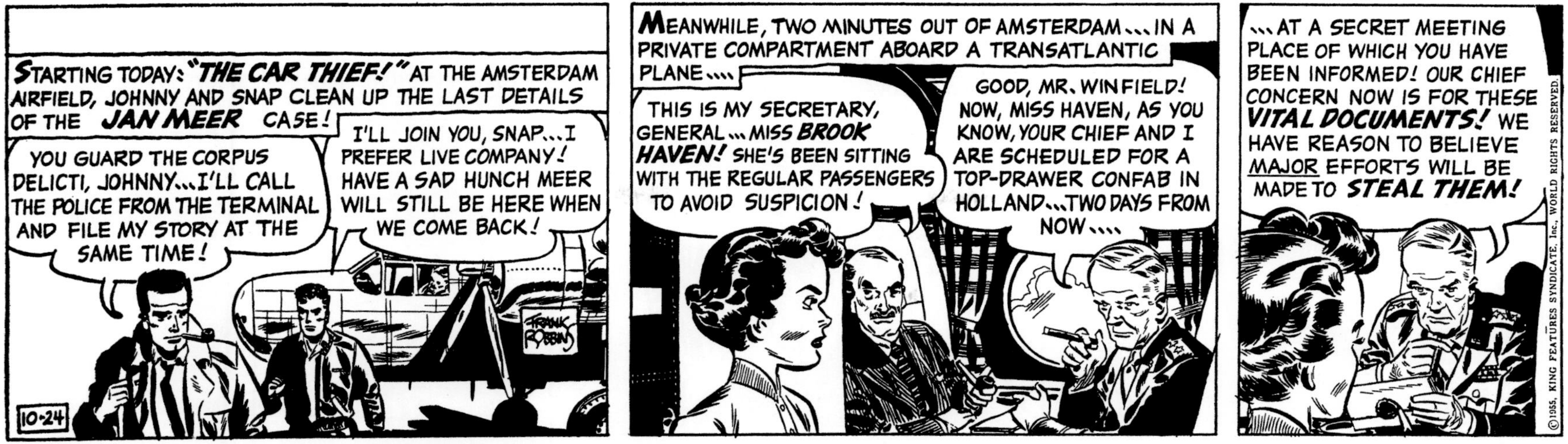
STARTING TODAY: "THE CAR THIEF!" AT THE AMSTERDAM AIRFIELD, JOHNNY AND SNAP CLEAN UP THE LAST DETAILS OF THE JAN MEER CASE!
YOU GUARD THE CORPUS DELICTI, JOHNNY...I'LL CALL THE POLICE FROM THE TERMINAL AND FILE MY STORY AT THE SAME TIME!
I'LL JOIN YOU, SNAP...I PREFER LIVE COMPANY! HAVE A SAD HUNCH MEER WILL STILL BE HERE WHEN WE COME BACK!
FRANK ROBBINS
10-24
MEANWHILE, TWO MINUTES OUT OF AMSTERDAM...IN A PRIVATE COMPARTMENT ABOARD A TRANSATLANTIC PLANE....
THIS IS MY SECRETARY, GENERAL...MISS BROOK HAVEN! SHE'S BEEN SITTING WITH THE REGULAR PASSENGERS TO AVOID SUSPICION!
GOOD, MR. WINFIELD! NOW, MISS HAVEN, AS YOU KNOW, YOUR CHIEF AND I ARE SCHEDULED FOR A TOP-DRAWER CONFAB IN HOLLAND...TWO DAYS FROM NOW....
...AT A SECRET MEETING PLACE OF WHICH YOU HAVE BEEN INFORMED! OUR CHIEF CONCERN NOW IS FOR THESE VITAL DOCUMENTS! WE HAVE REASON TO BELIEVE MAJOR EFFORTS WILL BE MADE TO STEAL THEM!
© 1955, KING FEATURES SYNDICATE, Inc., WORLD RIGHTS RESERVED.

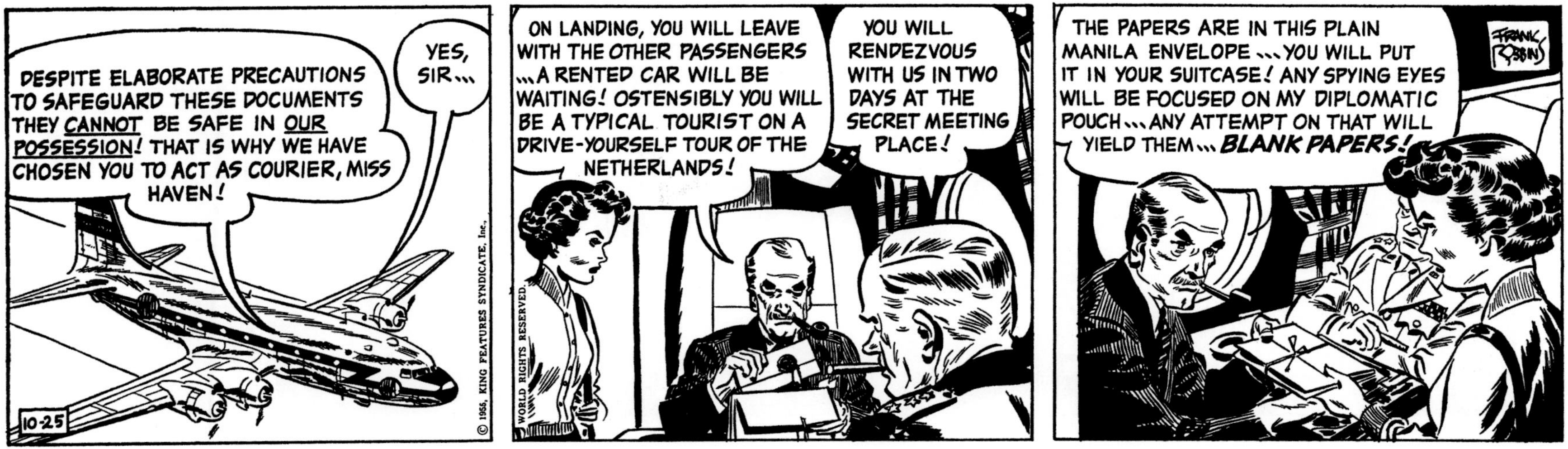
DESPITE ELABORATE PRECAUTIONS TO SAFEGUARD THESE DOCUMENTS THEY CANNOT BE SAFE IN OUR POSSESSION! THAT IS WHY WE HAVE CHOSEN YOU TO ACT AS COURIER, MISS HAVEN!
YES, SIR...
10-25
© 1955, KING FEATURES SYNDICATE, Inc., WORLD RIGHTS RESERVED.
ON LANDING, YOU WILL LEAVE WITH THE OTHER PASSENGERS ...A RENTED CAR WILL BE WAITING! OSTENSIBLY YOU WILL BE A TYPICAL TOURIST ON A DRIVE-YOURSELF TOUR OF THE NETHERLANDS!
YOU WILL RENDEZVOUS WITH US IN TWO DAYS AT THE SECRET MEETING PLACE!
THE PAPERS ARE IN THIS PLAIN MANILA ENVELOPE...YOU WILL PUT IT IN YOUR SUITCASE! ANY SPYING EYES WILL BE FOCUSED ON MY DIPLOMATIC POUCH...ANY ATTEMPT ON THAT WILL YIELD THEM...BLANK PAPERS!
FRANK ROBBINS

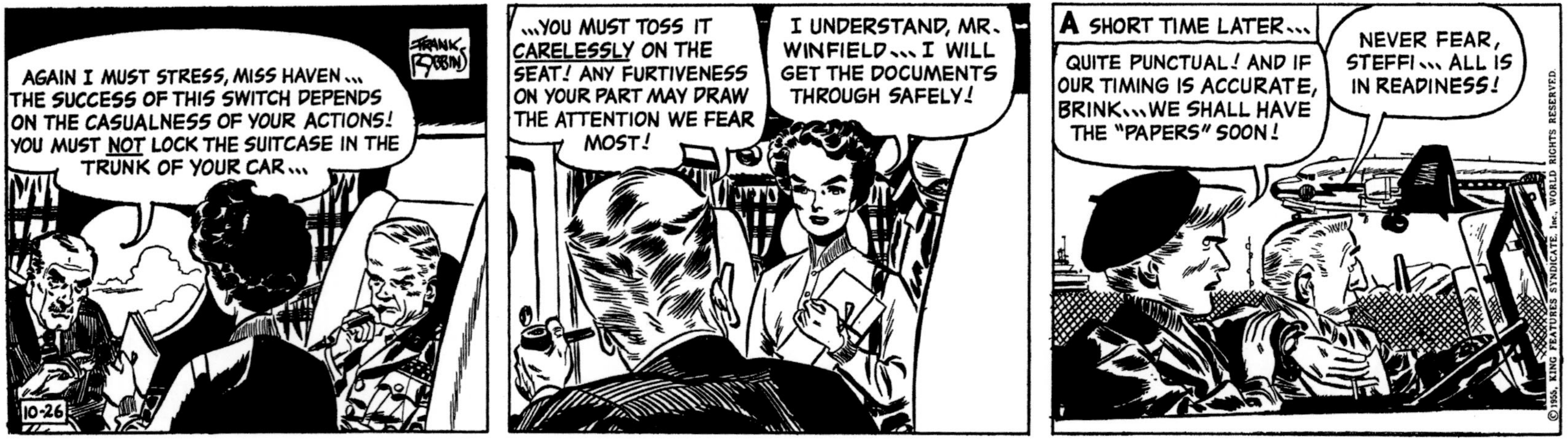
FRANK ROBBINS
AGAIN I MUST STRESS, MISS HAVEN... THE SUCCESS OF THIS SWITCH DEPENDS ON THE CASUALNESS OF YOUR ACTIONS! YOU MUST NOT LOCK THE SUITCASE IN THE TRUNK OF YOUR CAR...
10-26
...YOU MUST TOSS IT CARELESSLY ON THE SEAT! ANY FURTIVENESS ON YOUR PART MAY DRAW THE ATTENTION WE FEAR MOST!
I UNDERSTAND, MR. WINFIELD... I WILL GET THE DOCUMENTS THROUGH SAFELY!
A SHORT TIME LATER...
QUITE PUNCTUAL! AND IF OUR TIMING IS ACCURATE, BRINK...WE SHALL HAVE THE "PAPERS" SOON!
NEVER FEAR, STEFFI... ALL IS IN READINESS!
© 1955, KING FEATURES SYNDICATE, Inc., WORLD RIGHTS RESERVED.

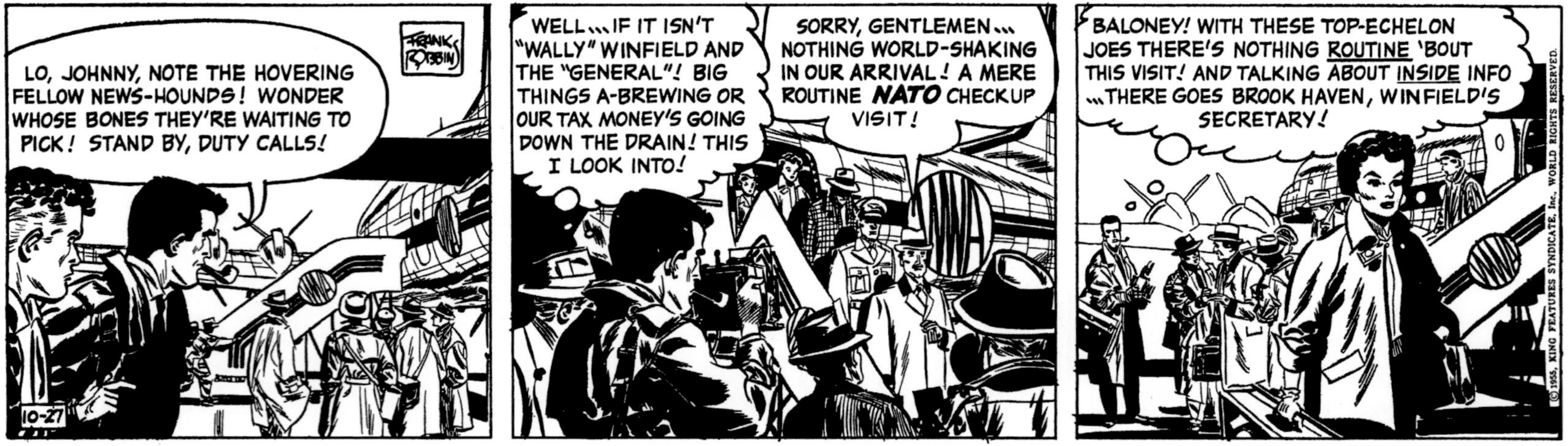
FRANK ROBBINS
LO, JOHNNY, NOTE THE HOVERING FELLOW NEWS-HOUNDS! WONDER WHOSE BONES THEY'RE WAITING TO PICK! STAND BY, DUTY CALLS!
10-27
WELL... IF IT ISN'T "WALLY" WINFIELD AND THE "GENERAL"! BIG THINGS A-BREWING OR OUR TAX MONEY'S GOING DOWN THE DRAIN! THIS I LOOK INTO!
SORRY, GENTLEMEN... NOTHING WORLD-SHAKING IN OUR ARRIVAL! A MERE ROUTINE NATO CHECKUP VISIT!
BALONEY! WITH THESE TOP-ECHELON JOES THERE'S NOTHING ROUTINE 'BOUT THIS VISIT! AND TALKING ABOUT INSIDE INFO ...THERE GOES BROOK HAVEN, WINFIELD'S SECRETARY!
© 1955, KING FEATURES SYNDICATE, Inc., WORLD RIGHTS RESERVED.

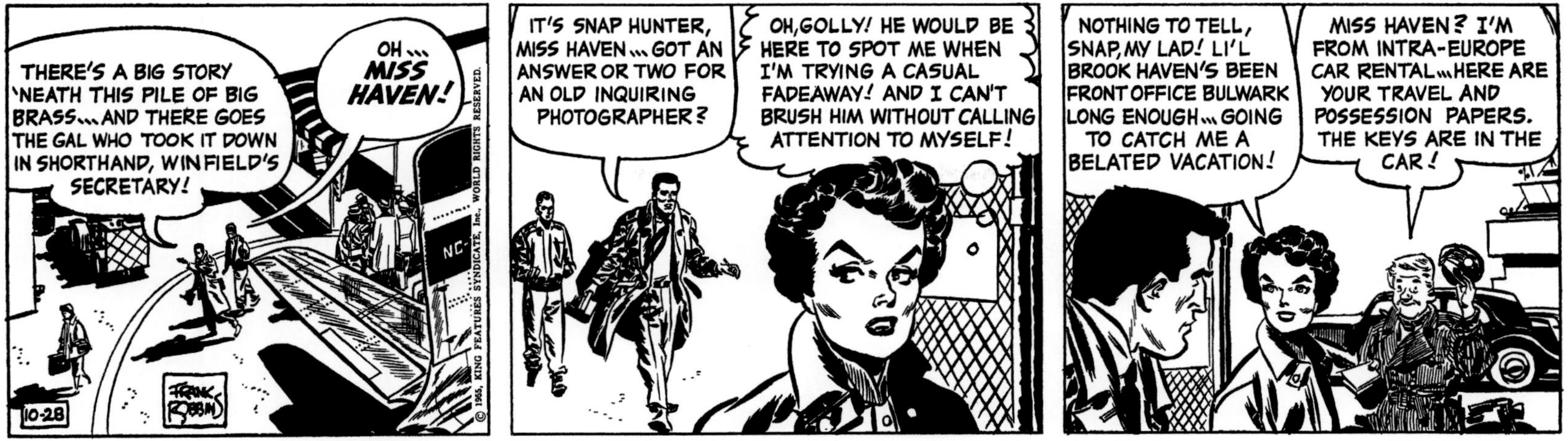
THERE'S A BIG STORY 'NEATH THIS PILE OF BIG BRASS... AND THERE GOES THE GAL WHO TOOK IT DOWN IN SHORTHAND, WINFIELD'S SECRETARY!
OH... MISS HAVEN!
NC-
FRANK ROBBINS
10-28
© 1955, KING FEATURES SYNDICATE, Inc., WORLD RIGHTS RESERVED.
IT'S SNAP HUNTER, MISS HAVEN... GOT AN ANSWER OR TWO FOR AN OLD INQUIRING PHOTOGRAPHER?
OH, GOLLY! HE WOULD BE HERE TO SPOT ME WHEN I'M TRYING A CASUAL FADEAWAY! AND I CAN'T BRUSH HIM WITHOUT CALLING ATTENTION TO MYSELF!
NOTHING TO TELL, SNAP, MY LAD! LI'L BROOK HAVEN'S BEEN FRONT OFFICE BULWARK LONG ENOUGH... GOING TO CATCH ME A BELATED VACATION!
MISS HAVEN? I'M FROM INTRA-EUROPE CAR RENTAL... HERE ARE YOUR TRAVEL AND POSSESSION PAPERS. THE KEYS ARE IN THE CAR!

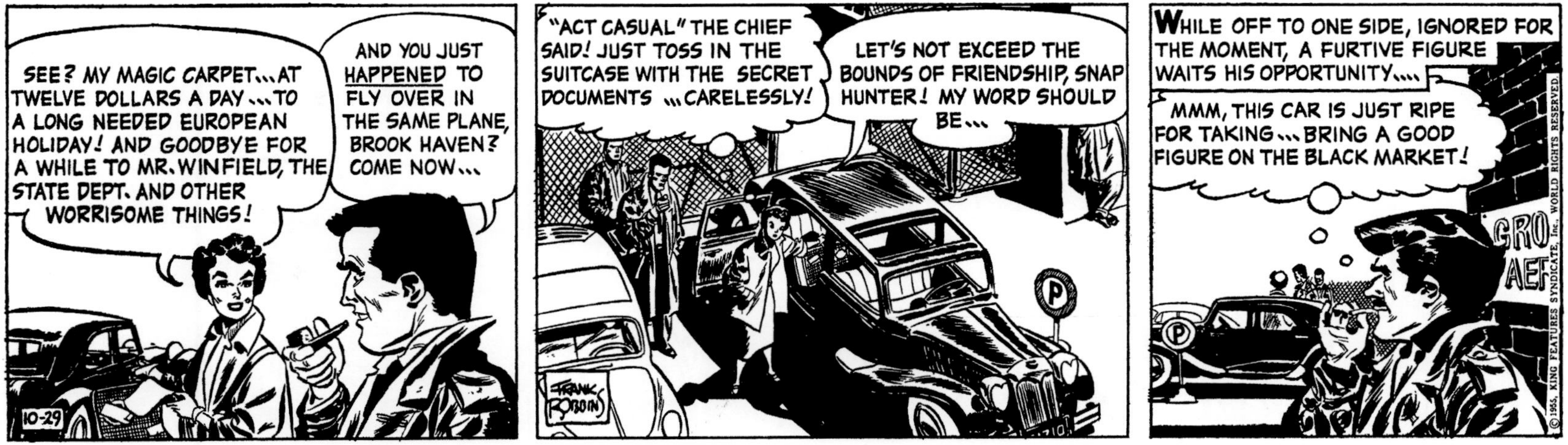
SEE? MY MAGIC CARPET... AT TWELVE DOLLARS A DAY... TO A LONG NEEDED EUROPEAN HOLIDAY! AND GOODBYE FOR A WHILE TO MR. WINFIELD, THE STATE DEPT. AND OTHER WORRISOME THINGS!
AND YOU JUST HAPPENED TO FLY OVER IN THE SAME PLANE, BROOK HAVEN? COME NOW...
10-29
"ACT CASUAL" THE CHIEF SAID! JUST TOSS IN THE SUITCASE WITH THE SECRET DOCUMENTS ... CARELESSLY!
LET'S NOT EXCEED THE BOUNDS OF FRIENDSHIP, SNAP HUNTER! MY WORD SHOULD BE...
FRANK ROBBINS
P
WHILE OFF TO ONE SIDE, IGNORED FOR THE MOMENT, A FURTIVE FIGURE WAITS HIS OPPORTUNITY....
MMM, THIS CAR IS JUST RIPE FOR TAKING... BRING A GOOD FIGURE ON THE BLACK MARKET!
GRO
AE
© 1955, KING FEATURES SYNDICATE, Inc., WORLD RIGHTS RESERVED.

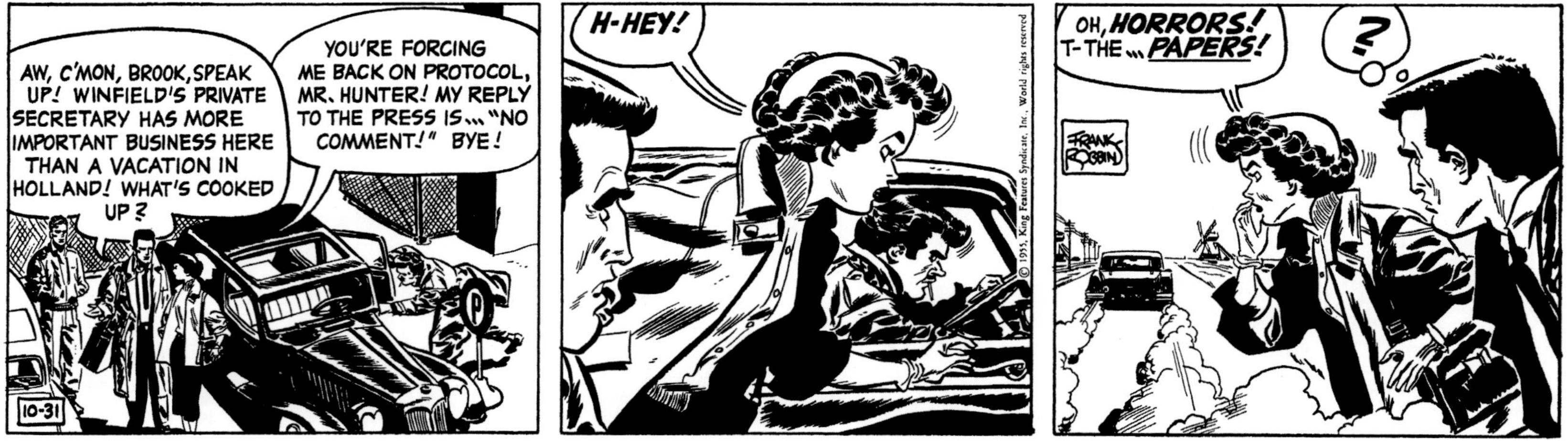
AW, C'MON, BROOK, SPEAK UP! WINFIELD'S PRIVATE SECRETARY HAS MORE IMPORTANT BUSINESS HERE THAN A VACATION IN HOLLAND! WHAT'S COOKED UP?
YOU'RE FORCING ME BACK ON PROTOCOL, MR. HUNTER! MY REPLY TO THE PRESS IS... "NO COMMENT!" BYE!
10-31
H-HEY!
© 1955, King Features Syndicate, Inc., World rights reserved
OH, HORRORS! T-THE... PAPERS!
?
FRANK ROBBIN

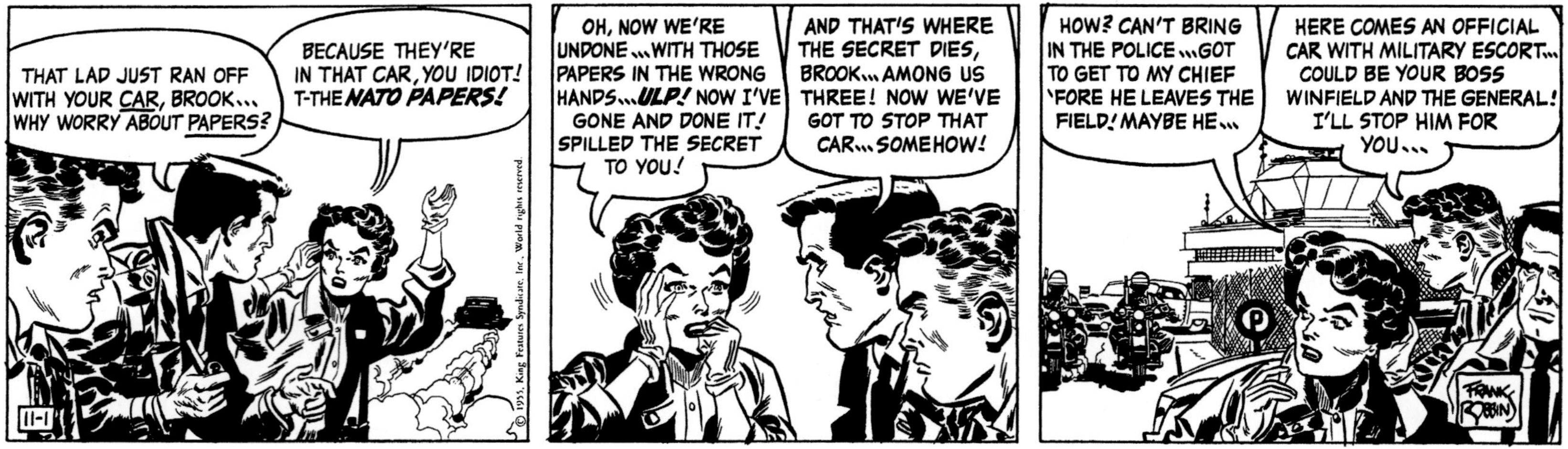
THAT LAD JUST RAN OFF WITH YOUR CAR, BROOK... WHY WORRY ABOUT PAPERS?
BECAUSE THEY'RE IN THAT CAR, YOU IDIOT! T-THE NATO PAPERS!
11-1
© 1955, King Features Syndicate, Inc., World rights reserved.
OH, NOW WE'RE UNDONE... WITH THOSE PAPERS IN THE WRONG HANDS... ULP! NOW I'VE GONE AND DONE IT! SPILLED THE SECRET TO YOU!
AND THAT'S WHERE THE SECRET DIES, BROOK... AMONG US THREE! NOW WE'VE GOT TO STOP THAT CAR... SOMEHOW!
HOW? CAN'T BRING IN THE POLICE... GOT TO GET TO MY CHIEF 'FORE HE LEAVES THE FIELD! MAYBE HE...
HERE COMES AN OFFICIAL CAR WITH MILITARY ESCORT... COULD BE YOUR BOSS WINFIELD AND THE GENERAL! I'LL STOP HIM FOR YOU...
FRANK ROBBINS

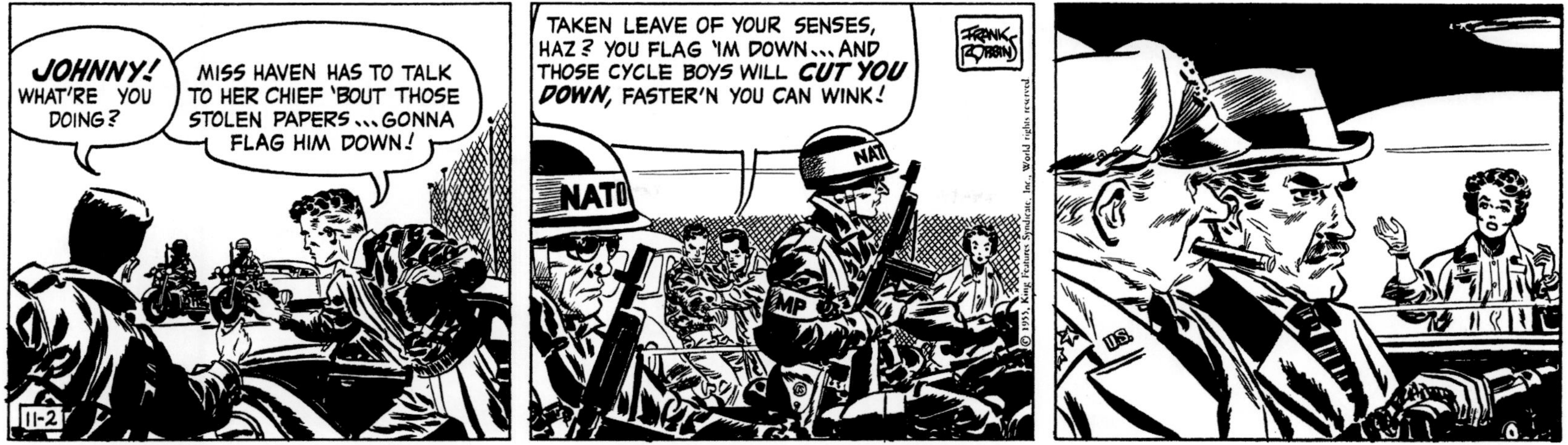
11-2
JOHNNY! WHAT'RE YOU DOING?
MISS HAVEN HAS TO TALK TO HER CHIEF 'BOUT THOSE STOLEN PAPERS ... GONNA FLAG HIM DOWN!
TAKEN LEAVE OF YOUR SENSES, HAZ? YOU FLAG 'IM DOWN ... AND THOSE CYCLE BOYS WILL CUT YOU DOWN, FASTER'N YOU CAN WINK!
FRANK ROBBINS
© 1955, King Features Syndicate, Inc., World rights reserved.
NATO
NATO
MP
U.S.

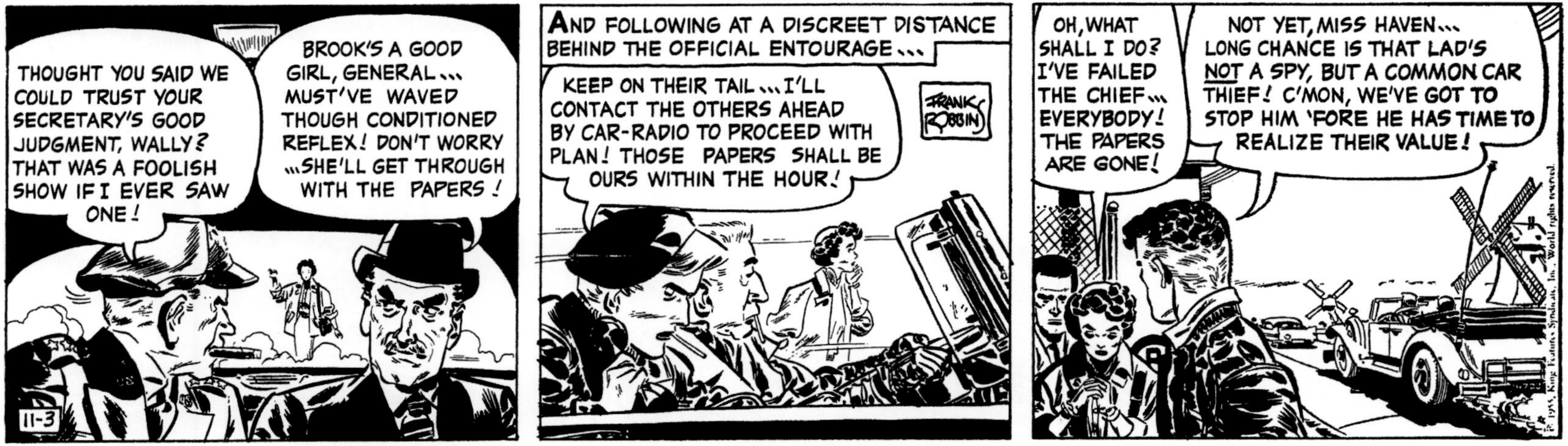
11-3
THOUGHT YOU SAID WE COULD TRUST YOUR SECRETARY'S GOOD JUDGMENT, WALLY? THAT WAS A FOOLISH SHOW IF I EVER SAW ONE!
BROOK'S A GOOD GIRL, GENERAL ... MUST'VE WAVED THOUGH CONDITIONED REFLEX! DON'T WORRY ... SHE'LL GET THROUGH WITH THE PAPERS!
AND FOLLOWING AT A DISCREET DISTANCE BEHIND THE OFFICIAL ENTOURAGE ...
KEEP ON THEIR TAIL ... I'LL CONTACT THE OTHERS AHEAD BY CAR-RADIO TO PROCEED WITH PLAN! THOSE PAPERS SHALL BE OURS WITHIN THE HOUR!
FRANK ROBBINS
OH, WHAT SHALL I DO? I'VE FAILED THE CHIEF ... EVERYBODY! THE PAPERS ARE GONE!
NOT YET, MISS HAVEN ... LONG CHANCE IS THAT LAD'S NOT A SPY, BUT A COMMON CAR THIEF! C'MON, WE'VE GOT TO STOP HIM 'FORE HE HAS TIME TO REALIZE THEIR VALUE!
© 1955, King Features Syndicate, Inc., World rights reserved.

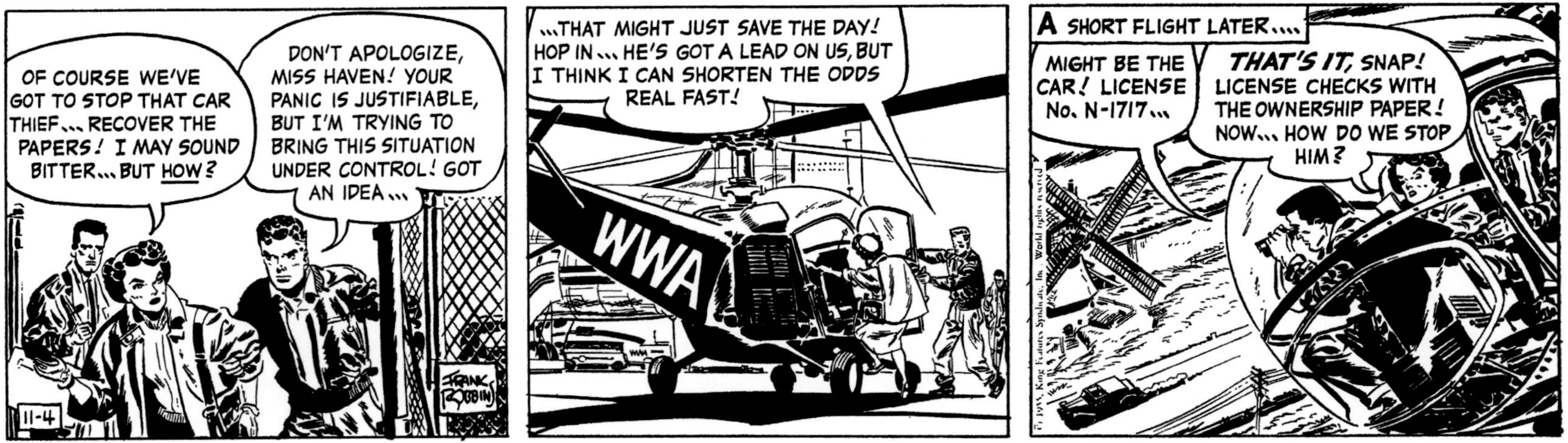
OF COURSE WE'VE GOT TO STOP THAT CAR THIEF... RECOVER THE PAPERS! I MAY SOUND BITTER... BUT HOW?
DON'T APOLOGIZE, MISS HAVEN! YOUR PANIC IS JUSTIFIABLE, BUT I'M TRYING TO BRING THIS SITUATION UNDER CONTROL! GOT AN IDEA...
FRANK ROBBINS
11-4
...THAT MIGHT JUST SAVE THE DAY! HOP IN... HE'S GOT A LEAD ON US, BUT I THINK I CAN SHORTEN THE ODDS REAL FAST!
WWA
A SHORT FLIGHT LATER....
MIGHT BE THE CAR! LICENSE No. N-1717...
THAT'S IT, SNAP! LICENSE CHECKS WITH THE OWNERSHIP PAPER! NOW... HOW DO WE STOP HIM?

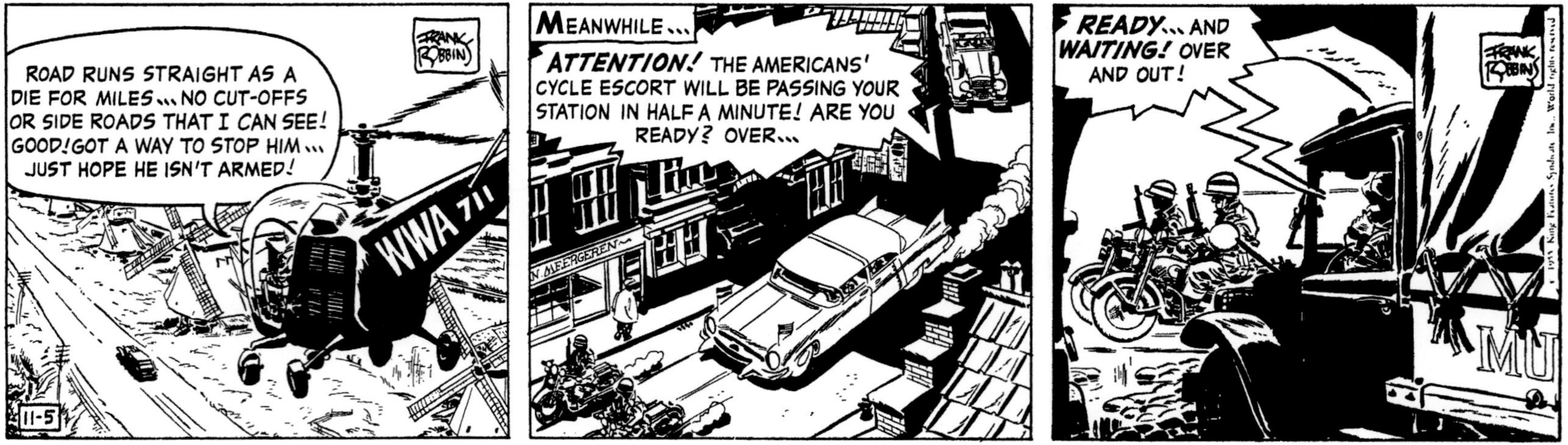
FRANK ROBBINS
ROAD RUNS STRAIGHT AS A DIE FOR MILES... NO CUT-OFFS OR SIDE ROADS THAT I CAN SEE! GOOD! GOT A WAY TO STOP HIM... JUST HOPE HE ISN'T ARMED!
WWA 711
11-5
MEANWHILE...
ATTENTION! THE AMERICANS' CYCLE ESCORT WILL BE PASSING YOUR STATION IN HALF A MINUTE! ARE YOU READY? OVER...
N MEERGEREN
READY... AND WAITING! OVER AND OUT!
FRANK ROBBINS
MU

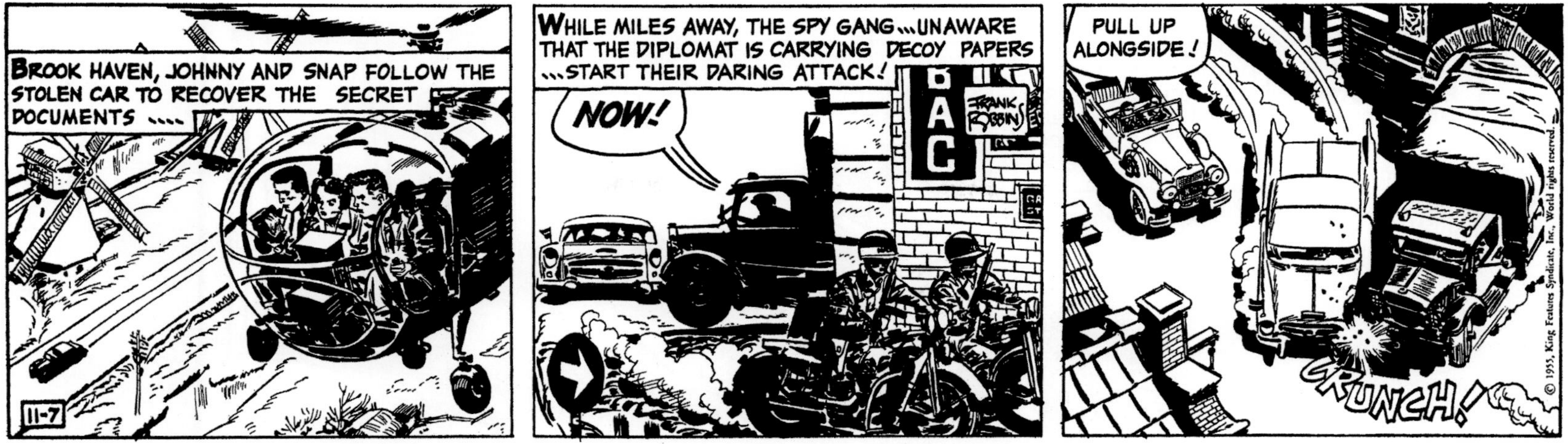
BROOK HAVEN, JOHNNY AND SNAP FOLLOW THE STOLEN CAR TO RECOVER THE SECRET DOCUMENTS ....
11-7
WHILE MILES AWAY, THE SPY GANG...UNAWARE THAT THE DIPLOMAT IS CARRYING DECOY PAPERS ...START THEIR DARING ATTACK!
NOW!
FRANK ROBBINS
PULL UP ALONGSIDE!
CRUNCH!
© 1955, King Features Syndicate, Inc., World rights reserved.

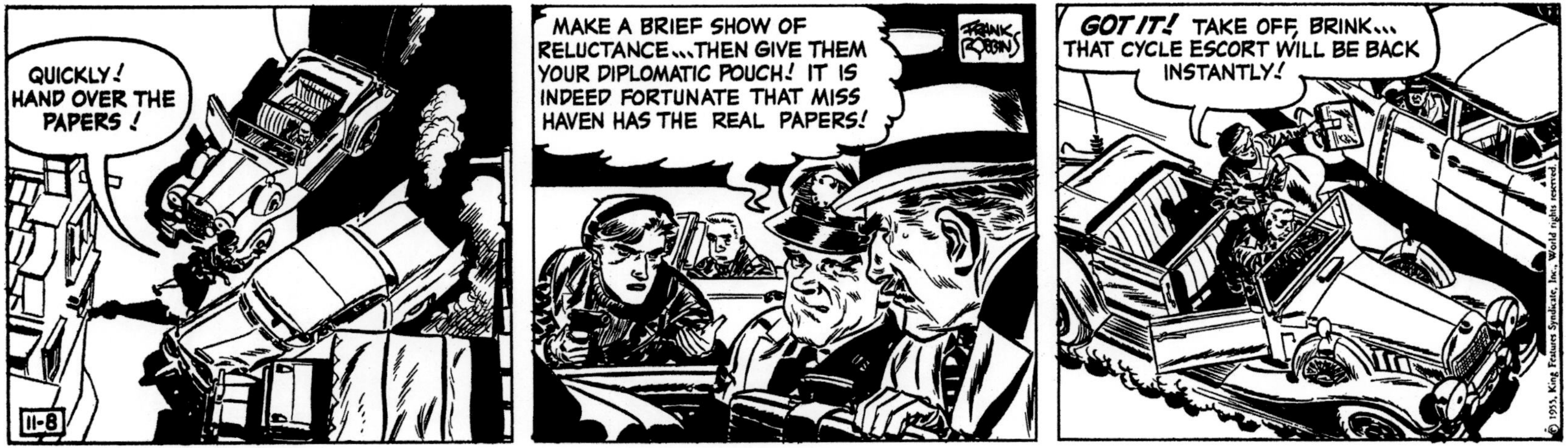
QUICKLY! HAND OVER THE PAPERS!
11-8
MAKE A BRIEF SHOW OF RELUCTANCE...THEN GIVE THEM YOUR DIPLOMATIC POUCH! IT IS INDEED FORTUNATE THAT MISS HAVEN HAS THE REAL PAPERS!
FRANK ROBBINS
GOT IT! TAKE OFF, BRINK... THAT CYCLE ESCORT WILL BE BACK INSTANTLY!
© 1955, King Features Syndicate, Inc., World rights reserved.

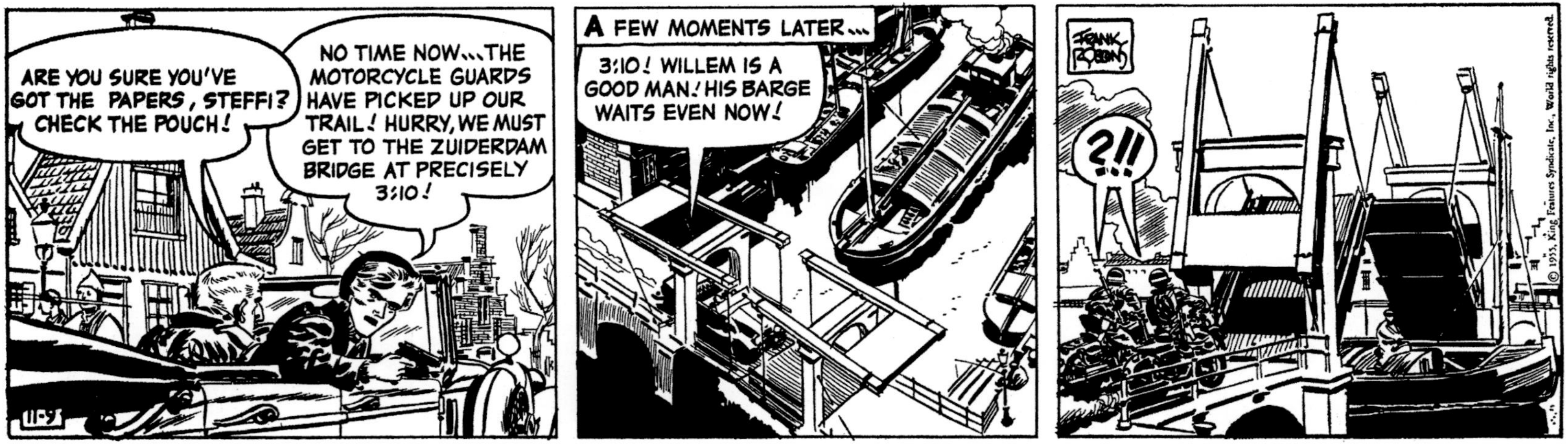
ARE YOU SURE YOU'VE GOT THE PAPERS, STEFFI? CHECK THE POUCH!
NO TIME NOW...THE MOTORCYCLE GUARDS HAVE PICKED UP OUR TRAIL! HURRY, WE MUST GET TO THE ZUIDERDAM BRIDGE AT PRECISELY 3:10!
11-9
A FEW MOMENTS LATER...
3:10! WILLEM IS A GOOD MAN! HIS BARGE WAITS EVEN NOW!
FRANK ROBBINS
?!!
© 1955, King Features Syndicate, Inc., World rights reserved.

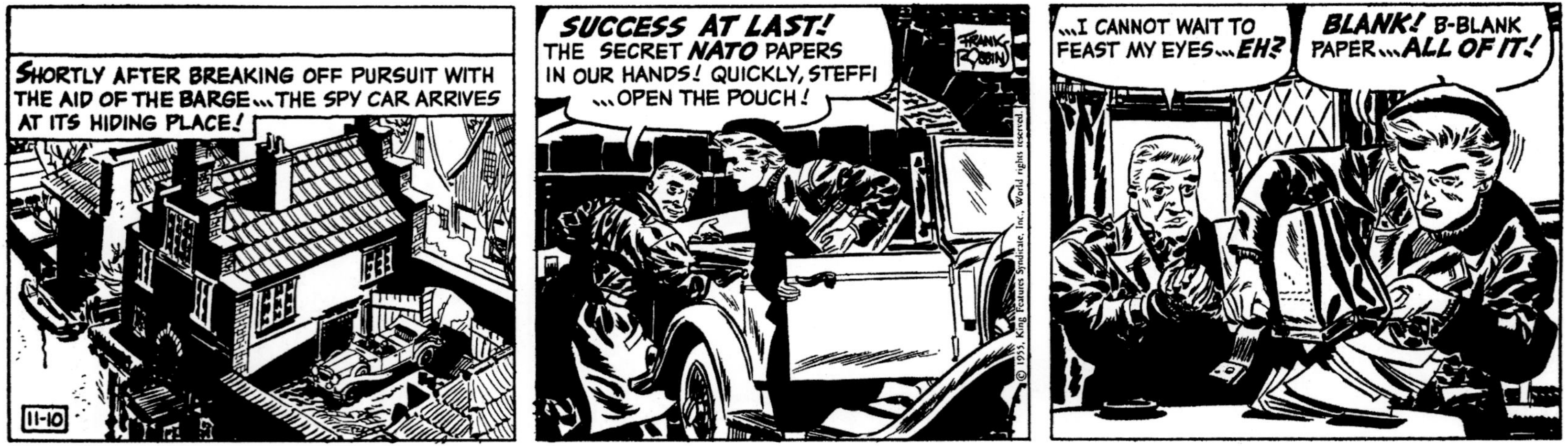
SHORTLY AFTER BREAKING OFF PURSUIT WITH THE AID OF THE BARGE...THE SPY CAR ARRIVES AT ITS HIDING PLACE!
11-10
SUCCESS AT LAST! THE SECRET NATO PAPERS IN OUR HANDS! QUICKLY, STEFFI ...OPEN THE POUCH!
FRANK ROBBINS
© 1955, King Features Syndicate, Inc., World rights reserved.
...I CANNOT WAIT TO FEAST MY EYES...EH?
BLANK! B-BLANK PAPER...ALL OF IT!

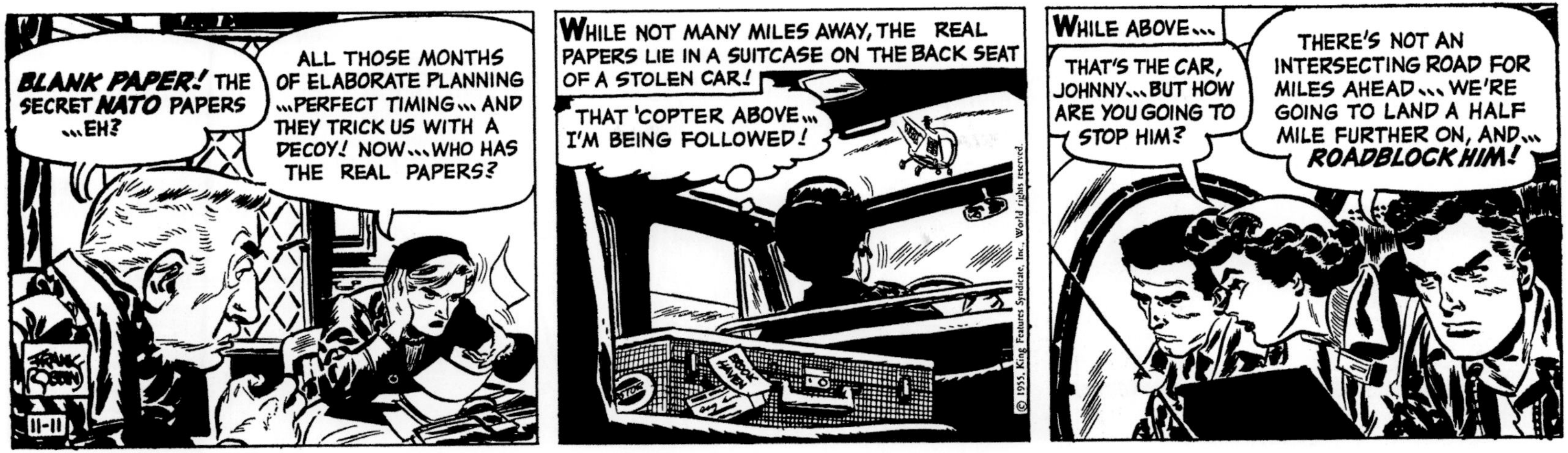

BLANK PAPER! THE SECRET NATO PAPERS ...EH?
ALL THOSE MONTHS OF ELABORATE PLANNING ...PERFECT TIMING... AND THEY TRICK US WITH A DECOY! NOW... WHO HAS THE REAL PAPERS?
FRANK ROBBIN
11-11
WHILE NOT MANY MILES AWAY, THE REAL PAPERS LIE IN A SUITCASE ON THE BACK SEAT OF A STOLEN CAR!
THAT 'COPTER ABOVE... I'M BEING FOLLOWED!
© 1955, King Features Syndicate, Inc., World rights reserved.
WHILE ABOVE...
THAT'S THE CAR, JOHNNY... BUT HOW ARE YOU GOING TO STOP HIM?
THERE'S NOT AN INTERSECTING ROAD FOR MILES AHEAD... WE'RE GOING TO LAND A HALF MILE FURTHER ON, AND... ROADBLOCK HIM!

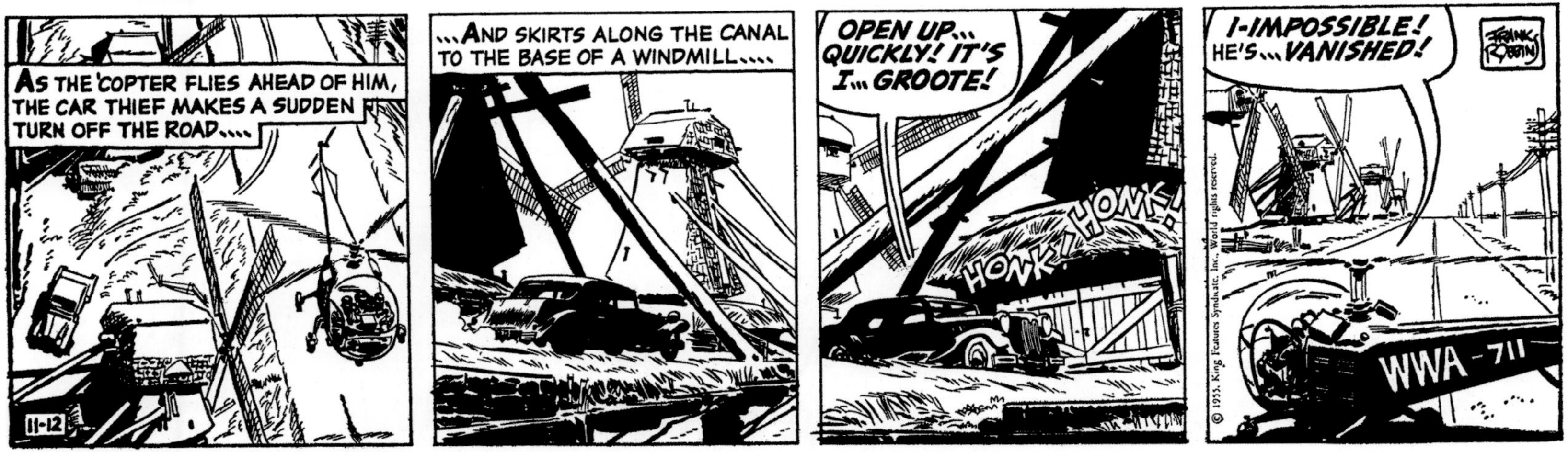

AS THE 'COPTER FLIES AHEAD OF HIM, THE CAR THIEF MAKES A SUDDEN TURN OFF THE ROAD....
11-12
...AND SKIRTS ALONG THE CANAL TO THE BASE OF A WINDMILL....
OPEN UP... QUICKLY! IT'S I... GROOTE!
HONK! HONK!
I-IMPOSSIBLE! HE'S... VANISHED!
FRANK ROBBIN
© 1955, King Features Syndicate, Inc., World rights reserved.
WWA-711

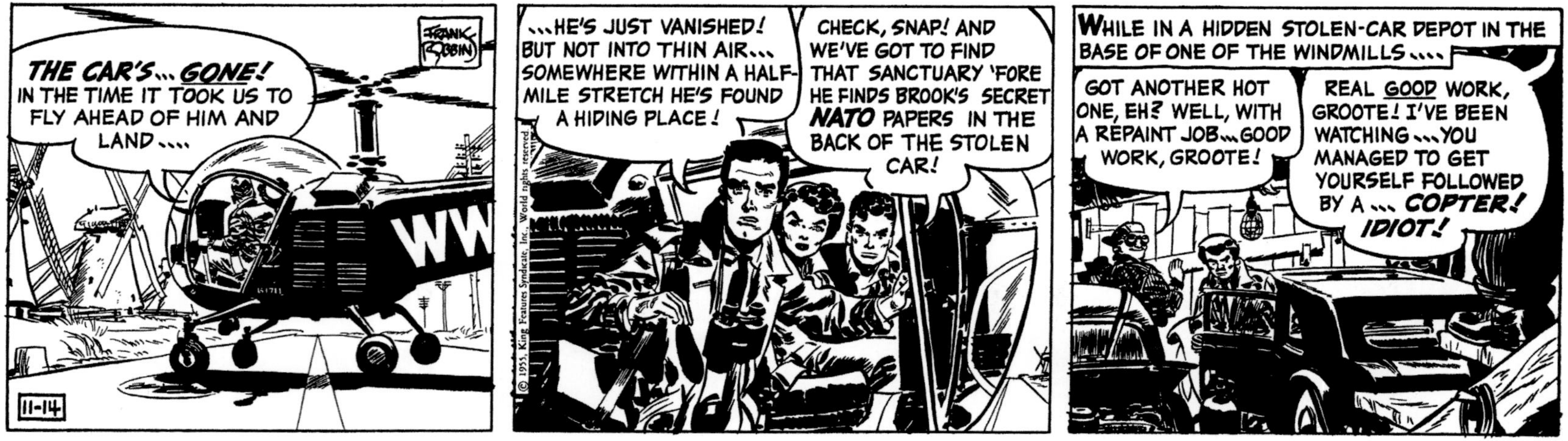
FRANK ROBBINS
THE CAR'S... GONE! IN THE TIME IT TOOK US TO FLY AHEAD OF HIM AND LAND....
11-14
© 1955, King Features Syndicate, Inc., World rights reserved.
...HE'S JUST VANISHED! BUT NOT INTO THIN AIR... SOMEWHERE WITHIN A HALF-MILE STRETCH HE'S FOUND A HIDING PLACE!
CHECK, SNAP! AND WE'VE GOT TO FIND THAT SANCTUARY 'FORE HE FINDS BROOK'S SECRET NATO PAPERS IN THE BACK OF THE STOLEN CAR!
WHILE IN A HIDDEN STOLEN-CAR DEPOT IN THE BASE OF ONE OF THE WINDMILLS....
GOT ANOTHER HOT ONE, EH? WELL, WITH A REPAINT JOB... GOOD WORK, GROOTE!
REAL GOOD WORK, GROOTE! I'VE BEEN WATCHING... YOU MANAGED TO GET YOURSELF FOLLOWED BY A... COPTER! IDIOT!

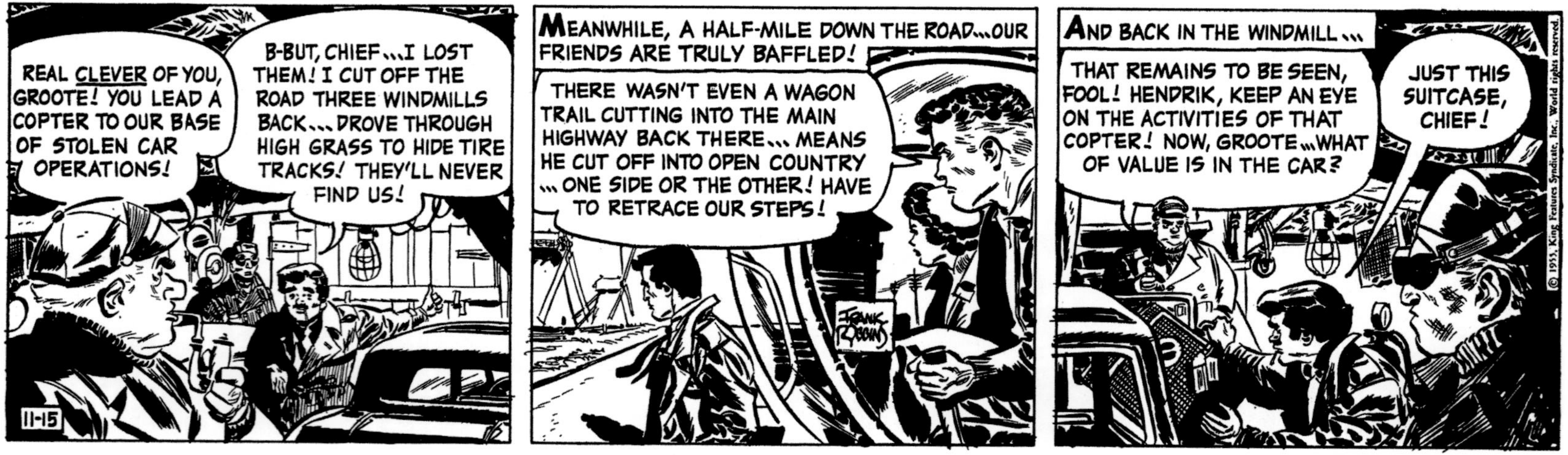
REAL CLEVER OF YOU, GROOTE! YOU LEAD A COPTER TO OUR BASE OF STOLEN CAR OPERATIONS!
B-BUT, CHIEF... I LOST THEM! I CUT OFF THE ROAD THREE WINDMILLS BACK... DROVE THROUGH HIGH GRASS TO HIDE TIRE TRACKS! THEY'LL NEVER FIND US!
11-15
MEANWHILE, A HALF-MILE DOWN THE ROAD... OUR FRIENDS ARE TRULY BAFFLED!
THERE WASN'T EVEN A WAGON TRAIL CUTTING INTO THE MAIN HIGHWAY BACK THERE... MEANS HE CUT OFF INTO OPEN COUNTRY ... ONE SIDE OR THE OTHER! HAVE TO RETRACE OUR STEPS!
FRANK ROBBINS
AND BACK IN THE WINDMILL...
THAT REMAINS TO BE SEEN, FOOL! HENDRIK, KEEP AN EYE ON THE ACTIVITIES OF THAT COPTER! NOW, GROOTE... WHAT OF VALUE IS IN THE CAR?
JUST THIS SUITCASE, CHIEF!
© 1955, King Features Syndicate, Inc., World rights reserved.

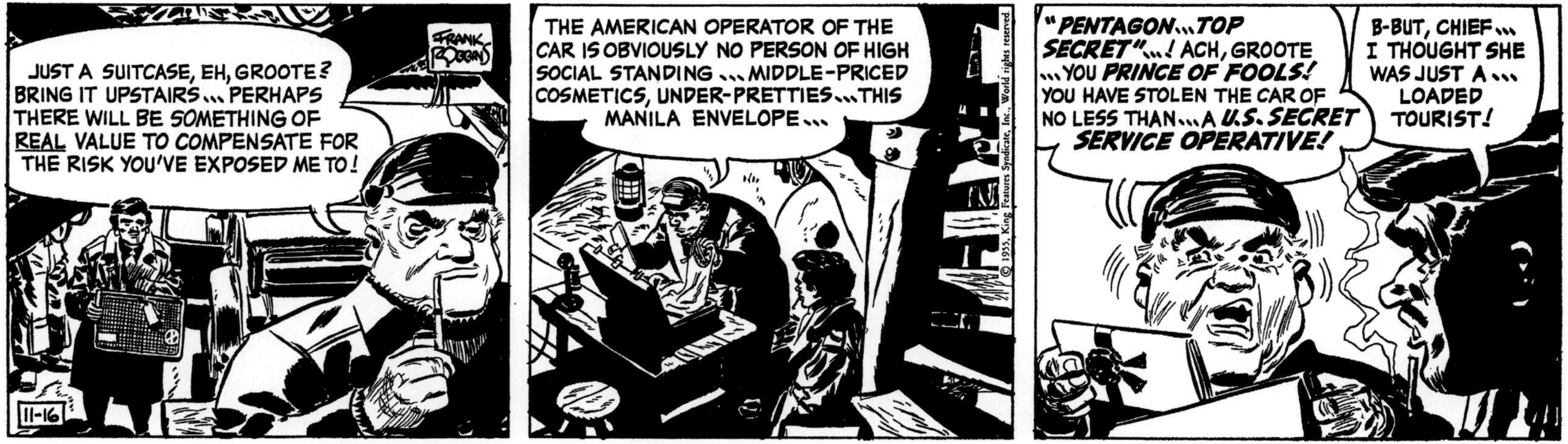

FRANK ROBBINS
JUST A SUITCASE, EH, GROOTE? BRING IT UPSTAIRS ... PERHAPS THERE WILL BE SOMETHING OF REAL VALUE TO COMPENSATE FOR THE RISK YOU'VE EXPOSED ME TO!
11-16
THE AMERICAN OPERATOR OF THE CAR IS OBVIOUSLY NO PERSON OF HIGH SOCIAL STANDING ... MIDDLE-PRICED COSMETICS, UNDER-PRETTIES ... THIS MANILA ENVELOPE ...
© 1955, King Features Syndicate, Inc., World rights reserved.
"PENTAGON ... TOP SECRET" ...! ACH, GROOTE ... YOU PRINCE OF FOOLS! YOU HAVE STOLEN THE CAR OF NO LESS THAN ... A U.S. SECRET SERVICE OPERATIVE!
B-BUT, CHIEF ... I THOUGHT SHE WAS JUST A ... LOADED TOURIST!

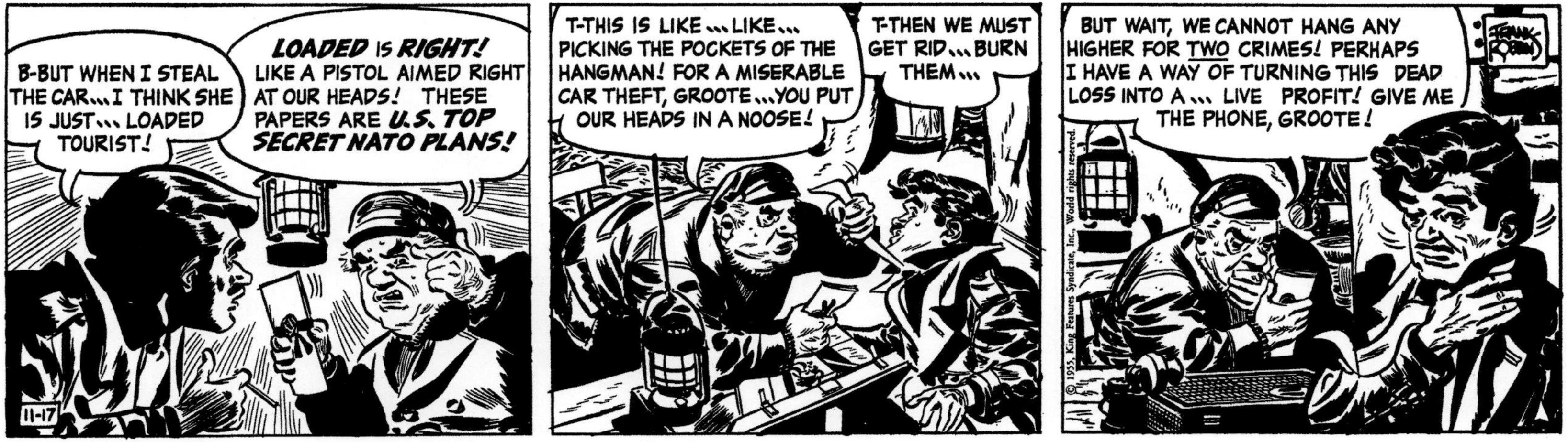

B-BUT WHEN I STEAL THE CAR ... I THINK SHE IS JUST ... LOADED TOURIST!
LOADED IS RIGHT! LIKE A PISTOL AIMED RIGHT AT OUR HEADS! THESE PAPERS ARE U.S. TOP SECRET NATO PLANS!
11-17
T-THIS IS LIKE ... LIKE ... PICKING THE POCKETS OF THE HANGMAN! FOR A MISERABLE CAR THEFT, GROOTE ... YOU PUT OUR HEADS IN A NOOSE!
T-THEN WE MUST GET RID ... BURN THEM ...
BUT WAIT, WE CANNOT HANG ANY HIGHER FOR TWO CRIMES! PERHAPS I HAVE A WAY OF TURNING THIS DEAD LOSS INTO A ... LIVE PROFIT! GIVE ME THE PHONE, GROOTE!
FRANK ROBBINS
© 1955, King Features Syndicate, Inc., World rights reserved.

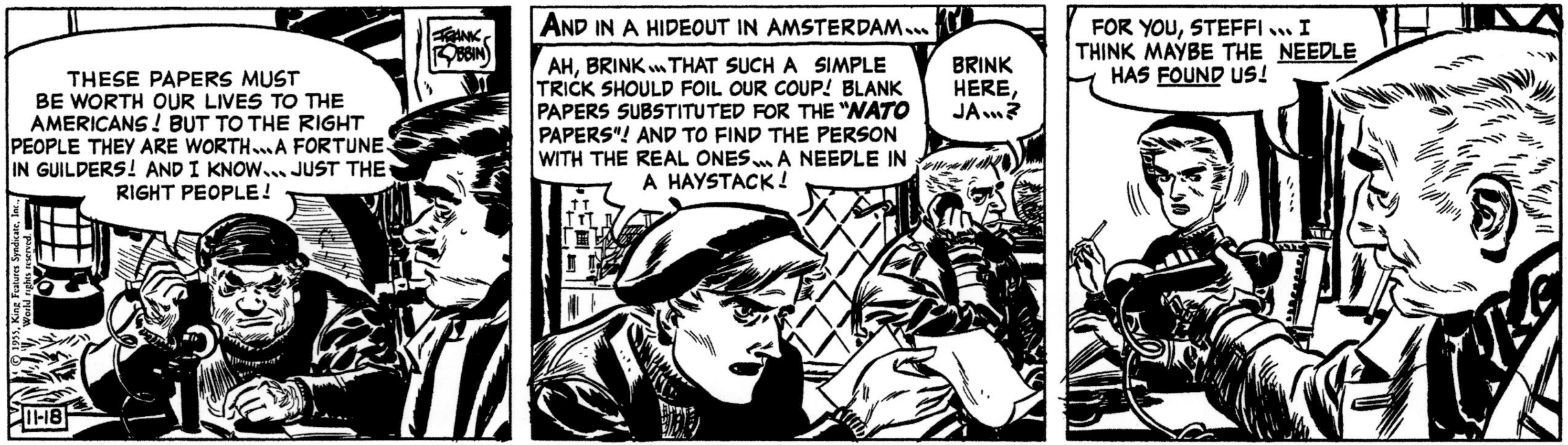
FRANK ROBBIN
THESE PAPERS MUST BE WORTH OUR LIVES TO THE AMERICANS! BUT TO THE RIGHT PEOPLE THEY ARE WORTH... A FORTUNE IN GUILDERS! AND I KNOW... JUST THE RIGHT PEOPLE!
© 1955, King Features Syndicate, Inc., World rights reserved.
11-18
AND IN A HIDEOUT IN AMSTERDAM...
AH, BRINK... THAT SUCH A SIMPLE TRICK SHOULD FOIL OUR COUP! BLANK PAPERS SUBSTITUTED FOR THE "NATO PAPERS"! AND TO FIND THE PERSON WITH THE REAL ONES... A NEEDLE IN A HAYSTACK!
BRINK HERE, JA...?
FOR YOU, STEFFI... I THINK MAYBE THE NEEDLE HAS FOUND US!

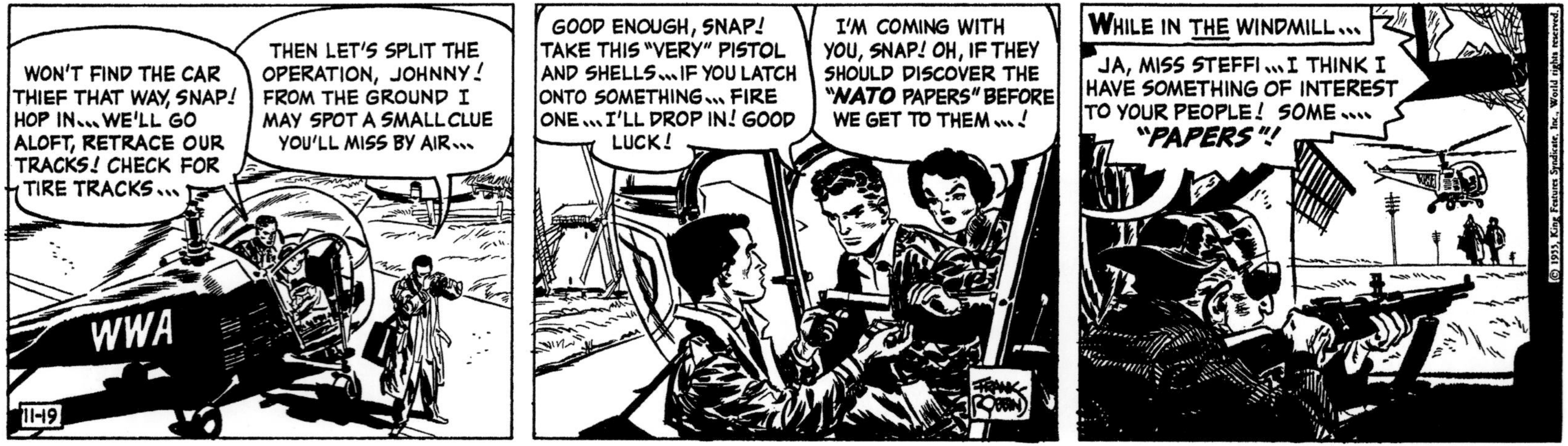
WON'T FIND THE CAR THIEF THAT WAY, SNAP! HOP IN... WE'LL GO ALOFT, RETRACE OUR TRACKS! CHECK FOR TIRE TRACKS...
THEN LET'S SPLIT THE OPERATION, JOHNNY! FROM THE GROUND I MAY SPOT A SMALL CLUE YOU'LL MISS BY AIR...
WWA
11-19
GOOD ENOUGH, SNAP! TAKE THIS "VERY" PISTOL AND SHELLS... IF YOU LATCH ONTO SOMETHING... FIRE ONE... I'LL DROP IN! GOOD LUCK!
I'M COMING WITH YOU, SNAP! OH, IF THEY SHOULD DISCOVER THE "NATO PAPERS" BEFORE WE GET TO THEM...!
FRANK ROBBIN
WHILE IN THE WINDMILL...
JA, MISS STEFFI... I THINK I HAVE SOMETHING OF INTEREST TO YOUR PEOPLE! SOME.... "PAPERS"!
© 1955, King Features Syndicate, Inc., World rights reserved.

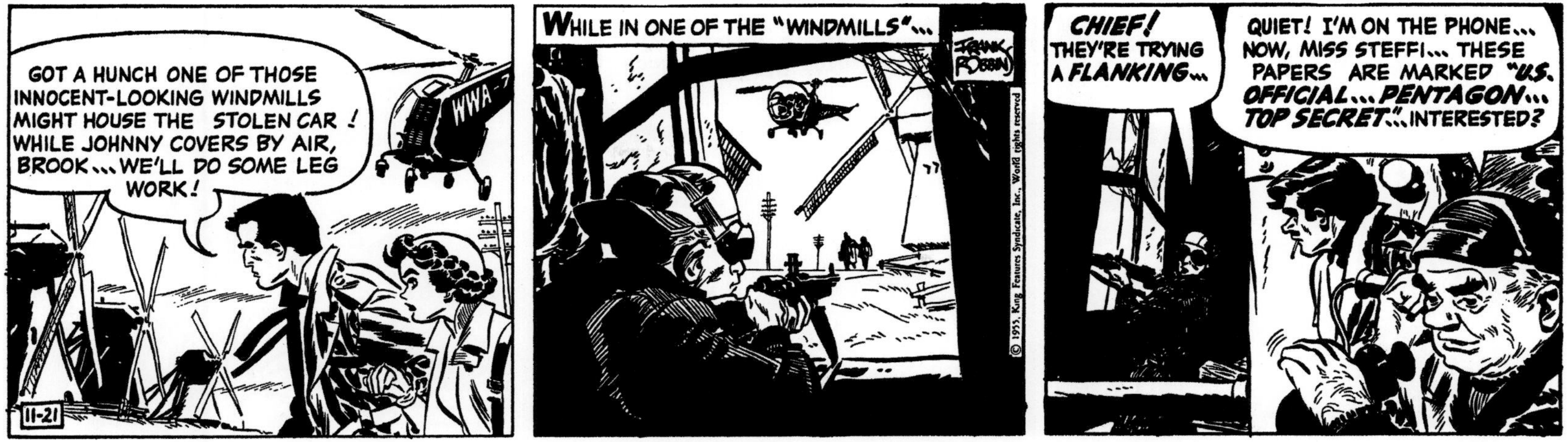
GOT A HUNCH ONE OF THOSE INNOCENT-LOOKING WINDMILLS MIGHT HOUSE THE STOLEN CAR! WHILE JOHNNY COVERS BY AIR, BROOK... WE'LL DO SOME LEG WORK!
WWA-7
11-21
WHILE IN ONE OF THE "WINDMILLS"...
FRANK ROBBIN
© 1955, King Features Syndicate, Inc., World rights reserved
CHIEF! THEY'RE TRYING A FLANKING...
QUIET! I'M ON THE PHONE... NOW, MISS STEFFI... THESE PAPERS ARE MARKED "U.S. OFFICIAL... PENTAGON... TOP SECRET"... INTERESTED?

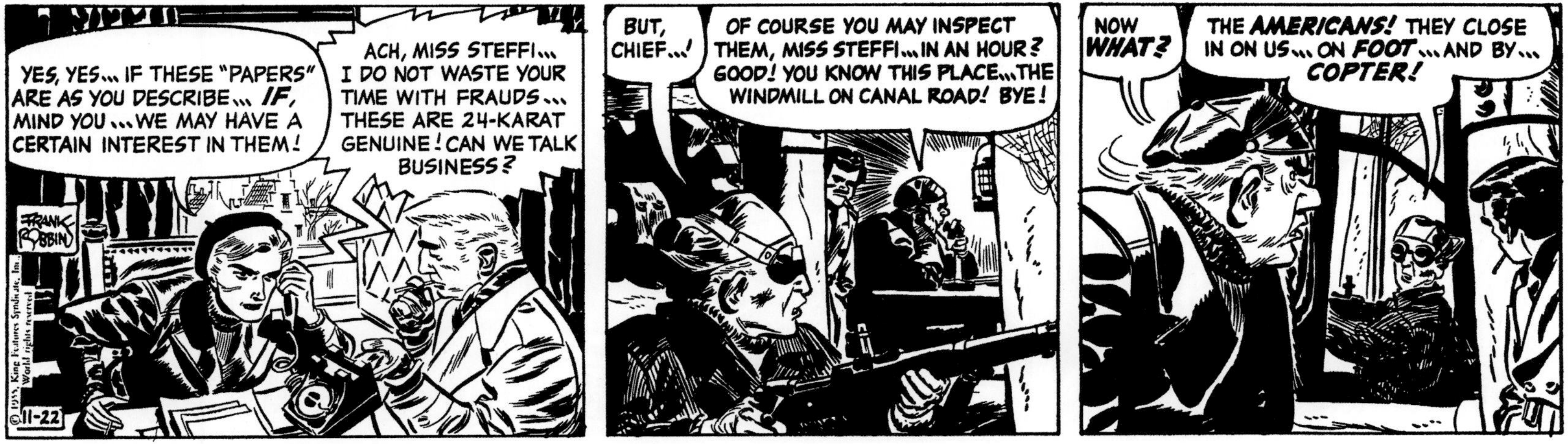
YES, YES... IF THESE "PAPERS" ARE AS YOU DESCRIBE... IF, MIND YOU... WE MAY HAVE A CERTAIN INTEREST IN THEM!
ACH, MISS STEFFI... I DO NOT WASTE YOUR TIME WITH FRAUDS... THESE ARE 24-KARAT GENUINE! CAN WE TALK BUSINESS?
FRANK ROBBIN
© 1955, King Features Syndicate, Inc., World rights reserved
11-22
BUT, CHIEF...!
OF COURSE YOU MAY INSPECT THEM, MISS STEFFI... IN AN HOUR? GOOD! YOU KNOW THIS PLACE... THE WINDMILL ON CANAL ROAD! BYE!
NOW WHAT?
THE AMERICANS! THEY CLOSE IN ON US... ON FOOT... AND BY... COPTER!

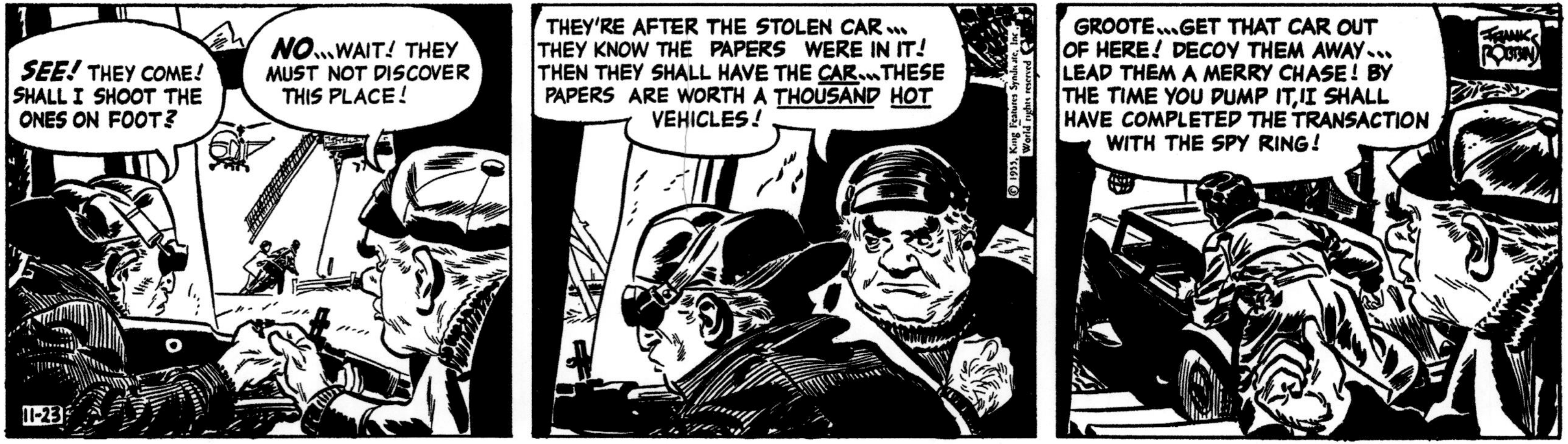
11-23
SEE! THEY COME! SHALL I SHOOT THE ONES ON FOOT?
NO...WAIT! THEY MUST NOT DISCOVER THIS PLACE!
THEY'RE AFTER THE STOLEN CAR... THEY KNOW THE PAPERS WERE IN IT! THEN THEY SHALL HAVE THE CAR...THESE PAPERS ARE WORTH A THOUSAND HOT VEHICLES!
© 1955, King Features Syndicate, Inc., World rights reserved
GROOTE...GET THAT CAR OUT OF HERE! DECOY THEM AWAY... LEAD THEM A MERRY CHASE! BY THE TIME YOU DUMP IT, I SHALL HAVE COMPLETED THE TRANSACTION WITH THE SPY RING!

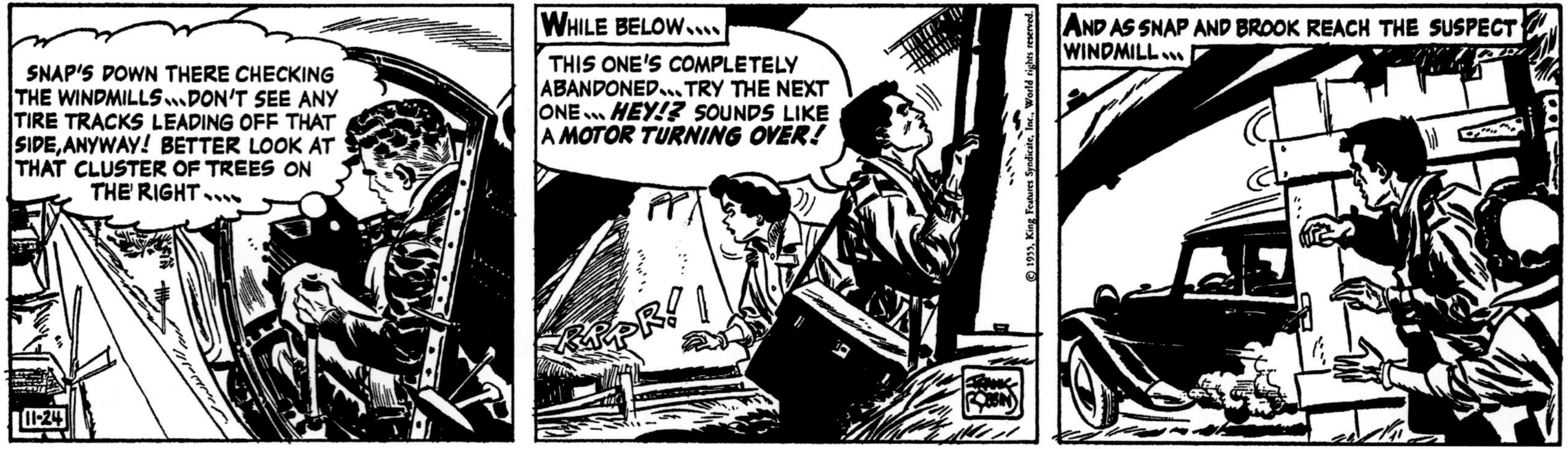
11-24
SNAP'S DOWN THERE CHECKING THE WINDMILLS...DON'T SEE ANY TIRE TRACKS LEADING OFF THAT SIDE, ANYWAY! BETTER LOOK AT THAT CLUSTER OF TREES ON THE RIGHT....
WHILE BELOW....
THIS ONE'S COMPLETELY ABANDONED...TRY THE NEXT ONE... HEY!? SOUNDS LIKE A MOTOR TURNING OVER!
RRRR!
© 1955, King Features Syndicate, Inc., World rights reserved.
AND AS SNAP AND BROOK REACH THE SUSPECT WINDMILL...

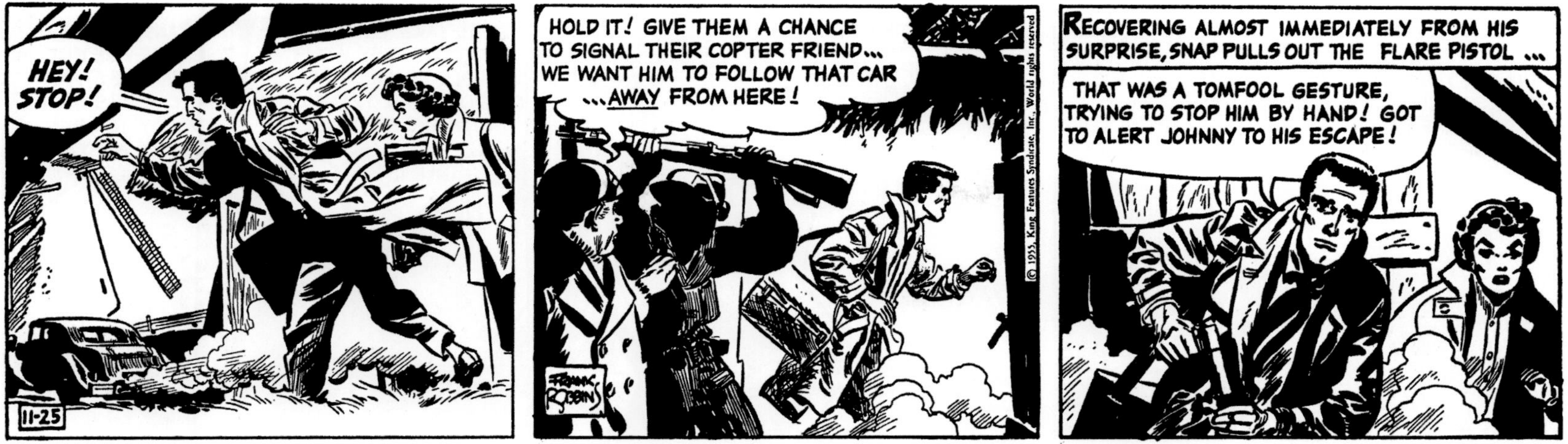
HEY! STOP!
HOLD IT! GIVE THEM A CHANCE TO SIGNAL THEIR COPTER FRIEND... WE WANT HIM TO FOLLOW THAT CAR ...AWAY FROM HERE!
RECOVERING ALMOST IMMEDIATELY FROM HIS SURPRISE, SNAP PULLS OUT THE FLARE PISTOL ...
THAT WAS A TOMFOOL GESTURE, TRYING TO STOP HIM BY HAND! GOT TO ALERT JOHNNY TO HIS ESCAPE!
11-25
© 1955, King Features Syndicate, Inc., World rights reserved
FRANK ROBBINS

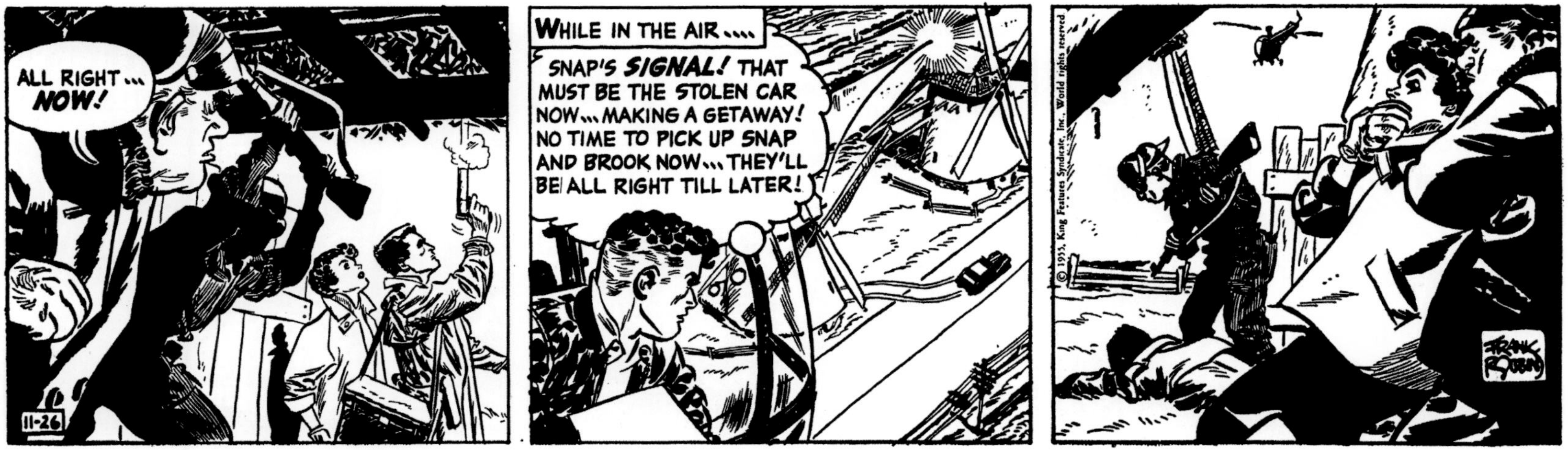
ALL RIGHT ... NOW!
WHILE IN THE AIR ....
SNAP'S SIGNAL! THAT MUST BE THE STOLEN CAR NOW... MAKING A GETAWAY! NO TIME TO PICK UP SNAP AND BROOK NOW... THEY'LL BE ALL RIGHT TILL LATER!
11-26
© 1955, King Features Syndicate, Inc., World rights reserved
FRANK ROBBINS

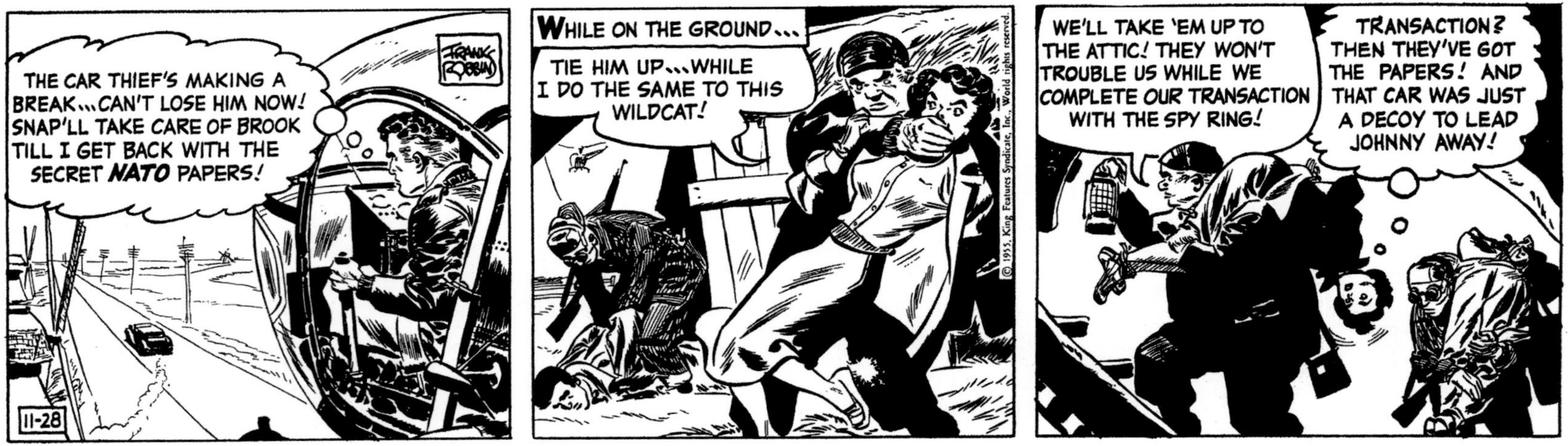
FRANK ROBBINS
THE CAR THIEF'S MAKING A BREAK...CAN'T LOSE HIM NOW! SNAP'LL TAKE CARE OF BROOK TILL I GET BACK WITH THE SECRET NATO PAPERS!
11-28
WHILE ON THE GROUND...
TIE HIM UP...WHILE I DO THE SAME TO THIS WILDCAT!
© 1955, King Features Syndicate, Inc., World rights reserved.
WE'LL TAKE 'EM UP TO THE ATTIC! THEY WON'T TROUBLE US WHILE WE COMPLETE OUR TRANSACTION WITH THE SPY RING!
TRANSACTION? THEN THEY'VE GOT THE PAPERS! AND THAT CAR WAS JUST A DECOY TO LEAD JOHNNY AWAY!

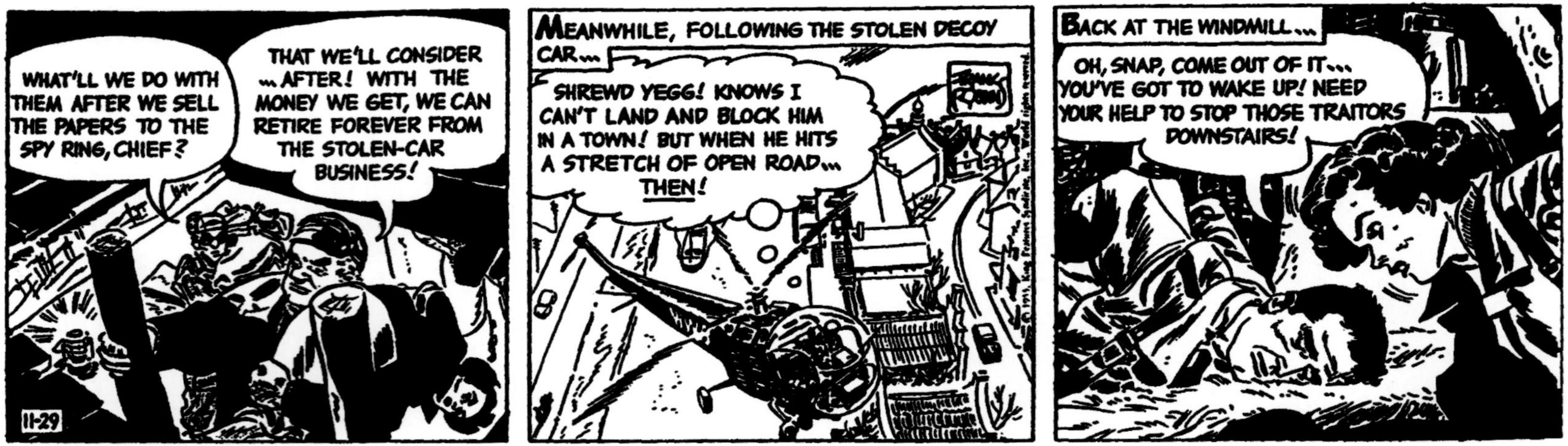
WHAT'LL WE DO WITH THEM AFTER WE SELL THE PAPERS TO THE SPY RING, CHIEF?
THAT WE'LL CONSIDER ...AFTER! WITH THE MONEY WE GET, WE CAN RETIRE FOREVER FROM THE STOLEN-CAR BUSINESS!
11-29
MEANWHILE, FOLLOWING THE STOLEN DECOY CAR...
FRANK ROBBINS
SHREWD YEGG! KNOWS I CAN'T LAND AND BLOCK HIM IN A TOWN! BUT WHEN HE HITS A STRETCH OF OPEN ROAD... THEN!
BACK AT THE WINDMILL...
OH, SNAP, COME OUT OF IT... YOU'VE GOT TO WAKE UP! NEED YOUR HELP TO STOP THOSE TRAITORS DOWNSTAIRS!

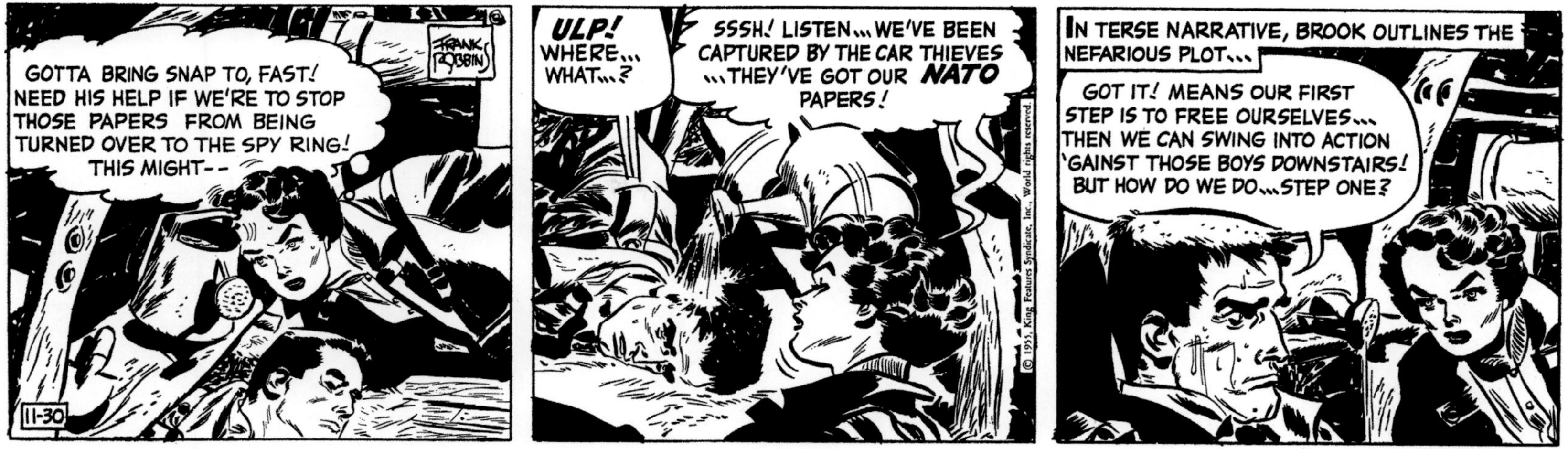
FRANK ROBBIN
11-30
GOTTA BRING SNAP TO, FAST! NEED HIS HELP IF WE'RE TO STOP THOSE PAPERS FROM BEING TURNED OVER TO THE SPY RING! THIS MIGHT- -
ULP! WHERE... WHAT...?
SSSH! LISTEN... WE'VE BEEN CAPTURED BY THE CAR THIEVES ...THEY'VE GOT OUR NATO PAPERS!
© 1955, King Features Syndicate, Inc., World rights reserved.
IN TERSE NARRATIVE, BROOK OUTLINES THE NEFARIOUS PLOT...
GOT IT! MEANS OUR FIRST STEP IS TO FREE OURSELVES... THEN WE CAN SWING INTO ACTION 'GAINST THOSE BOYS DOWNSTAIRS! BUT HOW DO WE DO...STEP ONE?

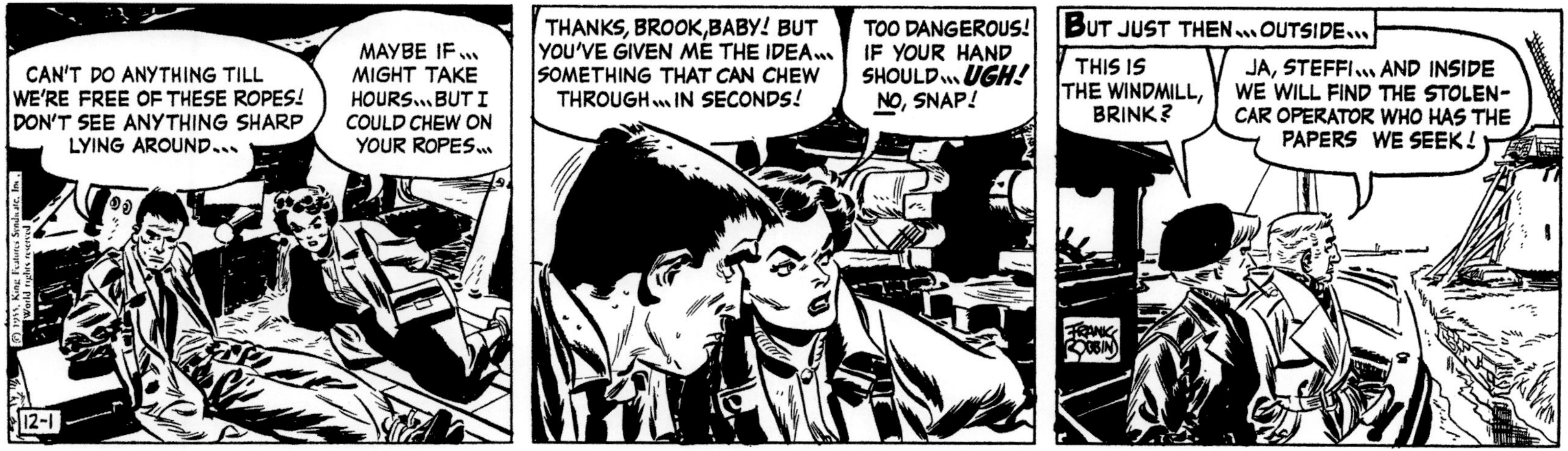
12-1
CAN'T DO ANYTHING TILL WE'RE FREE OF THESE ROPES! DON'T SEE ANYTHING SHARP LYING AROUND...
MAYBE IF... MIGHT TAKE HOURS...BUT I COULD CHEW ON YOUR ROPES...
© 1955, King Features Syndicate, Inc., World rights reserved
THANKS, BROOK, BABY! BUT YOU'VE GIVEN ME THE IDEA... SOMETHING THAT CAN CHEW THROUGH... IN SECONDS!
TOO DANGEROUS! IF YOUR HAND SHOULD... UGH! NO, SNAP!
BUT JUST THEN...OUTSIDE...
THIS IS THE WINDMILL, BRINK?
JA, STEFFI... AND INSIDE WE WILL FIND THE STOLEN-CAR OPERATOR WHO HAS THE PAPERS WE SEEK!
FRANK ROBBIN

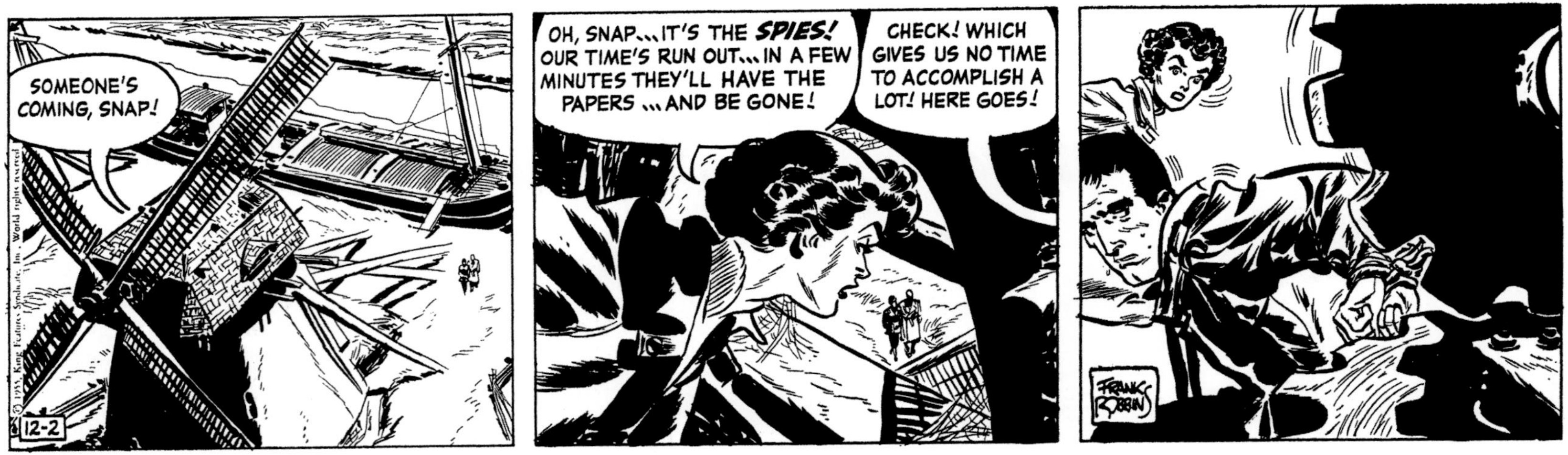
SOMEONE'S COMING, SNAP!
© 1955, King Features Syndicate, Inc., World rights reserved
12-2
OH, SNAP... IT'S THE SPIES! OUR TIME'S RUN OUT... IN A FEW MINUTES THEY'LL HAVE THE PAPERS ... AND BE GONE!
CHECK! WHICH GIVES US NO TIME TO ACCOMPLISH A LOT! HERE GOES!
FRANK ROBBINS

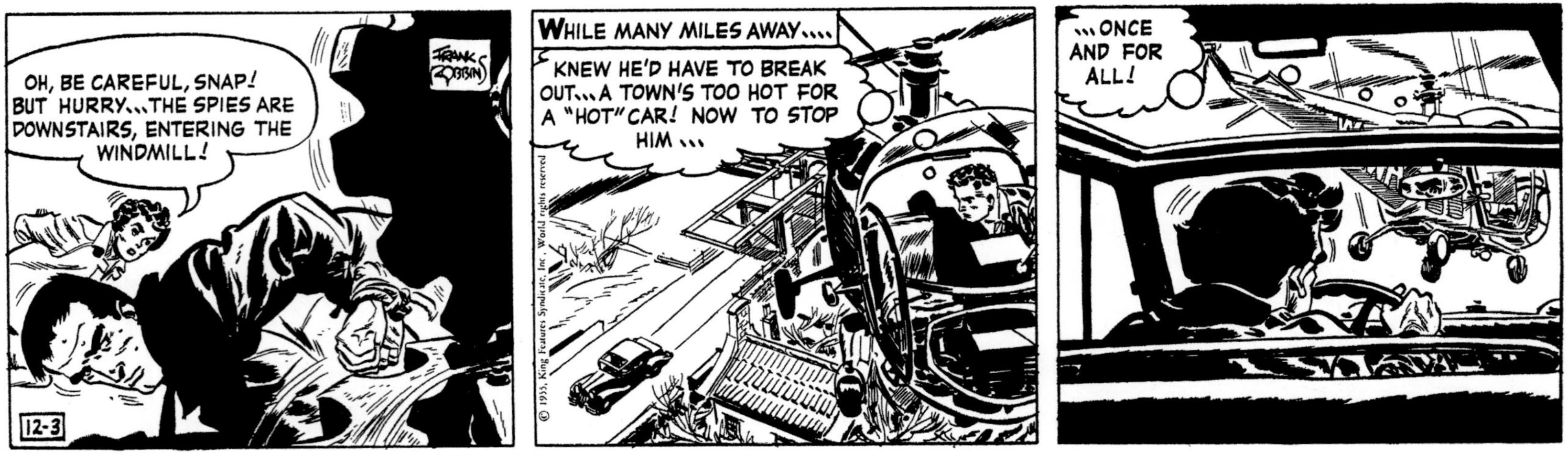
FRANK ROBBINS
OH, BE CAREFUL, SNAP! BUT HURRY... THE SPIES ARE DOWNSTAIRS, ENTERING THE WINDMILL!
12-3
WHILE MANY MILES AWAY....
KNEW HE'D HAVE TO BREAK OUT... A TOWN'S TOO HOT FOR A "HOT" CAR! NOW TO STOP HIM ...
© 1955, King Features Syndicate, Inc., World rights reserved
... ONCE AND FOR ALL!

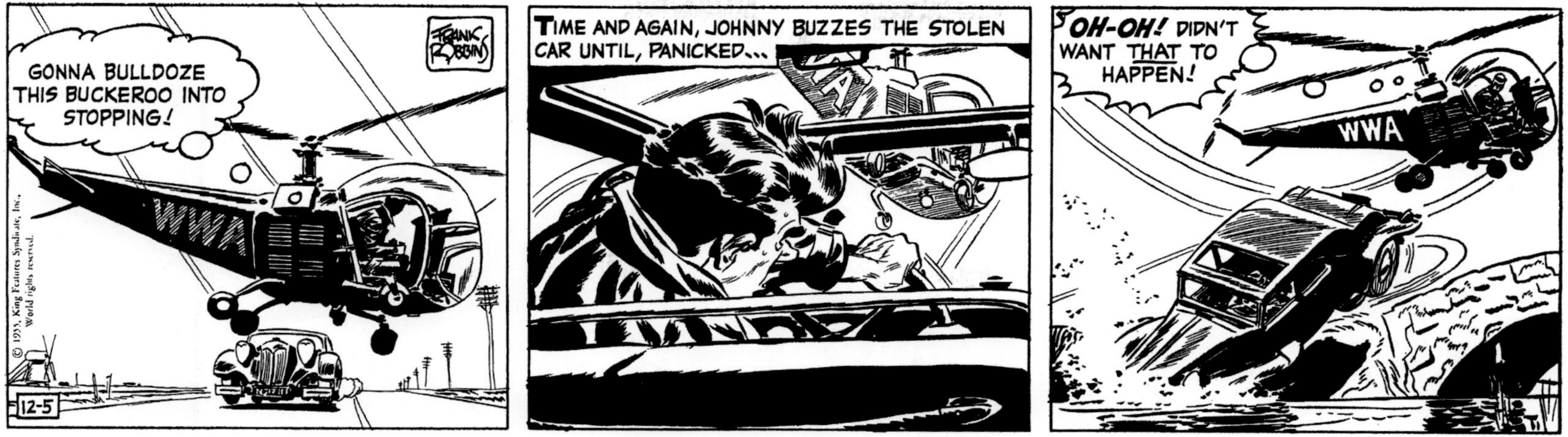
FRANK ROBBINS
GONNA BULLDOZE THIS BUCKEROO INTO STOPPING!
© 1955, King Features Syndicate, Inc., World rights reserved.
12-5
WWA
TIME AND AGAIN, JOHNNY BUZZES THE STOLEN CAR UNTIL, PANICKED...
OH-OH! DIDN'T WANT THAT TO HAPPEN!
WWA

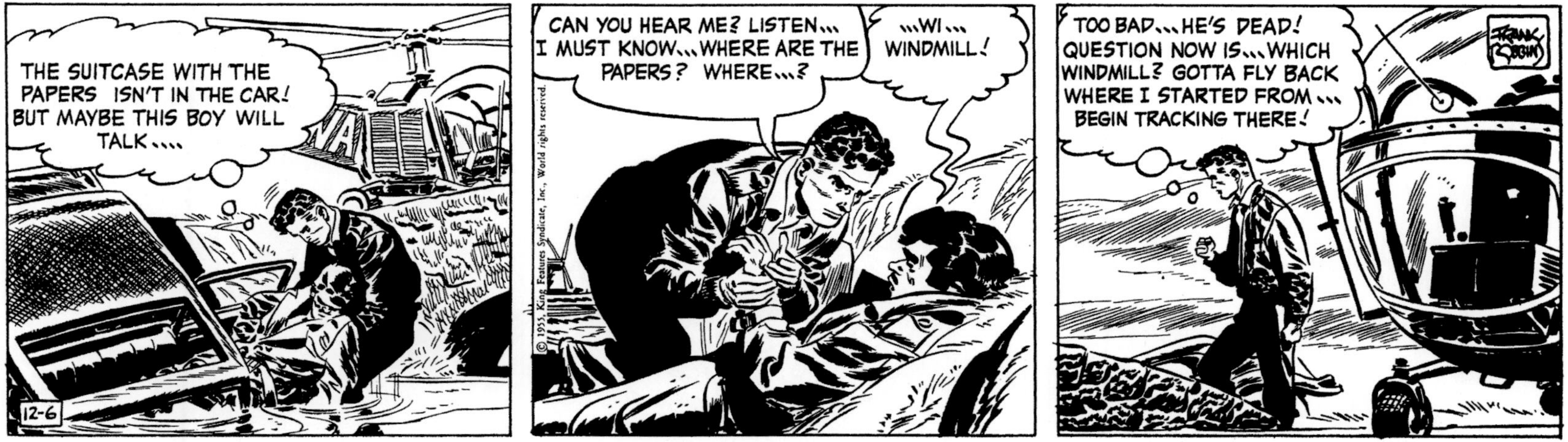
THE SUITCASE WITH THE PAPERS ISN'T IN THE CAR! BUT MAYBE THIS BOY WILL TALK....
12-6
CAN YOU HEAR ME? LISTEN... I MUST KNOW... WHERE ARE THE PAPERS? WHERE...?
...WI... WINDMILL!
© 1955, King Features Syndicate, Inc., World rights reserved.
TOO BAD... HE'S DEAD! QUESTION NOW IS... WHICH WINDMILL? GOTTA FLY BACK WHERE I STARTED FROM... BEGIN TRACKING THERE!
FRANK ROBBINS

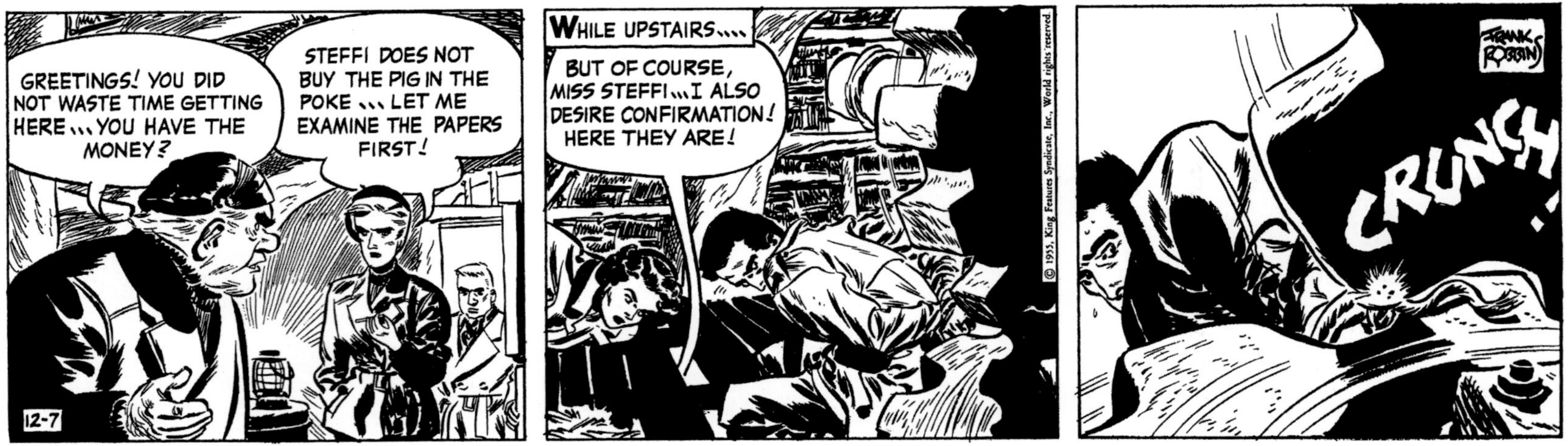
GREETINGS! YOU DID NOT WASTE TIME GETTING HERE ... YOU HAVE THE MONEY?
STEFFI DOES NOT BUY THE PIG IN THE POKE ... LET ME EXAMINE THE PAPERS FIRST!
12-7
WHILE UPSTAIRS....
BUT OF COURSE, MISS STEFFI ... I ALSO DESIRE CONFIRMATION! HERE THEY ARE!
© 1955, King Features Syndicate, Inc., World rights reserved.
FRANK ROBBINS
CRUNCH!

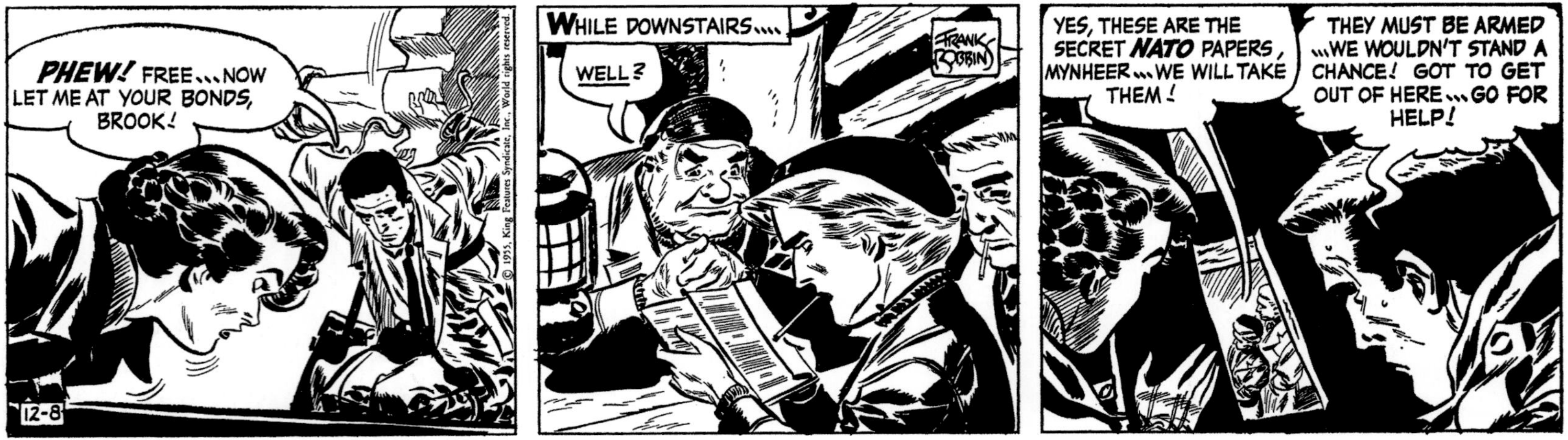
PHEW! FREE ... NOW LET ME AT YOUR BONDS, BROOK!
© 1955, King Features Syndicate, Inc., World rights reserved.
12-8
WHILE DOWNSTAIRS....
FRANK ROBBINS
WELL?
YES, THESE ARE THE SECRET NATO PAPERS, MYNHEER ... WE WILL TAKE THEM!
THEY MUST BE ARMED ... WE WOULDN'T STAND A CHANCE! GOT TO GET OUT OF HERE ... GO FOR HELP!

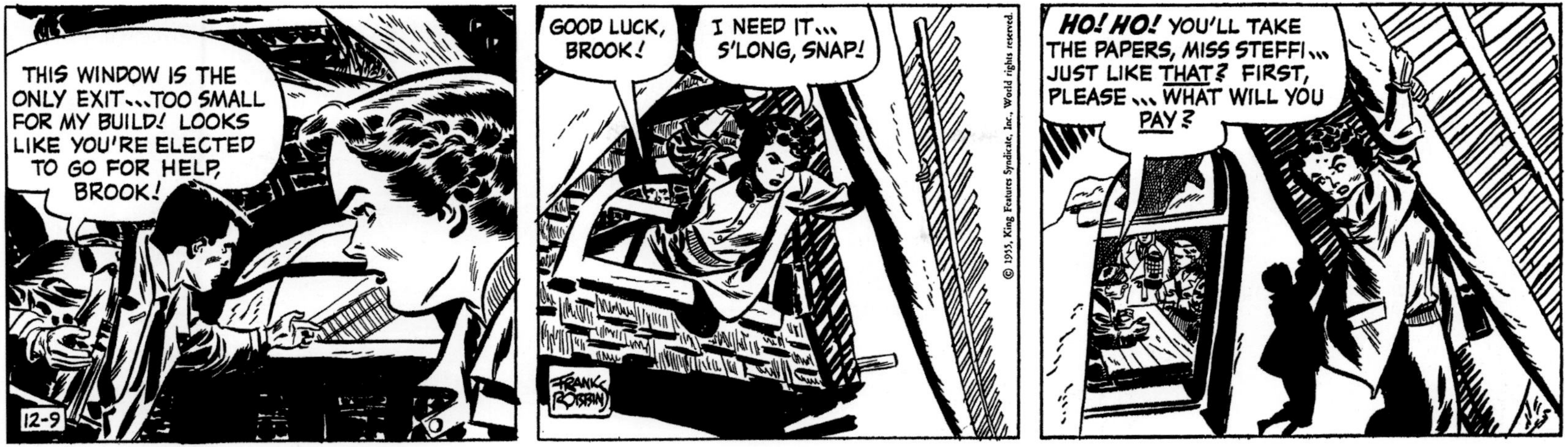
12-9
THIS WINDOW IS THE ONLY EXIT...TOO SMALL FOR MY BUILD! LOOKS LIKE YOU'RE ELECTED TO GO FOR HELP, BROOK!
GOOD LUCK, BROOK!
I NEED IT... S'LONG, SNAP!
© 1955, King Features Syndicate, Inc., World rights reserved.
HO! HO! YOU'LL TAKE THE PAPERS, MISS STEFFI... JUST LIKE THAT? FIRST, PLEASE... WHAT WILL YOU PAY?

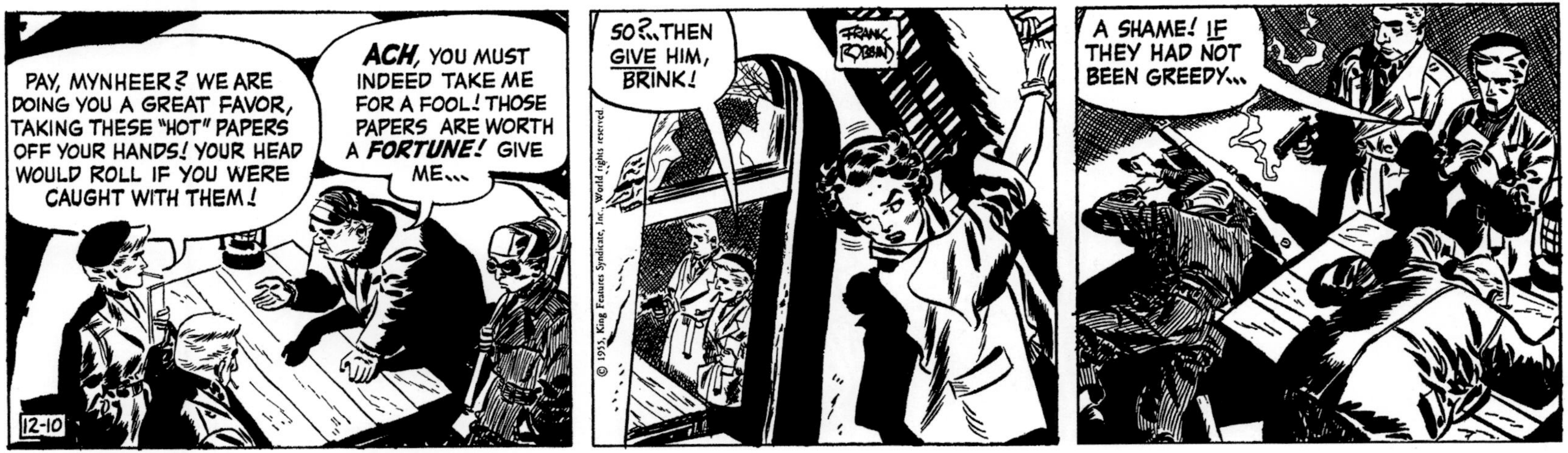
12-10
PAY, MYNHEER? WE ARE DOING YOU A GREAT FAVOR, TAKING THESE "HOT" PAPERS OFF YOUR HANDS! YOUR HEAD WOULD ROLL IF YOU WERE CAUGHT WITH THEM!
ACH, YOU MUST INDEED TAKE ME FOR A FOOL! THOSE PAPERS ARE WORTH A FORTUNE! GIVE ME...
SO?...THEN GIVE HIM, BRINK!
© 1955, King Features Syndicate, Inc., World rights reserved.
A SHAME! IF THEY HAD NOT BEEN GREEDY...

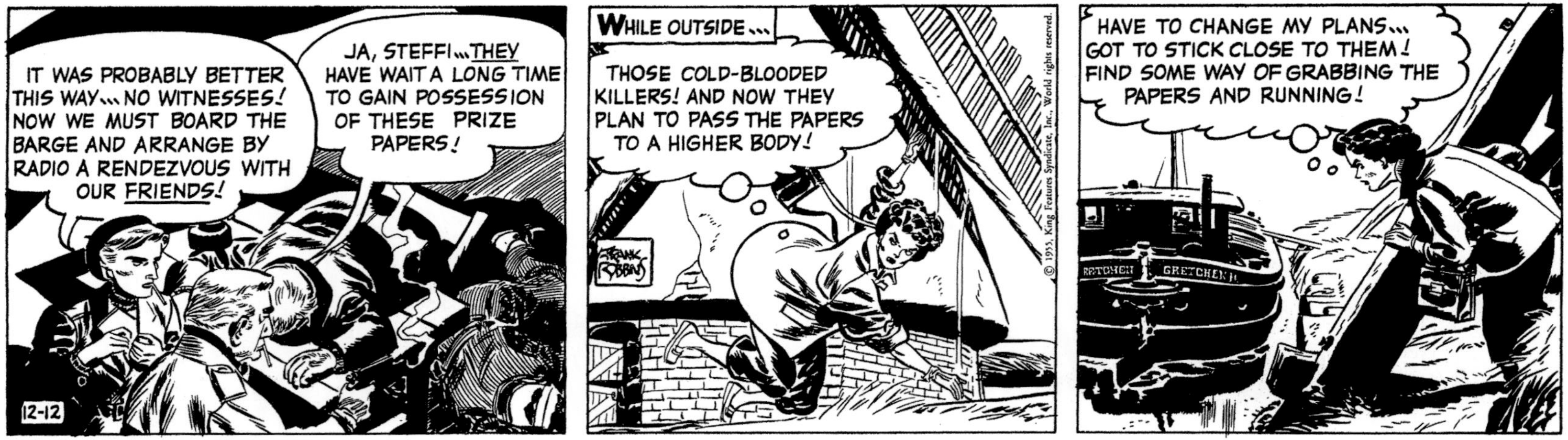
IT WAS PROBABLY BETTER THIS WAY... NO WITNESSES! NOW WE MUST BOARD THE BARGE AND ARRANGE BY RADIO A RENDEZVOUS WITH OUR FRIENDS!
JA, STEFFI... THEY HAVE WAIT A LONG TIME TO GAIN POSSESSION OF THESE PRIZE PAPERS!
12-12
WHILE OUTSIDE...
THOSE COLD-BLOODED KILLERS! AND NOW THEY PLAN TO PASS THE PAPERS TO A HIGHER BODY!
FRANK ROBBINS
© 1955, King Features Syndicate, Inc., World rights reserved.
HAVE TO CHANGE MY PLANS... GOT TO STICK CLOSE TO THEM! FIND SOME WAY OF GRABBING THE PAPERS AND RUNNING!
GRETCHEN

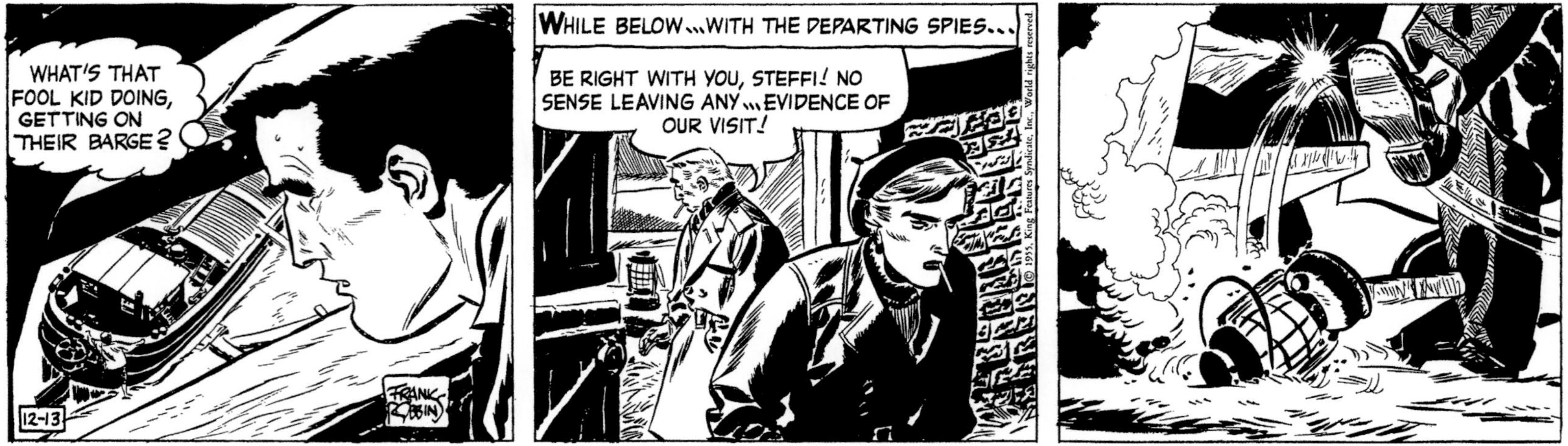
WHAT'S THAT FOOL KID DOING, GETTING ON THEIR BARGE?
FRANK ROBBINS
12-13
WHILE BELOW... WITH THE DEPARTING SPIES...
BE RIGHT WITH YOU, STEFFI! NO SENSE LEAVING ANY... EVIDENCE OF OUR VISIT!
© 1955, King Features Syndicate, Inc., World rights reserved.

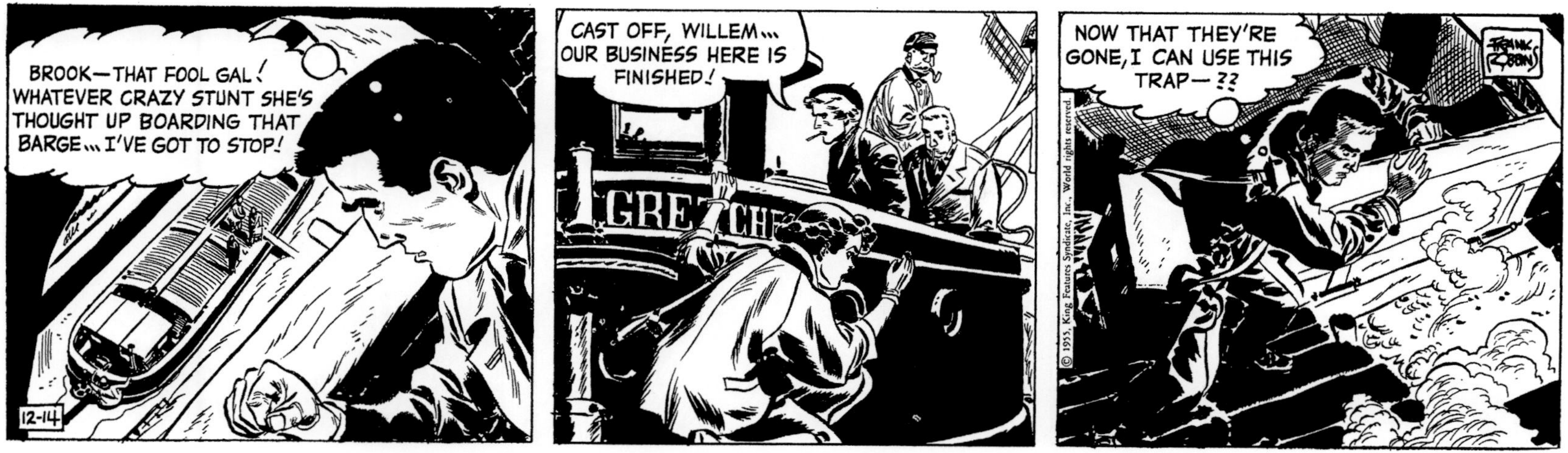
BROOK—THAT FOOL GAL! WHATEVER CRAZY STUNT SHE'S THOUGHT UP BOARDING THAT BARGE... I'VE GOT TO STOP!
12-14
CAST OFF, WILLEM... OUR BUSINESS HERE IS FINISHED!
GRETCH
NOW THAT THEY'RE GONE, I CAN USE THIS TRAP—??
FRANK ROBBINS
© 1955, King Features Syndicate, Inc., World rights reserved.

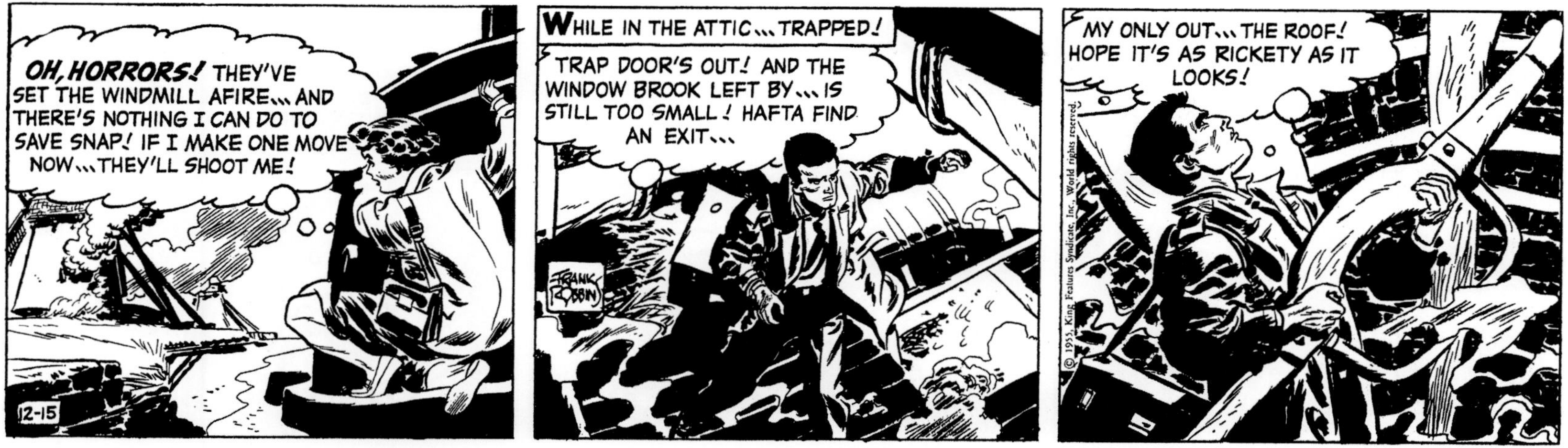
OH, HORRORS! THEY'VE SET THE WINDMILL AFIRE... AND THERE'S NOTHING I CAN DO TO SAVE SNAP! IF I MAKE ONE MOVE NOW... THEY'LL SHOOT ME!
12-15
WHILE IN THE ATTIC... TRAPPED!
TRAP DOOR'S OUT! AND THE WINDOW BROOK LEFT BY... IS STILL TOO SMALL! HAFTA FIND AN EXIT...
FRANK ROBBINS
MY ONLY OUT... THE ROOF! HOPE IT'S AS RICKETY AS IT LOOKS!
© 1955, King Features Syndicate, Inc., World rights reserved.

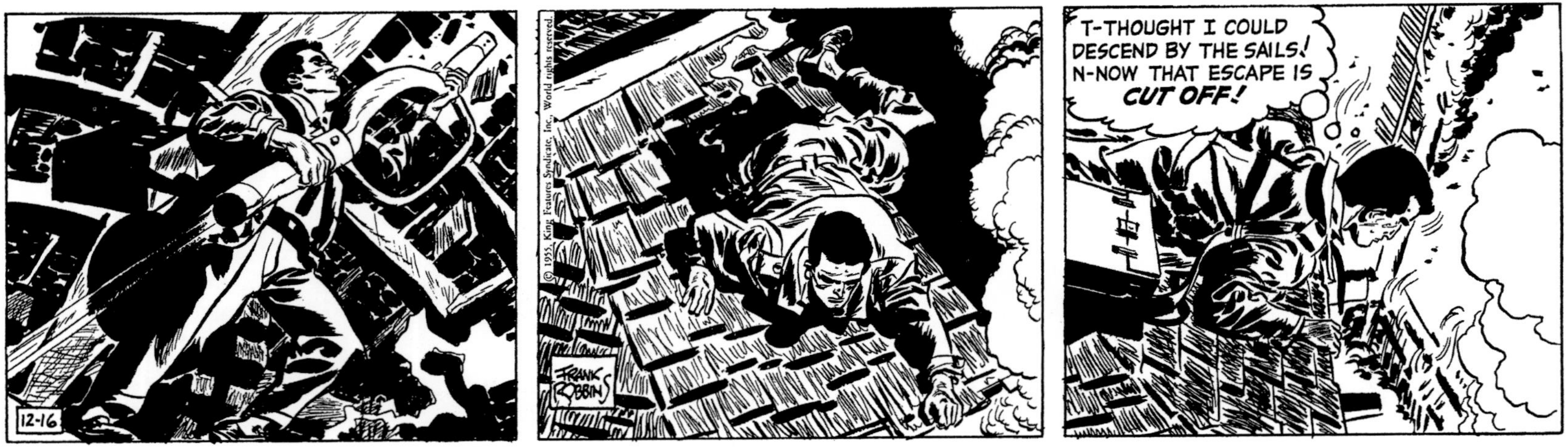
12-16
© 1955, King Features Syndicate, Inc., World rights reserved.
FRANK ROBBINS
T-THOUGHT I COULD DESCEND BY THE SAILS! N-NOW THAT ESCAPE IS *CUT OFF!*

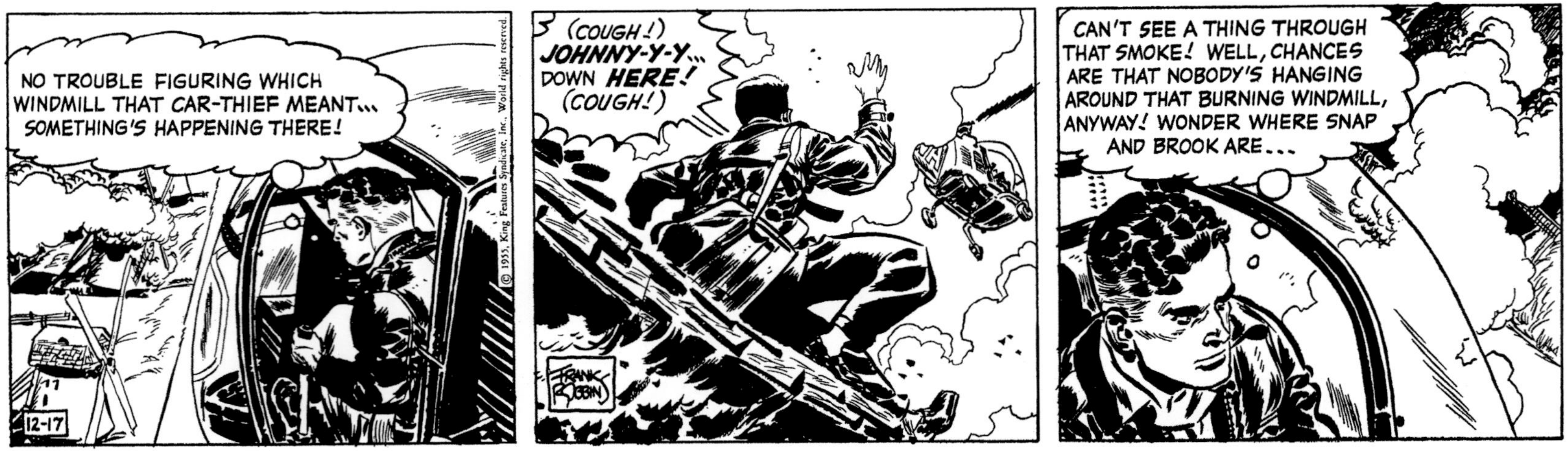
NO TROUBLE FIGURING WHICH WINDMILL THAT CAR-THIEF MEANT... SOMETHING'S HAPPENING THERE!
12-17
© 1955, King Features Syndicate, Inc., World rights reserved.
(COUGH!) *JOHNNY-Y-Y*... DOWN *HERE!* (COUGH!)
FRANK ROBBINS
CAN'T SEE A THING THROUGH THAT SMOKE! WELL, CHANCES ARE THAT NOBODY'S HANGING AROUND THAT BURNING WINDMILL, ANYWAY! WONDER WHERE SNAP AND BROOK ARE...

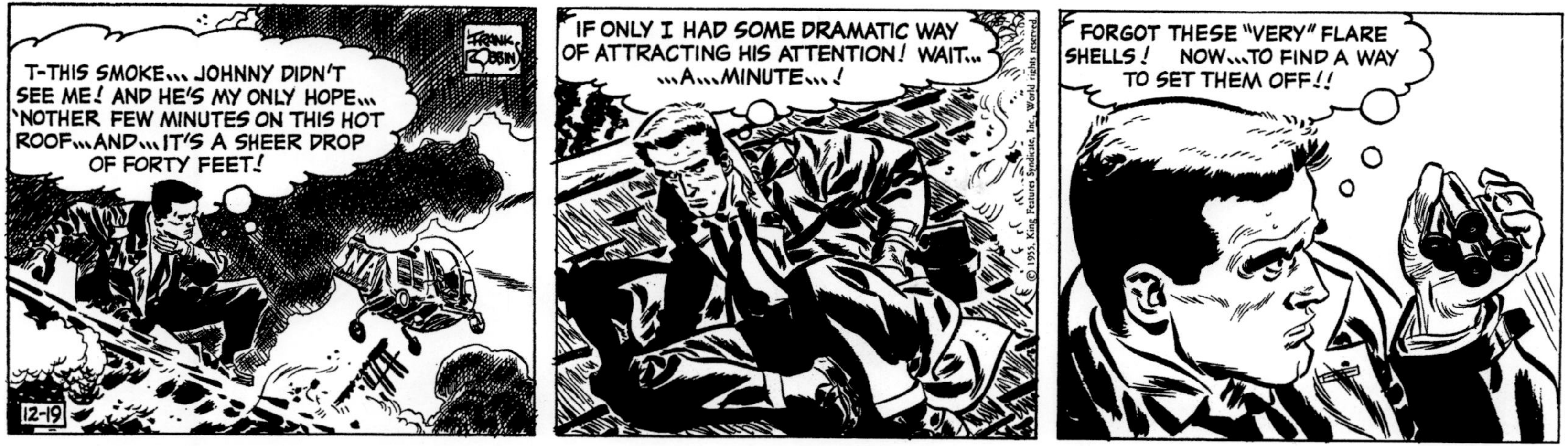
FRANK ROBBINS
T-THIS SMOKE... JOHNNY DIDN'T SEE ME! AND HE'S MY ONLY HOPE... 'NOTHER FEW MINUTES ON THIS HOT ROOF... AND... IT'S A SHEER DROP OF FORTY FEET!
12-19
IF ONLY I HAD SOME DRAMATIC WAY OF ATTRACTING HIS ATTENTION! WAIT... ...A... MINUTE... !
© 1955, King Features Syndicate, Inc., World rights reserved.
FORGOT THESE "VERY" FLARE SHELLS! NOW... TO FIND A WAY TO SET THEM OFF!!

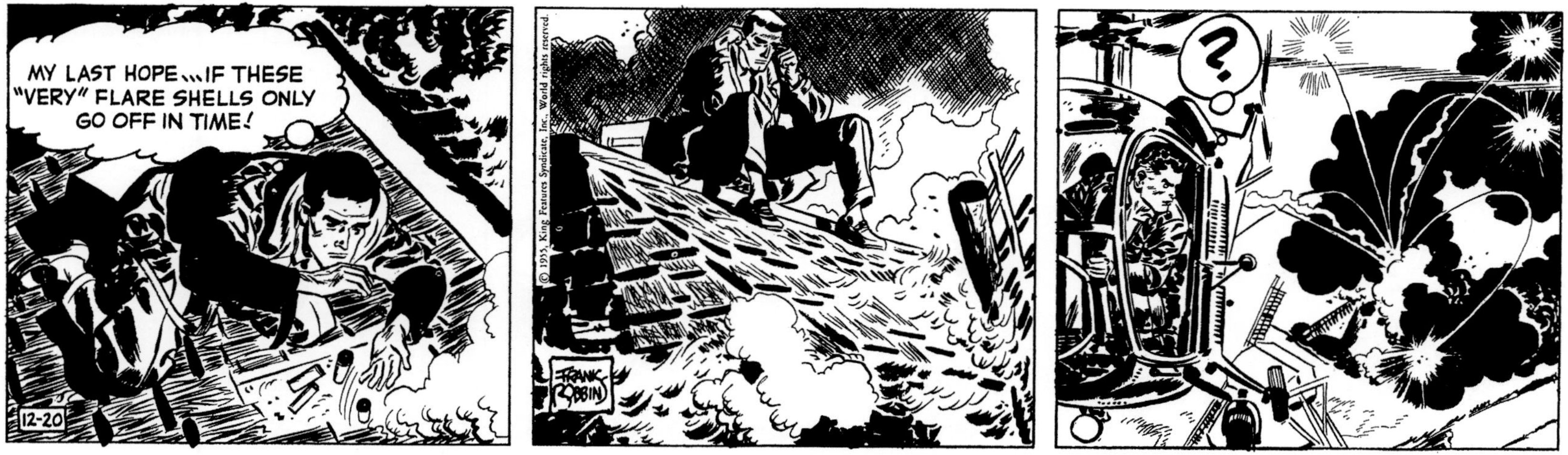
MY LAST HOPE... IF THESE "VERY" FLARE SHELLS ONLY GO OFF IN TIME!
12-20
© 1955, King Features Syndicate, Inc., World rights reserved.
FRANK ROBBINS
?

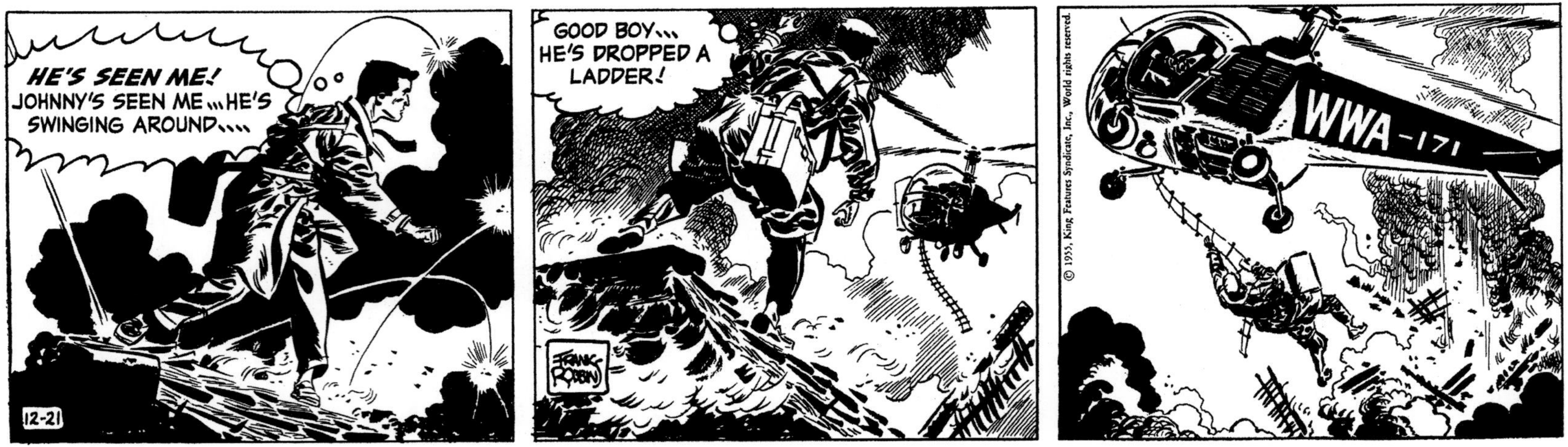
12-21
HE'S SEEN ME! JOHNNY'S SEEN ME...HE'S SWINGING AROUND....
GOOD BOY... HE'S DROPPED A LADDER!
WWA-171
© 1955, King Features Syndicate, Inc., World rights reserved.

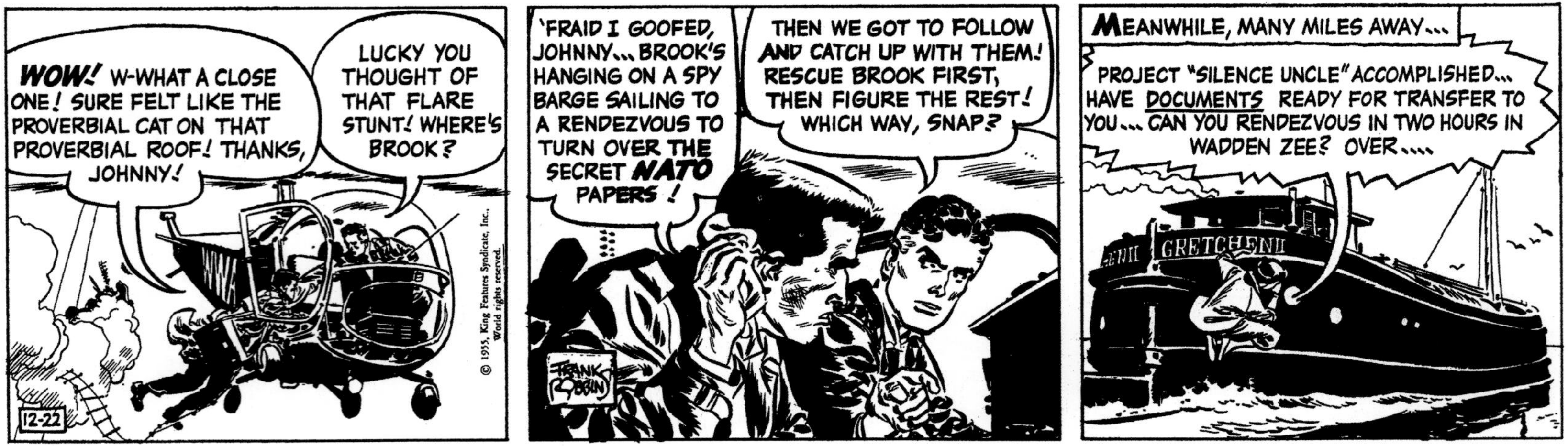
12-22
WOW! W-WHAT A CLOSE ONE! SURE FELT LIKE THE PROVERBIAL CAT ON THAT PROVERBIAL ROOF! THANKS, JOHNNY!
LUCKY YOU THOUGHT OF THAT FLARE STUNT! WHERE'S BROOK?
© 1955, King Features Syndicate, Inc., World rights reserved.
'FRAID I GOOFED, JOHNNY... BROOK'S HANGING ON A SPY BARGE SAILING TO A RENDEZVOUS TO TURN OVER THE SECRET NATO PAPERS!
THEN WE GOT TO FOLLOW AND CATCH UP WITH THEM! RESCUE BROOK FIRST, THEN FIGURE THE REST! WHICH WAY, SNAP?
MEANWHILE, MANY MILES AWAY...
PROJECT "SILENCE UNCLE" ACCOMPLISHED... HAVE DOCUMENTS READY FOR TRANSFER TO YOU... CAN YOU RENDEZVOUS IN TWO HOURS IN WADDEN ZEE? OVER....
GRETCHEN II

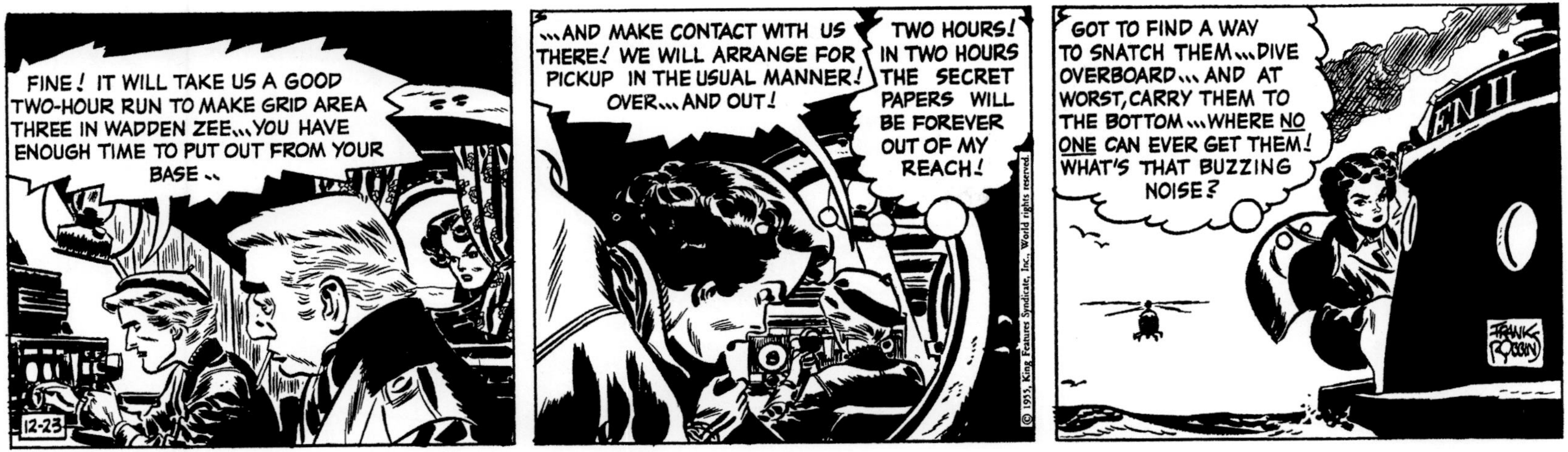
FINE! IT WILL TAKE US A GOOD TWO-HOUR RUN TO MAKE GRID AREA THREE IN WADDEN ZEE... YOU HAVE ENOUGH TIME TO PUT OUT FROM YOUR BASE..
12-23
...AND MAKE CONTACT WITH US THERE! WE WILL ARRANGE FOR PICKUP IN THE USUAL MANNER! OVER... AND OUT!
TWO HOURS! IN TWO HOURS THE SECRET PAPERS WILL BE FOREVER OUT OF MY REACH!
© 1955, King Features Syndicate, Inc., World rights reserved.
GOT TO FIND A WAY TO SNATCH THEM... DIVE OVERBOARD... AND AT WORST, CARRY THEM TO THE BOTTOM... WHERE NO ONE CAN EVER GET THEM! WHAT'S THAT BUZZING NOISE?
EN II
FRANK ROBBINS

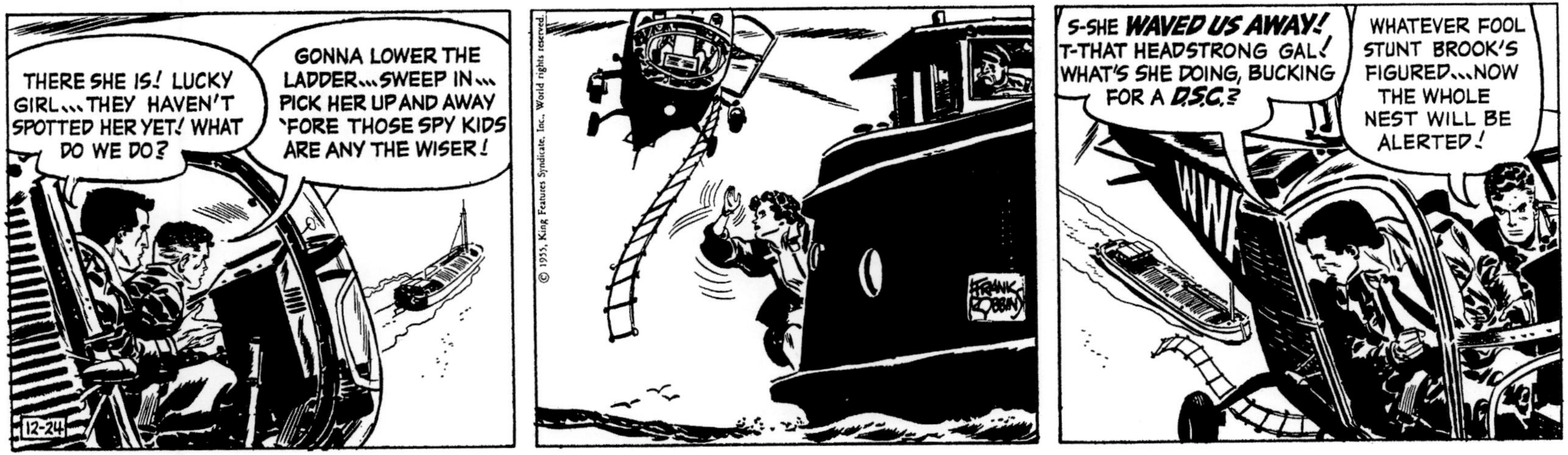
THERE SHE IS! LUCKY GIRL... THEY HAVEN'T SPOTTED HER YET! WHAT DO WE DO?
GONNA LOWER THE LADDER... SWEEP IN... PICK HER UP AND AWAY 'FORE THOSE SPY KIDS ARE ANY THE WISER!
12-24
© 1955, King Features Syndicate, Inc., World rights reserved.
FRANK ROBBINS
S-SHE WAVED US AWAY! T-THAT HEADSTRONG GAL! WHAT'S SHE DOING, BUCKING FOR A D.S.C.?
WHATEVER FOOL STUNT BROOK'S FIGURED... NOW THE WHOLE NEST WILL BE ALERTED!

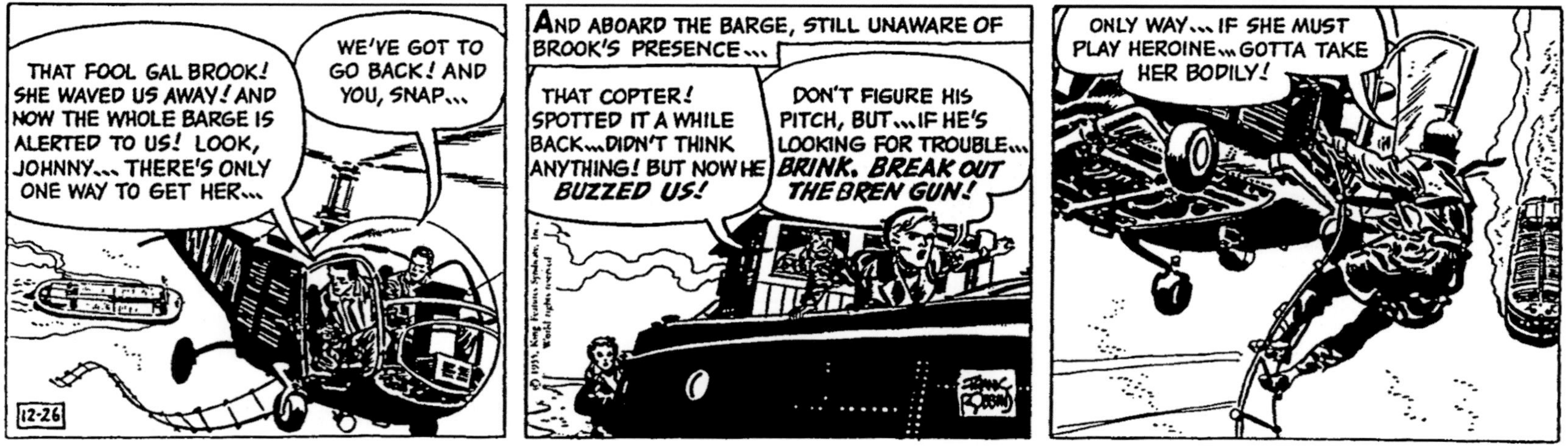
12-26
THAT FOOL GAL BROOK! SHE WAVED US AWAY! AND NOW THE WHOLE BARGE IS ALERTED TO US! LOOK, JOHNNY... THERE'S ONLY ONE WAY TO GET HER...
WE'VE GOT TO GO BACK! AND YOU, SNAP...
AND ABOARD THE BARGE, STILL UNAWARE OF BROOK'S PRESENCE...
THAT COPTER! SPOTTED IT A WHILE BACK...DIDN'T THINK ANYTHING! BUT NOW HE BUZZED US!
DON'T FIGURE HIS PITCH, BUT...IF HE'S LOOKING FOR TROUBLE... BRINK. BREAK OUT THE BREN GUN!
FRANK ROBBINS
ONLY WAY... IF SHE MUST PLAY HEROINE...GOTTA TAKE HER BODILY!

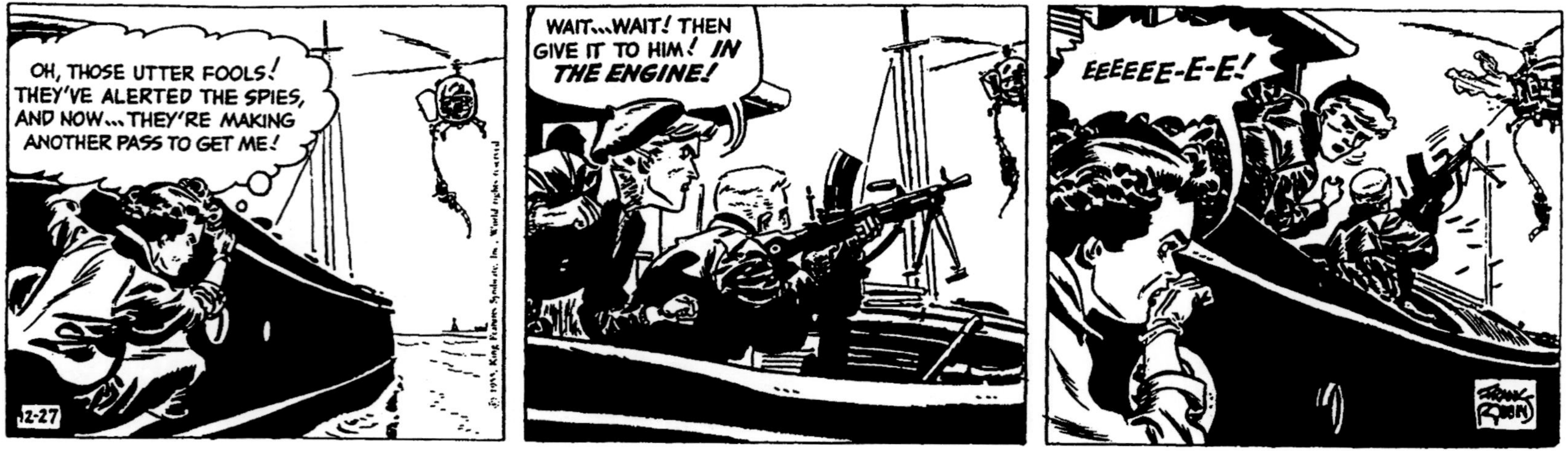
12-27
OH, THOSE UTTER FOOLS! THEY'VE ALERTED THE SPIES, AND NOW...THEY'RE MAKING ANOTHER PASS TO GET ME!
WAIT...WAIT! THEN GIVE IT TO HIM! IN THE ENGINE!
EEEEEE-E-E!
FRANK ROBBINS

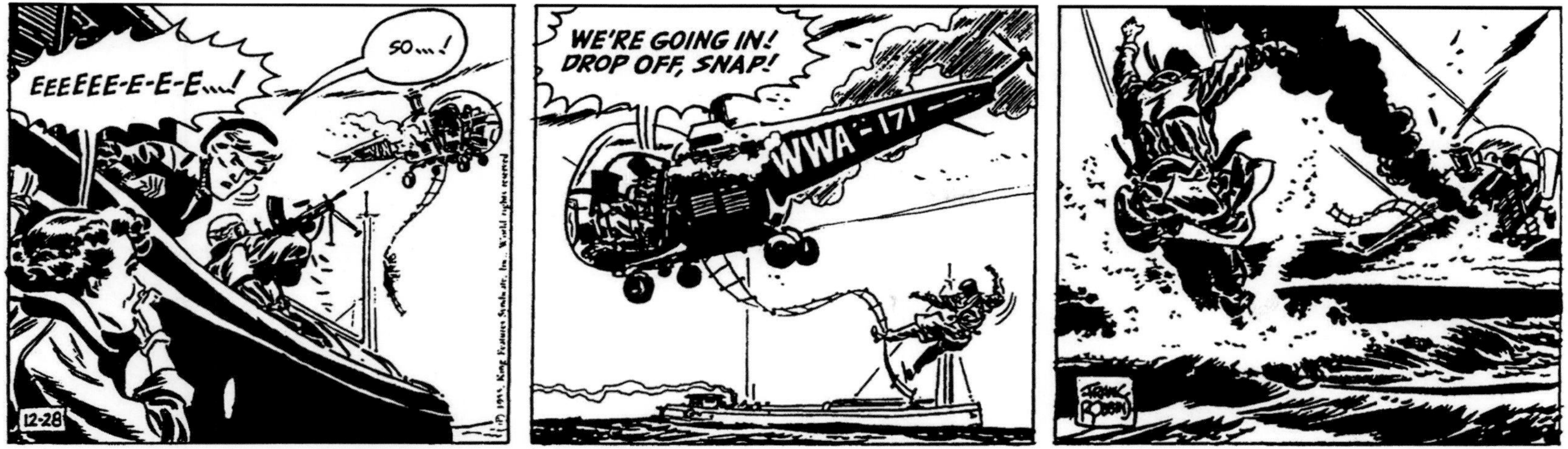
EEEEEE-E-E-E...!
SO...!
12-28
WE'RE GOING IN! DROP OFF, SNAP!
WWA-171
FRANK ROBBINS

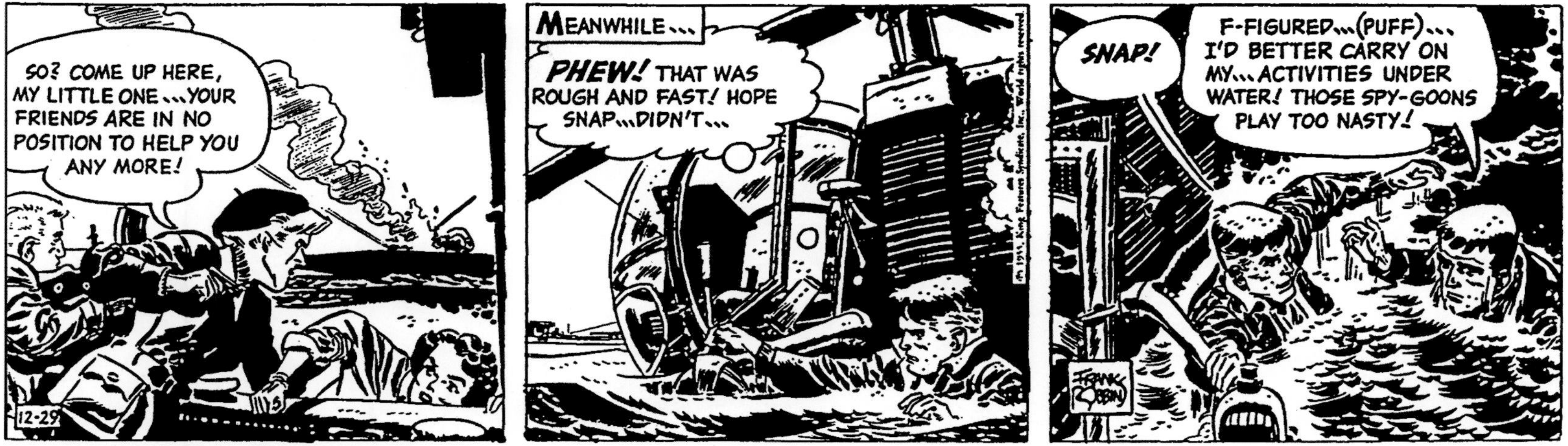
SO? COME UP HERE, MY LITTLE ONE...YOUR FRIENDS ARE IN NO POSITION TO HELP YOU ANY MORE!
12-29
MEANWHILE...
PHEW! THAT WAS ROUGH AND FAST! HOPE SNAP...DIDN'T...
SNAP!
F-FIGURED...(PUFF)... I'D BETTER CARRY ON MY...ACTIVITIES UNDER WATER! THOSE SPY-GOONS PLAY TOO NASTY!
FRANK ROBBINS

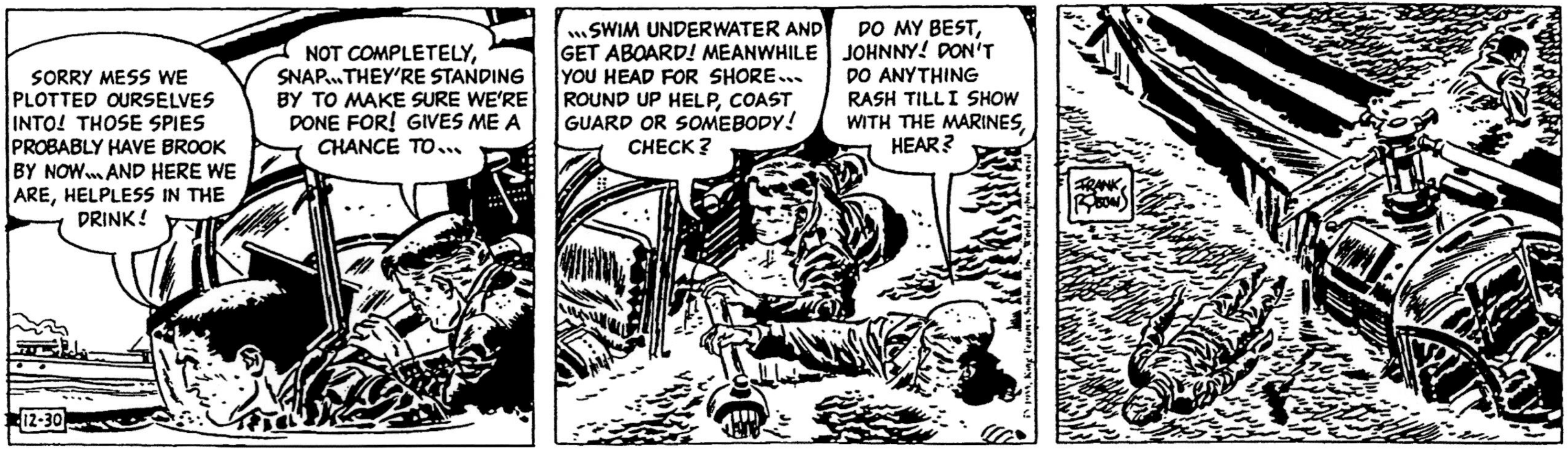
SORRY MESS WE PLOTTED OURSELVES INTO! THOSE SPIES PROBABLY HAVE BROOK BY NOW... AND HERE WE ARE, HELPLESS IN THE DRINK!
NOT COMPLETELY, SNAP... THEY'RE STANDING BY TO MAKE SURE WE'RE DONE FOR! GIVES ME A CHANCE TO...
12-30
...SWIM UNDERWATER AND GET ABOARD! MEANWHILE YOU HEAD FOR SHORE... ROUND UP HELP, COAST GUARD OR SOMEBODY! CHECK?
DO MY BEST, JOHNNY! DON'T DO ANYTHING RASH TILL I SHOW WITH THE MARINES, HEAR?
FRANK ROBBINS

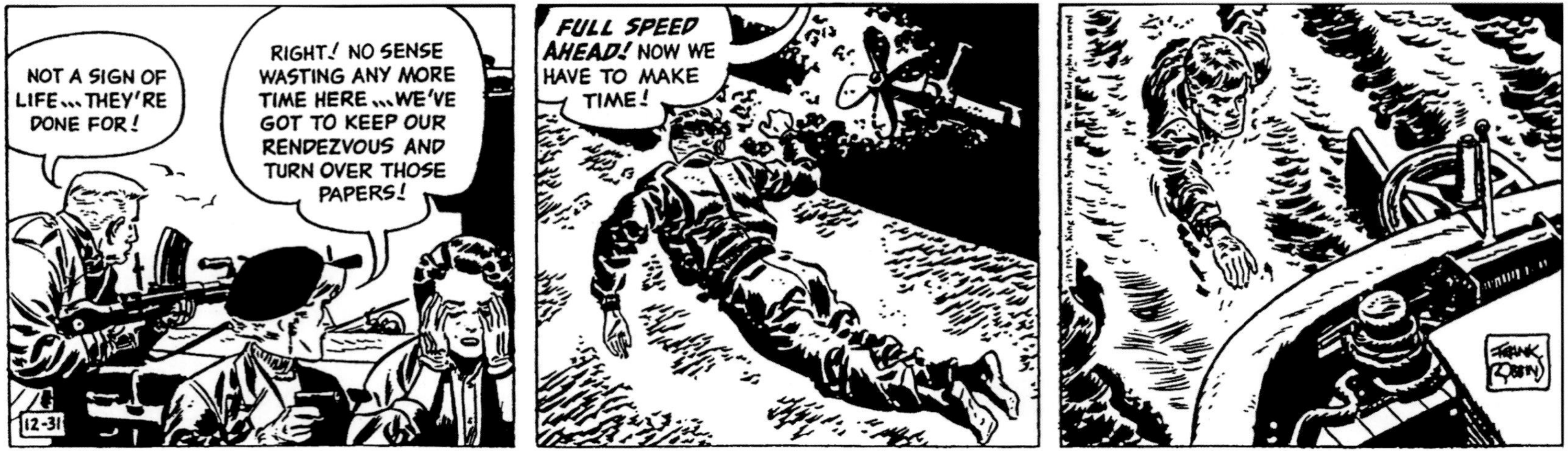
NOT A SIGN OF LIFE... THEY'RE DONE FOR!
RIGHT! NO SENSE WASTING ANY MORE TIME HERE... WE'VE GOT TO KEEP OUR RENDEZVOUS AND TURN OVER THOSE PAPERS!
12-31
FULL SPEED AHEAD! NOW WE HAVE TO MAKE TIME!
FRANK ROBBINS

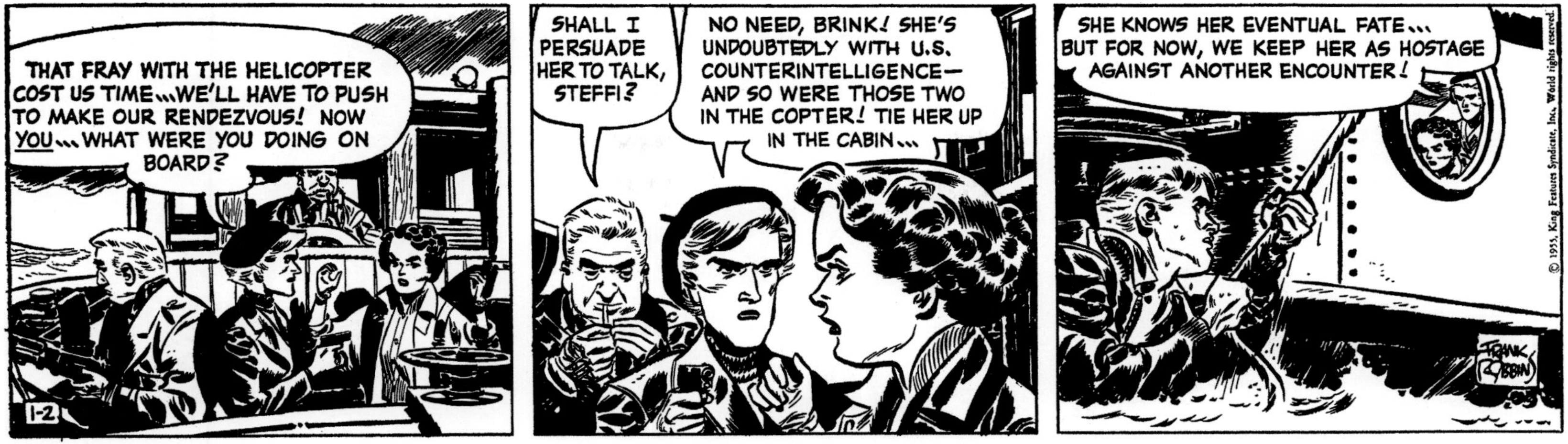
1-2
THAT FRAY WITH THE HELICOPTER COST US TIME... WE'LL HAVE TO PUSH TO MAKE OUR RENDEZVOUS! NOW YOU... WHAT WERE YOU DOING ON BOARD?
SHALL I PERSUADE HER TO TALK, STEFFI?
NO NEED, BRINK! SHE'S UNDOUBTEDLY WITH U.S. COUNTERINTELLIGENCE— AND SO WERE THOSE TWO IN THE COPTER! TIE HER UP IN THE CABIN...
SHE KNOWS HER EVENTUAL FATE... BUT FOR NOW, WE KEEP HER AS HOSTAGE AGAINST ANOTHER ENCOUNTER!
FRANK ROBBINS
© 1955, King Features Syndicate, Inc., World rights reserved.

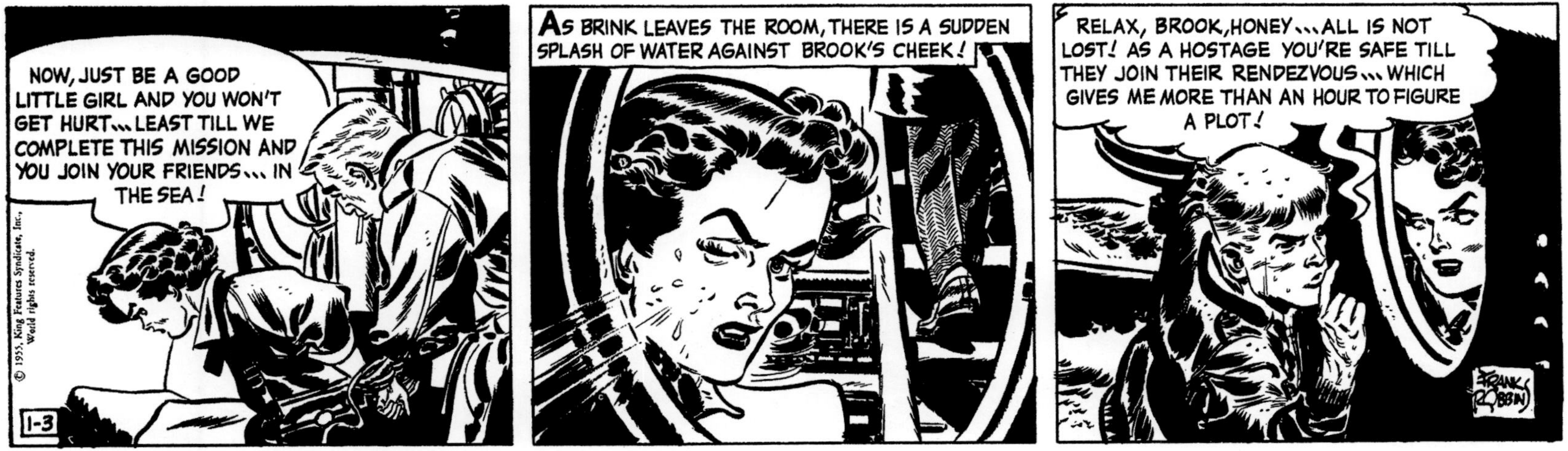
1-3
NOW, JUST BE A GOOD LITTLE GIRL AND YOU WON'T GET HURT... LEAST TILL WE COMPLETE THIS MISSION AND YOU JOIN YOUR FRIENDS... IN THE SEA!
© 1955, King Features Syndicate, Inc., World rights reserved.
AS BRINK LEAVES THE ROOM, THERE IS A SUDDEN SPLASH OF WATER AGAINST BROOK'S CHEEK!
RELAX, BROOK, HONEY... ALL IS NOT LOST! AS A HOSTAGE YOU'RE SAFE TILL THEY JOIN THEIR RENDEZVOUS... WHICH GIVES ME MORE THAN AN HOUR TO FIGURE A PLOT!
FRANK ROBBINS

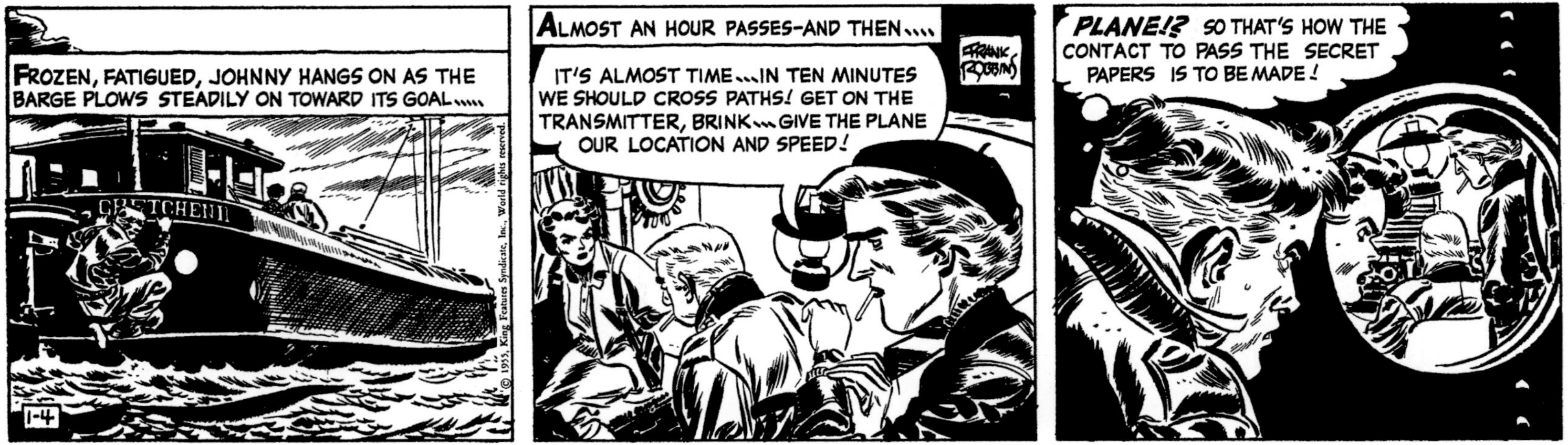
FROZEN, FATIGUED, JOHNNY HANGS ON AS THE BARGE PLOWS STEADILY ON TOWARD ITS GOAL.....
GRETCHEN II
© 1955, King Features Syndicate, Inc., World rights reserved.
1-4
ALMOST AN HOUR PASSES—AND THEN....
FRANK ROBBINS
IT'S ALMOST TIME....IN TEN MINUTES WE SHOULD CROSS PATHS! GET ON THE TRANSMITTER, BRINK....GIVE THE PLANE OUR LOCATION AND SPEED!
PLANE!? SO THAT'S HOW THE CONTACT TO PASS THE SECRET PAPERS IS TO BE MADE!

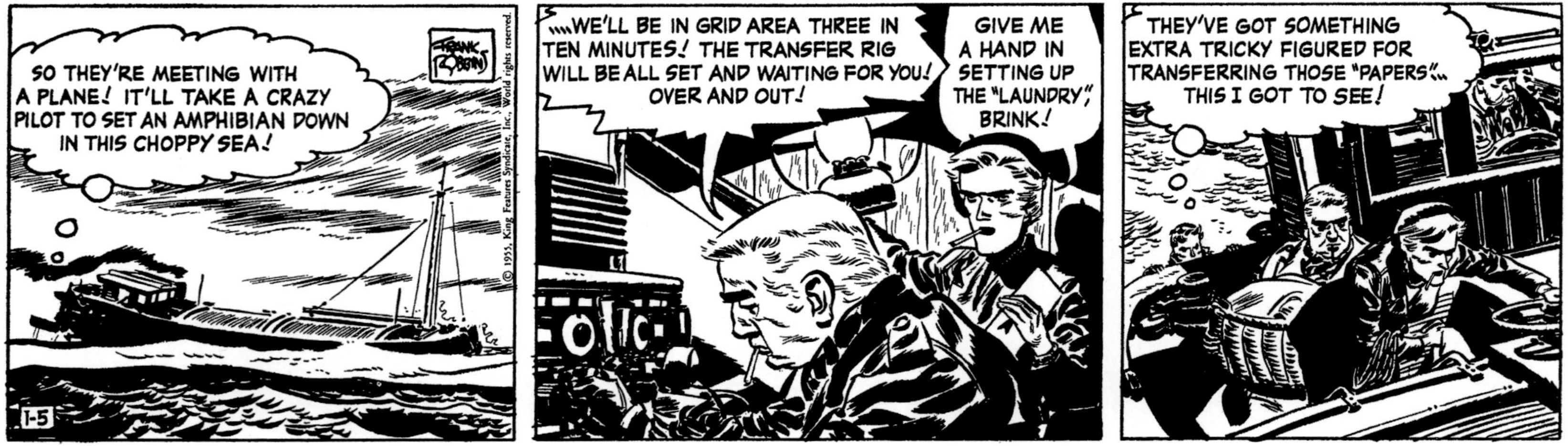
FRANK ROBBINS
SO THEY'RE MEETING WITH A PLANE! IT'LL TAKE A CRAZY PILOT TO SET AN AMPHIBIAN DOWN IN THIS CHOPPY SEA!
© 1955, King Features Syndicate, Inc., World rights reserved.
1-5
....WE'LL BE IN GRID AREA THREE IN TEN MINUTES! THE TRANSFER RIG WILL BE ALL SET AND WAITING FOR YOU! OVER AND OUT!
GIVE ME A HAND IN SETTING UP THE "LAUNDRY", BRINK!
THEY'VE GOT SOMETHING EXTRA TRICKY FIGURED FOR TRANSFERRING THOSE "PAPERS"... THIS I GOT TO SEE!

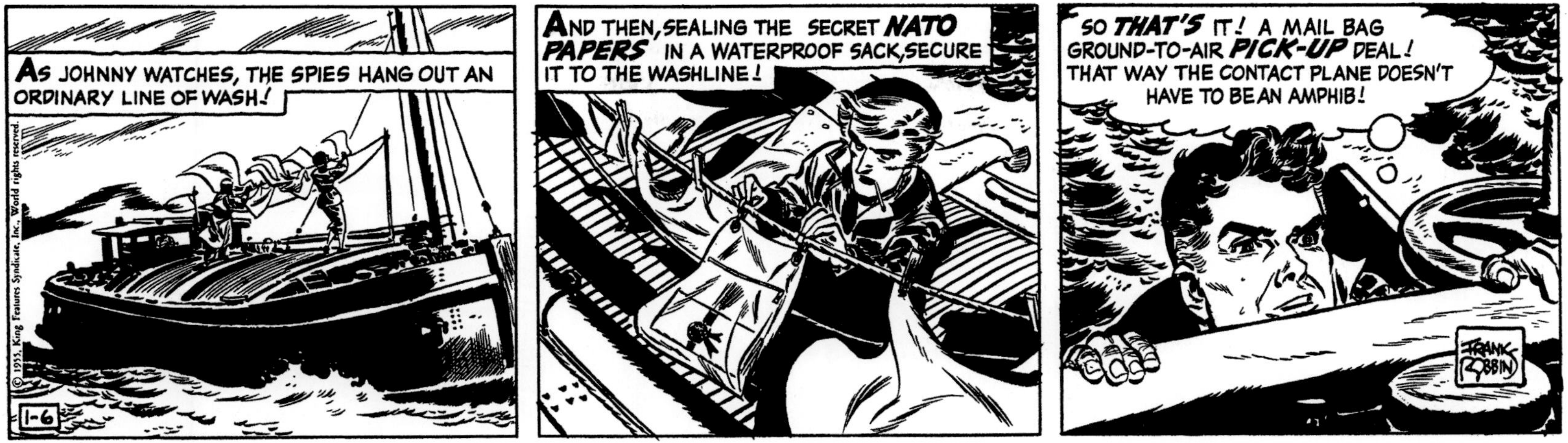
AS JOHNNY WATCHES, THE SPIES HANG OUT AN ORDINARY LINE OF WASH!
© 1955, King Features Syndicate, Inc., World rights reserved.
1-6
AND THEN, SEALING THE SECRET NATO PAPERS IN A WATERPROOF SACK, SECURE IT TO THE WASHLINE!
SO THAT'S IT! A MAIL BAG GROUND-TO-AIR PICK-UP DEAL! THAT WAY THE CONTACT PLANE DOESN'T HAVE TO BE AN AMPHIB!
FRANK ROBBINS

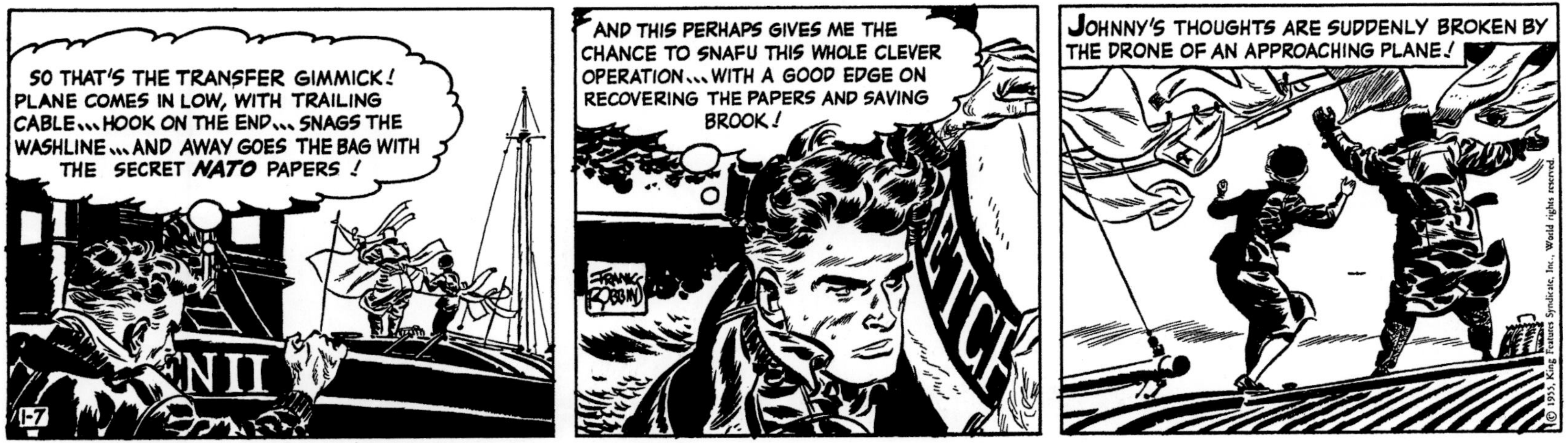
SO THAT'S THE TRANSFER GIMMICK! PLANE COMES IN LOW, WITH TRAILING CABLE... HOOK ON THE END... SNAGS THE WASHLINE... AND AWAY GOES THE BAG WITH THE SECRET NATO PAPERS!
1-7
AND THIS PERHAPS GIVES ME THE CHANCE TO SNAFU THIS WHOLE CLEVER OPERATION... WITH A GOOD EDGE ON RECOVERING THE PAPERS AND SAVING BROOK!
FRANK ROBBINS
JOHNNY'S THOUGHTS ARE SUDDENLY BROKEN BY THE DRONE OF AN APPROACHING PLANE!
© 1955, King Features Syndicate, Inc., World rights reserved.

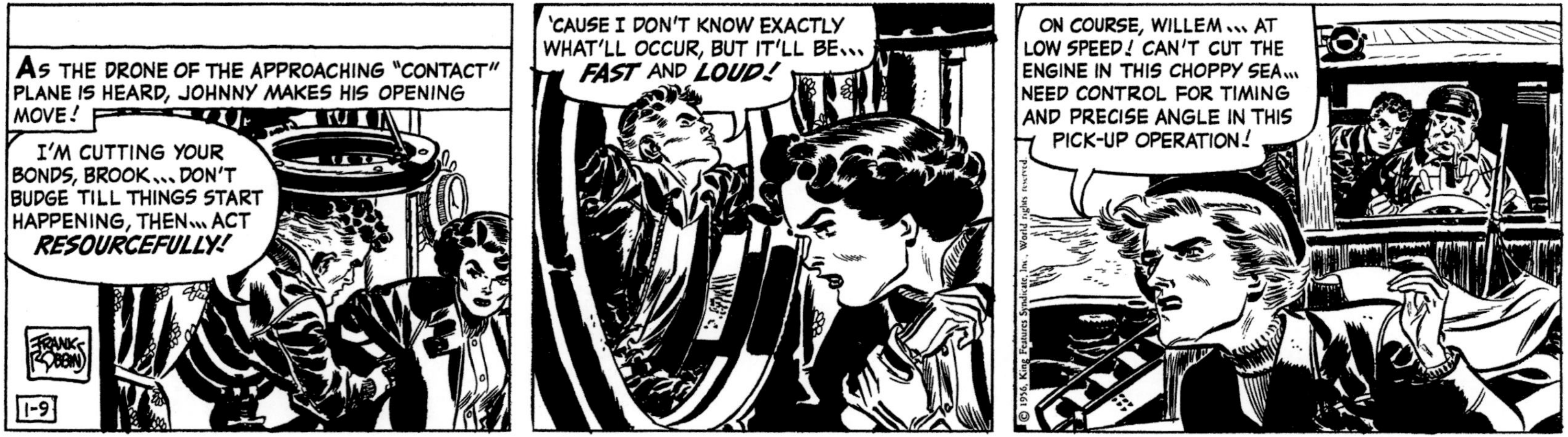
AS THE DRONE OF THE APPROACHING "CONTACT" PLANE IS HEARD, JOHNNY MAKES HIS OPENING MOVE!
I'M CUTTING YOUR BONDS, BROOK... DON'T BUDGE TILL THINGS START HAPPENING, THEN... ACT RESOURCEFULLY!
FRANK ROBBINS
1-9
'CAUSE I DON'T KNOW EXACTLY WHAT'LL OCCUR, BUT IT'LL BE... FAST AND LOUD!
ON COURSE, WILLEM... AT LOW SPEED! CAN'T CUT THE ENGINE IN THIS CHOPPY SEA... NEED CONTROL FOR TIMING AND PRECISE ANGLE IN THIS PICK-UP OPERATION!
© 1956, King Features Syndicate, Inc., World rights reserved.

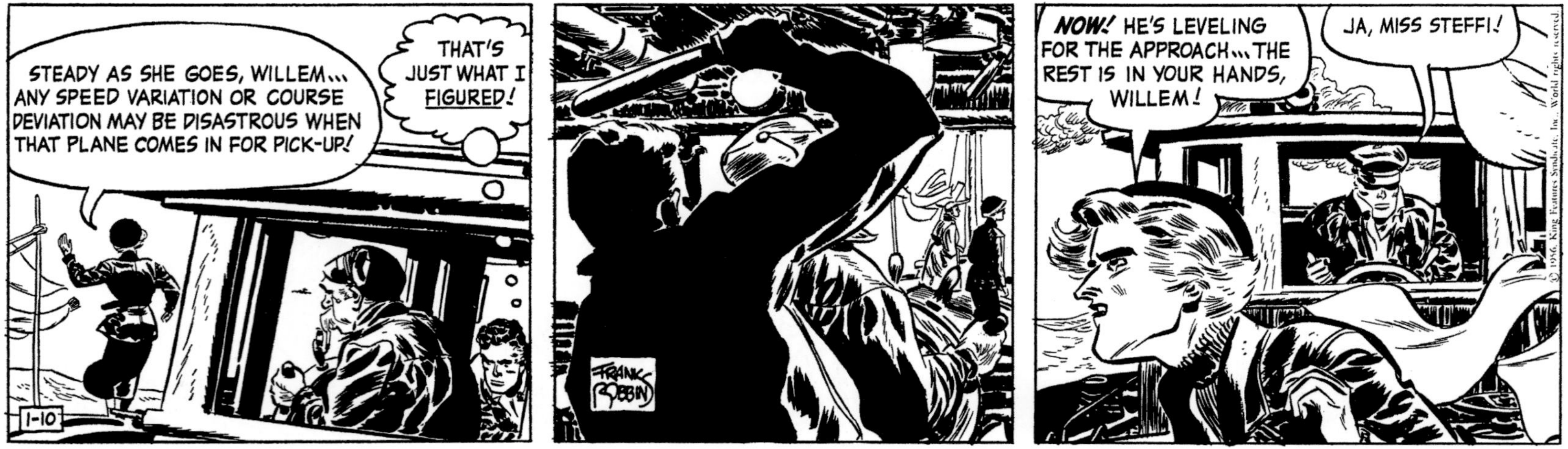
STEADY AS SHE GOES, WILLEM... ANY SPEED VARIATION OR COURSE DEVIATION MAY BE DISASTROUS WHEN THAT PLANE COMES IN FOR PICK-UP!
THAT'S JUST WHAT I FIGURED!
1-10
FRANK ROBBINS
NOW! HE'S LEVELING FOR THE APPROACH... THE REST IS IN YOUR HANDS, WILLEM!
JA, MISS STEFFI!
© 1956, King Features Syndicate, Inc., World rights reserved.

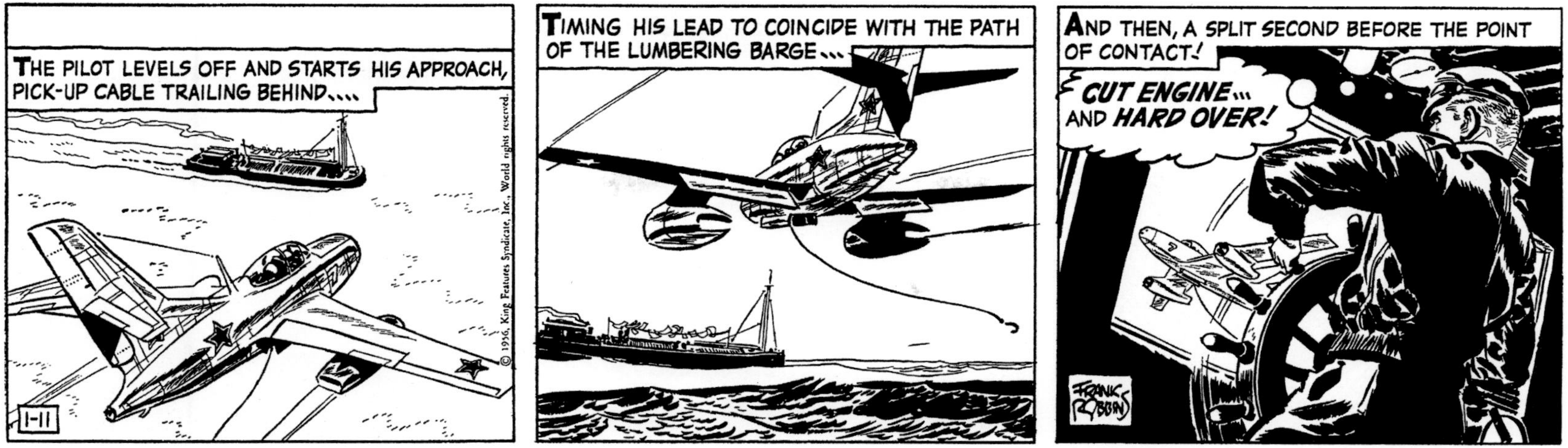
THE PILOT LEVELS OFF AND STARTS HIS APPROACH, PICK-UP CABLE TRAILING BEHIND....
© 1956, King Features Syndicate, Inc., World rights reserved.
1-11
TIMING HIS LEAD TO COINCIDE WITH THE PATH OF THE LUMBERING BARGE...
AND THEN, A SPLIT SECOND BEFORE THE POINT OF CONTACT!
CUT ENGINE... AND HARD OVER!
FRANK ROBBINS

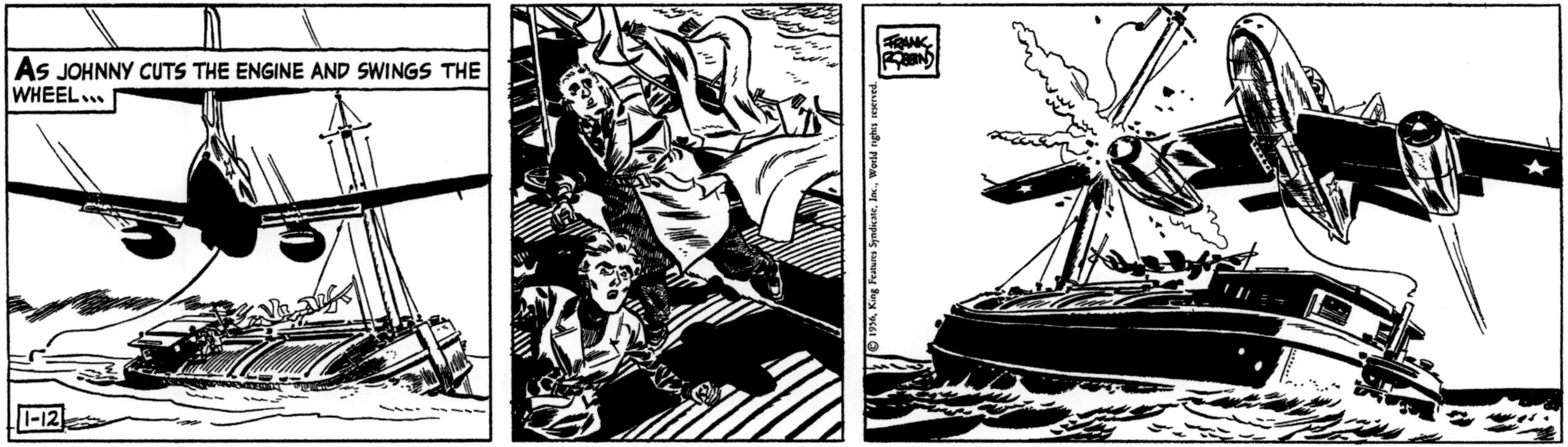
AS JOHNNY CUTS THE ENGINE AND SWINGS THE WHEEL...
1-12
© 1956, King Features Syndicate, Inc., World rights reserved.
FRANK ROBBINS

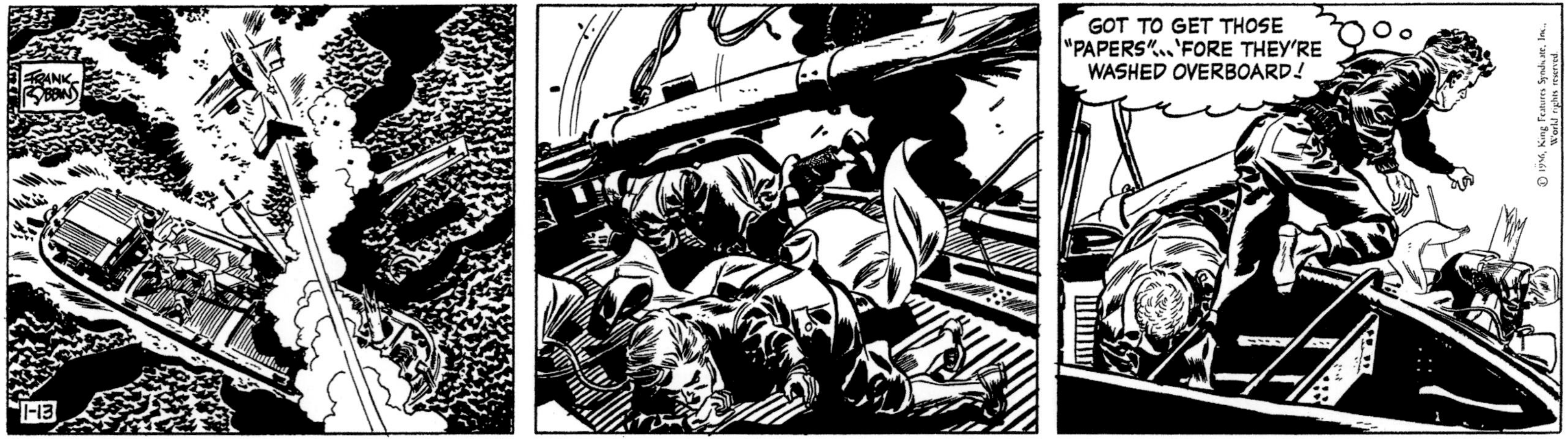
FRANK ROBBINS
1-13
GOT TO GET THOSE "PAPERS"... 'FORE THEY'RE WASHED OVERBOARD!
© 1956, King Features Syndicate, Inc., World rights reserved.

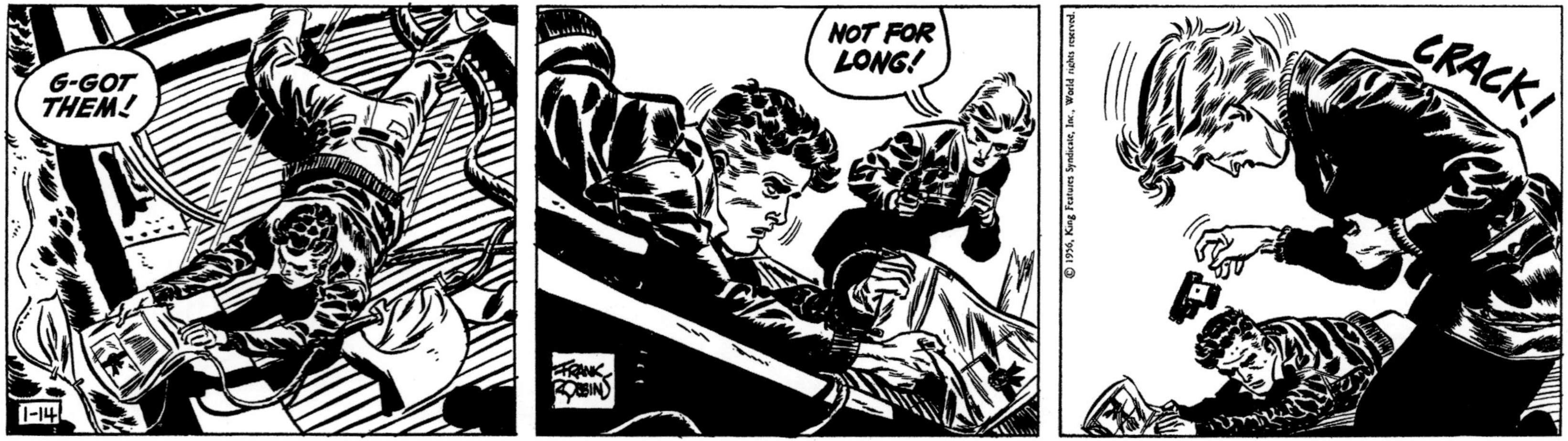
G-GOT THEM!
1-14
NOT FOR LONG!
FRANK ROBBINS
© 1956, King Features Syndicate, Inc., World rights reserved.
CRACK!

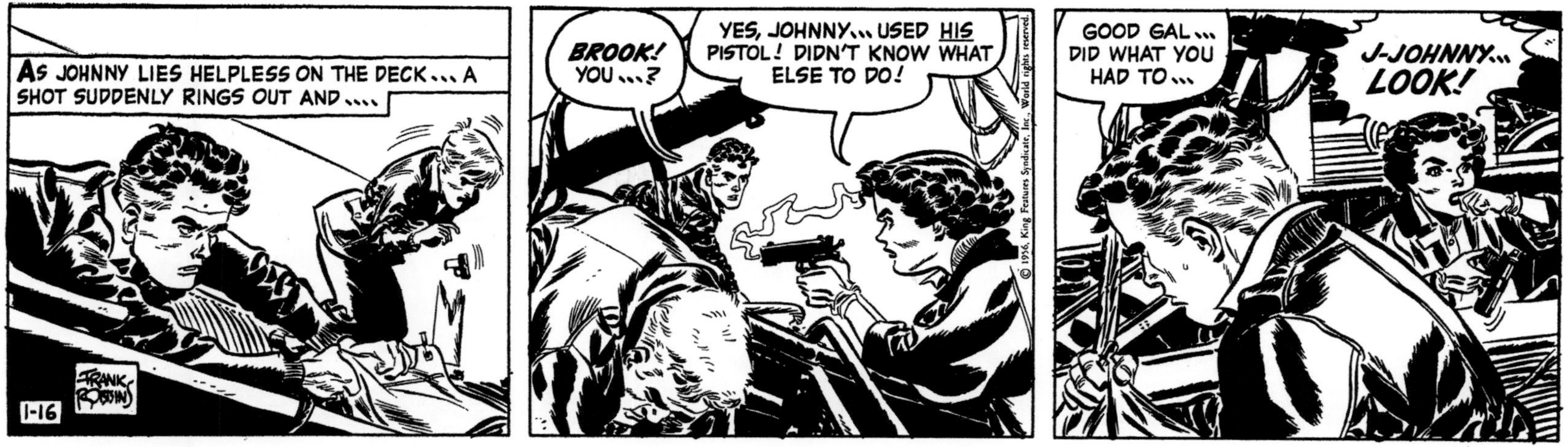
AS JOHNNY LIES HELPLESS ON THE DECK... A SHOT SUDDENLY RINGS OUT AND....
FRANK ROBBINS
1-16
BROOK! YOU...?
YES, JOHNNY... USED HIS PISTOL! DIDN'T KNOW WHAT ELSE TO DO!
© 1956, King Features Syndicate, Inc., World rights reserved.
GOOD GAL... DID WHAT YOU HAD TO...
J-JOHNNY... LOOK!

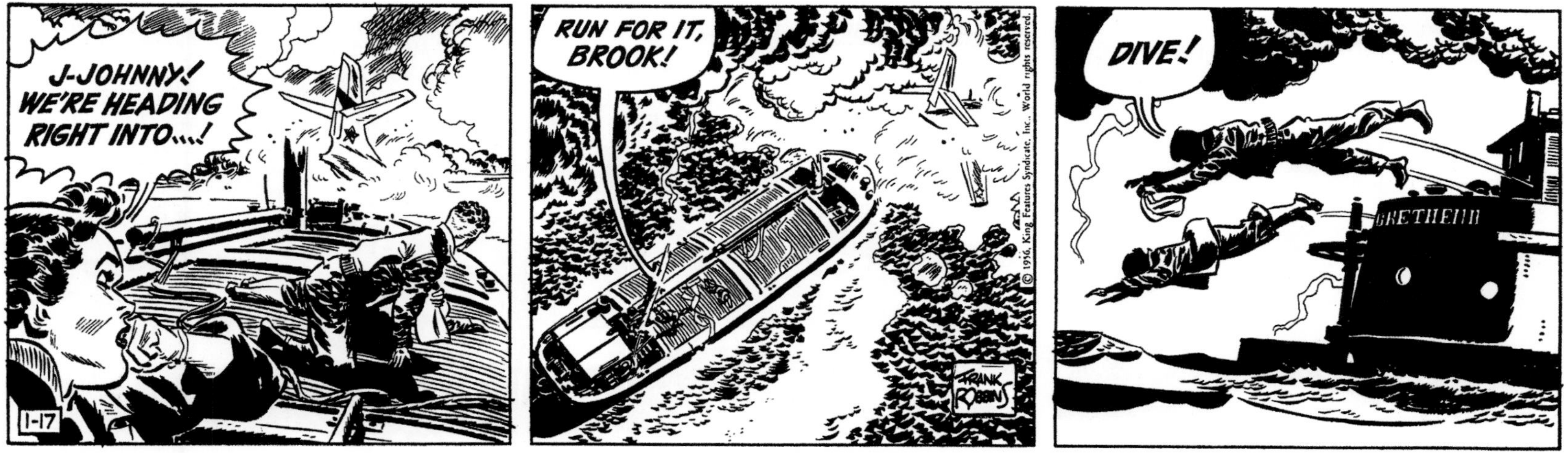
J-JOHNNY! WE'RE HEADING RIGHT INTO...!
1-17
RUN FOR IT, BROOK!
© 1956, King Features Syndicate, Inc., World rights reserved.
FRANK ROBBINS
DIVE!

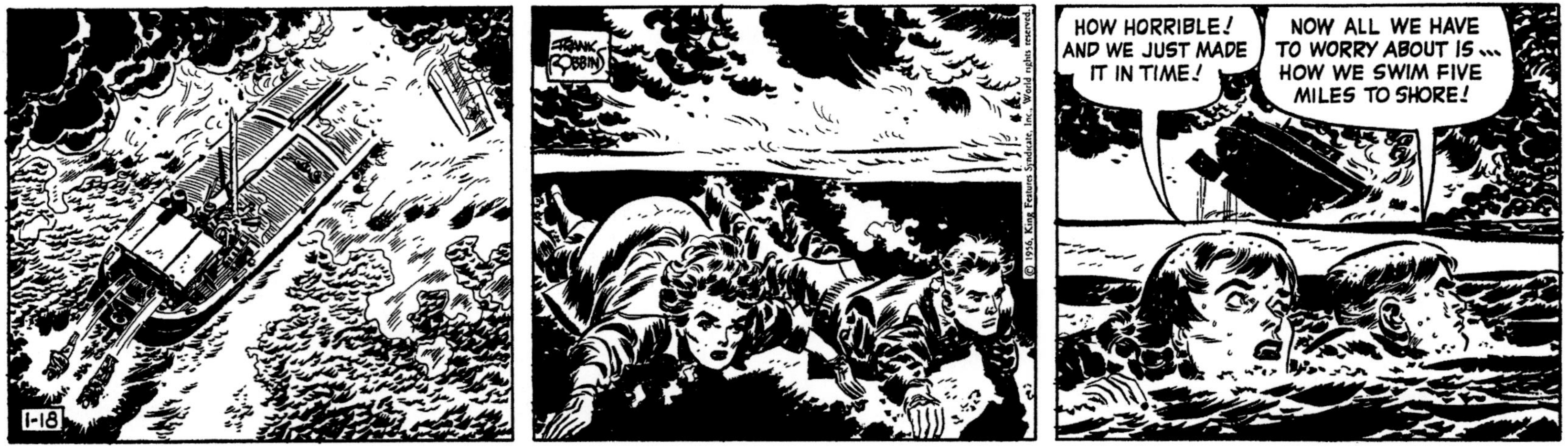
1-18
FRANK ROBBINS
© 1956, King Features Syndicate, Inc., World rights reserved.
HOW HORRIBLE! AND WE JUST MADE IT IN TIME!
NOW ALL WE HAVE TO WORRY ABOUT IS... HOW WE SWIM FIVE MILES TO SHORE!

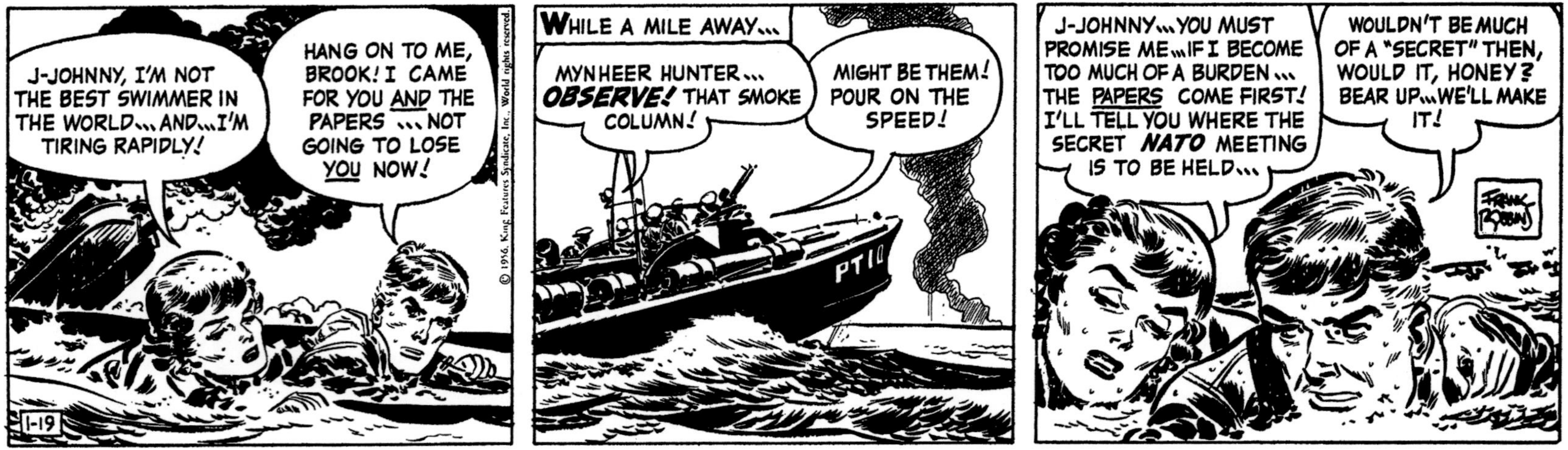
J-JOHNNY, I'M NOT THE BEST SWIMMER IN THE WORLD... AND... I'M TIRING RAPIDLY!
HANG ON TO ME, BROOK! I CAME FOR YOU AND THE PAPERS ... NOT GOING TO LOSE YOU NOW!
© 1956, King Features Syndicate, Inc., World rights reserved.
1-19
WHILE A MILE AWAY...
MYNHEER HUNTER... OBSERVE! THAT SMOKE COLUMN!
MIGHT BE THEM! POUR ON THE SPEED!
PT1
J-JOHNNY... YOU MUST PROMISE ME... IF I BECOME TOO MUCH OF A BURDEN ... THE PAPERS COME FIRST! I'LL TELL YOU WHERE THE SECRET NATO MEETING IS TO BE HELD...
WOULDN'T BE MUCH OF A "SECRET" THEN, WOULD IT, HONEY? BEAR UP... WE'LL MAKE IT!
FRANK ROBBINS

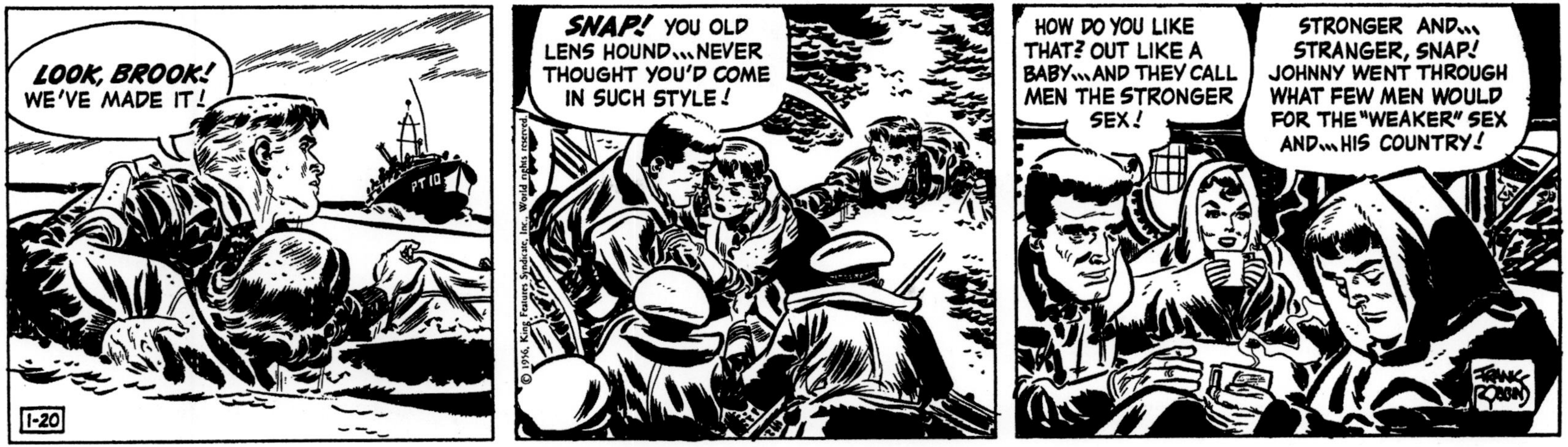
LOOK, BROOK! WE'VE MADE IT!
PT 10
1-20
SNAP! YOU OLD LENS HOUND... NEVER THOUGHT YOU'D COME IN SUCH STYLE!
© 1956, King Features Syndicate, Inc., World rights reserved.
HOW DO YOU LIKE THAT? OUT LIKE A BABY... AND THEY CALL MEN THE STRONGER SEX!
STRONGER AND... STRANGER, SNAP! JOHNNY WENT THROUGH WHAT FEW MEN WOULD FOR THE "WEAKER" SEX AND... HIS COUNTRY!
FRANK ROBBINS

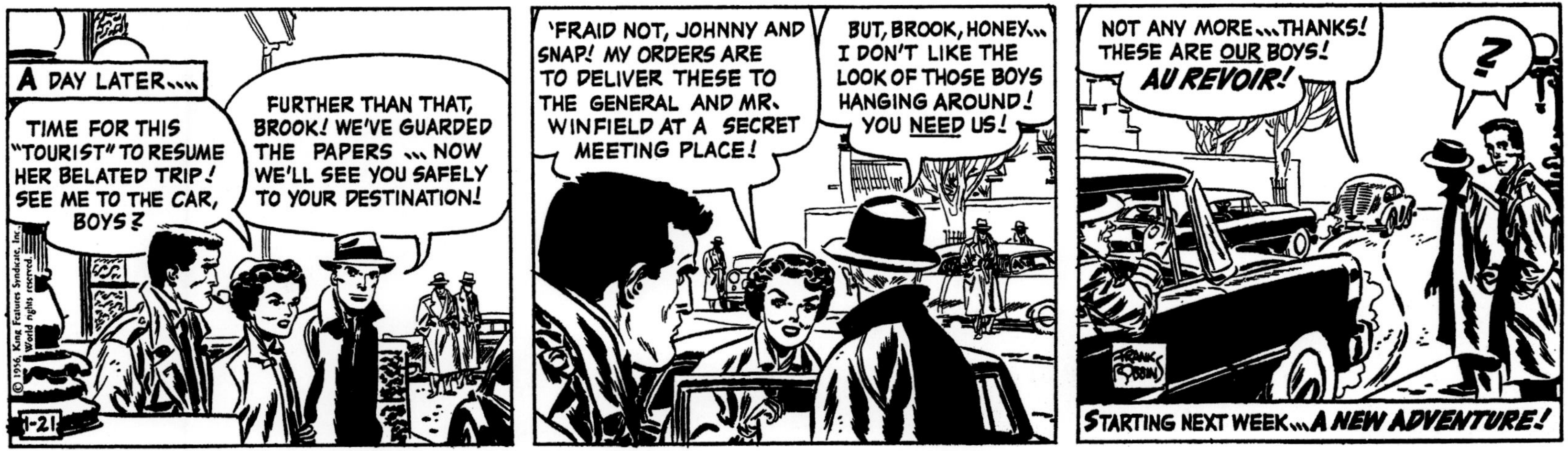
A DAY LATER....
TIME FOR THIS "TOURIST" TO RESUME HER BELATED TRIP! SEE ME TO THE CAR, BOYS?
FURTHER THAN THAT, BROOK! WE'VE GUARDED THE PAPERS ... NOW WE'LL SEE YOU SAFELY TO YOUR DESTINATION!
© 1956, King Features Syndicate, Inc., World rights reserved.
1-21
'FRAID NOT, JOHNNY AND SNAP! MY ORDERS ARE TO DELIVER THESE TO THE GENERAL AND MR. WINFIELD AT A SECRET MEETING PLACE!
BUT, BROOK, HONEY... I DON'T LIKE THE LOOK OF THOSE BOYS HANGING AROUND! YOU NEED US!
NOT ANY MORE...THANKS! THESE ARE OUR BOYS! AU REVOIR!
?
FRANK ROBBINS
STARTING NEXT WEEK...A NEW ADVENTURE!

JOHNNY HAZARD

Chapter Seven: Project Heat-Barrier

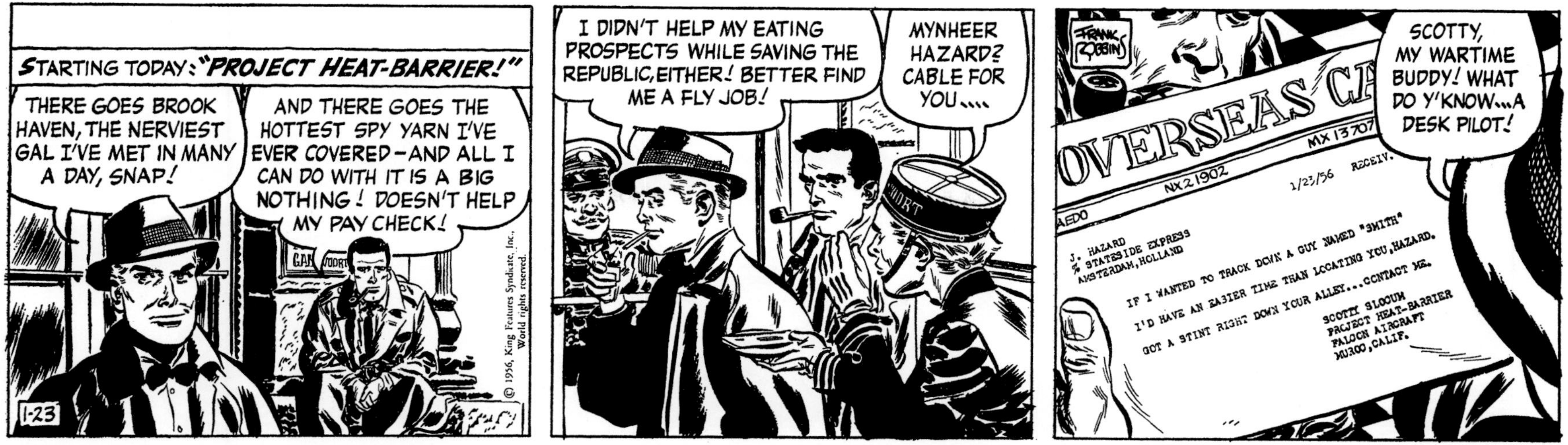
STARTING TODAY: "PROJECT HEAT-BARRIER!"
THERE GOES BROOK HAVEN, THE NERVIEST GAL I'VE MET IN MANY A DAY, SNAP!
AND THERE GOES THE HOTTEST SPY YARN I'VE EVER COVERED—AND ALL I CAN DO WITH IT IS A BIG NOTHING! DOESN'T HELP MY PAY CHECK!
1-23
© 1956, King Features Syndicate, Inc., World rights reserved.
I DIDN'T HELP MY EATING PROSPECTS WHILE SAVING THE REPUBLIC, EITHER! BETTER FIND ME A FLY JOB!
MYNHEER HAZARD? CABLE FOR YOU....
FRANK ROBBINS
OVERSEAS CA
NX2 1902
MX 13707
1/23/56 RECEIV.
J. HAZARD
% STATESIDE EXPRESS
AMSTERDAM, HOLLAND
IF I WANTED TO TRACK DOWN A GUY NAMED "SMITH"
I'D HAVE AN EASIER TIME THAN LOCATING YOU, HAZARD.
GOT A STINT RIGHT DOWN YOUR ALLEY...CONTACT ME.
SCOTTY SLOCUM
PROJECT HEAT-BARRIER
FALCON AIRCRAFT
MUROC, CALIF.
SCOTTY, MY WARTIME BUDDY! WHAT DO Y'KNOW...A DESK PILOT!

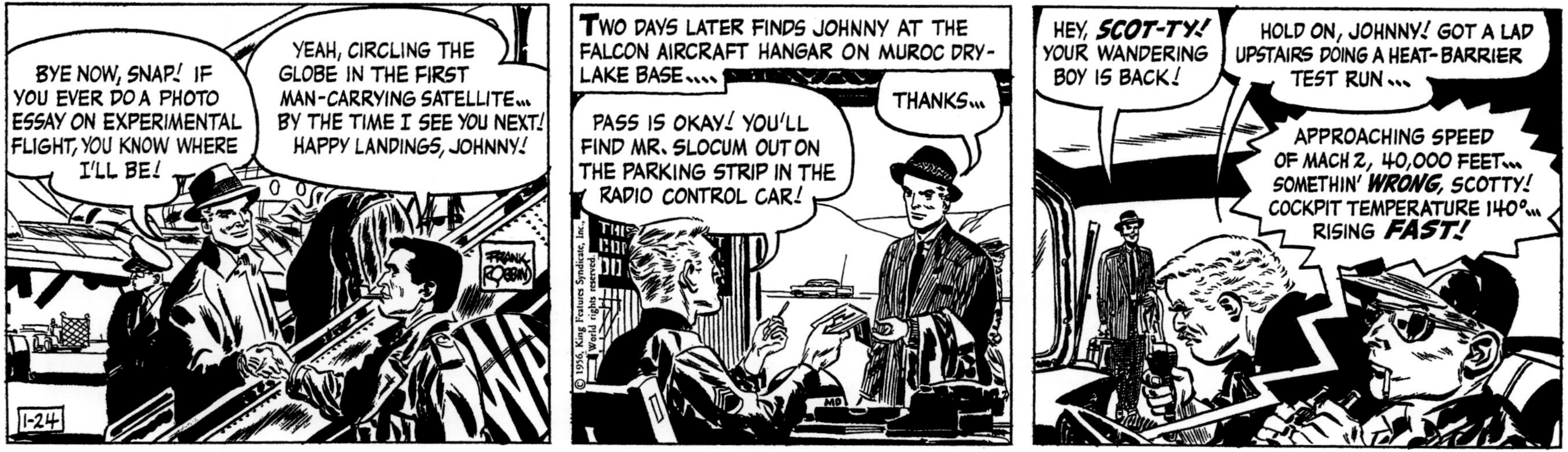
BYE NOW, SNAP! IF YOU EVER DO A PHOTO ESSAY ON EXPERIMENTAL FLIGHT, YOU KNOW WHERE I'LL BE!
YEAH, CIRCLING THE GLOBE IN THE FIRST MAN-CARRYING SATELLITE... BY THE TIME I SEE YOU NEXT! HAPPY LANDINGS, JOHNNY!
FRANK ROBBINS
1-24
TWO DAYS LATER FINDS JOHNNY AT THE FALCON AIRCRAFT HANGAR ON MUROC DRY-LAKE BASE....
PASS IS OKAY! YOU'LL FIND MR. SLOCUM OUT ON THE PARKING STRIP IN THE RADIO CONTROL CAR!
THANKS...
© 1956, King Features Syndicate, Inc., World rights reserved.
HEY, SCOT-TY! YOUR WANDERING BOY IS BACK!
HOLD ON, JOHNNY! GOT A LAD UPSTAIRS DOING A HEAT-BARRIER TEST RUN...
APPROACHING SPEED OF MACH 2, 40,000 FEET... SOMETHIN' WRONG, SCOTTY! COCKPIT TEMPERATURE 140°... RISING FAST!

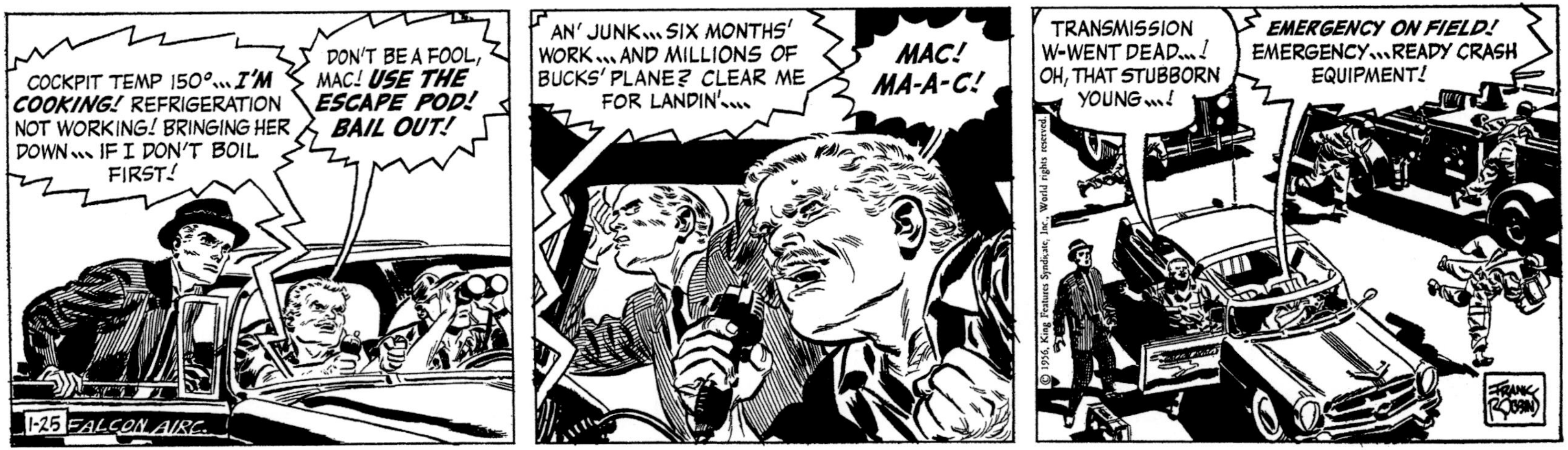
COCKPIT TEMP 150°... I'M COOKING! REFRIGERATION NOT WORKING! BRINGING HER DOWN... IF I DON'T BOIL FIRST!
DON'T BE A FOOL, MAC! USE THE ESCAPE POD! BAIL OUT!
1-25
FALCON AIRC.
AN' JUNK... SIX MONTHS' WORK... AND MILLIONS OF BUCKS' PLANE? CLEAR ME FOR LANDIN'....
MAC! MA-A-C!
TRANSMISSION W-WENT DEAD...! OH, THAT STUBBORN YOUNG...!
EMERGENCY ON FIELD! EMERGENCY... READY CRASH EQUIPMENT!
© 1956, King Features Syndicate, Inc., World rights reserved.
FRANK ROBBINS

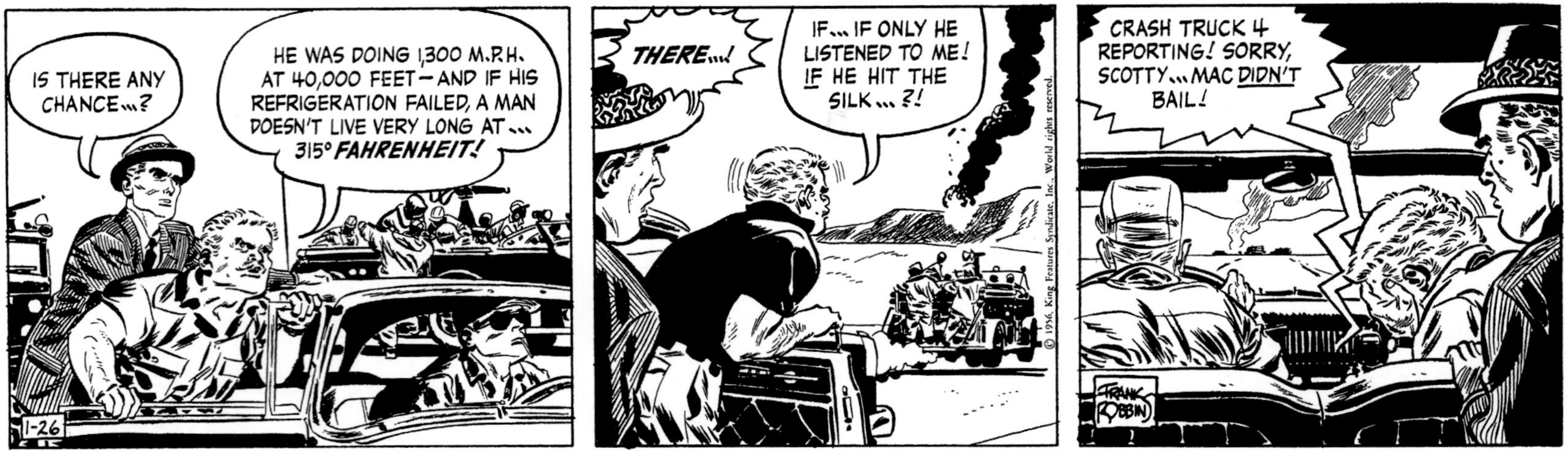
IS THERE ANY CHANCE...?
HE WAS DOING 1,300 M.P.H. AT 40,000 FEET—AND IF HIS REFRIGERATION FAILED, A MAN DOESN'T LIVE VERY LONG AT... 315° FAHRENHEIT!
1-26
THERE...!
IF... IF ONLY HE LISTENED TO ME! IF HE HIT THE SILK...?!
© 1956, King Features Syndicate, Inc., World rights reserved.
CRASH TRUCK 4 REPORTING! SORRY, SCOTTY... MAC DIDN'T BAIL!
FRANK ROBBINS

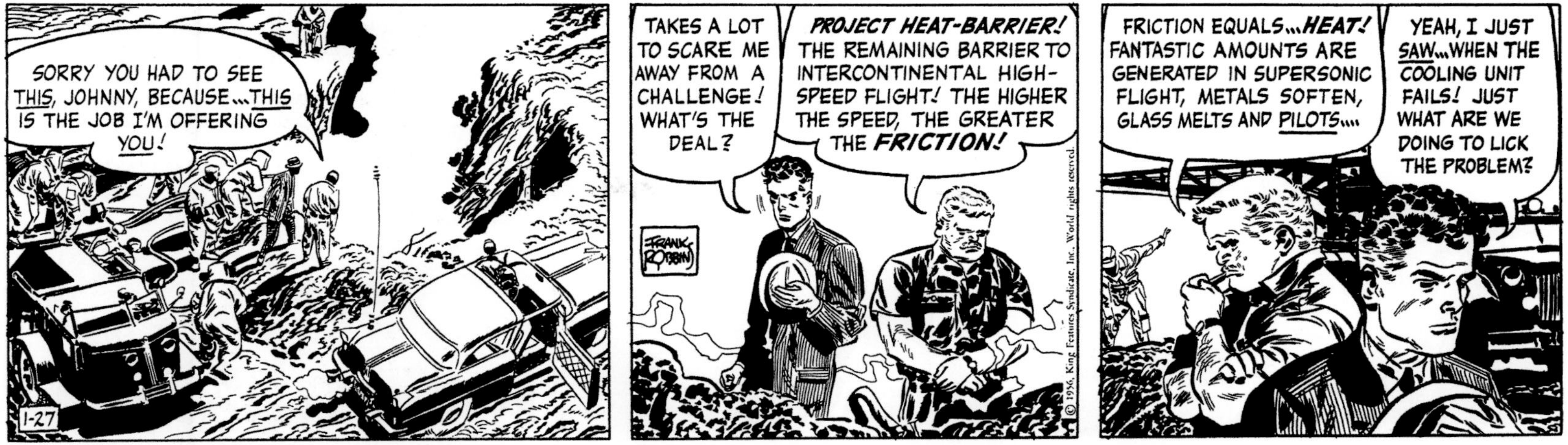
1-27
SORRY YOU HAD TO SEE THIS, JOHNNY, BECAUSE... THIS IS THE JOB I'M OFFERING YOU!
TAKES A LOT TO SCARE ME AWAY FROM A CHALLENGE! WHAT'S THE DEAL?
PROJECT HEAT-BARRIER! THE REMAINING BARRIER TO INTERCONTINENTAL HIGH-SPEED FLIGHT! THE HIGHER THE SPEED, THE GREATER THE FRICTION!
FRANK ROBBINS
© 1956, King Features Syndicate, Inc. World rights reserved.
FRICTION EQUALS... HEAT! FANTASTIC AMOUNTS ARE GENERATED IN SUPERSONIC FLIGHT, METALS SOFTEN, GLASS MELTS AND PILOTS....
YEAH, I JUST SAW... WHEN THE COOLING UNIT FAILS! JUST WHAT ARE WE DOING TO LICK THE PROBLEM?

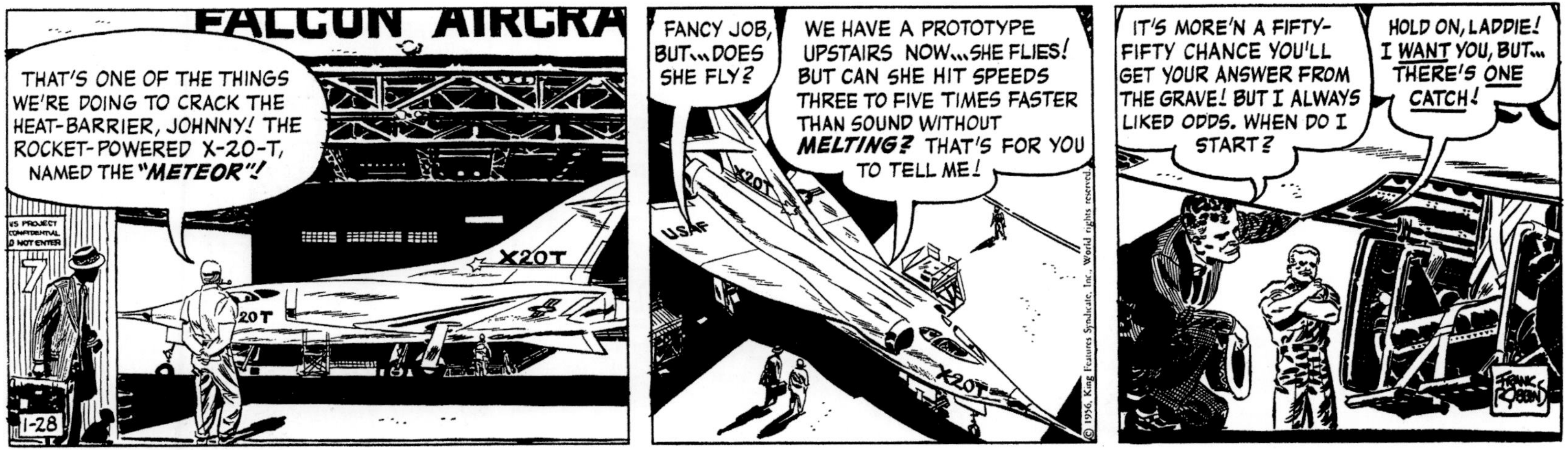
FALCON AIRCRA
THAT'S ONE OF THE THINGS WE'RE DOING TO CRACK THE HEAT-BARRIER, JOHNNY! THE ROCKET-POWERED X-20-T, NAMED THE "METEOR"!
X20T
1-28
FANCY JOB, BUT... DOES SHE FLY?
WE HAVE A PROTOTYPE UPSTAIRS NOW... SHE FLIES! BUT CAN SHE HIT SPEEDS THREE TO FIVE TIMES FASTER THAN SOUND WITHOUT MELTING? THAT'S FOR YOU TO TELL ME!
USAF
X20T
© 1956, King Features Syndicate, Inc. World rights reserved.
IT'S MORE'N A FIFTY-FIFTY CHANCE YOU'LL GET YOUR ANSWER FROM THE GRAVE! BUT I ALWAYS LIKED ODDS. WHEN DO I START?
HOLD ON, LADDIE! I WANT YOU, BUT... THERE'S ONE CATCH!
FRANK ROBBINS

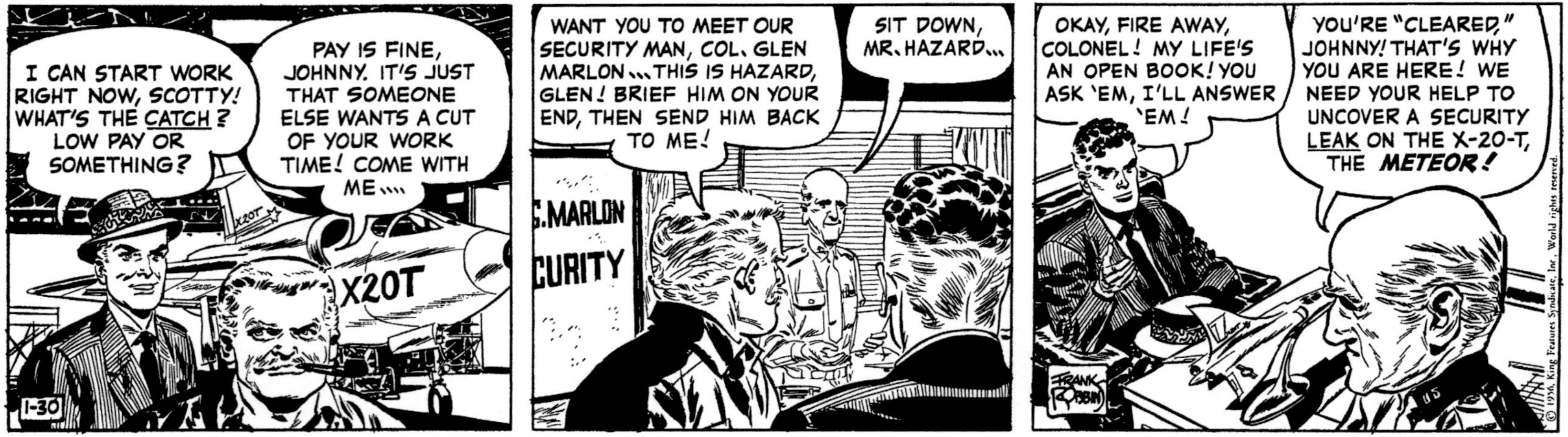
1-30
I CAN START WORK RIGHT NOW, SCOTTY! WHAT'S THE CATCH? LOW PAY OR SOMETHING?
PAY IS FINE, JOHNNY. IT'S JUST THAT SOMEONE ELSE WANTS A CUT OF YOUR WORK TIME! COME WITH ME....
X20T
WANT YOU TO MEET OUR SECURITY MAN, COL. GLEN MARLON ... THIS IS HAZARD, GLEN! BRIEF HIM ON YOUR END, THEN SEND HIM BACK TO ME!
SIT DOWN, MR. HAZARD...
G. MARLON
CURITY
OKAY, FIRE AWAY, COLONEL! MY LIFE'S AN OPEN BOOK! YOU ASK 'EM, I'LL ANSWER 'EM!
YOU'RE "CLEARED," JOHNNY! THAT'S WHY YOU ARE HERE! WE NEED YOUR HELP TO UNCOVER A SECURITY LEAK ON THE X-20-T, THE METEOR!
FRANK ROBBINS
© 1956, King Features Syndicate, Inc. World rights reserved.

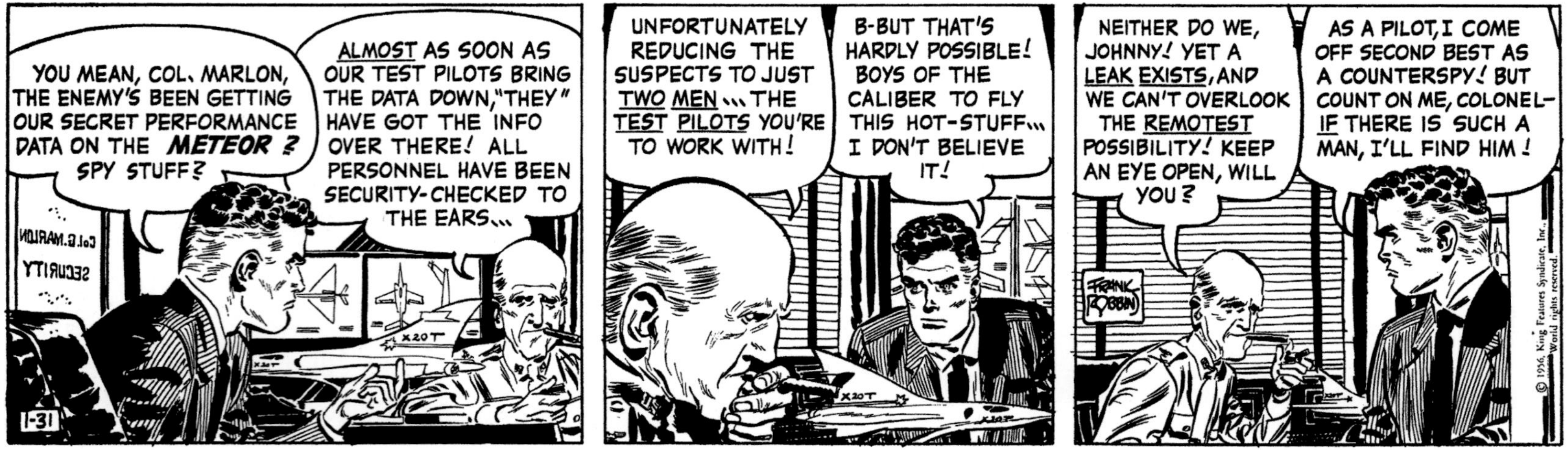
YOU MEAN, COL. MARLON, THE ENEMY'S BEEN GETTING OUR SECRET PERFORMANCE DATA ON THE METEOR? SPY STUFF?
ALMOST AS SOON AS OUR TEST PILOTS BRING THE DATA DOWN, "THEY" HAVE GOT THE INFO OVER THERE! ALL PERSONNEL HAVE BEEN SECURITY-CHECKED TO THE EARS...
1-31
UNFORTUNATELY REDUCING THE SUSPECTS TO JUST TWO MEN ... THE TEST PILOTS YOU'RE TO WORK WITH!
B-BUT THAT'S HARDLY POSSIBLE! BOYS OF THE CALIBER TO FLY THIS HOT-STUFF... I DON'T BELIEVE IT!
NEITHER DO WE, JOHNNY! YET A LEAK EXISTS, AND WE CAN'T OVERLOOK THE REMOTEST POSSIBILITY! KEEP AN EYE OPEN, WILL YOU?
AS A PILOT, I COME OFF SECOND BEST AS A COUNTERSPY! BUT COUNT ON ME, COLONEL— IF THERE IS SUCH A MAN, I'LL FIND HIM!
FRANK ROBBINS
© 1956, King Features Syndicate, Inc., World rights reserved.

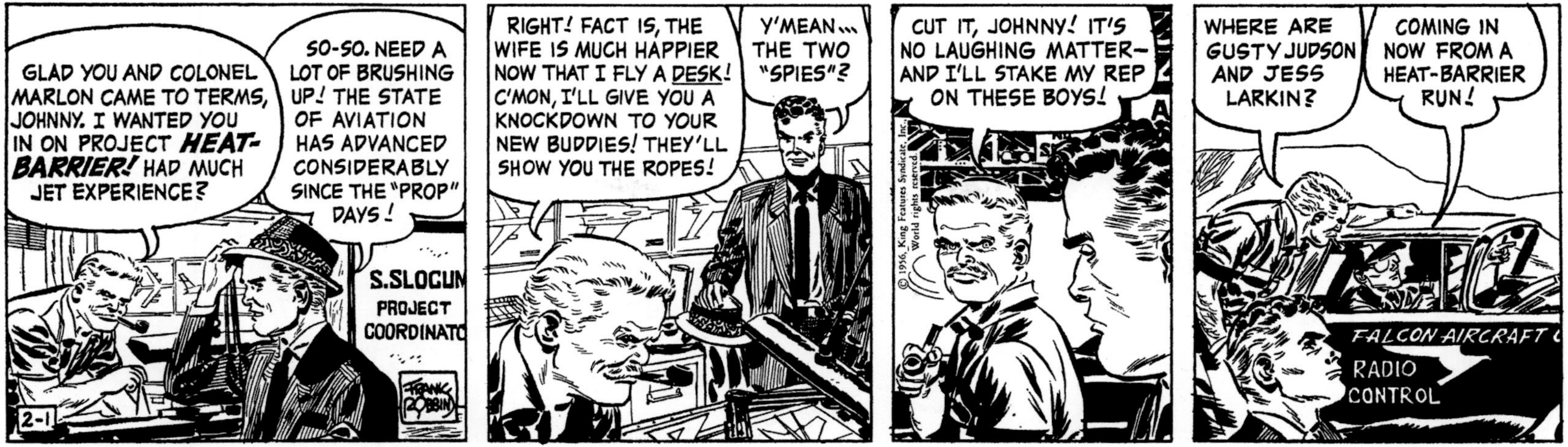
GLAD YOU AND COLONEL MARLON CAME TO TERMS, JOHNNY. I WANTED YOU IN ON PROJECT HEAT-BARRIER! HAD MUCH JET EXPERIENCE?
SO-SO. NEED A LOT OF BRUSHING UP! THE STATE OF AVIATION HAS ADVANCED CONSIDERABLY SINCE THE "PROP" DAYS!
S.SLOGUM
PROJECT COORDINATO
FRANK ROBBIN
2-1
RIGHT! FACT IS, THE WIFE IS MUCH HAPPIER NOW THAT I FLY A DESK! C'MON, I'LL GIVE YOU A KNOCKDOWN TO YOUR NEW BUDDIES! THEY'LL SHOW YOU THE ROPES!
Y'MEAN... THE TWO "SPIES"?
CUT IT, JOHNNY! IT'S NO LAUGHING MATTER— AND I'LL STAKE MY REP ON THESE BOYS!
© 1956, King Features Syndicate, Inc., World rights reserved.
WHERE ARE GUSTY JUDSON AND JESS LARKIN?
COMING IN NOW FROM A HEAT-BARRIER RUN!
FALCON AIRCRAFT
RADIO CONTROL

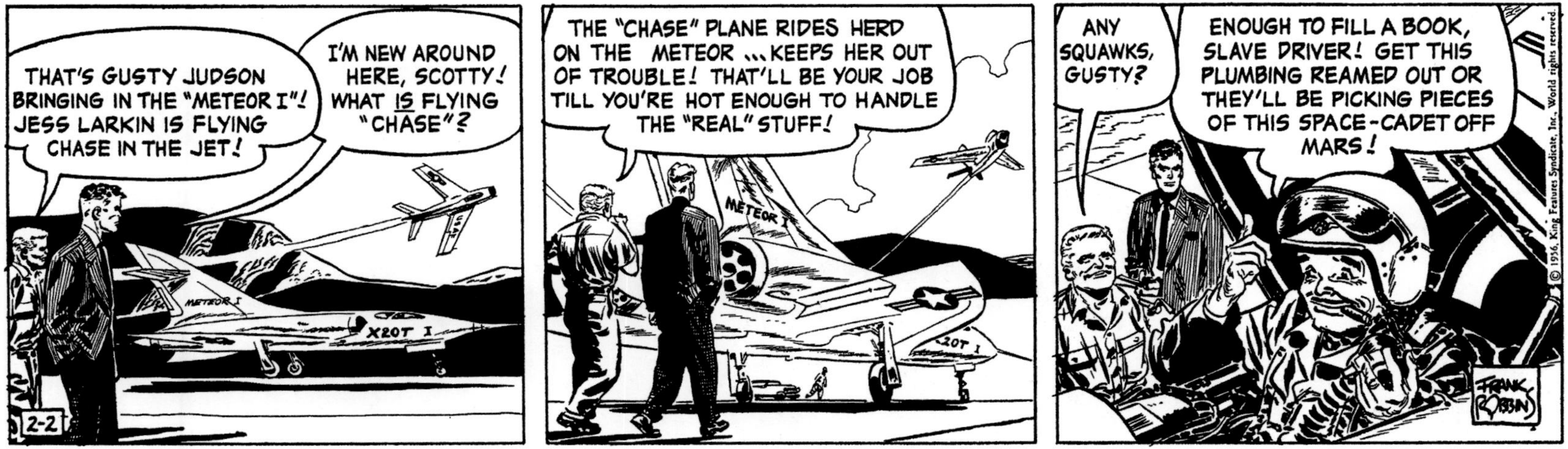
THAT'S GUSTY JUDSON BRINGING IN THE "METEOR I"! JESS LARKIN IS FLYING CHASE IN THE JET!
I'M NEW AROUND HERE, SCOTTY! WHAT IS FLYING "CHASE"?
METEOR I
X20T I
2-2
THE "CHASE" PLANE RIDES HERD ON THE METEOR ... KEEPS HER OUT OF TROUBLE! THAT'LL BE YOUR JOB TILL YOU'RE HOT ENOUGH TO HANDLE THE "REAL" STUFF!
ANY SQUAWKS, GUSTY?
ENOUGH TO FILL A BOOK, SLAVE DRIVER! GET THIS PLUMBING REAMED OUT OR THEY'LL BE PICKING PIECES OF THIS SPACE-CADET OFF MARS!
© 1956, King Features Syndicate, Inc., World rights reserved.
FRANK ROBBIN

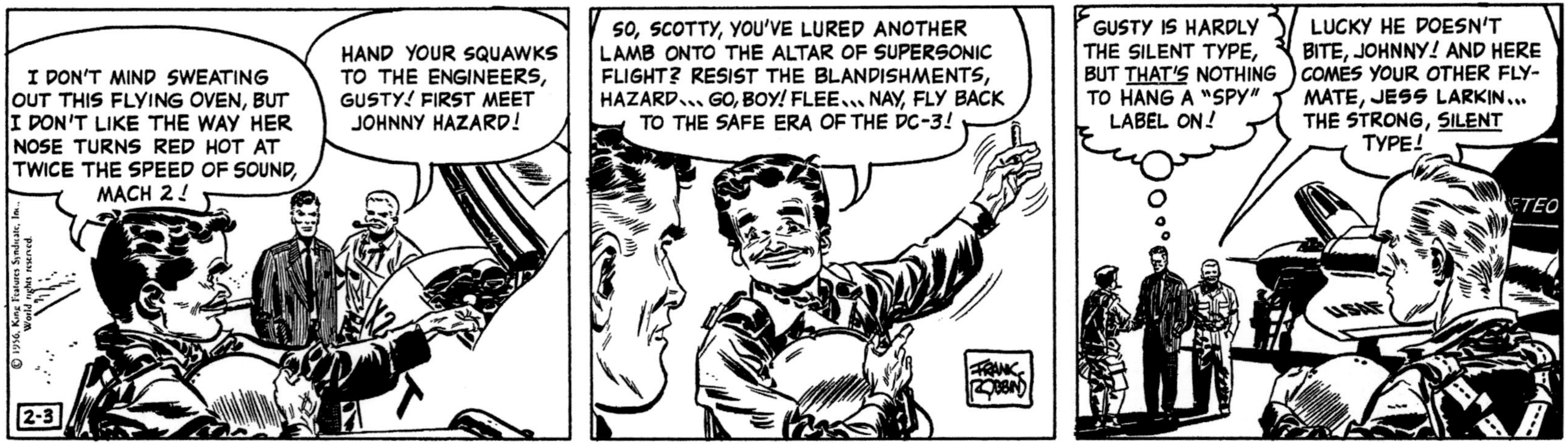
2-3
I DON'T MIND SWEATING OUT THIS FLYING OVEN, BUT I DON'T LIKE THE WAY HER NOSE TURNS RED HOT AT TWICE THE SPEED OF SOUND, MACH 2!
HAND YOUR SQUAWKS TO THE ENGINEERS, GUSTY! FIRST MEET JOHNNY HAZARD!
© 1956, King Features Syndicate, Inc., World rights reserved.
SO, SCOTTY, YOU'VE LURED ANOTHER LAMB ONTO THE ALTAR OF SUPERSONIC FLIGHT? RESIST THE BLANDISHMENTS, HAZARD... GO, BOY! FLEE... NAY, FLY BACK TO THE SAFE ERA OF THE DC-3!
FRANK ROBBINS
GUSTY IS HARDLY THE SILENT TYPE, BUT THAT'S NOTHING TO HANG A "SPY" LABEL ON!
LUCKY HE DOESN'T BITE, JOHNNY! AND HERE COMES YOUR OTHER FLY-MATE, JESS LARKIN... THE STRONG, SILENT TYPE!
USAF

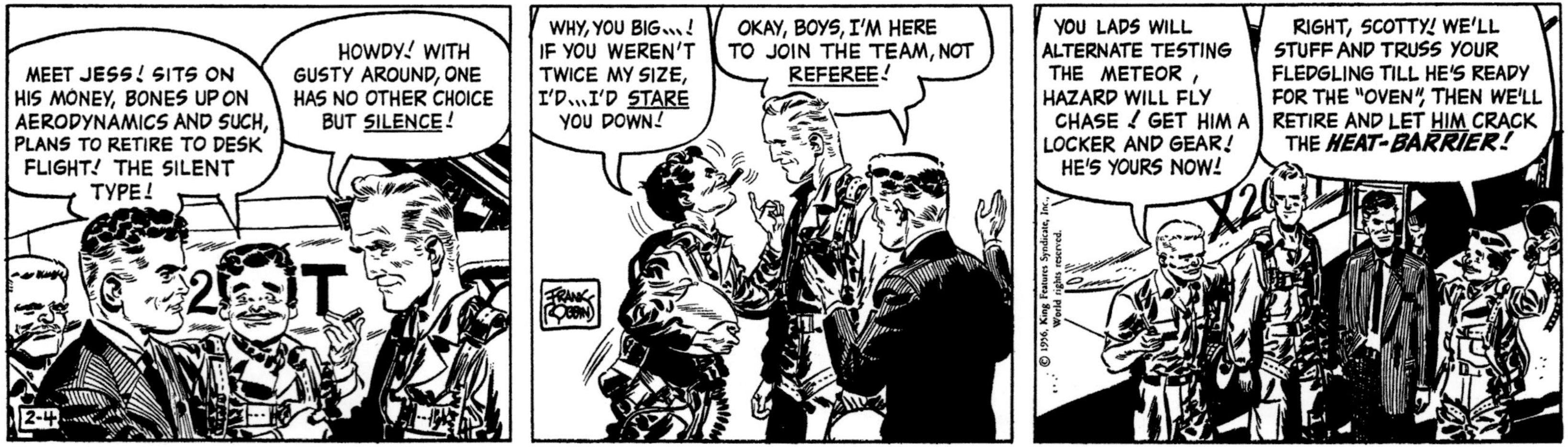
2-4
MEET JESS! SITS ON HIS MONEY, BONES UP ON AERODYNAMICS AND SUCH, PLANS TO RETIRE TO DESK FLIGHT! THE SILENT TYPE!
HOWDY! WITH GUSTY AROUND, ONE HAS NO OTHER CHOICE BUT SILENCE!
WHY, YOU BIG...! IF YOU WEREN'T TWICE MY SIZE, I'D...I'D STARE YOU DOWN!
OKAY, BOYS, I'M HERE TO JOIN THE TEAM, NOT REFEREE!
FRANK ROBBINS
YOU LADS WILL ALTERNATE TESTING THE METEOR, HAZARD WILL FLY CHASE! GET HIM A LOCKER AND GEAR! HE'S YOURS NOW!
RIGHT, SCOTTY! WE'LL STUFF AND TRUSS YOUR FLEDGLING TILL HE'S READY FOR THE "OVEN", THEN WE'LL RETIRE AND LET HIM CRACK THE HEAT-BARRIER!
© 1956, King Features Syndicate, Inc., World rights reserved.

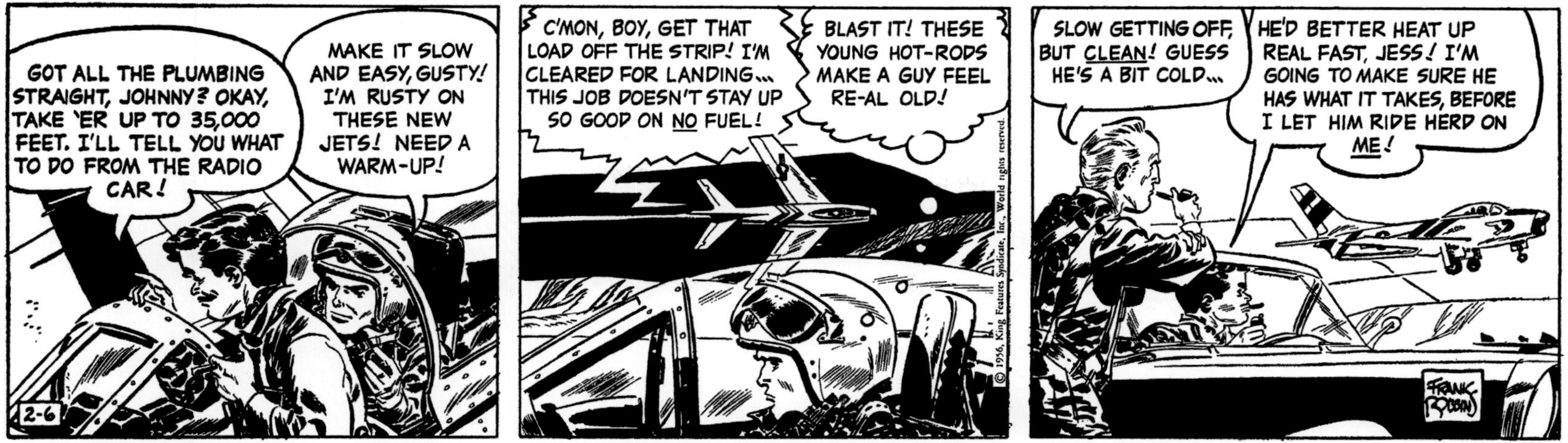
GOT ALL THE PLUMBING STRAIGHT, JOHNNY? OKAY, TAKE 'ER UP TO 35,000 FEET. I'LL TELL YOU WHAT TO DO FROM THE RADIO CAR!
MAKE IT SLOW AND EASY, GUSTY! I'M RUSTY ON THESE NEW JETS! NEED A WARM-UP!
2-6
C'MON, BOY, GET THAT LOAD OFF THE STRIP! I'M CLEARED FOR LANDING... THIS JOB DOESN'T STAY UP SO GOOD ON NO FUEL!
BLAST IT! THESE YOUNG HOT-RODS MAKE A GUY FEEL RE-AL OLD!
© 1956, King Features Syndicate, Inc., World rights reserved.
SLOW GETTING OFF, BUT CLEAN! GUESS HE'S A BIT COLD...
HE'D BETTER HEAT UP REAL FAST, JESS! I'M GOING TO MAKE SURE HE HAS WHAT IT TAKES, BEFORE I LET HIM RIDE HERD ON ME!
FRANK ROBBINS

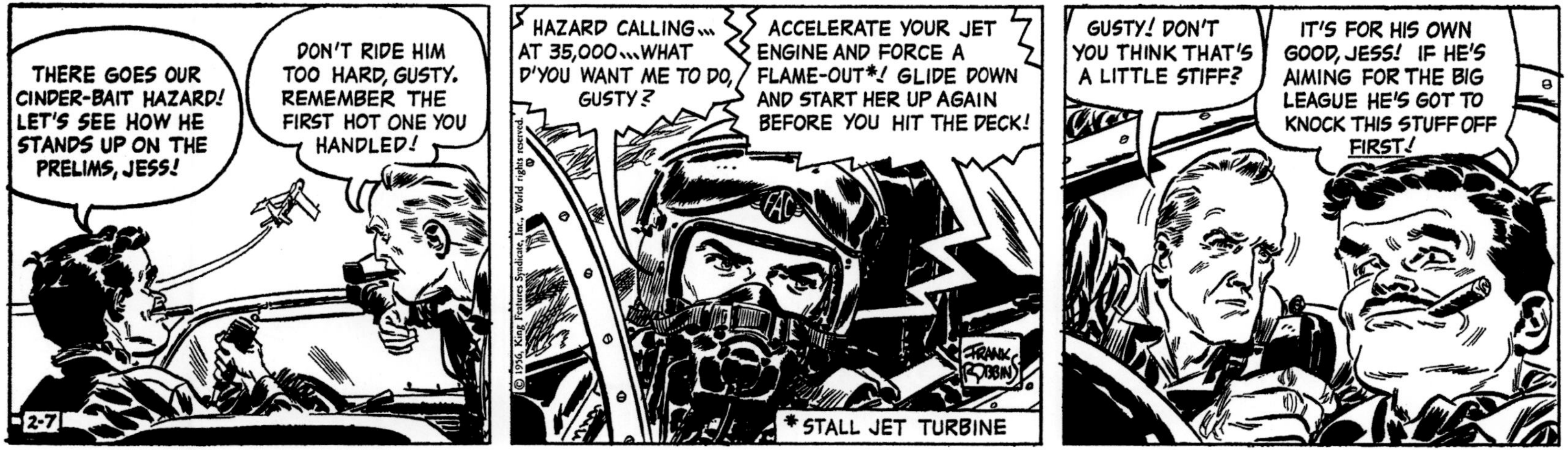
THERE GOES OUR CINDER-BAIT HAZARD! LET'S SEE HOW HE STANDS UP ON THE PRELIMS, JESS!
DON'T RIDE HIM TOO HARD, GUSTY. REMEMBER THE FIRST HOT ONE YOU HANDLED!
2-7
HAZARD CALLING... AT 35,000...WHAT D'YOU WANT ME TO DO, GUSTY?
ACCELERATE YOUR JET ENGINE AND FORCE A FLAME-OUT*! GLIDE DOWN AND START HER UP AGAIN BEFORE YOU HIT THE DECK!
© 1956, King Features Syndicate, Inc., World rights reserved.
FRANK ROBBINS
* STALL JET TURBINE
GUSTY! DON'T YOU THINK THAT'S A LITTLE STIFF?
IT'S FOR HIS OWN GOOD, JESS! IF HE'S AIMING FOR THE BIG LEAGUE HE'S GOT TO KNOCK THIS STUFF OFF FIRST!

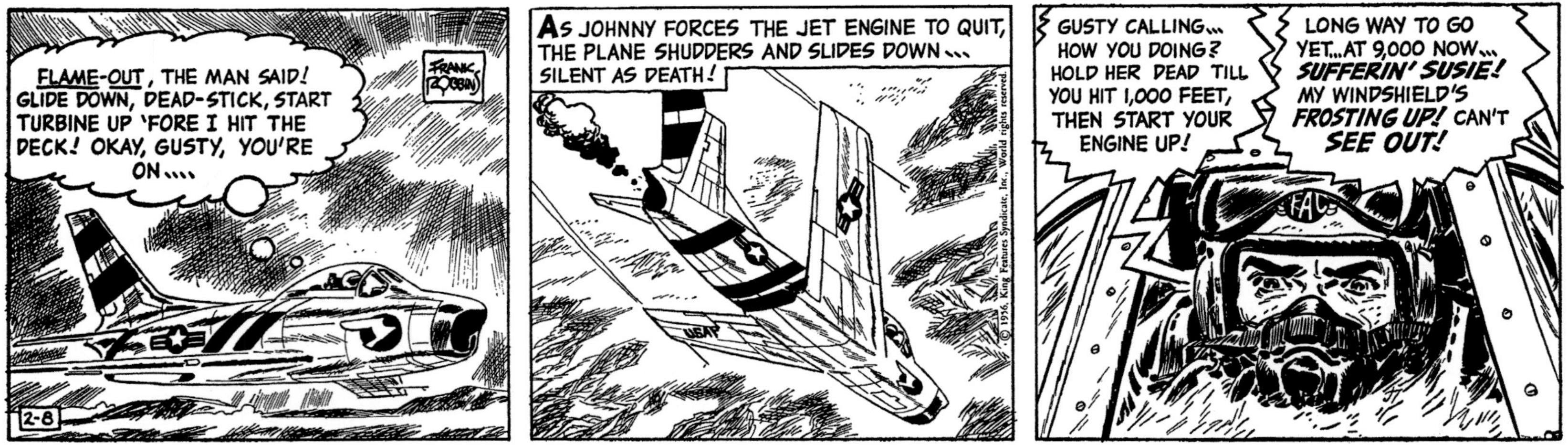
FLAME-OUT, THE MAN SAID! GLIDE DOWN, DEAD-STICK, START TURBINE UP 'FORE I HIT THE DECK! OKAY, GUSTY, YOU'RE ON....
FRANK ROBBINS
2-8
AS JOHNNY FORCES THE JET ENGINE TO QUIT, THE PLANE SHUDDERS AND SLIDES DOWN... SILENT AS DEATH!
© 1956, King Features Syndicate, Inc., World rights reserved.
GUSTY CALLING... HOW YOU DOING? HOLD HER DEAD TILL YOU HIT 1,000 FEET, THEN START YOUR ENGINE UP!
LONG WAY TO GO YET...AT 9,000 NOW... SUFFERIN' SUSIE! MY WINDSHIELD'S FROSTING UP! CAN'T SEE OUT!

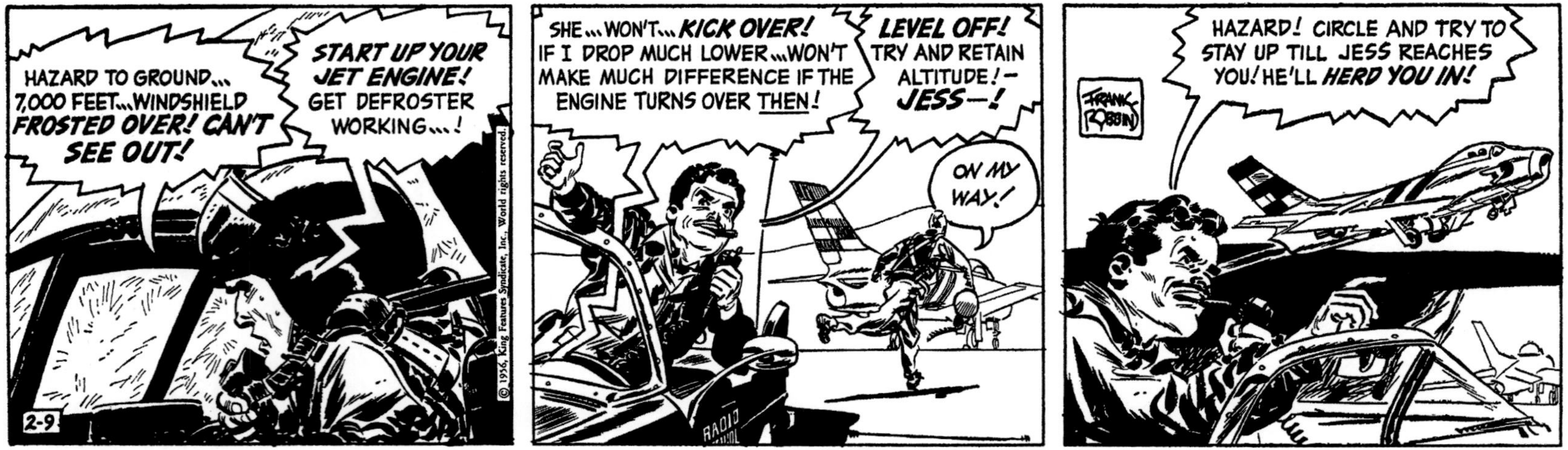
HAZARD TO GROUND... 7,000 FEET...WINDSHIELD FROSTED OVER! CAN'T SEE OUT!
START UP YOUR JET ENGINE! GET DEFROSTER WORKING...!
2-9
© 1956, King Features Syndicate, Inc., World rights reserved.
SHE...WON'T...KICK OVER! IF I DROP MUCH LOWER...WON'T MAKE MUCH DIFFERENCE IF THE ENGINE TURNS OVER THEN!
LEVEL OFF! TRY AND RETAIN ALTITUDE!—JESS—!
ON MY WAY!
FRANK ROBBINS
HAZARD! CIRCLE AND TRY TO STAY UP TILL JESS REACHES YOU! HE'LL HERD YOU IN!

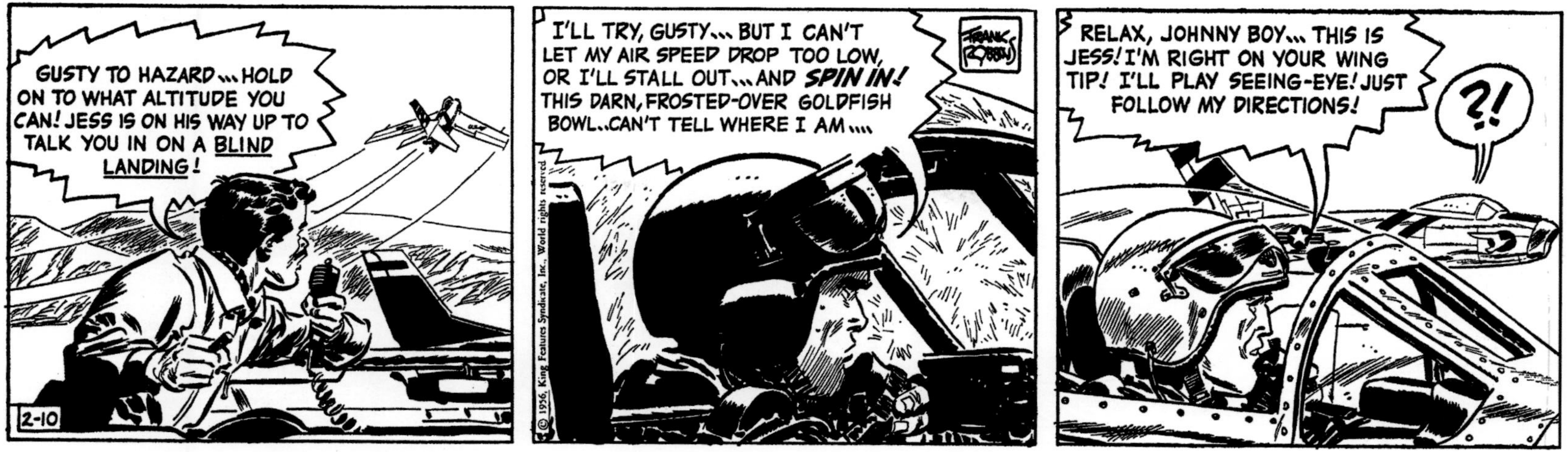
2-10
GUSTY TO HAZARD... HOLD ON TO WHAT ALTITUDE YOU CAN! JESS IS ON HIS WAY UP TO TALK YOU IN ON A BLIND LANDING!
I'LL TRY, GUSTY... BUT I CAN'T LET MY AIR SPEED DROP TOO LOW, OR I'LL STALL OUT... AND SPIN IN! THIS DARN, FROSTED-OVER GOLDFISH BOWL..CAN'T TELL WHERE I AM....
FRANK ROBBINS
© 1956, King Features Syndicate, Inc., World rights reserved
RELAX, JOHNNY BOY... THIS IS JESS! I'M RIGHT ON YOUR WING TIP! I'LL PLAY SEEING-EYE! JUST FOLLOW MY DIRECTIONS!
?!

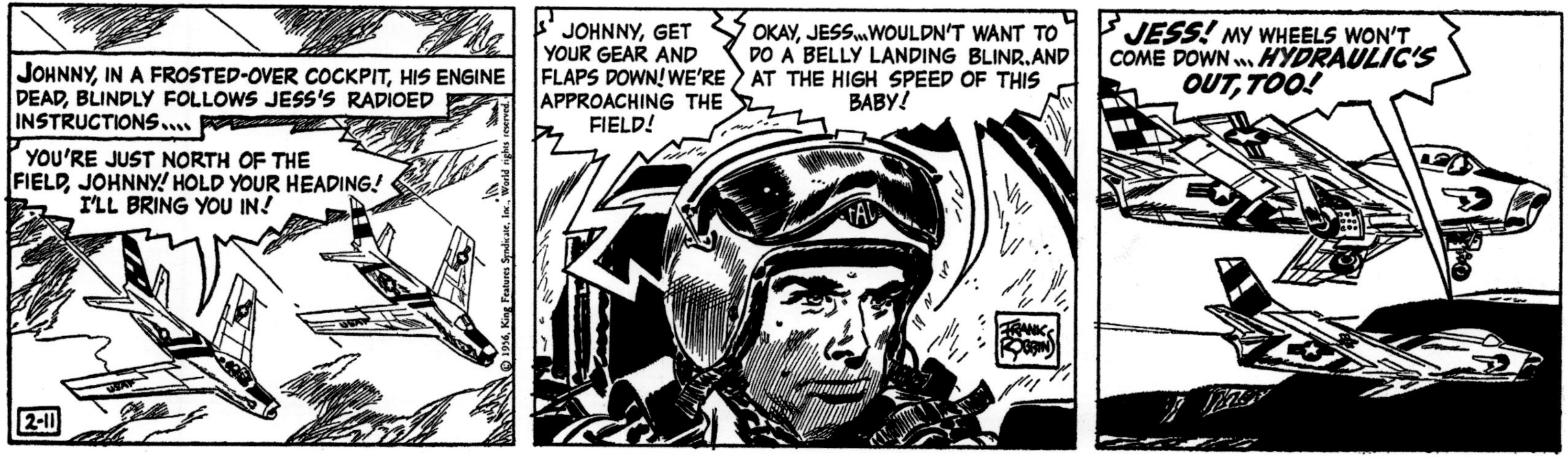
JOHNNY, IN A FROSTED-OVER COCKPIT, HIS ENGINE DEAD, BLINDLY FOLLOWS JESS'S RADIOED INSTRUCTIONS....
YOU'RE JUST NORTH OF THE FIELD, JOHNNY! HOLD YOUR HEADING! I'LL BRING YOU IN!
2-11
© 1956, King Features Syndicate, Inc., World rights reserved.
JOHNNY, GET YOUR GEAR AND FLAPS DOWN! WE'RE APPROACHING THE FIELD!
OKAY, JESS... WOULDN'T WANT TO DO A BELLY LANDING BLIND..AND AT THE HIGH SPEED OF THIS BABY!
FRANK ROBBINS
JESS! MY WHEELS WON'T COME DOWN... HYDRAULIC'S OUT, TOO!

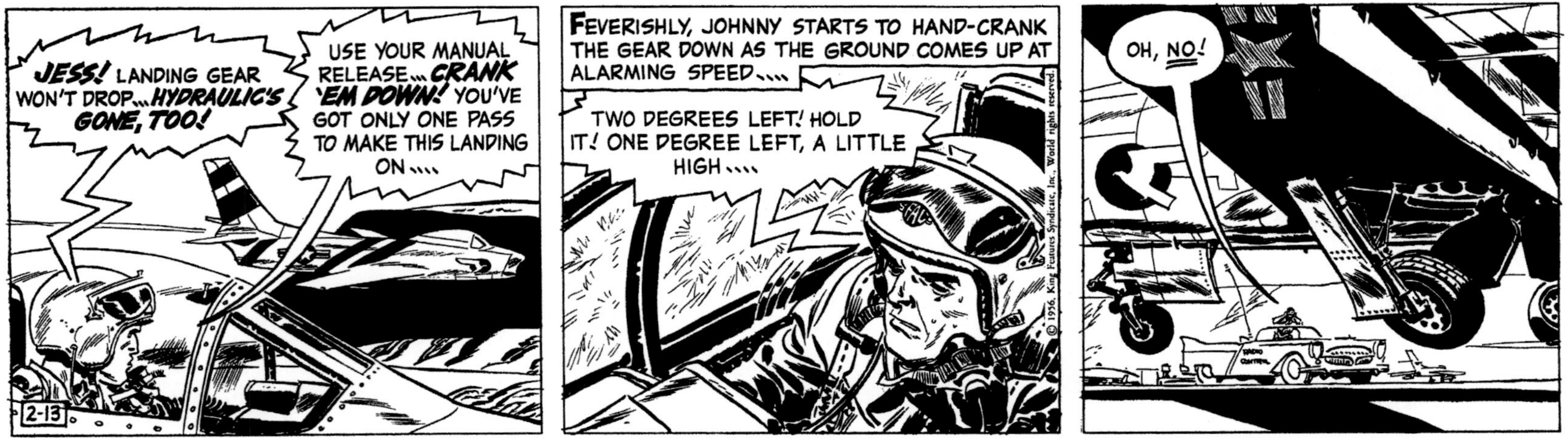

JESS! LANDING GEAR WON'T DROP... HYDRAULIC'S GONE, TOO!
USE YOUR MANUAL RELEASE... CRANK 'EM DOWN! YOU'VE GOT ONLY ONE PASS TO MAKE THIS LANDING ON....
2-13
FEVERISHLY, JOHNNY STARTS TO HAND-CRANK THE GEAR DOWN AS THE GROUND COMES UP AT ALARMING SPEED....
TWO DEGREES LEFT! HOLD IT! ONE DEGREE LEFT, A LITTLE HIGH....
© 1956, King Features Syndicate, Inc., World rights reserved.
OH, NO!

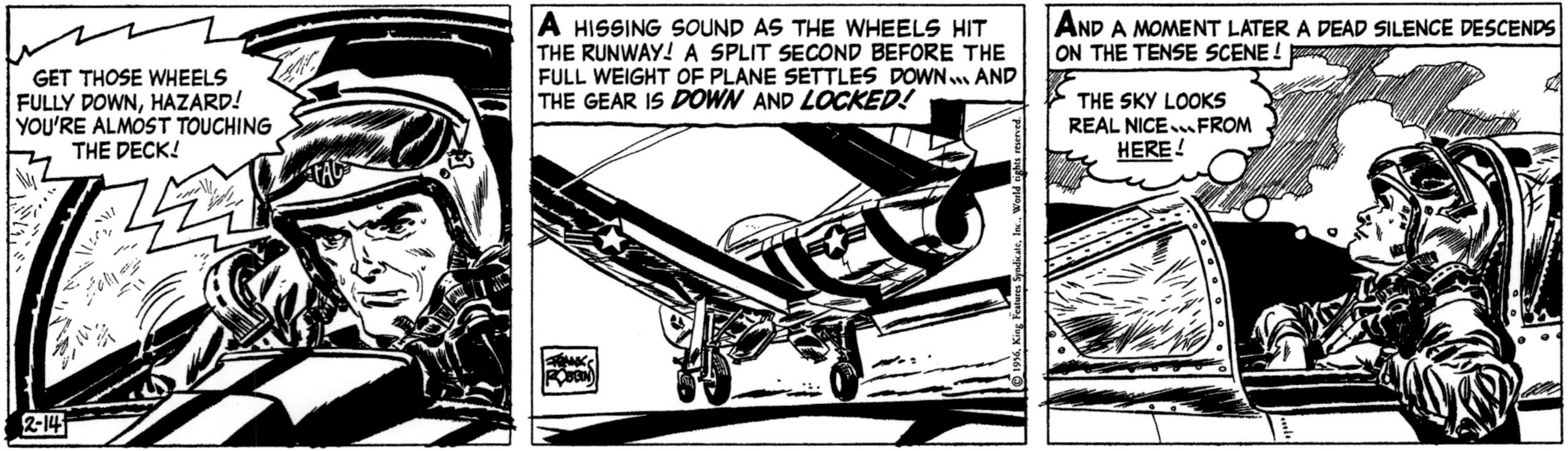

GET THOSE WHEELS FULLY DOWN, HAZARD! YOU'RE ALMOST TOUCHING THE DECK!
2-14
A HISSING SOUND AS THE WHEELS HIT THE RUNWAY! A SPLIT SECOND BEFORE THE FULL WEIGHT OF PLANE SETTLES DOWN... AND THE GEAR IS DOWN AND LOCKED!
© 1956, King Features Syndicate, Inc., World rights reserved.
AND A MOMENT LATER A DEAD SILENCE DESCENDS ON THE TENSE SCENE!
THE SKY LOOKS REAL NICE... FROM HERE!

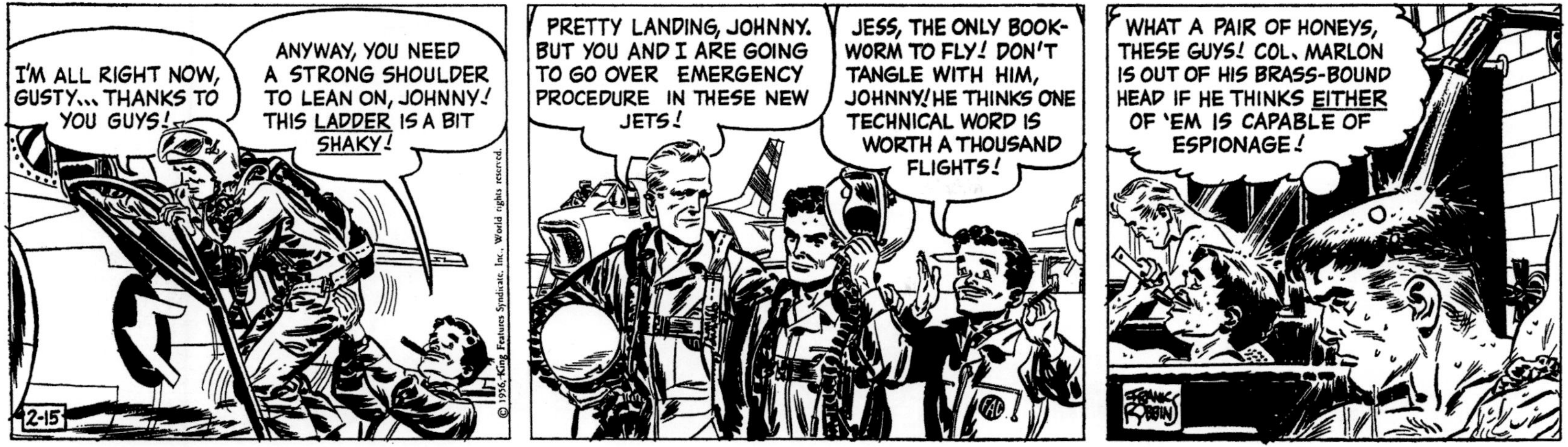
I'M ALL RIGHT NOW, GUSTY... THANKS TO YOU GUYS!
ANYWAY, YOU NEED A STRONG SHOULDER TO LEAN ON, JOHNNY! THIS LADDER IS A BIT SHAKY!
2-15
© 1956, King Features Syndicate, Inc., World rights reserved.
PRETTY LANDING, JOHNNY. BUT YOU AND I ARE GOING TO GO OVER EMERGENCY PROCEDURE IN THESE NEW JETS!
JESS, THE ONLY BOOK-WORM TO FLY! DON'T TANGLE WITH HIM, JOHNNY! HE THINKS ONE TECHNICAL WORD IS WORTH A THOUSAND FLIGHTS!
WHAT A PAIR OF HONEYS, THESE GUYS! COL. MARLON IS OUT OF HIS BRASS-BOUND HEAD IF HE THINKS EITHER OF 'EM IS CAPABLE OF ESPIONAGE!
FRANK ROBBINS

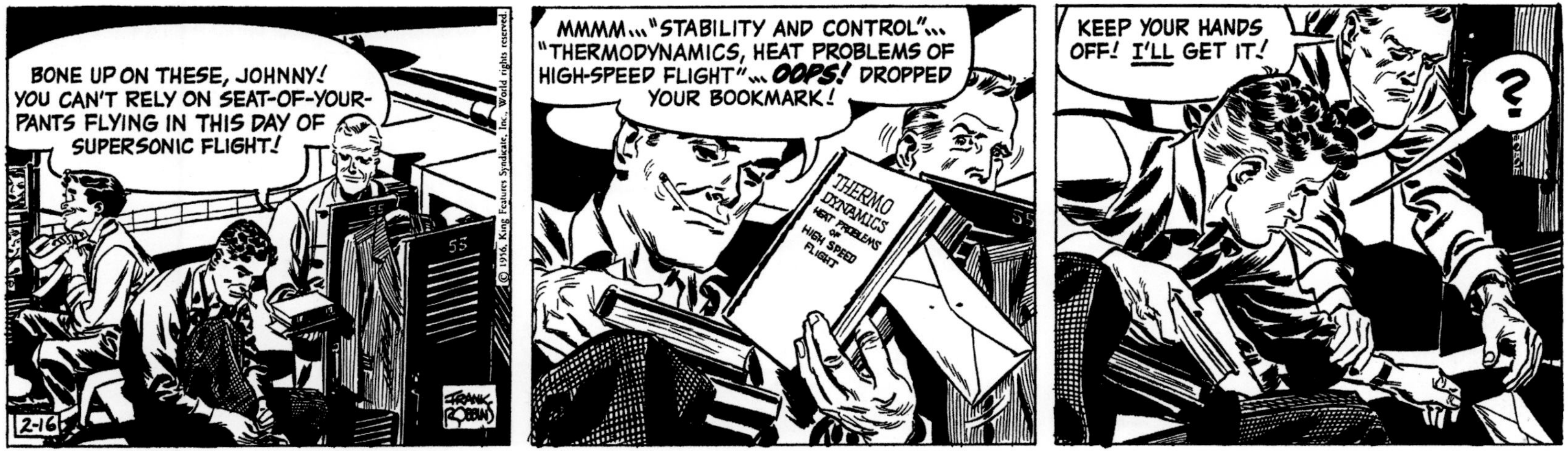
BONE UP ON THESE, JOHNNY! YOU CAN'T RELY ON SEAT-OF-YOUR-PANTS FLYING IN THIS DAY OF SUPERSONIC FLIGHT!
2-16
© 1956, King Features Syndicate, Inc., World rights reserved.
FRANK ROBBINS
MMMM... "STABILITY AND CONTROL"... "THERMODYNAMICS, HEAT PROBLEMS OF HIGH-SPEED FLIGHT"... OOPS! DROPPED YOUR BOOKMARK!
THERMO DYNAMICS HEAT PROBLEMS OF HIGH SPEED FLIGHT
KEEP YOUR HANDS OFF! I'LL GET IT!
?

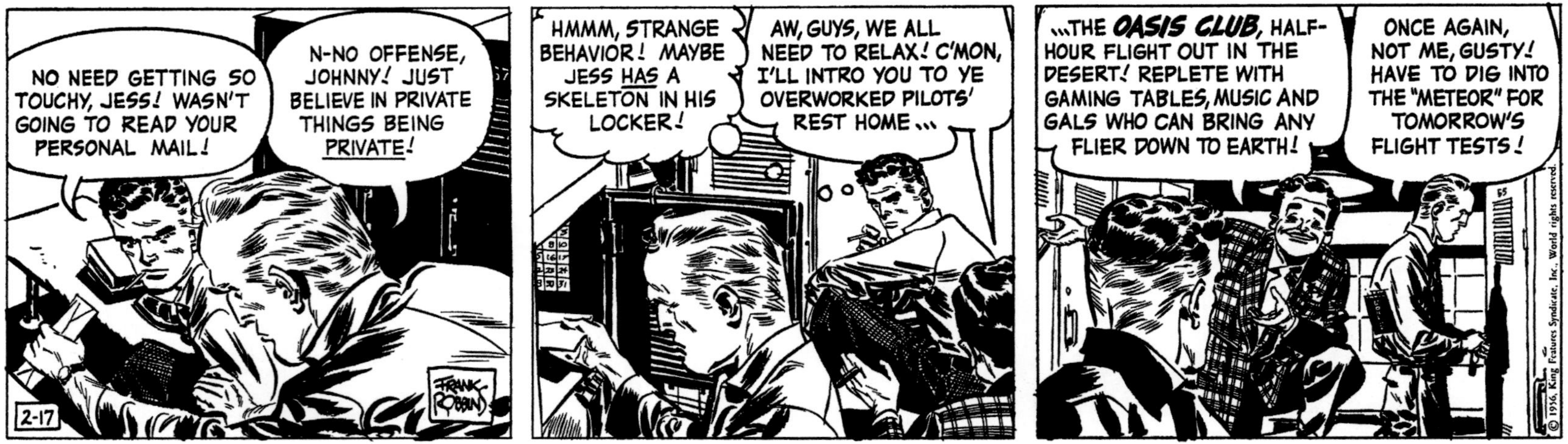
NO NEED GETTING SO TOUCHY, JESS! WASN'T GOING TO READ YOUR PERSONAL MAIL!
N-NO OFFENSE, JOHNNY! JUST BELIEVE IN PRIVATE THINGS BEING PRIVATE!
FRANK ROBBINS
2-17
HMMM, STRANGE BEHAVIOR! MAYBE JESS HAS A SKELETON IN HIS LOCKER!
AW, GUYS, WE ALL NEED TO RELAX! C'MON, I'LL INTRO YOU TO YE OVERWORKED PILOTS' REST HOME....
...THE OASIS CLUB, HALF-HOUR FLIGHT OUT IN THE DESERT! REPLETE WITH GAMING TABLES, MUSIC AND GALS WHO CAN BRING ANY FLIER DOWN TO EARTH!
ONCE AGAIN, NOT ME, GUSTY! HAVE TO DIG INTO THE "METEOR" FOR TOMORROW'S FLIGHT TESTS!
© 1956, King Features Syndicate, Inc., World rights reserved.

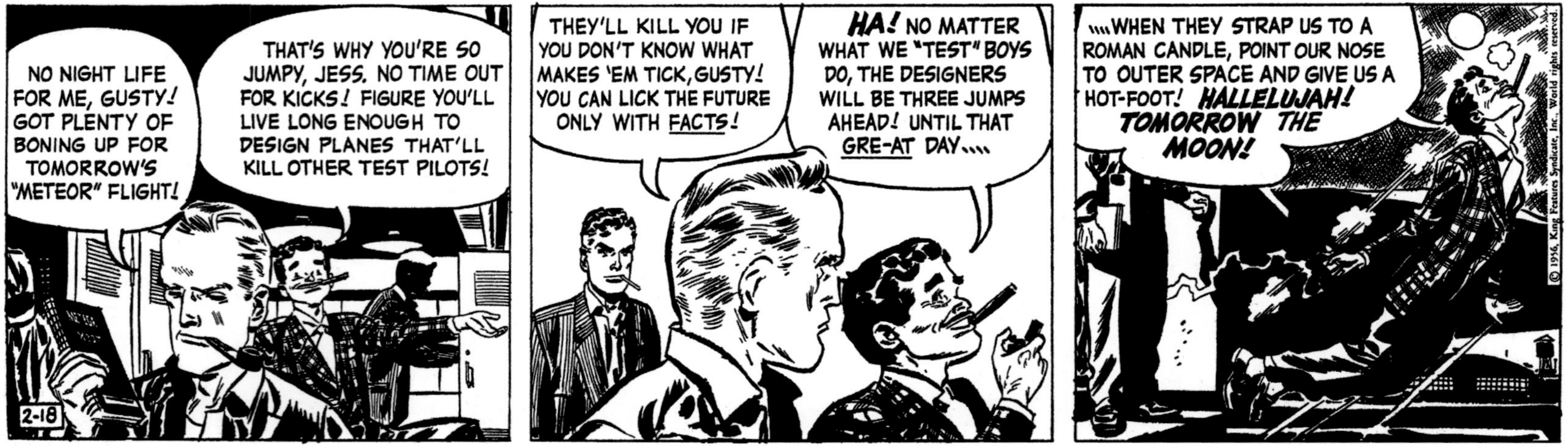
NO NIGHT LIFE FOR ME, GUSTY! GOT PLENTY OF BONING UP FOR TOMORROW'S "METEOR" FLIGHT!
THAT'S WHY YOU'RE SO JUMPY, JESS. NO TIME OUT FOR KICKS! FIGURE YOU'LL LIVE LONG ENOUGH TO DESIGN PLANES THAT'LL KILL OTHER TEST PILOTS!
2-18
THEY'LL KILL YOU IF YOU DON'T KNOW WHAT MAKES 'EM TICK, GUSTY! YOU CAN LICK THE FUTURE ONLY WITH FACTS!
HA! NO MATTER WHAT WE "TEST" BOYS DO, THE DESIGNERS WILL BE THREE JUMPS AHEAD! UNTIL THAT GRE-AT DAY....
....WHEN THEY STRAP US TO A ROMAN CANDLE, POINT OUR NOSE TO OUTER SPACE AND GIVE US A HOT-FOOT! HALLELUJAH! TOMORROW THE MOON!
© 1956, King Features Syndicate, Inc., World rights reserved.

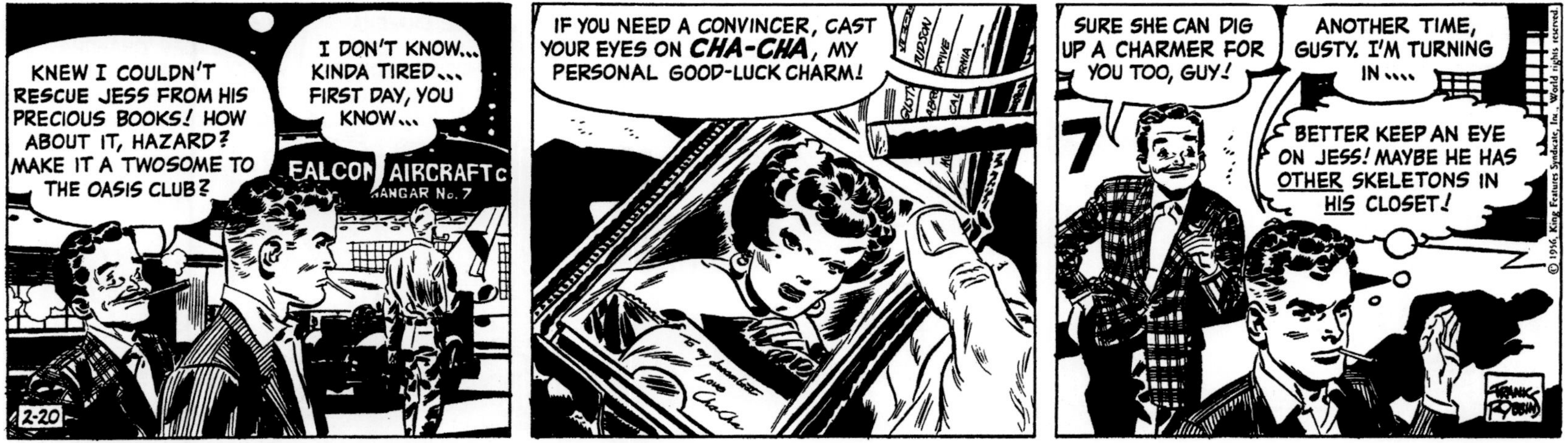
2-20
KNEW I COULDN'T RESCUE JESS FROM HIS PRECIOUS BOOKS! HOW ABOUT IT, HAZARD? MAKE IT A TWOSOME TO THE OASIS CLUB?
I DON'T KNOW... KINDA TIRED... FIRST DAY, YOU KNOW...
IF YOU NEED A CONVINCER, CAST YOUR EYES ON CHA-CHA, MY PERSONAL GOOD-LUCK CHARM!
SURE SHE CAN DIG UP A CHARMER FOR YOU TOO, GUY!
ANOTHER TIME, GUSTY. I'M TURNING IN....
BETTER KEEP AN EYE ON JESS! MAYBE HE HAS OTHER SKELETONS IN HIS CLOSET!
© 1956, King Features Syndicate, Inc., World rights reserved.
FRANK ROBBINS

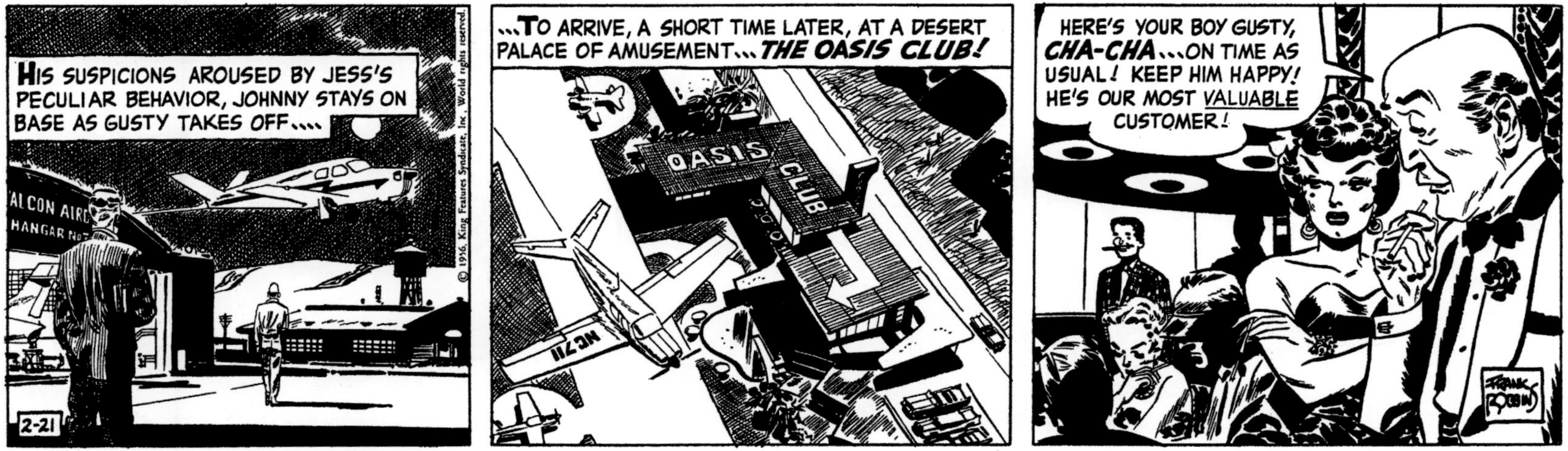
HIS SUSPICIONS AROUSED BY JESS'S PECULIAR BEHAVIOR, JOHNNY STAYS ON BASE AS GUSTY TAKES OFF....
© 1956, King Features Syndicate, Inc., World rights reserved.
2-21
...TO ARRIVE, A SHORT TIME LATER, AT A DESERT PALACE OF AMUSEMENT... THE OASIS CLUB!
OASIS CLUB
HERE'S YOUR BOY GUSTY, CHA-CHA...ON TIME AS USUAL! KEEP HIM HAPPY! HE'S OUR MOST VALUABLE CUSTOMER!
FRANK ROBBINS

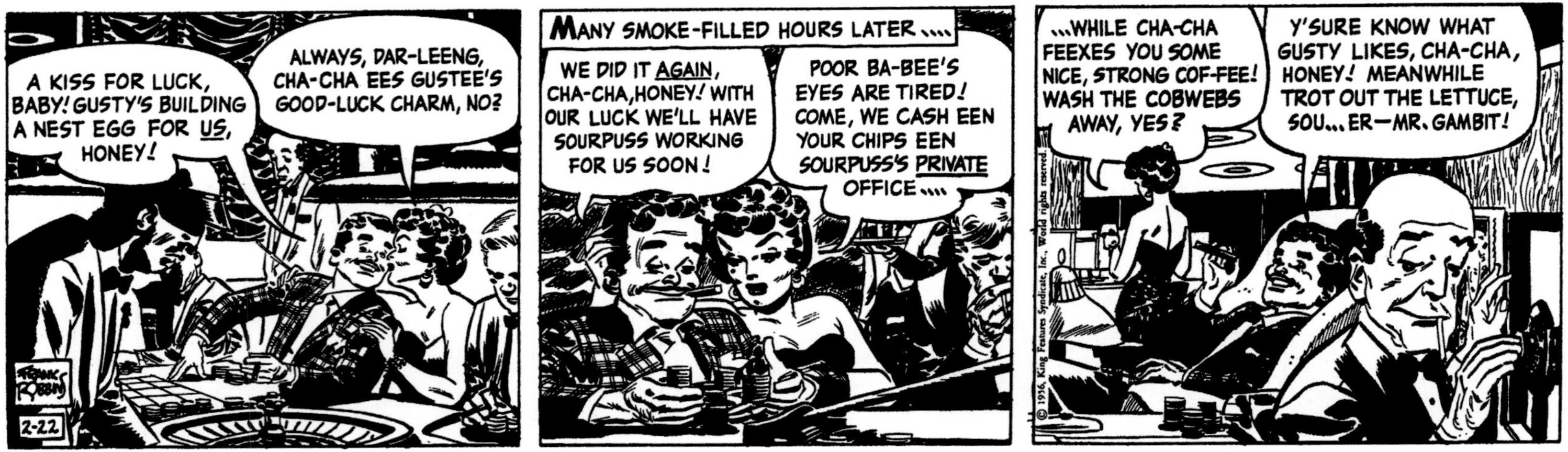

A KISS FOR LUCK, BABY! GUSTY'S BUILDING A NEST EGG FOR US, HONEY!
ALWAYS, DAR-LEENG, CHA-CHA EES GUSTEE'S GOOD-LUCK CHARM, NO?
FRANK ROBBINS
2-22
MANY SMOKE-FILLED HOURS LATER....
WE DID IT AGAIN, CHA-CHA, HONEY! WITH OUR LUCK WE'LL HAVE SOURPUSS WORKING FOR US SOON!
POOR BA-BEE'S EYES ARE TIRED! COME, WE CASH EEN YOUR CHIPS EEN SOURPUSS'S PRIVATE OFFICE....
...WHILE CHA-CHA FEEXES YOU SOME NICE, STRONG COF-FEE! WASH THE COBWEBS AWAY, YES?
Y'SURE KNOW WHAT GUSTY LIKES, CHA-CHA, HONEY! MEANWHILE TROT OUT THE LETTUCE, SOU... ER—MR. GAMBIT!
© 1956, King Features Syndicate, Inc., World rights reserved.

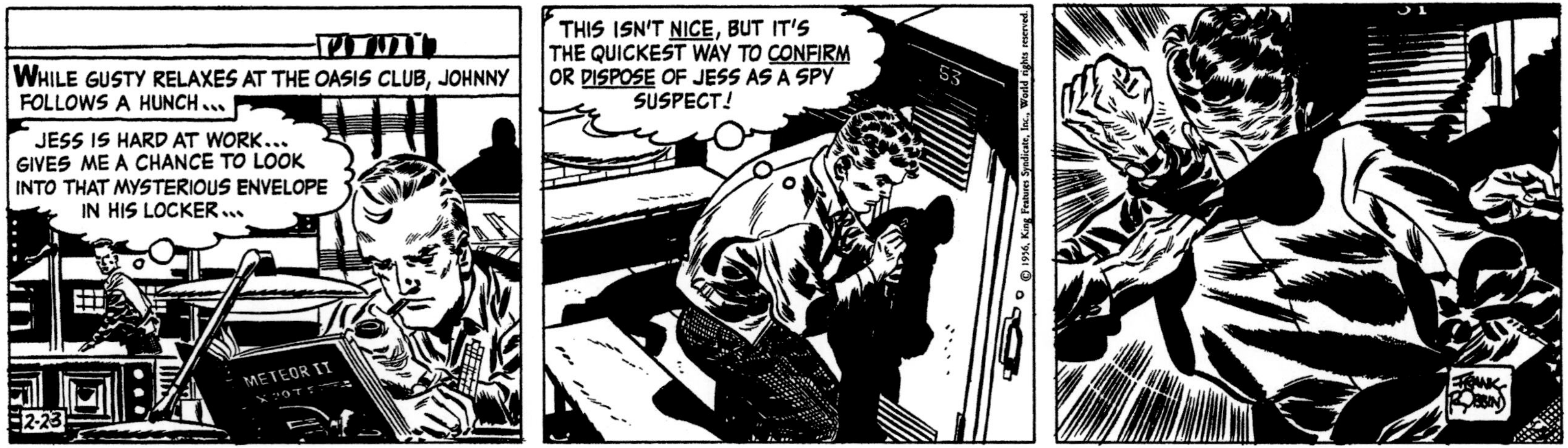

WHILE GUSTY RELAXES AT THE OASIS CLUB, JOHNNY FOLLOWS A HUNCH...
JESS IS HARD AT WORK... GIVES ME A CHANCE TO LOOK INTO THAT MYSTERIOUS ENVELOPE IN HIS LOCKER...
METEOR II
2-23
THIS ISN'T NICE, BUT IT'S THE QUICKEST WAY TO CONFIRM OR DISPOSE OF JESS AS A SPY SUSPECT!
53
© 1956, King Features Syndicate, Inc., World rights reserved.
FRANK ROBBINS

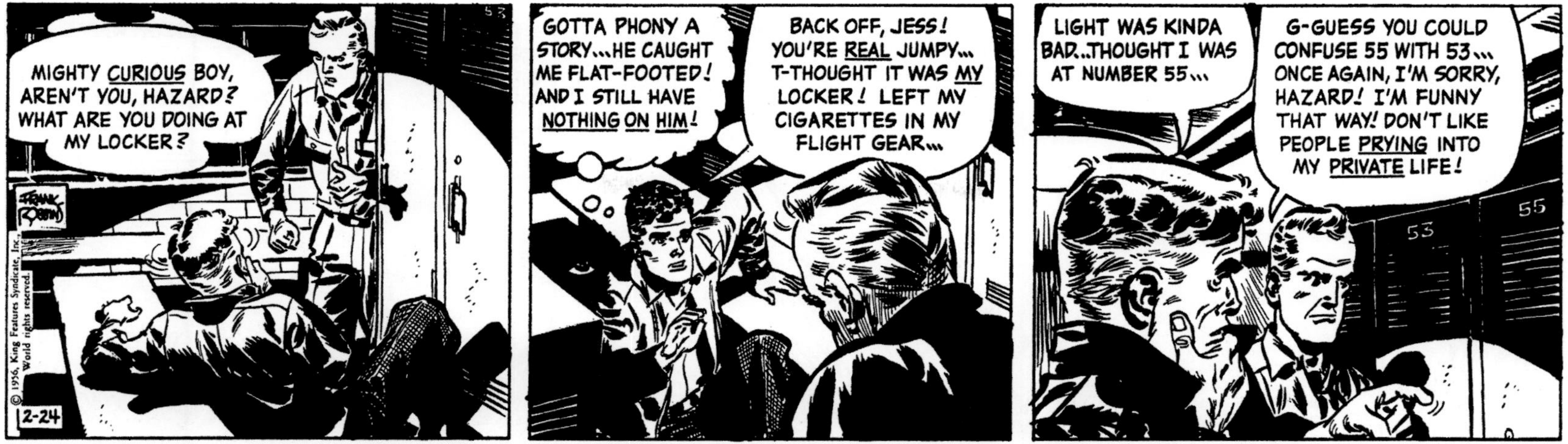
MIGHTY CURIOUS BOY, AREN'T YOU, HAZARD? WHAT ARE YOU DOING AT MY LOCKER?
FRANK ROBBINS
© 1956, King Features Syndicate, Inc., World rights reserved
2-24
GOTTA PHONY A STORY... HE CAUGHT ME FLAT-FOOTED! AND I STILL HAVE NOTHING ON HIM!
BACK OFF, JESS! YOU'RE REAL JUMPY... T-THOUGHT IT WAS MY LOCKER! LEFT MY CIGARETTES IN MY FLIGHT GEAR...
LIGHT WAS KINDA BAD...THOUGHT I WAS AT NUMBER 55...
G-GUESS YOU COULD CONFUSE 55 WITH 53... ONCE AGAIN, I'M SORRY, HAZARD! I'M FUNNY THAT WAY! DON'T LIKE PEOPLE PRYING INTO MY PRIVATE LIFE!
53
55

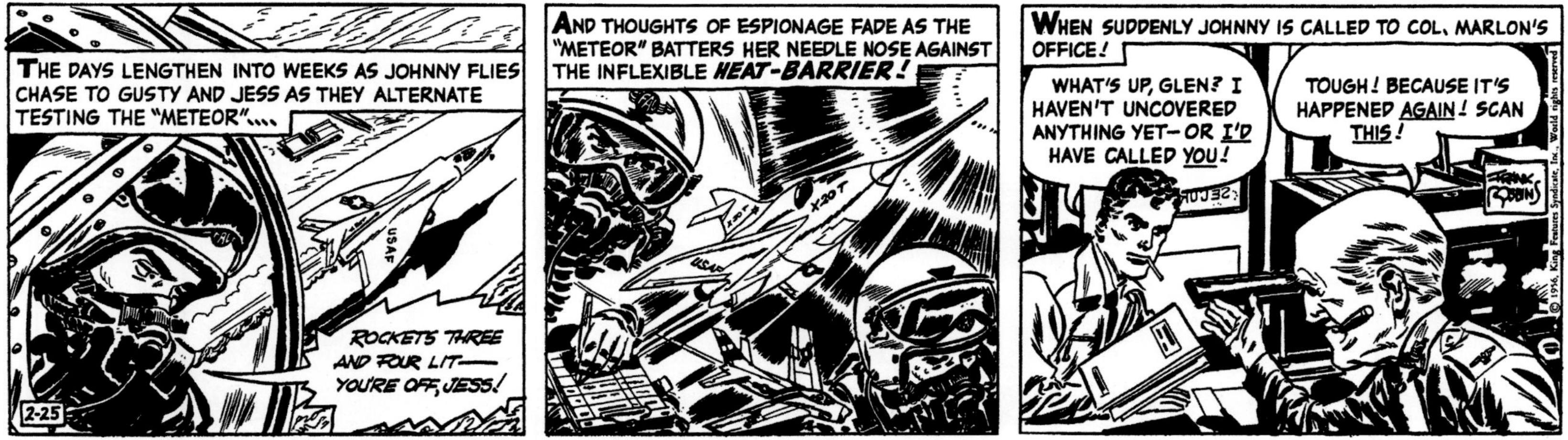
THE DAYS LENGTHEN INTO WEEKS AS JOHNNY FLIES CHASE TO GUSTY AND JESS AS THEY ALTERNATE TESTING THE "METEOR"....
USAF
ROCKETS THREE AND FOUR LIT— YOU'RE OFF, JESS!
2-25
AND THOUGHTS OF ESPIONAGE FADE AS THE "METEOR" BATTERS HER NEEDLE NOSE AGAINST THE INFLEXIBLE HEAT-BARRIER!
X-20T
USAF
WHEN SUDDENLY JOHNNY IS CALLED TO COL. MARLON'S OFFICE!
WHAT'S UP, GLEN? I HAVEN'T UNCOVERED ANYTHING YET—OR I'D HAVE CALLED YOU!
TOUGH! BECAUSE IT'S HAPPENED AGAIN! SCAN THIS!
FRANK ROBBINS
© 1956, King Features Syndicate, Inc., World rights reserved

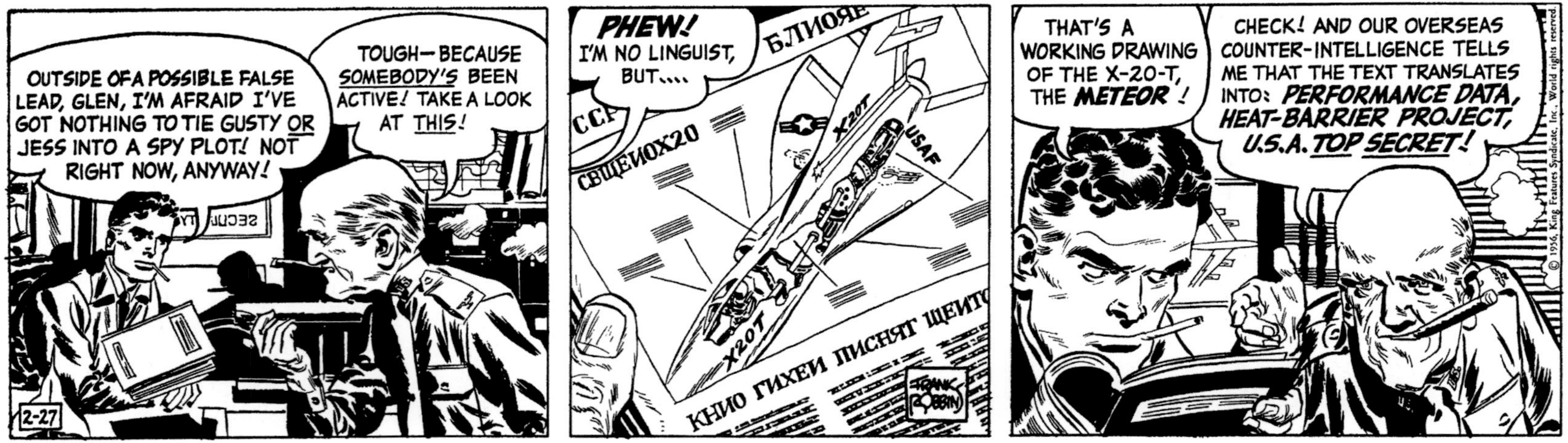
2-27
OUTSIDE OF A POSSIBLE FALSE LEAD, GLEN, I'M AFRAID I'VE GOT NOTHING TO TIE GUSTY OR JESS INTO A SPY PLOT! NOT RIGHT NOW, ANYWAY!
TOUGH—BECAUSE SOMEBODY'S BEEN ACTIVE! TAKE A LOOK AT THIS!
PHEW! I'M NO LINGUIST, BUT....
БЛИОЯЕ
СВЩЕИОХ20
X20T
USAF
КНИО ГИХЕИ ПИСНЯТ ЩЕИТО
FRANK ROBBIN
THAT'S A WORKING DRAWING OF THE X-20-T, THE METEOR!
CHECK! AND OUR OVERSEAS COUNTER-INTELLIGENCE TELLS ME THAT THE TEXT TRANSLATES INTO: PERFORMANCE DATA, HEAT-BARRIER PROJECT, U.S.A. TOP SECRET!
© 1956, King Features Syndicate, Inc., World rights reserved.

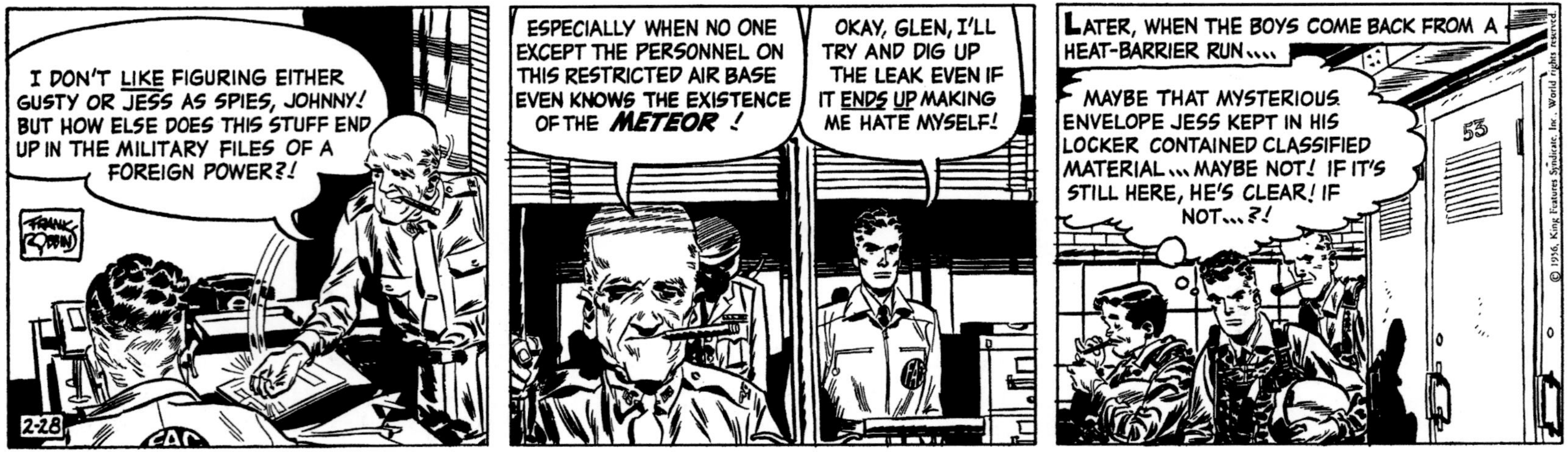
2-28
I DON'T LIKE FIGURING EITHER GUSTY OR JESS AS SPIES, JOHNNY! BUT HOW ELSE DOES THIS STUFF END UP IN THE MILITARY FILES OF A FOREIGN POWER?!
FRANK ROBBIN
ESPECIALLY WHEN NO ONE EXCEPT THE PERSONNEL ON THIS RESTRICTED AIR BASE EVEN KNOWS THE EXISTENCE OF THE METEOR!
OKAY, GLEN, I'LL TRY AND DIG UP THE LEAK EVEN IF IT ENDS UP MAKING ME HATE MYSELF!
LATER, WHEN THE BOYS COME BACK FROM A HEAT-BARRIER RUN....
MAYBE THAT MYSTERIOUS ENVELOPE JESS KEPT IN HIS LOCKER CONTAINED CLASSIFIED MATERIAL... MAYBE NOT! IF IT'S STILL HERE, HE'S CLEAR! IF NOT...?!
53
© 1956, King Features Syndicate, Inc., World rights reserved.

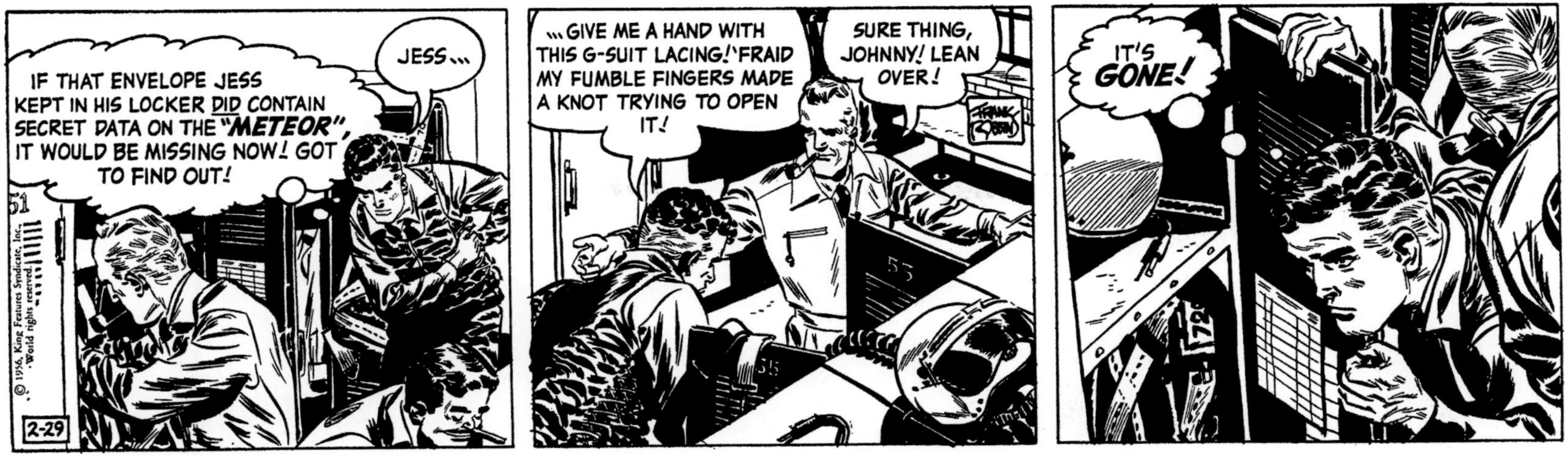
IF THAT ENVELOPE JESS KEPT IN HIS LOCKER DID CONTAIN SECRET DATA ON THE "METEOR", IT WOULD BE MISSING NOW! GOT TO FIND OUT!
JESS...
...GIVE ME A HAND WITH THIS G-SUIT LACING! 'FRAID MY FUMBLE FINGERS MADE A KNOT TRYING TO OPEN IT!
SURE THING, JOHNNY! LEAN OVER!
IT'S GONE!
© 1956, King Features Syndicate, Inc. World rights reserved.
2-29
FRANK ROBBIN

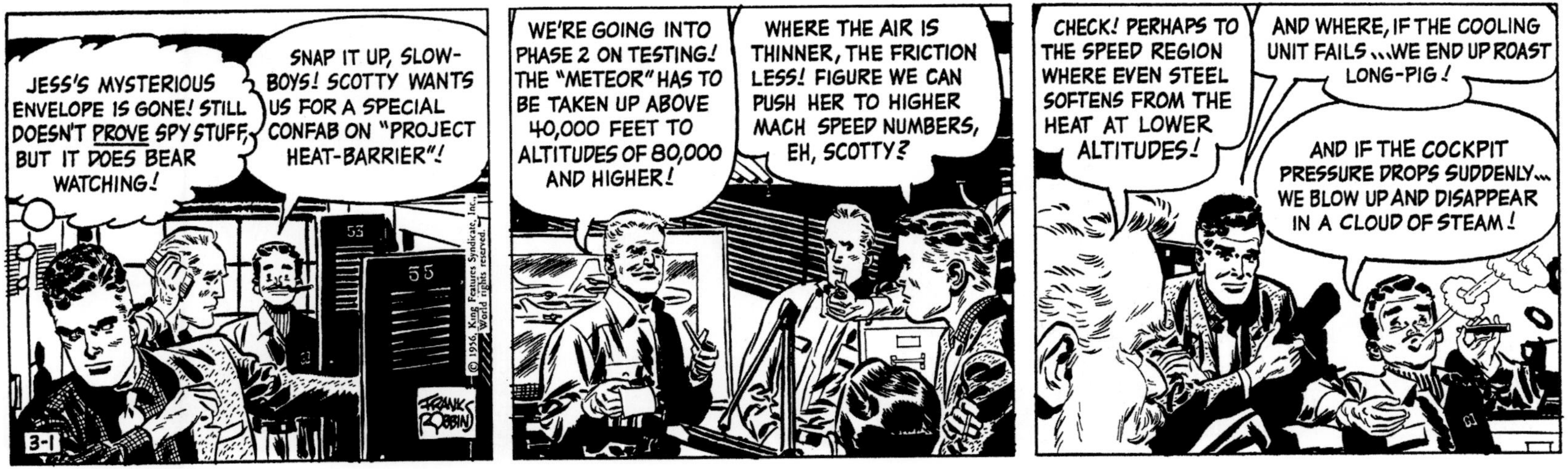
JESS'S MYSTERIOUS ENVELOPE IS GONE! STILL DOESN'T PROVE SPY STUFF, BUT IT DOES BEAR WATCHING!
SNAP IT UP, SLOW-BOYS! SCOTTY WANTS US FOR A SPECIAL CONFAB ON "PROJECT HEAT-BARRIER"!
WE'RE GOING INTO PHASE 2 ON TESTING! THE "METEOR" HAS TO BE TAKEN UP ABOVE 40,000 FEET TO ALTITUDES OF 80,000 AND HIGHER!
WHERE THE AIR IS THINNER, THE FRICTION LESS! FIGURE WE CAN PUSH HER TO HIGHER MACH SPEED NUMBERS, EH, SCOTTY?
CHECK! PERHAPS TO THE SPEED REGION WHERE EVEN STEEL SOFTENS FROM THE HEAT AT LOWER ALTITUDES!
AND WHERE, IF THE COOLING UNIT FAILS...WE END UP ROAST LONG-PIG!
AND IF THE COCKPIT PRESSURE DROPS SUDDENLY... WE BLOW UP AND DISAPPEAR IN A CLOUD OF STEAM!
© 1956, King Features Syndicate, Inc. World rights reserved.
3-1
FRANK ROBBIN

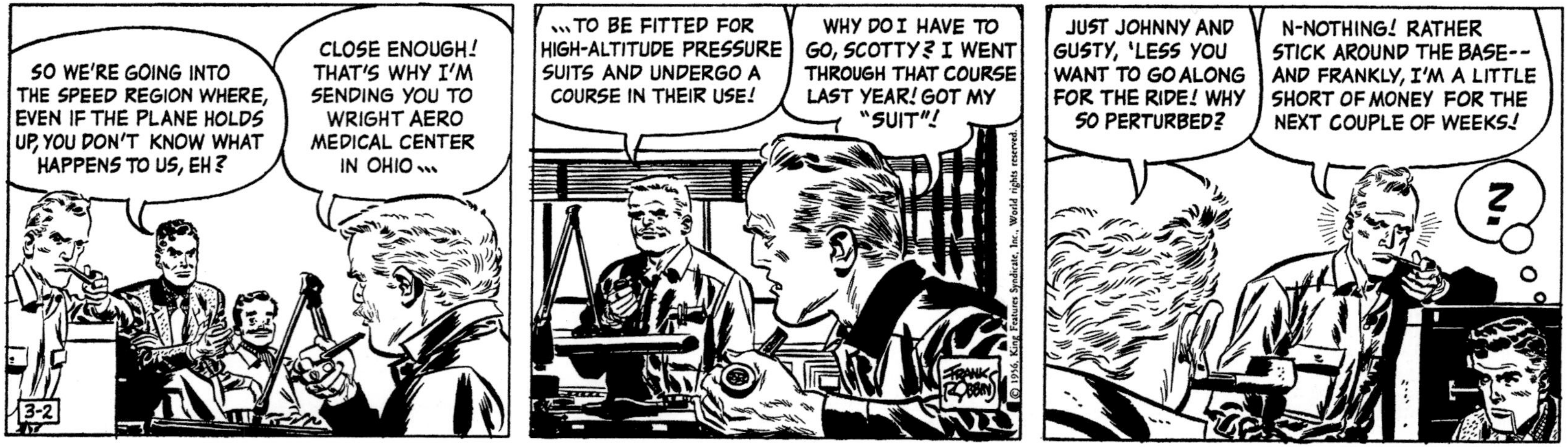
3-2
SO WE'RE GOING INTO THE SPEED REGION WHERE, EVEN IF THE PLANE HOLDS UP, YOU DON'T KNOW WHAT HAPPENS TO US, EH?
CLOSE ENOUGH! THAT'S WHY I'M SENDING YOU TO WRIGHT AERO MEDICAL CENTER IN OHIO...
...TO BE FITTED FOR HIGH-ALTITUDE PRESSURE SUITS AND UNDERGO A COURSE IN THEIR USE!
WHY DO I HAVE TO GO, SCOTTY? I WENT THROUGH THAT COURSE LAST YEAR! GOT MY "SUIT"!
FRANK ROBBINS
© 1956, King Features Syndicate, Inc., World rights reserved.
JUST JOHNNY AND GUSTY, 'LESS YOU WANT TO GO ALONG FOR THE RIDE! WHY SO PERTURBED?
N-NOTHING! RATHER STICK AROUND THE BASE-- AND FRANKLY, I'M A LITTLE SHORT OF MONEY FOR THE NEXT COUPLE OF WEEKS!
?

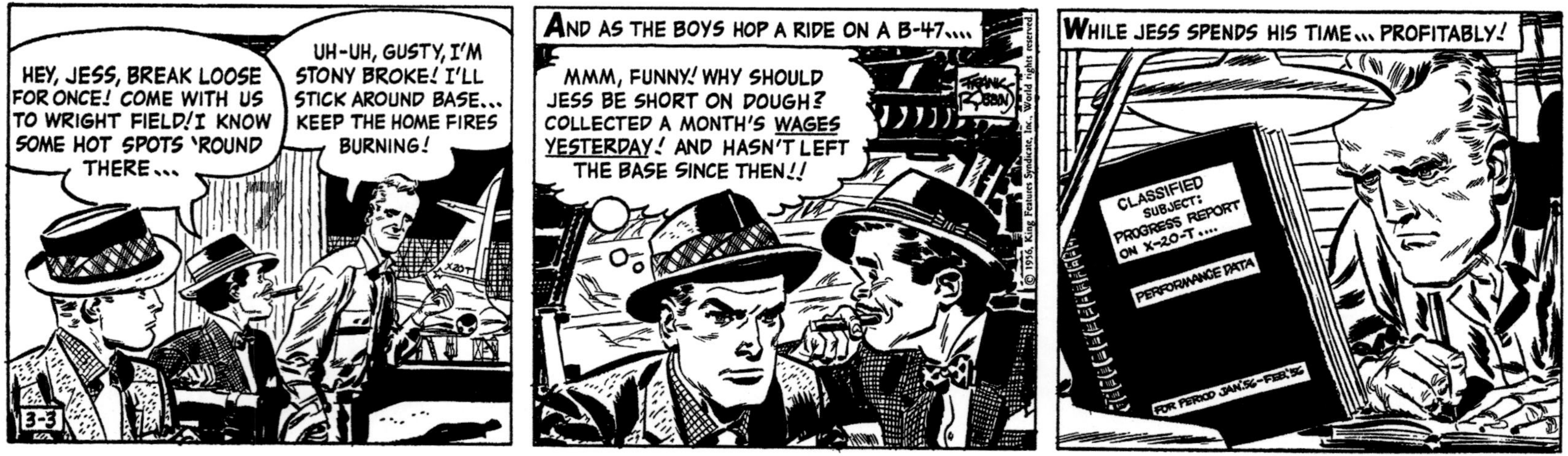
3-3
HEY, JESS, BREAK LOOSE FOR ONCE! COME WITH US TO WRIGHT FIELD! I KNOW SOME HOT SPOTS 'ROUND THERE...
UH-UH, GUSTY, I'M STONY BROKE! I'LL STICK AROUND BASE... KEEP THE HOME FIRES BURNING!
X-20T
AND AS THE BOYS HOP A RIDE ON A B-47....
MMM, FUNNY! WHY SHOULD JESS BE SHORT ON DOUGH? COLLECTED A MONTH'S WAGES YESTERDAY! AND HASN'T LEFT THE BASE SINCE THEN!!
FRANK ROBBINS
© 1956, King Features Syndicate, Inc., World rights reserved.
WHILE JESS SPENDS HIS TIME... PROFITABLY!
CLASSIFIED SUBJECT: PROGRESS REPORT ON X-20-T....
PERFORMANCE DATA
FOR PERIOD JAN.'56-FEB.'56

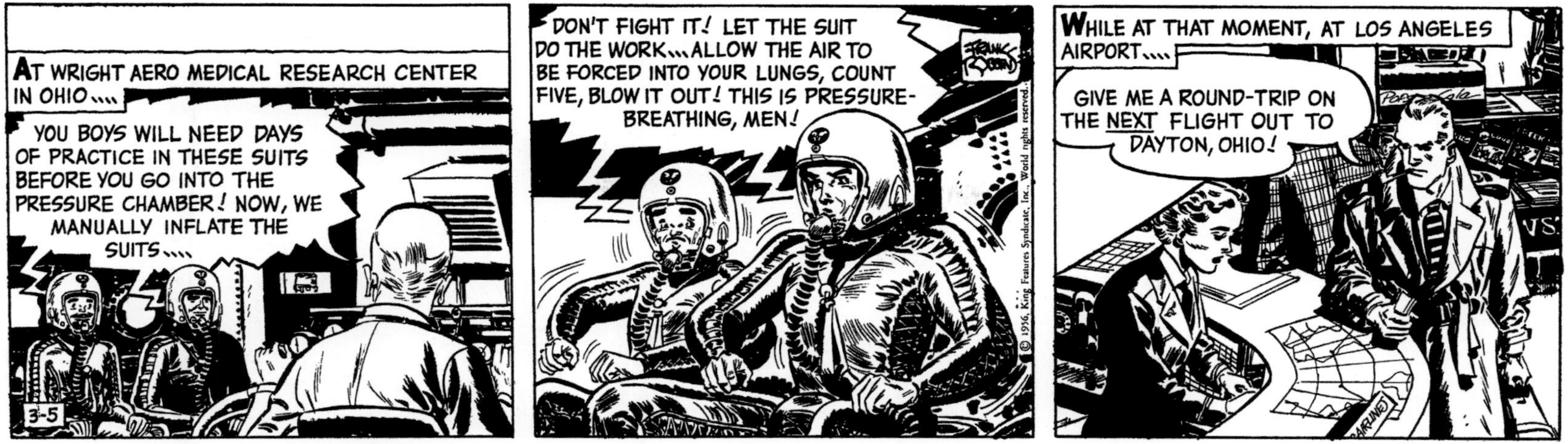
AT WRIGHT AERO MEDICAL RESEARCH CENTER IN OHIO....
YOU BOYS WILL NEED DAYS OF PRACTICE IN THESE SUITS BEFORE YOU GO INTO THE PRESSURE CHAMBER! NOW, WE MANUALLY INFLATE THE SUITS....
3-5
DON'T FIGHT IT! LET THE SUIT DO THE WORK....ALLOW THE AIR TO BE FORCED INTO YOUR LUNGS, COUNT FIVE, BLOW IT OUT! THIS IS PRESSURE-BREATHING, MEN!
© 1956, King Features Syndicate, Inc., World rights reserved.
WHILE AT THAT MOMENT, AT LOS ANGELES AIRPORT....
GIVE ME A ROUND-TRIP ON THE NEXT FLIGHT OUT TO DAYTON, OHIO!

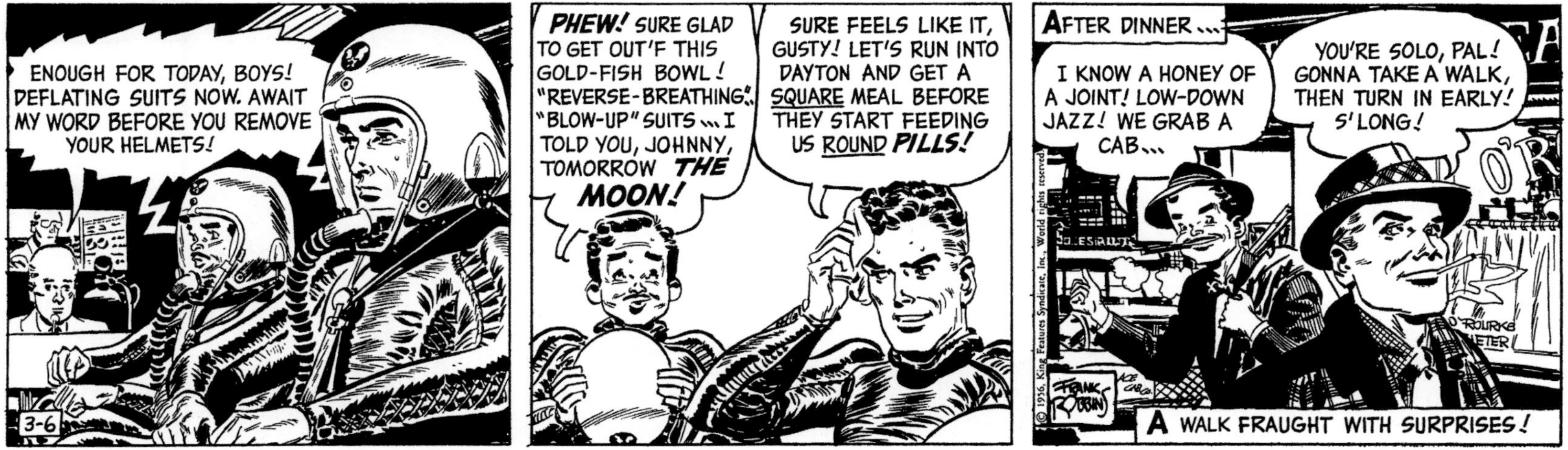
ENOUGH FOR TODAY, BOYS! DEFLATING SUITS NOW. AWAIT MY WORD BEFORE YOU REMOVE YOUR HELMETS!
3-6
PHEW! SURE GLAD TO GET OUT'F THIS GOLD-FISH BOWL! "REVERSE-BREATHING", "BLOW-UP" SUITS ... I TOLD YOU, JOHNNY, TOMORROW THE MOON!
SURE FEELS LIKE IT, GUSTY! LET'S RUN INTO DAYTON AND GET A SQUARE MEAL BEFORE THEY START FEEDING US ROUND PILLS!
AFTER DINNER....
I KNOW A HONEY OF A JOINT! LOW-DOWN JAZZ! WE GRAB A CAB...
YOU'RE SOLO, PAL! GONNA TAKE A WALK, THEN TURN IN EARLY! S'LONG!
© 1956, King Features Syndicate, Inc., World rights reserved.
A WALK FRAUGHT WITH SURPRISES!

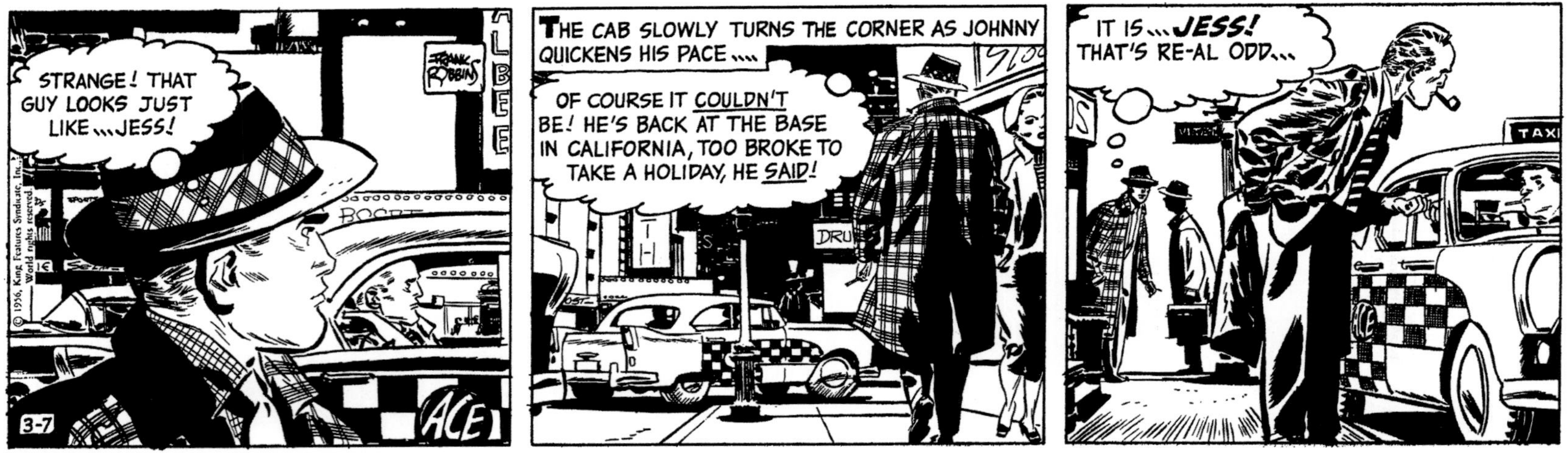
STRANGE! THAT GUY LOOKS JUST LIKE....JESS!
FRANK ROBBINS
© 1956, King Features Syndicate, Inc., World rights reserved.
3-7
ACE
THE CAB SLOWLY TURNS THE CORNER AS JOHNNY QUICKENS HIS PACE....
OF COURSE IT COULDN'T BE! HE'S BACK AT THE BASE IN CALIFORNIA, TOO BROKE TO TAKE A HOLIDAY, HE SAID!
IT IS....JESS! THAT'S RE-AL ODD...
TAXI

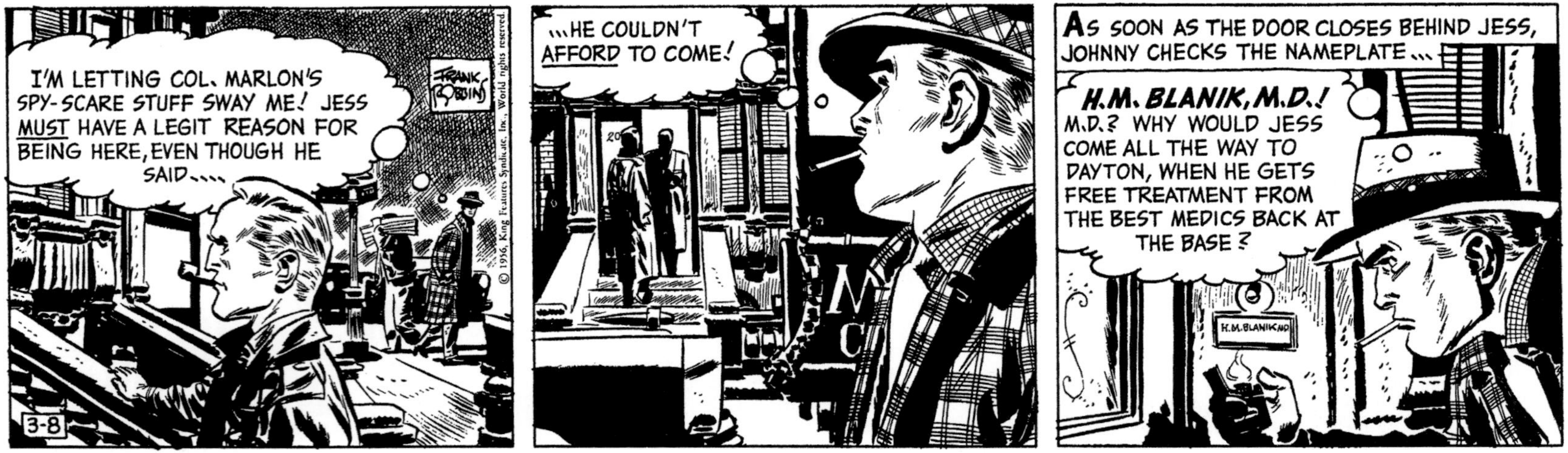
I'M LETTING COL. MARLON'S SPY-SCARE STUFF SWAY ME! JESS MUST HAVE A LEGIT REASON FOR BEING HERE, EVEN THOUGH HE SAID....
FRANK ROBBINS
© 1956, King Features Syndicate, Inc., World rights reserved.
3-8
...HE COULDN'T AFFORD TO COME!
AS SOON AS THE DOOR CLOSES BEHIND JESS, JOHNNY CHECKS THE NAMEPLATE....
H.M. BLANIK, M.D.! M.D.? WHY WOULD JESS COME ALL THE WAY TO DAYTON, WHEN HE GETS FREE TREATMENT FROM THE BEST MEDICS BACK AT THE BASE?
H.M. BLANIK MD

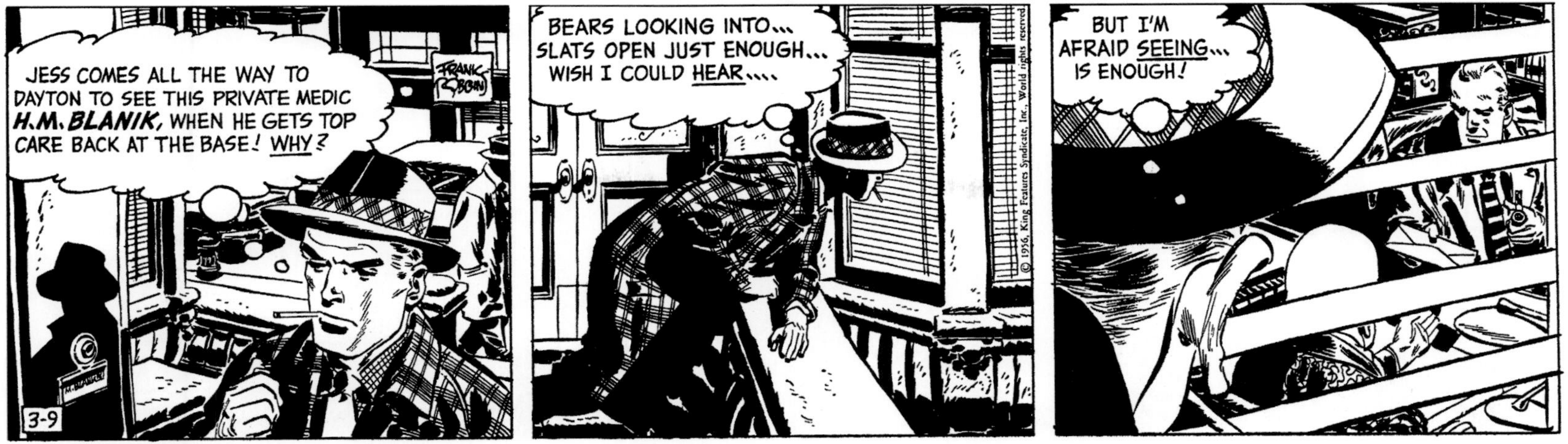
JESS COMES ALL THE WAY TO DAYTON TO SEE THIS PRIVATE MEDIC H.M. BLANIK, WHEN HE GETS TOP CARE BACK AT THE BASE! WHY?
FRANK ROBBIN
3-9
BEARS LOOKING INTO... SLATS OPEN JUST ENOUGH... WISH I COULD HEAR....
© 1956, King Features Syndicate, Inc., World rights reserved.
BUT I'M AFRAID SEEING... IS ENOUGH!

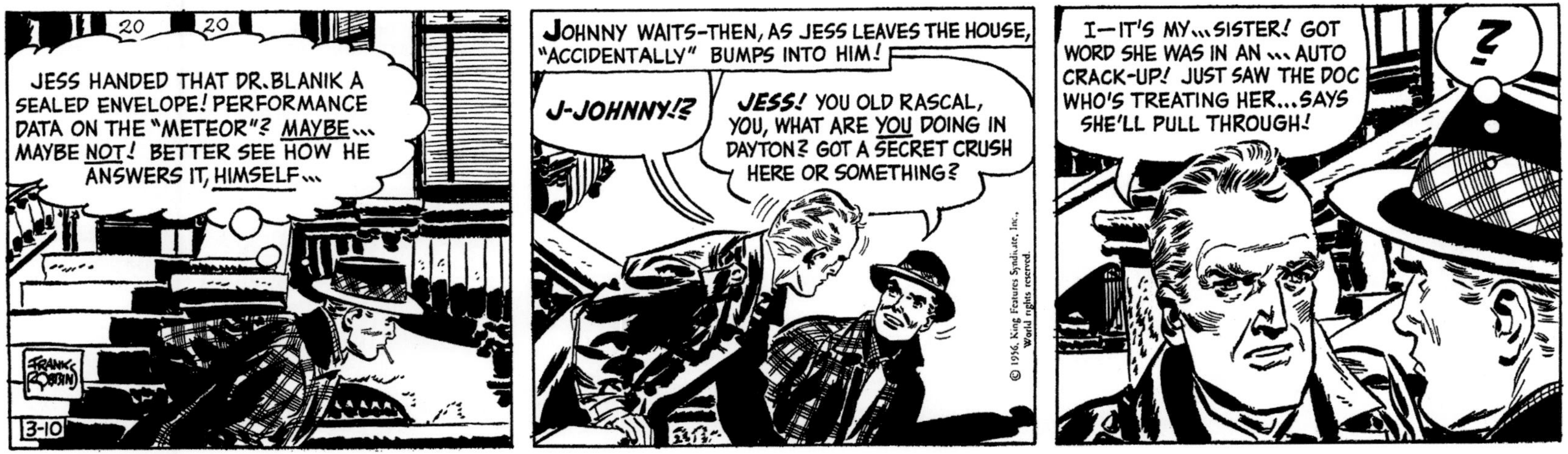
20 20
JESS HANDED THAT DR. BLANIK A SEALED ENVELOPE! PERFORMANCE DATA ON THE "METEOR"? MAYBE... MAYBE NOT! BETTER SEE HOW HE ANSWERS IT, HIMSELF...
FRANK ROBBIN
3-10
JOHNNY WAITS—THEN, AS JESS LEAVES THE HOUSE, "ACCIDENTALLY" BUMPS INTO HIM!
J-JOHNNY!?
JESS! YOU OLD RASCAL, YOU, WHAT ARE YOU DOING IN DAYTON? GOT A SECRET CRUSH HERE OR SOMETHING?
© 1956, King Features Syndicate, Inc., World rights reserved.
I—IT'S MY... SISTER! GOT WORD SHE WAS IN AN ... AUTO CRACK-UP! JUST SAW THE DOC WHO'S TREATING HER... SAYS SHE'LL PULL THROUGH!
?

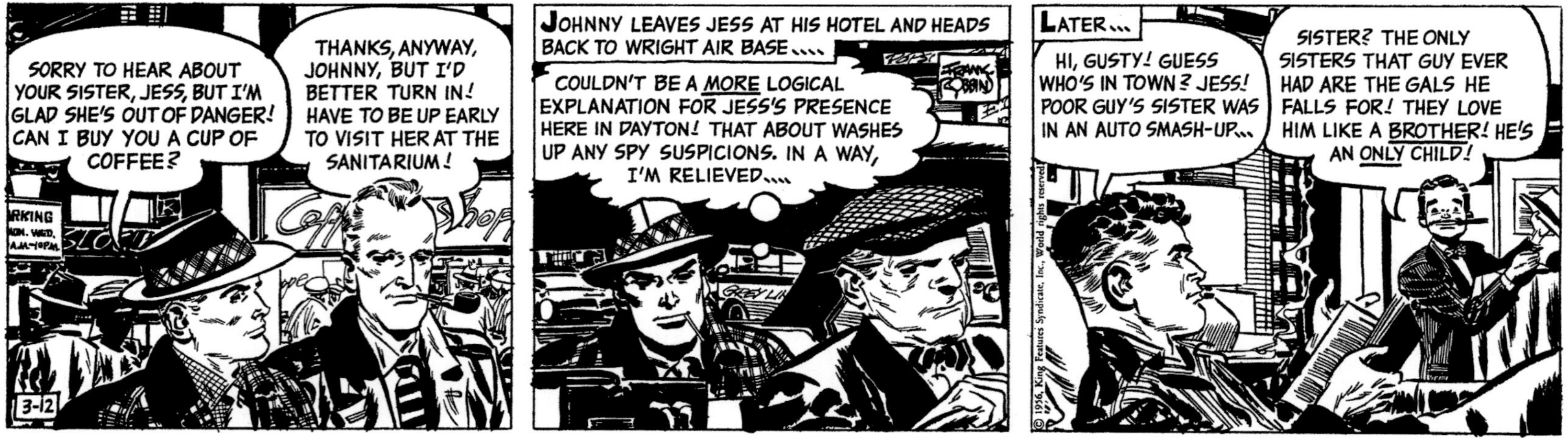
SORRY TO HEAR ABOUT YOUR SISTER, JESS, BUT I'M GLAD SHE'S OUT OF DANGER! CAN I BUY YOU A CUP OF COFFEE?
THANKS, ANYWAY, JOHNNY, BUT I'D BETTER TURN IN! HAVE TO BE UP EARLY TO VISIT HER AT THE SANITARIUM!
3-12
JOHNNY LEAVES JESS AT HIS HOTEL AND HEADS BACK TO WRIGHT AIR BASE....
COULDN'T BE A MORE LOGICAL EXPLANATION FOR JESS'S PRESENCE HERE IN DAYTON! THAT ABOUT WASHES UP ANY SPY SUSPICIONS. IN A WAY, I'M RELIEVED....
FRANK ROBBINS
LATER...
HI, GUSTY! GUESS WHO'S IN TOWN? JESS! POOR GUY'S SISTER WAS IN AN AUTO SMASH-UP...
SISTER? THE ONLY SISTERS THAT GUY EVER HAD ARE THE GALS HE FALLS FOR! THEY LOVE HIM LIKE A BROTHER! HE'S AN ONLY CHILD!
© 1956, King Features Syndicate, Inc., World rights reserved.

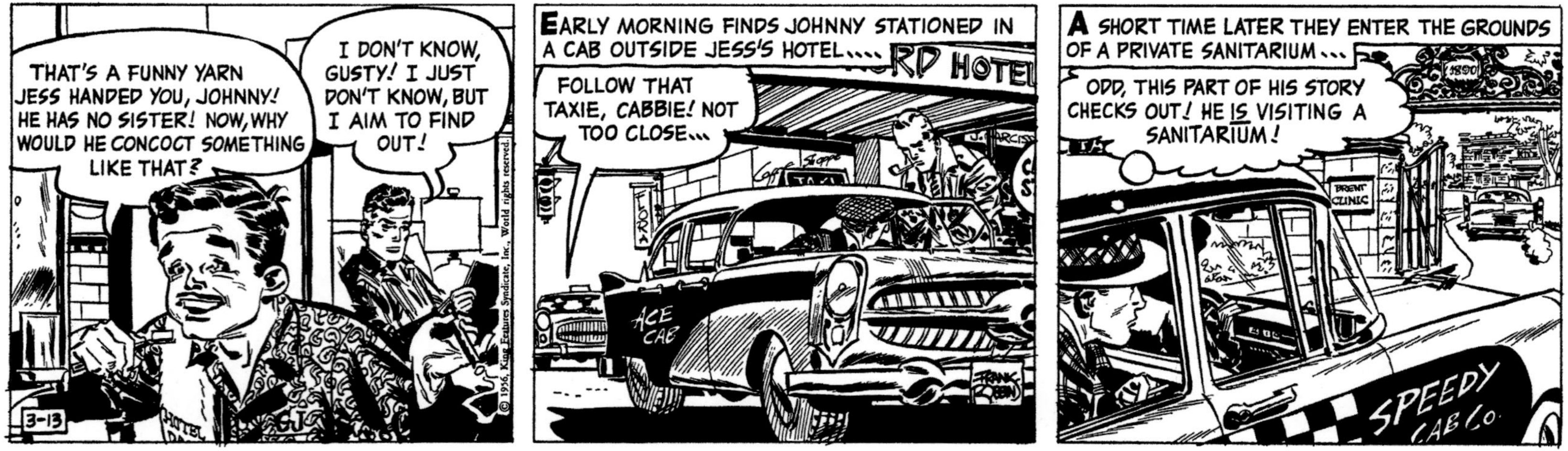
THAT'S A FUNNY YARN JESS HANDED YOU, JOHNNY! HE HAS NO SISTER! NOW, WHY WOULD HE CONCOCT SOMETHING LIKE THAT?
I DON'T KNOW, GUSTY! I JUST DON'T KNOW, BUT I AIM TO FIND OUT!
3-13
© 1956, King Features Syndicate, Inc., World rights reserved.
EARLY MORNING FINDS JOHNNY STATIONED IN A CAB OUTSIDE JESS'S HOTEL....
FOLLOW THAT TAXIE, CABBIE! NOT TOO CLOSE...
HOTEL
ACE CAB
FRANK ROBBINS
A SHORT TIME LATER THEY ENTER THE GROUNDS OF A PRIVATE SANITARIUM...
ODD, THIS PART OF HIS STORY CHECKS OUT! HE IS VISITING A SANITARIUM!
1890
BRENT CLINIC
SPEEDY CAB CO.

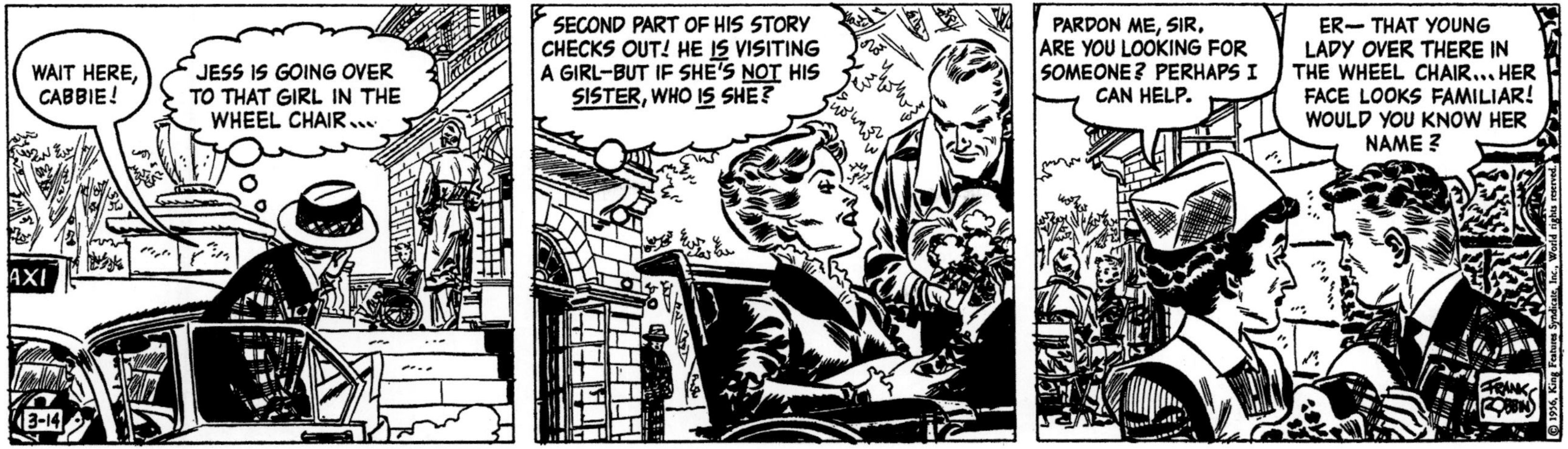
3-14
WAIT HERE, CABBIE!
JESS IS GOING OVER TO THAT GIRL IN THE WHEEL CHAIR...
SECOND PART OF HIS STORY CHECKS OUT! HE IS VISITING A GIRL—BUT IF SHE'S NOT HIS SISTER, WHO IS SHE?
PARDON ME, SIR. ARE YOU LOOKING FOR SOMEONE? PERHAPS I CAN HELP.
ER— THAT YOUNG LADY OVER THERE IN THE WHEEL CHAIR... HER FACE LOOKS FAMILIAR! WOULD YOU KNOW HER NAME?
FRANK ROBBINS
© 1956, King Features Syndicate, Inc., World rights reserved.

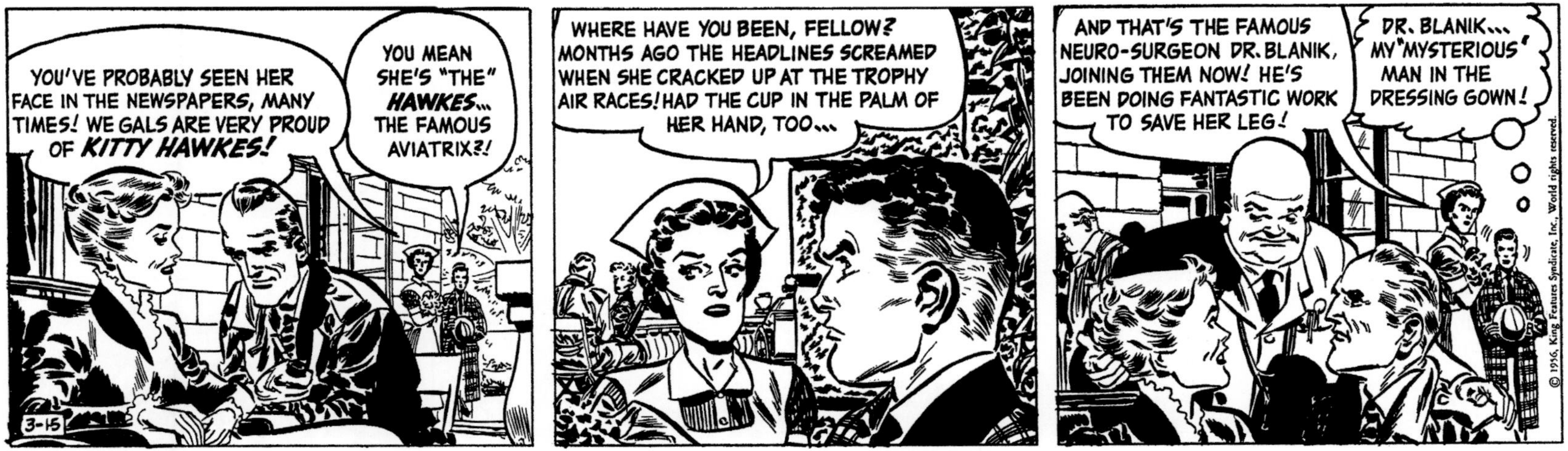
3-15
YOU'VE PROBABLY SEEN HER FACE IN THE NEWSPAPERS, MANY TIMES! WE GALS ARE VERY PROUD OF KITTY HAWKES!
YOU MEAN SHE'S "THE" HAWKES... THE FAMOUS AVIATRIX?!
WHERE HAVE YOU BEEN, FELLOW? MONTHS AGO THE HEADLINES SCREAMED WHEN SHE CRACKED UP AT THE TROPHY AIR RACES! HAD THE CUP IN THE PALM OF HER HAND, TOO...
AND THAT'S THE FAMOUS NEURO-SURGEON DR. BLANIK, JOINING THEM NOW! HE'S BEEN DOING FANTASTIC WORK TO SAVE HER LEG!
DR. BLANIK... MY "MYSTERIOUS" MAN IN THE DRESSING GOWN!
© 1956, King Features Syndicate, Inc., World rights reserved.

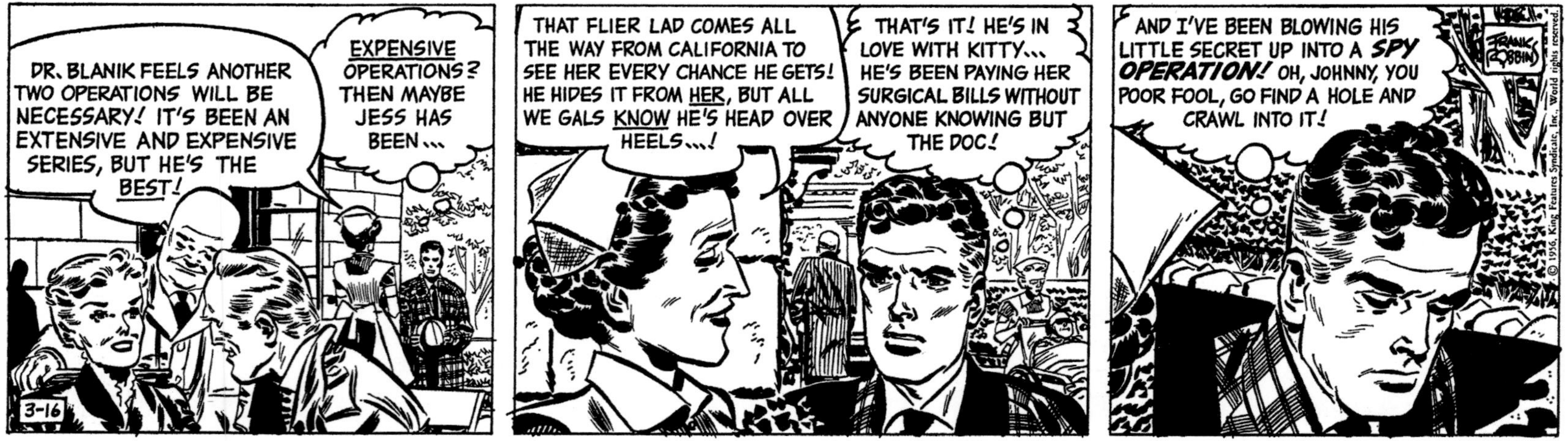
3-16
DR. BLANIK FEELS ANOTHER TWO OPERATIONS WILL BE NECESSARY! IT'S BEEN AN EXTENSIVE AND EXPENSIVE SERIES, BUT HE'S THE BEST!
EXPENSIVE OPERATIONS? THEN MAYBE JESS HAS BEEN...
THAT FLIER LAD COMES ALL THE WAY FROM CALIFORNIA TO SEE HER EVERY CHANCE HE GETS! HE HIDES IT FROM HER, BUT ALL WE GALS KNOW HE'S HEAD OVER HEELS...!
THAT'S IT! HE'S IN LOVE WITH KITTY... HE'S BEEN PAYING HER SURGICAL BILLS WITHOUT ANYONE KNOWING BUT THE DOC!
AND I'VE BEEN BLOWING HIS LITTLE SECRET UP INTO A SPY OPERATION! OH, JOHNNY, YOU POOR FOOL, GO FIND A HOLE AND CRAWL INTO IT!
FRANK ROBBINS
© 1956, King Features Syndicate, Inc., World rights reserved.

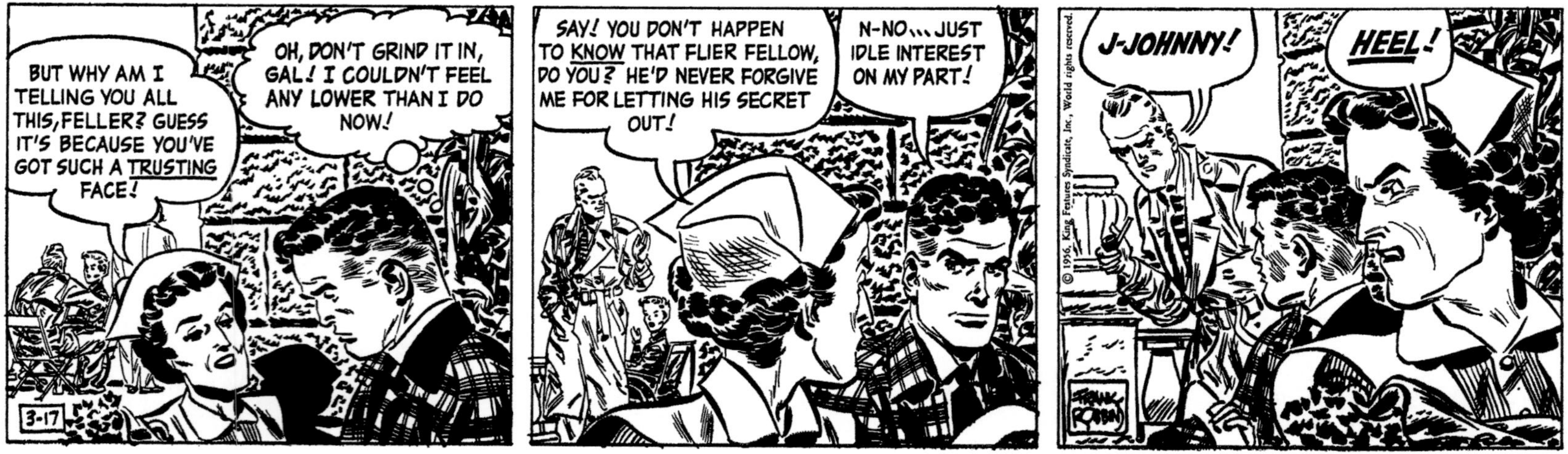
3-17
BUT WHY AM I TELLING YOU ALL THIS, FELLER? GUESS IT'S BECAUSE YOU'VE GOT SUCH A TRUSTING FACE!
OH, DON'T GRIND IT IN, GAL! I COULDN'T FEEL ANY LOWER THAN I DO NOW!
SAY! YOU DON'T HAPPEN TO KNOW THAT FLIER FELLOW, DO YOU? HE'D NEVER FORGIVE ME FOR LETTING HIS SECRET OUT!
N-NO... JUST IDLE INTEREST ON MY PART!
© 1956, King Features Syndicate, Inc., World rights reserved.
J-JOHNNY!
HEEL!
FRANK ROBBINS

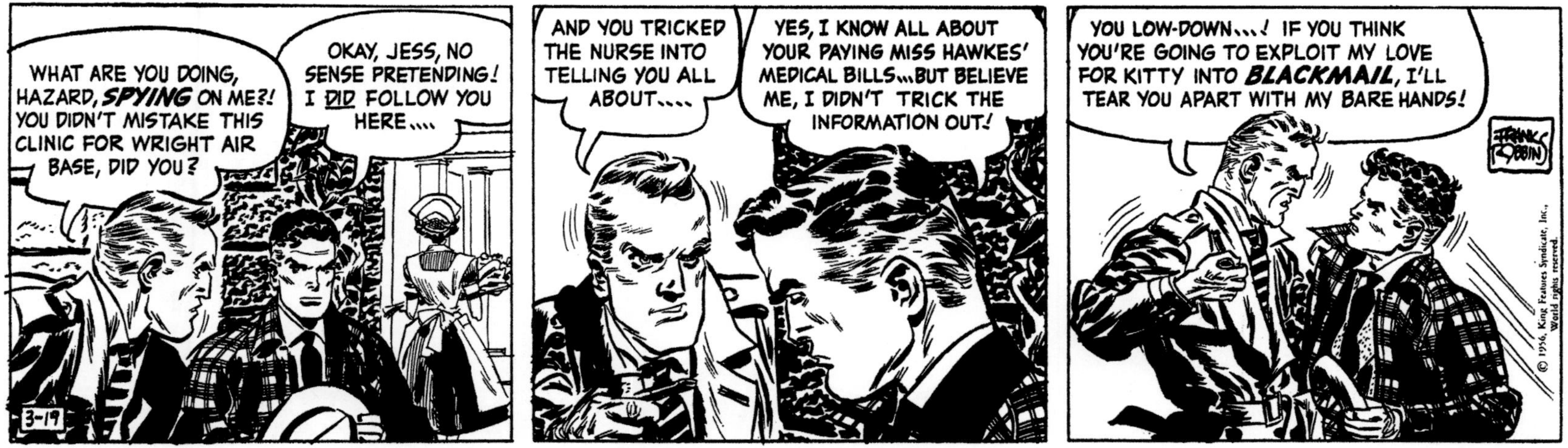
WHAT ARE YOU DOING, HAZARD, SPYING ON ME?! YOU DIDN'T MISTAKE THIS CLINIC FOR WRIGHT AIR BASE, DID YOU?
OKAY, JESS, NO SENSE PRETENDING! I DID FOLLOW YOU HERE....
3-19
AND YOU TRICKED THE NURSE INTO TELLING YOU ALL ABOUT....
YES, I KNOW ALL ABOUT YOUR PAYING MISS HAWKES' MEDICAL BILLS...BUT BELIEVE ME, I DIDN'T TRICK THE INFORMATION OUT!
YOU LOW-DOWN....! IF YOU THINK YOU'RE GOING TO EXPLOIT MY LOVE FOR KITTY INTO BLACKMAIL, I'LL TEAR YOU APART WITH MY BARE HANDS!
© 1956, King Features Syndicate, Inc., World rights reserved.

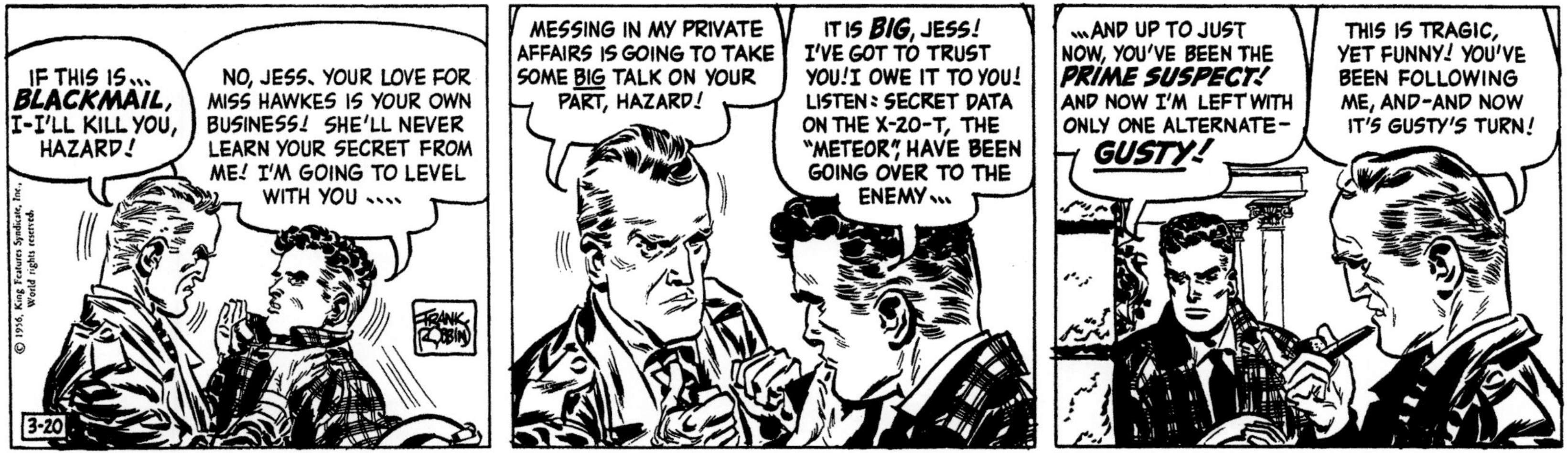
IF THIS IS... BLACKMAIL, I-I'LL KILL YOU, HAZARD!
NO, JESS. YOUR LOVE FOR MISS HAWKES IS YOUR OWN BUSINESS! SHE'LL NEVER LEARN YOUR SECRET FROM ME! I'M GOING TO LEVEL WITH YOU ....
© 1956, King Features Syndicate, Inc., World rights reserved.
3-20
MESSING IN MY PRIVATE AFFAIRS IS GOING TO TAKE SOME BIG TALK ON YOUR PART, HAZARD!
IT IS BIG, JESS! I'VE GOT TO TRUST YOU! I OWE IT TO YOU! LISTEN: SECRET DATA ON THE X-20-T, THE "METEOR", HAVE BEEN GOING OVER TO THE ENEMY...
...AND UP TO JUST NOW, YOU'VE BEEN THE PRIME SUSPECT! AND NOW I'M LEFT WITH ONLY ONE ALTERNATE—GUSTY!
THIS IS TRAGIC, YET FUNNY! YOU'VE BEEN FOLLOWING ME, AND-AND NOW IT'S GUSTY'S TURN!

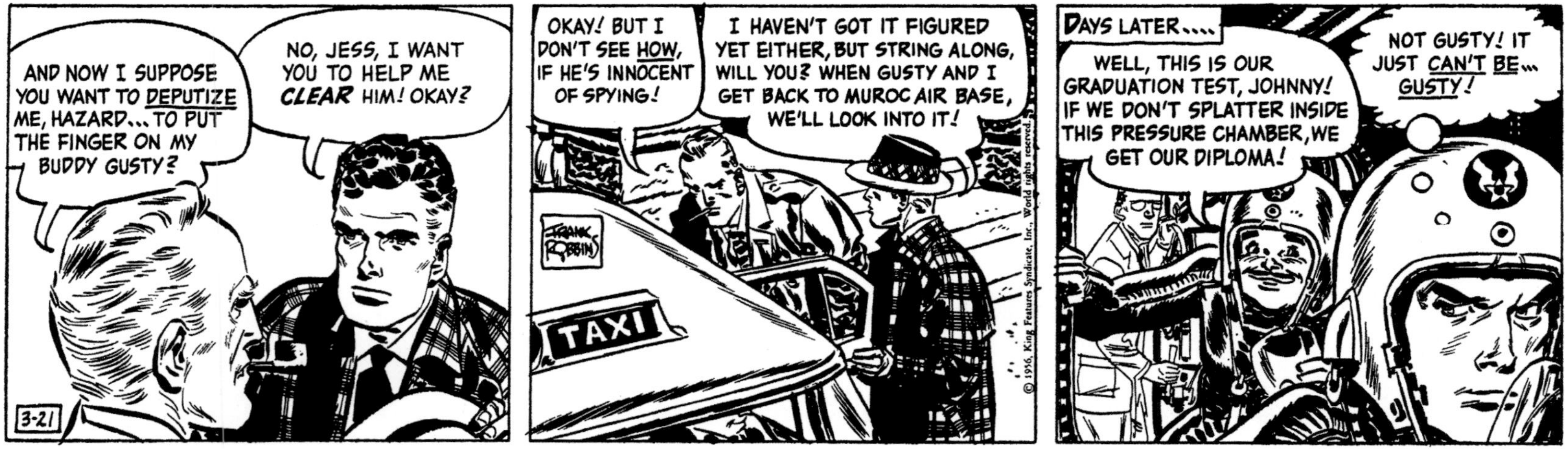
AND NOW I SUPPOSE YOU WANT TO DEPUTIZE ME, HAZARD... TO PUT THE FINGER ON MY BUDDY GUSTY?
NO, JESS, I WANT YOU TO HELP ME CLEAR HIM! OKAY?
3-21
OKAY! BUT I DON'T SEE HOW, IF HE'S INNOCENT OF SPYING!
I HAVEN'T GOT IT FIGURED YET EITHER, BUT STRING ALONG, WILL YOU? WHEN GUSTY AND I GET BACK TO MUROC AIR BASE, WE'LL LOOK INTO IT!
FRANK ROBBINS
TAXI
© 1956, King Features Syndicate, Inc., World rights reserved.
DAYS LATER....
WELL, THIS IS OUR GRADUATION TEST, JOHNNY! IF WE DON'T SPLATTER INSIDE THIS PRESSURE CHAMBER, WE GET OUR DIPLOMA!
NOT GUSTY! IT JUST CAN'T BE... GUSTY!

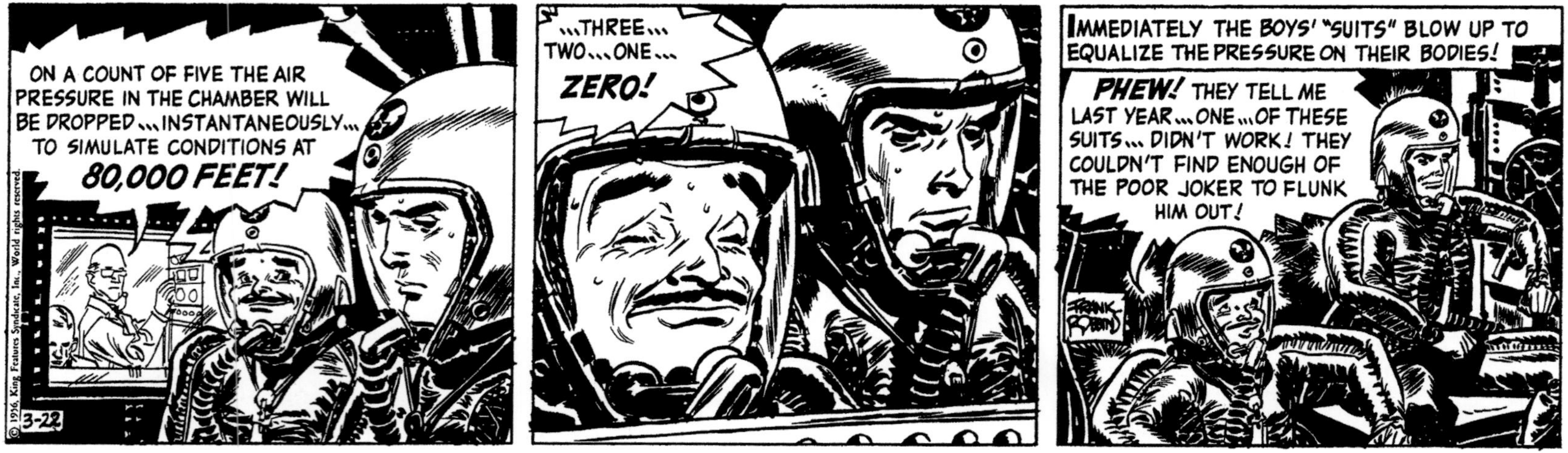
ON A COUNT OF FIVE THE AIR PRESSURE IN THE CHAMBER WILL BE DROPPED... INSTANTANEOUSLY... TO SIMULATE CONDITIONS AT 80,000 FEET!
© 1956, King Features Syndicate, Inc., World rights reserved.
3-22
...THREE... TWO... ONE... ZERO!
IMMEDIATELY THE BOYS' "SUITS" BLOW UP TO EQUALIZE THE PRESSURE ON THEIR BODIES!
PHEW! THEY TELL ME LAST YEAR... ONE... OF THESE SUITS... DIDN'T WORK! THEY COULDN'T FIND ENOUGH OF THE POOR JOKER TO FLUNK HIM OUT!
FRANK ROBBINS

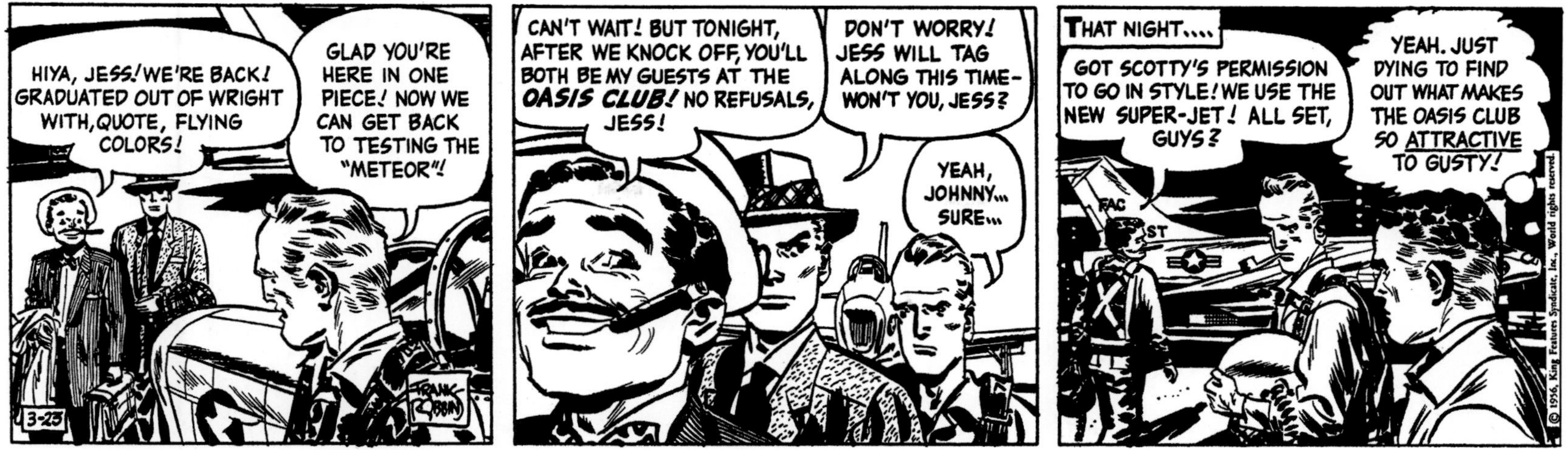
HIYA, JESS! WE'RE BACK! GRADUATED OUT OF WRIGHT WITH, QUOTE, FLYING COLORS!
GLAD YOU'RE HERE IN ONE PIECE! NOW WE CAN GET BACK TO TESTING THE "METEOR"!
FRANK ROBBINS
3-23
CAN'T WAIT! BUT TONIGHT, AFTER WE KNOCK OFF, YOU'LL BOTH BE MY GUESTS AT THE OASIS CLUB! NO REFUSALS, JESS!
DON'T WORRY! JESS WILL TAG ALONG THIS TIME– WON'T YOU, JESS?
YEAH, JOHNNY... SURE...
THAT NIGHT....
GOT SCOTTY'S PERMISSION TO GO IN STYLE! WE USE THE NEW SUPER-JET! ALL SET, GUYS?
YEAH. JUST DYING TO FIND OUT WHAT MAKES THE OASIS CLUB SO ATTRACTIVE TO GUSTY!
© 1956, King Features Syndicate, Inc., World rights reserved.

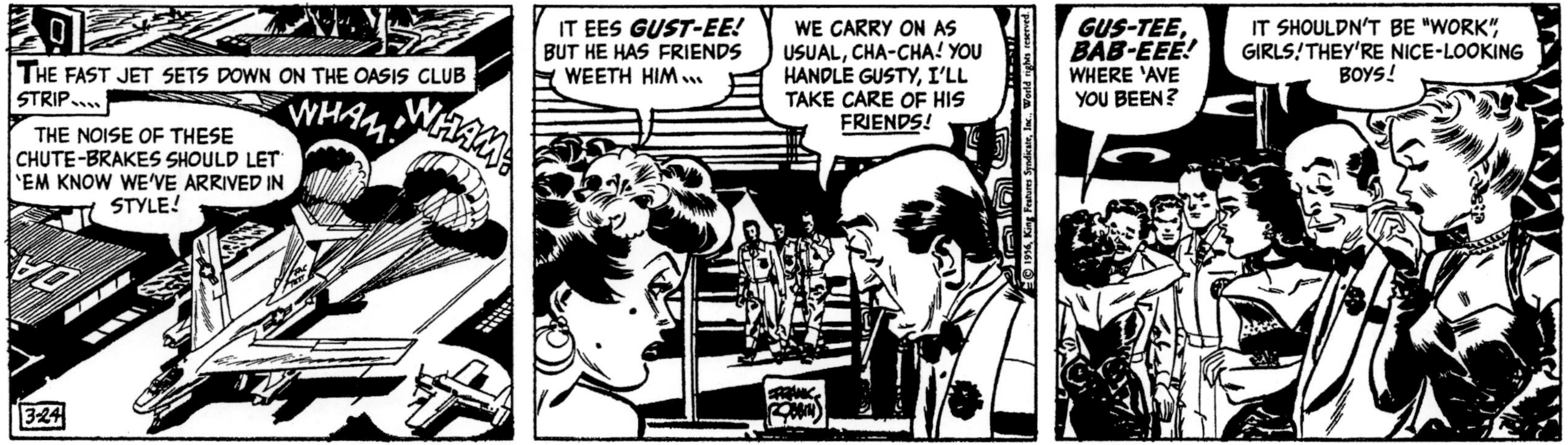
THE FAST JET SETS DOWN ON THE OASIS CLUB STRIP....
THE NOISE OF THESE CHUTE-BRAKES SHOULD LET 'EM KNOW WE'VE ARRIVED IN STYLE!
WHAM! WHAM!
3-24
IT EES GUST-EE! BUT HE HAS FRIENDS WEETH HIM...
WE CARRY ON AS USUAL, CHA-CHA! YOU HANDLE GUSTY, I'LL TAKE CARE OF HIS FRIENDS!
© 1956, King Features Syndicate, Inc., World rights reserved.
FRANK ROBBINS
GUS-TEE, BAB-EEE! WHERE 'AVE YOU BEEN?
IT SHOULDN'T BE "WORK", GIRLS! THEY'RE NICE-LOOKING BOYS!

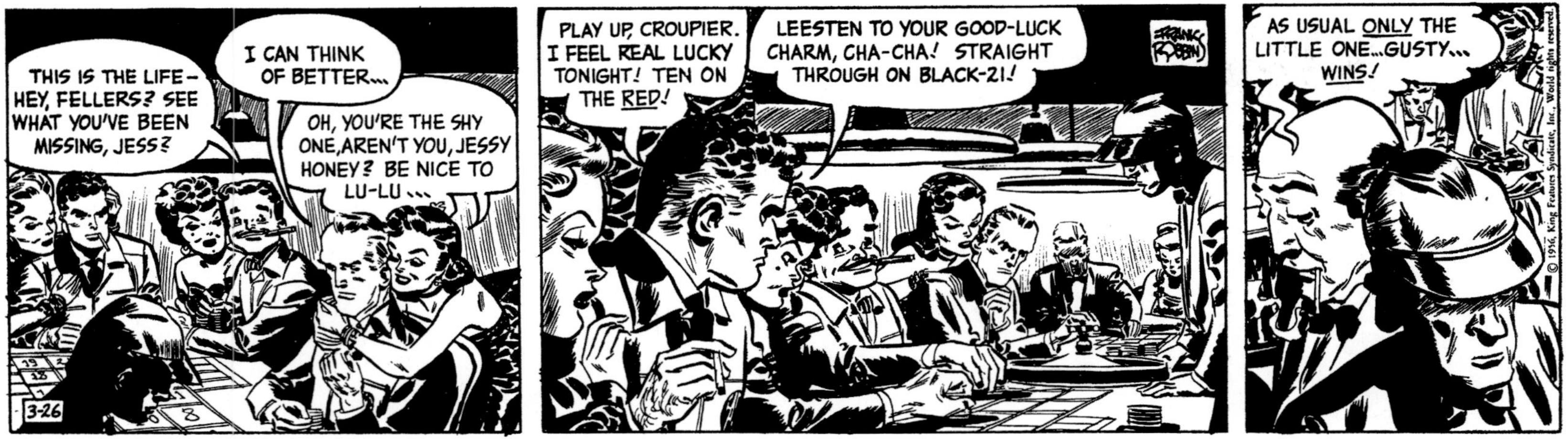
3-26
THIS IS THE LIFE—HEY, FELLERS? SEE WHAT YOU'VE BEEN MISSING, JESS?
I CAN THINK OF BETTER...
OH, YOU'RE THE SHY ONE, AREN'T YOU, JESSY HONEY? BE NICE TO LU-LU...
PLAY UP, CROUPIER. I FEEL REAL LUCKY TONIGHT! TEN ON THE RED!
LEESTEN TO YOUR GOOD-LUCK CHARM, CHA-CHA! STRAIGHT THROUGH ON BLACK-21!
FRANK ROBBINS
AS USUAL ONLY THE LITTLE ONE...GUSTY... WINS!
© 1956, King Features Syndicate, Inc., World rights reserved.

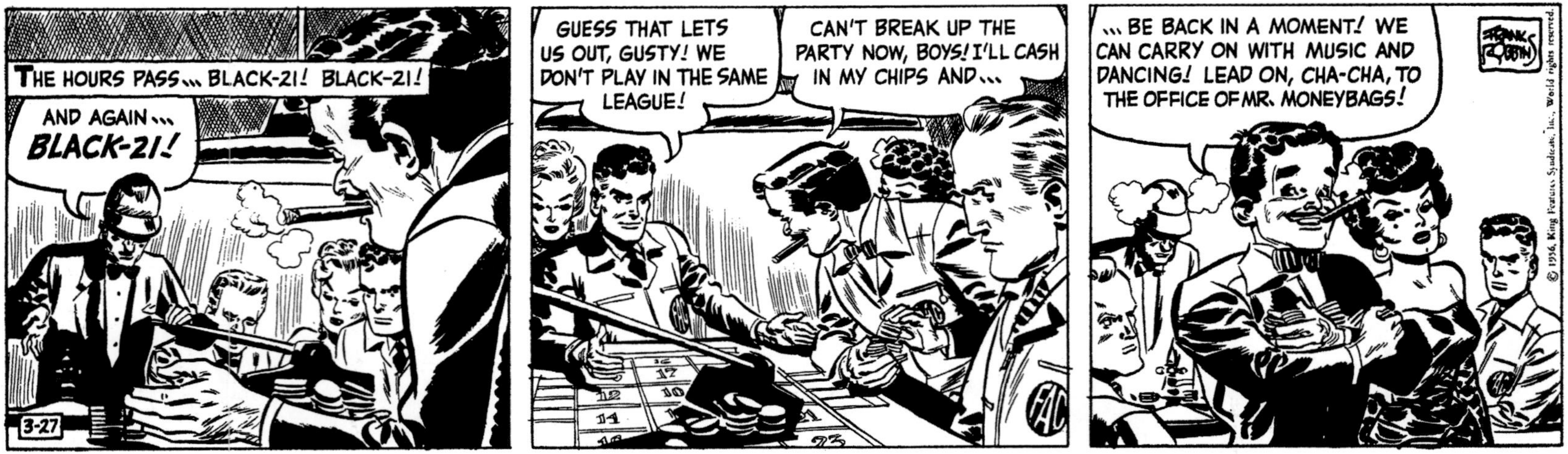
3-27
THE HOURS PASS... BLACK-21! BLACK-21!
AND AGAIN... BLACK-21!
GUESS THAT LETS US OUT, GUSTY! WE DON'T PLAY IN THE SAME LEAGUE!
CAN'T BREAK UP THE PARTY NOW, BOYS! I'LL CASH IN MY CHIPS AND...
...BE BACK IN A MOMENT! WE CAN CARRY ON WITH MUSIC AND DANCING! LEAD ON, CHA-CHA, TO THE OFFICE OF MR. MONEYBAGS!
FRANK ROBBINS
© 1956, King Features Syndicate, Inc., World rights reserved.

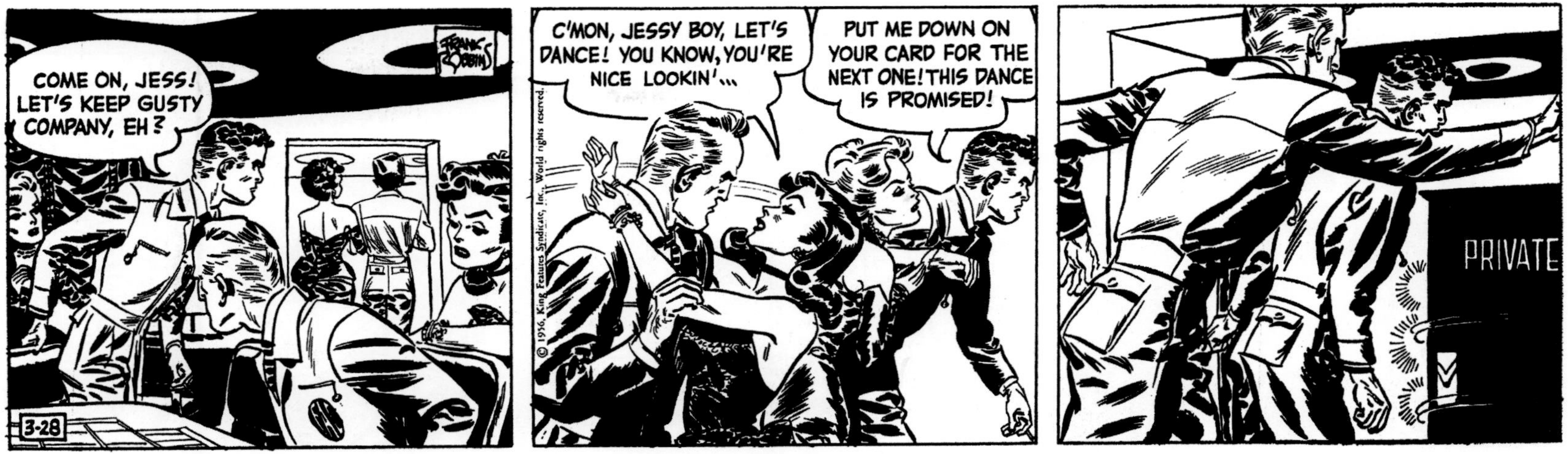
FRANK ROBBINS
COME ON, JESS! LET'S KEEP GUSTY COMPANY, EH?
3-28
C'MON, JESSY BOY, LET'S DANCE! YOU KNOW, YOU'RE NICE LOOKIN'...
PUT ME DOWN ON YOUR CARD FOR THE NEXT ONE! THIS DANCE IS PROMISED!
© 1956, King Features Syndicate, Inc., World rights reserved.
PRIVATE

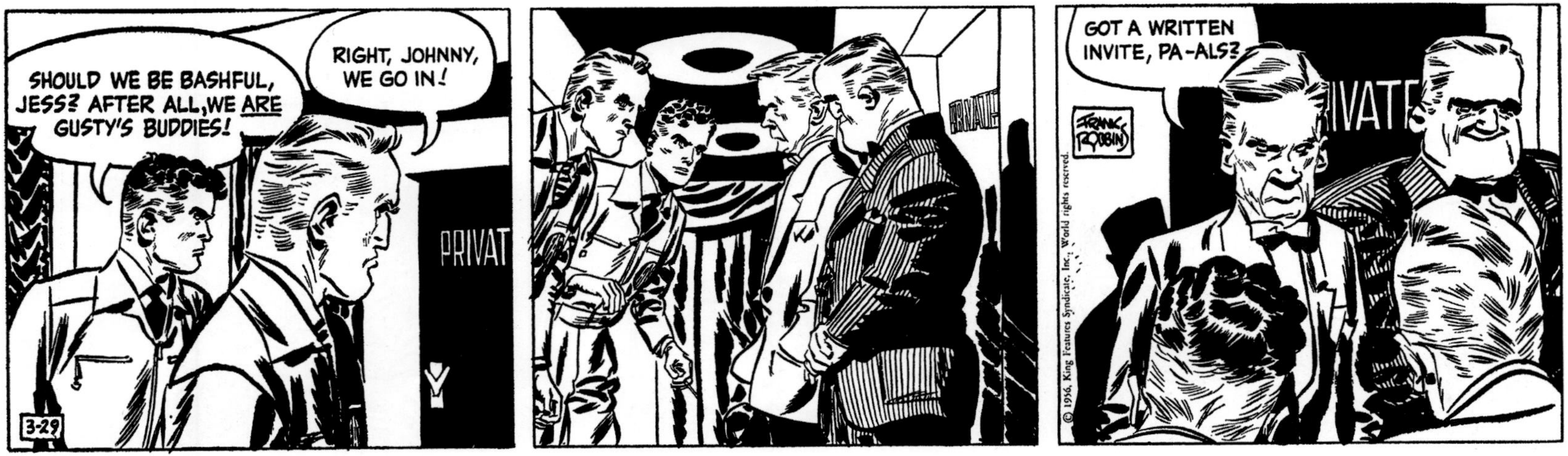
SHOULD WE BE BASHFUL, JESS? AFTER ALL, WE ARE GUSTY'S BUDDIES!
RIGHT, JOHNNY, WE GO IN!
PRIVAT
3-29
GOT A WRITTEN INVITE, PA-ALS?
FRANK ROBBINS
© 1956, King Features Syndicate, Inc., World rights reserved.

SHOULD WE, JOHNNY?

NO SENSE BARGING IN WHERE WE'RE NOT INVITED, JESS! WE'LL WAIT OUTSIDE IN THE CLUB!

WHY DIDN'T WE TAKE 'EM ON, JOHNNY? ONLY TWO OF 'EM!

WE'LL GIVE GUSTY A DECENT AMOUNT OF TIME TO CASH IN HIS CHIPS—AND THEN, IF HE DOESN'T SHOW......!

FRANK ROBBIN

© 1956, King Features Syndicate, Inc., World rights reserved.

WHILE INSIDE MR. GAMBIT'S PRIVATE OFFICE .....

DREENK THIS, GUSTEE! CHA-CHA FEEX IT SPECIAL FOR YOU LIKE ALWAYS!

© 1956, King Features Syndicate, Inc., World rights reserved.

HAVEN'T GOT TIME FOR COFFEE TONIGHT, CHA-CHA! MY BUDDIES ARE WAITING OUTSIDE! CASH IN MY CHIPS, MR. GAMBIT.....

OH-H, GUST-EE, YOU 'AVE TIME FOR ONE LITTLE SIP, NO? CHA-CHA BREWED EET SPECIAL.....

OKAY, JUST ONE.... GLOP!

FRANK ROBBIN

GOOD! IN HOT COFFEE THIS DRUG WORKS INSTANTLY! WHEN HE WAKES HE WILL NOT KNOW HE WAS "OUT"! WE BEGIN THE QUESTIONING.....SWITCH ON THE RECORDER!

© 1956, King Features Syndicate, Inc., World rights reserved.

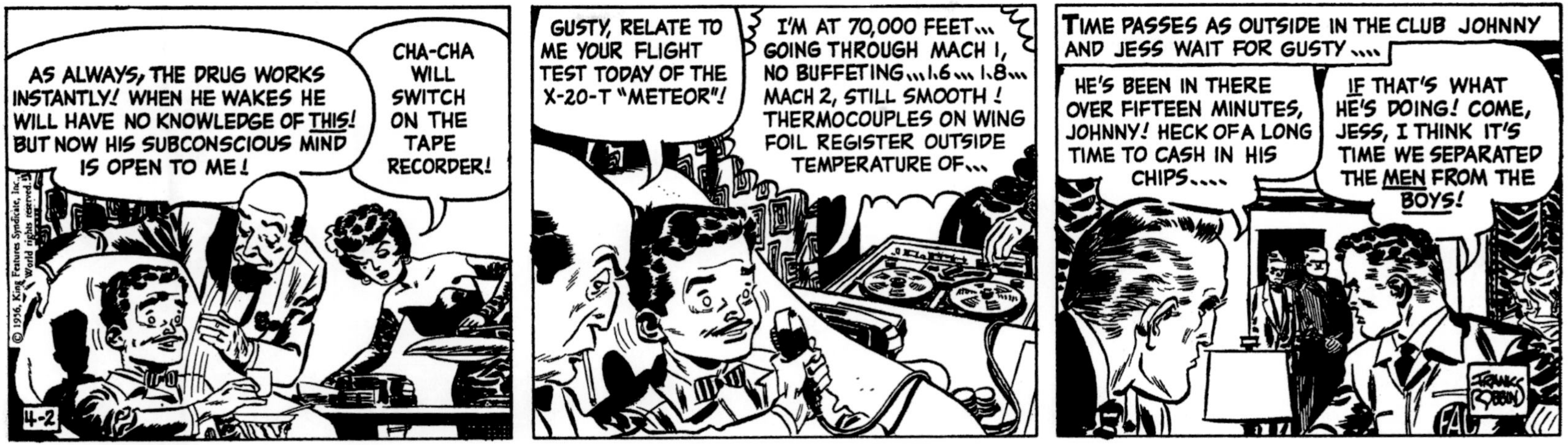
AS ALWAYS, THE DRUG WORKS INSTANTLY! WHEN HE WAKES HE WILL HAVE NO KNOWLEDGE OF THIS! BUT NOW HIS SUBCONSCIOUS MIND IS OPEN TO ME!
CHA-CHA WILL SWITCH ON THE TAPE RECORDER!
© 1956, King Features Syndicate, Inc., World rights reserved.
4-2
GUSTY, RELATE TO ME YOUR FLIGHT TEST TODAY OF THE X-20-T "METEOR"!
I'M AT 70,000 FEET... GOING THROUGH MACH 1, NO BUFFETING... 1.6... 1.8... MACH 2, STILL SMOOTH! THERMOCOUPLES ON WING FOIL REGISTER OUTSIDE TEMPERATURE OF...
TIME PASSES AS OUTSIDE IN THE CLUB JOHNNY AND JESS WAIT FOR GUSTY....
HE'S BEEN IN THERE OVER FIFTEEN MINUTES, JOHNNY! HECK OF A LONG TIME TO CASH IN HIS CHIPS....
IF THAT'S WHAT HE'S DOING! COME, JESS, I THINK IT'S TIME WE SEPARATED THE MEN FROM THE BOYS!
FRANK ROBBINS

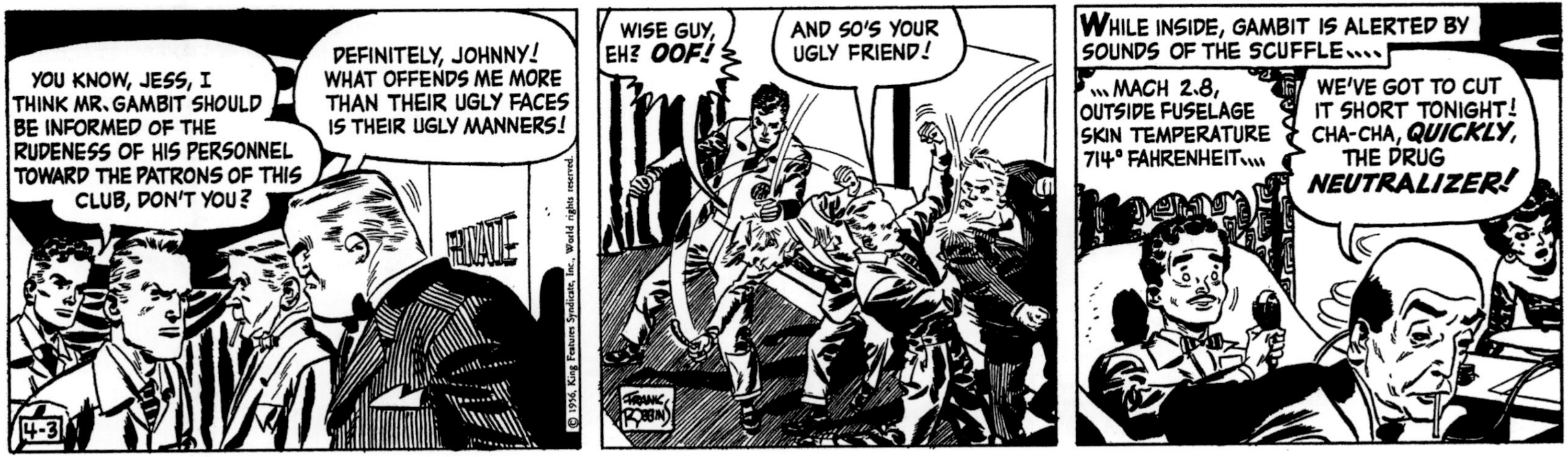
YOU KNOW, JESS, I THINK MR. GAMBIT SHOULD BE INFORMED OF THE RUDENESS OF HIS PERSONNEL TOWARD THE PATRONS OF THIS CLUB, DON'T YOU?
DEFINITELY, JOHNNY! WHAT OFFENDS ME MORE THAN THEIR UGLY FACES IS THEIR UGLY MANNERS!
PRIVATE
4-3
© 1956, King Features Syndicate, Inc., World rights reserved.
WISE GUY, EH? OOF!
AND SO'S YOUR UGLY FRIEND!
FRANK ROBBINS
WHILE INSIDE, GAMBIT IS ALERTED BY SOUNDS OF THE SCUFFLE....
...MACH 2.8, OUTSIDE FUSELAGE SKIN TEMPERATURE 714° FAHRENHEIT....
WE'VE GOT TO CUT IT SHORT TONIGHT! CHA-CHA, QUICKLY, THE DRUG NEUTRALIZER!

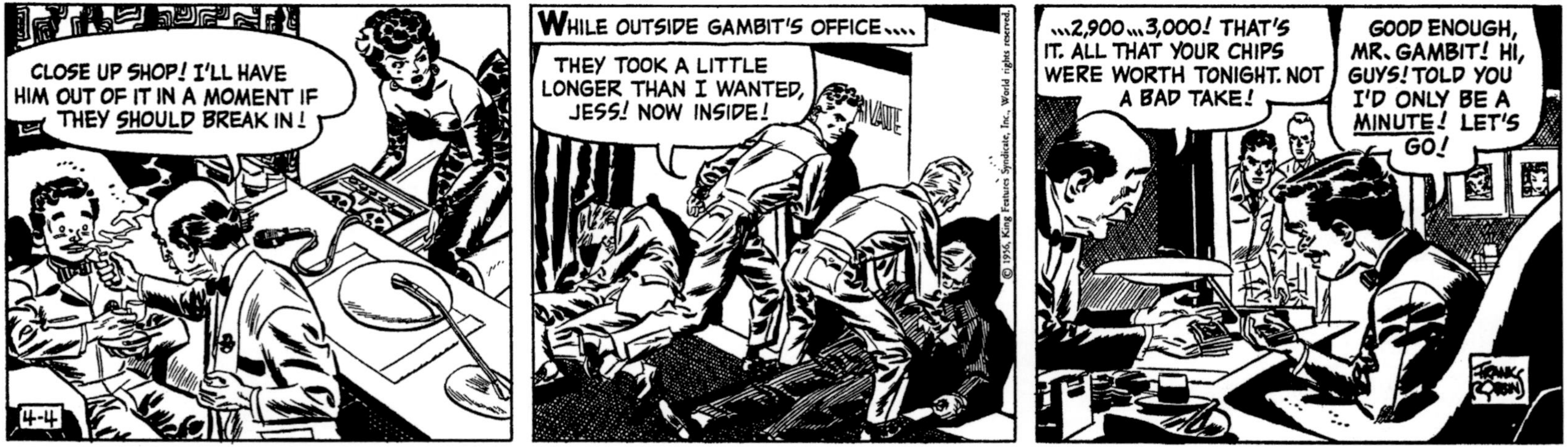
CLOSE UP SHOP! I'LL HAVE HIM OUT OF IT IN A MOMENT IF THEY SHOULD BREAK IN!
4-4
WHILE OUTSIDE GAMBIT'S OFFICE....
THEY TOOK A LITTLE LONGER THAN I WANTED, JESS! NOW INSIDE!
PRIVATE
© 1956, King Features Syndicate, Inc., World rights reserved.
...2,900...3,000! THAT'S IT. ALL THAT YOUR CHIPS WERE WORTH TONIGHT. NOT A BAD TAKE!
GOOD ENOUGH, MR. GAMBIT! HI, GUYS! TOLD YOU I'D ONLY BE A MINUTE! LET'S GO!
FRANK ROBBINS

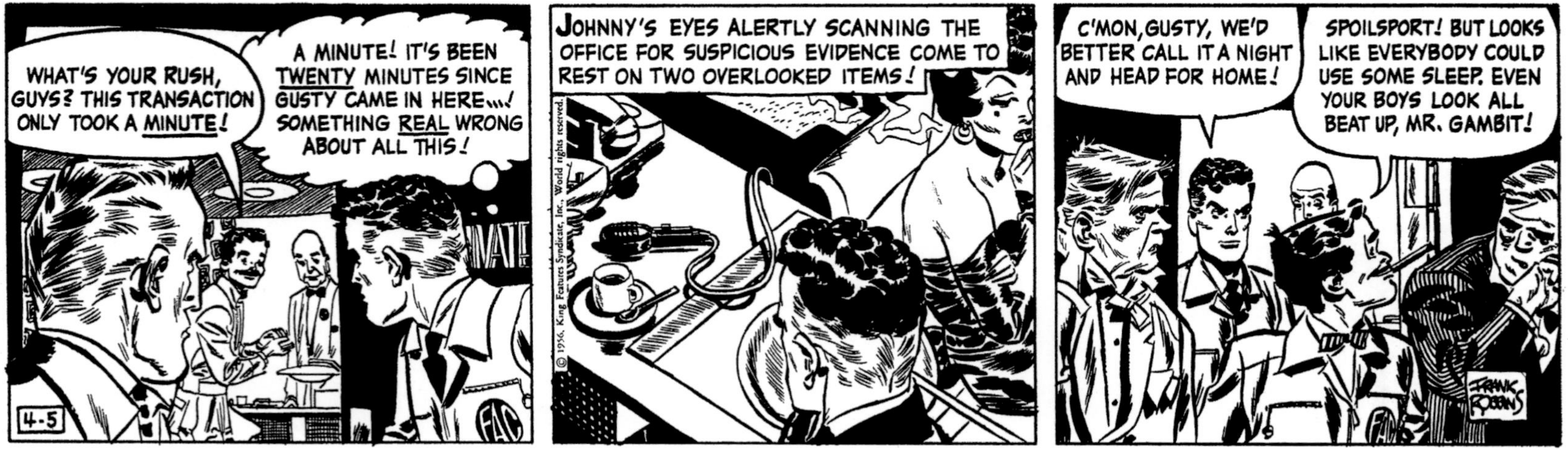
WHAT'S YOUR RUSH, GUYS? THIS TRANSACTION ONLY TOOK A MINUTE!
A MINUTE! IT'S BEEN TWENTY MINUTES SINCE GUSTY CAME IN HERE...! SOMETHING REAL WRONG ABOUT ALL THIS!
4-5
JOHNNY'S EYES ALERTLY SCANNING THE OFFICE FOR SUSPICIOUS EVIDENCE COME TO REST ON TWO OVERLOOKED ITEMS!
© 1956, King Features Syndicate, Inc., World rights reserved.
C'MON, GUSTY, WE'D BETTER CALL IT A NIGHT AND HEAD FOR HOME!
SPOILSPORT! BUT LOOKS LIKE EVERYBODY COULD USE SOME SLEEP. EVEN YOUR BOYS LOOK ALL BEAT UP, MR. GAMBIT!
FRANK ROBBINS

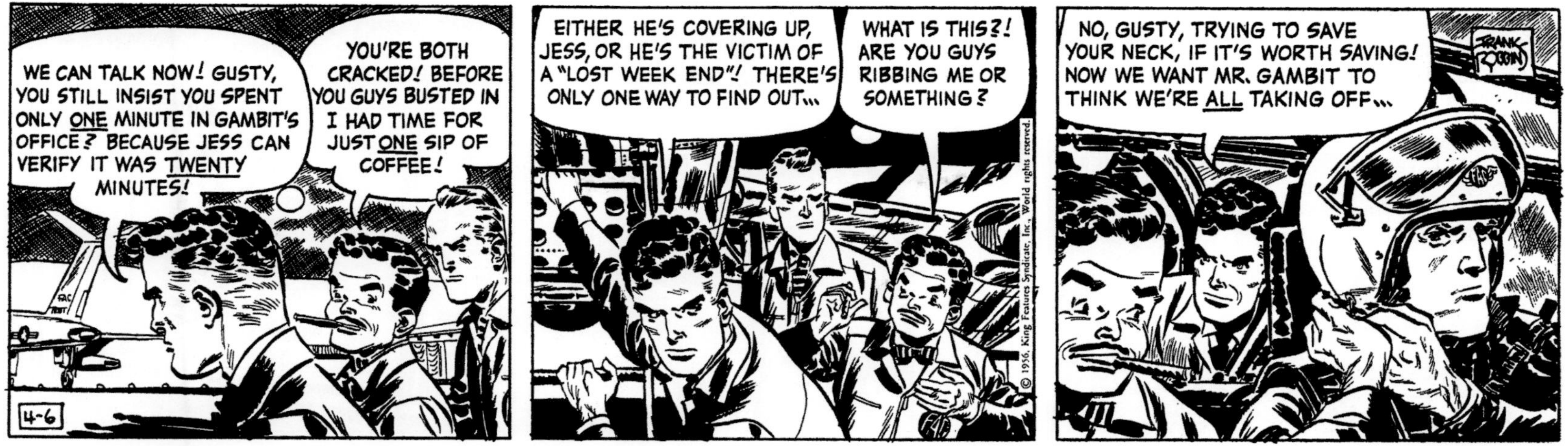
WE CAN TALK NOW! GUSTY, YOU STILL INSIST YOU SPENT ONLY ONE MINUTE IN GAMBIT'S OFFICE? BECAUSE JESS CAN VERIFY IT WAS TWENTY MINUTES!
YOU'RE BOTH CRACKED! BEFORE YOU GUYS BUSTED IN I HAD TIME FOR JUST ONE SIP OF COFFEE!
4-6
EITHER HE'S COVERING UP, JESS, OR HE'S THE VICTIM OF A "LOST WEEK END"! THERE'S ONLY ONE WAY TO FIND OUT...
WHAT IS THIS?! ARE YOU GUYS RIBBING ME OR SOMETHING?
© 1956, King Features Syndicate, Inc., World rights reserved.
NO, GUSTY, TRYING TO SAVE YOUR NECK, IF IT'S WORTH SAVING! NOW WE WANT MR. GAMBIT TO THINK WE'RE ALL TAKING OFF...

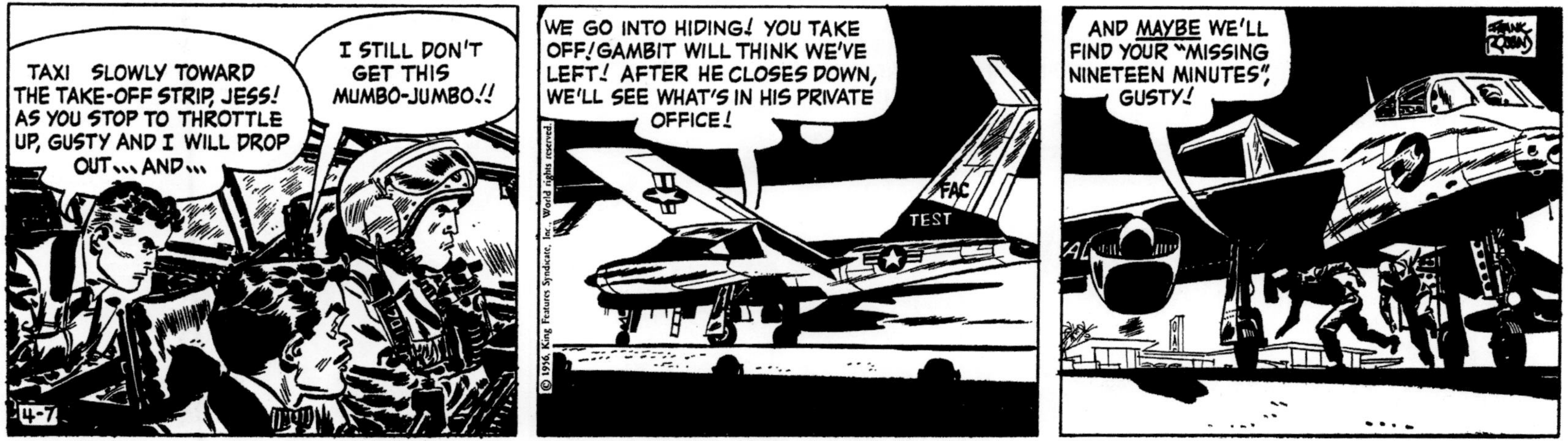
TAXI SLOWLY TOWARD THE TAKE-OFF STRIP, JESS! AS YOU STOP TO THROTTLE UP, GUSTY AND I WILL DROP OUT... AND...
I STILL DON'T GET THIS MUMBO-JUMBO!!
4-7
© 1956, King Features Syndicate, Inc., World rights reserved.
WE GO INTO HIDING! YOU TAKE OFF! GAMBIT WILL THINK WE'VE LEFT! AFTER HE CLOSES DOWN, WE'LL SEE WHAT'S IN HIS PRIVATE OFFICE!
FAC
TEST
AND MAYBE WE'LL FIND YOUR "MISSING NINETEEN MINUTES", GUSTY!

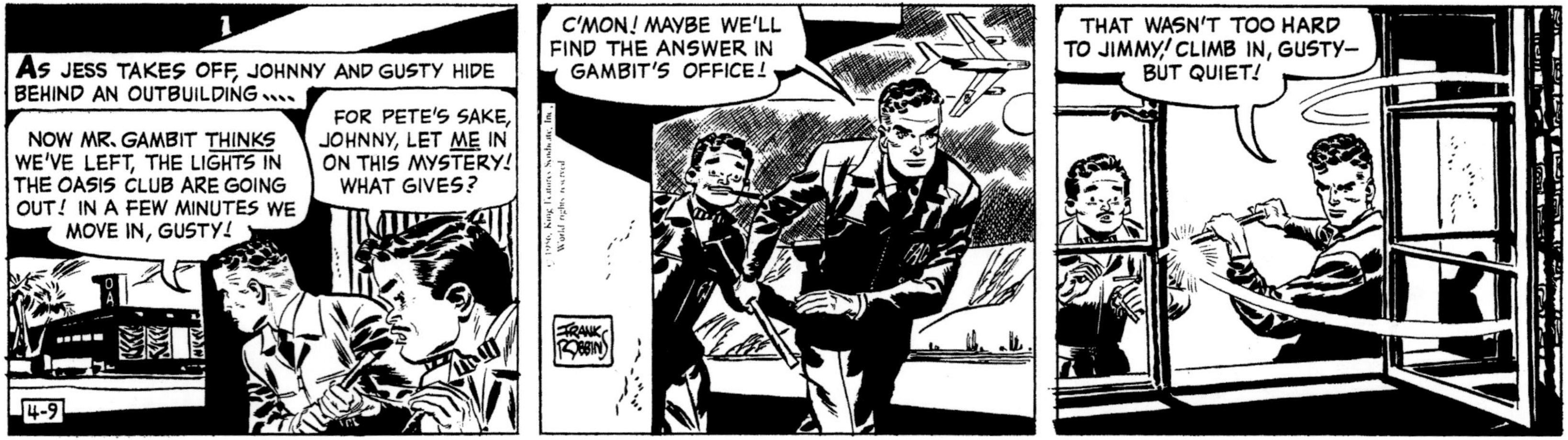
AS JESS TAKES OFF, JOHNNY AND GUSTY HIDE BEHIND AN OUTBUILDING....
NOW MR. GAMBIT THINKS WE'VE LEFT, THE LIGHTS IN THE OASIS CLUB ARE GOING OUT! IN A FEW MINUTES WE MOVE IN, GUSTY!
FOR PETE'S SAKE, JOHNNY, LET ME IN ON THIS MYSTERY! WHAT GIVES?
4-9
C'MON! MAYBE WE'LL FIND THE ANSWER IN GAMBIT'S OFFICE!
© 1956, King Features Syndicate, Inc., World rights reserved
FRANK ROBBINS
THAT WASN'T TOO HARD TO JIMMY! CLIMB IN, GUSTY— BUT QUIET!

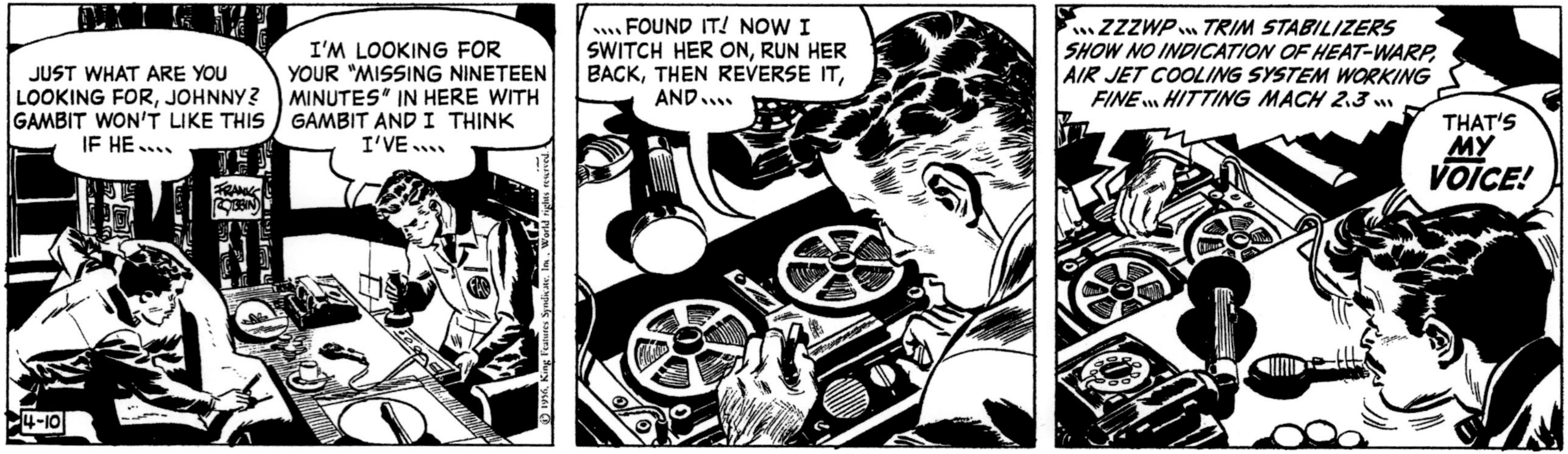
JUST WHAT ARE YOU LOOKING FOR, JOHNNY? GAMBIT WON'T LIKE THIS IF HE....
I'M LOOKING FOR YOUR "MISSING NINETEEN MINUTES" IN HERE WITH GAMBIT AND I THINK I'VE....
FRANK ROBBINS
© 1956, King Features Syndicate, Inc., World rights reserved
4-10
....FOUND IT! NOW I SWITCH HER ON, RUN HER BACK, THEN REVERSE IT, AND....
...ZZZWP... TRIM STABILIZERS SHOW NO INDICATION OF HEAT-WARP, AIR JET COOLING SYSTEM WORKING FINE... HITTING MACH 2.3...
THAT'S MY VOICE!

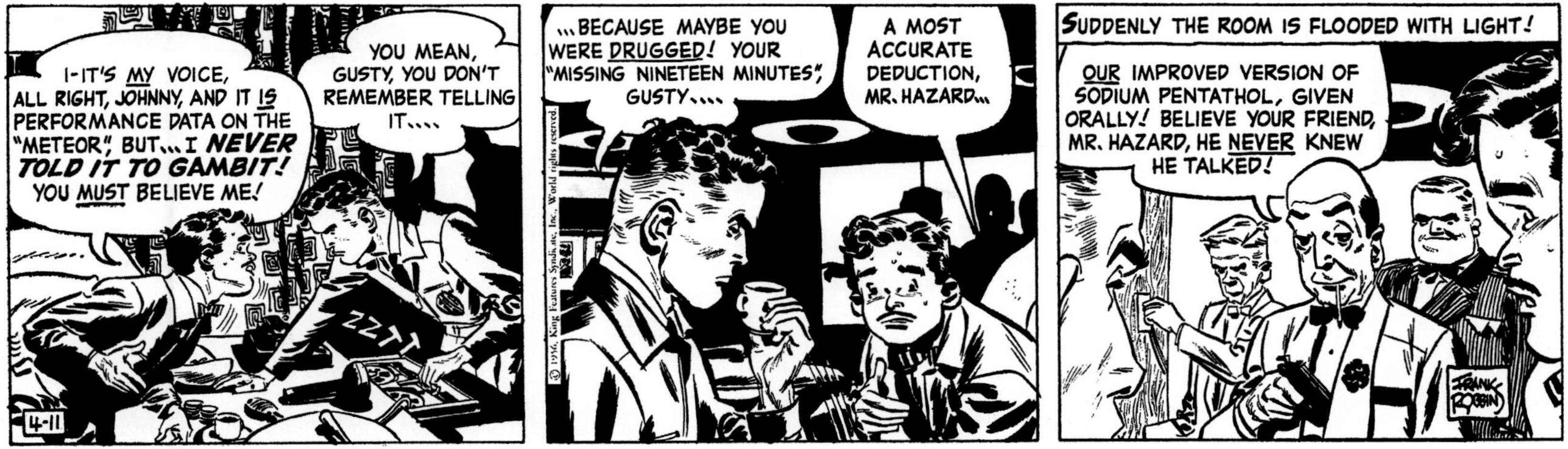
4-11
I-IT'S MY VOICE, ALL RIGHT, JOHNNY, AND IT IS PERFORMANCE DATA ON THE "METEOR", BUT...I NEVER TOLD IT TO GAMBIT! YOU MUST BELIEVE ME!
YOU MEAN, GUSTY, YOU DON'T REMEMBER TELLING IT....
ZZT
...BECAUSE MAYBE YOU WERE DRUGGED! YOUR "MISSING NINETEEN MINUTES", GUSTY....
A MOST ACCURATE DEDUCTION, MR. HAZARD...
© 1956, King Features Syndicate, Inc., World rights reserved.
SUDDENLY THE ROOM IS FLOODED WITH LIGHT!
OUR IMPROVED VERSION OF SODIUM PENTATHOL, GIVEN ORALLY! BELIEVE YOUR FRIEND, MR. HAZARD, HE NEVER KNEW HE TALKED!
FRANK ROBBINS

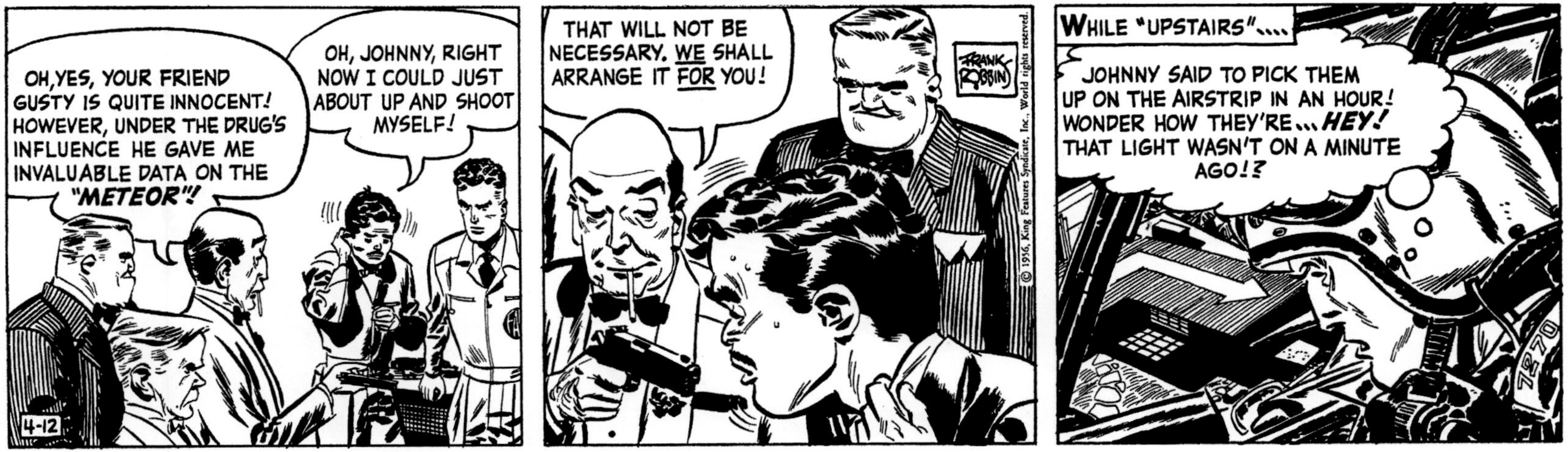
4-12
OH, YES, YOUR FRIEND GUSTY IS QUITE INNOCENT! HOWEVER, UNDER THE DRUG'S INFLUENCE HE GAVE ME INVALUABLE DATA ON THE "METEOR"!
OH, JOHNNY, RIGHT NOW I COULD JUST ABOUT UP AND SHOOT MYSELF!
THAT WILL NOT BE NECESSARY. WE SHALL ARRANGE IT FOR YOU!
FRANK ROBBINS
© 1956, King Features Syndicate, Inc., World rights reserved.
WHILE "UPSTAIRS"....
JOHNNY SAID TO PICK THEM UP ON THE AIRSTRIP IN AN HOUR! WONDER HOW THEY'RE...HEY! THAT LIGHT WASN'T ON A MINUTE AGO!?
7270

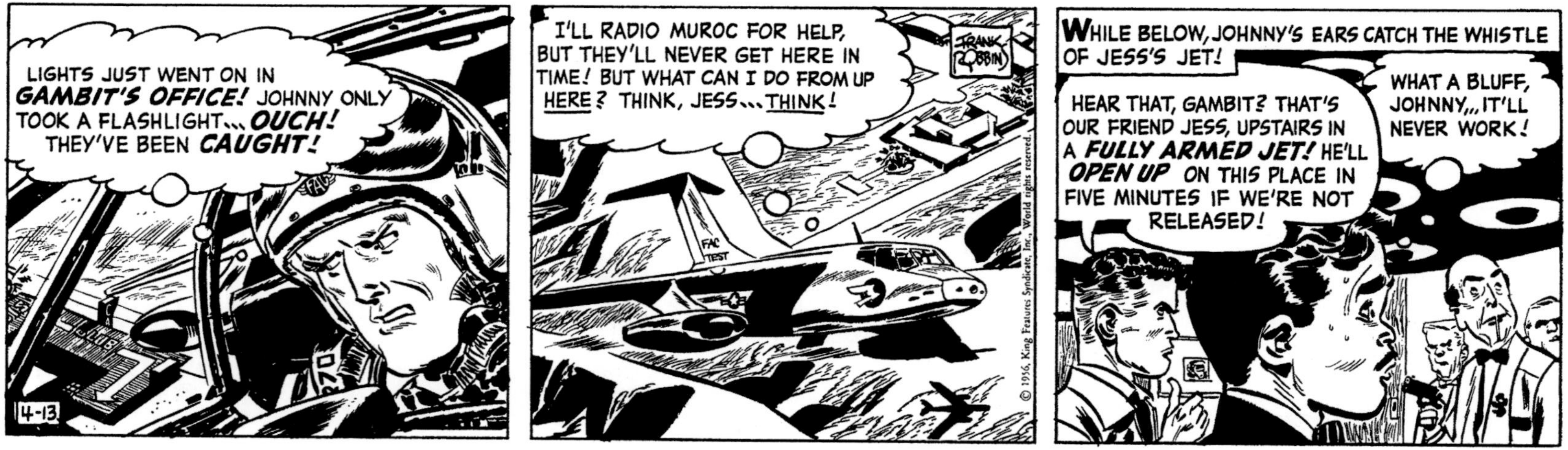
4-13
LIGHTS JUST WENT ON IN GAMBIT'S OFFICE! JOHNNY ONLY TOOK A FLASHLIGHT... OUCH! THEY'VE BEEN CAUGHT!
I'LL RADIO MUROC FOR HELP, BUT THEY'LL NEVER GET HERE IN TIME! BUT WHAT CAN I DO FROM UP HERE? THINK, JESS... THINK!
FRANK ROBBIN
FAC TEST
© 1956, King Features Syndicate, Inc., World rights reserved.
WHILE BELOW, JOHNNY'S EARS CATCH THE WHISTLE OF JESS'S JET!
HEAR THAT, GAMBIT? THAT'S OUR FRIEND JESS, UPSTAIRS IN A FULLY ARMED JET! HE'LL OPEN UP ON THIS PLACE IN FIVE MINUTES IF WE'RE NOT RELEASED!
WHAT A BLUFF, JOHNNY... IT'LL NEVER WORK!

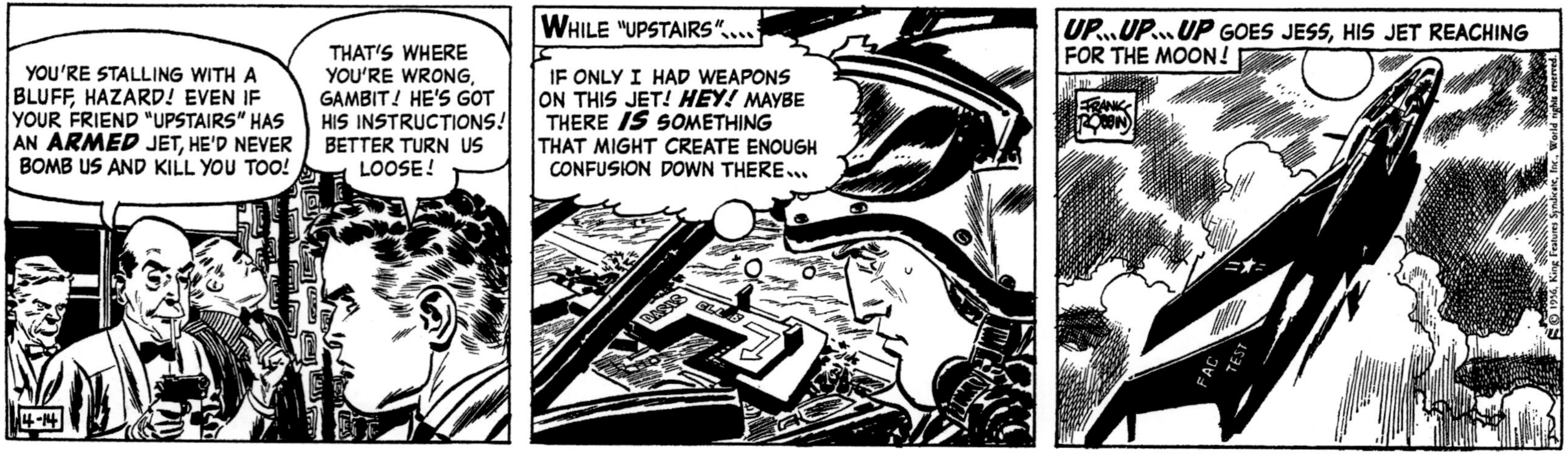
4-14
YOU'RE STALLING WITH A BLUFF, HAZARD! EVEN IF YOUR FRIEND "UPSTAIRS" HAS AN ARMED JET, HE'D NEVER BOMB US AND KILL YOU TOO!
THAT'S WHERE YOU'RE WRONG, GAMBIT! HE'S GOT HIS INSTRUCTIONS! BETTER TURN US LOOSE!
WHILE "UPSTAIRS"....
IF ONLY I HAD WEAPONS ON THIS JET! HEY! MAYBE THERE IS SOMETHING THAT MIGHT CREATE ENOUGH CONFUSION DOWN THERE...
OASIS CLUB
UP...UP...UP GOES JESS, HIS JET REACHING FOR THE MOON!
FRANK ROBBIN
FAC TEST
© 1956, King Features Syndicate, Inc., World rights reserved.

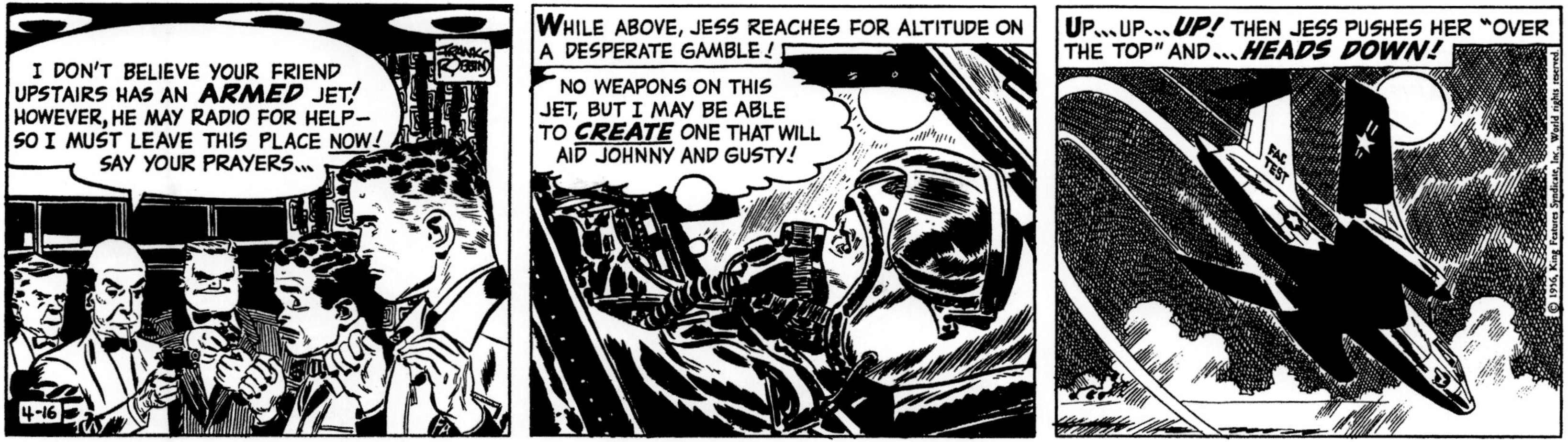
FRANK ROBBIN
I DON'T BELIEVE YOUR FRIEND UPSTAIRS HAS AN **ARMED** JET! HOWEVER, HE MAY RADIO FOR HELP— SO I MUST LEAVE THIS PLACE NOW! SAY YOUR PRAYERS...
4-16
WHILE ABOVE, JESS REACHES FOR ALTITUDE ON A DESPERATE GAMBLE!
NO WEAPONS ON THIS JET, BUT I MAY BE ABLE TO **CREATE** ONE THAT WILL AID JOHNNY AND GUSTY!
UP...UP...**UP!** THEN JESS PUSHES HER "OVER THE TOP" AND...**HEADS DOWN!**
FAC TEST
© 1956, King Features Syndicate, Inc., World rights reserved.

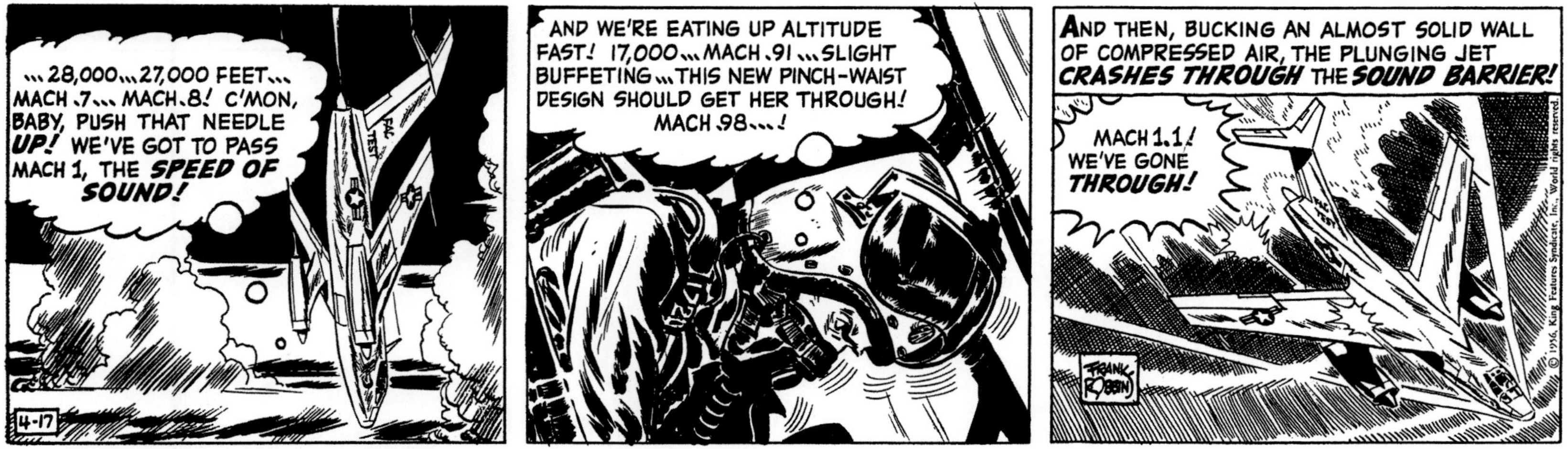
...28,000...27,000 FEET... MACH .7... MACH .8! C'MON, BABY, PUSH THAT NEEDLE **UP!** WE'VE GOT TO PASS MACH 1, THE **SPEED OF SOUND!**
FAC TEST
4-17
AND WE'RE EATING UP ALTITUDE FAST! 17,000... MACH .91 ...SLIGHT BUFFETING... THIS NEW PINCH-WAIST DESIGN SHOULD GET HER THROUGH! MACH .98...!
AND THEN, BUCKING AN ALMOST SOLID WALL OF COMPRESSED AIR, THE PLUNGING JET **CRASHES THROUGH** THE **SOUND BARRIER!**
MACH 1.1! WE'VE GONE **THROUGH!**
FAC TEST
FRANK ROBBIN
© 1956, King Features Syndicate, Inc., World rights reserved.

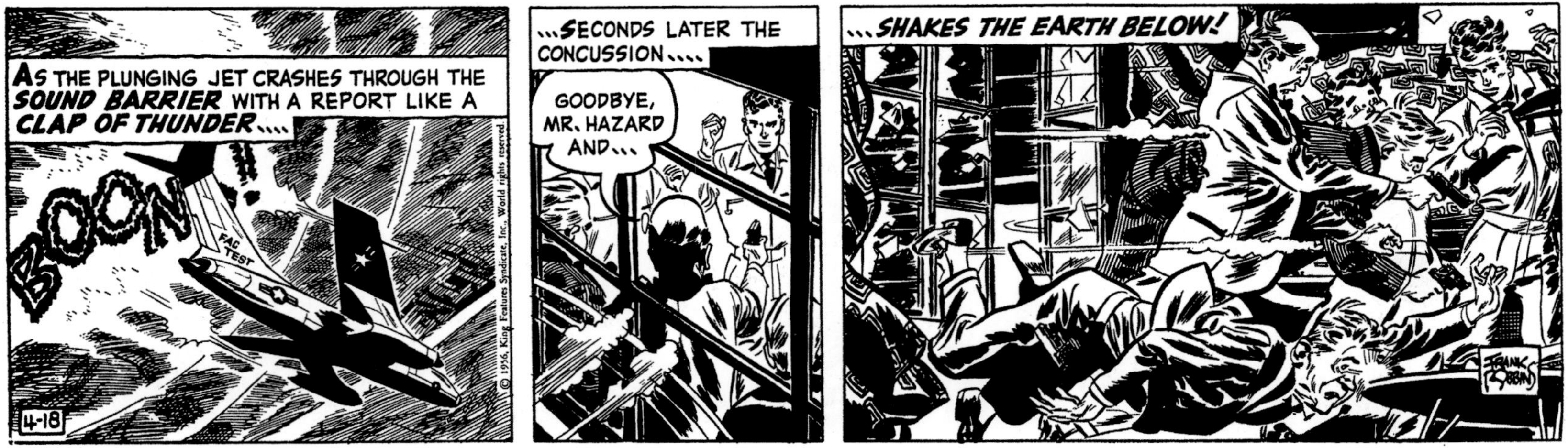
AS THE PLUNGING JET CRASHES THROUGH THE SOUND BARRIER WITH A REPORT LIKE A CLAP OF THUNDER....
BOOOM!
FAC TEST
© 1956, King Features Syndicate, Inc., World rights reserved.
4-18
...SECONDS LATER THE CONCUSSION....
GOODBYE, MR. HAZARD AND...
...SHAKES THE EARTH BELOW!
FRANK ROBBINS

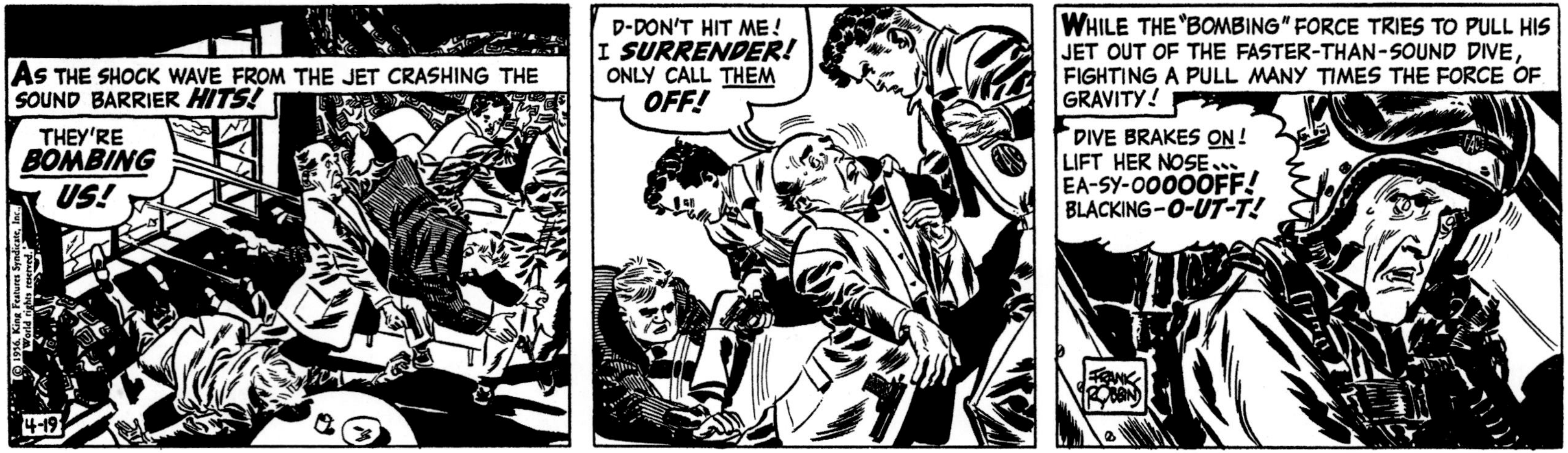
AS THE SHOCK WAVE FROM THE JET CRASHING THE SOUND BARRIER HITS!
THEY'RE BOMBING US!
© 1956, King Features Syndicate, Inc., World rights reserved.
4-19
D-DON'T HIT ME! I SURRENDER! ONLY CALL THEM OFF!
WHILE THE "BOMBING" FORCE TRIES TO PULL HIS JET OUT OF THE FASTER-THAN-SOUND DIVE, FIGHTING A PULL MANY TIMES THE FORCE OF GRAVITY!
DIVE BRAKES ON! LIFT HER NOSE... EA-SY-OOOOOFF! BLACKING-O-UT-T!
FRANK ROBBINS

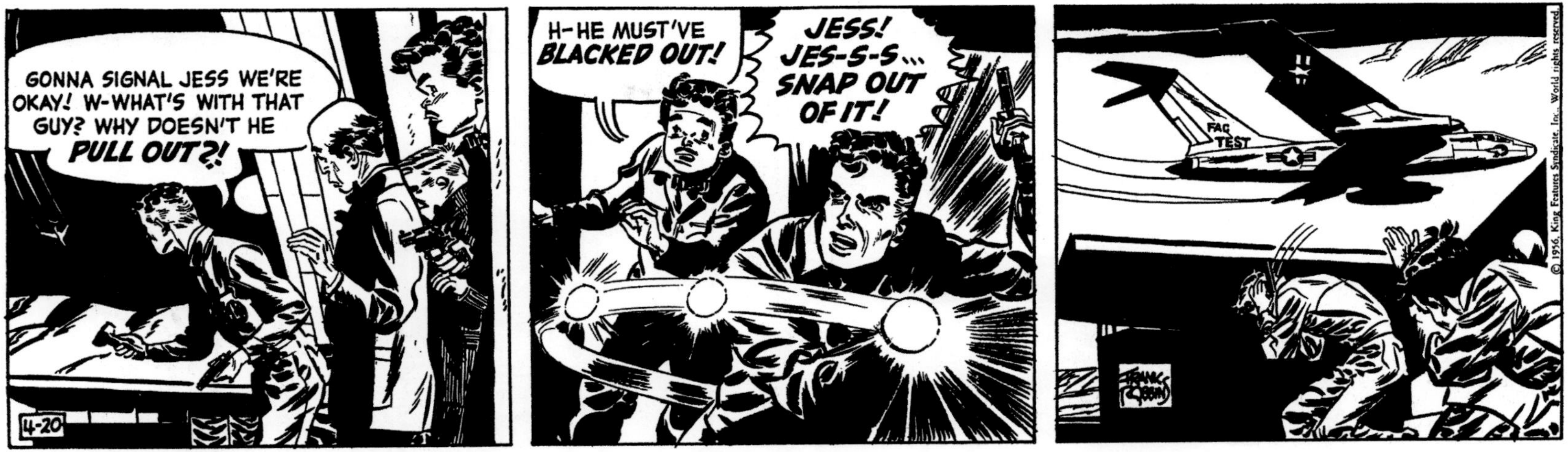
4-20
GONNA SIGNAL JESS WE'RE OKAY! W-WHAT'S WITH THAT GUY? WHY DOESN'T HE PULL OUT?!
H-HE MUST'VE BLACKED OUT!
JESS! JES-S-S... SNAP OUT OF IT!
FAC TEST
© 1956, King Features Syndicate, Inc., World rights reserved.

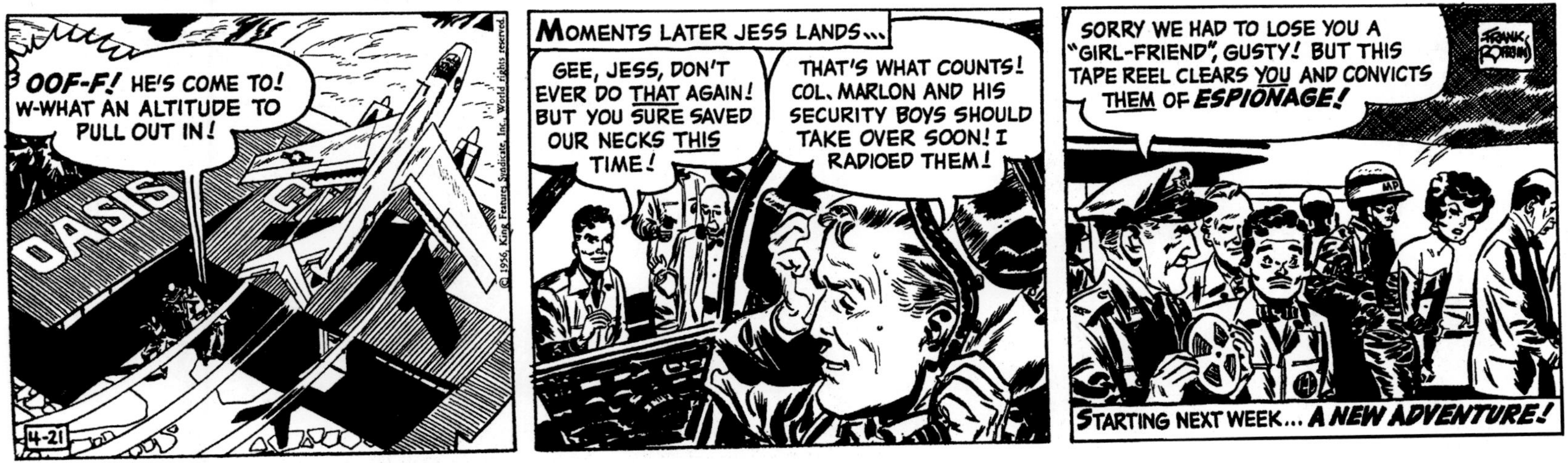
4-21
OOF-F! HE'S COME TO! W-WHAT AN ALTITUDE TO PULL OUT IN!
OASIS
© 1956, King Features Syndicate, Inc., World rights reserved.
MOMENTS LATER JESS LANDS...
GEE, JESS, DON'T EVER DO THAT AGAIN! BUT YOU SURE SAVED OUR NECKS THIS TIME!
THAT'S WHAT COUNTS! COL. MARLON AND HIS SECURITY BOYS SHOULD TAKE OVER SOON! I RADIOED THEM!
SORRY WE HAD TO LOSE YOU A "GIRL-FRIEND", GUSTY! BUT THIS TAPE REEL CLEARS YOU AND CONVICTS THEM OF ESPIONAGE!
MP
STARTING NEXT WEEK... A NEW ADVENTURE!

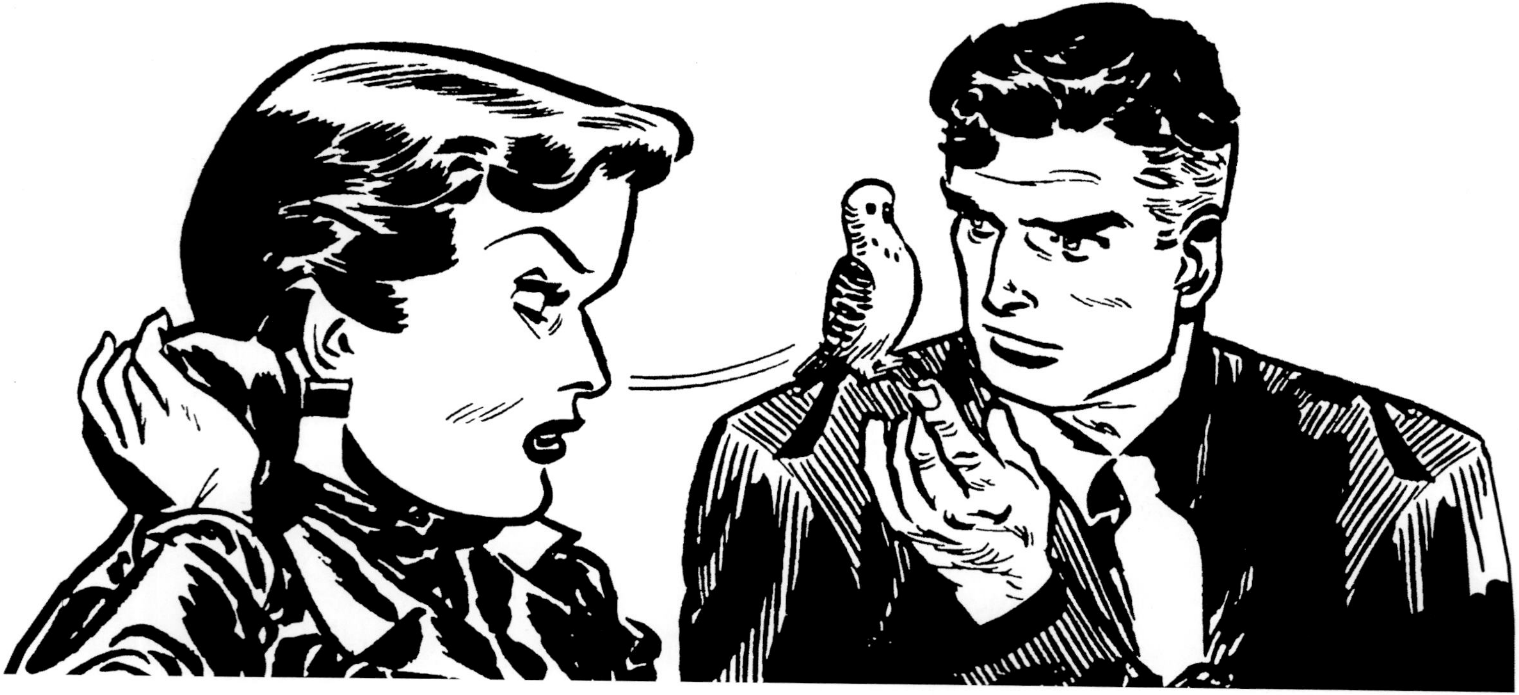